The Reception of Jesus in the First Three Centuries

3

Editors
Chris Keith, Helen Bond and Jens Schröter

The Gospel of Tatian

Exploring the Nature and Text of the Diatessaron

Edited by
Matthew R. Crawford and Nicholas J. Zola

LONDON • NEW YORK • OXFORD • NEW DELHI • SYDNEY

T&T CLARK
Bloomsbury Publishing Plc
50 Bedford Square, London, WC1B 3DP, UK
1385 Broadway, New York, NY 10018, USA
29 Earlsfort Terrace, Dublin 2, Ireland

BLOOMSBURY, T&T CLARK and the T&T Clark logo are trademarks of
Bloomsbury Publishing Plc

First published in Great Britain 2019
This paperback edition published in 2021

Copyright © Matthew R. Crawford, Nicholas J. Zola and contributors, 2019

Matthew R. Crawford and Nicholas J. Zola have asserted their right under the Copyright,
Designs and Patents Act, 1988, to be identified as Editors of this work.

For legal purposes the Acknowledgments on p. xi constitute an
extension of this copyright page.

Cover design: Tjaša Krivec
Cover image: The Good Shepherd, fresco (3rd century) in the Catacomb of
Priscilla, Rome, Lazio, Italy © De Agostini / G. Cargagna / Getty Images.

All rights reserved. No part of this publication may be reproduced or
transmitted in any form or by any means, electronic or mechanical,
including photocopying, recording, or any information storage or retrieval
system, without prior permission in writing from the publishers.

Bloomsbury Publishing Plc does not have any control over, or responsibility for, any
third-party websites referred to or in this book. All internet addresses given in this book
were correct at the time of going to press. The author and publisher regret any
inconvenience caused if addresses have changed or sites have ceased to exist,
but can accept no responsibility for any such changes.

A catalogue record for this book is available from the British Library.

Library of Congress Cataloging-in-Publication Data
Names: Crawford, Matthew R., editor. | Zola, Nicholas J., editor.
Title: The gospel of Tatian : exploring the nature and text of the
Diatessaron / edited by Matthew R. Crawford and Nicholas J. Zola.
Description: London ; New York : T&T Clark, 2019. |
Series: The reception of Jesus in the first three centuries ; volume 3 |
Includes bibliographical references and index.
Identifiers: LCCN 2019009769 | ISBN 9780567679888 (hardback) |
ISBN 9780567679918 (epub) | ISBN 9780567679895 (epdf)
Subjects: LCSH: Bible. Gospels. Syriac Diatessaron–Versions–Criticism,
interpretation, etc. | Tatian, approximately 120–173.
Classification: LCC BS2550.T2 G67 2019 | DDC 226/.1–dc23
LC record available at https://lccn.loc.gov/2019009769

ISBN: HB: 978-0-5676-7988-8
PB: 978-0-5677-0034-6
ePDF: 978-0-5676-7989-5
ePUB: 978-0-5676-7991-8

Series: The Reception of Jesus in the First Three Centuries, volume 3

Typeset by Newgen KnowledgeWorks Pvt. Ltd., Chennai, India

To find out more about our authors and books visit www.bloomsbury.com
and sign up for our newsletters.

For Tjitze Baarda,
in memoriam,
a pioneer in the Tatiankultus

Contents

List of Illustrations	ix
List of Contributors	x
Acknowledgments	xi
List of Abbreviations	xii
Introduction *Matthew R. Crawford and Nicholas J. Zola*	1

Part 1 The Sources of Tatian's Gospel

1. The Diatessaron and Its Beginning: A Twofold Statement of Tatian *Tjitze Baarda* — 13

2. Diatessaron, Diapente, Diapollon? Exploring the Nature and Extent of Extracanonical Influence in Tatian's Diatessaron *Charles E. Hill* — 25

3. Tatian's Sources and the Presentation of the Jewish Law in the Diatessaron *Jan Joosten* — 55

Part 2 The Nature of Tatian's Gospel

4. Harmony or Gospel? On the Genre of the (So-Called) Diatessaron *Francis Watson* — 69

5. What Justin's Gospels Can Tell Us about Tatian's: Tracing the Trajectory of the Gospel Harmony in the Second Century and Beyond *Nicholas Perrin* — 93

6. Tatian's Diatessaron and the Proliferation of Gospels *James W. Barker* — 111

Part 3 The Witnesses to Tatian's Gospel

7. The Wrong Harmony: Against the Diatessaronic Character of the Dura Parchment *Ian N. Mills* — 145

8. Before and After: Some Notes on the Pre- and Post-History of Codex
   Fuldensis *Ulrich B. Schmid*   171

9. The Use of Tatian's Diatessaron in the Textual Criticism of the Gospels
   and the Future of Diatessaronic Studies *Nicholas J. Zola*   191

Bibliography   239
Index of Ancient Sources   259
Index of Modern Authors   270
Index of Subjects   273

Illustrations

Plates

1 Dura Parchment 24 (recto)
2 Dura Parchment 24 (verso)

Figures

6.1	The proliferation of LXX recensions	121
6.2	The proliferation of Gospels	139

Tables

5.1	Parallels between Matt 5:40–6:1 and Justin, *1 Apol.* 15.9, 10, 13, 17	104
7.1	Joseph of Arimathea in the Dura Fragment, as Outlined by Jan Joosten	149
7.2	Text of the Dura Fragment and Its Canonical Parallels	150
7.3	Joosten's Element B in the Dura Fragment and Western Parallels	152
7.4	Joosten's Element F in the Dura Fragment and Western Parallels	153
7.5	Sequence of Dura, Fuldensis, Liège, and Venetian Harmonies	155
7.6	Placement of the Lance Piercing in Dura and Fuldensis	157
7.7	Luke 23:51 in Dura, Fuldensis, and the Syriac Peshitta	161
7.8	Sequence of Pseudo-Ephrem, Dura, Fuldensis, and Arabic	165
7.9	Luke 23:51 in Dura, Pseudo-Ephrem, and the Old Syriac	166
7.10	Joosten's Element B in the Dura Fragment and Arabic Diatessaron	168
7.11	Joosten's Element F in the Dura Fragment and Arabic Diatessaron	169
7.12	Subdivision of NA^{28} Gospel Texts that Overlap with Dura	170
9.1	Diatessaronic Sigla in Merk, 4th ed. (1942) to 11th ed. (1992)	214
9.2	Diatessaronic Sigla in UBS$^{1-3}$ (1966–83)	220
9.3	Diatessaronic Sigla in UBS$^{4-5}$ (1993–2014)	226

Contributors

Tjitze Baarda
Emeritus Professor of New Testament Studies
Vrije Universiteit Amsterdam, Netherlands

James W. Barker
Assistant Professor of New Testament
Western Kentucky University, USA

Charles E. Hill
John R. Richardson Professor of New Testament and Early Christianity
Reformed Theological Seminary, USA

Jan Joosten
Regius Professor of Hebrew
University of Oxford, UK

Ian Mills
PhD Candidate
Duke University, USA

Nicholas Perrin
Franklin S. Dyrness Professor of Biblical Studies
Wheaton Graduate School, USA

Ulrich B. Schmid
Associate Professor of Church History
Kirchliche Hochschule Wuppertal/Bethel, Germany

Francis Watson
Research Chair in Early Christian Literature
Durham University, UK

Nicholas J. Zola
Associate Professor of Religion
Pepperdine University, USA

Acknowledgments

This project has been well over three years in the making. It began as an idea we had in 2015 to rekindle the conversation on the Diatessaron, which led to two sessions in the Development of Early Christian Theology section at back-to-back annual meetings of the Society of Biblical Literature (2016 in San Antonio and 2017 in Boston). We would especially like to thank Mark DelCogliano, the program unit chair, along with the rest of the program unit committee, for supplying us with the space and support to convene these sessions, without which this volume would not likely have happened.

The volume would be nothing without our contributors, who are masters in their respective fields and who were remarkably quick to respond to requests and revisions. We thank each of you for your dedication to the volume and your willingness to trust us with the task. A special and poignant thank you is due to Fokke Baarda, the son of Tjitze Baarda, who graciously gave us permission to publish his father's essay after Tjitze passed away unexpectedly in August 2017 and who worked with us to ensure that we had the latest version. We pray Tjitze's memory is honored by our work.

The editing process was made easier by the work of Matt's research assistants, Carolyn Alsen and Clift Ward, whom we heartily thank for their steady labor and attention to detail. We are grateful to the Beinecke Rare Book & Manuscript Library at Yale University for making available the images of Dura Parchment 24. The editorial team at Bloomsbury has been wonderfully supportive along the way, and we thank especially Dominic Mattos, Meredith Benson, and Sarah Blake for their guidance. Likewise, we are grateful to Chris Keith, Helen Bond, and Jens Schröter for accepting the volume into their "The Reception of Jesus in the First Three Centuries" series, of which we are proud to be a part.

Finally, we each thank our spouse and children, respectively, without whose sacrifices and support we could not have completed the work at hand—or complete any work. Thank you for indulging our devotion to this esoteric discipline.

Abbreviations

Standard abbreviations are employed from *The SBL Handbook of Style* (second edition). Bibliographic abbreviations that do not appear in that handbook are listed below, along with a selection of specialized terms.

Ar	Arabic Diatessaron
cap.	*capitulum*
Comm. (Diat.)	Ephrem, *Commentary on the Diatessaron*
CSIC	Consejo Superior de Investigaciones Cientificas
D	Diatessaron evangelist
Dem.	Aphrahat, *Demonstrations*
EC	*Early Christianity*
Ephr	Ephrem, *Commentary on the Diatessaron*
F	Codex Fuldensis
F^{cap}	*capitulum* in Codex Fuldensis
FGNK	Forschungen zur Geschichte des neutestamentlichen Kanons und der altkirchlichen Literatur
it	Old Latin
JSJSup	Supplements to the Journal for the Study of Judaism
Lat	Latin Diatessaron
MS(S)	manuscript(s)
NT	New Testament
om.	omit(s)
OT	Old Testament
SSLL	Studies in Semitic Languages and Linguistics
Str-B	Hermann Strack and Paul Billerbeck, *Kommentar zum Neuen Testament aus Talmud und Midrasch*
syr^c	Curetonian Old Syriac Gospel
syr^{NF}	Old Syriac Sinai New Finds palimpsest Gospel (see S. Brock, "Two Hitherto Unattested Passages of the Old Syriac Gospels" in the Bibliography)
syr^p	Syriac Peshitta
syr^s	Sinaitic Old Syriac Gospel
VCSup	Supplements to Vigiliae Christianae
VKNAW	Verhandelingen der Koninklijke Nederlandse Akademie van Wetenschappen

Introduction
Matthew R. Crawford and Nicholas J. Zola

On May 17, 1934, following Kirsopp Lake's announcement that a Greek fragment of Tatian's Diatessaron had been unearthed in the excavations underway at the Roman frontier town of Dura-Europos (see Plates 1 and 2), F. C. Burkitt, Norrisian Professor of Divinity at the University of Cambridge and "indisputably the greatest New Testament textual critic of [his] time,"[1] wrote a letter to *The Times* expressing great enthusiasm about the discovery. He concluded on a note of hopeful expectation: "the discovery is of the greatest interest and may throw some light on the genesis of the Diatessaron itself. The main question about the Diatessaron is whether we should regard it as the last attempt to make a new Gospel, or as the first attempt to translate the Canonical Four."[2] The current volume takes up and expands upon this very question—hence our intentionally probing title, "The Gospel of Tatian."

What Burkitt called "the main question about the Diatessaron" is what we refer to in our subtitle as the "nature" of Tatian's text. It is a line of inquiry on which no scholarly consensus has yet emerged. Of course, identifying the "nature" of Tatian's Diatessaron, or "Gospel" if that is how it was originally known, requires detailed attention to the text that he produced, insofar as it can be reconstructed on the basis of surviving witnesses. It is this endeavor that forms the remainder of our subtitle. These twin foci (the "nature" and "text" of the Diatessaron) reflect the origin of the present volume in two invited panels at the annual meetings of the Society of Biblical Literature in 2016 and 2017. Organized by the two editors and hosted under the auspices of the Development of Early Christian Theology program unit, these sessions had as their themes "The Diatessaron and the Fourfold Gospel" and "Tatian and the Text of the Gospels." Eight of the volume's nine contributors participated in those panels and have produced revised chapters for inclusion in the current collection.

---

[1] The description is that of Alexander Souter in "Francis Crawford Burkitt," *JTS* 36 (1935): 225–54, at 227.
[2] F. C. Burkitt, "Tatian's Diatessaron," *The Times*, May 21, 1934, 11. Cf. Kirsopp Lake, "Tatian's Diatessaron," *The Times*, May 16, 1934, 17. In a brief note published posthumously just over a year later, Burkitt answered the question he had posed after having examined the edition of the Dura fragment published by C. H. Kraeling. He repeated a position he had staked out in an earlier issue of the same journal: "I see no reason to withdraw my conjecture about the origin of [Tatian's] famous Harmony, that it was not a rival to the Gospels themselves, but rather the first of the versions" ("The Dura Fragment of Tatian," *JTS* 36 [1935]: 255–9, at 257). Burkitt goes on to cite extensively from his earlier study: "Tatian's Diatessaron and the Dutch Harmonies," *JTS* 25 (1924): 113–30.

The ninth contributor deserves special mention. It is with a note of melancholy that we report that the volume's opening chapter is the final publication of Tjitze Baarda, who has contributed more to Diatessaronic studies than perhaps anyone else over the past half-century. Tjitze's poor health prevented him from accepting our invitation to participate in the aforementioned SBL sessions, but he nevertheless expressed enthusiasm that the Diatessaron continued to be a topic of scholarly inquiry, and he graciously offered to let us include in the volume a paper he had written in September 2016 and presented to the Faculty of Theology at Vrije Universiteit Amsterdam. Sadly, Tjitze passed away in August of the following year; thus we are publishing his essay posthumously.[3] The range of linguistic expertise Tjitze possessed was legendary and is not likely to be seen again any time soon in any single scholar of early Christianity. Moreover, the judiciousness of his scholarly conclusions and the precision of his method will no doubt ensure that his many publications related to the Diatessaron continue to be read for decades to come. Indeed, his works are cited repeatedly in the chapters that follow, indicating that our contributors recognize them as essential starting points for any new research on the topic. Thanks to the kindness of the Baarda family in allowing us to publish Tjitze's work, the present volume points to both the past and the future of Diatessaronic studies, including a chapter from the leading scholar of the last generation as well as one from a doctoral student currently writing a dissertation on the topic. As such, the volume indicates both where the field has been and where it is headed.

Keeping the field moving is in fact one of the aims of this collection, since the discipline of Diatessaronic studies is unusually esoteric and can appear intimidating to outsiders. Nowhere has this point been made more clearly than in the monumental summary of scholarship published in 1994 by the late William L. Petersen, the only scholar whose influence over the past three decades might rival that of Baarda. Describing his own motivation for undertaking doctoral studies on the Diatessaron, Petersen says he was attracted to its inherent diversity: "At the same time that it drew one into arcane byways and the study of minutiae, it also forced one to study the entire antique world, for Diatessaronic witnesses crop up in places as diverse as Britain and China."[4] He chose to begin the body of his tome by pointing out that there are "significant obstacles to using the Diatessaron," including the breadth of languages required to access the essential primary and secondary literature; the "nature of the work," which consists of an attempt to identify short snippets of text that can only be reconstructed after much painstaking labor with no guarantee of any positive outcome; and finally the lack of an agreed-upon "method" that would ensure that the results of this tedious labor could be trusted. Summing up the state of affairs just prior to his own scholarly interventions, Petersen claimed, "Put charitably, the field was seen as too problematic, too abstruse, and too difficult; less charitably, it was seen as idiosyncratic,

---

[3] We express sincere gratitude to Tjitze's son, Fokke Baarda, for granting us permission to publish Tjitze's last essay here and for working with us to ensure we had the latest revisions.
[4] William L. Petersen, *Tatian's Diatessaron: Its Creation, Dissemination, Significance, and History in Scholarship*, VCSup 25 (Leiden: Brill, 1994), xiii.

chaotic, and lacking norms and controls."[5] Although the intent of Petersen's book was to provide an aid to students seeking to overcome these daunting obstacles and join what Adolf Jülicher called the "Tatiankultus,"[6] one wonders if it in fact had the opposite effect. If the necessary expertise requires so long to develop and if the task is, at least potentially, so unrewarding, why should one even bother? Might this overriding emphasis on the complexity and difficulty of Diatessaronic studies account at least partially for the relative scarcity of studies on the topic in the past quarter of a century? Whatever the case, one of the aims of the present collection of chapters is to convey the message that the study of the Diatessaron is a rewarding discipline and that one does not have to be a Petersen or a Baarda to make a meaningful contribution to it. This aim has been helped by what must surely be the most significant development in the field since the publication of Petersen's book—the shift in methodology led in part by Ulrich Schmid (one of the volume's contributors), culminating in what Schmid has called the "new perspective on the Diatessaron."[7] Not all of our contributors agree with Schmid's "new perspective," as will be clear in the pages that follow, but even the debate around this issue indicates that the field is alive and well, that much work remains to be done, and that exciting discoveries can yet be made.

Despite the original two-pronged approach of the SBL sessions, we have rebalanced the current volume into a tripartite scheme, corresponding to three overarching questions in the field: (1) what sources did Tatian use to compile his Gospel? (2) What is the nature of Tatian's Gospel? (3) How do we properly identify and employ the surviving witnesses to Tatian's Gospel? Of course, some of the answers to these questions are mutually entailing, with the consequence that more than one of the chapters transgress the boundaries of the book's structure. For this reason, the remaining aim of this introduction is first to lay out the argument of each chapter and then to set them in synthetic dialogue with one another, in order to gesture toward where the field of Diatessaronic studies might go next.

The first three chapters concern the sources of Tatian's Gospel. We open with Tjitze Baarda's appropriately titled chapter, "The Diatessaron and its Beginning: A Twofold Statement of Tatian," in which Baarda draws theological import from Tatian's incorporation of the Gospel of John as a framework for his own work at a time when John's Gospel was not embraced in all circles (and in a way that is not apparent in the writings of his teacher Justin). Tatian intentionally elevated the Fourth Gospel to the level of the other three, ensuring that his work could be called at least a Diatessaron (and not a Diatrion).

The next chapter then tackles the question of how many *additional* sources Tatian employed. In "Diatessaron, Diapente, Diapollon? Exploring the Nature and Extent of Extracanonical Influence in Tatian's Diatessaron," Charles Hill challenges the

---

[5] Petersen, *Tatian's Diatessaron*, 4–6.
[6] Adolf Jülicher, "Der echte Tatiantext," *JBL* 63 (1924): 132. Cited also in Petersen, *Tatian's Diatessaron*, 6.
[7] Ulrich B. Schmid, "The Diatessaron of Tatian," in *The Text of the New Testament in Contemporary Research: Essays on the Status Quaestionis*, ed. Bart D. Ehrman and Michael W. Holmes, 2nd ed. (Leiden: Brill, 2013), 115–42.

standard line advanced by Petersen and others that there is direct evidence for Tatian's incorporation of "extracanonical" Gospels. Hill interrogates some of the most common textual touchstones for such a position and finds them all wanting. His stark conclusion is that there is no direct evidence for Tatian's incorporation of "extracanonical" sources in the Diatessaron.

By contrast, in "Tatian's Sources and the Presentation of the Jewish Law in the Diatessaron," Jan Joosten advocates for the position that Tatian not only employed sources beyond the canonical four, but also that we can trace Tatian's use of a preexisting western Aramaic Gospel as part of the basis of his compilation. Joosten, while aware of the complexities of the field, still argues that a careful comparison of Diatessaronic witnesses (with emphasis on the eastern witnesses) can provide glimpses into a pre-canonical form of the gospel text. On this point, Joosten stands in continuity with the traditional approach of Diatessaronic studies but diverges with several of the other chapters in the volume.

The next three chapters concern the "nature" of Tatian's Gospel, encompassing both its genre and its intended purpose. We open the section with Francis Watson's "Harmony or Gospel? On the Genre of the (so-called) Diatessaron," in which he problematizes the labeling of Tatian's work as a "gospel harmony." Watson contends that Tatian stands in continuity with the "canonical" gospel-writers who came before him, rewriting and reworking his sources to create a new Gospel in its own right, just as they did. As a Gospel that revised and incorporated earlier texts, Tatian's work is therefore subject to redaction criticism, which Watson initiates by comparing the opening sequences of the Arabic and Latin versions, uncovering two distinct streams of the Diatessaron. Later in the volume, both Schmid and Zola will advocate for a sequence-comparison approach as the key to future work in the field.

On the other hand, in the next chapter Nicholas Perrin identifies the Diatessaron squarely as a "harmony" meant to work alongside (and not to replace) the canonical four. In his chapter entitled, "What Justin's Gospels Can Tell Us about Tatian's: Tracing the Trajectory of the Gospel Harmony in the Second Century and Beyond," Perrin argues that a text's function is signaled by its genre and reception. Building from the theory that Justin employed a gospel harmony, Perrin locates the Diatessaron in a line of early harmonies that presumably served the same function. Since Justin ostensibly employed his harmony in subservience to the "canonical" Gospels (the "memoirs"), Tatian would have had the same intent and expectation for his own harmony. The Diatessaron, therefore, was designed to supplement—not supplant—the fourfold gospel.

In the section's third chapter, James Barker arrives at a similar conclusion by different means. In "Tatian's Diatessaron and the Proliferation of Gospels," Barker explores the Jewish, Greek, and Roman pattern of composing fresh texts that would logically compete with what came before but which ultimately settle side by side with their potential competition (such as Luke being read alongside Mark). Barker argues that authors (including Tatian) would be aware of this precedent and would therefore be unlikely to expect their newly minted works to replace either their sources or their competition; rather, authors would expect audiences to collect and compare multiple texts on the same topic. Barker desires to move the question beyond one of supplement or supplant to one of how Gospels proliferate and interact, a pertinent point for the many derivatives of the Diatessaron.

Accordingly, the last section of the volume concerns the witnesses to Tatian's Gospel, addressing not only how to identify them but also how to use them in the reconstruction of Tatian's text (if we can). The section opens with Ian Mills's provocative piece, "The Wrong Harmony: Against the Diatessaronic Character of the Dura Parchment," in which he contests the status of what some consider the only extant fragment of the Diatessaron in Greek (the same fragment on which we cited Burkitt above). Mills performs a meticulous line-by-line analysis of the Dura fragment and concludes that the arguments put forward in the past to establish its connection with Tatian's Diatessaron are faulty, both under Petersen's older methodology and Schmid's revised approach. The sequential parallels are only conceptual, not verbally precise; and the sequence itself does not match what Mills reconstructs for this section of Tatian's work. Mills contends that the Dura parchment is not a fragment of Tatian's Diatessaron but of some other gospel harmony entirely, calling into question what would otherwise be the earliest surviving witness to Tatian's Gospel and his text.

The next chapter is a sustained examination of another famous Diatessaronic witness, Codex Fuldensis. In "Before and After: Some Notes on the Pre- and Post-History of Codex Fuldensis," Ulrich Schmid analyzes what can be determined about the sources Victor used to produce his sixth-century Latin Diatessaron, focusing especially on the Eusebian canon tables and the prefatory *capitula*. Then Schmid extends that analysis to what can be determined about the adoption and adaptation of Fuldensis in the following centuries. Schmid maintains the position that all western Diatessaronic witnesses (both Latin and vernaculars) ultimately derive from Fuldensis. The most solid means of testing that genealogical relationship, says Schmid, is a diachronic comparison of sequences that isolates incremental editorial changes made from copy to copy across the centuries. Schmid's emphasis on sequential comparison agrees with Watson's pursuits earlier in the volume and is in keeping with the recommendations of the volume's final chapter.

The final chapter of the volume also functions as its conclusion. In "The Use of Tatian's Diatessaron in the Textual Criticism of the Gospels and the Future of Diatessaronic Studies," Nicholas Zola (also one of the volume's coeditors) traces how the Diatessaron has been used in the critical apparatus of printed Greek New Testaments from the early modern period to today. Zola notes that as more and more Diatessaronic witnesses came to light over the last three centuries, the Diatessaron's position in the text-critical apparatus rapidly grew in prominence; but the discoveries outpaced the methodology. A close examination of the Diatessaronic data reported in the apparatuses often reveals conflicting, misleading, and even erroneous evidence. In a series of seven recommendations for the future of the field, Zola proposes foremost that the critical apparatus of the Greek New Testament should *stop* citing the Diatessaron until a full genealogical stemma of all the surviving Diatessaronic witnesses can be established, a stemma that will reveal both their relation to each other and their relative weight for reconstructing what we can of Tatian's text. Zola also proposes the creation of a central online repository of information on Tatian's Diatessaron, in order to make the field more accessible and inviting to those who wish to contribute.

Although written independently, the volume's chapters enter into a natural dialogue with each other over the state of the field and its future. One point about which all of our contributors seem to agree is that high on the agenda for the next stage of Diatessaronic research is analysis of the sequence of various supposed witnesses. Schmid himself ended his 2013 essay on the *status quaestionis* by highlighting "the issue of harmony sequence, which has the potential to produce new insights into harmonies as gospel narratives."[8] In his contribution to the present volume he points out that an examination of "sequence" can be pursued in two ways, either at the level of macrostructure, that is, the order of pericopes one after another, or at the level of microstructure, that is, the arrangement of words from various Gospels in a conflated version of a single pericope. Schmid is not alone in proposing a turn toward sequence. In his 2003 article defending the Diatessaronic status of the Dura parchment, Jan Joosten made his argument primarily based upon the microlevel sequence of elements from various Gospels within a single pericope across several witnesses in the western and eastern tradition,[9] while Ian Mills, in his chapter for the present volume, uses the same microlevel sequential evidence, with added macrolevel data, to argue *against* Dura's Diatessaronic status.

Whether or not the Dura parchment is indeed Diatessaronic—no doubt the debate is not over—Joosten's and Mills's textual analysis of the fragment in terms of the micro- and macrolevel sequence is a model of how future research might proceed. One specific task in this line of inquiry, heralded by the present volume, is the comparison of intra-pericope sequence for other episodes in Fuldensis and the Arabic tradition. Mills is skeptical that Fuldensis can offer much of Tatian's original sequence on the intra-pericope level in light of its heavy vulgatization. Schmid contends that Fuldensis is the sole parent of the entire western Diatessaronic tradition. The combined inference of these two claims is that there is no recoverable intra-pericope Tatianic sequence in any of the western witnesses. If true, this is a major blow to efforts to reconstruct Tatian's text. It is imperative, then, that the field moves next to a systematic comparison of pericopes in Fuldensis and the Arabic version, in order to test these hypotheses.

Evidence suggests that the macrolevel sequence of one pericope after another is likely to be more stable than the microlevel sequence of one word after another, since in the transmission of harmonies it takes a minor editorial intervention to rearrange the words within an episode but a major intervention to relocate an entire episode somewhere else in the narrative sequence. Analysis of macrolevel sequence may therefore hold the key to unlocking a number of genealogical relationships between supposed Diatessaronic witnesses. Both Schmid and Watson engage in such macrolevel analysis, but come to provocatively different conclusions on which sequence is likely to be more original for the same pericope (the Wedding at Cana)—the Arabic (so Schmid) or the Latin (so Watson). Their two chapters thus simultaneously provide models for this kind of analysis and demonstrate the need for additional research at the macrolevel. The method holds tremendous promise for unraveling the mysterious relationship between the eastern and western branches of the Diatessaron.[10]

---

[8] Schmid, "The Diatessaron of Tatian," 138.
[9] Jan Joosten, "The Dura Parchment and the Diatessaron," *VC* 57 (2003): 159–75.
[10] A helpful place to begin in this regard would be L. Leloir's early study of several Diatessaronic sequences, based on the order of Ephrem's citations, which first appeared in his article "Le Diatessaron de Tatien," *OrSyr* 1 (1956): 208–31, and was then reproduced in his *Le témoignage*

If it were possible to reconstruct Tatian's sequence with a sufficient degree of plausibility, it would finally be possible to speculate about Tatian's own editorial techniques and strategies. Baarda's contribution to this volume represents just such an approach. One fact about which there is no disagreement is that Tatian began his work with the opening section of the Johannine prologue, a feature that Baarda interprets as indicating his desire to appeal to a philosophically minded audience. Likewise, elsewhere in the volume Joosten, Perrin, and Barker each attempt in part to reach behind Tatian's Gospel in order to deduce some of Tatian's motivation and intent.

This point raises the question of Tatian's second-century context and how his composition fits into the larger history of the writing and reception of gospel literature in early Christianity. These issues have wide relevance for scholars studying other areas of early Christianity, which is no doubt why Burkitt considered the "main question about the Diatessaron" to be whether it was a new Gospel or the first attempt to translate the four. Wrapped up in this debate is the question of what sources Tatian used for his composition. As already noted, there is direct disagreement in this volume between the chapters of Hill and Joosten, with the former arguing against the presence of any material from beyond the four "canonical" Gospels and the latter continuing to hold to Tatian's use of at least one "extracanonical" Gospel source. Either conclusion has broader implications for the history of early Christian gospel literature. Perhaps, here the macrolevel approach to sequence introduced above can contribute a useful perspective. None of the surviving Diatessaronic witnesses contains an entire pericope derived from a source other than the canonical four. Presuming that the macrolevel content of these witnesses is generally intact (an assumption that could be debated), this state of affairs suggests that even if Tatian availed himself of other sources they did not play the same role as the Gospels we know as Matthew, Mark, Luke, and John.

The next question to answer is whether the mid-second-century editions of these four Gospels to which Tatian had access differed in any way from the editions that have come down to us in the earliest extant manuscripts. This long-standing query forms the basis for the Diatessaron's historically influentially role in the textual criticism of the Gospels. Undergirding such a pursuit is the unstated premise that Tatian strove always to maintain the text of his sources with perfect fidelity, an assumption that Watson's chapter calls into question with his classification of Tatian's work as a Gospel outright, not merely a harmony. Zola brings the issue to its logical end in his concluding chapter: until we understand better the nature of Tatian's Gospel and the relationship between its surviving witnesses, the Diatessaron does not belong in the apparatus of the Greek New Testament.

This point brings us to the heart of the matter. What exactly was Tatian trying to do? Who did he imagine his readers would be? What ambitions did he have for his project vis-à-vis his (at minimum) four sources? If he did allow himself some editorial license

---

d'Éphrem sur le Diatessaron (Louvain: Secrétariat du CorpusSCO, 1962), 1–11. One should also not forget that the western and eastern traditions, with all their differences, might in fact both go back to Tatian. If he originally composed his work in Greek and then translated it into Syriac himself, he could certainly have made further editorial changes in the process of translating it, essentially producing not just a strict translation but a revised second edition.

to modify his sources, how often did he exploit this authorial freedom (a task for which he surely was well equipped in light of his evident rhetorical training)? How one answers these questions depends partly upon where one imagines Tatian composing his work. Burkitt (like Petersen after him) posited that Tatian's work came into existence in the east as an aid to his own missionary efforts among Syriac speakers. However, two chapters in our volume take a different approach and shed light on the question by considering Tatian's context in Rome. Perrin draws inferences about Tatian's access to and use of gospel literature on the basis of Justin's precedent, since Tatian's attachment to Justin's school in Rome is one of the few firm facts we know about his life. Barker draws conclusions about Tatian's ambitions in light of the "competitive textualization" evident in book culture of the Greco-Roman world. Just as Plutarch wrote his *Cato the Younger* with no expectation of displacing the other eight lives of Cato already in circulation, so Tatian would have expected his Greco-Roman audience to continue reading his sources alongside his composite work. Both contributors agree that Tatian had no intent of supplanting the four.

These attempts are surely on the right track in their assumption that Tatian's work should be viewed in light of the world he inhabited. Yet one of the few other undisputed historical details about Tatian is that he hailed from the east and likely returned there sometime after Justin's martyrdom. If he composed his work while active in the east, he might have had access to different versions of the Gospels (so Joosten in the current volume), and could have been operating with different cultural expectations about how books circulated and competed with one another. In other words, while Tatian's hybrid identity as both an "Assyrian" and a "Greek" make him a fascinating historical figure, it also complicates the scholarly task by presenting two possible contexts for the composition and circulation of his Gospel. In the end, choosing between them may not be necessary, since it may be the case that they each provide some explanation of the circumstances surrounding the origin and dissemination of his work.[11]

Nevertheless, it is a remarkable coincidence (or is it?) that Tatian, at least for a time, inhabited the same city in which occurred the other famous second-century attempt to redact an existing Gospel into a more suitable form, namely the Gospel that Marcion composed only a few decades prior to the Diatessaron. The analogy between Marcion and Tatian is intriguing, though it is hard to know how far to press it, since the evidence for the Gospels they each produced is so patchy. What we can say is that they both witness to a time when Christians in the imperial capital felt free to apply their editorial skills to existing gospel literature in order to modify and improve upon it. Yet that time did not last long, for only a decade or so after Tatian, Irenaeus made his similarly famous declaration that the Gospels are no more and no fewer in number than four.

To return then to Burkitt's question that we posed at the outset of this introduction, was Tatian's Diatessaron a "new Gospel" or "the first of the versions"? Maybe what is

---

[11] E.g., the fact that later Syriac Christians used his Gospel as their primary text could have been a mere accident of history, with Tatian's version attaining dominance by default in the absence of a Syriac translation of the separated Gospels. In other words, whatever Tatian imagined his readers doing with his text in Rome, something altogether different might have happened back east.

most significant about the Diatessaron is precisely the fact that it can be interpreted as either. Both chronologically and conceptually, Tatian's Diatessaron lies somewhere between Marcion's one authoritatively edited Gospel and Irenaeus's exclusively authoritative fourfold gospel, which might suggest that the dichotomy presumed in Burkitt's question is alien to the transitional stage that Tatian occupied in the history of gospel writing and reception. In other words, his Gospel may testify to a fleeting moment in the second-century reception of the Jesus tradition when all four Gospels were viewed as being indispensable but not yet irreducible. In that liminal space, Tatian composed his "one Gospel through four," a Diatessaron that would reverberate throughout the Christian world for the next two millennia.

Part One

The Sources of Tatian's Gospel

1

The Diatessaron and Its Beginning

A Twofold Statement of Tatian

Tjitze Baarda

Abstract

This chapter explores the opening line of Tatian's Diatessaron, focusing on the eastern tradition. There is ample evidence that Tatian began his Gospel with the words of John 1:1: "In the beginning was the Word." The witnesses are reviewed alongside Tatian's context, and two reasons are proposed for Tatian's choice. The first reason was to demonstrate to pagan critics of Christianity that here was a complete "Life of Jesus" that not only removed the discrepancies between the Gospels but also one that embedded itself in a philosophical texture (the Logos) as its fundamental starting point. The second reason was to exhort his fellow Christians to embrace the Gospel of John alongside the other three, at a time when not all circles accepted the Fourth Gospel and there was a multiplicity of other Gospels circulating. By beginning with John 1:1, Tatian is making a twofold (philosophical and theological) statement. The chapter ends with an addendum on the evidence for the opening of the Diatessaron in the western tradition.

1. The Beginning of the Gospel of Our Lord

While studying the Armenian translation of Aphrahat's *Demonstrations*, I was struck again by the following interesting quotation in *Demonstration* 1.10[1]:

> as it is also written in the beginning of *the Gospel of our Lord*:
> "*From* the beginning was the Word" (ի սկզբանէ էր բանն).

---

[1] G. Lafontaine, *La version Arménienne des oeuvres d'Aphraate le Syrien, I* (Louvain: CSCO, 1977), 9.

The preposition "from" is a particularity of the Armenian translator or perhaps of the scribe of one of the two extant Armenian manuscripts,[2] because we know that the original Syriac text[3] reads here, in agreement with the Greek text ('Ἐν ἀρχῇ ἦν ὁ λόγος): ܪܫܝܬ ܒܣܒܪܬܗ ܕܡܪܢ: ܒܪܫܝܬ ܐܝܬܘܗܝ ܗܘܐ ܡܠܬܐ, "in the beginning of the Gospel of our Savior: '*In* the beginning was the Word.'" One might ask what the author meant with this "Gospel of our Savior." Elsewhere Aphrahat quotes other sayings of Jesus from "His Gospel" (ܣܒܪܬܗ).[4] He even suggests several times that Jesus himself *wrote* (ܟܬܒ) the words of *that* Gospel.[5]

This reminds us of a similar idea held by those who revered the "Gospel of Marcion" as the *only* true Gospel, *which Christ had written*. A certain Megethius, who is portrayed as a follower of Marcion's doctrines, declared that there are not *four* true Gospels, but only *one* (ἕν ἐστι τὸ εὐαγγέλιον). When he was asked, "Who wrote that Gospel which you claim to be one (ὃ ἔφης εἶναι ἕν)," his answer was clear: Ὁ Χριστός![6] This Gospel was, as has been proven, more or less a creation of Marcion himself. From reconstructions of its text[7] it becomes clear that it was mainly a specific edition and adaptation of Luke's Gospel.

"The Gospel" to which Aphrahat refers here was most probably not the Gospel of John, but the *Diatessaron* of Tatian,[8] a harmony in which the four Gospels were combined. In circles in which Aphrahat was living in the fourth century it was apparently not strange to speak of the Diatessaron of Tatian as a Gospel of which Christ himself was the *auctor primarius,* just as the Marcionites did with the Gospel that Marcion had created.

2. The Diatessaron of Tatian

Eusebius, in his *History of the Church*,[9] tells us about this harmony: ὁ μέντοι γε πρότερος αὐτῶν ἀρχηγὸς ὁ Τατιανὸς συνάφειάν τινα καὶ συναγωγὴν οὐκ οἶδ' ὅπως τῶν εὐαγγελίων συνθείς, τὸ διὰ τεσσάρων τοῦτο προσωνόμασεν ὃ καὶ παρά τισιν εἰσέτι νῦν φέρεται, that is, "Their first leader[10] then, Tatian, composed—I do not know how—a

---

[2] See §4 (cf. also T. Baarda, *The Gospel Quotations of Aphrahat the Persian Sage*, 2 vols. [Meppel: Krips Repro, 1975] 55–9).

[3] J. Parisot, *Aphraatis Sapientis Persae Demonstrationes*, PS 1 (Paris: Firmin-Didot, 1894), 22 (*Dem.* 1.1).

[4] Parisot, *Demonstrationes*, 14.31 (1:653); 20.11 (1:909); 22.18 (1:1028). The number in parentheses is the volume and page number in Parisot.

[5] Parisot, *Demonstrationes*, 4.10 (1:160); 8.3 (1:365); 14.9 (1:591); 21.1 (1:932); 23.1 (2:4); 23.53 (2:101).

[6] Cf. W. H. van de Sande Bakhuyzen, *Der Dialog des Adamantius* (Leipzig: Hinrichs, 1901), 16.

[7] E.g., in A. von Harnack, *Marcion: Das Evangelium vom fremden Gott*, 2nd ed. (Leipzig: Hinrichs, 1924). [Editors' note: most recently, see Dieter T. Roth, *The Text of Marcion's Gospel*, NTTSD 49 (Leiden: Brill, 2015).]

[8] See, among others, Baarda, *Gospel Quotations*, 1:55–9; M.-J. Pierre, *Aphraate le Sage Persan: Les Exposés*, SC 349 (Paris: Les Éditions du Cerf, 1988), 1:139–42; A. Lehto, *The Demonstrations of Aphrahat, the Persian Sage* (New York: Piscataway, 2010), 75n. 46.

[9] Eusebius, *Hist. eccl.* 4.29.6, in the edition of E. Schwartz and T. Mommsen, *Eusebius Werke 2: Die Kirchengeschichte* (Leipzig: Hinrichs, 1903), 1:392.

[10] Eusebius suggests here that Tatian belonged to the first chiefs of what he sees as the Encratite heresy.

sort of a combination and assemblage of the Gospels and gave it the title Diatessaron, (a work) that is still circulating among some."[11] This is the first mentioning of this "harmony" that we know of. One has the impression that Eusebius did not himself have a clear knowledge of its text, but he seems only have heard about it. When the Greek text of Eusebius's work was translated into Syriac we read a remarkably different text: "But he, this Tatianos, their first chief, collected and combined and composed *a Gospel* (ܐܘܢܓܠܝܘܢ) and called it *Diatessaron*, that is [that] of the Mixed (ܗܘ ܕܡܚܠܛܐ), which is in the possession of *many* up to this day."[12] The first difference between the Syriac and its Greek model is that "of the Mixed" is not a literal rendering of Diatessaron; the translator was apparently used to the custom of his time (fourth century) to distinguish between a "Gospel of the Mixed" (ܐܘܢܓܠܝܘܢ ܕܡܚܠܛܐ) and a "Gospel of the Separated" (ܐܘܢܓܠܝܘܢ ܕܡܦܪܫܐ), that is, a collection of the separate Gospels. The second difference might be that he interpreted the Greek "among *some*" as "among *many*,"[13] which might imply that he lived in a Syrian region in which the Diatessaron was not a rare gospel text. It reminds us of the statement of Theodoret of Cyrrhus that he had found more than two hundred copies in his own diocese.[14]

The name "Diatessaron" was apparently well-known in Syria.[15] In contrast with the "Gospel of the Separated"—that is, the Gospel in which Matt-Mark-Luke-John were separate—the Diatessaron could be identified as the "Gospel of the Mixed."[16] Its usual name was, however, merely "the Gospel," as we can deduct from the treatises of Aphrahat.[17]

3. The Beginning of the Diatessaron Gospel, John 1:1

The observation of Aphrahat that the opening sentence of the Diatessaron was "In the beginning was the Word" was not something that was new for scholars when

---

[11] The phrase παρά τισιν is interpreted differently: e.g., "in some quarters" (J. R. Harris, *The Diatessaron of Tatian, A Preliminary Study* [London: C. J. Clay and Sons, 1890], 10); "in the hands of some [or: many]" (W. L. Petersen, *Tatian's Diatessaron: Its Creation, Dissemination, Significance, and History in Scholarship* [Leiden: Brill, 1994], 36).

[12] Petersen, *Tatian's Diatessaron*, 36.

[13] Technically speaking παρά τισιν could be interpreted as "with or in the possession of several persons." In Rufinus's translation (cf. Petersen, *Tatian's Diatessaron*, 57) we read *qui etiam nunc habetur a multis*, which might suggest that this interpretation was not unusual, unless Rufinus knew that there were also several Greek or perhaps Latin harmonies around.

[14] See *Haer. fab.* 1.20: εὗρον δὲ κἀγὼ πλείους ἢ διακοσίας βίβλους τοιαύτας ἐν ταῖς παρ' ἡμῖν ἐκκλησίαις τετιμημένας.

[15] For the name, see Petersen, *Tatian's Diatessaron*, 42 (Rabbula), 51 (Theodorus bar Koni), 52–3 (Isho'dad), 53–4 (Isho' bar Ali), 54–5 (Bar Bahlul), 55–6 (Bar Kepha), 57–8 (Chronicle of Se'ert), 59–61 (Dionysius bar Ṣalibi), 61 (Michael the Syrian), 62–4 (Bar Hebraeus), 64–5 ('Abd Iso'), 65 (Mari ibn Sulaiman).

[16] Cf. Petersen, *Tatian's Diatessaron*, 52–3 (Isho'dad), 53–4 (Isho' bar Ali), 59–61 (Dionysius bar Ṣalibi), 61 (Michael the Syrian), 62–4 (Bar Hebraeus).

[17] "The Gospel of Christ" (*Dem.* 1.8, col. 20:7), "the Gospel of our Savior" (*Dem.* 1.10, col. 21:18), "the Gospel of our Redeemer" (*Dem.* 6.1, col. 244:7), "His Gospel" (*Dem.* 14.31, col. 653:4; *Dem.* 20.11, col. 909:25; *Dem.* 22.18, col. 1028:7). It is possible that Paul's reference to *the Gospel* (e.g., "I have preached the Gospel of the Messiah free of charge" in 2 Cor 11:7; cf. 1 Cor 9:18) may have been of influence (cf. *Dem.* 23.9, Vol. II. col. 25:14-16). [Editors' note: the column references are to Parisot's edition; see n. 3.]

his treatises were printed. For it was already known through an observation of the medieval author Dionysius bar Ṣalibi. In his commentary bar Ṣalibi wrote about the Diatessaron: ܪܫܝܬܐ ܗܘܐ ܐܝܬܘܗܝ ܕܝܢ ܒܪܫܝܬ ܗܘܐ ܐܝܬܘܗܝ ܡܠܬܐ, "Its beginning, then, was: 'In the beginning was the Word.'"[18] It was repeated in the great commentary of the famous Bar Hebraeus who wrote ܪܫܝܬܐ ܗܘܐ ܐܝܬܘܗܝ ܒܪܫܝܬ ܡܠܬܐ, "Its beginning: 'In the beginning was the Word.'"[19]

The discovery of an Armenian version of the gospel commentary of Mar Ephrem the Syrian, who lived also in the fourth century, led to the first edition published by the Mechitarists of Venice in 1836. It remained unnoticed among theologians until Aucher's Latin translation was published by G. Moesinger in 1876.[20] It was this work that served as a source for the reconstruction of the Diatessaron by that great German scholar Theodor Zahn.[21] In Zahn's reconstruction the first section comprises John 1:1-5, and the beginning of the Diatessaron is therefore *In principio erat verbum*,[22] just as was reported by Aphrahat and later Syrian authors.

Not long after Zahn's reconstruction of the Diatessaron a new discovery was made, which gave another proof of this beginning of the harmony, the publication of the *Arabic* translation of the Diatessaron of Tatian by a renowned Vatican orientalist, Augusto Ciasca.[23] It was in this late Arabic version of the Syriac Diatessaron that—just as in Ephrem's *Commentary*—its first section contained John 1:1-5, and so the beginning of this harmony presents us with the words في البدء كان الكلمة, "in the beginning was the Word."

In 1951, a Persian Harmony[24] was published which, though not being a direct off-spring of the Syriac Diatessaron, may have preserved many elements of the Diatessaronic tradition. It also opens (in agreement with these witnesses to the Diatessaron) with the text of John 1:1-5 (beginning with در اغاز کلمه بود, "In the beginning the Word was"), but here it is preceded by sort of a heading that refers to Mark 1:1: "Beginning of the Gospel of Jesus Christ, Son of God."[25]

---

[18] Petersen, *Tatian's Diatessaron*, 59. This text was already known to the scholarly world since the eighteenth century.

[19] Petersen, *Tatian's Diatessaron*, 63.

[20] J. B. Aucher and G. Moesinger, *Evangelii concordantis expositio facta a Sancto Ephraemo Doctore Syro* (Venice: Mechitarist Monastery of S. Lazzaro, 1876). The Armenian text (with Latin translation) was published by a magnificent scholar, L. Leloir, *Saint Éphrem: Commentaire de l'Évangile concordant, version arménienne* (Leuven: Imprimerie Orientaliste L. Durbecq, 1953); his Latin translation appeared in 1954.

[21] Theodor Zahn, *Tatian's Diatessaron*, FGNK 1 (Erlangen: Andreas Deichert, 1881).

[22] Zahn, *Tatian's Diatessaron*, 113. Zahn refers both to Aphrahat and Ephrem, moreover to Dionysius bar Ṣalibi.

[23] A. Ciasca, *Tatiani Evangeliorum harmoniae arabice* (Rome: Typographia Polyglotta, 1888); in 1883 Ciasca published already an article on the text and its importance (apparently prompted by the reconstruction of Zahn in 1881).

[24] G. Messina, *Diatessaron Persiano*, BibOr 14 (Rome: Pontifical Biblical Institute, 1951); cf. Petersen, *Tatian's Diatessaron*, 259–63.

[25] See the references of Dionysius and Bar Hebraeus, "Its beginning: 'In the beginning.'" Could that be a reminiscence of a rubric title before the first words of the Diatessaron (i.e., Mark 1:1 or part of it)? [Editors' note: scribal prefaces to both recensions of the Arabic Diatessaron (B-E-O and A) include preambles that also refer to Mark 1:1 in similar language. For the text, see the English translation of Hope W. Hogg, "The Diatessaron of Tatian," in *The Ante-Nicene Fathers*, vol. 9, ed. Alan Menzies (New York: Charles Scribner's Sons, 1896), 42.]

Two later discoveries brought to the scholarly world the greater part of the *Syriac* text of Ephrem's *Commentary on the Diatessaron*.[26] It is clear from the comparison of what is left of chapter one that the Syriac text had the same beginning as the Armenian version, namely John 1:1: ܒܪܫܝܬ ܐܝܬܘܗܝ ܗܘܐ ܡܠܬܐ, "In the beginning was the Word." The Syriac text is here in agreement with MS B of the Armenian which reads һ uկզբանն, "*In* the beginning"; this differs from the reading in MS A that was adopted in the editions.[27] One might consider the possibility that MS B has, indeed, preserved the original reading.

4. The Author of the Diatessaron

Tatian[28] was "born in the land of the Assyrians" (γεννηθεὶς μὲν ἐν τῇ τῶν Ἀσσυρίων γῇ),[29] which is a rather vague indication, for it could refer to the eastern part of present Turkey and the regions of present Syria and beyond, most likely in an area where Syriac was the vernacular language. However, as someone of "good birth" (τὴν εὐγένειαν οὐ σεμνύνομαι, *Or. Graec.* 11.1) he had enjoyed a "Greek" education (παιδευθεὶς πρῶτον τὰ ὑμέτερα, *Or. Graec.* 42.1; cf. 35.1). His own works, of which only the Λόγος πρὸς Ἕλληνας has been preserved, were apparently written in Greek.[30] And, in my view, the "Diatessaron" that was reckoned as one of his great achievements was also composed in Greek, most likely during the time when he taught in the school of Rome after his teacher Justin died.

Before Tatian was challenged to create this harmony of the Gospels he first had traveled a lot through the world (πολλὴν δὲ ἐπιφοιτήσας γῆν, *Or. Graec.* 35.1); he tells us also that he had been initiated in religious practices and mysteries (μυστηρίων μεταλαβὼν κτλ., *Or. Graec.* 29.1) before and/or after he came to Rome. Rome, like Alexandria, attracted many orientals either for study or for employment.[31]

When Tatian was still seeking for what was really worth attention (περινοοῦντι δέ μοι τὰ σπουδαῖα, *Or. Graec.* 29.2), it happened that he became acquainted with what

---

[26] L. Leloir, *Saint Éphrem: Commentaire de l'Évangile concordant, texte syriaque (MS Chester Beatty 709)*, CBM 8 (Dublin: Hodges Figgis, 1963); *Saint Éphrem: Commentaire de l'Évangile concordant, texte syriaque (MS Chester Beatty 709): Folios additionnels*, CBM 8(b) (Leuven: Peeters, 1990). The text of John 1:1 in the edition of 1963 appears at ch. 1.3, page 3 (line 11); ch. 1.4, page 4 (lines 3, 10); ch. 1.5, page 4 (lines 14–15).

[27] MS A reads һ uկզբանէ էր բանն, "*From* the beginning was the Word." L. Leloir, *Saint Éphrem: Commentaire, version arménienne*, ch. 1.2, p. 2 (line 26); ch. 1.3, p. 3 (line 18); ch. 1.4, p. 4 (line 8); ch. 1.5, p. 4 (lines 20, 23). Leloir follows the choice of Aucher(-Moesinger) in following the text of MS A, which agrees with the Armenian Vulgate of John 1:1. In the Armenian Vulgate, the words һ uկզբանէ also render ἀπ' ἀρχῆς in Luke 1:2.

[28] Cf. William L. Petersen, "Tatian the Assyrian," in *A Companion to Second-Century Christian "Heretics,"* ed. A. Marjanen and P. Luomanen, VCSup 67 (Leiden: Brill, 2005), 125–58; repr. in *Patristic and Text-Critical Studies: The Collected Essays of William L. Petersen*, ed. J. Krans and J. Verheyden (Leiden: Brill, 2012), 437–69.

[29] J. Trelenberg, *Tatianos, Oratio ad Graecos* (Tübingen: Mohr Siebeck, 2012), 1; cf. Petersen, *Tatian's Diatessaron*, 68.

[30] For his other works see Trelenberg, *Oratio*, 3–4.

[31] Cf. e.g., Franz Cumont, *Oriental Religions in Roman Paganism* (Chicago, IL: The Open Court Publishing Company, 1911), 1–19 ("Rome and the Orient").

he calls "some barbaric writings" (συνέβη γραφαῖς τισιν ἐντυχεῖν βαρβαρικαῖς, ibid.) that impressed him because of their antiquity.[32] He converted then to Christianity (*Or. Graec.* 29.2-3), and either already was or soon became a student of Justin whom he greatly admired (ὁ θαυμασιώτατος Ἰουστῖνος, *Or. Graec.* 18.6). There is reason to assume that in this Roman school the goal was to defend the new *philosophy*—Christianity—against the attacks from the side of Jewish and pagan authors. His teacher Justin, for example, engaged himself in a debate with a Jewish scholar (*Dialogue with Trypho*) and also defended his new faith against the authorities (his so-called *First Apology* and *Second Apology*).[33]

5. Christian Groups in Rome in the Second Century

When Tatian arrived in Rome—that is, in the fifties or sixties of the second century—Christianity seems to have acquired a relatively strong position in the city. Christian faith was only one of the foreign cults of the Orient that had invaded Rome,[34] but it was perhaps the most contested among them. Rulers of the Roman Empire were confronted with the question whether Christians should be tolerated or not. Besides some political actions of the government against Christians[35] there was especially a strong opposition of philosophers. One of them was a certain Crescens, a philosopher who had threatened Tatian's teacher Justin—"who proclaimed the truth"—with death.[36] Justin had opposed this Cynic philosopher who had labeled the Christians as pure atheists and impious people.[37] It was perhaps this Crescens who was accessory to the martyrdom of Justin.[38]

Christianity in Rome, in the second century, was not an "orthodox" unity under the bishop of Rome, but it was strongly divided into groups with different views concerning specific theological issues. Celsus, who lived and worked in Rome in the same period as Tatian, was aware of tensions between the various dissenting parties in Christianity. Once he speaks of the great church (μεγάλη ἐκκλησία),[39] but then he also mentions the diversity among the Christian believers, of which some are labeled

---

[32] It seems that he speaks here of the Old Testament, because he lays stress on their antiquity ("older than the Greek doctrines") and on the fact that these books present a good understanding of the creation, show insight in future things, and offer instructions.

[33] I still use the edition of J. K. Th. von Otto, *Ivstini Philosophi et Martyris Opera*, 4 vols. (Jena: Dufft, 1876–81).

[34] See Cumont, *Oriental Religions,* for examples.

[35] See, e.g., H. D. Stöver, *Christenverfolgung im Römischen Reich* (Düsseldorf/Vienna: Antiquariat Walter Nowak, 1984), 102–15, for the period of the emperor Marcus Aurelius.

[36] Tatian, *Or. Graec.* 19.2 (…ὡς καὶ Ἰουστῖνον τῷ θανάτῳ περιβαλεῖν πραγματεύεσθαι).

[37] Justin, *2 Apol.* 3.

[38] It was Eusebius (*Hist. eccl.* 4.16) who seems to suggest that Crescens had actually been involved in the martyrdom of Justin (cf. Jerome, *Vir. ill.* 23).

[39] See M. Borret, *Origène: Contre Celse, Tome III: Livres V-VI,* SC 147 (Paris: Les Éditions du Cerf, 1969), 160 (5.59); *1 Clement* (of Rome; ca. 97 CE) opens with the phrase: Ἡ ἐκκλησία τοῦ θεοῦ ἡ παροικοῦσα Ῥώμην . . . , which seems to imply a certain authority, the more so because the letter is directed to the church in Corinth to strengthen the believers there and to address some of the difficulties in that church.

as supporters of Valentinus[40]—who was active in Rome when Tatian lived there[41]—and also the followers of Marcion and Apelles, whom Origen tells us that Celsus mentions by name.[42]

6. The Beginning of Gospel Writing

In the earliest decades of our Christian history there was no need of a written history of Jesus, for the believers lived with the oral stories of the eyewitnesses and their successors.[43] The "Scriptures" (i.e., our Old Testament) were their only holy book, which testified about Jesus and proved that he was the one chosen by God to redeem humanity. Further, they lived with the traditions that started with the eyewitnesses (οἱ ἀπ' ἀρχῆς αὐτόπται, Luke 1:2) "of the events that happened among us," until the need for a written documentation was felt by believers, which led some of them to put the early traditions in writing. However, not everyone was waiting for written documents about Jesus—his life and his teaching—as we can conclude from a remark of Papias (ca. 110 CE) that the information about Jesus and his preaching in books was not so profitable as what was preserved in a living tradition.[44] Although we know that Papias was acquainted with at least the Gospels of Mark and Matthew—which he could certainly appreciate—he himself preferred to collect what he could hear from "the Elders," and to comment on these oral traditions in a five-volume opus.[45] The fact that he himself favored the oral traditions did not hinder him from writing an opus magnum about the words of Jesus and their meaning. One might ask whether his work implicitly contains a criticism of earlier attempts at collecting the words and deeds of Jesus.[46] If the πολλοί of which Luke spoke (1:1) is not an exaggeration,

---

[40] So Origen (Borret, *Origène: Contre Celse, Tome III*, 166 (5.61): οἶμαι δ' αὐτὸν λέγειν τοὺς ἀπὸ Οὐαλεντίνου.

[41] So Irenaeus, *Haer*. 3.4.3: Οὐαλεντῖνος μὲν γὰρ ἦλθεν εἰς Ῥώμην ἐπὶ Ὑγίνου· ἤκμασε δὲ ἐπὶ Πίου καὶ παρέμεινεν ἕως Ἀνικήτου. According to Epiphanius, Valentinus was still seen as an orthodox believer in Rome, but no longer when he was at Cyprus (*Pan*. 31.7.1-2). For the presence of Valentinians in Rome, cf. P. Lampe, *Die Stadtrömischen Christen in den ersten beiden Jahrhunderten*, WUNT 2/18 (Tübingen: Mohr Siebeck, 1982), 251-68.

[42] See Borret, *Origène: Contre Celse, Tome III*, 168 (5.62): Ἐμνήσθη δ' ὁ Κέλσος καὶ Μαρκιωνιστῶν, προϊσταμένων Μαρκίωνα.

[43] Cf. T. Baarda, *VIER=EEN, Enkele bladzijden uit de geschiedenis van de harmonistiek der Evangeliën* (Kampen: J. H. Kok, 1969) and T. Baarda, "ΔΙΑΦΩΝΙΑ—ΣΥΜΦΩΝΙΑ: Factors in the Harmonization of the Gospels, Especially in the Diatessaron of Tatian," in *Gospel Traditions in the Second Century*, ed. William L. Petersen (Notre Dame: University of Notre Dame Press, 1989), 133-54. The latter study was reprinted in T. Baarda, *Essays on the Diatessaron*, CBET 11 (Kampen: Kok Pharos, 1994), 29-47. The page numbers from the reprint volume will be used in the current chapter. In these studies one will find references to the sources that I consulted.

[44] The full line is, οὐ γὰρ τὰ ἐκ τῶν βιβλίων τοσοῦτόν με ὠφελεῖν ὑπελάμβανον, ὅσον τὰ παρὰ ζώσης φωνῆς καὶ μενούσης. For the whole text of Papias, see Michael W. Holmes, *The Apostolic Fathers: Greek Texts and English Translations*, 3rd ed. (Grand Rapids: Baker, 2007), 734.

[45] Holmes, *The Apostolic Fathers*, 732: Τοῦ δὲ Παπία συγγράμματα πέντε τὸν ἀριθμὸν φέρεται, ἃ καὶ ἐπιγέγραπται λογίων κυριακῶν ἐξηγήσεως....

[46] One might think of such mild criticism as found in Luke's foreword (Luke 1:1-4). It is tempting to ask whether Papias's working method was inspired by this Lukan preface. In that case he did not only know the Gospels of Mark and Matthew, but also that of Luke.

one might consider the possibility that there were in the time of Papias several more books about the words and activity of Jesus around, which necessitated him to make a fresh compendium of traditions that he had acquired through the traditions of those who lived in the time when the first-hand memories were still alive. The loss of this voluminous work of Papias is one of the many unfortunate casualties that happened to books in ancient times, and it makes us aware that our reconstruction of antiquity is always a limited one.

7. The Problem of the Various Gospels in the Second Century

The existence of several Gospels beside one another could easily create a problem for some believers, especially when they were puzzled by the differences between these Gospels. If we think of second-century Rome, we meet first with Marcion[47]: he did not accept our *four* Gospels,[48] but chose only *one*, most likely because his favorite apostle, Paul, spoke of τὸ εὐαγγέλιον in the singular form.[49] It is assumed by some that he chose the Gospel of Luke, although he revised it by cleansing it from its Jewish elements. He may have preferred this Gospel, because Luke was a fellow traveler of his favorite apostle, Paul. Or was it because Luke had shown himself a real historian in his prologue (1:1-4)? Marcion created a Gospel with an anti-Jewish tendency, but there were also Jewish Gospels in the second century, such as the one according to the Hebrews, then the *Gospel of the Nazarenes*, and the *Gospel of the Ebionites*. Then there were other Gospels around, such as the *Gospel of the Egyptians* and the *Gospel of Peter*.[50] We do not know whether all of these Gospels were around in Rome in the first half of the second century.

The plurality of the Gospels became a real problem for some Christian groups. The Marcionites (who of course accepted Marcion's edition of Luke) laid emphasis on the incongruity of the Gospels (διαφωνοῦσι τὰ εὐαγγέλια) and their mutual divergencies (ἀντικεῖνται).[51] But also for "orthodox" believers it was not easy to deal with that problem. The erudite Origen has aptly expressed this problem: "if the διαφωνία cannot be solved, one has to give up one's [historical] trust with respect to the Gospels, since [if one would take them literally] they would not be true and not written by a more divine spirit, or would be just casual memorabilia"; and further,

---

[47] Harnack, *Marcion*, 35–73.
[48] The Marcionites held the conviction that the apostles did not write (ἐκήρυξαν ἀγράφως, cf. Harnack, *Marcion*, 40), a conviction that excluded the Gospel of Matthew and the Gospel of John.
[49] E.g., Rom. 1:1; Baarda, *VIER=EEN*, 11.
[50] See for the various gospels, J. K. Elliott, *The Apocryphal New Testament* (Oxford: Oxford University Press, 1993), 3–46.
[51] Van de Sande Bakhuyzen, *Der Dialog*, 14 (*Dial*. 1.7); cf. O. Cullmann, "Die Pluralität der Evangelien als theologisches Problem im Altertum (1945)," in *Vorträge und Aufsätze 1925–1962*, ed. K. Fröhlich (Tübingen: Mohr Siebeck, 1966), 552ff; Baarda, *VIER=EEN*, 11; ΔΙΑΦΩΝΙΑ—ΣΥΜΦΩΝΙΑ, 31–3.

if someone carefully studies the Gospels with respect to the ἀσυμφωνία in historical matters, . . . he gets dizzy and will either give up any attempt to establish the truth of [all four] Gospels, and—since he does not dare to fully deny his belief with respect to [the story of] our Lord—will at random choose one of them, or will accept that the truth of these four [Gospels] does not lie in the literal text.

Origen can thus maintain his thesis: τὸ ἀληθῶς διὰ τεσσάρων ἕν ἐστιν εὐαγγέλιον.[52]

Tatian was bothered by this very same problem of disharmony of the Gospels, but he did not seek the solution in allegorization, as Origen did after him. He once addressed the Greeks with the words Πείσθητέ μοι νῦν, ὦ ἄνδρες Ἕλληνες, μηδὲ τοὺς μύθους μηδὲ τοὺς θεοὺς ὑμῶν ἀλληγορήσητε, "O, you Greek men, may you be convinced by me: *you should not allegorize* either your fictions or your gods" (*Or. Graec.* 21.5). Tatian faults Greek historians for their lack of historical accuracy in their myths and stories. He blames the Greeks in the same way as Josephus did for their inaccuracy in historical matters.[53] For Tatian "symphony and harmony" are the hallmarks of truthfulness and reliability. In his pursuit of the truth,[54] he felt that he should create a new Gospel text: the various discrepancies between the Gospels needed the skill of a good historian who could create the true story of Jesus and his preaching.

His Diatessaron is, in fact, an attempt at creating such a *Life of Jesus* out of all the material in the records or memoirs of the apostles (ἀπομνημονεύματα), which were in use in the school of Justin. It is not impossible that this specific method of harmonizing was already applied in Justin's academy; it has, indeed, been suggested that kind of a harmony of Matthew-Mark-Luke had already been developed even before Tatian created his Diatessaron.[55] The newness of the latter's attempt was that he introduced the *Johannine* material in his work.

8. The Gospel of John in the Second Century

It is interesting that Tatian's teacher Justin—by the way, a Palestinian—never quoted from the Gospel of John in his extant works,[56] despite his great interest in the idea of the

---

[52] The Greek text of the three quotations may be found, respectively, in A. E. Brooke, *The Commentary of Origen on St. John's Gospel* (Cambridge: Cambridge University Press, 1896), 1:183 (line 29)–184 (line 1) (*Comm. Jo.* 10.3.2); 1:185 (lines 8–15) (*Comm. Jo.* 10.3.2); and 2:232 (lines 17–18) (from the fragments of *Comm. Jo.* 5.7); see, for literature on these passages, Baarda, ΔΙΑΦΩΝΙΑ—ΣΥΜΦΩΝΙΑ, 32–3. [Editors' note: the English translation here is Baarda's own.]
[53] Cf. Baarda, ΔΙΑΦΩΝΙΑ—ΣΥΜΦΩΝΙΑ, 41.
[54] See *Or. Graec.* 29; and Baarda, ΔΙΑΦΩΝΙΑ—ΣΥΜΦΩΝΙΑ, 39–41.
[55] Cf. William L. Petersen, "Textual Evidence of Tatian's Dependence upon Justin's ΑΠΟΜΝΗΜΟΝΕΥΜΑΤΑ," *NTS* 36 (1990): 512–34; repr. in *Patristic and Text-Critical Studies: The Collected Essays of William L. Petersen*, eds. J. Krans and J. Verheyden (Leiden: Brill, 2012), 130–51.
[56] A. J. Bellinzoni, *The Sayings of Jesus in the Writings of Justin Martyr* (Leiden: Brill, 1967), 140: "Justin's quotations . . . show absolutely no dependence on the Gospel of John." In my view, this does not necessarily mean that he did not know about the existence of this Gospel. W. Bauer, *Rechtgläubigkeit und Ketzerei im ältesten Christentum* (Tübingen: J. C. B. Mohr, 1934), 208–9, formulates it this

"Logos."⁵⁷ It is possible that this Gospel was not yet fully accepted in the Roman church. His pupil Tatian—in his *Oratio ad Graecos*—did hardly quote from any of the other Gospels, but he refers to the beginning verses of John's Gospel three times⁵⁸: θεὸς ἦν ἐν ἀρχῇ, τὴν δὲ ἀρχὴν λόγου δύναμιν παρειλήφαμεν κτλ. (*Or. Graec.* 5.1; cf. John 1:1f.); πάντα ὑπ' αὐτοῦ καὶ χωρὶς αὐτοῦ γέγονεν οὐδὲ ἕν (*Or. Graec.* 19.4; cf. John 1:3); and λόγος μέν ἐστι τὸ τοῦ θεοῦ φῶς (*Or. Graec.* 13.2; cf. John 1:9). Apparently, Tatian did not only know about the existence of this Gospel, but also saw it a source for his theological discourse.

This was perhaps quite new in Rome, where there was a tendency in some circles to reject the Fourth Gospel as heretical and false. Some Christians—who through Epiphanius are known as *Alogi*—even suggested that the author of the Fourth Gospel had bent the truth (ὁ δὲ Ἰωάννης ψεύδεται),⁵⁹ because its emphasis on the Logos was seen as heterodox. It was therefore amazing that both Justin and Tatian in their theology laid much emphasis on the idea of the Logos.

For them Logos was a word that opened up the possibility of claiming that Christianity was not just a sectarian movement but was indeed a meaningful philosophy. Both Justin and Tatian had their education in Greek philosophy and had been initiated in Platonism *and* Stoicism. In the latter ("atheistic") philosophy the Logos was the power through which the material "All" followed a reasonable course in all its cycles of change. Although it was originally thought of as an immanent power, a sort of "reason" that pervades the universe, it was not unusual that in the Stoa of Tatian's time it was identified as a divine power: God being "transcendent and immanent at the same time."⁶⁰ Justin and Tatian seem to have used the term in such a way that God, who was *in* the beginning, preceded the Logos, who in his turn was the beginning of the cosmos. It is very difficult for me—actually beyond my ability—to follow the reasonings of both apologists in their exposition about the relation between the absolute God and the functioning of the Logos, whom Tatian identifies as creator (δημιουργός) in a non-gnostic sense (because it is not an antagonist of God).

One finds here in the school of Justin and later in that of Tatian early attempts to create a theology that should convince the critics in the pagan world by emphasizing the idea of the Logos. In part of the Roman Christian world there was, however, quite a fear that by introducing this theme of the Fourth Gospel one would open up the ideas of Gnosticism that were gradually spread over the world by such eminent leaders as the Alexandrian Valentinus who was then also influencing the believers in Rome. This explains the

---

way: "Das Johannesevangelium hat Justin vielleicht gekannt, doch steht er ihm dann innerlich fremd gegenüber." He shares the Logos idea with John, but "er nimmt seine Beweise nicht aus dem vierten Evangelium. . . . Das Mindeste, was wir sagen müssen, ist dies, daß das Johannesevangelium bei Justin keinen spürbaren Eindruck hinterlassen hat."

[57] E. R. Goodenough, *The Theology of Justin Martyr* (Jena: Walter Beidermann, 1923), 139–75 (under ch. 5, "The Logos"). Justin had probably been influenced by the ideas of the first-century Alexandrian Jewish philosopher Philo, who, like Justin, was in debt to (Neo-)Platonism and Stoic philosophy.

[58] T. Baarda, "John 1:5 in the Oration and Diatessaron of Tatian, Concerning the Reading καταλαμβάνει," *VC* 47 (1993): 210; a fourth quotation appears in *Or. Graec.* 4.1 (John 4:24).

[59] Epiphanius, *Pan.* 51.21.15, in K. Holl, *Epiphanius, Ancoratus und Panarion II: Panarion haer. 34–64*, GCS 31 (Leipzig: Hinrichs, 1922), 2:281; the anti-Johannine mood was also present in the Christian groups known as Anti-Montanists who rejected the claims of the Asian "prophet" Montanus.

[60] Goodenough, *Theology of Justin*, 139.

resistance of the anti-Montanist Gaius and other "Alogi" against the Johannine literature. The Christian believers in Rome were then still divided about whether one should accept the Fourth Gospel as an authentic source of the words and works of Jesus.

9. John 1:1—A Twofold Statement

After this round trip through the world of second-century Christianity in Rome, I must eventually answer the question why I think that the beginning of the Diatessaron with John 1:1 was an important event in early Christian Rome. In my view, there were two reasons for Tatian to place this text up in front.

The *first* reason was to attract the attention of pagan critics to his edition of the "Gospel." His creation of the Life of Jesus not only gave a complete history in which the discrepancies between the Gospels were removed, but from the very start it made clear to the reader that this history of Jesus was embedded in a philosophical texture: the idea of the Logos as a fundamental starting point of a new philosophy—Christianity.

The *second* reason to create this entry for his Gospel was to make a clear statement to his fellow Christians that one should not refuse to accept the Fourth Gospel as an important source of knowledge about Jesus. It is as if he wants to say: "The opening sentence '*In the beginning was the Logos,* and the Logos was with God, and God is the Logos' is not casual, but it offers the key for understanding the whole story of Jesus as presented in the *four* Gospels, now so aptly combined in my Diatessaron." John's Gospel became the frame for the history of Jesus; it is its "beginning and end." The last verse—according to the Arabic version—is John 21:25: "And there are also many other things that Jesus has done, which if they were written—each of them—not even the world, in my view, could contain the books that should be written."[61] It is obvious that Tatian's harmony of the Gospels was not just the result of a good combination of the many pieces of a jigsaw puzzle—which in fact it was—but rather the result of a "theological" reconstruction of the life of Jesus.

10. Addendum: John 1:1 in the Western Diatessaronic Tradition

In this short study I have focused on the eastern Diatessaronic tradition. Our knowledge about the western tradition begins with the text of the harmony of the Gospels found in the Codex Fuldensis of the Vulgate.[62] In this codex the text of John 1:1-5 is preceded by the *prologue* of Luke's Gospel (1:1-4). However, it has been observed[63] that the order

---

[61] A.-S. Marmardji, *Diatessaron de Tatien: Texte arabe établi, traduit en français, collationné avec les anciennes versions syriaques* (Beyrouth: Imprimerie Catholique, 1935), 530. This was observed by Peter M. Head in "Tatian's Christology and Its Influence on the Composition of the Diatessaron," *TynBul* 43 (1992): 129: "Tatian locates the synoptic gospels within the Johannine framework."

[62] E. Ranke, *Codex Fuldensis: Novum Testamentum Latine Interprete Hieronymo ex Manuscripto Victoris Capuani* (Marburg: N. G. Elwert, 1868).

[63] Petersen, *Tatian's Diatessaron,* 128, 307, 435.

of pericopes in the *capitula* begins with "I. *In principio uerbum*," which seems to imply that the Lukan prologue was perhaps added by Victor of Capua or by the copyist of the manuscript that this bishop once happened to find at his desk (*Cum fortuito in manus meas incideret*).[64]

In the Dutch harmonies that are related to the Latin Diatessaron tradition there is no prologue of Luke; rather they begin with the harmony after a long introduction that ends with the words,

> Sente IJan de ewangeliste, die onder de vire ewangelisten sonderling*he* ghelijct es den vligenden are, om dat hi hoger uloegh met kinnisse ende met uerstannissen in de ombegrijpleke heimlekheit der gotheit dan dandre daden, hi beghint sine ewangelie aldus: In principio erat verbum. In den beghinne was dat wart, ende dat wart was met Gode, ende Got was dat wart.[65]

And in the Stuttgart manuscript of the Dutch harmony we find a similar prologue; then it starts with chapter "I: *Hier begennen de helege ewangelien. In principio erat. In den beginne was twoort ende twort was met Gode.*"[66] The same is true for the other Dutch harmonies—the Cambridge manuscript,[67] the Haaren manuscript[68]—and equally for the early German harmonies.[69] Even in the Pepysian harmony the opening paragraph is a paraphrase of the beginning of John's Gospel.[70] This seems to imply that the Latin *Vorlage* of these Dutch and German harmonies was most likely slightly different from the text that we now have in the Codex Fuldensis and some other Latin harmony texts.[71]

---

[64] Cf. Ranke, *Codex Fuldensis*, 29 (for Luke 1:1-4); 21 (for the first *capitulum*); and 1 (for Victor's description of his discovery).

[65] C. C. de Bruin, *Het Luikse Diatessaron*, trans. A. J. Barnouw (Leiden: Brill, 1970), 4. The English translation (p. 5) reads:

> Saint John the Evangelist, who among the four evangelists is especially compared to the flying eagle, because he flew higher with knowledge and with understanding into the unfathomable mystery of the Godhead than did the others, (he) begins his gospel thus: In principio erat verbum. In the beginning was the Word, and the Word was with God, and God was the Word.

[66] Jan Bergsma, *De levens van Jezus in het Middelnederlandsch*, 3 vols. (Leiden: Sijthoff, 1895-8), 1:4.

[67] C. C. de Bruin, *Diatessaron Cantabrigiense* (Leiden: Brill, 1970), 1: "*In principio*, I. *Johannes* In deme beghinne was dat wort."

[68] C. C. de Bruin, *Diatessaron Haarense* (Leiden: Brill, 1970), 1: "Inden beghinne was dat woert"; the Utrecht manuscript was defective in the beginning, cf. A. A. den Hollander, *Virtuelle Vergangenheit: Die Textrekonstruktion einer verlorenen Mittelnieder-ländischen Evangelienharmonie* (Leuven: Leuven University Press, 2007), 43.

[69] Christoph Gerhardt, *Diatessaron Theodiscum: Das Leben Jhesu* (Leiden: Brill, 1970), 2: "In principio erat verbum. In dem beginne was das wort vnd das wort was bi gotte"; some MSS have longer Latin texts; MS V reads "anbeginne."

[70] Margery Goates, ed., *The Pepysian Gospel Harmony* (London: Oxford University Press, 1922), 1 (§1): "Ovre suete lord Jhesu Crist vpe his godhede he was tofore all creatures, for whi he made alle creatures þorou3 his owen suete mi3th." [Editors' note: to this evidence should now be added the agreement of the recently published "Old French" exemplar of the Pepysian harmony, which also begins with a paraphrase of the beginning of John; see Brent A. Pitts, ed., *Estoire de l'Evangile* (Dublin, Christ Church Cathedral, MS. 6.1.1), Medium Ævum Monographs 28 (Oxford: Society for the Study of Medieval Languages and Literature, 2011), 11, 30.]

[71] Zahn, *Tatian's Diatessaron*, 300-3; D. Plooij, *A Primitive Text of the Diatessaron: The Liège Manuscript of a Mediæval Dutch Translation* (Leiden: A. W. Sijthoff, 1923), 10-11; cf. Petersen, *Tatian's Diatessaron*, 307.

2

Diatessaron, Diapente, Diapollon? Exploring the Nature and Extent of Extracanonical Influence in Tatian's Diatessaron

Charles E. Hill

Abstract

Scholars often take for granted that Tatian made use, possibly fairly extensive use, of extracanonical Gospels in producing the Diatessaron. Petersen saw the appropriations of these sources as proof that for Tatian "there was little or no distinction between canonical and extracanonical traditions." Claims have been made for Tatian's use of the *Gospel of Peter*, the *Gospel of Thomas*, the *Gospel of the Hebrews*, and others, including hypothesized lost Gospels. Many of these claims were made on the basis of what is now referred to as the Old Perspective on Diatessaronic studies and would be open to reinvestigation on that basis alone. This chapter offers a new review of what scholars have proposed to be the most indicative instances of Tatian's dependence on extracanonical Gospels. It concludes that in none of these instances is the hypothesis of Tatian's dependence on a noncanonical Gospel the most obvious or problem-free explanation, and in some it is demonstrably false. Even the most generous, realistic allowance for possible influence does not leave the hypothesis much basis for optimism. With little doubt, Tatian knew of other Gospels. But there are only four Gospels we know that Tatian used for his composition, and for that composition he used no other Gospel in the way in which he used each of the four.

1. Introduction: The Search for a Lost Source behind a Lost Source

What does Tatian's Diatessaron tell us about the status of Gospels ca. 160–180? The abstract for our 2016 SBL session offered a binary choice between understanding the Diatessaron as something that indicates "the canonical status of the fourfold gospel in the second half of the second century," or "as an argument for its ongoing fluidity and ambiguity"? Each position has certainly been held by scholars.¹ The path to an answer is determined by our session abstract to lie on the terrain of Tatian's intention. Did he intend his prodigious enterprise to serve as "merely a 'gospel harmony'"² or as a "'gospel' in its own right, comparable to other early Christian gospels." At the outset, I would want to say that even if we could ascertain Tatian's intention along these lines (and given the state of the evidence, it is at least doubtful that we can), this would not necessarily make a difference. The eminently quotable Bill Petersen believed he knew exactly what Tatian was attempting to accomplish: "*the Diatessaron was an attempt to create a single, definitive gospel—a 'super-gospel'—superseding all other gospels. It was, in that sense, a frontal assault on the four-gospel canon.*"³ Because people generally do not take the trouble to mount "frontal assaults" on things that do not already exist, if Petersen was right, the Diatessaron could have been both—an attempt to compose a new "gospel in its own right," and at the same time, evidence of a preexisting "canonical" status of the four. The mere existence of Tatian's work, no matter what his intention was, cannot be a determiner, for Gospels, or gospel-like compositions, continued to be written and rewritten even long after an exclusive four-Gospel collection is recognized. The question in any case would still remain, why did Tatian choose to mingle *these* four Gospels,⁴ particularly if there were others in circulation?

If convincing ourselves of Tatian's intention (whatever that may have been) is not likely to dispel the impression that his choice of source material implies a preexisting status for these four Gospels, one matter that could dispel it is the question of whether and to what extent Tatian's work really was, or could rightly be called, a Dia–*tessaron*. There is, of course, the curious notation of Victor of Capua that, according to Eusebius in his *Ecclesiastical History*, Tatian's name for his Gospel was *Diapente*.⁵ This has been taken to indicate a fifth major source, and therefore has generated no small amount of scholarly investigation. Yet no manuscript of Eusebius can be found in Greek or in

---

[1] E.g., see Everett Ferguson, "Factors Leading to the Selection and Closure of the New Testament Canon," in *The Canon Debate*, ed. Lee Martin McDonald and James A. Sanders (Peabody, MA: Hendrickson, 2008), 302n. 30, who believes the undertakings of Tatian, Theophilus, and Ammonius the Alexandrian "would seem to presuppose the special authority of the four gospels." In the same volume of essays, Harry Y. Gamble stresses that Tatian's handling of the four "shows both that the texts had not attained an inviolate or exclusive status and that the multiplicity of gospel documents was still felt to be problematic." See his "The New Testament Canon: Recent Research and the Status Quaestionis," in *The Canon Debate*, ed. Lee Martin McDonald and James A. Sanders (Peabody, MA: Hendrickson, 2008), 280.
[2] The use of the word "merely" might seem to suggest a predetermined answer.
[3] William L. Petersen, "The Diatessaron and the Fourfold Gospel," in *The Earliest Gospels: The Origins and Transmission of the Earliest Christian Gospels—The Contribution of the Chester Beatty Gospel Codex P45*, ed. Charles Horton (London: T&T Clark, 2004), 67, his emphasis.
[4] Bruce M. Metzger, *The Canon of the New Testament: Its Origin, Development, and Significance* (Oxford: Oxford University Press, 1987), 115.
[5] E.g., "It became clear to me also from his [Eusebius'] *History* that Tatian, a very learned man and famous orator of the time, combined one gospel out of the four, for which he composed the title 'Diapente' (*unum ex quattuor conpaginauerit euangelium cui titulum Diapente conposuit*)." Translation and text from William L. Petersen, *Tatian's Diatessaron: Its Creation, Dissemination, Significance, and History in Scholarship*, VCSup 25 (Leiden: Brill, 1994), 46-7. The famous Fulda manuscript, Bonifatianus 1 (Victor-Codex) may now be viewed at the Hochschul- und Landesbibliothek Fuldig website, available at http://fuldig.hs-fulda.de/viewer/image/PPN325289808/1/.

any version that says anything other than "Diatessaron," and Victor himself repeatedly states that the work was constructed out of the *four* Gospels.[6]

More to the point, then, is it not a long-established fact that scholars have discovered in numerous Diatessaronic witnesses portions of text that, on the one hand, have no parallel in our present Greek texts of any of the four Gospels, and on the other hand, do closely parallel elements of noncanonical Gospels? Some prominent scholars, indeed, have denied Tatian's use of other written Gospels,[7] but the opposite opinion is probably more common today. Original Diatessaronic elements have been claimed to derive from the *Gospel of Peter*[8]; the *Gospel of Thomas*[9]; the *Gospel of the Ebionites*, the *Gospel according to the Hebrews*,[10] or a lost Judaic-Christian Gospel akin to these;[11] the *Protevangelium of James*;[12] or from "several apocryphal works."[13] That Tatian borrowed substantially from noncanonical sources is often taken for granted by scholars.

For Petersen, to acknowledge Tatian's active use of extracanonical materials would mean that "at least for Tatian, there was little or no distinction between canonical and extra-canonical traditions: both seem to have had equal validity, and could be seamlessly combined without warning the reader."[14] Recently, Matthew Crawford has suggested that the name "Diatessaron" may be a misnomer: "Given the usage of these other texts which we now know as non-canonical, an inherent contradiction emerges

---

[6] For instance, in the "Diapente" statement itself (see note 5). For more on this see C. E. Hill, *Who Chose the Gospels? Probing the Great Gospel Conspiracy* (Oxford: Oxford University Press, 2010), 272–3.

[7] H. J. W. Drijvers says it was "extremely unlikely that Tatian made use of extracanonical material or even of an apocryphal gospel in composing his Diatessaron." See H. J. W. Drijvers, "Facts and Problems in Early Syriac-Speaking Christianity," *The Second Century* 2 (1982): 173n. 64. See also Metzger, *The Canon of the New Testament*, 115–16.

[8] Lee Martin McDonald, "The Gospels in Early Christianity: Their Origin, Use, and Authority," in *Reading the Gospels Today*, ed. Stanley E. Porter (Grand Rapids, MI: Eerdmans, 2004), 175.

[9] Matthew R. Crawford, "Diatessaron, a Misnomer? The Evidence from Ephrem's Commentary," *EC* 4 (2013): 383.

[10] A. Baumstark, *Geschichte der syrischen Literatur* (Bonn: A. Marcus und E. Webers Verlag, 1922); C. Peters, "Nachhall ausserkanonischer Evangelien-Überlieferung in Tatians Diatessaron," *Acta Orientalia* 16 (1938): 293–4; A. Vööbus, *Studies in the History of the Gospel Text in Syriac*, (Louvain: Peeters, 1951), 19; G. Quispel, "The Gospel of Thomas and the New Testament," *VC* 11 (1957): 189–207; and G. Quispel, "L'Évangile selon Thomas et le Diatessaron," *VC* 13 (1959): 87–117 (these references supplied by James H. Charlesworth, "Tatian's Dependence upon Apocryphal Traditions," *HeyJ* 15 [1974]: 7–8).

[11] Petersen, *Tatian's Diatessaron*, 41, 100, 347, 420, 427–8.

[12] See G. Messina, *Diatessaron Persiano* (Rome: Pontifical Biblical Institute, 1951), lxxxiv, who was countered by Bruce M. Metzger, *Chapters in the History of New Testament Textual Criticism* (Grand Rapids, MI: Eerdmans, 1963), 97–120 (this too is from Charlesworth, "Tatian's Dependence upon Apocryphal Traditions," 7–8).

[13] Geoffrey Mark Hahneman, *The Muratorian Fragment and the Development of the Canon* (Oxford: Clarendon Press, 1992), 99, citing Charlesworth, "Tatian's Dependence upon Apocryphal Traditions," 5–17. Charlesworth claimed, "There is no consensus regarding the sources employed by Tatian, except perhaps that Eusebius erred when he wrote that Tatian complied his harmony from 'the gospels' and called it the Diatessaron" (5). Charlesworth simply took it for granted that Tatian's sources were more than four and more than five.

[14] William L. Petersen, "The Genesis of the Gospel," in *New Testament Textual Criticism and Exegesis: Festschrift J. Delobel*, ed. A. Denaux (Leuven: Leuven University Press, 2002), 42–3.

between the title 'Diatessaron' ('From Four') and the actual gospel material that occurs in the work."[15]

The significance of Tatian's work for establishing that a notional, four-Gospel canon existed at the time would surely seem to be compromised if we were able to establish two things. The first, of course, is that he indeed used one or more noncanonical Gospels, and not simply untethered, oral tradition or exegetical expansions. The reason for saying this is that even the texts of the canonical Gospels were affected to a degree by minor accretions from unknown sources or exegetical/homiletical traditions, even well after the four were alone regarded as handed down from the apostles,[16] as *homolegoumena*,[17] and as "indisputable."[18] A number of passages in Codex Bezae, for instance, would meet this description.[19] Some scholars have concluded that Tatian, at points, may have altered the Gospel text before him in idiosyncratic ways that brought the resulting work into greater conformity with his own theological or ascetical proclivities.[20] These types of minor modifications or glosses, while they might be thought to imply something about what an individual was able to do with the text of the Gospels at the time, do not really touch deeply upon the question of whether there was a perception of the four as already holding primacy among churches in communion with one another throughout the empire.

The second thing we ought to be able to establish in order for us to say that for Tatian there were no distinctions between Gospels, and to argue seriously for discarding the word "Diatessaron," is that Tatian used one or more noncanonical Gospels in a way that closely resembled the way he used the four Gospels. To do this requires that we can ascertain two things: how Tatian used the four, and how he used any other Gospels (if indeed he used them).

2. The Shape of the Diatessaron and the Method of Its Construction

2.1 How Did Tatian Treat the Four Gospels?

Because only one small fragment of an early Greek copy survives (the Dura fragment; though see Chapter 7 by Ian Mills in this volume), trying to establish the precise wording of the original Diatessaron is filled with often insuperable challenges. But at the pericope level, the content and sequence of the Diatessaron appears to be more

---

[15] Crawford, "Diatessaron, a Misnomer?" 383–4.
[16] Irenaeus, *Haer.* 3.11.9; Clement, *Strom.* 3.13.93.
[17] Clement, *Quis div.* 1.5.
[18] Origen, *Comm. Matt.* in Eusebius, *Hist. eccl.* 6.25.4.
[19] The story about a woman caught in sin (John 7:53–8:11), in particular, which Eusebius (*Hist. eccl.* 3.39.17) said that Papias knew and which occurred in a *Gospel according to the Hebrews*, is an example. Codex Bezae has at least two sayings of Jesus not recorded in other copies of Luke or Mark: "Every sacrifice will be salted with salt," at Mark 9:49; "Man, if you know what you are doing, you are blessed; but if you do not know, you are cursed and a transgressor of the law," at Luke 6:4.
[20] As just one example, J. Rendel Harris, "Some Notes on the Gospel-Harmony of Zacharias Chrysopolitanus," *JBL* 43 (1924): 40.

definable. Besides the Dura fragment, we have Armenian and Syriac manuscripts of a late-fourth-century commentary on the Syriac version of the Diatessaron, a commentary long attributed to Ephrem (though recent scholarship has questioned the attribution).[21] From the twelfth century there are manuscripts of an Arabic translation made apparently in the eleventh century from the Syriac version,[22] which scholars believe gives a very close approximation of the original sequence of the pericopes. Finally, we have Codex Fuldensis (completed in 546) in a Vulgate or Vulgatized Latin. These may be considered "primary Diatessaronic witnesses." They are supplemented on the eastern side by quotations from Aphrahat, by MSS of the Old Syriac separated Gospels, and on the western side by MSS of the Old Latin Gospels and by a host of "Unum ex Quattuor" Gospels (along with commentary paraphernalia) in various Western languages that apparently descended ultimately from Fuldensis. From these sources a fairly reliable picture of the organization and contents of the Diatessaron has been claimed, though not for its particular wording.

According to John Granger Cook, Tatian may have used Matthew as the main guide for sequencing the major, middle part of the narrative, but in both the beginning and the concluding episodes of the Diatessaron, he followed Luke and John more closely.[23] This would be only natural, since both Luke and John[24] have significant additional material that pertains to the period before the main narratives of Matthew and Mark begin, and material that pertains to the time after Jesus's resurrection. What this tells us is that Tatian was seeking to construct his Gospel from at least three of the four Gospels.

We get a better picture of this when we consider the pericopes included. While, according to Theodoret,[25] the Diatessaron omitted some things that were contained in the four, specifically the genealogies, it did make a serious effort to include the great bulk of each of the four Gospels, even their unique passages. Victor of Capua went to

---

[21] See Christian Lange, *The Portrayal of Christ in the Syriac Commentary on the Diatessaron*, CSCO 616, Subsidia 118 (Leuven: Peeters, 2005). Simply for convenience, I shall here refer to the commentary as Ephrem's.

[22] All the Arabic manuscripts were copied in Egypt in a Coptic milieu, according to Peter Joosse, "From Antioch to Bagdad, from Bagdad to Cairo: Towards an Archetype of the Arabic Diatessaron," *Parole de l'Orient* 37 (2012): 76.

[23] John Granger Cook, "A Note on Tatian's Diatessaron, Luke, and the Arabic Harmony," ZAC 10 (2006): 464, 471.

[24] The Arabic Diatessaron and Ephrem begin with John 1:1-5.

[25] Theodoret, *Haer. fab.* 1.20. Theodoret also says that many of the orthodox used the Diatessaron "in their simplicity for its conciseness." Though Theodoret reports that he found more than 200 copies in reverential use in the churches of his diocese, which he collected and replaced with copies of the four separate Gospels, the Diocese of Cyrrhus consisted of about 800 churches (T. Baarda, "Tatian's Diatessaron and the Greek Text of the Gospels," in *The Early Text of the New Testament*, ed. Charles E. Hill and Michael J. Kruger [Oxford: Oxford University Press, 2012], 338n. 18). It is of course possible that Theodoret could not collect all the copies of the Diatessaron in the area. But the fact that he found only 200 in use among around 800 churches indicates that the use of the four separate Gospels must have been more customary in eastern Syria than we are often led to believe (e.g., Hans von Campenhausen, *The Formation of the Christian Bible*, trans. J. A. Baker [Philadelphia, PA: Fortress Press, 1972], 175–6: "on his home ground of Syria, his harmony of the Gospel actually established itself as the canonical gospel of the Church, and this 'Gospel of the Mixed' was dislodged only at a late date, in the fifth and sixth centuries, and that with a deal of trouble, by the so-called 'Gospel of the Separated'"). Quite possibly even some churches that surrendered their copies of the Diatessaron may have also been using the four separate Gospels.

great trouble, in fact, to supply the harmonized Gospel text of Codex Fuldensis with the Ammonian Sections and Eusebian Canons.[26] Eusebius's tenth canon table listed passages unique to each of the four Gospels, listing sixty-two of these for Matthew, nineteen for Mark, seventy-two for Luke, and ninety-six for John. It is notable that the tenth canon table in Fuldensis also lists passages in the harmonized Gospel that were unique to each Gospel.[27] There are 83 places in the text of Fuldensis where one of the 62 unique sections of Matthew is accessed (because of the rearrangement of material, a given Ammonian section could be broken up and used more than once); there are 18 places where one of the 19 unique sections of Mark is accessed; 81 places where one of the 72 unique Lukan sections is accessed; and 109 places where one of the 96 unique sections of John is accessed.

The unique material from each of the four Gospels, then, is substantially reproduced in the Diatessaron tradition as represented by Fuldensis. While Tatian's original may have omitted certain materials (such as the genealogies) based on some principle or other, there was apparently no prejudice against any one of the four Gospels in this regard. Pericopes unique to each individual Gospel were included in the plan of the Diatessaron. Even Mark was integral.

Not only did Tatian include the special material of each of the four, but within a particular passage an exacting effort was made to integrate details from each Gospel that contained it—or one that was related to it. As Crawford says about the passage on Joseph of Arimathea preserved in the Dura fragment, "we should observe that he has succeeded in finding all four parallel descriptions of Joseph in the canonical gospels and has drawn distinct elements from each one."[28] Another example, this one from Fuldensis, is Jesus's saying about putting a light on a stand (Matt 5:14-16; Mark 4:21; Luke 8:16; 11:33), where all three Synoptic sources are integrated. As Zola says, "F[uldensis] manages to incorporate the objects of each instance into the Matthean form by supplying *neque* before each one, and by altering other small details."[29] The same technique is visible throughout the Arabic Diatessaron. For instance, its account of Jesus's baptism and subsequent temptation in the wilderness (chapter 4) interlaces details from each of the four Gospels. In passage after passage in Fuldensis and in the Arabic Diatessaron we observe the same procedure that is seen in the Greek Dura fragment, an attempt to consult and to incorporate relevant information from each of the four.

Both the breadth and the consistency of this procedure, found in each of these primary witnesses, are important because in any individual case it might be

---

[26] Ulrich B. Schmid, "The Diatessaron of Tatian," in *The Text of the New Testament in Contemporary Research: Essays on the Status Quaestionis*, 2nd ed., ed. Bart D. Ehrman and Michael W. Holmes (Leiden: Brill, 2013), 119–20: "We can be reasonably certain that it was Victor who appended the Eusebian tables and added the respective canon numbers to the harmony's text, simply because he says so in his preface. But we do not know whether he also added the set of 182 capitula we also find in Codex Fuldensis and if and to what extent he might have reworked the harmony's text."

[27] Canon X is on pp. 25:11r–28:12v, available at http://fuldig.hs-fulda.de/viewer/image/PPN325289808/1/.

[28] Matthew R. Crawford, "The Diatessaron, Canonical or Non-canonical? Rereading the Dura Fragment," *NTS* 62 (2016): 265–6.

[29] Nicholas J. Zola, "Tatian's Diatessaron in Latin: A New Edition and Translation of Codex Fuldensis" (PhD diss., Baylor University, 2014), 67.

possible to suggest an alternative explanation. Scholars have long noted a process of "Vulgatization" in the Diatessaronic tradition, that is, a tendency of Diatessaronic witnesses to be revised toward a current, local text of the canonical Gospels.[30] Thus, it is often possible to propose that an original Diatessaronic reading (or a sequencing of pericopes) has been "revised" to look more like a standard Gospel text in use in the reviser's locale. Yet, while details of vocabulary and sometimes sequencing may remain uncertain, because we find this intricate "intra-pericope" harmonization technique, involving each of the four separate Gospels, in each primary linguistic tradent of the Diatessaronic tradition—in the case of the Dura fragment, in a very early example,[31] and in the other two, consistently and pervasively—it is difficult to attribute the employment of the technique itself only to the work of later "Vulgatizers" and not to Tatian himself.[32] Tatian, then, appears to have made a systematic attempt to include the pericopes of all four canonical Gospels, and for each pericope included, all four were consulted for details.

2.2 How Did Tatian Treat Noncanonical Gospels?

How, then, does Tatian's integration of extracanonical gospel material compare with the way he integrated material from the four? Specifically, (1) did he attempt to incorporate pericopes from any other Gospels that are unique to those Gospels? Then, (2) in pericopes shared with one or more of the four, did Tatian attempt consistently or systematically to include details from that Gospel?

We need only return to the Dura fragment for a moment for a partial test case. We have observed that in the presentation of Joseph of Arimathea's request for the body of Jesus after the crucifixion, distinct elements from each of the four Gospels are preserved. In its version of this same incident, the *Gospel of Peter* states that "the Jews rejoiced and gave his body to Joseph that he might bury it, since he had seen what good things he had

---

[30] On Vulgatization, see Petersen, *Tatian's Diatessaron*, 127–9; 202, etc. Speaking of the creation of Codex Fuldensis, Petersen says, "readings from the by-then-standard Vulgate were, in the vast majority of cases, substituted for the original 'Diatessaronic' readings. In the jargon of Diatessaronic studies, this process is known as 'Vulgatization,' regardless of the language in which it occurs" (127). His short definition of the term is "the tendency to replace non-standard Diatessaronic readings with the 'standard' reading" (202).

[31] I am persuaded that the Dura fragment is Diatessaronic. If it is not, but represents another gospel harmony, perhaps the one by Theophilus, it would still not be without importance. In that case it would still provide very early, virtually contemporary evidence of a very similar enterprise to Tatian's which approached the texts of the Gospels in this manner.

[32] Also, while we know that Vulgatization occurred (particularly in the case of Fuldensis and in the later western harmonies), there are reasons for exercising caution before assuming it as the correct explanation in every case in which a deviating reading shows up somewhere in the tradition, lest the phenomenon devolve into a principle such as, "the 'wildest' form of the reading, the form most distant from the canonical text, would be the oldest form of the interpolation" (the principle baldly stated by Petersen, *Tatian's Diatessaron*, 418). That is, the wildest form of a reading may be assumed to be the oldest, and the tamer forms assumed to be the product of Vulgatization. Not only can such a principle not be proved, but it ignores the fact that, as we have noted above, well after Tatian's time minor accretions sometimes entered the textual traditions of the canonical Gospels themselves. It is quite likely that various traditions of the Diatessaron were at times affected by later, "less pure" forms of the canonical texts.

done" (*Gos. Pet.* 23). We can see here that the *Gospel of Peter* contributes at least three new details to the report: the Jews rejoicing, apparently over the death of Jesus; "the Jews," not Pilate, giving over the body to Joseph for burial; and Joseph's motivation for burying the body of Jesus, namely, because he had seen the good things Jesus had done. None of these details appears in the Dura fragment of the Diatessaron, in Ephrem's *Commentary*, in Fuldensis, or in the Arabic Harmony. If Tatian knew the *Gospel of Peter*'s account, he did not use it at this point.[33] But what about the actual examples that scholars have collected to demonstrate noncanonical Gospel influence on the Diatessaron?

3. Proposed Elements Taken from Noncanonical Gospels

3.1 Old Perspective Limbo

A fair number of examples of influence from noncanonical Gospels have been proposed in the history of Diatessaron research. Right away, however, it has to be said that many of these entered the discussion under the sponsorship of what has lately been termed the "old perspective" on Diatessaronic studies, and have not been subjected to the insights of the so-called "new perspective." The old perspective sought for variant readings in the later, western vernacular harmonies and then screened them against Codex Fuldensis. For any remaining elements not witnessed in Fuldensis a search was then conducted for possible parallels in eastern Diatessaronic witnesses. Any matches, or near matches, could then be claimed as belonging to the original Diatessaron. This method was predicated upon the assumption that these later vernacular harmony translations, bypassing Fuldensis, somehow had retained pre-Fuldensian readings stemming from a presumed Old Latin Diatessaron that was in turn assumed to be exceedingly close to the original Greek or Syriac Diatessaron.

Recent scholarship, however, has cast these assumptions and the resulting methodology into dubiety. The later, western vernacular harmonies, it turns out, have absorbed elements from many sources, particularly from the *Glossa Ordinaria* tradition, as well as from the commentary, homiletic, and textual translation streams.[34] Ulrich Schmid now proposes that "in all likelihood only one Western witness has an

---

[33] Is it possible that elements from the *Gos. Pet.* were edited out of Tatian's work due to Vulgatization? (I do not know of anyone who has suggested this, but the question may certainly be raised.) This would have to depend upon a denial that the Dura fragment is a fragment of the Diatessaron, or that it represents at this point something very close to its original. If the Dura fragment has been "Vulgatized" to conform to current, canonical Greek Gospel texts, this revision must have been done very soon after the original. The Syriac/Arabic and the Old Latin/Fuldensis traditions also independently had to delete the same materials. One might also find it too convenient that Ephrem, who presumably would not have been concerned with, or possibly even aware of, noncanonical elements in his copy of the Diatessaron, failed to reference any of them—though given the selectivity of Ephrem's comments, such omissions may have little force. In any case, faced with such issues, and in the absence of any positive evidence, any suggestion of independent censorship of a presumed Tatianic text at this point would have to show it was relying on something more than mere conjecture.

[34] Joose, "From Antioch to Bagdad," 69n. 2, exclaims, "It is over, folks: hand in your guns! Bury the 'Old Perspective' and let the adherents of the 'New Perspective' do their work, because only then the Eastern sources can have their independent say and resilient results can flow therefrom!"

independent voice, and that is Codex Fuldensis itself. Forget about the rest, if you want to reconstruct Tatian's Diatessaron."[35]

What we have now is a situation in which much of the evidence formerly seen as establishing Tatian's use of noncanonical materials has become marginalized, at least until it can make a better defense.

Consider now a set of stellar witnesses. In his review of past research Petersen claimed that C. A. Phillips, in a short article written in 1931, "had uncovered more—and better—specific references to the Judaic-Christian gospel tradition in Diatessaronic witnesses than any other scholar, before or since."[36] Phillips identified six readings which he believed argued that "Tatian's Gospel sources were to some extent really five."[37] Briefly summarized (they will be discussed further below), the six are as follows.

1. Two middle-Dutch Harmonies, Liège (ca. 1280)[38] and Stuttgart (1332),[39] and a Jewish-Christian Gospel known to Jerome add, with respect to the man with a withered hand at Mark 3:1-6 or at Matt 12:9-14, that the man could not work with his hand.
2. The Liège Harmony and a marginal gloss in the ninth-century Greek manuscript 566 of Matthew attributed to τὸ Ἰουδαϊκόν ("the Jewish [Gospel]") replace the reference to the "holy city" at Matt 4:5 with a reference to Jerusalem/the city of Jerusalem.
3. The Syrians Aphrahat and Ephrem and a Jewish-Christian Gospel known to Jerome combine Matt 18:21f and Luke 17:3f, in Peter's question to Jesus about how many times "in one day" one ought to forgive a repenting brother.
4. The *capitularia* (table of contents) in some MSS of Zacharias Chrysopolitanus's (d. 1155) Commentary on an *In unum ex quattuor* harmony (though not the commentary itself) and a Jewish-Christian Gospel known to Jerome add "son of Joiade" to "son of Barachiah" at Matt 23:35.
5. The *capitularia* in some MSS of Zacharias Chrysopolitanus's Commentary on an *In unum ex quattuor* harmony (though, again, not the commentary itself) and a Jewish-Christian Gospel known to Jerome add to the narrative of Matt 27:51 that the "lintel of the temple" was split at the time of the crucifixion.
6. The Arabic Diatessaron and a Hebrew Gospel mentioned in an interpolation in the Latin translation of Origen's *Commentary on Matthew* presuppose the same arrangement of Gospel episodes concerning rich men.

At least four of these six alleged Diatessaronic readings identified by Phillips (numbers 1, 2, 4, and 5 above) and endorsed by Petersen,[40] however, would not pass

---

[35] Schmid, "The Diatessaron of Tatian," 137.
[36] Petersen, *Tatian's Diatessaron*, 259, referring to C. A. Phillips, "Diatessaron—Diapente," *Bulletin of the Bezan Club* 9 (1931): 6–8. Elsewhere Petersen calls Phillips's article "[t]he most important study of apocryphal traditions in the Diatessaron" (Petersen, *Tatian's Diatessaron*, 31n. 77).
[37] Phillips, "Diatessaron—Diapente," 8.
[38] Petersen, *Tatian's Diatessaron*, 145. According to Petersen, it is a revision of an earlier Middle Dutch archetype, translated ultimately from a *Vetus Latina* harmony.
[39] Petersen, *Tatian's Diatessaron*, 175, in some way related to the Liège, but more Vulgatized.
[40] Ibid., 257–8.

"new perspective" muster. All four are elements of later western vernacular traditions without support from Fuldensis.

Strictly speaking, these four do not even meet both of the normal criteria of an old perspective witness. They meet the first criterion of being readings found somewhere in the western, vernacular harmony tradition that do not occur in Fuldensis. But they have no support in eastern Diatessaronic witnesses. Their ancient support comes instead from an alleged Jewish-Christian Gospel that is presumed by some scholars to lie *behind* Tatian's Diatessaron as one of its sources. The new perspective on Diatessaronic studies would ask, since these four readings have no support either from Fuldensis or from any ancient eastern Diatessaron witness, whether it is not more likely that they entered the later harmony tradition through some more proximate source.

As to the ancient Jewish-Christian Gospel presumed to lie behind the Diatessaron, its existence is deduced from two main sources: several of Jerome's references to a Hebrew Gospel or a Gospel that the Nazarenes use; and scholia in the margins of a number of medieval Greek NT manuscripts that give readings from something they call τὸ Ἰουδαϊκόν, apparently a "Jewish" Gospel. Petersen, along with scholars such as Schmidtke, Vielhaur, and Klijn, believed all of these are references to the same Gospel, the Gospel they and others have called the *Gospel of the Nazarenes*.[41] For Petersen, this Gospel was related to an even earlier Jewish-Christian Gospel that must have been used by Tatian.[42]

There has long been debate, however, over the number of early Jewish-Christian Gospels that were extant in the early centuries, whether one, two, or three. Some scholars believe that all the ancient testimonies can be accounted for by the hypothesis of a single Jewish-Christian Gospel.[43] But the existence of at least two, a *Gospel according to the Hebrews* attested by Clement, Origen, Jerome, and others, and a *Gospel of the Ebionites* attested by Epiphanius, is more widely acknowledged. More questionable is whether several of Jerome's more ambiguous references, combined with the τὸ Ἰουδαϊκόν glosses in five medieval Greek Gospel manuscripts (there is one, but only one, overlap with one of Jerome's reports), can certify the existence of a third, distinct Gospel, one used by the Nazarenes (and, in one of Jerome's references, the Ebionites) and thus commonly labeled the *Gospel of the Nazarenes*.

In his recent and authoritative book on the *Gospel according to the Hebrews* and the *Gospel of the Ebionites*, Andrew Gregory joins a number of other scholars who dispute the existence of a third Jewish Gospel. Gregory believes that Jerome knew only one independent, Jewish-Christian Gospel, namely, the better attested *Gospel according to the Hebrews*, to which he refers on many occasions. The references we are concerned with here, however, relate to "a second text," which Gregory believes "is better understood as an Aramaic version of Matthew than as a different gospel with a

---

[41] Petersen, *Tatian's Diatessaron*, 31, 41.
[42] Ibid., 29–31, 39–41, 347, 420, 427–8.
[43] Besides Petersen (see previous note), see, e.g., James R. Edwards, *The Hebrew Gospel and the Development of the Synoptic Tradition* (Grand Rapids, MI: Eerdmans, 2009).

distinct identity of its own."⁴⁴ This Aramaic version would have been a translation from the Greek. Speaking of the medieval manuscripts that refer to a Ἰουδαϊκόν, Gregory continues,

> the marginal readings attributed to a 'Jewish [gospel]' are also best understood as witnesses to an Aramaic version of Matthew, translated from the Greek text of his gospel (the language in which it was composed). They may reflect the same Aramaic version that was known to Jerome, but there is no reason to identify it as a distinct gospel in its own right, let alone as a third 'Jewish-Christian' gospel.⁴⁵

We return then to Phillips's alleged Diatessaronic readings. Given the concerns raised by the new perspective, it ought to be investigated whether these elements found in the later western harmonies are attested outside the harmony tradition in, for example, the *Glossa Ordinaria* or in medieval commentaries. But since the report that they occurred in a Jewish Gospel comes from Jerome, and since Jerome's writings were known, valued, and *accessible* throughout the middle ages, one has to ask whether Jerome himself might be a more likely conduit through which these readings entered the later western vernacular harmony traditions than an otherwise lost, pre-Vulgate, Latin harmony, which (1) preserved Tatian's lost Syriac or Greek Diatessaron that got the readings from a lost Judaic Gospel in the second century, but (2) whose original Diatessaronic readings were also bypassed by Ephrem and Aphrahat and successfully edited out of both the later Latin (Fuldensis) and the Arabic Diatessaronic traditions.⁴⁶

In fact, we can easily be more certain in the cases of Phillips's numbers 4 and 5 above. For number 4, Petersen presents the evidence of the *capitularia* in certain MSS⁴⁷ of Zacharias Chrysopolitanus's twelfth-century commentary (for ch. 141)⁴⁸ as a case of

---

⁴⁴ Andrew Gregory, *The Gospel According to the Hebrews and the Gospel of the Ebionites* (Oxford: Oxford University Press, 2017), 269. Petri Luomanen, *Recovering Jewish-Christian Sects and Gospels*, VCSup 110 (Leiden: Brill, 2012), esp. 236–9, thinks that the references to Jewish or Hebrew Gospels refer to texts deriving from a harmonized, post-synoptic Gospel in Syria that predated Tatian's Diatessaron.
⁴⁵ Gregory, *The Gospel According to the Hebrews*, 269. Many questions have been raised about the source of the notations attributed to "the Jewish Gospel" in manuscripts 566 and 1424.
⁴⁶ Similar is Jan Joosten's statement, summarizing the work of Schmid and den Hollander, "That a thirteenth-century Dutch cleric should have consulted such glosses while translating a gospel harmony from Latin into the vernacular surely is more likely than that he possessed a now lost Old Latin Diatessaron transmitting second-century readings" (Jan Joosten, "The *Gospel of Barnabas* and the Diatessaron," *HTR* 95 [2002]: 78).
⁴⁷ See Phillips, "Diatessaron—Diapente," 7; Petersen, *Tatian's Diatessaron*, 258. This and the following example do not occur in J. P. Migne's 1834 edition of Zacharias (see PG 186:1). The relevant MSS are said to be Bodleian 209; British Library, Harley 1915; and the Winchester Cathedral MS of Zechariah's work.
⁴⁸ In his third preface (cols. 37–40), Zacharias seems to trace his Harmony to Ammonius of Alexandria, though he also mentions that Tatian too constructed an *unum ex quatuor . . . Evangelium*. The language in this preface shows dependence, whether firsthand or secondhand, on Victor of Capua's preface. The Harmony used by Zacharias is also shown to be a descendent of Fuldensis by its 181 chapters, the chapter titles, and the marginal and interlinear numbers linking the passages to the individual Gospels. Fuldensis has 182 *capitula*, but, as Schmid, "The Diatessaron of Tatian," 119, notes, these contain certain oddities of counting (doublets and mismatches), so that among the descendants of Fuldensis there are two versions of the *capitula* list, some that rework the 182 *capitula* to 181, others that rework it into 184.

addition, translating its *pro filio barachi filium Ioiade* as "to the son of Barachaia, son of Joiade." This interprets the chapter heading as intending to supply by the words *filium Ioiade* another generation of the genealogy of the priest Zechariah in Matt 23:35. But the case endings are odd. *Pro filio barachi filium Ioiade* would instead seem to mean "for 'son of Barachaia,' (read) son of Joiade," that is, "son of Joiade" is intended as a replacement for "son of Barachaia." And in fact, this is the precise wording (apart from a variation of the spelling of the names) of Jerome in his *Commentary on Matthew* 23:35 when he is reporting what he found in a Gospel used by the Nazarenes:

> *In evangelio quo utuntur Nazareni pro filio Barachiae filium Ioiadae scriptum reperimus.*
>
> In the gospel that the Nazarenes use we find that there is written "son of Ioiada" for "son of Barachia."[49]

This seems to point directly to Jerome as the source of the supposedly Diatessaronic relic in some manuscripts of the *capitularia* of Zacharias's commentary. We know that Jerome was one of the writers Zacharias quoted most and that he even paid attention to Jerome's notices of Hebrew Gospels![50] And as Gregory notes, the substitution of Joiade (Jehoiada) for Berachaia is known to other medieval interpreters, namely Paschasius Radbertus in the ninth century and Petrus Comestor in the twelfth.[51] Radbertus even specifies that Jerome was his source for the reading and, as Gregory says, "Comestor probably depends on him as well."[52]

So much for Phillips's number 4. The situation is even worse for number 5, the splitting of the temple lintel at the time of the crucifixion. In this case, not only does the syntax of the chapter title for ch. 170 in some MSS of Zacharias's commentary[53] again match that of Jerome in his *Commentary on Matthew* 27:51,[54] Petersen even inadvertently lets the cat out of the bag by acknowledging that Zacharias in the commentary itself *actually quotes Jerome's report of the Hebrew Gospel's reading!*[55] Yet Petersen still cites this instance as an example of a noncanonical Gospel variant preserved in a Diatessaronic witness (i.e., Zacharias's commentary on an *In unum ex quattuor*). Nor does Petersen mention that four medieval authors[56] also cited the

---

[49] Text and translation taken from Gregory, *The Gospel According to the Hebrews*, 154.
[50] Harris, "Zacharias Chysopolitanus," 41: "through Jerome, who knows Hebrew as well as Greek, he gets some bits of Hebrew lore, and some of the best known of Jerome's quotations from the *Gospel according to the Hebrews*."
[51] Gregory, *The Gospel According to the Hebrews*, 155.
[52] Ibid. Also, as Nick Zola has pointed out to me, Comestor was himself the author of a harmony in the Diatessaronic tradition.
[53] Again, this variant does not occur in Migne's edition.
[54] With two minor changes that are probably scribal errors:

> Jerome: *superliminare templi infinitae magnitudinis fractum esse*;
> Zacharias: *supraliminare templi infine magnitudinis fractum esse*.

The text of Jerome I have taken from Gregory, *The Gospel According to the Hebrews*, 158; the text of Zacharias is from Petersen, *Tatian's Diatessaron*, 258.
[55] Petersen, *Tatian's Diatessaron*, 258n. 155.
[56] Christian of Stavelot, ninth century; Petrus Comestor, twelfth century; Hugo of St. Cher, thirteenth century; the author of the *Historia passionis Domini*, fourteenth century; all reproduced in A. F. J. Klijn, *Jewish-Christian Gospel Tradition*, VCSup 17 (Leiden: Brill, 1992), 94–5.

tradition of a breaking lintel, probably in dependence upon Jerome.[57] Thus, even if Zacharias did not get this tradition from Jerome directly, it is a tradition that was well known in the middle ages. This makes it special pleading to insist instead on a theory that the variant chapter title preserves independently the wording of a pre-Fuldensian, Old Latin Diatessaron.

Phillips's *first* example is a variant in the thirteenth-century Liège and the fourteenth-century Stuttgart harmonies that adds a detail about the man with a withered hand (Mark 3:1-6/Matt 12:9-14) that he could not work with his hand. This is said to be related to one of Jerome's reports of a Jewish Gospel, which states that the man was a mason who asks Jesus for healing so that he would not have to beg. Jerome's version, however, as Gregory notes, is known to Rabanus Maurus (ninth century) and Paschasius Radbertus (ninth century), who each identify it as coming from a Gospel used by the Nazarenes, information they obviously derived from Jerome.[58] The variant is also, now not surprisingly, found in Zacharias's twelfth-century commentary.[59] Klijn thought the short variant in Liège could be explained from the canonical text alone and was not related to the expansion in the *Gos. Naz.*[60] Even if it was, it would be another element which made its way into the western harmony tradition, one that is claimed to be a remnant from a lost Old Latin Diatessaron, which turns out to be a more widely known tradition traceable to Jerome.

Phillips's *second* example has (finally) no connection to Jerome. It comes instead from one of the marginal glosses in a medieval Greek Gospel manuscript, the ninth-century MS 566. At Matt 4:5, where Satan takes Jesus "into the holy city," a scribe reports that instead of "into the holy city" (εἰς τὴν ἁγίαν πόλιν), τὸ Ἰουδαϊκόν has "to Jerusalem" (ἐν ἰλημ). This is a near coincidence with the Liège Harmony, which at Matt 4:5 has "into the city of Jerusalem."[61] Even though these are not quite the same, they are close enough for Petersen to claim support for the theory that the original Diatessaron must have taken this substitution from a now-lost Judaic-Christian Gospel that was "known to Tatian" in the second century.[62]

The substitution in the Liège Harmony may also have come, like other of its variant readings, from a source in the late Gospel gloss tradition that was familiar with the same reading in τὸ Ἰουδαϊκόν. Alternatively, this near agreement with the reading of τὸ Ἰουδαϊκόν could have been coincidental. It is, after all, a virtual one-word substitution/clarification, and the same variant occurs in Liège and in the Himmelgarten Fragments at Matt 27:53,[63] though it does *not* occur at that point in 566 or in any other witness to τὸ Ἰουδαϊκόν. And even if the reading in Liège and Stuttgart came from an Old Latin Diatessaron, it may have had nothing to do with a lost Judaic Gospel. If Gregory is

---

[57] Cf. Gregory, *The Gospel According to the Hebrews*, 158–9.
[58] Ibid., 107; Klijn, *Jewish-Christian Gospel Tradition*, 88–9.
[59] See Klijn, *Jewish-Christian Gospel Tradition*, 89.
[60] Ibid., 90.
[61] Petersen, *Tatian's Diatessaron*, 31.
[62] Ibid.
[63] Ibid., 252n. 128.

correct, τὸ Ἰουδαϊκόν mentioned in MS 566 was an Aramaic translation of Matthew made sometime well after Tatian.[64]

3.2 Remaining Possibilities

This leaves us with two of the stellar examples from C. A. Phillips's seminal article, relied upon by Petersen, that are not marginalized, and in fact disproved, by the new perspective (and compromised by a questionable hypothesis of a third Jewish-Christian Gospel). In this section we shall consider these two remaining examples and three more examples sometimes claimed as proving Tatian's use of noncanonical Gospels.

3.2.1 "Seven Times in One Day"

With Phillips's *third* example of influence on the Diatessaron from a Jewish-Christian Gospel we are once again in the company of Jerome, but unlike the three such examples treated above, this one has a real connection with eastern representatives of the Diatessaron. Petersen says,

> Aphrahat, *Dem.* XIV.44 and Ephrem, *Comm.* IX.22 [*sic*; XIV.22 is correct] stress "how many times <u>in one day</u>" should one forgive one's brother. This same stress, and the same combination of Matt 18.21f. with Luke 17.3f., is found in Jerome's *adv. Pelag.* III.2, in a passage Jerome says is drawn from the "Gospel according to the Hebrews" which is used by the Nazoraeans.[65]

The supposition here is that Tatian must have used the *Gos. Heb.* for this combination and that both Aphrahat and Ephrem must have been using a Diatessaron text that, at this point, still looked more like the *Gos. Heb.* than like the currently attested Latin and Arabic texts, which, apparently, do not preserve the same stress upon "how many times in one day" one should forgive. At this point we may even mention the possibility that the work Jerome here calls the *Gospel according to the Hebrews* is actually a copy of the Diatessaron (an idea mentioned by Epiphanius, *Pan.* 46.1).

Here are the relevant texts.

Matthew 18:21-22

> Then Peter came and said to him, "Lord, how often shall my brother sin against me, and I forgive him? As many as seven times?" Jesus said to him, "I do not say to you seven times, but seventy times seven."[66] (RSV)

---

[64] Gregory, *The Gospel According to the Hebrews*, 269–74; see p. 266: "there is no firm evidence that any Hebrew or Aramaic gospel that may have been known in the fourth century was known prior to that period."
[65] Petersen, *Tatian's Diatessaron*, 258 (underlining original).
[66] Τότε προσελθὼν ὁ Πέτρος εἶπεν αὐτῷ· κύριε, ποσάκις ἁμαρτήσει εἰς ἐμὲ ὁ ἀδελφός μου καὶ ἀφήσω αὐτῷ; ἕως ἑπτάκις; λέγει αὐτῷ ὁ Ἰησοῦς· οὐ λέγω σοι ἕως ἑπτάκις ἀλλ' ἕως ἑβδομηκοντάκις ἑπτά.

Luke 17:4

And if he sins against you seven times in the day, and turns to you seven times, and says, "I repent," you must forgive him.[67] (RSV)

***Gos. Heb.* (*apud* Jerome, *Pelag.* 3.2)**

And in the same volume: If your brother has sinned with a word, he said, and has made amends to you, accept him seven times a day. Simon his disciple said to him, "Seven times a day?" The Lord answered, and said to him, "Even, I say to you, as much as seventy-seven times. For even among the prophets, after they were anointed with the Holy Spirit, a word of sin was found."[68]

Aphrahat, *Dem.* 14.44

On the contrary, the Lord says, "If an offender offends you seventy times seven times, forgive him in one day."[69]

Ephrem, *Comm.* 14.22, *lemma*

If someone sins against me, how many times should I forgive him? Seven times? But he said to him, "More than seventy-seven times seven."[70]

The *Gos. Heb.* knows both Gospel accounts, either directly or indirectly, for though it may be closer structurally to Matthew,[71] the "seven times a day" element is from Luke. Yet while its text is conflational, it does not seem concerned to preserve the vocabulary or sequencing of the sources, such as we typically see in our representatives of Tatian's Diatessaron. It is instead simply a loose retelling of the incident(s), beginning with Luke's account (17:4), and with certain elements of each source omitted and some major elements added. Aphrahat's paraphrastic text is not a quotation of the *Gos. Heb.* as we know it, but appears instead to be a free adaptation of Luke 17:4 that incorporates (perhaps by confusion?) Matthew's "seventy times seven." The *lemma* in Ephrem's *Commentary* offers a third configuration. It looks rather more like it is taken

---

Matthew's ἑβδομηκοντάκις ἑπτά is rendered in modern English translations as either "seventy times seven" or "seventy-seven times" (cf. Gen 4:24; *T. 12 Patr.*, *T. Benj.* 7.4).

[67] καὶ ἐὰν ἑπτάκις τῆς ἡμέρας ἁμαρτήσῃ εἰς σὲ καὶ ἑπτάκις ἐπιστρέψῃ πρὸς σὲ λέγων· μετανοῶ, ἀφήσεις αὐτῷ.

[68] Translation from Gregory, *The Gospel According to the Hebrews*, 125. See that page as well for Jerome's Latin.

[69] Translation from Adam Lehto, *The Demonstrations of Aphrahat, the Persian Sage* (Piscataway, NJ: Gorgias Press, 2010), 354. Syriac text and Latin translation may be found in J. Parisot, *Aphraatis Sapientis Persae Demonstrationes*, 2 vols. (Paris: Firmin-Didot, 1894–1907), 1:709–10.

[70] The translation of Carmel McCarthy, *Saint Ephrem's Commentary on Tatian's Diatessaron: An English Translation of Chester Beatty Syriac MS 709 with Introduction and Notes* (Oxford: Oxford University Press, 1993), 224.

[71] Gregory, *The Gospel According to the Hebrews*, 127.

straight from Matt 18:21-22, with some omissions,[72] and begins with Peter's words, not those of Jesus. But unlike *Gos. Heb.* and Aphrahat, Ephrem's version shows arguably no influence from Luke 17:4 (unless it be simply the use of a conditional). The "one-day" element from Luke 17:4 is not found in the lemma but only in the subsequent commentary.[73] This at least shows that both Matthean and Lukan elements must have been contained somewhere in Ephrem's copy of the Diatessaronic text, but on the other hand, neither in the lemma nor in the commentary does Ephrem repeat any of the distinctive "noncanonical" elements of the *Gos. Heb.*: its prominent addition of the material relating to sins among the prophets,[74] its specification that the sin in question is a sin "in word," or any of its minor details, like the change of "Peter" to "Simon" or "Jesus" to "Lord" or "if he repents" (Luke; Matthew, "if he hears you") to "and has made amends to you." Nor do any of these details appear in the Arabic Diatessaron or in Fuldensis, or its later tradents.

At this point, one could again appeal (as presumably Petersen would have done) to the process of Vulgatization for an explanation: every foreign (noncanonical) element of the *Gos. Heb.*'s version was edited out of each branch of the Diatessaron, except for the (in this case) one harmonistic detail that was already available in the canonical sources. But in the present instance, at least, such a suggestion seems ill suited to the problem. Here it is hardly simply a matter of noncanonical elements being edited out and the vocabulary of the remainder adapted to a contemporary Gospel text. The Arabic Diatessaron does not blend the two Gospel texts together into a free paraphrase, as does *Gos. Heb.*, but presents intact the saying of Jesus from Luke 17:3-4 (in which Peter is not involved), followed by the larger Matthean passage consisting of 18:15-22, which includes Jesus's teaching on church discipline and ends with the exchange with Peter.[75] It is difficult to conceive of how one could move from something like the wording of the *Gos. Heb.* to something like the wording of the Arabic Diatessaron, or even the Latin Fuldensis. What we have would represent a complete rewriting, in both linguistic traditions, based directly on the canonical Gospels. While this is not, of course, impossible, the term "Vulgatization" does not seem like a good one to describe the process. "Starting from scratch" would be more accurate. This is also what renders problematic the theory that the *Gospel according to the Hebrews* and the Diatessaron

---

[72] On Ephrem's scriptural (Diatessaronic) citations, and his tendency to abbreviate or paraphrase, see McCarthy, *Saint Ephrem's Commentary*, 35-6.

[73] Peter "did not concede even one day to [anger] . . . [f]or anger injures" and "[f]or who could commit all these transgressions in *one single day?*" (McCarthy, *Saint Ephrem's Commentary*, 224). Ephrem seems also to have Eph 4:26, "Do not let the sun go down on your anger," already in mind, which he goes on to reference in the next paragraph.

[74] It is, in fact, only this distinctive, "uncanonical" portion of *Gos. Heb.*'s account which was preserved, in Greek, in marginal attributions to τὸ Ἰουδαϊκόν in MSS 566 and 899. See Gregory, *The Gospel According to the Hebrews*, 125–30; Klijn, *Jewish-Christian Gospel Tradition*, 105–7.

[75] Chapter 27 in the Arabic harmony actually begins with Matt 18:23-35, splices in Luke 17:3-4, then continues with Matt 18:15-22; Luke 12:47-50; Matt 18:10-11; John 7:1; Luke 13:1-17. Perhaps significantly, Aphrahat also cites Matt 18:15-17 in the context leading up to his conflational citation of Matt 18:22/Luke 17:4. Fuldensis at this point follows a sequence that is similar, though the Lukan portion incorporated into the beginning of its citation of Matt 18:15-35 contains only Luke 17:3 without Luke 17:4. Thus it does not preserve the "in one day" element from Luke 17:4 but apparently regards it as "covered" by the later incorporation of Matt 18:22.

are the same thing, based on Epiphanius's report in *Pan.* 46.1 that some called the Diatessaron *According to the Hebrews*. Like every other snippet of the *Gos. Heb.* that has come down to us, the wording of this one is quite different from the wording not only of our current texts of the Diatessaron but even from the citations or allusions in Ephrem and Aphrahat assumed to be based on a Diatessaronic text. The "Diatessaron as *Gospel according to the Hebrews*" theory has to rely at almost every point on a theory of mass Vulgatization. Again, this does not render it impossible, though the extent of rewriting necessitated by the theory is at least suspicious, and leaves one with very little positive evidence on which to rest the case. In the present case all we are left with is the combined use of Matt 19:22 with Luke 17:4 by the *Gos. Heb.* and the two fourth-century Syrian authors Aphrahat and Ephrem (though in three significantly different ways).

On the other hand, the evidence of all three may be more economically explained by their own distinctive, synthetic uses of a Diatessaron text that looked very much like the Arabic Diatessaron.[76] In other words, it seems easier to view the *Gos. Heb.*, Aphrahat, and Ephrem as dependent upon the Diatessaron, than to view the Diatessaron as a "Vulgatization" of the *Gos. Heb.* or to view them as one and the same. While we cannot of course claim certainty here, the next example, I believe, will provide us with even more reason to conclude that this is the direction of dependence.

3.2.2 "Another Rich Man"

Phillips's *sixth* example concerns a late (fourth- or fifth-century) interpolation in the Latin translation of Origen's *Commentary on Matthew*. The passage does not occur in the Greek text of Origen and is, therefore, according to the common opinion of experts not original. It is inserted in Origen's *Commentary* (15.14) on Matt 19:16–30, the parable of the rich young ruler.[77] Here the interpolator reports that a "Hebrew Gospel" begins, "And another rich man." This mention of "another rich man" agrees with the order of pericopes in the Arabic Diatessaron (chs. 28–29), which places in succession three stories concerning rich men that were not in succession in the synoptic Gospels: the parable of the rich fool (Luke 12:13–21), the story of the rich young ruler (Matt 19:16–22; Mark 10:17–22; Luke 18:18–23), and the parable of Lazarus and the rich man (Luke 16:19–31).[78]

---

[76] Common to Ephrem and the Arabic Diatessaron alone is the presence of two "sevens" in the text following "seventy times." This is rendered in McCarthy's text of Ephrem as "seventy-seven times seven" and in Hogg's translation (*ANF* 9:85) of the Vatican MS of the Arabic ("following the Syriac versions") as "seventy times seven, seven."

[77] For text and translation of this passage, see Gregory, *The Gospel According to the Hebrews*, 130–1, along with his comments, 131–40. A. F. J. Klijn, "The Question of the Rich Young Man in a Jewish-Christian Gospel," *NovT* 8 (1966): 152, reports that Justin Martyr in his use of the rich young ruler passage in *1 Apol.* 16.7 and *Dial.* 101.2 shows no awareness of the characteristics of this Hebrew Gospel's version, nor does Clement of Alexandria, nor do the Clementine Homilies.

[78] Ephrem's *Commentary*, however, does not have the three episodes involving rich men in sequence, only the last two (15.1–11; 15.12–13). If we accept that the Arabic preserves the original order,

There clearly seems to be a relationship between this Hebrew Gospel and the Diatessaron. The Arabic Diatessaron itself, however, does *not* introduce the second episode with "another rich man." This is the wording of the Hebrew Gospel. And this means that the Hebrew Gospel *presupposes* the harmonizing rearrangement of the Gospel material that is found in the Diatessaron (unless, of course, this Hebrew Gospel *is* the Diatessaron; see below). In fact, while Petersen uses the correlation between these sources as evidence for Tatian's use of a lost Judaic-Christian Gospel, he does not report what Phillips actually determined about the direction of dependence: "if Pseudo-Origen on St. Matt. quotes correctly," wrote Phillips, "the 'Hebrew' itself shows traces of Diatessaron influence."[79] Luomanen agrees: "Dependence on the *Diatessaron* makes understandable the expression 'another' for which there is no reason in the synoptic narratives."[80]

The evidence provided by the "another rich man" example is important, for it virtually establishes that at least one "Hebrew Gospel" known in antiquity was dependent upon the Diatessaron (or a similar Gospel harmony),[81] rather than the other way around.

An escape from this conclusion might be found if, reverting to Epiphanius's report in *Pan.* 46.1, we could establish that this Hebrew Gospel was in fact a more primitive form of the Diatessaron itself. One problem with such a theory however is that, according to Luomanen, this Hebrew Gospel shows the influence not only of the Diatessaron, but also, and even primarily, of the Old Syriac translations of the separate Gospels. Such agreement "suggests that Origen's passage was composed in a context where the Old Syriac translations and the *Diatessaron* were available."[82] Luomanen concludes that "almost every expression in the story of Origen that can be compared with the synoptic versions finds a corresponding expression in the Old Syriac translations and (other) Diatessaronic witnesses."[83] If we are to imagine that the Hebrew Gospel in question is the original Diatessaron, this does not accord with the usual supposition that the Diatessaron was composed before the Syriac Gospels were available.[84] To my

---

then the Syriac Diatessaron known to the author of the Syriac commentary near the end of the fourth century had undergone revision. This appears to be another sign that the Diatessaron used by Ephrem had been revised at least once; cf. the similar conclusion coming from the study of the Dura fragment (Crawford, "The Diatessaron, Canonical or Non-canonical?" 274), where it is shown that the Dura fragment agrees with the Arabic but not with Ephrem or Fuldensis.

[79] Phillips, "Diatessaron—Diapente," 8.

[80] See Petri Luomanen, "Where Did Another Rich Man Come from? The Jewish-Christian Profile of the Story about a Rich Man in the '*Gospel of the Hebrews*' (Origen, *Comm. in Matth.* 15.14)," *VC* 57 (2003): 255.

[81] Perhaps the equation between the two works reported by Epiphanius in *Pan.* 46.1 was made because a Gospel used by the Ebionites—said to be a copy of Matthew in Hebrew but also called *According to the Hebrews*—was indeed based on the Diatessaron (cf. *Pan.* 20.3.7; 13.2; 14.3, where it is noted that the Ebionites' Matthew cut out Matthew's genealogy). Alternatively, the equation may have been made simply because the Diatessaron was known to be written in Syriac.

[82] Luomanen, "Where Did Another Rich Man Come from?" 253–4.

[83] Ibid., 257. The same may be said for the addition, "do the law," which occurs in the interpolator's account as well as in the Old Syriac of Mark's version of Jesus's response to the rich young ruler, as well as in Ephrem and Aphrahat.

[84] If Tatian's original Diatessaron was in Greek and was not translated into Syriac until, let us say, the early third century, early forms of the individual Syriac Gospels may have been available.

mind, at least as problematic for this theory is that, as with our previous example, the Arabic Diatessaron (Fuldensis too) then appears not merely to be a "Vulgatized" version of the Hebrew Gospel/Diatessaron, but essentially a new composition begun from scratch. The account in the Arabic does not look like the Hebrew Gospel with revised wording and the noncanonical elements (of which there are many) cleaned out. Instead, it is a carefully integrated harmony of Matthew's, Mark's,[85] and Luke's versions of the story of the Rich Young Ruler—which is to say that it shows in this passage the same characteristics it has throughout the composition. The Hebrew Gospel looks to be something different.

Gregory considers this fragment to be part of the *Gospel according to the Hebrews*. If this is valid, it would have significant implications. For one, looking back to Phillips's third example, it now seems even more likely that the combined use of Matt 18:21 and Luke 17:4 in Aphrahat and Ephrem also originated with the Diatessaron, which was also used by the creator, or by a later editor, of this *Gospel according to the Hebrews* cited by Jerome.

3.2.3 "The Fire/Light at the Baptism," Ephrem, Comm. 4.5

Perhaps the most frequently cited example of Tatian's alleged use of a noncanonical Gospel is the "fire/light at the baptism" variant. The witnesses consist of a number of similar to not-so-similar expressions in a variety of sources, in no two of which is the wording the same. We may in fact be dealing with two separate traditions having to do with Jesus's baptism in the Jordan. There is variation about whether it was a fire or a light;[86] and whether the light shines from the water, from Jesus, from heaven, or on the water; whether it shines around or just shines; whether it happens as Jesus enters the water or after he has left it, and even after the Holy Spirit descends and a voice from heaven speaks.

The tradition of some sort of theophanic manifestation of fire or light at the time of Jesus's baptism would become very widespread, witnessed in numerous sources from the second century and throughout the middle ages, and not just in Diatessaronic tradents. Are all these witnesses best explained by the theory that they come ultimately from a noncanonical Gospel, either from that Gospel directly, or indirectly through Tatian's original Diatessaron or some other intermediary? We have space to introduce here, and only very briefly, the most pertinent witnesses.[87]

3.2.3.1 Justin

Probably the earliest exponent of the tradition is Justin's *Dial.* 88.3:

---

[85] I find nothing distinctively Markan in the Origen interpolation, in contrast to the Arabic Diatessaron.
[86] Because the Syriac words for fire and light are very similar and are homonyms, some have suggested that confusion between them was the cause of the bifurcation in the traditions. This is highly doubtful, however. Justin (*Dial.* 88.3) also uses the verb ἀνάπτω, which goes with fire but does not go with light (cf. Ps 77:21 LXX).
[87] For more of them, see Petersen, *Tatian's Diatessaron*, 14–22.

[A]nd when He had stepped into the water, a fire was kindled in the Jordan ([καὶ] πῦρ ἀνήφθη ἐν τῷ Ἰορδάνῃ); and when He came out of the water, the Holy Spirit lighted on Him like a dove, [as] the apostles of this very Christ of ours wrote.[88]

Justin's statement makes it unclear whether what he is attributing to the writings of the apostles includes the fire in the Jordan, or just the Holy Spirit alighting on Christ like a dove. In any case, his version may have been the result of an exegetical gloss that may have no close relationship to the "light" incident. In Matt 3:11/Luke 3:16, John announces that Jesus will baptize with the Holy Spirit and with fire. A fire kindled in the Jordan, then, is a fitting analogue to the descent of the Holy Spirit as a dove. John's announcement that Jesus would baptize with the Spirit and with fire would be memorialized rhetorically in a statement like Justin's "and a fire was kindled in the Jordan."[89]

3.2.3.2 Two Old Latin Manuscripts

The fourth-century Vetus Latina MS *a* (Vercellensis)[90] inserts before Matt 3:16

> *et cum baptizaretur, lumen ingens circumfulsit de aqua;*
> *ita ut timerent omnes qui advenerant*

> And when he was baptized, a momentous light shone about from the water,
> so that all who had come were afraid.[91]

Similarly, MS g¹ (Codex Sangermanensis) from the ninth[92] century has

> *et cum baptizaretur Iesus lumen magnum fulgebat de aqua,*
> *ita ut timerent omnes qui congregati erant;*

---

[88] The translation of Alexander Roberts and James Donaldson, *ANF* 1:243 (slightly adapted); Greek text from Miroslav Marcovich, *Iustini Martyris Apologiae pro Christianis, Dialogus cum Tryphone*, PTS 47 (Berlin: de Gruyter, 2005).

[89] In the sixth-century, poetic composition of Romanos Melodos (*First Hymn on the Epiphany*, XVI.14.7–10), the fire in the Jordan is Jesus himself:

> And seeing again in the middle of the streams
> The one who appeared in the midst of the three youths,
> The dew in the fire, and the fire in the Jordan,
> Shining, springing forth, the unapproachable Light.
> (See Petersen, *Tatian's Diatessaron*, 19, for the Greek text.) Romanos seems to know both traditions, the fire and the light.

[90] This is VL3 in Houghton's notation; see H. A. G. Houghton, *The Latin New Testament: A Guide to its Early History, Texts, and Manuscripts* (Oxford: Oxford University Press, 2016), 26, 211.

[91] Text taken from J. Belsheim, *Codex Vercellensis. Quatuor evangelia ante hieronymum latine translata ex reliquiis codices vercellensis, saeculo ut videtur quarto scripti et ex editione iriciana principe* (Christiania: Libraria Mallingiana, 1894), 3.

[92] This is VL7 in Houghton's notation, see Houghton, *The Latin New Testament*, 213–14. Houghton reports that this ninth-century MS "goes back to a pandect assembled in the fifth century, probably in Rome" (213).

And when Jesus was baptized, a great light began to shine from the water,
> so that all who had gathered were afraid.[93]

These manuscripts show that a variant reading, which included a report about a *light* at the baptism, had entered some portion of the textual tradition of Matthew, at least in Latin if not also in Greek, by at least some point in the fourth century. We cannot say just how early this variant is.

3.2.3.3 "Ephrem"

The only primary Diatessaronic witness to the tradition is a passage in Ephrem's *Commentary* 4.5, extant only in the Armenian recension (in the Syriac there is a hiatus).[94]

> When he saw, from the splendour of the light which appeared on the water, and the voice which came from heaven.[95]

This notice comes not from Ephrem's exposition of Jesus's baptism, where he made no mention of the light,[96] but from his comments on Jesus's temptation in the wilderness following his baptism. The subject of Ephrem's sentence is not Jesus or John, but Satan. It is part of Ephrem's attempt to furnish a reason for why Satan had not tempted Jesus before his thirtieth year. Ephrem's use of the tradition does not give us the actual text of the Diatessaron. If the source of his allusion was the Diatessaronic text of the baptism, and not some other tradition, we have no clear idea of the wording of the text.

3.2.3.4 *The Gospel of the Ebionites (Epiphanius, Pan. 30.13)*

Epiphanius adduces passages from a Gospel he says was used by the Ebionites, the Hebraic ([τὸ] Ἑβραϊκιον), which scholars today usually identify as the *Gospel of the Ebionites*. This was a harmonistic Gospel that sought to combine at least Matthew and Luke and probably Mark. Petersen calls it "a harmony of the *synoptic* gospels."[97] The author's method, according to Gregory, "seems to have been to conflate the synoptic accounts, lengthening the tradition by including the sayings found in each of the three Synoptics, and some but not all of the other details that might be culled from all three accounts."[98]

---

[93] Text and translation from Houghton, *The Latin New Testament*, 158. Charlesworth, "Tatian's Dependence upon Apocryphal Traditions," 14–15, suggests that the element of the fear of those present also went back to Tatian.
[94] See McCarthy, *Saint Ephrem's Commentary*, 84n. 3. This lacuna covers part of the baptism and temptation sections, 4.2–6 in the commentary.
[95] The translation of McCarthy, *Saint Ephrem's Commentary*, 85.
[96] This is perhaps why Charlesworth, "Tatian's Dependence upon Apocryphal Traditions," 12, mistakenly said that the passage did not occur in either the Syriac or Armenian manuscripts of the commentary.
[97] Petersen, *Tatian's Diatessaron*, 30; cf. Andrew Gregory, "Jewish Christian Gospels," in *The Non-canonical Gospels*, ed. Paul Foster (London: T&T Clark, 2008), 54–67; Andrew Gregory, "Prior or Posterior? The Gospel of the Ebionites and the Gospel of Luke," *NTS* 51 (2005): 351–4; Gregory, *The Gospel According to the Hebrews*, 226–40. Like the Diatessaron, this Gospel is said by Epiphanius to have lacked the genealogies and is said to have begun with Jesus's baptism.
[98] Gregory, "Prior or Posterior?" 355.

Its account of Jesus's baptism includes the words, "and immediately a great light shone around the place" (καὶ εὐθὺς περιέλαμψε τὸν τόπον φῶς μέγα).[99] But it also presents many more additions that have no parallel in Ephrem. This version of Jesus's baptism in fact seeks to incorporate and harmonize elements from two or, more probably, all three synoptic sources. In my opinion, it executes this harmonization by also incorporating elements from Paul's conversion story in Acts.

The author first gives the heavenly approbation in the words of Mark and Luke, "*You are* my beloved son, in whom I am well pleased," and then adds, "And again, "This day I have begotten you," the famous phrase from Psalm 2:7 that occurs in seven manuscripts of the Old Latin at Luke 3:22, as well as in Codex Bezae's Luke (both columns),[100] as well as being attested in Justin (*Dial.* 103).

At this point, a light shines about the place and John asks Jesus a question that is in none of the canonical accounts: "Who are you, Lord?" (σὺ τίς εἶ κύριε;). His question is answered not by Jesus himself but by another heavenly voice, this time giving the divine approbation in the exact wording of Matthew, "*This is* my beloved son, in whom I am well pleased." The question John put to Jesus (σὺ τίς εἶ κύριε;) is the same one Paul asked the risen Jesus on the road to Damascus (minus only the emphatic σύ) in Acts 9:5; 22:8; 26:15. In the Lukan story of Paul's conversion his question was preceded by the appearance of a great light: "a light . . . that shone around (περιλάμψαν) me and those who journeyed with me" (Acts 26:13). Luke's word περιλάμπω is the same word used by the author of the *Gos. Eb.* in his account of Jesus's baptism.[101]

The light at the baptism incident in the harmonistic *Gos. Eb.* could be viewed as the origination of the variant. If so, the shining light and John's subsequent question appear to function as a rationale for fitting in the wording of Matthew's version of the heavenly voice along with Mark's and Luke's. Alternatively, perhaps the author of the *Gos. Eb.* had a manuscript of Matthew which, like Vercellensis or Sangermanensis, already contained the variant. In either case, that the author of the *Gos. Eb.* seems to restrict himself to canonical sources for his Gospel pastiche is intriguing.

So, how did such a variant enter the Diatessaronic textual stream by the time of the commentary attributed to Ephrem? Although Petersen lists several possibilities, he ultimately invokes Westcott's little-known, text-critical canon that "the combination of the oldest types of the Syriac and Latin texts can outweigh the combination of the primary Greek texts," and from this he argues that (some form of) this incident was part of the original text of Matthew.[102] If Petersen is correct—or if the reading was,

---

[99] Petersen, *Tatian's Diatessaron*, 15.
[100] Gregory, "Prior or Posterior?" 356.
[101] It is used but one more time in the NT, at Luke 2:9.
[102] Petersen, *Tatian's Diatessaron*, 21. Petersen reiterated this position in at least one later publication, Petersen, "The Diatessaron and the Fourfold Gospel," 67n. 38. Here, however, he offers the reader a choice between concluding that the text of the canonical Gospels at the time Tatian wrote (ca. 175) "was significantly different from the text we have before us today" and "had not yet finished evolving" or that Tatian used other "extra- or non-canonical traditions, either oral or (more likely) written," showing that "some Christians—including, apparently, Syrians, Armenians, and others—had no problem conflating what we regard as extra-canonical traditions with what we today regard as canonical traditions."

let us say, not in the original text of Matthew but was in a copy of Matthew used by Tatian—then it did not come from any noncanonical Gospel.[103]

There are certainly other possible explanations. The reading could have originated in

1. an original text of Matthew (Petersen),
2. an interpolated text of Matthew that was used by Tatian,
3. a noncanonical Judaic Gospel that was used by Tatian,
4. an insertion into the Syriac Diatessaron (perhaps from a variant text of Matthew) at the time of its translation from Greek (late second to mid-third century),[104]
5. a revision of the Syriac Diatessaron sometime before Ephrem,[105]
6. a non-Diatessaronic written source known to Ephrem, perhaps the *Gos. Eb.* or something else,
7. oral lore or exegetical tradition.[106]

The plurality of possible explanations is precisely the problem. The solution that requires us to posit that a notice of a light (or fire?) at the baptism of Jesus was indeed part of Tatian's original composition, *and* that Tatian's source for the variant was a now-lost, noncanonical Gospel is only one of several. It could be the right one but is not obviously so (it is not the one Petersen ultimately favored, despite his innuendos elsewhere). And if we choose it, we are faced with further questions. If Tatian used the *Gos. Eb.*, the only known, noncanonical Gospel that contains it, we shall wonder why Tatian selected only this detail from the many others in the text. We then practically require a further hypothesis, that Epiphanius's *Gos. Eb.* is a later expansion of a lost harmonized Gospel that had many fewer noncanonical details. And then we shall have to ask why this detail was preserved only in the Syriac Diatessaron known to Ephrem and was edited out of both Fuldensis and the Arabic. If we wish to attribute this to Vulgatization, the act of conforming copies of the Diatessaron to a current, local text of

---

[103] It may of course have entered the textual tradition of Matthew from an existing Gospel, but we cannot presume that Tatian would have known this.

[104] Sebastian Brock, *The Bible in the Syriac Tradition*, 2nd ed. (Piscataway, NJ: Gorgias Press, 2006), 32, suggests this path for two other variants in the Syriac Diatessaron. Though many date the translation of the separate Gospels after the Diatessaron, this is very uncertain and dates have been given ranging from the late second to the early fourth century (Brock, *The Bible in the Syriac Tradition,* 33). The Dura fragment of the Diatessaron, evidently in use in eastern Syria when Dura was destroyed in 256-7, is in *Greek*, not Syriac. If the Greek Diatessaron was not translated into Syriac until sometime in the third century, the translator may have been influenced by an existing Syriac translation of the separate Gospels. In this case, influence from the Old Latin, perhaps through the Old Syriac, would be possible as well.

[105] We know that the copy used for Ephrem's *Commentary* had been revised at least once from the original (Crawford, "The Diatessaron, Canonical or Non-canonical?" 273-4) and that our copy of the Syriac commentary attributed to Ephrem was revised at least once (Lange, *The Portrayal of Christ*, 42, 51, 52).

[106] If so, it might be viewed much like, for instance, the detail in Ephrem's *Commentary* at 4.2: "Because John had confessed, *I am not worthy to untie the thongs of his sandals*, our Lord took John's right hand and placed it on his head [saying], *Permit that we may fulfil justice now*" (McCarthy, *Saint Ephrem's Commentary*, 84). No ancient source I am aware of tells us that Jesus took John's right hand and placed it on his head before uttering those famous Matthean words. Was this too in the Diatessaron, or was it simply based on Ephrem's mental picture of what must have happened at the time?

the canonical Gospels, it should be kept in mind that by the time of Ephrem we know there was an analogous reading in the Old Latin text of Matthew. So, it could be that such a variant, canonical source was actually the conduit by which this reading entered into the Diatessaron, and this would even qualify as "Vulgatization." Though some have suggested that the Diatessaron was the source for this variant in the Old Latin, Hugh Houghton thinks it and other variants "are more likely to have been incorporated as part of ongoing tradition rather than from any direct influence of the Diatessaron or Syriac sources."[107]

3.2.4 "The Woes at the Crucifixion"

Another oft-cited example of possible noncanonical Gospel influence, also contained in "Ephrem," is the "woes" uttered by the Jerusalemites at the time of Jesus's crucifixion, which some have thought Tatian derived from the *Gospel of Peter*.[108] Petersen regards the passage as one more demonstration of "the incorporation of apocryphal traditions into the Diatessaron,"[109] though he does not consider it to have come from the *Gos. Pet.*

3.2.4.1 *Ephrem*, Comm. 20.28

The only primary Diatessaronic witness to this passage is Ephrem's *Commentary* (20.28 Armenian; Syriac is vacant);[110] it does not appear in the Arabic Harmony or in Fuldensis, nor even in the vernacular harmonies.[111] After commenting on the darkness in the land until the ninth hour on the day of the crucifixion, as recorded in Luke 23:44, Ephrem reports that those who crucified Christ had their spiritual darkness lifted to the extent that they could utter the words, "Woe, woe to us, this was the Son of God."

A little later in the same chapter Ephrem says that the darkening of the natural sun "revealed the imminence of the destruction of their city," and then cites words that seem easily attributable to the same people who pronounced the woes: "Behold the judgements concerning the destruction of Jerusalem have come and are here."

3.2.4.2 *Doctrina Addai*

Both the woes and the proclamation of the desolation of Jerusalem are alluded to in a passage in the *Doctrina Addai*, though the order is switched: "For, behold, except they who crucified Him knew that He was the Son of God, they would not have

---

[107] Houghton, *The Latin New Testament*, 26. It is possible for scholars to claim "Vulgatization" of deviating Diatessaron texts, or "Diatessaronization" of deviating canonical texts in order to argue that a reading is Diatessaronic.

[108] E.g., Crawford, "Diatessaron, a Misnomer?" 383: "A passage from the *Gospel of Peter* appears in witnesses to Tatian's gospel ([Ephrem,] C*Diat* XX.28)."

[109] Petersen, *Tatian's Diatessaron*, 420. He also regards it as a demonstration of the dependence of the separate Syriac Gospels upon the Diatessaron "rather than the reverse."

[110] Translations from McCarthy, *Saint Ephrem's Commentary*, 308.

[111] Petersen, *Tatian's Diatessaron*, 418.

proclaimed the desolation of their city, also they would not have brought down woes upon themselves."[112]

3.2.4.3 Aphrahat, Dem. 14.26

In Aphrahat there is something similar: "Woe to us! What has befallen us, who have left the Law and the ones from us who glory in iniquity?"[113] It should be noted, however, that Aphrahat does not place these words in the mouths of anyone at the time of the crucifixion of Jesus, but attributes them to unfaithful Christian shepherds in his own day. There is no indication that he is citing any source.

3.2.4.4 The Textual Tradition of Luke

As the "light at the baptism" variant did with Matthew, this episode has left its traces in the textual tradition of Luke. After Luke 23:48, "And when all the crowds who had gathered there for this spectacle saw what had taken place, they returned home, beating their breasts," both the Sinaitic (fourth century) and Curetonian (fifth century) manuscripts of Syriac Luke add the following expansion: "and saying: 'Woe to us! What hath befallen us? Woe to us from our sins!'"[114]

Similarly, a single Latin manuscript of Luke, the ninth-century Sangermanensis mentioned above,[115] contains an interpolation after Luke 23:48 that critics have assigned to the Old Latin. The crowd's lament is different yet: "Woe to us who have today, on account of our sins, hastened the desolation of Jerusalem."[116]

3.2.4.5 The Gospel of Peter

According to Petersen, the only other ancient source to include this interpolation is the *Gospel of Peter* 7: "Then the Jews and the elders and the priests, when they perceived how great evil they had done themselves, began to lament and to say: 'Woe unto our sins; the judgment and the end of Jerusalem is drawn near.'"[117]

Petersen, who assumed that a form of the variant was in the text Tatian produced, denied that Tatian got it from *Gos. Pet.* Observing that "[w]hile agreements between

---

[112] Translation from George Phillips, *The Doctrine of Addai, the Apostle* (London: Trübner, 1876), 27 (cf. Petersen, *Tatian's Diatessaron*, 415).
[113] This is the translation of Petersen, *Tatian's Diatessaron*, 415, made apparently by himself from the Syriac text in Parisot, *Aphraatis Sapientis*, 1:640. Lehto, *The Demonstrations*, translates, "Woe to us! What have we become when the Law is forsaken and some among us adorn themselves with wickedness?"
[114] Translation from Petersen, *Tatian's Diatessaron*, 414.
[115] Sangermanensis's text of Matthew (which contain the "light at the baptism" variant), known as g¹, is Old Latin. Its text of Luke is Vulgate, but this interpolation after Luke 23:48 is considered an Old Latin remnant. See Houghton, *The Latin New Testament*, 213–14 on Codex Sangermanensis (primus), denoted VL7, and Houghton's mention of this variant on p. 164. Other interpolations in other Old Latin MSS of Luke are mentioned on pp. 163–4.
[116] Translation from Petersen, *Tatian's Diatessaron*, 415: *uae uobis quae facta sunt hodiae propter peccata nostra, adpropinquauit enim desolatio hierusalem.*
[117] Translation from Petersen, *Tatian's Diatessaron*, 416.

Peter and the Diatessaron exist, they are few and minor,"[118] he concluded that "direct dependence in either direction seems unlikely."[119] We may refer again to the lack of any details from the *Gos. Pet.* in the Joseph of Arimathea passage in the Greek Dura fragment, or, for that matter, in any number of other Diatessaronic passages in other witnesses. Instead, Petersen proposes that "both Tatian and *Peter* took the variant from the same [lost] Judaic-Christian gospel,"[120] and that the Diatessaron became the source for all the remaining witnesses.[121]

As with the light/fire at the baptism variant, a number of other options exist. The witnesses for this variant would fit Westcott's formula for an original Lukan reading, though Petersen does not invoke that formula here. It might have crept into an altered copy of Luke that Tatian came in contact with; it could have entered the Syriac Diatessaronic tradition from a glossed Latin or Syriac translation of Luke at the time of the Diatessaron's original translation into Syriac, or during a later revision before the time of Ephrem and Aphrahat (assuming that Aphrahat's witness is relevant). Alternatively, because of the wide variation in its forms, could it have been simply a fairly common exegetical gloss on Luke's narrative? The point again is that the proposal that this variant was in Tatian's original Diatessaron (despite its absence from all primary Diatessaronic witnesses except Ephrem's *Commentary*) *and* that Tatian obtained it from a noncanonical Gospel now lost to us may be plausible, but it is neither obviously correct nor free of difficulty.

3.2.5 *"Where there is One, there I am"*

Crawford cites one last example from Ephrem's *Commentary*, a saying attributed to Jesus, "Where there is one, there I am" (Ephrem, *Comm.* 14.24), which Crawford thinks comes from the *Gospel of Thomas* 30.[122] Petersen did not treat this particular parallel but was fairly emphatic in his denial of the idea that Tatian was dependent on the *Gos. Thom.*, because the parallels were only of the synoptic type, because they were too few, and because "[n]one of *Thomas'* striking *agrapha* crop up in the Diatessaron."[123] Petersen's preference, once again, was for a hypothetical Judaic-Christian Gospel that was the source of both Tatian and *Thomas*.[124] In any case, in the present instance neither of the two forms of this Thomasine saying (the Coptic or the Greek of P.Oxy. 1) matches the words or the context of Ephrem's *Commentary* very well.

---

[118] Petersen, *Tatian's Diatessaron*, 417.
[119] Ibid., 419.
[120] Ibid., 420.
[121] Ibid., 417–18.
[122] Crawford, "Diatessaron, a Misnomer?" 383.
[123] Petersen, *Tatian's Diatessaron*, 298. For the first of these points he cites A. F. J. Klijn, *A Survey of the Researches into the Western Text of the Gospels and Acts. Part Two: 1949–1969* (Brill: Leiden, 1969), 8–9.
[124] See his long review of the work of Gilles Quispel and its aftermath in Petersen, *Tatian's Diatessaron*, 272–300, particularly his review of Jacques-É. Ménard (296–7).

Gos. Thom. 30[125]

Coptic: "Jesus said, 'Where there are three gods, they are gods; where there are two or one, I am with him.'"

Greek of P.Oxy. 1: "Jesus says, 'Wherever there are [three] they are without God and where there is one alone I say I am with him. Lift the stone and there you will find me; cleave the wood and I am there.'"

Ephrem, *Comm.* 14.24

Just as the Messiah took care of his flock in every necessity, so too he offered consolation with regard to the sadness of loneliness, when he said, *Where there is one, I [am there]*, lest all those who are solitary be sad. For he is our joy, and he is with us. *Where there are two, I [am there]*. His grace gives us protection. And *when there are three*, it is like when we are assembled in the Church, which is the perfect body, the seal of the Messiah. *Their angels in heaven see the face of my Father*, that is, [through] their prayers.[126]

In my opinion, the most probable explanation for Ephrem's words is found in neither version of the *Gos. Thom.* but emerges instead when we compare the entire passage in Ephrem's *Commentary* with the sequence of elements preserved in the Arabic Diatessaron. In the Arabic Diatessaron, Matt 18:20 ("For where two or three are gathered in my name, I am there among them") precedes 18:10 ("Take care that you do not despise one of these little ones; for, I tell you, in heaven their angels continually see the face of my Father in heaven"). Ephrem seems to be offering a harmonizing meditation on Christ's solution to loneliness by flowing from the "one" in "one of these little ones" of 18:10, to the "two" and then the "three" who may gather in Jesus's name in 18:20, then coming back again to 18:10 with a reference to the angels of the little ones, who see the Father's face in heaven. This solution offers, I think, a much better accounting of Ephrem's text than does the theory that it is based on a hypothetical Diatessaronic text that looked more like the (Greek?) *Gospel of Thomas*.

4. Conclusion: Diatessaron, not Diapente or Diapollon

Most of the supposed examples of Tatian's dependence upon a lost Judaic Gospel (four of Phillips's six) can instead be traced back with virtual certainty to the notices of Jerome, which we know were eagerly sought out by medieval interpreters. In another example, the dependence actually goes the other way, with the Hebrew Gospel of the Origen interpolator showing dependence upon the same rearrangement of synoptic stories that is present in the Diatessaron. Tatian's use of a noncanonical Gospel or

---

[125] The translations of both Coptic and Greek texts are from J. K. Elliott, *The Apocryphal New Testament: A Collection of Apocryphal Christian Literature in an English Translation* (Oxford: Clarendon Press, 1993), 139.

[126] Translation from McCarthy, *Saint Ephrem's Commentary*, 225.

Gospels may remain a possibility in a small handful of instances. But in no instance that I am aware of is this possibility clearly the most probable one, let alone a proven one. I would have to judge that none of the elements claimed to have come from noncanonical Gospels can be shown to have occurred in Tatian's original composition.

But let us suppose that this judgment is mistaken. Let us say that one (maybe the "woes") or two (the "light at the baptism") were in Tatian's original work. And let us say he got these elements not from contemporary copies of Luke and Matthew, and not from unwritten exegetical or homiletical custom, but from another written Gospel or Gospels. And, it is always possible that we might have missed something,[127] so let us double the number from two to four. And to be overly cautious, let us triple the number to six. The ancient text, of course, did not have our modern versification. But a study of the Arabic Diatessaron by George Foote Moore published in 1890 reported that 2,769 of the 3,780 total modern verses in the four Gospels were represented.[128] If we were to allow for six interpolations of approximately a verse in length, even though most of those that have been suggested are not nearly as long as a typical Gospel verse, the extracanonical material would account for 0.21668472 percent of the Diatessaron (six out of 2,769), which we might round upward to an even 0.22 percent. If there are only two such interpolations instead of six, they would take up 0.07 percent of the text of the Diatessaron. And, again, none of these can be established.

But it is not just the paucity of additions or the small amount of text they represent that deserves to be stressed here. These are not new episodes in the life of Jesus but expansions on canonical ones. We hear nothing of Jesus passing through the seven heavens on his earthly descent, no clay pigeons coming to life, no sprinkling miracle at the Jordan, no talking cross at the resurrection, to cite just a few of the many possibilities. While Tatian shows a clear concern to reproduce "special Matthew," "special Mark," "special Luke," and "special John," there is no concern to reproduce "special Peter," "special Thomas," "special Egerton," or "special lost, Judaic-Christian."

One can understand how the theory of a lost, Ur-Judaic Gospel would be attractive to Petersen and others. If all the disparate, suggested noncanonical elements could be imagined as tributaries flowing from a single Jewish-Christian Gospel spring, this would make it look like Tatian came to draw from this source more often.[129] But it now

---

[127] For instance, at the 2016 SBL session, Nick Zola rightly mentioned the variant of the "flying Jesus" found in Aphrahat and identified by T. Baarda as coming from the Syriac Diatessaron (T. Baarda, "'The Flying Jesus': Luke 4:29–30 in the Syriac Diatessaron," *VC* 40 (1986): 313–41). Even though this possible variant in the Diatessaron probably did not come from an alternative Gospel (Baarda thought it arose from a corruption in Tatian's text of Luke, or else from Tatian's misunderstanding of the text, possibly influenced by knowledge of Marcion's Gospel; in my opinion, it could also have come to the Syriac from a misunderstanding of the Greek text of the Diatessaron, or of Luke), it does illustrate the possibility that Tatian's original work could have contained a number of "extraneous" elements. It is a reminder that, in our present state of knowledge, we cannot entirely rule out the possibility that original elements from noncanonical, written sources could have been eliminated from the textual traditions of the Diatessaron through Vulgatization.

[128] George Foote Moore, "Tatian's Diatessaron and the Analysis of the Pentateuch," *JBL* 9 (1890): 203. The numbers for the individual Gospels are John, 847 of 880 verses; Matthew, 821 of 1,071; Mark, 340 of 678; Luke, 761 of 1,151.

[129] Charlesworth, "Tatian's Dependence upon Apocryphal Traditions," 16, criticizes Peters's proposal that the lost fifth source was the *Gospel according to the Hebrews* as circular, because "we end up

seems that the fountainhead has nearly gone dry, thanks in part to the desiccating rays of Jerome's wide influence, and there are no sure signs that Tatian ever visited the proposed site.

This leaves us, then, with Matthew, Mark, Luke, and John as the only written Gospels we can be sure that Tatian used for constructing his Diatessaron Gospel. These four are the only Gospels he used consistently and the only Gospels he used in a programmatic way, incorporating unique passages from each and, for their common passages, seeking to combine what each had to contribute. Tatian does the same for no other Gospel. If Tatian knew any other Gospels, and surely he must have, he did not treat any of them in the same way he treated these four. On the most generous allowance that certain details entered his composition from a noncanonical source or sources, it will be difficult to argue that he regarded it or them as having "equal validity" with the four.

Did Tatian intend to replace the four Gospels, and all others, with his impressive, integrating composition? We do not know. But it seems fair to assume that his decision to unite these four Gospels (no more and no less), one of which was the highly distinctive Gospel of John, tells us something about the Christian environment in which he worked, or the one from which he emerged. That the four he chose to unify are the same four that are distinguished from all others in various ways in multiple second-century authors[130] precludes the option that his choice was random.

---

compiling GH from noncanonical elements in the Diatessaron and then employ this fabricated source to explain the origin of Tatian's apocryphal traditions." This same critique strikes Petersen's approach with just as much force. His lost Judaic-Christian Gospel is essentially what results when we combine all the noncanonical elements that are attributed to the original Diatessaron.

[130] Irenaeus (*Haer.* 3.11.9, cf. 3.1.1; 3.11.8); Clement of Alexandria (*Strom.* 3.13.93; *Quis div.* 1.5); the *Muratorian Fragment*; the four-Gospel *Harmony* of Theophilus. All four, though not named, are arguably known as a collection in the works of earlier writers: Justin (see G. N. Stanton, "The Fourfold Gospel," *NTS* 43 [1997]: 330–1; Oskar Skarsaune, "Justin and His Bible," in *Justin Martyr and His Worlds*, ed. Sara Parvis and Paul Foster [Minneapolis, MN: Fortress Press, 2007], 72); the *Ep. Apos.* (see Darrell D. Hannah, "The Four-Gospel 'Canon' in the *Epistula Apostolorum*," *JTS* 59 [2008]: 598–633); and Papias (see Charles E. Hill, *The Johannine Corpus in the Early Church* [Oxford: Oxford University Press, 2004], 383–96, 407–16). See also Charles E. Hill, "A Four-Gospel Canon in the Second Century? Artifact and Arti-fiction," *EC* 4 (2013): 310–34.

3

Tatian's Sources and the Presentation of the Jewish Law in the Diatessaron

Jan Joosten

Abstract

This chapter consists of two parts, a methodological survey and a case study. The Diatessaron has for the most part come down to us indirectly, in quotations and translations that are much more recent than the original writing. Even these indirect witnesses attest many interesting variants, although not all of them can go back to Tatian's harmony. In the first part of the chapter I plead for a method that gives pride of place to the eastern witnesses—quotations in Aphrahat, Ephrem, and other authors; Old Syriac and Peshitta versions of the Gospels; and the Arabic Diatessaron. The Syriac texts are written in the language Tatian almost certainly used in composing his harmony, and all the eastern witnesses come to us from a region where the impact of the Diatessaron was strongest. Western witnesses are valuable, but second in rank. In the second part of the chapter, I seek to illustrate the value of Diatessaronic research for the textual history and early development of the gospel text. In certain cases, the refractions of the Diatessaron appear to give access to pre-canonical forms of sayings incorporated in the Greek gospel text. The absence of a base-text makes working with the Diatessaron difficult. New Testament textual critics and historical-critical exegetes should nevertheless continue to engage in Diatessaronic research: even the refractions of its text in later sources will in certain cases illuminate the textual history of the Gospels.

1. Method in Diatessaron Studies

The central problem in studying the Diatessaron is the lack of a base text. There are many indirect witnesses, but no one can tell how well they represent the original harmony.[1] Even determining whether a given text reflects the Diatessaron at all may

---

[1] For a list of witnesses, see William L. Petersen, *Tatian's Diatessaron: Its Creation, Dissemination, Significance and History in Scholarship*, VCSup 25 (Leiden: Brill, 1994), 445–89. An important additional witness identified more recently is the *Gospel of Barnabas*; see Jan Joosten, "The Date and Provenance of the *Gospel of Barnabas*," *JThS* 61 (2010): 200–15.

lead to heated arguments. Consequently, Diatessaronic studies have been dominated by methodological issues. Saying anything at all about the textual history of the Diatessaron implies multiple layers of argument, each of which is open to discussion. One builds a house of cards—not impossible, but difficult, precarious, and always at the mercy of someone pounding on the table. In the compass of the present chapter, it will not be possible to demonstrate the soundness of the approach underlying it. But a quick tour of its principal methodological moorings will be helpful.[2]

1.1 The Diatessaron as a Syriac Text

Several independent lines of evidence indicate that the Diatessaron began its career in the east. Tatian, the probable author of the Diatessaron,[3] designates himself as an Assyrian in his *Oration to the Greeks*.[4] After leaving Rome, in the middle of the second half of the second century CE, we hear nothing more of him, and it is a plausible hypothesis that he returned to his homeland beyond the Euphrates and published the Diatessaron there. Although Greek was of course used in Mesopotamia, the language of the church of the east was Syriac from its beginnings. This makes it likely Tatian wrote his harmony in that language. Much indirect evidence confirms the Syriac origin of the Diatessaron. The Diatessaron is widely quoted in Syriac writings until the beginning of the fifth century.[5] Meanwhile, Greek authors know it only from hearsay, if at all.[6] Tatian's harmony influenced the Syriac gospel text profoundly, particularly in its earliest, Old Syriac stage, but also in the Peshitta.[7] A "vulgatized," or rather "peshitta-ized," form of the Diatessaron was translated into Arabic in the Islamic period. All these data confirm that the early Diatessaron was a Syriac text.

The earliest textual witness of the Diatessaron, it is true, is written in Greek: the famous fragment from Dura Europos, dating from the first half of the third century (or

---

[2] Petersen's monograph of 1994 (see previous note) remains fundamental to Diatessaron research. I will simply refer to this monograph for much of the relevant data, tracing out in more detail only the areas where I go beyond his approach or differ from it.

[3] This has been contested, most recently by Naomi Koltun-Fromm, "Re-imagining Tatian: The Damaging Effects of Polemical Rhetoric," *JECS* 16 (2008): 1–30. On the whole, however, the connection between Tatian and the Diatessaron remains likely. See, e.g., Matthew R. Crawford, "'Reordering the Confusion': Tatian, the Second Sophistic, and the so-called Diatessaron," *ZAC* 19 (2015): 209–36.

[4] See Petersen, *Tatian's Diatessaron*, 68, and more extensively Nathanael Andrade, "Assyrians, Syrians and the Greek Language in the Late Hellenistic and Roman Imperial Periods," *JNES* 73 (2014): 299–317, in particular 311–16, for more precise information on the geographical definition of Assyria in the second century.

[5] For a useful collection of possible quotations from the Diatessaron in Syriac writings, see Ignacio Ortiz de Urbina, *Vetus evangelium Syrorum et exinde excerptum Diatessaron Tatiani*, Biblia Polyglotta Matritensia VI (Madrid: CSIC, 1967).

[6] See Petersen, *Tatian's Diatessaron*, 35–8 (Eusebius), 39–41 (Epiphanius), 41–5 (Theodoret of Cyrrhus). Theodoret of Cyrrhus does have first-hand knowledge of the Diatessaron, but only of the Syriac version.

[7] For a recent review of the question, see Jean-Claude Haelewyck, "Les Vieilles versions syriaques des Évangiles," in *Le Nouveau Testament en syriaque*, ed. Jean-Claude Haelewyck, Études Syriaques 14 (Paris: Geuthner, 2017), 67–113. See also section 1.3 of this chapter.

even slightly before).⁸ It is to be recognized, however, that this early witness stands quite isolated among Greek manuscripts. Dura hardly warrants the view that the harmony was created in Greek. Another enigmatic phenomenon is the Diatessaron's posterity in the west. But this again should simply be accepted as a complicating factor. The western branch may have sprouted from a unique Syriac-Latin contact. Admittedly, we know nothing about this contact, except that it must have happened before 546, the date of the earliest Latin version of the Diatessaron.

In the last quarter of the second century CE, the fourfold gospel was only just coming into its own in the Greek-speaking church. It is therefore next to unthinkable that a Syriac translation of the four Gospels existed when Tatian produced the Diatessaron. The Diatessaron must have been the first Syriac version of the gospel. This strongly suggests that the goal of Tatian's undertaking was to provide the Syriac-speaking church with a version of the Tetra-evangelion. In later times and in other places the Diatessaron functioned alongside the canonical Gospels, but in Mesopotamia between the late second and early fifth century, the Diatessaron simply represented the gospel.⁹

1.2 Tatian's Sources

A more direct argument in favor of the Syriac origin of Tatian's harmony comes from a consideration of its sources. No one doubts the Diatessaron was based on Greek exemplars of the four Gospels that would soon come to be regarded as canonical. But Greek Matthew, Mark, Luke, and John cannot have been the only sources used in weaving together the harmony.

To begin with, Tatian most probably drew on the Peshitta Old Testament while composing the Diatessaron.¹⁰ In many Old Testament quotations, the Old Syriac and, to a lesser degree, the Peshitta Gospels diverge from the Greek tradition and follow the wording of the Old Testament Peshitta. The same phenomenon has been observed in Ephrem's text of the Diatessaron, although it must be said the material there is much less abundant. Because the overall tendency in the history of Syriac gospel translations is toward ever-greater adherence to the Greek tradition, the divergences under the influence of the Old Testament Peshitta can with some confidence be attributed to the earliest stage, meaning to the Diatessaron.

Much evidence shows that the Diatessaron contained phrases and passages from an extracanonical gospel tradition.¹¹ For instance, the Diatessaron probably included

---

⁸ See Petersen, *Tatian's Diatessaron*, 196–203. The connection between the Dura fragment and the Diatessaron has been contested but needs to be upheld; see Jan Joosten, "The Dura Parchment and the Diatessaron," *VC* 57 (2003): 159–75. For a counter-argument, see Chapter 7 by Ian Mills in the current volume.

⁹ Cf. Matthew R. Crawford, "The Diatessaron, Canonical or Non-canonical? Rereading the Dura Fragment," *NTS* 62 (2016): 253–77.

¹⁰ See Jan Joosten, "Tatian's *Diatessaron* and the Old Testament Peshitta," *JBL* 120 (2001): 501–23, with extensive discussion of earlier literature.

¹¹ See Petersen, *Tatian's Diatessaron*, passim (cf. *Index rerum s.v.* "extra-canonical traditions"). The term extracanonical is shorthand for traditions that were not transmitted in the Gospels that became canonical later in the Christian church. Tatian and the community he was writing for probably

the exclamation, not mentioned in any Greek text of the Gospels: "Woe to us, what has befallen us," said by the crowds at the crucifixion.[12] Many scholars from Hugo Grotius onward have conjectured Tatian's additional source to be a Semitic Gospel.[13] The use of an Aramaic gospel would account for the use of words and expressions that are not typical of classical Syriac:[14]

Luke 2:35

Greek: καὶ σοῦ αὐτῆς τὴν ψυχὴν διελεύσεται ρομφαία

English: "and a sword will pierce through your own soul"

syr^s (cf. Ephrem, *Comm.* 21.27[15]): ܘܢܦܩܐ ܕܠܚܪ ܬܒܙܥܝܘܗܝ ܠܢܦܫܟܝ

English: "and a spear will pierce your own soul"

Here syr^s renders the Greek well,[16] but the suffixed verbal form is not representative of Syriac. The insertion of a *nun* between the imperfect and the suffix is unknown in Syriac. It appears to reflect western Aramaic, where the use of such a *nun* is normal.[17]

There are some twenty items like this in the Old Syriac Gospels, many of which are found also in the Peshitta Gospels.[18] A few of them (including the present example) can be confirmed for the Diatessaron from Ephrem or Aphrahat. Taken together, they suggest that Tatian took account of a gospel text or tradition formulated in a western

---

regarded these traditions as authentic gospel testimonies. For a counter-argument, see Chapter 2 by Charles Hill in the current volume.

[12] See Petersen, *Tatian's Diatessaron*, 414–20.

[13] For Grotius, see Petersen, *Tatian's Diatessaron*, 89–90.

[14] The Greek text of the Gospels is quoted after NA[28]. The Old Syriac and Peshitta Gospels are quoted from George Anton Kiraz, *Comparative Edition of the Syriac Gospels*, 4 vols. (Leiden: Brill, 1996). In the citations that follow, syr^s refers to the Sinaitic Old Syriac Gospel, syr^c refers to the Curetonian Old Syriac Gospel, and syr^p refers to the Syriac Peshitta.

[15] For quotations from Ephrem's *Commentary* (abbreviated as *Comm.*) on the Diatessaron I have used Louis Leloir, *Saint Éphrem: Commentaire de l'Évangile concordant, text syriaque* (*MS Chester Beatty 709*), CBM 8 (Dublin: Hodges Figgis, 1963) and Louis Leloir, *Saint Éphrem: Comnmentaire de l'Évangile concordant, texte syriaque* (*MS Chester Beatty 709*): *Folios additionnels*, CBM 8(b) (Leuven: Peeters, 1990). Ephrem's quotation of Luke 2:35 has been independently transmitted also by Isho'dad; see J. Rendel Harris, *Fragments of the Commentary of Ephrem Syrus on the Diatessaron* (London: C. J. Clay, 1895), 34. The form of the quotation varies somewhat, and varies from syr^s, but the verbal form with epenthetic *nun* appears in both attestations.

[16] The normal meaning of the word ܪܘܡܚܐ is "lance," not "sword," but this apparent divergence cannot be discussed here.

[17] Burkitt has sought to justify the Syriac text by arguing that the verbal form is not 3fs ("it will pierce") but 2fs in the causative stem ("you will make to pierce"). See Francis Crawford Burkitt, *Evangelion Da-Mepharreshe: The Curetonian Version of the Four Gospels with the Readings of the Sinai Palimpsest and the Early Syriac Patristic Evidence*, 2 vols. (Cambridge: Cambridge University Press, 1904), 2:66. This is a possible parsing of the verbal form, but the contextual meaning is peculiar. Also, the interpretation postulated by Burkitt does not agree with the Greek.

[18] See Jan Joosten, "West Aramaic Elements in the Old Syriac and Peshitta Gospels," *JBL* 110 (1991): 271–89; Jan Joosten, "Two West Aramaic Elements in the Old Syriac and Peshitta Gospels," *BN* 61 (1992): 17–21; Jan Joosten, *Language and Textual History of the Syriac Bible: Collected Studies*, TS 9 (Piscataway, NJ: Gorgias, 2013), 127–219.

dialect of Aramaic that was perhaps circulating among Syriac-speaking Christians at the end of the second century.

As mentioned above, the original motivation for the creation of the Diatessaron would have been to provide Syriac-speaking Christians with a version of the gospel. If so, the Old Testament Peshitta and the western Aramaic gospel tradition may both have been known among the intended readers of the Diatessaron. The use of these additional sources would have enhanced the acceptability of the harmony in this milieu.

In any event, the use of these additional sources confirms that the Diatessaron was from the start composed in Syriac. Neither the use of the Old Testament Peshitta, nor that of an Aramaic gospel tradition would have been possible had the Diatessaron been created originally in Greek. Several scholars have recently pleaded again for a Greek origin, arguing that it would have been difficult or unnatural to create a Syriac harmony out of Greek sources.[19] But the textual data indicate that the Diatessaron was conceived as a Syriac writing, a Syriac Gospel, addressed to a Syriac readership in an eastern context. Historical data show that this conception was successful.[20]

1.3 The Syriac Textual Evidence

These considerations should lead anyone interested in the original text of the Diatessaron to privilege the eastern, and in particular the Syriac, textual evidence over all other material. Quotations in early Syriac authors, foremost Ephrem and Aphrahat, stand relatively close in time to the autograph. They present all the problems of quotations, but otherwise they provide evidence of high quality. The Old Syriac and Peshitta Gospels also offer good prospects. Much evidence suggests that the Old Syriac and Peshitta Gospels—the former more than the latter—show influence of the Diatessaron and echo its wording. The strongest evidence is the frequent agreement between these versions and quotations of the Diatessaron in Ephrem or Aphrahat:

Mark 10:21

Greek: ὁ δὲ Ἰησοῦς ἐμβλέψας αὐτῷ ἠγάπησεν αὐτὸν

English: "Jesus, looking at him, loved him"

syr^s (= Ephrem, *Comm.* 15.6, 7, 8): ܘܚܪ ܒܗ ܝܫܘܥ ܚܒܝܒܐܝܬ

English: "And Jesus looked upon him lovingly"

The transformation of a finite verb into an adverb is unusual in the translation technique of early Syriac gospel translations. The Syriac is not a straightforward

---

[19] See Ulrich Schmid, "The Diatessaron of Tatian," in *The Text of the New Testament in Contemporary Research: Essays on the Status Quaestionis*, 2nd ed., ed. Bart D. Ehrman and Michael W. Holmes (Leiden: Brill, 2013), 115–42, in particular 115–16n. 5; Francis Watson, "Towards a Redaction-Critical Reading of the Diatessaron Gospel," *EC* 7 (2016): 95–112.

[20] See the more detailed discussion in Jan Joosten, "Le Diatessaron syriaque," in *Le Nouveau Testament en syriaque*, ed. Jean-Claude Haelewyck, Études Syriaques 14 (Paris: Geuthner, 2017), 55–66.

rendering of the Greek. Perhaps the divergence is merely stylistic. Possibly, however, there is a theological point to it. The Greek text suggests that Jesus, before this moment in the story, had not loved the rich man. For a Syriac translator with a high Christology this may have seemed problematic. The Syriac version implies that the way Jesus looked upon the man expressed the love he antecedently felt for him. Whatever the nature of the divergence, the agreement between syrˢ and Ephrem's quotation almost certainly reflects direct borrowing of one source from the other. Agreements between the Old Syriac and Peshitta Gospels and early quotations of the Syriac Diatessaron are frequent. Other evidence also shows that the Old Syriac and Peshitta Gospels depend on the Diatessaron to some degree. Occasionally, the Old Syriac and Peshitta Gospels agree with texts in the Diatessaronic tradition in matters of sequence.[21] And even where the Syriac versions of the Gospels find no parallels in the later harmonies they are intensely harmonistic in a way that suggests dependence on a gospel harmony.

In my dissertation on the Syriac versions of Matthew, I argued in some detail that, at least in this Gospel, the Old Syriac and the Peshitta are not successive stages of a single translation, with the latter a revision of the former, but independent, though typologically similar, translations.[22] Both the Old Syriac and the Peshitta render a Greek text of the four Gospels while borrowing much of their wording from Tatian's version. If this is true, agreements between these two Syriac versions against the attested Greek text-forms are to be attributed to the Diatessaron:

Matt 19:10

Greek: εἰ οὕτως ἐστὶν ἡ αἰτία τοῦ ἀνθρώπου μετὰ τῆς γυναικός, οὐ συμφέρει γαμῆσαι.

English: "If the case of the man be so with his wife, it is not good to marry." (KJV)

syrᵖ (substantially similar in syrˢᶜ):

ܐܢ ܗܟܢܐ ܐܝܬ ܥܕܠܝܐ ܒܝܢܝ ܓܒܪܐ ܠܐܢܬܬܐ ܠܐ ܦܩܚ ܠܡܣܒ ܐܢܬܬܐ

English: "If thus there is *censure* between a man and a woman, it is not profitable to take wife."

The rendering of ἡ αἰτία as "blame, censure" is tendentious in this verse, and may reflect Encratite views of the type held by Tatian. Although to the best of my knowledge the reading is not found elsewhere (except in the Arabic Diatessaron, as expected),[23] it may well represent the text of the Diatessaron.

---

[21] For a striking example of this phenomenon, see Joosten, "Dura Parchment," 169.

[22] Jan Joosten, *The Syriac Language of the Peshitta and Old Syriac Versions of Matthew: Syntactic Structure, Inner-Syriac Developments and Translation Technique*, SSLL 22 (Leiden: Brill, 1996), 17–21.

[23] The Arabic Diatessaron (25.40) has *malâmaʰ* ("blame, reproof"): *in kâna bayna l-rajuli wa-l-marʾaʰ miṯla haḏihi l-malâmaʰ*.

1.4 The Use of Western Witnesses in Reconstructions of the Diatessaron

The Diatessaron started out as a Syriac writing. Its reconstruction and analysis should therefore be based first and foremost on the Syriac sources: Ephrem's quotations in his commentary, other quotations in early Syriac authors, the Old Syriac and Peshitta Gospels. But what about the western harmonies? Since Daniel Plooij, most specialists of the Diatessaron have given equal authority to western sources. Quispel and Petersen went as far as postulating that Diatessaronic origin can only be established if a reading is attested in eastern *and* western sources.[24]

The most interesting western sources—the Liège Diatessaron, the Venetian harmony, Hebrew Matthew—hail from the twelfth century or later. How Diatessaronic readings may have come to them is unknown. Recent work by August den Hollander and Ulrich Schmid has identified a number of false positives: readings claimed as Diatessaronic on the basis of their alleged attestation only in eastern and western witnesses of the harmony, but which later were found to exist also in western exegetical writings.[25] There is every reason therefore to exert caution.

Nevertheless, it seems to me today as in the past that the similarity between Diatessaronic readings in east and west is simply too striking to ignore. The reading from Mark 10:21, "Jesus looked upon him lovingly" signaled above, is attested not only in syr^s and Ephrem's *Commentary*, but also in two distinct branches of the western Diatessaronic tradition:

Liège: *Doe sach ihc lieflec op hem* ("Then Jesus looked upon him lovingly")[26]
Pepysian: *And Jesus bihelde hym amyablelich*[27]

Perhaps these Middle Dutch and Middle English readings reflect the same type of exegesis as the Syriac one and the agreement between east and west is due to coincidence. But it is hard to believe this scenario, particularly when similar agreements, against all Greek and Latin textual material, occur repeatedly.

In an article published in 2001, I argued in contradistinction to Quispel and Petersen that precedence should be conceded to the eastern sources in research on the original Diatessaron. At the same time, against Schmid and den Hollander, I argued that western corroboration is nevertheless appreciable.[28]

---

[24] Petersen, *Tatian's Diatessaron*, 357–435.
[25] See notably August den Hollander and Ulrich Schmid, "Middeleeuwse bronnen van het Luikse 'Leven van Jezus,'" *Queeste* 6 (1999): 127–46; Ulrich B. Schmid, *Unum ex Quattuor: Eine Geschichte der lateinischen Tatianüberlieferung*, AGLB 37 (Freiburg im Breisgau: Herder, 2005).
[26] D. Plooij, A. J. Barnouw, C. A. Phillips, and A. H. A. Bakker, *The Liège Diatessaron*, 8 vols., VKNAW 31.1-8 (Amsterdam: Koninklijke Akademie van Wetenschappen, 1929–70), 347. This edition incorporates an English translation by A. J. Barnouw, which has been followed in the present study.
[27] M. Goates, *The Pepysian Gospel Harmony* (London: Oxford University Press, 1922; repr., New York: Kraus, 1971), 68.
[28] Joosten, "Tatian's *Diatessaron* and the Old Testament Peshitta."

2. A Case Study: The Jewish Law in the Diatessaron

The investigation of the Diatessaron is complex and controversial. So why bother? I will try to show why by the help of an example.

William Petersen argued that the Diatessaron contained a positive reference to the Jewish law in a passage corresponding to Matt 8:4:[29]

Matt 8:4

Greek: ὕπαγε σεαυτὸν δεῖξον τῷ ἱερεῖ καὶ προσένεγκον τὸ δῶρον ὃ προσέταξεν Μωϋσῆς

English: "Go, show yourself to the priest, and offer the gift that Moses commanded"

Ephrem, *Comm.* 12.21, 23: ܐܝܙܠ ܚܘܐ ܢܦܫܟ ܠܟܗܢܐ ܘܡܠܝ ܢܡܘܣܐ

English: "Go, show yourself to the priests and *fulfill the law*"

Romanos the Melodist:[30] ὕπαγε, <u>νόμον πλήρωσον</u> καὶ ἑαυτὸν δεῖξαι ... τῷ ἱερεῖ

English: "Go, <u>fulfill the Law</u> and [hasten] to show yourself to the priest"

Venetian[31] (cf. Liège): *va et monstrate a li prevedi e fa l'oferta che comanda la leçe*

English: "Go and show [yourself] to the overseers and make the offering that the law commands"

For Petersen, the double attestation, in east and west, is what gives certainty as to the Diatessaronic nature of the reference to the law in this passage. But one can only observe that the agreement between the eastern and western texts is not exact. The criterion of double attestation does not really work in this case. The witness of Ephrem is impressive, however.[32] On the basis of our earlier orientation privileging eastern sources, the reading may be cautiously accepted. Unless this should be a case of gross paraphrase on the part of Ephrem, the reading "fulfill the law" would seem to reflect the Diatessaron.

Petersen argued that the Diatessaron in this passage gives access to a lost Greek text of Matthew that had not yet been adapted to the antinomian theology characterizing mainstream Christianity from the second century onward. This is of course a possibility. The "orthodox corruption of scripture" affected several other gospel passages. Here are a few possible examples from the Gospel of John:

John 10:34

Greek: οὐκ ἔστιν γεγραμμένον ἐν τῷ νόμῳ ὑμῶν ὅτι ἐγὼ εἶπα· θεοί ἐστε;

English: "Is it not written in your law: 'I said you are gods'?"

om. ὑμῶν $\mathfrak{P}^{45}$ ℵ* D Θ syr^s it

---

[29] Petersen, *Tatian's Diatessaron*, 22–4.
[30] Ibid., 23.
[31] Venanzio Todesco, Alberto Vaccari, and Marco Vattasso, eds., *Il Diatessaron in Volgare Italiano*, StT 81 (Vatican City: Biblioteca Apostolica Vaticana, 1938).
[32] Romanos may have adopted the reading directly or indirectly from Ephrem.

A strong field of ancient witnesses has Jesus say: "Is it not written in *the* law." Possibly, the majority reading (which includes the personal pronoun) is a later correction depicting Jesus as distancing himself from the Jewish scriptures.

John 15:25

Greek: ἀλλ᾽ ἵνα πληρωθῇ ὁ λόγος ὁ ἐν τῷ νόμῳ αὐτῶν γεγραμμένος ὅτι *ἐμίσησάν με δωρεάν*

English: "It was to fulfill the word that is written in their law: 'They hated me without a cause.'"

om. αὐτῶν 𝔓⁶⁶*vid

In this case only a single witness omits the pronoun, thus having Jesus say: "It was to fulfill the word that is written in *the* law." Still, the presence of this reading in a very early witness is compatible with the view that, here, too, the majority text (which includes the personal pronoun) is the result of a later correction. The motivation for the addition of the pronoun would have been the same as in the previous example.

John 8:17

Greek: καὶ ἐν τῷ νόμῳ δὲ τῷ ὑμετέρῳ γέγραπται ὅτι δύο ἀνθρώπων ἡ μαρτυρία ἀληθής ἐστιν.

English: "In your law it is written that the testimony of two witnesses is valid."
(No variants in ancient witnesses.)

The absence of variants in this verse may show that the pronouns ὑμῶν in 10:34 and αὐτῶν in 15:25 are Johannine after all. But it is also possible to reverse the argument. The other cases suggest that there was a tendency to add such pronouns where Jesus refers to the Jewish law. Perhaps then in the present passage the pronoun was added secondarily, and the addition spread to all textual witnesses. A third possibility, of course, is that the original text of the Gospel of John was not consistent on this point.

None of our manuscripts of Matthew reach back to the time when Tatian put together his harmony. Tatian may well have been able to consult exemplars that had a more primitive, less de-Judaized, text of the Gospel. Petersen's approach to Matt 8:4 is theoretically viable.

I will nevertheless propose a different approach. As it happens, Matt 8:4 is not the only gospel passage where the Diatessaron appears to enhance references to the Jewish law. A comparable example is found in another context having to do with the observation of the law:

Matt 15:2 (//Mark 7:5, cf. Mark 7:3)

Greek: διὰ τί οἱ μαθηταί σου παραβαίνουσιν τὴν παράδοσιν τῶν πρεσβυτέρων

English: "Why do your disciples transgress the tradition of the elders?"

syr^{sc}: ܠܡܢܐ ܬܠܡܝܕܝܟ ܥܒܪܝܢ ܥܠ ܦܘܩܕܢܐ ܕܩܫܝܫܝܢ

English: "Why do your disciples transgress the *commandments of our elders*?"[33]

Zürich[34] (cf. Liège; Tuscan): war vmbe vbergent dine iungere die gebot vnsere fordern

English: "Why do your disciples transgress the *commandments of our elders*?"

This is a case where the Quispel–Petersen approach—triangulating back to the original Diatessaron on the basis of readings attested in eastern and western witness—works well. The Old Syriac diverges from the Greek tradition in three ways:

1. "Commandments" diverges lexically from "tradition."
2. It differs grammatically by the use of the plural.
3. "*Our* elders" comes instead of "*the* elders."

All three divergences turn up in exactly the same way in the western harmonies (though the Tuscan harmony does not have "*our* elders"). Attributing this agreement between east and west to chance is possible, but ill-advised. In any case, even if one should reject the testimony of the western texts out of principle, as Ulrich Schmid would propose to do, the reading may be considered Diatessaronic. The fact that the Old Syriac has all three elements of the divergent text in both Matthew (syr^{sc} as indicated above) and Mark (syr^s only, syr^c being absent in this passage) makes it likely that the reading goes back to the Diatessaron.

While the expression "tradition of the elders" is proper to the Greek Gospels, the notion of "commandments of the elders" is well represented in Jewish sources.[35] Thus, the discourse on the Law in this passage of the Diatessaron seems to be more attuned to Jewish customs than the Greek textual tradition of both Matthew and Mark. Perhaps this too is a case where an earlier, more Jewish, Greek text was adapted to later Christian doctrine and consequently disappeared completely—except in Diatessaronic witnesses. But the absence of the putatively earlier reading from all Greek manuscripts, exactly as in Matt 8:4 discussed above, weighs against this possibility.

How then do we explain these readings? Do they show us "what Tatian did" to the second-century Greek text he received? This can hardly be the case. Tatian had some heretical traits: he was an Encratite, and may have had sympathy for certain forms of Gnosticism. But in his relation to Judaism he is a representative of the mainstream Christianity of his time:[36] although he venerates the Old Testament (as is clear from the *Oratio ad Graecos*), he is utterly indifferent to the Jews. Picturing him as one who would Judaize, or re-Judaize, the text of the Gospels is very hard. If so, what are our other options? It seems that the solution in this case is to attribute the Judaizing

---

[33] Neither Ephrem nor Aphrahat quote Matt 15:2 or Mark 7:5, but the divergences from the Greek in the Old Syriac strongly suggest that the latter are influenced here by the Diatessaron.

[34] Christoph Gerhardt, *Diatessaron Theodiscum: Das Leben Jhesu* (Leiden: Brill, 1970), 65–6.

[35] See, e.g., b. Sukkah 46a מצות זקנים. Cf. Str-B 1:691.

[36] See Theodor Zahn, *Tatian's Diatessaron*, FGNK 1 (Erlangen: Andreas Deichert, 1881), 263–8.

readings to an extracanonical source. If it is true that Tatian made use of a western Aramaic Gospel—whether in written form, or as a collection of oral traditions—this source would almost certainly go back to a Jewish-Christian milieu. Perhaps then this same source also led to the changes we have observed in the text of Matt 8:4 and 15:2 and parallels.

This of course is just speculation. But it is not unthinkable. Let us inspect a third example:

Matt 19:16 (//Mark 10:17; Luke 18:18)

Greek: τί ἀγαθὸν ποιήσω ἵνα σχῶ ζωὴν αἰώνιον;

English: "What good thing must I do to gain eternal life?"

Ephrem, *Comm.* 15.1: ܟܐܕ ܓܠ ܐܟܪ ܐܟܪ

English: "What shall I do to live?"

Gospel of the Hebrews (apud Origen):[37] *Magister, quid bonum faciens vivam*

English: "What good thing must I do to live?"

The variant "that I may live" instead of "that I may have/inherit eternal life" has not attracted much attention. Among witnesses to the text of the Synoptics it is, as far as I can tell, attested only in Ephrem's quotation. It may therefore simply reflect Ephrem's paraphrase. Several factors weigh against this possibility, however. In the comparison between "to have eternal life" and "to live" the former is clearly more profiled theologically. It is not obvious that an interpreter would feel free to simplify it to what we read in Ephrem's *Commentary*. One should at least explore the possibility that the text quoted represents Ephrem's gospel text, that is, the Diatessaron.

If we imagine, for the sake of argument, that this reading is indeed Ephrem's gospel text, we will soon understand that it makes perfect sense—better sense, in fact, than that of the Synoptic Gospels. Although "eternal life" is a biblical phrase, it does not really belong in the context of a discussion on the practice of the law. "Eternal life" is an eschatological notion at home in discourse on the end of time. It is fitting in the vision of the judgment of the Son of Man in Matt 25:46. It combines felicitously with the phrase "in the world to come" as in Mark 10:30. And, of course, it suits the Gospel of John with its realized eschatology, where it is found sixteen times. In our passage, however, Jesus's interlocutor simply wants advice on what to do in his earthly life. Jesus's answer picks up on the question by referring to the commandments. In this, he follows a well-rehearsed biblical formula: if you want to live, do the commandments! (cf. "You shall keep my statutes and my ordinances; which if a man does, he shall live in them" [Lev 18:5]). This biblical logic favors the reading "that I may live" more than the canonical reading.[38] In other words, like our earlier examples, this is a case where a potentially Diatessaronic reading on the Law is closer to Jewish sources than the received gospel text.

---

[37] For the fragment of the putative *Gospel of the Hebrews*, see A. F. J. Klijn, "The Question of the Rich Young Man in a Jewish-Christian Gospel," *NovT* 8 (1966): 149–55.

[38] Note that Luke 10:28, in a similar context, has "live" alongside "have eternal life" (v. 25).

If our line of argument is sound, it would seem to be highly significant to observe that the Jewish-Christian gospel fragment quoted in Origen's *Commentary on Matthew* agrees with the reading in Ephrem's quotation of the Diatessaron.[39] With due caution it seems possible to conjecture two things: first, that the Jewish-Christian fragment in this reading reflects a relatively early phase in the tradition history of the gospel text; and second, that the Diatessaron received the reading from extracanonical tradition. To postulate that a similar process explains the presence of the two readings presented earlier, in Matt 8:4 and 15:2, is of course an additional step. But in the light of the present case it does not seem to be particularly far-fetched.

3. Conclusions

The absence of a base-text makes working with the Diatessaron difficult, not to say perilous. There are few hard data that one can securely build on. Nevertheless, some paths are well tried, and although one should not follow them blindly, following them lucidly may lead to results worth having. I have traced one such path and have tried to illustrate its merits with one particularly interesting example.

---

[39] For other agreements between the fragment quoted by Origen and the Diatessaron, see Klijn, "The Question of the Rich Young Man."

Part Two

The Nature of Tatian's Gospel

4

Harmony or Gospel? On the Genre of the (So-Called) Diatessaron

Francis Watson

Abstract

The so-called Diatessaron is normally viewed as a gospel harmony, the first in a long line of attempts to show that the canonical gospel texts do not contradict one another but can be blended together into a single coherent narrative. This chapter seeks to further the view that the Diatessaron is a Gospel in its own right, one that treats earlier instances of gospel writing as sources to be rewritten and reworked into a new and authoritative text. Thus the Diatessaron represents a continuation of Matthew and Luke's procedure with their own sources some decades earlier. The assumption that the Diatessaron is a gospel harmony compiled by Tatian stems from Eusebius, but its main users—Syriac-speaking Christian communities of the second to the fifth centuries—regarded it as the definitive version of the gospel itself, preserving the old tradition of anonymous gospel composition as representing collective apostolic authorship and authority. As a Gospel whose sources are largely known to us, the Diatessaron is therefore open to redaction-critical investigation. Although there are serious difficulties in recovering its precise wording from later Latin and Arabic sources, it is probable that the sequences in which older gospel material is incorporated remain largely intact, providing a promising opening for redaction criticism. Where the sequence of the Arabic differs from that of the Latin, a plausible explanation may be found in the hypothesis that a Greek original was subjected to significant revision when translated into Syriac.

The "Diatessaron" is historically and hermeneutically important both in its own right and for the light it sheds on its more successful rival, the four-gospel collection. The aim of this chapter is to explore the possibility of a redaction-critical approach to the Diatessaron, on the double assumption (1) that this largely lost text is still partially accessible, and (2) that it is more appropriately seen as a gospel than as a gospel harmony. The first task must be to clarify the difference between these two genres—although, as we shall see, the relationship is in practice a fluid one.

A "gospel harmony" is subordinate to authoritative canonical texts, seeking to show how they may best be coordinated. It is a supplement to the canonical gospels, not a substitute for them. A "gospel" is a text that aspires to a role as authoritative scripture in its own right. It may resemble a gospel harmony in drawing from and coordinating prior texts, but these are here viewed as sources or resources out of which the new text is to be constructed. The aim is not to demonstrate *that* these sources may be coordinated, in order to safeguard their reputation for absolute reliability, but rather to present existing gospel material in a more effective form. A gospel can afford to be selective in its use of its sources. Though dependent on them, it is not bound by them; new material may be added or old material may be presented with a new slant. In contrast, a gospel harmony seeks in principle to be comprehensive. No part of the canonical literature is to be rejected or passed over, for the point is to vindicate its absolute authority and truthfulness. Gospel harmonizers differ among themselves about how far this point is to be taken. They must consider whether or not it is important to show that the *sequence* of each gospel is historically reliable, and, if that is the case, how it is that so many almost identical incidents seem to take place at different points in Jesus's career.[1] One gospel harmony will report two different occasions on which Jesus expels moneychangers from the temple, once near the beginning of his ministry and once toward the end. Another will assume that literary rather than historical factors have shaped the order of events in the respective gospels.[2] Either way, the ongoing authority of the canonical texts is assumed; indeed, it is precisely this that one seeks to promote. A new gospel is under no such obligation. If its sources subsequently disappear from sight, that may well work to its advantage by ridding it of potential competitors. The "problem" of harmonizing Matthew with Mark would never have arisen if the newer and more comprehensive gospel had been understood as a more-than-adequate *replacement* for its most important source. In incorporating so much of Mark and other source material, Matthew has no great stake in its survival in its original form. As he draws on Mark and other sources, Matthew is no "harmonizer" but part editor and part author.

The question is whether, and how far, this may also be the case with the compiler of the Diatessaron. The balance between editing and authoring will no doubt be different in the two cases. Yet it may still be possible to view the respective editor-authors as

---

[1] A gospel harmony with a rigorous concern to preserve gospel sequences is promised in the title of Andreas Osiander's work, dating from 1537: *Harmoniae Evangelicae libri quatuor, in quibus Evangelica historia ex quatuor Evangelistis ita in unum est contexta, ut nullius verbum ullum omissum, nihil alienum immixtum, nullius ordo turbatus, nihil non suo loco positum: omnia vero litteris et notis ita distincta sunt, ut quid cujusque Evangelistae proprium, quid cum aliis, et cum quibus commune sit, primo aspectu deprehendere queas* (Basel: H. Froben and N. Episcopius). A later example is James MacKnight's *Harmony of the Four Gospels, in Which the Natural Order of Each Is Preserved*, 2 vols. (London: [Printed for the Author], 1756), reissued in no fewer than five editions. According to McKnight, "the best method of producing a perfect Harmony is to preserve the thread of [the gospels'] several narrations entire, because seeming contradictions will thus be removed, the whole will be rendered consistent, the credit of the evangelists as historians will be better secured, and our faith built upon the most solid foundation" (1:iii, in the 5th ed., 1819).

[2] The less rigorous approach can appeal to the example of Augustine, who asks: "What does it matter where any of [the evangelists] locates a particular story?" (*Cons.* 2.21.51). On gospel harmonies, see my *Gospel Writing: A Canonical Perspective* (Grand Rapids, MI: Eerdmans, 2013), 28–61, 78–91.

confronted with the same problem: that of finding the most suitable literary form for prior written and oral traditions about Jesus. If so, the assumption that gospel production ceases when the so-called "fourth evangelist" lays down his pen will have to be revised. So too will the related assumption that those who continued to reshape the gospel material can be regarded as an aberration. The fourfold canonical gospel was not inevitable, and it did not just happen of its own accord. It had to be constructed, and it had to prevail over its rivals. One such rival was the text known in Greek as the "Diatessaron" and in Syriac as the "Gospel."

1. Greek Diatessaron and Syriac Gospel

Two versions of an ancient gospel harmony have survived, a sixth-century edition of an older Latin text and an eleventh-century Arabic translation of a text in Syriac. The Latin version occurs in the single-volume copy of the New Testament known as *Codex Fuldensis*, where it takes the place of the individual gospels.[3] Its editor, Victor of Capua, assumes that readers also have access to individual gospels, and he equips his text with Eusebian section numbers and canon tables to make it possible to refer back to the source of any given passage. In that sense this harmony is a supplement to the canonical gospels rather than a substitute. Similarly, Arabic manuscripts use *sigla* within the text to indicate an origin in Matthew (*M*), Mark (*R*), Luke (*Q*), or John (*Ḥ*).[4] These or other *sigla* were probably already present in the translator's Syriac exemplar,[5] and they acknowledge the work's subordination to the separate gospels of "Matthew the Elect," "Mark the Chosen," "Luke the Favored," and "John the Beloved."[6]

Both gospel harmonies claim to represent a work known as the "Diatessaron." In a preface to one of the Arabic recensions, the scribe announces his intention of writing "the holy gospel and the beautiful garden known as *Diyātāsarōn*," adding that "the explanation of this term is *by-four*."[7] We are told that this composite work was translated from Syriac by the learned priest Abu-l-Faraj Abdullah ibn-aṭ-Ṭayyib and originally compiled by "Tîtyānōs the Greek." Victor finds no title or

---

[3] E. Ranke, *Codex Fuldensis: Novum Testamentum Latine Interprete Hieronymo ex Manuscripto Victoris Capuani* (Marburg: N. G. Elwert, 1868). A new edition is under preparation by Nicholas Zola.

[4] MSS B, O, E, Sbath 1020, Sbath 1280; MS A uses the *sigla* MT, MR, LW, YW (so William L. Petersen, *Tatian's Diatessaron: Its Creation, Dissemination, Significance, and History in Scholarship*, VCSup 25 [Leiden: Brill, 1994], 135–7). The Preface cited here occurs in MSS of the first group.

[5] Identified in the colophon to MS B as the work of the ninth-century lexicographer Isā ibn ʿAlī (see T. Baarda, "On the Author of the Arabic Diatessaron," in *Miscellanea Neotestamentica, Volume I*, ed. T. Baarda, A. F. J. Klijn, and W. C. van Unnik [Leiden: Brill, 1978], 61–103).

[6] Augustinus Ciasca, *Tatiani Evangeliorum harmoniae arabice*, 2 vols. (Rome: Typographia Polyglotta, 1888), 1:1 (Latin), 2:1 (Arabic); A.-S. Marmardji, *Diatessaron de Tatien: Texte arabe établi, traduit en français, collationné avec les anciennes versions syriaques* (Beyrouth: Imprimerie Catholique, 1935), 2–3 (Arabic and French). On these editions, see Petersen, *Tatian's Diatessaron*, 133–8. H. W. Hogg's English translation of Ciasca's edition is available in ANF 9:42–130; note also the dated but still valuable introduction (9:35–41) and the cross-references to the separated gospels (9:131–38).

[7] Marmardji, *Diatessaron de Tatien*, 2. Here and throughout this chapter translations are my own.

author specified in his Latin exemplar, but he considers it most likely that this is the work of *Tatianus vir eruditissimus et orator . . . clarus*.[8] Unfortunately, Tatian was also a heretic, and yet:

> *Tatianus quoque licet profanis inplicatus erroribus non inutile tamen exhibens studiosis exemplum hoc evangelium ut mihi videtur sollerti conpaginatione disposuit.*[9]
>
> Although implicated in ungodly errors, Tatian provided the learned with a text that is not without value, compiling a gospel characterized (in my view) by its skillfully-constructed connections.

Victor claims, falsely but interestingly, that Tatian entitled his work not *Diatessaron* but *Diapente*.[10] Assembled out of four gospels, the Diatessaron in effect represents a fifth. Four-from-one, *unum ex quattuor*, becomes four-plus-one. Victor draws all his information about Tatian from Eusebius, and must be aware that the Greek word Eusebius uses is not *Diapente* but *Diatessaron*.

The Arabic and Latin editors are dependent on Eusebius for both the work's title and its author. Eusebius himself has three sources of information about Tatian. The first is Tatian's *Oratio ad Graecos*, which Eusebius regards as the "best and most useful" (κάλλιστός τε καὶ ὠφελιμώτατος) of his many surviving works.[11] The second is the negative assessment of Irenaeus, who tells of Tatian's lapse into the Encratite heresy after the martyrdom of his teacher Justin.[12] The third is an anonymous, perhaps oral, source from which Eusebius has heard about Tatian's paraphrases of Paul and his "Diatessaron." About the latter he has this to say,

> ὁ Τατιανὸς συνάφειάν τινα καὶ συναγωγὴν οὐκ οἶδ' ὅπως τῶν εὐαγγελίων συνθεὶς τὸ διὰ τεσσάρων τοῦτο προσωνόμασεν ὃ καὶ παρά τισιν εἰσέτι νῦν φέρεται.[13]
>
> Tatian composed—I do not know how—a combination and compilation from the gospels, and he named it *The Fourfold*, which is still extant among some.[14]

Eusebius has unrivalled knowledge of gospel parallels, as his canon tables demonstrate. "I do not know how" must mean that no copy of Tatian's text has reached Eusebius, not that he had studied it but failed to grasp its logic.[15] His own work on gospel parallels was inspired by Ammonius of Alexandria, another

---

[8] Ranke, *Codex Fuldensis*, 1.
[9] Ibid., 2.
[10] Ibid., 1.
[11] *Hist. eccl.* 4.29.7; cf. 4.16.7, where Eusebius quotes from this work a passage about Justin. (The edition of the *Historia Ecclesiastica* used here is *Eusebius Werke 2: Die Kirchengeschichte*, ed. E. Schwartz and Theodor Mommsen, GCS 9.1–3 [Leipzig: Hinrichs, 1903–9].)
[12] *Hist. eccl.* 4.29.2, citing Irenaeus, *Haer.* 3.23.
[13] *Hist. eccl.* 4.29.6.
[14] For the translation of τὸ διὰ τεσσάρων as "The Fourfold," see M. Crawford, "Ammonius of Alexandria, Eusebius of Caesarea and the Origins of Gospel Scholarship," *NTS* 61 (2015): 8–13.
[15] So Petersen, *Tatian's Diatessaron*, 36.

scholar who worked on τὸ διὰ τεσσάρων εὐαγγέλιον—although that study of gospel interrelations was a Matthew-based synopsis rather than a harmony.[16] The coincidence of terminology is nevertheless striking, and it suggests that Eusebius uses the term *Diatessaron* generically. Any work that assembles the four Gospels into one may be regarded as a "Diatessaron," whether arranged in distinct columns or as a connected narrative. Eusebius must also assume that a work with such a title was composed in Greek, like the *Oratio ad Graecos* and the rest of Tatian's literary output. In contrast, Epiphanius reports that some identify the Diatessaron with the mysterious Gospel "according to the Hebrews," which may imply an awareness of the Syriac version of Tatian's work.[17]

If the title "Diatessaron" seems self-evident to Eusebius, that was not the case for others. Centuries later, the Arabic scribe still has to explain the strange loanword, ܕܝܛܣܪܘܢ. Back in the fourth century the term was evidently unknown in Syriac-speaking contexts, precisely the area where the text itself was most widely used. This is evident from the Syriac translation of Eusebius, in which it is said that Tatian, founder of the Encratite heresy,

> ܚܒܪ ܘܚܠܛ ܘܣܡ ܐܘܢܓܠܝܘܢ ܘܩܪܝܗܝ ܕܝܛܣܪܘܢ ܗܘ ܕܝܢ ܕܡܚܠܛܐ ܕܠܘܬ
> ܣܓܝܐܐ ܒܗܕܐ ܠܝܘܡܢܐ ܐܝܬܘܗܝ
>
> collected and connected and composed a Gospel and called it *Diyatessarōn*, that is, *Of the Connected*, and it is extant among many to this day.[18]

Here, three finite verbs (ܚܒܪ, ܚܠܛ, ܣܡ) render two Greek substantives and a participle (συνάφεια, συναγωγή, συνθείς), with the second Syriac verb (ܚܠܛ) representing the first Greek substantive (συνάφεια). The explanation of the loanword (ܕܝܛܣܪܘܢ i.e., ܕܡܚܠܛܐ) is a participial construction derived from ܚܠܛ (= συνάφεια), and need not imply that ܐܘܢܓܠܝܘܢ ܕܡܚܠܛܐ is already familiar terminology that contrasts the Diatessaron as the "Gospel of the Mixed" with the ܐܘܢܓܠܝܘܢ ܕܡܦܪܫܐ, the "Gospel of the Separated." The latter expression is attested in the colophon of the Sinaitic Syriac and the inscriptio of the Curetonian,[19] and refers to the four distinct and named gospels arranged in sequence. This expression may be derived from ܐܘܢܓܠܝܘܢ ܕܡܚܠܛܐ, itself derived not from general usage but specifically from Eusebius in translation.

16 See Eusebius's letter to Carpianus, written as a preface to an edition of the four gospels featuring Eusebius's new canon tables (Barbara Aland, et al., *Novum Testamentum Graece*, 28th ed. [Stuttgart: Deutsche Bibelgesellschaft, 2012], 89*–90*). Eusebius speaks of Ammonius as composing τὸ διὰ τεσσάρων εὐαγγέλιον, τῷ κατὰ Ματθαῖον τὰς ὁμοφώνους τῶν λοιπῶν εὐαγγελιστῶν περικοπὰς παραθείς, with the result that the sequence of the non-Matthean texts was disrupted. Origen's *Hexapla* may have been an antecedent for Ammonius's work.

17 Epiphanius, *Pan.* 46.1.9; see K. Holl, *Epiphanius: Ancoratus und Panarion, Vol. II: Panarion haer. 34–64*, GCS 31 (Leipzig: Hinrichs, 1922); English translation in Frank Williams, trans., *The Panarion of Epiphanius of Salamis*, 2 vols., 2nd ed. (Leiden: Brill, 2000).

18 W. Wright and N. McLean, eds., *The Ecclesiastical History of Eusebius in Syriac* (Cambridge: Cambridge University Press, 1898), 243; cited by Petersen, *Tatian's Diatessaron*, 36. Petersen notes that the oldest MS of the Syriac Eusebius dates from 462.

19 George Anton Kiraz, *Comparative Edition of the Syriac Gospels*, 4 vols. (Leiden: Brill, 1996), 4:369 (John); 1:1 (Matthew).

According to the translator, Tatian's work is itself an ܐܘܢܓܠܝܘܢ. It is now said to be "extant among *many* to this day," and not just among *some* as in the Greek. Presuming a familiarity with it, the translator omits Eusebius's confession of ignorance. A reversal has taken place: Eusebius knows the name and authorship of the Diatessaron but not the text itself; his Syriac readers know the text but must learn from Eusebius who compiled it and what he called it. This suggests that it is a mistake to envisage a Syriac "Diatessaron" functioning as a mere supplement to the four distinct gospels. For Ephrem, who composed a commentary on the (so-called) Diatessaron in around the 360s, the text on which he was commenting was "the gospel" and its author "the evangelist."[20] While its attribution to Tatian is not implausible, it rests solely on Eusebius's informant or source and may have been unknown in Syriac Christian circles—until Eusebius communicated the unwelcome news that the cherished vernacular gospel was in fact the work of a heretic. That was probably the major reason for the fifth-century campaign to eradicate the old gospel text and replace it with the distinct gospels of Matthew, Mark, Luke, and John. Theodoret, bishop of Cyrrhus from 423 to 457, explicitly appeals to Tatian's heretical status to justify his removal from the churches in his diocese of two hundred copies of the text that, following Eusebius, he now knows as "the Diatessaron." These two hundred composite gospels had to be *replaced* by copies of the four distinct gospels. Rabbula, bishop of Edessa from ca. 412 to 435, insists that each church must possess and read from a copy of the ܐܘܢܓܠܝܘܢ ܕܡܦܪܫܐ.[21]

The difference between a gospel and a gospel harmony is in part a matter of perspective. Where the separate gospels attributed to Matthew, Mark, Luke, and John are well established, it will be clear that the "Diatessaron" is a composite work combining four familiar texts—a gospel harmony. But where the composite work functions liturgically as gospel, and where most churches do not possess, need, or even know the separate gospels, then the work in question is no longer a gospel harmony but simply "the gospel." This conclusion only seems perverse or eccentric from a Eusebian standpoint in which the four named evangelists—two of them apostles, two disciples of apostles—are self-evidently superior to the disciple of Justin who later deviated from orthodoxy.

The integrity of the composite Syriac gospel becomes clear on the premise of the original anonymity of the tradition of gospel writing.

2. Gospels and Anonymity

The Syriac exemplar used by the Arabic translator was clearly identified as Tatian's Diatessaron.[22] That was not the case with its Latin opposite number. Victor's Preface opens as follows:

---

[20] On this, see the presentation and analysis of the terminological evidence in Matthew R. Crawford, "Diatessaron, A Misnomer? The Evidence of Ephrem's Commentary," *EC* 4 (2013): 366–70. Later Syriac references to "the Diatessaron" all derive from Eusebius (373–7).
[21] Greek and Syriac texts with translations are provided by Petersen, *Tatian's Diatessaron*, 41–3.
[22] See the discussion above, and the colophons to MSS E and B in Marmardji, *Diatessaron de Tatien*, 536. The scribes' confidence about the identity of their text must go back to the translator and his exemplar.

Cum fortuito in manus meas incideret unum ex quattuor euangelium conpositum et absente titulo non invenirem nomen auctoris, diligenter inquirens quis gesta vel dicta domini et salvatoris nostri euangelica lectione discreta in ordinem quo se consequi videbantur, non minimo studii labore redegerit repperi Ammonium quemdam Alexandrinum[23]

When by chance there came into my hands a single gospel composed out of the four, and I found it lacking not only a title but also its author's name, I investigated carefully who might have arranged the acts and sayings of our Lord and Savior, as recorded in the separate gospels, in the order in which they occurred. I discovered that a certain Ammonius of Alexandria had directed no little scholarly labor [to this matter]

Victor's researches lead him not only to Eusebius's letter to Carpianus but also to the *Historia Ecclesiastica* in Rufinus's Latin translation, where he finds the name of Tatian and concludes that he is a stronger candidate than Ammonius for authorship of the anonymous *unum ex quattuor euangelium*.[24] As if in passing, Victor also indicates why he considers this text to be so extraordinarily significant. In it the old problem of sequence—recognized already by Luke and Papias—is resolved.[25] In the singular gospel we can at last read about what the Lord did and said in the true historical order. All this gospel lacks is an author, the Eusebian section enumeration, and Jerome's Latin text; Victor sets himself to supply these deficiencies.[26]

Why did Victor's old gospel manuscript lack an author? While it is possible that Tatian's name was suppressed, it is at least as likely that this anonymity is an archaic feature that this manuscript shared with Syriac gospel manuscripts whose users were unaware of their gospel's odd Greek name or its alleged heretical compiler.[27] The

---

[23] Ranke, *Codex Fuldensis*, 1.
[24] Victor's *unum ex quattuor euangelium conpositum* echoes Rufinus's paraphrastic rendering of Eusebius: *Tatianus conlationem quandam faciens evangeliorum nescio quomodo conposuit euangelium unum ex quattuor quod Diatessaron nominavit, quod etiam nunc habetur a multis.* (*Hist. eccl.* 4.29.6; Schwartz and Mommsen, *Eusebius Werke 2*, 1:393). Victor's adaptation of Rufinus's *unum ex quattuor* later became standard terminology for the Latin harmony tradition. On this, see Ulrich B. Schmid, *Unum ex Quattuor: Eine Geschichte der lateinischen Tatianüberlieferung* (Freiburg im Breisgau: Herder, 2005), 177–82. Schmid, however, finds the origin of the phrase in Victor's Latin citation from Eusebius's letter to Carpianus, where *unum ex quattuor nobis reliquit euangelium* renders τὸ διὰ τεσσάρων καταλέλοιπεν εὐαγγέλιον (180–1). Since Latin texts of the *ad Carpianum* normally refer to *unum nobis pro quattuor evangeliis* (181), it is clear that the application of the *unum ex quattuor* formula to Ammonius is derived from Rufinus. This is confirmed by the echo of Rufinus's *conposuit* in Victor's *conpositum*.
[25] Compare Luke 1:3 (ἀκριβῶς, καθεξῆς) with Papias on Mark, who wrote ἀκριβῶς . . . οὐ μέντοι τάξει (*apud* Eusebius, *Hist. eccl.* 3.39.15). Like Victor, Augustine too is on occasion interested in the possibility that gospel harmonization will combine disparate events "into a single narrative . . . as these events may actually have taken place [*quemadmodum geri potuerint*]" (*Cons.* 3.24.69; see F. Weihrich, ed. Augustine, *De consensu evangelistarum*, CSEL 43 [Vienna: Österreichische Akademie der Wissenschaften, 1904]).
[26] In his Preface Victor discusses the first two issues but not the third. It was most likely Victor who brought an Old Latin gospel text into line with Jerome's, in the course of integrating the Eusebian section enumeration obtained from a second, Jerome-influenced exemplar.
[27] Summing up his analysis of early Syriac terminology, Crawford writes: "Originally, as reflected in Aphrahat, Ephrem, and Aba, it was simply 'the Gospel'; later, as the fourfold gospel came into use,

contrast between Syriac anonymity and Eusebian naming has an interesting analogy in Tertullian. Here an anonymous gospel text is attributed not to Tatian but to Marcion, and is played off against the named canonical authors—with the added complication that the Marcionite gospel is based on Luke, the authority of which must therefore be relativized. Here apostolic authority is closely correlated with authorship:

> *Constituimus inprimis evangelicum instrumentum apostolos auctores habere, quibus hoc munus evangelii promulgandi ab ipso domino sit impositum. Si et apostolicos, non tamen solos, sed cum apostolis et post apostolos, quoniam praedicatio discipulorum suspecta fieri posset de gloriae studio, si non adsistant illi auctoritas magistrorum immo Christi, quae magistros apostolos fecit. Denique nobis fidem ex apostolis Ioannes et Matthaeus insinuant, ex apostolicis Lucas et Marcus instaurant*[28]

> We assert in the first place that the gospel record has apostles as its authors, to whom the task of promulgating the gospel was entrusted by the Lord himself. If this role is extended to apostolic followers, they act not on their own but with apostles and after apostles; for the preaching of disciples might be suspected of concern for personal glory if unaccompanied by the authority of their teachers—or rather of Christ, who established the apostles as teachers. Of the apostles, then, it is John and Matthew who initiate us into the faith; of the apostolic followers, Luke and Mark who renew it.

Mark is the disciple of Peter, Luke of Paul, so that the authority of Peter and Paul stands behind their gospels to complement the direct authority and authorship of Matthew and John. What matter—Tertullian adds, sidestepping a potentially significant issue—if there are variations between their accounts, when the apostolic texts unanimously proclaim one and the same apostolic faith. Against this display of prestigious names, an anonymous gospel—related to a canonical one but composed by a notorious heretic—has little chance:

> *Contra Marcion evangelio, scilicet suo, nullum adscribit auctorem, quasi non licuerit illi titulum quoque affingere, cui nefas non fuit ipsum corpus evertere. Et possem hic iam gradum fiere, non agnoscendum contendens opus quod non erigat frontem, quod nullam constantiam praeferat, nullam fidem repromittat de plenitudine tituli et professione debita auctoris*[29]

> In contrast, Marcion assigns no author to the gospel—*his* gospel—as if he were not permitted to attach a title to it when he saw nothing wrong in subverting its entire content. I might make an issue of this, arguing that a work should not

---

it was designated as the 'Gospel of the Mixed', as seen in the Syriac Eusebius; and finally where Eusebius's *Church History* exercised its influence, or where other Greek sources touched the Syriac world, it was also known as the 'Diatessaron'" ("Diatessaron, A Misnomer?," 377). I have suggested above that "Gospel of the Mixed" may itself derive from the Syriac Eusebius.

[28] Tertullian, *Marc.* 4.2.1-2; see Ernest Evans, *Tertullian: Adversus Marcionem*, OECT (Oxford: Clarendon Press, 1972).

[29] Tertullian, *Marc.* 4.2.3.

be acknowledged that does not hold its head up high, that does not display the integrity or guarantee the trustworthiness represented by a full title and a due acknowledgment of the author.

In this case, title and authorship belong together: for the full title Tertullian has in view is the now established *euangelion kata* . . . plus evangelist's name, and the inadequate title that speaks of deviousness and deceit is the anonymous *euangelion*. Yet what Tertullian here objects to is traditional usage. Citations are regularly introduced by formulae such as, "As the Lord says in the gospel," and evangelists are typically named only on occasions when one is being differentiated from another.[30] In the early tradition it is what Jesus says and does that matters, not what a specific named evangelist says. Thus the texts later attributed to Mark and Matthew contain no indications of any authorial persona, and even in Luke and John there are only slight deviations from this absolute anonymity (cf. Luke 1:3; John 21:24). The *Gospel of Peter*'s ἐγὼ δὲ Σίμων Πέτρος (14.60) is an indication of precisely the link between gospel and named apostle on which Tertullian insists, and it represents a departure from the written gospel's traditional anonymity.

The convention of anonymity may also be reflected in the first attested use of the plural "gospels," in Justin's *First Apology*. Here a composite version of the eucharistic words of institution derived from Matthew and Luke is introduced with the words,

οἱ γὰρ ἀπόστολοι ἐν τοῖς γενομένοις ὑπ' αὐτῶν ἀπομνημονεύμασιν, ἃ καλεῖται εὐαγγέλια, οὕτως παρέδωκαν ἐντετάλθαι αὐτοῖς τὸν Ἰησουν[31]

For the apostles, in the memoirs produced by them that are called "gospels," handed down what Jesus commanded them

Justin's terminology implies a concept of collective apostolic authorship, and the composite citation that follows confirms his lack of interest in differentiating one gospel from another.[32] Elsewhere he can speak of "the gospel" as the customary title of a single anonymous text: Trypho refers to the precepts contained ἐν τῷ λεγομένῳ εὐαγγέλιῳ.[33] Here, however, Justin acknowledges that the plural εὐαγγέλια is also in general use. The simplest explanation for the plural usage is that it reflects an awareness that texts circulating under the same title, τὸ εὐαγγέλιον, are not in fact identical.[34]

---

[30] On this, see Watson, *Gospel Writing*, 428–36, with particular reference to Clement of Alexandria.
[31] Justin, *1 Apol.* 66.3.
[32] In the citation the acts and words of institution are presented as Jesus's command to his followers to do likewise: (1) λαβόντα ἄρτον, (2) καὶ εὐχαριστήσαντα εἰπεῖν, (3) Τοῦτο ποιεῖτε εἰς τὴν ἀνάμνησίν μου, (4) τοῦτό ἐστι τὸ σῶμά μου, (5) καὶ τὸ ποτήριον ὁμοίως λαβόντα καὶ εὐχαριστήσαντα εἰπεῖν, (6) Τοῦτο ἐστι τὸ αἷμά μου (*1 Apol.* 66.3). The passage is derived from (1) Matt 26:26, (2) Luke 22:19a, (3) Luke 22:19c, (4) Matt 26:26 = Luke 22:19ba, (5) Matt 26:27 (cf. Luke 22:20, ὡσαύτως), (6) Matt 26:28. There is nothing distinctively Markan here. Text in M. Marcovich, ed., *Iustini Martyris Apologiae pro Christianis, Dialogus cum Tryphone*, PTS 47 (Berlin: de Gruyter, 2005).
[33] *Dial.* 10.2.
[34] Cf. also Celsus's complaint (Origen, *Cels.* 2.27) that Christians "have revised the gospel in its first written form three, four, or many times" (μεταχαράττειν ἐκ τῆς πρώτης γραφῆς τὸ εὐαγγέλιον τριτῇ καὶ τετραχῇ καὶ πολλαχῇ).

Authorial names are added in order to differentiate one "gospel" from another.³⁵ Whether the name is apostolic (Matthew, John, Peter), post-apostolic (Mark, Luke), or later still (Marcion, Tatian), the name shifts the focus onto the textual mediation of the gospel tradition and makes it important to discern which names guarantee an authentic mediation of gospel truth and which do not. Conversely, the absence of a name seems to promise direct unmediated access to Jesus. It is one thing for an individual named Tatian to compile a text called "the Diatessaron" from the four distinct gospels attributed to Matthew, Mark, Luke, and John. It is another thing to produce a gospel text that provides a single comprehensive form for earlier partial attempts to write the gospel tradition. In a certain sense, Tatian and Marcion share a single concern with Irenaeus, the great theorizer of the fourfold gospel: all three figures seek to provide the gospel tradition with a definitive textual form. The difference is that Tatian and Marcion—or the anonymous editors those names may represent—preserve the traditional association of gospel writing with anonymity. It is Irenaeus who is the innovator here, naming individual evangelists and so asserting the irreducibly plural mediation of gospel truth.³⁶

In spite of powerful endorsement from Tertullian and Eusebius, Irenaeus's claim that "the gospels cannot be more or fewer in number than they actually are" is—to say the least—debatable.³⁷ Indeed, it is precisely the apparent vulnerability of this claim that makes it theologically and hermeneutically interesting. A singular gospel comprehending all that was best in earlier texts might be attractive for at least two reasons. As already noted, Victor of Capua produces his new edition of a singular gospel in the belief that it provides at last a true sequential account of what the Lord said and did. A second, more pragmatic concern is recognized by Theodoret, reflecting on his discussions with officials in those two hundred churches that possess a "Diatessaron" compiled by a heretic but no true gospels. Theodoret acknowledges that this book is used far beyond the confines of Tatian's own sect, by people who are absolutely loyal to apostolic doctrine. Such people "use this book all too naively *as an abridgement*" (ὡς συντόμῳ).³⁸ Naive or otherwise, their point can be illustrated by referring to the Eusebian canons that feature prominently in post-Diatessaronic Syriac gospel books.³⁹

These canons or lists identify material that occurs in all four gospels (Canon I), in three (Canons II–IV), in two (Canons V–IX), or in one (Canon X). For a few intellectuals

---

[35] The εὐαγγέλιον κατά . . . title seems to be first attested in Irenaeus, who uses it in connection with different groups' respective preferences for Matthew (Ebionites), Mark (adoptionists), Luke (Marcionites), and John (Valentinians) (*Haer.* 3.11.7; cf. 1.26.2, 3.12.12). The title's primary context is the four gospel codex: see the excellent survey by Simon J. Gathercole, "The Titles of the Gospels in the Earliest New Testament Manuscripts," *ZNW* 104 (2013): 33–76.

[36] While it is true that two evangelists—Mark and Matthew—are earlier named by Papias (*Hist. eccl.* 3.39.15–16), he does so in a context where written texts are disparaged and there is as yet no fourfold gospel (cf. *Hist. eccl.* 3.39.4). Nor does Papias suggest that the texts he attributes to Mark and Matthew were already circulating under the title εὐαγγέλιον κατά (+ name). Martin Hengel overlooks key pieces of evidence in claiming that this formulation is original and that the gospels never circulated anonymously (*The Four Gospels and the One Gospel of Jesus Christ* [London: SCM, 2000], 48–56).

[37] Irenaeus, *Haer.* 3.11.8: *Neque autem plura numero quam haec sunt, neque rursus pauciora capit esse evangelia.*

[38] Theodoret of Cyrrhus, *Haer. fab.* 1.20 (cited by Petersen, *Tatian's Diatessaron*, 41–2).

[39] E.g., the Rabbula Gospels.

the canons represent a major new scholarly resource, useful both in identifying parallel passages, whose differences must be defended against charges of contradiction or exploited in the interests of edification, and in clarifying how and where each gospel makes its own unique contribution. For a less deep-thinking majority, the canons merely illustrate the high level of redundancy inevitable in a fourfold retelling of the same story. In depicting redundancy, they may seem redundant themselves. That is perhaps why such an extraordinary effort is often made to present them in a visually appealing way. Canon tables may enhance the authority of the fourfold gospel more by their artistry than by their usefulness as a reference tool, which is in any case severely limited by the tendency to incorporate all necessary enumeration into the margins of the text itself.[40] Arguably, however, redundant text and redundant artwork are not especially desirable in a gospel book. An "abridgement" that preserved important differences but eliminated pointless repetition would be useful indeed—not least in purely economic terms, in cutting the labor and material costs of book production.[41] Theologically, its anonymity might seem a more appropriate expression of the common apostolic faith than Theodoret's replacement codices with their individual authorial names and perspectives. That may help to explain why, a century or so after Theodoret replaced τὸ διὰ τεσσάρων καλούμενον εὐαγγελίον with τὰ τῶν τεσσάρων εὐαγγελιστῶν εὐαγγέλια,[42] Victor of Capua appears to contemplate a move in the opposite direction.

3. Two Editions

Where a "Diatessaron" is used liturgically and with little or no awareness of distinct named gospels, it is no longer a gospel harmony but simply "the Gospel." In it a collective apostolic voice speaks anonymously and without the potential idiosyncrasies of named individuals. If that gospel's original sources are recovered and brought into prominence, it may be downgraded to the subservient role of a "gospel harmony" as priority is conceded to the "gospels" that are "harmonized" in it. It may, however, regain its status as "gospel" if it seems to present the full content of the individual gospels in a more advantageous form—avoiding redundancy, arranging the events of Jesus's life in true historical sequence. Whether a text is best viewed as a gospel or as a harmony is dependent not just on its internal characteristics but also on its *perceived* relationship to its sources. As the contrasting cases of Theodoret and Victor indicate, this relationship is a variable one. Here as elsewhere, literary genre is determined in part by context and perspective.

---

[40] Like other Latin gospel manuscripts of its time, *Codex Fuldensis* includes not only section and canon numbers in its margins, as prescribed by Eusebius and Jerome but also section number of the parallels in other gospels. This enables the user to refer directly to the parallel passages without recourse to the canon tables.

[41] In its present form the Arabic Diatessaron is around 25 percent shorter than the four individual gospels combined.

[42] Theodoret, *Haer. fab.* 1.20.

The relationship between a gospel and its sources is also the province of the scholarly procedure known as redaction criticism. Here evangelists are viewed not just as editors (as in source criticism) nor just as authors (as in narrative criticism), but as both. These author-editors may add entirely new material of their own, but interest is focused primarily on their treatment of their sources; more specifically, on their *reorganizing* and *rewording* of their source material. Reorganizing includes both *juxtaposition* (deciding which item will follow which), and *selection* (deciding which of the available items will be incorporated and which omitted). Rewording includes both the addition of new words and the omission of old ones. These authorial or editorial activities are summed up in the concept of *rewriting*. An evangelist is one who rewrites the gospel tradition.

In the case of the *dia tessarōn* Gospel, the extant evidence makes it easier to study juxtaposition or sequence than wording. Juxtaposition may survive after originally distinctive wording has been assimilated to that of the separate gospels in what is held to be their normative form. That appears to be the case with both the Arabic and the Latin Diatessaron. It is indeed their common sequence that makes it clear that their translators or editors were right to conclude that their exemplar represented the so-called Diatessaron.

There are, however, significant exceptions to this common sequence, and divergences between the two texts may shed light on their history. Indeed, a third text must also be brought into play at this point. There are several discrepancies between the contents of the *Codex Fuldensis* gospel text and the *capitula* or list of section headings that precede it.[43] This table of contents, or list of section headings, must have been copied directly from the exemplar without the necessary revisions. Thus, Victor chooses to begin his text with the Lukan prologue (Luke 1:1-4), followed by the opening of John (John 1:1-5). The first of the *capitula* refers only to John: *In principio verbum, deus apud deum, per quem facta sunt omnia*. The Lukan prologue is also absent from the Arabic manuscripts,[44] and its inclusion is probably Victor's editorial decision. Similarly, *cap.* v identifies the section *de generationem* [sic] *vel nativitate Christi*, probably referring to passages derived from Matt 1:18-25 (*Christi autem generatio sic erat*) and Luke 2:1-7. In the main text, however, *cap.* v also covers the Matthean genealogy and the section of the Lukan one that reaches back from Abraham to Adam and God (Matt 1:1-16; Luke 3:34-38). It is true that the Latin genealogy speaks of itself as a *liber generationis*, and might be included within the *capitula* heading. Yet Theodoret claims that the Syriac Diatessaron lacked both genealogies, implicating it in its compiler's alleged docetism,[45] and in most Arabic manuscripts the genealogies are provided only as an appendix.[46]

---

[43] Codex Fuldensis confusingly lists its 182 *capitula* under the heading of *Praefatio* (Ranke, *Codex Fuldensis*, 21-8).

[44] Marmardji, *Diatessaron de Tatien*, 2-3. Aphrahat (fourth century), Dionysius Bar Salibi (twelfth century), and Bar Hebraeus (thirteenth century) all assert that the Diatessaron—known to Aphrahat as "the Gospel of our Saviour"—opened with, "In the beginning was the Word" (Petersen, *Tatian's Diatessaron*, 45, 50, 63).

[45] Theodoret, *Haer. fab.* 1.20: Tatian compiled the Diatessaron τάς τε γενεαλογίας περικόψας καὶ τὰ ἄλλα ὅσα ἐκ σπέρματος Δαβὶδ κατὰ σάρκα τὸν κύριον δείκνυσιν.

[46] MSS B, O, E, Sbath 1020. MS A places the genealogies at the appropriate Matthean and Lukan locations within the main text. See Petersen, *Tatian's Diatessaron*, 135-6.

It may have been Victor who added them to the Latin Diatessaron.[47] Yet a tendency to expand the text was already present in his exemplar, which included the pericope of the woman taken in adultery (John 8:1-11). This is a latecomer to the Johannine text and is absent from the Arabic/Syriac Diatessaron.[48]

Turning now to the relationship between the Latin and the Arabic sequence, it is normally possible to correlate the two—sometimes approximately but often quite precisely. Yet there are major exceptions, the most significant of which occurs in the transition from the call of the first disciples (Matt 4:18-22//Luke 5:1-11) to the "inaugural sermon" (Matt 5:1-7:27//Luke 6:17-49). In Matthew the transition occurs very rapidly, with only a summary passage about healing activity intervening (Matt 4:23-25). Luke places the sermon much later, prioritizing the Markan sequence from Luke 4:31-37 (exorcism in Nazareth//Mark 1:21-28) through to 6:12-16 (the appointment of the Twelve//Mark 3:13-19). Thus incidents that occur before the sermon in Luke occur after it in Matthew: for example, the healing of Peter's mother-in-law (Matt 8:14-16//Luke 4:38-39), the paralytic let down through the roof (Matt 9:1-8//Luke 5:17-26), and the call of Matthew/Levi and the feast that follows (Matt 9:9-13//Luke 5:27-32). The Latin Diatessaron follows an essentially Matthean trajectory. Between the call of the first disciples (*Lat* xvi–xx, including Johannine and Lukan material) and the inaugural sermon (*Lat* xxii–xliii), the only major non-Matthean item is John 3:22–4:2 (*Lat* xxi).[49] In contrast, the Arabic Diatessaron follows the more extended Lukan route between the call of the disciples and the inaugural sermon. Here the sequence from the exorcism at Nazareth through to the appointment of the Twelve is largely intact (*Ar* 6.40–8.25). Additional Johannine material is also included.

It is therefore possible to identify distinct Matthean and Lukan/Johannine recensions of this material, and to speculate that the first may go back to an original Greek Diatessaron, ancestor of the Latin version, while the second goes back to the original Syriac translation. In both versions a broadly Matthean sequence is perceptible through much of the text, but in the Syriac/Arabic version more weight is given to Luke's claim to narrate events in their proper chronological sequence (cf. Luke 1:1-3). Confirmation that the different sequences derive from "western" and "eastern"

---

[47] Later, the section enumeration in the main text (here, F + no.) diverges slightly from that of the *capitula* (F^{cap} + no.). F xxi (John 3:22–4:3) is added between F^{cap} xx and xxi, and the discrepancy is increased to two when F lxix (Matt 12:1-8) is added between F^{cap} lxvii and lxviii. Thus F^{cap} lxviii corresponds to F lxx. It is unlikely that these passages were absent from Victor's source, and more probable that he has adjusted its enumeration but failed to update its *capitula*. The discrepancy is reduced to one at F^{cap} lxxii, where there is no corresponding section enumeration in the main text, and the two sequences synchronize again at F/F^{cap} clviii (John 14), after F has omitted F^{cap} clvii. It should be noted that these editorial changes relate only to the enumeration systems, not to the content of the text. Victor is however responsible for transpositions at F lxxxvii + lxxxviii (= F^{cap} lxxxvii + lxxxvi) and at F ciii + civ + cv (= F^{cap} civ + cii + ciii), which restore connections between Markan and Lukan passages previously separated by Johannine ones.

[48] F^{cap} cxx = F cxxi, inserted after the Nicodemus episode.

[49] *Lat* = Latin Diatessaron, differentiating it from *Ar* = Arabic Diatessaron. In n. 47 and 48 above, F (+ no.) and F^{cap} (+ no.) refer, respectively, to the enumeration system in the main text and to the numbered *capitula*. F^{cap} is retained in the analysis that follows, F is dropped.

recensions is provided by Ephrem, whose commentary on the Diatessaron follows the Arabic order rather than the Latin one.[50]

In the overview below, *Lat* + number refers to the section numbers provided in the main text of *Codex Fuldensis*, while F[cap] refers to its 182 *capitula*. (Citations from the latter retain its inconsistent use of upper and lower case.) Manuscripts of the Arabic Diatessaron (*Ar*) use an unrelated chapter system, dividing the text into fifty-four sections of approximately equal length. Verse numbers have been added by modern editors. Bold numerals designate the common sequence, while bold numerals with added letters designate the supplementary material present in the Syriac/Arabic recension. The listing of gospel passages has been simplified slightly and does not include all supplementary details derived from the parallels. While references to these are sometimes placed in parentheses, the main concern here is with sequences rather than with the precise construction of each pericope. Ephrem's *Commentary* indicates that the Syriac exemplar underlying the Arabic translation preserves an order that goes back at least to the fourth century, although the wording may have been changed very considerably. References to Ephrem's *Commentary* (below, Ephr + chapter and section number) list the passages he selectively cites, which do not represent the full text from which he is working.

1. Baptism of Jesus and testimony of John (F[cap] xiv *ubi ihesus baptizatur ab iohanne*)
   Lat xiv: Matt 3:13, Luke 3:23,   Matt 3:14-17 (Luke 3:21-22),
                    John 1:33-34
   Ar 4.28–41:   Matt 3:13, Luke 3:23, John 1:29-31,   Matt 3:14-17 (Luke 3:21-22),
                    John 1:32-34
   Syr Ephr 4.1–5:   Luke 3:23,   Matt 3:14-15 (Luke 3:21,
                       John 1:34)

2. The temptations (F[cap] xv *ubi ihesus ductus est ab spiritu in deserto*)
   Lat xv: Matt 4:1-11 (Mark 1:12)
   Ar 4.42–5.3:   Matt 4:1-11 (Mark 1:12; Luke 4:5-6)
   Syr Ephr 4.4–16: Matt 4:1-11,   Luke 4:6

3. Jesus joined by his first disciples (F[cap] xvi *ubi duo discipuli iohannis secuti sunt ihesum* / xvii *de philippo et de nathanahel*)
   Lat xvi–xvii: John 1:35-51, Luke 4:14-15
   Ar 5.4–20:   John 1:35-51, Luke 4:14a
   Syr Ephr 4.17–20: John 1:35-37, 41, 46-47

---

[50] Owing to the complicated circumstances of its modern recovery, Ephrem's commentary has been edited in three separate works by L. Leloir, with Latin translations: (1) *Saint Éphrem: Commentaire de l'Évangile concordant, version arménienne*, 2 vols. (Leuven: Imprimerie Orientaliste L. Durbecq; Peeters, 1953–4); (2) *Saint Éphrem: Commentaire de l'Évangile concordant, texte syriaque (MS Chester Beatty 709)* (Dublin: Hodges Figgis, 1963); (3) *Saint Éphrem: Commentaire de l'Évangile concordant, texte syriaque (MS Chester Beatty 709): Folios additionels* (Leuven: Peeters, 1990). See also (4) *L'Évangile d'Éphrem d'après les oeuvres éditées: Recueil des textes* (Leuven: Secrétariat du CorpusSCO, 1958); (5) *Le témoignage d'Éphrem sur le Diatessaron* (Leuven: Secrétariat du CorpusSCO, 1962). For an English translation, see Carmel McCarthy, *Saint Ephrem's Commentary on the Diatessaron: An English Translation of Chester Beatty Syriac MS 709*, JSSSup 2 (Oxford: Oxford University Press, 1993).

3A. The first sign: miracle at Cana
Ar 5.21–32:   John 2:1-11, Luke 4:14b-15
Syr Ephr 5.1–12:   John 2:1-10

4. Jesus reads from Isaiah in Nazareth (F^cap xviii *ubi Iesus in synagoga legit librum esaiae*)
Lat xviii: Luke 4:14-22, Matt 4:17//Mark 1:14-15
Ar 5.33–43:   Luke 4:14-22, Matt 4:17//Mark 1:14-15
Syr Ephr 5.13:   Mark 1:15

5. Jesus calls his first disciples (F^cap xix *Ubi ihesus vocavit Petrum et andream, iacobum et iohannem* / xx *Ubi ihesus vocavit mattheum publicanum*)
Lat xix-xx: Matt 4:18-22, Luke 5:1-11, Matt 9:9
Ar 5.44–6.4:   Matt 4:18-22, Luke 5:1-11
Syr Ephr 5.18:   Luke 5:2, 5, 7

6. John testifies to Jesus's increase and his own decrease—and is arrested by Herod (F^cap om.)
Lat xxi: John 3:22–4:3   (Matt 4.12)
Ar 6.5–25:   John 3:22–4:3, Luke 3:19-20, Matt 4:12

   6A. The second sign: healing of royal official's son
   Ar 6.25–35:   John 4:46-54

7. Jesus's move from Nazareth to Capernaum (F^cap xxi *Ubi ihesus audiens quo iohannes traditus esset, secessit in finibus zabulon et nepthalim*)
Lat xxii: Matt 4:12-16
Ar 6.36–39:   Matt 4:13-16
Syr Ephr 1.7:   Matt 4:15-16

   7A. Sabbath exorcism in Capernaum
   Ar 6.40–45:   Luke 4:31-38//Mark 1:21-28

   7B. Call of Matthew
   Ar 6.46:   Matt 9:9
   Syr Ephr 5.17a: Matt 9:9-10

   7C. Healing of Peter's mother-in-law, summary of Capernaum healings
   Ar 6.47–54:   Luke 4:38-41//Mark 1:29-34[51]

   7D. Jesus announces his preaching tour
   Ar 7.1–6:   Luke 4:42-44//Mark 1:35-39

8. Summary of preaching tour and healings (F^cap xxii/a *Ubi ihesus circumibat omnes regiones ...*)
Lat xxiii/a: Matt 4:23-25, Luke 4:42-43
Ar 7.7–10:   Matt 4:23-24 (Mark 2:14)

---

[51] Markan parallels to this and other Lukan passages are listed to indicate the common sequence. Matthean parallels are omitted, in view of the interest here in sequence rather than wording.

8A. Healing of the paralytic
Ar 7.11–24:   Luke 5:17-26//Mark 2:1-12
Syr Ephr 5.19–20b: Luke 5:20, 22-23

8B. Call of Levi, feast
Ar 7.25–30:   Luke 5:27-32//Mark 2:13-17
Syr Ephr 5.21: Luke 5:30, 32-33

8C. Fasting
Ar 7.31–36:   Luke 5:33-39//Mark 2:18-22
Syr Ephr 5.22: Mark 2:19

8D. Sabbath eating
Ar 7.37–46:   Luke 6:1-5//Matt 12:1-8//   Mark 2:23-28, Mark 3:21
Syr Ephr 5.23–24:   Matt 12:1, 2, 5,   Mark 2:27

8E. Sabbath healing, the Isaianic servant
Ar 7.47–53:   Luke 6:6-12//Mark 3:1-6, Matt 12:11-12

9. Appointment of the Twelve (F[cap] xxii/b ... *et sedes in monte elegit xii discipulos* ...)
   Lat xxiii/b: Matt 5:1, Mark 3:13-14,   Luke 6:13-16
   Ar 8.9–25:   Mark 3:7-12, 14, Luke 6:12-17

10. Beatitudes (F[cap] xxii/c ... *et docuit eos de beatitudinem regni caelorum et quae secuntur*)
    Lat xxiii/c: Matt 5:3-12 (Luke 6:22)
    Ar 8.26–36:   Matt 5:3-12 (Luke 6:22)
    Syr Ephr 6.1a-1b: Matt 5:3-11 (Luke 6:23)

11. Woes (F[cap] xxiii *Increpatio divitum*)
    Lat xxiv: Luke 6:24-26
    Ar 8.37–39:   Luke 6:24-26
    Syr Ephr 6.2:   Luke 6:24

Tabulated in this format, the evidence for the Diatessaron's two editions is clear. One follows the Matthean sequence, taking the shorter route from the call of the disciples to the inaugural sermon. The other follows the Lukan (and Markan) sequence, with additional Johannine elements. Both sequences reflect conscious editorial strategies rather than arbitrary displacements, and the decisions as to which gospel sequence to prioritize are each, in their own terms, intelligible and defensible.

It is likely that the "Matthean" edition is the earlier of the two. Both Ammonius of Alexandria in his synopsis and Eusebius in his canons take Matthew as their base text, partly because of Matthew's established position as the "first" and fundamental gospel but also to reduce the considerable technical difficulties presented by their respective scholarly projects.[52] These considerations would also apply to a comprehensive

---

[52] Justin, too, tends to give Matthew priority over his other main gospel source, Luke; see my *Gospel Writing*, 473–7.

composite gospel. Once established, it would be relatively easy to reintroduce elements of Lukan or Johannine sequence into a framework which remains, overall, essentially Matthean. If so, then the Latin or western Diatessaron predates the Syriac/Arabic or eastern one. If the Latin is translated from Greek, we should envisage two "original" editions, in Greek and Syriac, surviving in translations from further west and further east, respectively. Both original versions might plausibly be ascribed to the author variously known as "Tatian the Greek" and "Tatian the Syrian,"[53] who studied in Rome with Justin (an author with a marked interest in coordinating individual gospel traditions), and who may have returned to his Syriac-speaking homeland later in his career.[54] While the identity of the author(s) must remain uncertain, however, evidence for the existence of a Greek Diatessaron is compelling. The odd and barely translatable name "Diatessaron" strongly implies a Greek text, stemming as it does from Eusebius's discussion of a prolific Christian author who may also have written in Syriac but who certainly wrote in Greek.[55] The Dura Europos gospel fragment shows close affinities with the extant versions of the Diatessaron.[56]

4. Uncovering Redactional Strategies

Significant elements of overall redactional strategy emerge from this identification of the two editions, with their common and distinctive features. (In the analyses that follow, numbers in bold refer back to the enumeration in the previous section. D = Diatessaron evangelist.)

4.1 Resolving the Conflict of Traditions

1. D detaches the Lukan statement about Jesus's age and supposed paternity (Luke 3:23) from the genealogy which in Luke it serves to introduce (Luke 3:23-38). D omits the genealogy altogether, not because it conflicts with the Matthean one (also omitted) but because it is only an *apparent* genealogy: Jesus was "the son, *as was believed*, of Joseph [son] of Heli, [son] of Matthat." In both Luke and Matthew the inclusion of a genealogy creates a tension between Jesus's miraculous conception through Mary and his Davidic descent through Joseph. The problem is acknowledged by Eusebius (as cited by Ambrose):

> *Cur autem Ioseph magis quam Mariae generatio describatur, cum Maria de sancto spiritu generaverit Christum et Ioseph a generatione domini videatur alienus,*

---

[53] For "Tatian the Greek," see the Arabic preface (Marmardji, *Diatessaron de Tatien*, 2–3); for "Tatian the Syrian," Clement, *Strom.* 3.12.81.
[54] Cf. Epiphanius, *Pan.* 46.1.6–9.
[55] Eusebius, *Hist. eccl.* 4.29.7.
[56] Carl H. Kraeling, *A Greek Fragment of Tatian's Diatessaron from Dura* (London: Christophers, 1935). Doubts about Kraeling's identification have been refuted by Jan Joosten, "The Dura Parchment and the Diatessaron," *VC* 57 (2003): 159–75. Petersen's discussion of the Dura fragment is notable for its sustained hostility to the harmless idea of an original Greek Diatessaron, and for its unsubstantiated attribution of basic methodological errors to the so-called "pro-Greek camp" (*Tatian's Diatessaron*, 196–203). For the most recent treatment, see Chapter 7 by Ian Mills in the current volume.

dubitare possemus, nisi consuetudo nos instrueret scripturarum, quae semper viri originem quaerit.[57]

Why it is Joseph rather than Mary whose generation [*i.e.* genealogy] is recorded, when Mary generated [gave birth to] Christ and Joseph seems a stranger to the Lord's generation, might cause us some perplexity unless we are instructed by scriptural convention, which always investigates the male descent.

Eusebius's appeal to scriptural convention is of course no solution to the problem at issue. D resolves it by claiming that Mary too was descended from David. At Luke 2:4-5 D's rewriting is preserved by the Old Syriac Sinaiticus (syr^s) and by Ephrem. (Italics indicate differences of wording or order.)

And Joseph too went up *from Nazareth, a city of Galilee*, to Judea, to the city of David which is called Bethlehem, because *both of them were* from the house [] of David—*he and* Mary his *wife*, who was pregnant. *And there they were enrolled*. (Luke 2:4-5 in syr^s)[58]

At this point, D's (Greek) Lukan source most probably read:

And Joseph too went up *from Galilee, from the city of Nazareth*, to Judea, to the city of David which is called Bethlehem, because *he was* from the house *and family* [καὶ πατριᾶς] of David, *to be enrolled with* Mary his *betrothed*, who was pregnant.

The motif of Mary's Davidic descent is attested in Justin.[59] Links of this kind between D and Justin would strengthen the case for identifying D with Tatian.[60] Omitting the genealogies serves to harmonize the conflicting traditions of miraculous conception and Davidic descent, and it also eliminates the notorious problem of conflict between the genealogies recorded in the separate Greek gospels.[61] In rearranging, rewriting,

---

[57] Roger Pearse, ed., *Eusebius of Caesarea, Gospel Problems and Solutions* (Ipswich: Chieftain Publishing, 2010), 260. The double sense of *generatio* corresponds exactly to that of γένεσις in Matt 1:1, 18.

[58] Cf. *Lat* v, *Ar* 2.12–13, where the D wording has been absorbed back into the Lukan one. Commenting on the reference to Elizabeth as Mary's relative (Luke 1:36), Ephrem denies that this makes Mary a member of the tribe of Levi, reminding his reader that "he [the evangelist] says of Joseph and Mary that 'they were both from the house of David'" (ܐܝܬ ܠܗ ܠܝܘܣܦ ܘܡܪܝܡ ܕܡܢ ܒܝܬ ܕܘܝܕ ܗܘܘ ܬܪܝܗܘܢ, Ephrem, *Comm.* 1.25, cf. also 1.26). The underlined words correspond exactly to the Sinaitic Syriac. On interpolations in Ephrem, *Comm.* 1.25–26 that refer to the Matthean genealogy, see Crawford, "Diatessaron, A Misnomer?," 368 n. 18; Matthew R. Crawford, "The Fourfold Gospel in the Writings of Ephrem the Syrian," *Hugoye* 18 (2015): 19–22.

[59] Justin says of Christ that he became incarnate and was born διὰ τῆς παρθένου ταύτης τῆς ἀπὸ τῆς γένους τοῦ Δαυίδ (*Dial.* 45.4; cf. 100.4).

[60] Note also D's assimilation of Luke 1:31 to Matt 1:21: "and you [Mary] shall call his name Jesus, *for he will save his people from their sins*" (Ephrem, *Comm.* 1.25; cf. Justin, *1 Apol.* 33.5, *Prot. Jas.* 11.3; no Old Syriac text is available at Luke 1:31).

[61] See Pearse, *Eusebius of Caesarea, Gospel Problems and Solutions*, 28–39, 135–45, 261–71 (listed as questions 3–4 to Stephanus). See also H. Merkel, *Die Widersprüche zwischen den Evangelien: Ihre polemische und apologetische Behandlung in der Alten Kirche bis zu Augustin*, WUNT 13 (Tübingen: Mohr Siebeck, 1971), 125–36.

supplementing, and omitting various components of his source material, D acts as an evangelist rather than a harmonizer.[62]

4.2 Coordinating Adjacent Narratives

1–3. In the synoptic gospels the sequel to Jesus's baptism and the descent of the Spirit is the temptation narrative. In John, the descent of the Spirit is narrated indirectly as part of the testimony of John the Baptist, and there is no reference either to Jesus's baptism or to the temptations. As analyzed by Origen, the Johannine testimony of John has six components, each with its own introduction:[63]

i. "John bore witness about him and cried out, saying" (John 1:15-18).
ii. "Now this is the testimony of John, when the Jews sent from Jerusalem priests and Levites" (John 1:19-23).
iii. "And there were [some] sent from the Pharisees" (John 1:24-28).
iv. "On the next day he saw Jesus coming to him and said, 'Behold the Lamb of God who takes away the sin of the world! This is he of whom I said'" (John 1:29-31).
v. "And John bore witness, saying, 'I saw the Spirit descend as a dove'" (John 1:32-34).
vi. "On the next day again John was standing with two of his disciples and seeing Jesus walking said, 'Behold the Lamb of God!'" (John 1:35-37).

Among early readers of the gospels opinion was divided as to whether or how this passage is compatible with the synoptic temptation narrative. Writing ca. 200 CE, an author who is probably Gaius of Rome points out that in John the sequel to Jesus's encounter with John the Baptist is his departure to Galilee with his new disciples, followed by the wedding at Cana. Precisely because the Johannine narrative is so coherent, there is no room for the period of temptations in the wilderness which, according to the otherwise unanimous gospel testimony, was the true sequel of Jesus's baptism.[64] Gaius's conclusion is stark: "The Gospel that goes under the name of John is lying [τὸ δὲ εὐαγγέλιον τὸ εἰς ὄνομα Ἰωάννου ψεύδεται]."[65] In opposition to Gaius,

---

[62] In **1.**, supplementation is illustrated by D's statement that, when the heavens were opened at Jesus's baptism, the descent of the Spirit was preceded or followed by light shining upon the water (cf. Ephrem, *Comm.* 4.5 [Arm.; Syr. missing here]). Compare Justin's claim that fire was kindled in the Jordan as Jesus entered it, while the Spirit descended as he emerged from it. As for the attestation, "his apostles wrote this about this our Christ" (*Dial.* 88.3).

[63] Origen, *Comm. Jo.* 2.29–30; see A. E. Brooke, ed., *The Commentary of Origen on St. John's Gospel*, 2 vols. (Cambridge: Cambridge University Press, 1896); English translation available in *ANF* 9:297–408. References to the Brooke edition are to the bracketed section enumeration system, which corresponds to the *ANF* translation.

[64] Epiphanius, *Pan.* 51.4.7–10. Although Epiphanius refers to a group, whom he calls the *Alogi*, he has in mind the figure of "Gaius the heretic" known from the later Syriac writer Dionysius bar Salibi (see my *Gospel Writing*, 477–90). In his *The Johannine Corpus in the Early Church* (Oxford: Oxford University Press, 2004), 172–204, Charles E. Hill attempts unsuccessfully to disprove the reality of an anti-Johannine tendency in the early Roman church.

[65] Epiphanius, *Pan.* 51.18.1.

Hippolytus of Rome and Epiphanius of Salamis suggest that **iv** is actually Jesus's *second* encounter with John the Baptist, occurring *after* the period in the wilderness; hence the retrospective nature of the Baptist's testimony at John 1:30 ("This was the one of whom I said") and 1:32 ("I saw the Spirit descending like a dove").[66]

Origen offers a radical contribution to the Gaius-Hippolytus debate, arguing on the basis of the hermeneutical distinction between letter and spirit that the Johannine and synoptic accounts remain historically irreconcilable yet without detriment to their spiritual value.[67] The Hippolytan solution will not work because it is operating within the wrong interpretative paradigm. It treats the chronology of John 1 and the synoptic temptation narrative as a self-contained issue, whereas the plurality of the fourfold gospel narrative generates countless such problems:

> καὶ ἐπὶ ἄλλων τῶν πλειόνων, εἴ τις ἐπιμελῶς ἐξετάζοι τὰ εὐαγγέλια περὶ τῆς κατὰ τὴν ἱστορίαν ἀσυμφωνίας . . . , σκοτοδεινιάσας ἤτοι ἀποστήσεται τοῦ κυροῦν τὰ εὐαγγέλια, καὶ ἀποκληρωτικῶς ἑνὶ αὐτῶν προσθήσεται, μὴ τολμῶν πάντη ἀθετεῖν τὴν περὶ τοῦ κυρίου ἡμῶν πίστιν, ἢ προσιέμενος τὰ τέσσαρα εἶναι ἀληθὲς αὐτῶν οὐκ ἐν τοῖς σωματικοῖς χαρακτῆρσιν.[68]

> In view of the many other such cases, anyone who seriously investigates the gospels for their disagreement in relation to history . . . will either despair of the attempt to vindicate the truth of the gospels and select just one of them at random (not wishing to write off all information about our Lord)—or else accept that the truth of the four does not lie in their outward sense.

Like Hippolytus and unlike Origen, D believes that a reliable account of the life of Jesus is available to us. Like Origen and unlike Hippolytus, D does not consider that such an account is available from the sources as they stand. D places his baptism account after **iv** and his temptation narrative after **v**. The result is a straightforward narrative sequence which, unlike Hippolytus's proposal, allows space for Jesus's baptism within the framework of the narrative. As Jesus emerges from the baptismal water, the Spirit descends and John immediately bears witness to that event. The introduction to **v**, redundant in its Johannine context since it is already John who is speaking in **iv**, now serves to mark the transition from the narrator's voice to John's. After **v** comes the temptation episode, there is a return to John and the Jordan at **vi**, and the forty-day interval explains why the acclamation of Jesus as "the Lamb of God" is repeated (John 1:35, cf. v. 29). Yet the crucial difference between D and Hippolytus lies not in the preferred solution to a specific problem but in D's decision to regard the texts in question

---

[66] Hippolytus's account is summarized in an excerpt from Bar Salibi's commentary on John published by J. Rendel Harris ("Presbyter Gaius and the Fourth Gospel," in his *Hermas in Arcadia and Other Essays* [Cambridge: Cambridge University Press, 1896], 43–57; 47–8). The summary corresponds closely to Epiphanius's refutation of the same anti-Johannine argument (*Pan.* 51.12.1–21.17). Epiphanius is clearly dependent on Hippolytus here, although the proposal that Jesus returns to John via Nazareth seems to be his own contribution.

[67] Origen, *Comm. Jo.* 10.1-2. Origen visited Rome early in his career (Eusebius, *Hist. eccl.* 6.14.10) and met Hippolytus there (Jerome, *Vir. ill.* 54, 61).

[68] Origen, *Comm. Jo.* 10.2.

as sources open to editorial manipulation rather than finished and authoritative gospels. For D, the problematic nature of the texts as they stand means that the work of gospel production must continue. Insofar as Hippolytus is right about the possibility of harmonizing gospel narratives, the task must be to turn that possibility into reality. The plural sources must be reduced to a singular form that will mirror the unique course of the life of Jesus. "Gospels" must again become "the Gospel."

4.3 Reconstructing the Life of Jesus

4. In *Lat* xvii–xviii the evangelist retraces the journey from the Jordan to Galilee (John 1:43-51) but brings Jesus and his first four disciples not to Cana, as in John, but to Nazareth (Luke 4:14-21).[69] There Jesus reads from Isaiah 61 in the synagogue, announces the fulfillment of its prophecy, rolls up the book, and embarks on a ministry not of reading the scriptures but of proclaiming his own message (cf. Luke 4:16-21). This initial success leads him to undertake the more extensive preaching ministry briefly summarized in Mark 1:14-15//Matt 4:17. The connection from Luke to Mark and Matthew is seamless, whether the report in Luke 4:22 of an initial favorable reception is omitted (*Lat* xviii) or included (*Ar* 4.41):

> *Et cum plicuisset librum reddidit ministro et sedit, et omnium in synagoga oculi erant intendentes in eum. Coepit autem dicere ad illos quod hodie impleta est haec scriptura in auribus vestris. Exinde coepit Ihesus praedicare et dicere quoniam impletum est tempus, paenitentiam agite et credite in evangelio, adpropinquavit enim regnum caelorum.*[70]

> And when he had rolled up the book he handed it back to the attendant and sat down, and everyone's eyes in the synagogue were fixed on him. And he began to say to them, "Today this scripture is fulfilled in your hearing." After that Jesus began to preach and to say, "The time is fulfilled, repent and believe in the gospel—for the kingdom of heaven has drawn near!"

Scripture is fulfilled, the book is restored to its place and gives way to the word of proclamation. This is not "harmonization" so much as the creation of new meaning potential by juxtaposing material from different sources. The juxtaposition is also a substitution, however. In Luke 4:21-24 the narrative continues as follows:

> "Today this scripture is fulfilled in your hearing." And all bore witness to him and were amazed at the words of grace that came forth from his mouth. And they were saying, "Is this not Joseph's son?" And he said to them, "No doubt you will quote to me this proverb: 'Doctor, heal yourself!' What we have heard has happened in

---

[69] On Tatian's redaction of this passage, see further M. Crawford, "Rejection at Nazareth in the Gospels of Matthew, Mark, Luke—and Tatian," in *Connecting Gospels: Beyond the Canonical/Non-canonical Divide*, ed. Francis Watson and Sarah Parkhouse (Oxford: Oxford University Press, 2018), 97–124.
[70] Ranke, *Codex Fuldensis*, 42–3, where *Lat xviii* combines parts of Luke 4:20-21, Matt 4:17, and Mark 1:14-15.

Capernaum, do here in your own home!'" And he said, "Amen I say to you: no prophet is acceptable in his own home."

Jesus's prophecy becomes self-fulfilling as he is dragged from the synagogue to the edge of a cliff (Luke 4:28-29). Understandably, D finds it impossible to accept that his source provides a credible account of a singular historical event. In Luke 4:16-30 in its original context, Jesus has done nothing as yet in Capernaum because he has never been there. There is not the slightest reason for Jesus to speculate about a possible challenge to repeat what he has not yet done. In addition, the shift from the initially positive reaction to murderous hatred is too abrupt and extreme to follow plausibly from Jesus's remark about the fate of the prophet or the supporting evidence from the careers of Elijah and Elisha (Luke 4:25-27). On the other hand, Luke 4:23-30 fits perfectly into the Matthean/Markan account of a later visit to Nazareth. The Lukan "Is this not Joseph's son?" (Luke 4:22) is obviously an abbreviated version of the Matthean "Is this not the son of the carpenter, and is Mary not his mother?" (Matt 13:55), enabling another seamless connection (*Lat* lxxix; *Ar* 17.36–53). In this new context, Nazareth's jealousy of Capernaum makes perfect sense. Early in his ministry Jesus moved his residence from Nazareth to Capernaum (7, above) and was active there as an exorcist and healer (*Ar* **6A, 7A, 7C, 8A**, with *Lat* equivalents).[71] On his return to Nazareth, Jesus might well anticipate the complaint that he has favored his adopted home at the expense of his place of origin. D's purpose in this critical dissection of Luke 4:16-30 is the historical reconstruction of one significant aspect of Jesus's career, his relationship with those among whom he grew up. On this account, the historical Jesus announced his ministry in Nazareth, but his reputation there later became entangled in violent local political antagonisms.[72]

4.4 The Johannine Problem

3A, 6, and 6A. The various sections of John 1 play a prominent role in the Diatessaron's opening sections, from the starting point "in the beginning" to the selection of the first disciples (*Lat* i–xvii = *Ar* 1.1–5.21). There is also agreement between the underlying Greek and Syriac versions over the placement of John 3:22-36, which tells of events in Judea prior to John the Baptist's arrest (**6**). Other components of John 2–6 are widely dispersed, especially in *Lat*. Here the link is broken between the journey to Galilee (John 1:43-51; *Lat* xvii) and the miracle at Cana (2:1-11; *Lat* xlvi). D's Johannine source also includes a further miracle that Jesus performed at Cana while its beneficiary was in Capernaum (4:46-54; *Lat* lvi), and the two stories are explicitly coordinated with one another as "the first of his signs" (2:11) and "the second sign that Jesus did when

---

[71] By the time of the second visit to Nazareth Jesus has performed a number of miracles in Capernaum, healing (1) the royal official's son (**6A** = *Lat* lvi: Cana/Capernaum), (2) the centurion's servant (*Ar* 11.4-16 = *Lat* xlviii), (3) Peter's mother-in-law, and others (**7C** = *Lat* xlix), and (4) the paralytic let down through the roof (**8A** = *Lat* lv). **7A** (exorcism in Capernaum synagogue) is non-Matthean and absent from *Lat*.

[72] According to a well-attested Diatessaronic reading eliminated in the revisions underlying *Ar* and *Lat*, the inhabitants of Nazareth actually succeeded in throwing Jesus over a cliff, and yet he did not fall but flew (Ephrem, *Comm.* 11.23, 26, 27). See T. Baarda, "'The Flying Jesus': Luke 4:29-30 in the Syriac Diatessaron," *VC* 40 (1986): 313–41; repr. in T. Baarda, *Essays on the Diatessaron* (Kampen: Kok Pharos, 1994), 59–85.

he came from Judea to Galilee" (4:54). In *Lat*, both miracles are postponed until after the inaugural sermon (xxiii–xliv, cf. Matt 5–7) and the missionary discourse that immediately follows it (xlv, cf. Matt 10). All this confirms that much of this gospel so far has been based on a Matthean template (*Lat* xv–lxiii, cf. Matt 4–10). Even the relocation of Matthew 10 to a position immediately after Matthew 5–7 serves to strengthen the conceptual link between the two discourses. In the missionary discourse the same twelve disciples who were chosen at the start of the inaugural sermon are sent out to begin their work of preaching and healing (*Lat* xxiii, xlv; cf. Luke 6:12-16, Matt 10:1-4). The wedding-at-Cana story follows immediately, opening a sequence based on Matthew 8–9 (*Lat* xlvi–lxii) into which a limited amount of non-Matthean material is incorporated—also including the raising of the widow's son at Nain (Luke 7:11-17; *Lat* l) and the healing of the royal official's son (John 4:46-54; *Lat* lvi). Eusebius's description of Ammonius's gospel synopsis is also broadly applicable to the Diatessaron in its Greek and Latin guise: the base text is Matthew, and additional material from the other gospels must therefore be detached from its original contexts. While the sequence is Matthean, however, individual stories still include numerous non-Matthean elements drawn from the Lukan and/or Markan parallels. Dependence on a source for its sequence does not entail an equal dependence on its wording.

In the Syriac recension reflected in *Ar* and attested also by Ephrem, the two enumerated Johannine signs are extracted from their subordinate roles within a Matthean context and reconnected with their Johannine source text. **3A** (wedding at Cana, John 2:1-11) is reattached to **3** (journey to Galilee, John 1:43-51), and **6A** (royal official's son, John 4:45-54) is attached to **6** (the Baptist's final testimony, John 3:22–4:3). Thus John 4:54 is omitted from *Lat* lvi but included at *Ar* 6.34: "This is the second sign that Jesus did when he returned from Judea to Galilee." Indeed, this statement may fit its new context better than its earlier Johannine one, for *Ar* 6.5-34 (= John 3:22–4:3 + 4:46-54) speaks more clearly of a (second) return from Judea to Galilee after D has transferred the intervening Samaria episode (John 4:4-42) to a later context. In conjunction with the new emphasis on Lukan sequence (**7ACD, 8A–E**), the transposition of the first two Johannine signs represents an attempt to break the dominance of the Matthean sequence and to maintain the even-handed treatment of the three main sources—Matthew, Luke, and John—that characterizes the earlier sections of this gospel.

5. Conclusion

In editing and re-editing his source material, D is apparently concerned to arrive at the best possible reconstruction of the actual course of Jesus's life as attested in his four main texts. These texts are viewed as sources that offer reliable access to the life of Jesus if subjected to appropriate critical judgments and procedures. As sources they are not themselves authoritative *gospels*—distinct literary embodiments of the one true gospel, attributed to named authors, normative in their current form. D is not a harmonizer of gospels, he is an evangelist editing his sources as his predecessors had edited theirs: selecting and omitting, shaping sequences and adjusting wording, so as to create a more comprehensive and adequate account of "what has taken place among us" than anything previously available. Only so will readers such as Luke's Theophilus attain the well-founded certainty for which they long. Like Luke, D aspires to produce the single definitive gospel that draws most of its material from earlier sources but presents it in new ways and with new editorial emphases.

Yet a text cannot finally determine its own reception or even its own genre. Where its sources are themselves acknowledged as "gospels"—irreducibly plural, normative even in their divergences—then a text that had subordinated them to its own exclusive claim to be "the gospel" may become something else: a gospel harmony. In the hands of its Syriac and Latin editors, it is made to conform to the wording of the plural gospels in their authorized vernacular forms. Indications of its derivation from each of them are carefully inserted throughout. Thus it is prepared for a relationship to the fourfold canonical gospel that will remain ambiguous and problematic.

5

What Justin's Gospels Can Tell Us about Tatian's

Tracing the Trajectory of the Gospel Harmony in the Second Century and Beyond

Nicholas Perrin

Abstract

While it is indisputable *that* Tatian composed a fourfold gospel harmony later identified as the Diatessaron, it is still not entirely clear *why* he did so or *how* he expected that harmony to function in the life of the Assyrian church. This chapter seeks to make a contribution to this question by drawing generic comparisons between Tatian's Diatessaron and a gospel harmony theoretically used by his predecessor Justin Martyr. The argument proceeds in three stages. First, building on a long-standing supposition that at least some of Justin's harmonized gospel traditions are to be explained by the prior existence of a now-lost gospel harmony, it will be maintained that the genre of gospel harmonies (like the Diatessaron and the one purportedly used by Justin) seem to have been well established in the second century, reaching as far back as *2 Clement*. Second, it will further be claimed that despite recent arguments that Justin used a *testimonium* for his mixed gospel quotations, at least one stretch of Justin's text (*1 Apology* 15–16) reflects the apologist's dependence on a gospel harmony, just as a prior generation of scholarship had theorized. Third, even if Justin presented his gospel citations—drawn from texts of various genres, including a gospel harmony as well as perhaps a *testimonium*—as authoritative, this does not negate the evidentiary significance of the Roman church's liturgical practices, which gave pride of place to the "memoirs," understood as the now-canonical gospels. Given Justin's prioritization of the now-canonical gospels over and against his own (hypothetical) gospel harmony, the application of contemporary genre theory would suggest that Tatian, in extending the genre of his mentor, maintained a similar distinction in drawing up his Diatessaron.

Although we know comparatively little about the first four centuries of Syriac Christianity, one thing we do know is that Tatian's Gospel harmony, the Diatessaron, was an extremely popular and influential text. Notwithstanding the introduction of the Old Syriac "separated gospels" several generations after the dissemination of the Diatessaron, these versions would remain under their older sibling's shadow for years to come. And for all we know the Diatessaron would have likely continued to reign as the de facto received text for the Syrian churches, were it not for the fifth-century bishop Theodoret's systematic confiscation of the harmony only to replace it with—what he deemed to be—the more appropriate fourfold gospel text. When Theodoret implemented his purge of the churches, the Diatessaron was still considered by the church's rank and file to be *the* standard gospel of the Syriac-speaking church, not the least inferior to the separated gospels (Matthew, Mark, Luke, and John) of the Old Syriac text.

Syriac Christianity's widespread and deep-seated admiration of the Diatessaron in the third, fourth, and fifth centuries CE raises the question as to whether the harmony had always been so highly regarded, that is, from its earliest days of circulation, following its composition around 170 CE.[1] On first blush, it would seem that we have only the slimmest of bases for answering this query. Given the paucity of witness to the Diatessaron's early reputation and range of influence, an audit of the harmony's *Rezeptionsgeschichte* could seemingly do little better than guess at the gospel harmony's first impress. On the other hand, insofar as our reconstruction of the Diatessaron's initial reception can be inferred from Tatian's intentions in composing the harmony in the first place (an issue which remains decidedly in play), I believe that more can be said on both fronts. To be more exact, on the assumption that the Diatessaron's earliest audiences' esteem for the gospel harmony had at least some relation to its intended function, a clearer understanding of Tatian's compositional motivations holds promise for yielding insight into its initial reception.

While there have been several important and insightful investigations into the Assyrian's motivations for cobbling together his gospel harmony, more work remains to be done in this area.[2] Along these lines, I would suggest that because a text's initial reception is normally constrained by its purported function, and function in turn is signaled by genre, our best start in gauging the earliest perceptions of the Diatessaron's weightiness—its originally ascribed authority vis-à-vis the scriptures and the now-canonical gospel texts—is by attending to its *Gattung*. Of course, this approach would be problematic were the Diatessaron in fact the first of its kind (sui generis). But since a respectable swathe of scholarship has located the Syriac harmony within a preexistent trajectory of harmonies, this affords possibilities for exploring its intended authority.

---

[1] On the dating of the Diatessaron, see William L. Petersen, *Tatian's Diatessaron: Its Creation, Dissemination, Significance, and History in Scholarship*, VCSup 25 (Leiden: Brill, 1994), 426–7.

[2] To date, various motivations have been mooted. These have ranged from a philosophical bent toward unity (Elze), to more pragmatic concerns of evangelism (Plooij, Jülicher) and apologetics (Preuschen), to a pedagogical concern for those within the church (Zahn), to name a handful of possibilities. For the most thorough explorations of the issue, see Matthew R. Crawford, "'Reordering the Confusion': Tatian, the Second Sophistic, and the So-Called *Diatessaron*," ZAC 19 (2015): 209–36; Tjitze Baarda, "ΔΙΑΦΩΝΙΑ—ΣΥΜΦΩΝΙΑ: Factors in the Harmonization of the Gospels, Especially in the Diatessaron of Tatian," in *Gospel Traditions in the Second Century: Origins, Recensions, Text, and Transmission*, ed. William L. Petersen (Notre Dame: University of Notre Dame Press, 1989), 133–54.

In this chapter my argument will proceed in three parts. First, I will renew and extend the long-standing (but as yet far from definitive) argument that Justin's harmonized quotations are in part to be explained by the existence of a gospel harmony, one which also had decisive shaping influence on the one later to be drawn up by Tatian. Second, toward sustaining this point, I will maintain the merits of hypothesizing a gospel harmony despite the claims of a leading competitor paradigm that suggests that Justin's harmonizations are to be traced to one or more testimony collections. Finally, I will argue that though this gospel harmony naturally retained a high degree of authority, it nevertheless did not garner the same esteem that the mid-second-century Roman congregants ascribed to another written gospel tradition, the "memoirs" of the apostles, which I take to be the "separated gospels" we know as Matthew, Mark, Luke, and John. From here, drawing on contemporary genre theory, I will maintain that the generic analogy between the Diatessaron and its prototype, Justin's harmonized *Grundschrift*, suggests a corresponding analogy of ascribed authority. If Tatian formally modeled his own composition on Justin's vade mecum, and if too this precursor text was widely assumed to be at a remove from the more robustly authoritative texts known to us as the "separated gospels," it appears that Tatian intended his harmony not as an outright replacement for the now-canonical gospels but—like Justin before him—as a provisional apparatus relatively efficient for catechetical purposes. Thus, although both Justin and Tatian probably maintained a highly nuanced, if not hermeneutically complex, understanding of their own harmonies in relation to the fourfold gospel, both figures likely admitted a principal distinction between the two which served to privilege the latter.

1. The Hypothesis of Justin's Gospel Harmony

The presence of harmonizations in Justin's gospel quotations has been long noted in the scholarly literature, prompting a variety of explanations. In the first half of the nineteenth century, K. A. Credner was the first to propose that the synoptic citations' blended quality was attributable to Justin's use of the *Gospel of Peter* if not other extracanonical gospels.[3] Around the same time, Karl Semisch would credit the conflations to Justin's foggy memory, a judgment later seconded by Theodor Zahn.[4] Meanwhile, in Zahn's day, William Sanday and Mortiz von Engelhardt, later followed by E. Lippelt, suggested Justin's use of a post-synoptic gospel harmony.[5] Against this

---

[3] K. A. Credner, *Beiträge zur Einleitung in die biblischen Schriften*, 2 vols. (Halle: Buchhandlung des Waisenhauses, 1832-8), 1:92-267. The same position was adopted by Adolf Hilgenfeld, *Kritische Untersuchungen über die Evangelien Justin's, der Clementinischen Homilien und Marcion's* (Halle: Schwetschke, 1850), 128-38.

[4] Karl G. Semisch, *Die apostolischen Denkwürdigkeiten des Märtyrers Justinus: Zur Geschichte und Aechtheit der Kanonis* (Hamburg: Perthes, 1848), 389-92; Theodor Zahn, *Geschichte des neutestamentlichen Kanons*, 2 vols. (Erlangen: Andreas Deichert, 1888-92), 1:463-585.

[5] William Sanday, *The Gospels in the Second Century: An Examination of the Critical Part of a Work Entitled Supernatural Religion* (London: Macmillan, 1876), 36-8; Moritz von Engelhardt, *Das Christentum Justin Märtyrers: Eine Untersuchung über die Anfänge katholischen Glaubenslehre* (Erlangen: Deichert, 1878), 335-48; E. Lippelt, *Quae fuerint Justini Martyris*

position, Wilhelm Bousset posited a much earlier source for Justin and attributed the apologist's harmonizing tendencies to pre-synoptic traditions.[6] Still others insisted that Justin directly depended on—with modifications of course—the synoptic gospels, primarily Matthew.[7] Thus, for the bulk of the twentieth century, five live options remained for explaining Justin's harmonizations: (1) dependence on apocryphal gospels, (2) the church father's faulty memory, (3) a post-synoptic gospel harmony, (4) pre-synoptic traditions, and (5) direct dependence on the now-canonical gospels.[8]

The third aforementioned option, the theory of a post-synoptic gospel harmony, has received considerable support in twentieth-century scholarship, not least in Arthur J. Bellinzoni's still important published dissertation, completed under Helmut Koester, on Justin's gospel citations.[9] Following a thorough study of (1) sayings that occur multiple times in the Justinian corpus, (2) various sayings in *Apology* 15–17 and *Dial.* 35.3, and (3) miscellaneous synoptic sayings, Bellinzoni concluded that *Apology* 15–17 was "probably based on a primitive Christian catechism in use in Justin's school in Rome, and it is likely that this same catechism or a similar catechism was known to Clement of Alexandria, Origen, and to the author of the Pseudoclementine *Homilies*."[10] Meanwhile, the four sayings contained in *Dial.* 35.3 were extracted from a manual drawn up as an apologia against heresies.[11] On this basis Bellinzoni theorized "that the catechisms and church manuals used in Justin's school at Rome were the composition of Justin and his pupils. Justin and his pupils apparently used the synoptic gospels as their primary source and composed church catechisms and *vade mecums* by harmonizing material from the synoptic gospels."[12] On this finding, Justin made use of not one but at least two gospel traditions: the "separated" synoptic gospels and an abridged harmony of the same. Though Bellinzoni insisted that there is no evidence that Justin ever composed a full-fledged gospel harmony on the scale of the Diatessaron, he does maintain that the notion of a gospel harmony was already commonplace, as instantiated by one of Justin's source texts, well before Tatian took stylus to parchment.[13]

In due course, the thrust of Bellinzoni's findings (though not all its details) would be corroborated by later research. In his 1975 published dissertation, Leslie L. Kline

---

ΑΠΟΜΝΗΜΟΝΕΥΜΑΤΑ *quaque ratione cum forma Evangeliorum syro-latina cohaeserint* (Halle: Karras, 1901), 35.

[6] Wilhelm Bousset, *Die Evangeliencitate Justins des Märtyrers in ihrem wert für die Evangelienkritik* (Göttingen: Vandenhoeck & Ruprecht, 1891), 114–16.

[7] Aloys Baldus, *Das Verhältnis Justins des Märtyrers zu unsern synoptischen Evangelien* (Münster: Aschendorff, 1895), 98–9; B. F. Westcott, *A General Survey of the Canon of the New Testament* (London: Macmillan, 1870), 96–179; Edouard Massaux, "Le texte du sermon sur la montagne de Matthieu utilisé par Saint Justin: Contribution à la critique textuelle du premier évangile," *ETL* 28 (1952): 411–48.

[8] The case for Justin's recourse to a testimony collection only begins to emerge toward the end of the twentieth century; see Section 2 of this chapter.

[9] Arthur J. Bellinzoni, *The Sayings of Jesus in the Writings of Justin Martyr*, NovTSup 17 (Leiden: Brill, 1967).

[10] Bellinzoni, *Sayings of Jesus*, 140.

[11] Ibid., 140–1.

[12] Ibid., 141.

[13] Ibid., 140–1.

confirmed "the existence and influence of a harmonized sayings collection which was used by Justin and the [Pseudo-Clementine] Homilies."[14] Like Bellinzoni, Kline maintained that Justin's harmonizing source must have been the inspiration for Tatian, even as it was for other swathes of Christianity.[15] In a 1989 essay, Helmut Koester agreed with his student Bellinzoni regarding a preexisting harmony but differed on its intended purposes.[16] In one of his more recent treatments of the same topic, Koester writes,

> It seems to me that the way in which Justin's catechisms move from one saying to another suggests that he is not composing a catechism and at the same time harmonizing the readings of the two gospels for that particular purpose. Rather, the sayings he included in his catechism were already harmonized in his *Vorlage*. Whoever produced this *Vorlage*—and I am inclined to think that it was Justin himself or his "school"—did not intend to construct a catechism but was composing the *one* inclusive new gospel that would make its predecessors, Mathew and Luke (and possibly Mark), obsolete.[17]

While Bellinzoni, Kline, and Koester differed in regard to the motivations leading up to the creation of Justin's harmony, that there was a harmony of sorts in hand was little doubted. That this harmony also had a decided influence on Tatian was no less dubious.

In a 1990 article, William Petersen sought to clarify the nature of Justin's influence on Tatian by comparing harmonizations in the former with similar wording in his best reconstruction of the latter.[18] More exactly, Petersen alleged six parallels between Justin's harmonization and the phrasing preserved by the Diatessaronic traditions, in both their eastern and western attestations. Petersen also claimed to find additional supporting evidence in five more Justin-Tatian parallels, where the case for a Diatessaronic reading falls short of being cinched. On these grounds, Petersen concluded, "we may be quite certain that we have recovered the text of the Diatessaron."[19] While it is possible that these parallels shared by Justin and the Diatessaronic tradition trace themselves back to a gospel harmony belonging to the Assyrian's mentor, fundamental questions now surrounding Petersen's method

---

[14] Leslie Lee Kline, *The Sayings of Jesus in the Pseudo-Clementine Homilies*, SBLDS 14 (Missoula, MT: Scholars Press, 1975), 175; see also his "Harmonized Sayings of Jesus in the Pseudo-Clementine Homilies and Justin Martyr," ZNW 66 (1975): 223–41.
[15] Kline, *Sayings of Jesus*, 175.
[16] Helmut Koester, "From the Kerygma-Gospel to Written Gospels," NTS 35 (1989): 361–81. See also Helmut Koester, *Synoptische Überlieferung bei den Apostolischen Vätern*, TU 65 (Berlin: Akademie Verlag, 1957), 264–5.
[17] Helmut Koester, *From Jesus to the Gospels: Interpreting the New Testament in Its Context* (Minneapolis, MN: Fortress, 2007), 46–7.
[18] William L. Petersen, "Textual Evidence of Tatian's Dependence upon Justin's ΑΠΟΜΝΗΜΟΝΕΥΜΑΤΑ," NTS 36 (1990): 512–34.
[19] Petersen, "Textual Evidence," 529. In a later article, Petersen ("From Justin to Pepys: The History of the Harmonized Gospel Tradition," StPatr 30 [1997]: 71–96) would maintain that this gospel harmony standing behind both Justin and his protégé Tatian was in fact the *Gospel of the Hebrews*.

(which seeks to establish an assured reading on the basis of so-called eastern and western witnesses) limits the probative force of his argument.[20] Still, the scenario that Petersen seeks to reconstruct is hardly implausible, given Tatian's well-established relationship with his spiritual forebear, Justin.

The implications of the Bellinzoni/Kline/Koester/Petersen position, in its broad terms, have yet to be fully considered. If, for the better part of the past century, we have been content to suppose that Justin's harmony merely "inspired" Tatian (or something of the sort), Petersen's hypothesis of a pattern of variant parallels raises the theoretical possibility that the Assyrian convert materially depended on his mentor's harmony, which served as a significant precedent for Tatian as he contemplated his own compositional decisions. Yet the very feasibility of this scenario in turn would seem to call into question Bellinzoni's default assumption that the scope and scale of Justin's *Vorlage* fell far short of Tatian's.[21] Given the enormous task of editing a gospel harmony, it is difficult to imagine Tatian trolling through and then replicating portions of Justin's harmonizing text, if that precursor text did not at least *begin* to approach the Assyrian's envisioned project in scope and sequence. Indeed, without speculating too much on two texts that no longer exist, evidence of Tatian's indebtedness to Justin's *Vorlage* on both a formal and material level inclines us to think that the Diatessaron was no *novum*. More similar than they were different, the two texts must be seen as occupying the same genre category.[22]

There are also indications that Justin's harmony was not the first of its kind either. A generation or two before the Apologist's death we find evidence of a circulating composite gospel of sorts in *2 Clement*, one materially reminiscent of Justin's.[23] Such evidence proceeds in the first place from several instances where the same distinctive blending of Matthew and Luke shows up in both *2 Clement* and Justin. For example, if an analysis of *1 Apol.* 16.11 and *Dial.* 76.5 has revealed overlapping verbiage commonly rooted in a harmonization of Matt 7:22-23 and Luke 13:26-27, the very same harmonization also occurs in *2 Clem.* 4.5.[24] Similarly, Justin's composite of Matt 10:28 and its parallel Luke 12:4-5 seems to have been anticipated by *2 Clem.* 5.4.[25] Meanwhile, the author of *2 Clement* appears to have known not only the now-canonical gospels (Matthew, Luke, Mark, and probably John), but a compilation of

---

[20] See Ulrich B. Schmid, "The *Diatessaron* of Tatian," in *The Text of The New Testament in Contemporary Research: Essays on the Status Quaestionis*, 2nd ed., NTTSD 42, ed. Bart D. Ehrman and Michael W. Holmes (Leiden: Brill, 2013), 115–42.

[21] The last sentence of Bellinzoni's volume reads: "What is new in Tatian's *Diatessaron* and what is not found in Justin's writings is a full gospel harmony rather than one of limited scope and the incorporation into the gospel harmony of the Gospel of John" (*Sayings of Jesus*, 142).

[22] So also Petersen, *Tatian's Diatessaron*, 430–1.

[23] The dating of *2 Clement* has proven notoriously difficult. On the one extreme, Adolf von Harnack (*Die Geschichte der altchristlichen Literatur bis Eusebius*, 2 vols. [Leipzig: Hinrichs, 1897], 2:438–50) has assigned *2 Clement* a date of ca. 166–174 CE; on the other extreme, Karl P. Donfried (*The Setting of Second Clement in Early Christianity*, NovTSup 38 [Leiden: Brill, 1974], 1–15), following suit with Zahn and Lightfoot, has located it close to the turn of the first century. Contemporary opinions seem to have settled in around the median point between these two poles, namely a setting somewhere in the second quarter of the second century.

[24] Bellinzoni, *Sayings of Jesus*, 22–5.

[25] So Koester, *Synoptische Überlieferung*, 94–9; Bellinzoni, *Sayings of Jesus*, 108–11.

gospel texts, which seems also to have included sayings falling outside the synoptic and Johannine tradition. Evidence to this effect emerges in both his distinctive citation of Luke 16:10-12 and his introduction thereof:

> For the Lord says *in the gospel* (ἐν τῷ εὐαγγελίῳ), "If you do not keep what is small, who will give you what is great? For I say to you that the one who is faithful in what is very little is also faithful in much." (*2 Clem.* 8.5)

The phrase "in the gospel" is significant, for it strongly suggests a *written* deposit of (post-synoptic) gospel traditions.[26] Given the free citation of Luke 16:10-12, it is not impossible that "the gospel" simply refers to Luke's gospel. On the other hand, given the inclusion of patently apocryphal material, merged with the Lukan tradition but also occurring no less "in the gospel," it is improbable that Luke or indeed any of the now-canonical gospels is in view, that is, as *discrete texts*. While we cannot be certain, it is best to conclude with the majority of commentators on *2 Clement* that the community behind this text availed itself of a harmonized compendium of gospel traditions, recognizable as "the gospel." For all we know, this composite "gospel" is one and the same as "the gospel" which Aristides of Athens (*Apol.* 2.4 [Syriac]) invites Hadrian to read in 125 CE.[27] For all we know, too, the shared harmonizations between *2 Clement* and Justin witness to a direct genealogical link between Clement's "gospel" and Justin's harmony. In any case, well before Justin, we detect two textual modalities for the transmission of the Synoptic (and perhaps Johannine) traditions: one in which the now-canonical gospels were copied and esteemed as individual documents, one in which the gospels (and/or derivatives thereof) are somehow creatively spliced and recombined.[28]

Even if Justin did not depend on the Gospel of John to the extent that Tatian did, that Justin knew and used the Fourth Gospel (notwithstanding the judgments of Bellinzoni, Kline, and Koester) is, I think, a conclusion that is now safely beyond dispute.[29] Apart from any forthcoming and suspicious appeals to raise the bar of

---

[26] So Klaus Wengst, *Didache (Apostellehre), Barnabasbrief, Zweiter Klemensbrief, Schrift an Diognet*, Schriften des Urchristentums 2 (Munich: Kösel, 1984), 224; Andreas Lindemann, *Die Clemensbriefe* (Tübingen: Mohr Siebeck, 1992), 94; Egbert Scharb and Dieter Lührmann, *Fragmente apokryph gewordener Evangelien in griechischer und lateinischer Sprach*, MTS 50 (Marburg: Elwert, 2000), 134–7; C. M. Tuckett, *2 Clement: Introduction, Text, and Commentary*, Oxford Apostolic Fathers (Oxford: Oxford University Press, 2012), 41n. 25, 200. The traces of Matthean and Lukan redaction in *2 Clement* leave little question as to its relationship to the synoptic texts. Tuckett (*2 Clement*, 40) summarizes the consensus succinctly: "*2 Clement* is thus a witness to the post-synoptic development of the tradition of the saying of Jesus reflected here: it is not a witness to an earlier, pre-synoptic form of the tradition."

[27] When Aristides of Athens composes his *Apology* for Emperor Hadrian in around 125 CE, he invites the ruler to read "the Gospel," a document that Hill (*Who Chose the Gospels? Probing the Great Gospel Conspiracy* [Oxford: Oxford University Press, 2010], 181–2) takes to be a gospel collection.

[28] For other possible examples in this genre (e.g., Egerton Papyrus 2, *Gospel of the Hebrews*), see Petersen, *Tatian's Diatessaron*, 530–1.

[29] James W. Barker, "Written Gospel or Oral Tradition? Patristic Parallels to John 3:3, 5," *EC* 6 (2015): 543–58; Charles E. Hill, "'The Orthodox Gospel': The Reception of John in the Great Church Prior to Irenaeus," in *The Legacy of John: The Second Century Reception of the Fourth Gospel*, ed. T. Rasimus, NovTSup 132 (Leiden: Brill, 2010), 233–300; Charles E. Hill, "Was John's Gospel among Justin's Apostolic Memoirs?" in *Justin Martyr and His Worlds*, ed. Sara Parvis and

evidence, *1 Apol.* 61.4-5 alone, with its inclusion of redactional material from John 3:3-5, is evidence enough that Justin knew John. To be sure, while Justin's familiarity with the Gospel of John does nothing to establish its inclusion in his harmony, by the same token there are also no grounds for assuming that the Fourth Gospel went missing from the apologist's *Vorlage*. We simply do not know one way or another. John's slim appearance in Justin's writings (unless of course Justin's Logos theology was directly inspired by John, in which case the Fourth Gospel's presence is pervasive) can be accounted for by any one of a number of homiletical concerns (involving, say, the greater appropriateness of the synoptic material) or rhetorical concerns (pertaining to, say, the theological tastes and/or needs of his audience).[30] John's absence from the passage with the greatest concentration of harmonizations (*1 Apol.* 15-16) is even more easily explained by Justin's obvious interest in specific ethical teachings, a kind not found in John but scattered throughout the Sermon on the Mount. Modern-day source critics need to remember that ancient authors did not write with the intention of treating posterity to a sampler platter of authoritative texts, but to make a point. If Justin finds that John is relatively less useful for the purposes of his argument, this is no grounds for drawing inferences about the material content of his sources—either in his separated gospels or in his composite gospel. Did Justin's harmonized *Vorlage* include John? Again we can hardly be certain but it is more likely than not.

All this suggests that when Tatian first undertook the project of reducing all four gospels into one (at some time in the third quarter of the second century), he was self-consciously participating in a literary tradition that had already been well established for decades. Thus, even if the Diatessaron's first readers were unaware of this long-standing literary convention, it can only be the case that the Assyrian introduced his gospel harmony to the Syrian church as a generic extension of—and as an improvement on—similar precursor texts.[31] Working within the parameters of this literary convention, Tatian looked to Justin's harmonized text as his most immediate model.

2. The Challenge of the Testimony Hypothesis

At this point, a specific objection could be raised up against my argument: if, as has been vigorously argued by Oskar Skarsaune, Justin depended on a collection of

---

Paul Foster (Minneapolis, MN: Fortress, 2007), 88-94; Oskar Skarsaune, "Justin and His Bible," in *Justin Martyr and His Worlds*, ed. Sara Parvis and Paul Foster (Minneapolis, MN: Fortress, 2007), 53-76; G. N. Stanton, "The Fourfold Gospel," *NTS* 43 (1997): 317-46 (332). On the significant role of John in the *Diatessaron*, see John Granger Cook, "A Note on Tatian's *Diatessaron*, Luke, and the Arabic Harmony," *ZAC* 10 (2006): 462-71 (471); Nicholas Perrin, "The *Diatessaron* and the Second-Century Reception of the Gospel of John," in *The Legacy of John: The Second Century Reception of the Fourth Gospel*, ed. T. Rasimus, NovTSup 132 (Leiden: Brill, 2010), 301-18.

[30] On Justin's audience, see Jon Nilson, "To Whom is Justin's *Dialogue with Trypho* Addressed?" *TS* 38 (1977): 538-46.

[31] Historical reconstruction should not overstate the cultural distance between Rome and Edessa, as if the latter were a backwoods outlier. Edessa sat alongside a major Roman trade route reaching from Antioch to India, with no small evidence of economic and cultural interchange between the major cities; see W. Stewart McCullough, *A Short History of Syriac Christianity to the Rise of Islam* (Chico, CA: Scholars Press, 1982), 3-35.

harmonized *testimonia* for many of his citations, does this not militate against the possibility that he also drew on a harmony akin to the Diatessaron?[32] The objection is not altogether invalid, but serves less to undermine my argument for a Justinian harmony than, very helpfully, to qualify it in important ways. To be sure, while the principle of Occam's razor would prefer us to surmise fewer rather than more sources in explaining Justin's harmonizations, the evidence may leave us—especially if we are committed ahead of time to the *testimonium* hypothesis—little other choice. Of course, if we were to hypothesize a handful of gospel sources behind the apologist's citations, we would be in familiar territory. In the present *status quaestionis*, if there is any one explanation for the highly variegated character of Justin's LXX citations, it necessarily involves a plurality of textual sources. Skarsaune himself comments:

> Observing Justin's great familiarity with many of the non-LXX texts, especially in the Christological section of the apology, one can hardly escape the impression that they derive from sources which Justin had not just happened to read. And the quite complex relation proved to exist in regard to all known and hypothetical sources excludes, I think, every theory which claims a single—or even a couple of literary sources—as the all-explaining source behind Justin's non-LXX texts and his non-LXX exegesis.[33]

Of course, if this point holds true in relation to the LXX texts, the same principle may well apply—mutatis mutandis—to the gospel tradition. In other words, even if it were true, as Skarsaune argues, that Justin possessed a now-lost *testimonium* (*datum sed non concessum*), this would not preclude the possibility that he also availed himself of a gospel harmony not unlike Tatian's.[34]

Whatever the appeal of the *testimonium* hypothesis, the paradigm is not without its contraindications. For, on considering Justin's citations in *1 Apol.* 15–16, one of his more heavily harmonized passages, we are bound to infer his dependence on something quite different: an extended discourse-laden narrative, precisely as we might find it in something like a proto-Diatessaron.[35] Quoting extensively from the Sermon on the Mount/Plain (touching on roughly half of the pericopes in Matthew's version), *1 Apol.* 15–16 subdivides naturally into four sections that comprise smaller units (*logia*) generally connected by the conjunction καί and introduced with the

---

[32] *The Proof from Prophecy: A Study in Justin Martyr's Proof-Text Tradition: Text-Type, Provenance, Theological Profile*, NovTSup 56 (Leiden: Brill, 1987). While the "testimony hypothesis" has its advocates, Skarsaune's case is not without its weaknesses; see Jeffrey S. Siker, review of *The Proof from Prophecy: A Study in Justin Martyr's Proof-Text Tradition: Text-Type, Provenance, Theological Profile*, by Oskar Skarsaune, CBQ 52 (1990): 365–6.

[33] Skarsaune, *Proof from Prophecy*, 234.

[34] Though it might be argued that Justin's harmonizing quality is owed to his dependence on oral sources, this supposition poorly fits the apologist's recurring references to texts and reading; see Graham N. Stanton, "Jesus Traditions and Gospels in Justin Martyr and Irenaeus," in *The Biblical Canons*, ed. J.-M. Auwers and H. J. de Jonge, BETL 163 (Leuven: Leuven University Press, 2003), 356–65.

[35] Justin's citations reflect not only numerous blendings of Matthew and Luke but also clear signs of Mark: see, e.g., *1 Apol.* 15.2 (Mark 9:43); *1 Apol.* 16.6 (Mark 12:30).

transitional phrase περὶ μὲν or περὶ δὲ (*1 Apol.* 15.1, 9; 16.1, 5), with each section being devoted to a different theme: chastity (*1 Apol.* 15.1-8), love (*1 Apol.* 15.9-16), patience (*1 Apol.* 16.1-4), and swearing (*1 Apol.* 16.5-14). While the prominence of four neatly separated *topoi* in *1 Apol.* 15-16 may at first blush lend itself well to the theory of a supporting topical anthology, closer examination of the details in fact leads in a different direction. Indeed, on tracing the sequence and substance of Justin's citations, it becomes clear that within each section his flow of thought has been principally governed by a text closely resembling something like a Tatian-style Sermon on the Mount/Plain.

The occasional correspondence between Justin's sequence and the biblical order of material is unmistakable. For example, when the apologist introduces the issue of chastity, he does so with a citation of Matt 5:28 (*1 Apol.* 15.1); moves on to a text barely distinguishable from Matt 5:29-30, harmonized with Mark 9:43 (*1 Apol.* 15.2); only to alight on Matt 5:32, blended with Luke 16:18 (*1 Apol.* 15.3). All the while, the steady progression across material that comes down to us in Matthew in two discrete and clearly delineated pericopes (Matt 5:27-30 and 5:31-32) discourages the surmise that Justin is merely reproducing a short unit of text culled from a testimonial collection. If the case for a testimony collection has generally envisaged Justin's reliance on short snippets of text, passages like these weaken the case.

Although this pattern of Matthean sequencing is broken on the following saying (*1 Apol.* 15.4), recognizable as Matt 19:11-12, this does little to compromise the argument for a full-fledged narrative backdrop. The seeming jump from *1 Apol.* 15.3 (= Matt 5:32//Luke 16:18 ["Whoever marries a woman who has been divorced from another man commits adultery"]) to *1 Apol.* 15.4 (= Matt 19:11-12 ["There are some who have been made eunuchs by men, and some who were born eunuchs, and there are some who have made themselves eunuchs on account of the kingdom of heaven"]) is still best explained with the assumption that Justin used a gospel harmony. Whereas the hypothesis of a topically organized subtext cannot easily explain the abrupt transition from *1 Apol.* 15.3 to 15.4, a more promising paradigm emerges on the observation that the major terms of Matt 5:32 ("divorce" [ἀπολύων/ἀπολελυμένην], "marry" [γαμήσῃ], "commit adultery" [μοιχευθῆναι/μοιχᾶται]) are repeated in Matt 19:3-12.[36] The bottom

---

[36] That Justin uses a conflation of Matt 5:32 and Luke 16:18 here is indisputable; I only present the Greek verbal forms of Matt 5:32 for the sake of simplicity. The full text of Matt 19:3-12 (NRSV) reads as follows:

> Some Pharisees came to him, and to test him they asked, "Is it lawful for a man to divorce (ἀπολῦσαι) his wife for any cause?" He answered, "Have you not read that the one who made them at the beginning 'made them male and female,' and said, 'For this reason a man shall leave his father and mother and be joined to his wife, and the two shall become one flesh'? So they are no longer two, but one flesh. Therefore what God has joined together, let no one separate." They said to him, "Why then did Moses command us to give a certificate of dismissal and to divorce (ἀπολῦσαι) her?" He said to them, "It was because you were so hard-hearted that Moses allowed you to divorce (ἀπολῦσαι) your wives, but from the beginning it was not so. And I say to you, whoever *divorces* (ἀπολύσῃ) his wife, except for unchastity, and *marries* (γαμήσῃ) another commits *adultery* (μοιχᾶται). His disciples said to him, "If such is the case of a man with his wife, it is better not to *marry* (γαμῆσαι)." But he said to them, "Not everyone can accept this teaching, but only those to whom it is given.

line: applying the ancient principle of *scriptura sui ipsius interpres*, Justin seems to have brought Matt 19:11-12 (*1 Apol.* 15.4) to bear as a *pars pro toto* extension of Matt 19:3-12, a passage which in turn interpretatively extends Matt 5:32. Only Justin's familiarity with the full narrative of Matthew 19:3-12, as well as that narrative's potential as an intra-textual *explanans* for Matt 5:32 (not least by virtue of its sharing its key terms), makes the move from *1 Apol.* 15.3 to 15.4 explicable. The apologist gathers such knowledge, one imagines, as he pores over the length of the harmonized narrative.

The next and final citation in this section (*1 Apol.* 15.8 = Matt 9:13//Luke 5:32//Mark 2:17 ["I have come to call not the righteous but sinners to repentance"]) also arguably has its gravitational center in or around the narrative of the Sermon on the Mount/Plain. In preparation of his citation of Matt 9:13 par., Justin speaks of the "innumerable multitude" (ἀναρίθμητον πλῆθος) within the church who have converted out of a lifestyle of debauchery (*1 Apol.* 15.7). Here, one suspects, Justin identifies the second-century converts with Luke's "great crowd" (πλῆθος πολὺ) comprising the audience of Jesus's Sermon on the Plain (Luke 6:17; cf. Matt 5:1; 7:28; 8:1, 18; 9:8). The correlation makes sense if only because for Matthew and Luke the "crowd(s)" are also the human pool from which Jesus draws his more notorious converts; their encounters with Jesus are recorded by Matthew just after the Sermon (Matt 8–9), and by Luke just before it (Luke 5:1–6:19).[37]

In the next section, Justin moves from a citation of Matt 5:44, 46//Luke 6:28 (*1 Apol.* 15.9) to Matt 5:40//Luke 6:30, 34 (*1 Apol.* 15.10), which would be but a short step away in any reasonably constructed harmony. Here we also notice a few telling terms in the editorial transition leading up to the blended citation of Matt 5:40//Luke 6:30, 34 in *1 Apol.* 15.10: "Now in order that we might share with the needy and do nothing for glory (δόξαν), he said these things." Very clearly, Justin has in mind something like Matt 6:2, a text which introduces the concept of giving to the needy, even as it warns again the hypocrites who give alms in order that they might be "glorified" (δοξασθῶσιν) by others.[38] At the same time, the same section is loaded with texts familiar to us from Matthew 5 and 6 (and Luke 6). In Table 5.1, a simplified comparison of Justin's text with Matthew shows how the apologist has exegetically "camped out" in the end of Matthew 5 and the very beginning of Matthew 6. I use different underlinings to highlight the correspondences.[39]

> For there are eunuchs who have been so from birth, and there are eunuchs who have been made eunuchs by others, and there are eunuchs who have made themselves eunuchs for the sake of the kingdom of heaven. Let anyone accept this who can."

[37] I suspect that for Justin this same crowd is "innumerable" simply because its members are descendants from Abraham engaged in an Exodus of their own. Compare Heb 11:12 (NRSV): "Therefore from one person, and this one as good as dead, descendants were born, *as many as the stars of heaven and as the innumerable grains of sand by the seashore* (καθὼς τὰ ἄστρα τοῦ οὐρανοῦ τῷ πλήθει καὶ ὡς ἡ ἄμμος ἡ παρὰ τὸ χεῖλος τῆς θαλάσσης ἡ ἀναρίθμητος)."

[38] On Justin's pattern of providing such exegetical paraphrases as a lead up to an extended citation, see Philippe Bobichon, "Composite Features and Citations in Justin Martyr's Textual Composition," in *Composite Citations in Antiquity: Volume 1: Jewish, Graeco-Roman and Early Christian Uses*, ed. Sean A. Adams and Seth M. Ehorn, LNTS 525 (London: T&T Clark, 2016), 178–9.

[39] In Justin the text shows strong harmonization of Matthew and Luke. Yet again for simplicity's sake, I have omitted from consideration the Lukan verbal parallels which are in many cases stronger than

Table 5.1 Parallels between Matt 5:40–6:1 and Justin, *1 Apol.* 15.9, 10, 13, 17

Matt 5:40–6:1 (NRSV)	Justin, *1 Apol.* 15.9, 10, 13, 17
⁵:⁴⁰ "and if anyone wants to sue you and take your coat, give your cloak as well; ⁴¹ and if anyone forces you to go one mile, go also the second mile. ⁴² <u>Give to everyone who begs from you, and do not refuse anyone who wants to borrow from you.</u>"	And concerning love to all, he taught these things: "<u>If you love those that love you, what new thing are you doing? For even fornicators do this.</u> But I say unto you, 'Pray for your <u>enemies, and love those that hate you, and bless those that curse you, and pray for them that spitefully use you.</u>'" (1 *Apol.* 15.9)
⁴³ "You have heard that it was said, 'You shall love your neighbor and hate your enemy.' ⁴⁴ <u>But I say to you, Love your enemies and pray for those who persecute you,</u> ⁴⁵ so that you may be children of your Father in heaven; for <u>he makes his sun rise on the evil</u> and on the good, and sends rain on the righteous and on <u>the unrighteous.</u> ⁴⁶ <u>For if you love those who love you, what reward do you have? Do not even the tax collectors do the same?</u> ⁴⁷ And if you greet only your brothers and sisters, what more are you doing than others? Do not even the Gentiles do the same? ⁴⁸ Be perfect, therefore, as your heavenly Father is perfect."	And that we should share with the needy, and do nothing for glory, he said these things: "<u>Give to the one who asks, and do not turn away the one who would borrow.</u> For if you lend to those from whom you hope to receive, what new thing are you doing? Even the publicans do this." (1 *Apol.* 15.10) And, "Be kind and merciful, as your Father also is kind and merciful. And <u>he makes his sun to rise on sinners, and the unrighteous, and the wicked.</u>" (1 *Apol.* 15.13)
⁶:¹ "<u>Beware of practicing your piety before others in order to be seen by them; for then you have no reward from your Father in heaven.</u>"	And, "<u>Do not these things to be seen of people; otherwise ye have no reward from your Father who is in heaven.</u>" (1 *Apol.* 15.17)

The possibility that Justin's arrangement is driven by topical concerns, as might be reflected in a testimony collection, is decisively weakened by the fact that *1 Apol.* 15.17 (= Matt 6:1) marks an entirely new train of thought, but one which is nonetheless reflected in both Matthew's passage and in the apologist's reflections. Much the same exercise could easily be repeated for *1 Apol.* 15.14, 15, and 16, since these three consecutive sayings draw on Matt 6:25, Matt 6:32, and Matt 6:26, respectively.

A final strand of evidence may be useful, this time in connection with *1 Apol.* 16.5–7. In my view, the wording and arrangement of the citations presupposes a logic that can only be explained by a full-length narrative of the gospels:

> 5. And in regards to our not swearing at all, and always speaking the truth, he exhorted as follows: "Swear not at all; but let your 'yes' be 'yes', and your 'no,' 'no'; anything beyond this is from the evil one (τοῦ πονηροῦ)" [Matt 5:34, 37].
>
> 6a. And that it is necessary to <u>worship God alone</u> (τὸν θεὸν μόνον <u>δεῖ προσκυνεῖν</u>) he persuaded us thus, saying:
>
> 6b. "The greatest commandment is 'You shall <u>worship</u> the Lord your <u>God</u>, and <u>only</u> serve him (Κύριον τὸν <u>θεόν</u> σου <u>προσκυνήσεις</u> καὶ αὐτῷ <u>μόνῳ</u> λατρεύσεις [Matt 4:10 = Luke 4:8]), with all your heart, and with all your strength, the Lord <u>God</u> (<u>θεόν</u>) who made you'" [Matt 22:37 par.].

Matthew's. My point has to do with Justin's range of texts, which seems to have been governed by the Matthean sequence.

7. And when a certain man came to him and said, "Good Master," He answered and said, "There is no one good but <u>God alone</u> (εἰ μὴ <u>μόνος</u> ὁ <u>θεός</u>), who made all things" [Matt 19:16, 17 par.].

In the midst of his disquisition on the Sermon on the Mount, Justin first cites a harmonized version of Matt 5:34, 37, which includes an admixture of a tradition appearing in James and certain patristic authors (*1 Apol.* 16.5), only suddenly to shift subjects to the necessity of monotheistic faith (*1 Apol.* 16.6a), the double commandment according to Matt 22:37 par. (*1 Apol.* 16.6b), and then to the beginning of a familiar gospel dialogue (cf. Matt 19:16 par.) infused with intimations of the *shema* (*1 Apol.* 16.7).[40] How this strange assemblage of verses came together is not apparent at first blush, but with some consideration of a narrative substratum it all begins to make sense. First, in citing Jesus's injunction against oaths, Justin preserves Matthew's wording regarding "the evil one" (τοῦ πονηροῦ), who here, as in a number of places in Matthew's gospel (Matt 4:10; 6:13; 13:19, 38), is identifiable as the Satan. Presumably, Justin was aware of this identification as well as the Matthean-Lukan temptation account (Matt 4:1-11//Luke 4:1-13). This explains the transition to *1 Apol.* 16.6a with its phrasing τὸν θεὸν μόνον δεῖ προσκυνεῖν, clearly an exegetical paraphrase of Jesus's final words to the "evil one" as recorded in Matthew and Luke: "Worship the Lord your God and serve him alone" (κύριον τὸν θεόν σου προσκυνήσεις καὶ αὐτῷ μόνῳ λατρεύσεις) (Matt 4:10b = Luke 4:8b). Seemingly, in Justin's mind, the refraining from oaths, insofar as it is a form of resistance to the evil one (Matt 5:34, 37), is not unrelated to another form of resistance instantiated in the temptation account: the worshiping of God alone (Matt 4:10 par.). Meanwhile the circumlocutory invocation of three terms "worship," "God," and "alone" from Matt 4:10b//Luke 4:8b becomes the exegetical basis for next invoking Matt 22:37, which matches the first two of these three key terms ("worship" and "God"), and then Matt 19:16 par., which lines up with the final two ("God" and "alone"). Notwithstanding the seeming disconnect between *1 Apol.* 16.5 and *1 Apol.* 16.6a, the two texts can be persuasively connected via the suppressed premise of the temptation narrative. Meanwhile, the exegetical correlating of Matt 4:10; 19:17; and 22:37 in *1 Apol.* 16.6b-7 is clarified on recognizing these as narratival variations of the *shema*: "only . . . God." If, as it has been convincingly argued, a composite quotation's tendency to run roughshod over the individual contexts of the cited passage is an indication of its having been derived from a *testimonium*, here the train of Justin's thought shows exquisite sensitivity to the gospel narrative context. This suggests that the collocation of heavily harmonized verses here hails not from a preexistent catalogue of proof texts; rather, before being set down together, these were connected in Justin's mind as he culled them from a preexisting harmony that sat out before his eyes.

Despite the possible impression that the series of sayings contained in *1 Apol.* 15-16 have been reproduced whole cloth by Justin as he drew on a *testimonium*, a closer examination shows that the apologist's sequencing and range of citations within

---

[40] On the parallels with James and later literature in *1 Apol.* 16.5, see Bellinzoni, *Sayings of Jesus*, 64-7.

discrete units is much more likely driven by his perusal of a *Vorlage* which blends the Sermon on the Mount (Matthew) and the Sermon on the Plain (Luke), all within a larger harmonized narrative. The same harmonized subtext also promises to explain several editorial transitions and intertextual connections within this Justinian text. This conclusion does not rule out the possibility that Justin did in fact make use of *testimonia*. Rather, my more modest proposal is that the evidence shows he did in fact possess—perhaps or perhaps not in addition to a testimony collection—something like a reduced-scale Diatessaron, even before Tatian put his hand to composing his own.

To summarize my argument thus far: where Justin availed himself of harmonized traditions, these seem to testify to a gospel harmony that (1) took its place within a well-established tradition of gospel harmonies, (2) was fairly extensive in scope, (3) may or may not have contained John, and (4) provided at least some grist for Tatian's mill as he set about his own harmonizing composition. On these considerations, there is every reason to believe that Tatian self-consciously modeled his Diatessaron on this same harmony. There is every reason to believe, as well, that the two texts shared the same genre.

3. The Use of Justin's Various Gospels and Implications for the Diatessaron

Justin's writings provide evidence that he belonged to a community that privileged the four gospels by putting them on par with the Hebrew scriptures. That Justin had access to the written Gospels of Matthew, Mark, Luke, and (yes) John as authoritative texts is a point which, I think, can no longer be denied outright. That these four "separated gospels" existed alongside Justin's gospel harmony, serving different purposes, even as the former collection must have been the basis for the latter, is more than plausible. Two texts are particularly telling in this regard. In *1 Apol.* 67.3, Justin comments that in the context of the weekly liturgy "the memoirs of the apostles or the writings of the prophets are read for as long as time permits." Unless there is reason to doubt the veracity of Justin's remark, the interchangeability of the prophets and the memoirs in mid-second-century liturgical practice can only mean that these same memoirs had attained a status akin to that of the inspired Hebrew scriptures. In the immediately preceding chapter of the *First Apology*, these same "memoirs" are designated as gospels (*1 Apol.* 66.3).[41] Certainly it is not impossible, as some scholars have suggested, that

---

[41] On this point, see E. L. Shodu, *La mémoire des origines chrétiennes selon Justin Martyr*, Paradosis 50 (Fribourg: Fribourg Academic Press, 2008), 59–66. According to Wally V. Cirafesi and Gregory P. Fewster ("Justin's Ἀπομνημονεύματα and Ancient Greco-Roman Memoirs," *EC* 7 [2016], 212), the memoirs do "not derive, at least primarily, from their status as scripture in the early church but rather from Justin's linking of them to the elite social status associated with the cultural relevance of literary and literate media." But this reading falters not only because it seems to over-interpret a term that was clearly used in an attempt to "translate" one less-known cultural datum with reference to a better-known cultural datum, but more fundamentally because it fails to take into account the memoirs' social context *in liturgy*.

this unique use of "gospels" in the Justinian corpus comes to us as a later insertion. But appealing to a theory of interpolation at *1 Apol.* 66.3 apart from supporting text-critical support not only comes perilously close to question-begging but also fails to do justice to the intriguing statement—our second text—at *Dial.* 103.8, where Justin mentions in passing that the memoirs were composed "by the apostles and those who followed them." Graham Stanton comments:

> The phrase "the memoirs of the apostles" could be taken to refer to the "one Gospel", but this is most unlikely ... Confirmation that in his reference to "the memoirs of the apostles" Justin has in mind more than one written Gospel is provided by two of the thirteen references to the memoirs in the Dialogue. At 103.8 an explanatory clause follows a reference to the memoirs: "which, I say, were composed by his apostles and those who followed them". This comment on the composition of the memoirs implies that they were written by more than one apostle, and more than one follower of an apostle, i.e. Justin accepts at least four Gospels, though unlike Irenaeus, he does not name them or discuss their differences. It is a natural, but not a necessary inference that Justin has in mind Gospels written by the apostles Matthew and John, and by followers of the apostles, Mark and Luke.[42]

While, as Stanton notes, the inference of four gospels is certainly not strictly required by the text, the coherence between this interpretation of *Dial.* 103.8 and the emerging picture of a *functional* fourfold gospel canon in the mid-second century is hard to resist. And why not? If there was a gospel harmony available to Justin in Rome, would we not virtually assume as a matter of course that the raw materials for the composition of that harmony were also available in the leading churches of the Great City?

Justin describes how the worshipping community assigned pride of place to the memoirs (i.e., the separated gospels) and the prophets. This does not altogether negate the possibility of other texts (a gospel harmony, for example) being read at the same gathering, but it does suggest that whenever such texts were read, they would be of subsidiary importance to the standard weekly readings. This leads to an important point. While we may not be able to discern exactly how Justin conceived of his gospel harmony's function, it appears that he shared his community's conviction that the same harmony was not worthy of sharing the same liturgical stage as the memoirs. Whatever practical purposes Justin's gospel harmony may have served, then, it was finally the so-called memoirs (and not Justin's harmonized *Vorlage*) that functioned as the church's *official* written Jesus traditions.[43] This supports earlier scholarly speculation

---

[42] Stanton, "Justin Martyr and Irenaeus," 361–2; cf. also Stanton, "Fourfold Gospel," 330.
[43] Again Stanton ("Justin Martyr and Irenaeus," 364–5) is imminently quotable in this regard:

> As we have seen, Justin's own comments confirm that he had a very high regard for Gospels "written by the apostles and their followers" (Dialogues 103,8). So his preference for one single harmonized Gospel is inherently unlikely. There is no reason at all why Justin should not have composed harmonized collections of sayings of Jesus for catechetical purposes and have used them alongside his use of written Gospels. Indeed, in my view, he almost certain did just that.

that the same harmony had been drawn up as an in-house narrative catechesis, so as to provide a less cumbersome and more unified summative account of Jesus's teachings and actions.

These findings on Justin position us to sharpen our understanding of the Diatessaron. I have been arguing that Justin did indeed have a gospel harmony and this served as the principal inspiration for Tatian's composition, in terms of both content and genre. Accordingly, although the composition of the Diatessaron doubtlessly involved no small measure of fresh and creative transposition, redaction, expansion, and finally translation, Tatian clearly thought of himself as redeploying a well-established text even as he worked within the constraints marked out by its genre. Any historical account of the Diatessaron's composition must accordingly be sensitive to the socio-rhetorical realities presupposed by Tatian's participation in this trajectory.

In applying contemporary genre theory to the ancient gospel harmonies, we are reminded that "a rhetorically sound definition of genre must be centered not on the substance or the form of discourse but on the action it is used to accomplish."[44] In other words, if a text's formal and material features are the leading indicators of its genre, genre in turn is indicative of a fairly fixed and socially embedded rhetorical function. All to say, as theorists within the Rhetorical Genre Studies school insist, continuity of genre implies a continuity of rhetorical function, especially within an analogous social situation. This cannot be easily reversed even through the intentional efforts of the author. As JoAnne Yates and Wanda Orlikowski put it, "one person cannot single-handedly effect the change of an institutionalized structure; other relevant participants must adopt and reinforce the attempted change for it to be implemented and sustained in practice."[45] Given the Diatessaron's shared generic trajectory with Justin's harmony and lacking any evidence that Tatian sought to reinvent the gospel harmony genre (even though he undoubtedly took on a theological identity different from Justin), it stands to reason that the Assyrian's project was beholden to "an institutionalized structure" that would have been all but determinative for how he would have expected his gospel harmony to function. From a correlation of genre we may—all things being equal—infer a correlative function, with correlative distinctions of authority.

Although we know little about Justin's intentions for his harmony, I believe we can at least infer two, mutually qualifying points. On the one hand, we know that Justin reproduces the text of his harmonized gospel sources, without any hint that his argument was any less credible for his having done so. On the basis of the gospel citations by themselves, we would never have guessed that Justin distinguished between the authority of his gospel harmony and the separated gospels. Consequently, on the principles of genre theory, whereby analogy of genre implies an analogy of social functionality, we might expect Tatian to have plied his Diatessaron as an alternative to or replacement for Matthew, Mark, Luke, and John. On the other hand, because Justin's gospel harmony never rose to the authoritative status of the memoirs/separated

---

[44] Carolyn R. Miller, "Genre as Social Action," *The Quarterly Journal of Speech* 70 (1984), 151.
[45] JoAnne Yates and Wanda Orlikowski, "Genre Systems: Chronos and Kairos in Communicative Action," in *The Rhetoric of Ideology and Ideology of Genre*, ed. Richard Coe, Lorelei Lingard, and Tatiana Teslenko (Cresskill, NJ: Hampton Press, 2002), 108.

gospels, which alone among gospel texts seem to have been reserved for worship settings, we suspect that Tatian likewise never intended his harmony as an outright replacement for, much less as a *"frontal assault on the four-gospel canon."*[46] Rather he presented his composition as an authoritative compendium of the same, in the final analysis subordinate to the fourfold gospel.[47]

4. Conclusion

By firmly locating Tatian's Diatessaron within the trajectory established by precursor gospel harmonies, not least the harmony used by Justin, I have sought to draw certain inferences (and rule out others) regarding the Assyrian's intentions. If Justin thought of his harmony as standing in for yet also being at a remove from the unrivaled separated gospels, then we are bound to assume—short of evidence to the contrary—that Tatian's harmony initially asked to be understood in the same vein. Such an assumption follows on the application of contemporary genre theory, whereby analogies of genre are presumed to be underwritten by corresponding social mappings, complete with their ascriptions of differentiated authority. In all likelihood, then, Tatian positioned his Diatessaron, much as presumably Justin's school had positioned its harmony before him, as a précis of the life and teachings of Jesus—a *relatively* authoritative document which would have had obvious pedagogical and apologetic value. Of course, texts have a way of taking on a life of their own far after the lifetime of their authors. Whatever Tatian's intentions, as the Diatessaron served as the Syriac church's one and only gospel, it was inevitable that it would acquire unparalleled authority in the Syriac-speaking church. How quickly this sea change might have taken place is impossible to know. In any event, the evidence of Justin's harmony suggests that the Diatessaron rose over time from ecclesial vade mecum to the one and only authoritative gospel, only to fall again centuries later when the church-sponsored separated gospels invaded the field.

---

[46] The phrase is from William L. Petersen, "The Diatessaron and the Fourfold Gospel," in *The Earliest Gospels: The Origins and Transmission of the Earliest Christian Gospels—The Contribution of the Chester Beatty Gospel Codex P45*, ed. Charles Horton (London: T&T Clark, 2004), 67 (emphasis original).

[47] In assertions like these, as well as in dialogues of friendly disagreement like those between myself ("Hermeneutical Factors in the Harmonization of the Gospel and the Question of Textual Authority," in *The Biblical Canons*, ed. J.-M. Auwers and H. J. de Jonge, BETL 163 [Leuven: Leuven University Press, 2003], 599–605) and Matthew R. Crawford ("The Diatessaron, Canonical or Non-Canonical? Rereading the Dura Fragment," *NTS* 62 [2016]: 275–6), there is inevitably some foundering on the philosophical difficulty as to what exactly is meant by terms like "authority," "canonical," "better edition," and the like. In one obvious sense, both Justin and Tatian regarded their harmony as superior to the separated gospels, otherwise they would not have been used or composed them at all. At the same time, this approach relies on the unexamined assumption that, so far as ancient gospel text is concerned, functionality and ontological status were interchangeable categories.

6

Tatian's Diatessaron and the Proliferation of Gospels

James W. Barker

Abstract

Previous scholarship on the Diatessaron has asked whether Tatian intended to supplement or replace the fourfold gospel. This chapter reconsiders the question by sketching a general theory of Gospel proliferation. Greek, Roman, and Jewish comparanda show that the proliferation and collection of similar works were common reading and writing practices. Accordingly, gospel writers would not likely discard their sources, and gospel readers would likely collect and compare multiple texts. On the supposition that ancient writers were attuned to their contemporary reading practices, Tatian likely would have expected the Diatessaron to be read alongside—not instead of—the fourfold gospel, as was the outcome over the next few centuries.

In composing the Diatessaron, Tatian meticulously harmonized the Gospels of Matthew, Mark, Luke, and John.[1] Many have taken up the question whether Tatian intended to supplement or replace the fourfold gospel. Matthew Crawford refers to the Diatessaron as a "rival to the fourfold gospel,"[2] intended as "a new and...better edition of the life of Jesus."[3] Crawford leaves open the question whether Tatian wanted his Gospel to be read alongside others, and so does Charles Hill in mentioning "whatever purpose Tatian had in producing the *Diatessaron*."[4] Nicholas Zola suggests that the

---

[1] My thanks to Sarah E. Rollens and Larry W. Hurtado as well as Matthew R. Crawford and Nicholas J. Zola for engaging and helpful comments on this chapter; I also acknowledge a Quick Turnaround Grant from Potter College of Arts & Letters at Western Kentucky University to present an earlier version at the 2016 Society of Biblical Literature meeting. Given Victor of Capua's nomenclature Diapente, Tatian might have drawn on more than these four; on this question, see Charles Hill's contribution (Chapter 2) to this volume.

[2] Matthew R. Crawford, "The Diatessaron, Canonical or Non-canonical? Rereading the Dura Fragment," *NTS* 62 (2016): 253–77, here 253.

[3] Crawford, "Diatessaron, Canonical or Non-canonical?" 275.

[4] Charles E. Hill, *The Johannine Corpus in the Early Church* (Oxford: Oxford University Press, 2004), 302.

question cannot be answered based on extant evidence.[5] Others assume a stronger position. William Petersen says that Tatian intended his gospel to be "the one, *definitive* description of Jesus' life."[6] Francis Watson echoes "the definitive Gospel,"[7] and Tjitze Baarda concludes that Tatian wanted not only to surpass his sources but also to replace them as *"the* Gospel."[8] To the contrary, David Dungan finds "no evidence that Tatian intended that his composition *replace* the original Greek Gospels."[9] Similarly, Nicholas Perrin argues that the Diatessaron does not supplant the earlier Gospels' authority.[10] It seemed to me too that I should ask this question,[11] but I have come to reject "supplement or replace" as a false dichotomy that mischaracterizes the nature of Gospel proliferation.

Drawing on studies of circles of authors, sociology of reading, and manuscript materiality, this chapter sketches a general theory of Gospel proliferation, a neutral term for the processes of composition, transmission, reception, and revision culminating in more than a dozen extant or attested Gospels appearing a century or two after Jesus's crucifixion. Writing a subsequent Gospel raises questions of authors' intentions, which are bound to questions of anticipated audience. Rather than assuming that each Gospel reinforces the beliefs and practices of a particular Christian community, Richard Bauckham argues that "the Gospels were written for general circulation," an implied audience of "any and every Christian community in the late-first-century Roman Empire";[12] as a mediating position, each evangelist could have written within a specific community while anticipating a wider readership.[13] Yet the very notion of

---

[5] Nicholas J. Zola, "Evangelizing Tatian: The *Diatessaron's* Place in the Emergence of the Fourfold Gospel Canon," *PRSt* 43 (2016): 399–414, here 399.

[6] William L. Petersen, "Canonicity, Ecclesiastical Authority, and Tatian's *Diatessaron*," in *Patristic and Text-Critical Studies: The Collected Essays of William L. Petersen*, NTTSD 40, ed. Jan Krans and Joseph Verheyden (Leiden: Brill, 2012), 509; English original of "Canonicité, autorité ecclésiastique et *Diatessaron* de Tatien," in *Le canon du Nouveau Testament: Regards nouveaux sur l'histoire de sa formation*, ed. Frédéric Amsler, Le monde de la Bible 54 (Geneva: Labor et Fides, 2005), 87–116.

[7] See Francis Watson's contribution (Chapter 4) to this volume.

[8] Tjitze Baarda, "ΔΙΑΦΩΝΙΑ—ΣΥΜΦΩΝΙΑ: Factors in the Harmonization of the Gospels, Especially in the Diatessaron of Tatian," in *Gospel Traditions in the Second Century: Origins, Recensions, Text, and Transmission*, ed. William L. Petersen (Notre Dame: University of Notre Dame Press, 1989), 133–54, here 154.

[9] David Laird Dungan, *A History of the Synoptic Problem: The Canon, the Text, the Composition, and the Interpretation of the Gospels*, ABRL (New York: Doubleday, 1999), 44.

[10] Nicholas Perrin, "Hermeneutical Factors in the Harmonization of the Gospels and the Question of Textual Authority," in *The Biblical Canons*, ed. J.-M. Auwers and H. J. de Jonge, BETL 163 (Leuven: Leuven University Press, 2003), 599–605, here 605.

[11] My essay for the Development of Early Christian Theology section's panel on the Diatessaron at the 2016 SBL meeting was entitled, "Did Tatian intend to supplement or to supplant the fourfold gospel?"

[12] Richard Bauckham, "Introduction," in *The Gospels for All Christians: Rethinking the Gospel Audiences*, ed. Richard Bauckham (Grand Rapids, MI: Eerdmans, 1998), 1–7.

[13] E.g., Craig L. Blomberg, "The Gospels for Specific Communities *and* All Christians," in *The Audience of the Gospels: The Origin and Function of the Gospels in Early Christianity*, ed. Edward W. Klink III, LNTS 353 (New York: T&T Clark, 2010), 111–33; Margaret M. Mitchell, "Patristic Counter-Evidence to the Claim that 'The Gospels Were Written for All Christians,'" *NTS* 51 (2005): 36–79; David C. Sim, "The Gospels for All Christians? A Response to Richard Bauckham," *JSNT* 84 (2001): 3–27; Daniel W. Ulrich, "The Missional Audience of the Gospel of Matthew," *CBQ* 69 (2007): 64–83. Bauckham ("For Whom Were the Gospels Written?" in *The Gospels for All Christians*, 9–48, here 45–6) anticipated and rejected such a compromise, however.

"community" can be problematic,[14] and I am persuaded by studies conceptualizing the evangelists within literary networks.[15] Also, Matthew D. C. Larsen helpfully shows how publication and circulation—even post-publication revision—lay largely beyond an author's control.[16] As books circulated, material artifacts offer ample evidence of readers collecting and studying multiple works on the same topic.[17] By extension, writers were aware of reading practices, so Tatian likely expected the Diatessaron to be read alongside—not instead of—the earlier Gospels.

The chapter divides into three main parts. First are Greek, Roman, and Jewish examples showing the proliferation of highly similar works. Second is an overview of Gospel production and reception before and after Tatian. Third is a reexamination of the Diatessaron in light of the preceding analogies. Overall, I find no strong evidence for literary replacement. Source texts did not disappear by being absorbed into subsequent Gospels. Also, although there is occasional evidence for the exclusive use of a single Gospel, exclusivity is the exception rather than the norm, and the Diatessaron never appears to have been used exclusively. Instead, the Diatessaron was read alongside the fourfold gospel for centuries, as would have been Tatian's most reasonable expectation when composing his Gospel.

1. Analogies to the Proliferation of Gospels

This section adduces examples of Greco-Roman literature and Jewish biblical texts. Similar works would proliferate, but subsequent works would not replace their predecessors. The "supplement or replace" question begins to break down as soon as

---

[14] Stanley Stowers, "The Concept of Community and the History of Early Christianity," *MTSR* 23 (2011): 238–56.
[15] E.g., Loveday Alexander, "Ancient Book Production and the Circulation of the Gospels," in *The Gospels for All Christians: Rethinking the Gospel Audiences*, ed. Richard Bauckham (Grand Rapids, MI: Eerdmans, 1998), 71–105, here 91–3; E. Earle Ellis, *The Making of the New Testament Documents*, Biblical Interpretation (Leiden: Brill, 1999); Chris Keith, "The Competitive Textualization of the Jesus Tradition in John 20:30–31 and 21:24–25," *CBQ* 78 (2016): 321–37; Richard Last, "Communities that Write: Christ-Groups, Associations, and Gospel Communities," *NTS* 58 (2012): 173–98; Richard Last, "The Social Relationships of Gospel Writers: New Insights from Inscriptions Commending Greek Historiographers," *JSNT* 37 (2015): 223–52; Robyn Faith Walsh, "Q and the 'Big Bang' Theory of Christian Origins," in *Redescribing the Gospel of Mark*, ed. Barry S. Crawford and Merrill P. Miller, SBLECL 22 (Atlanta, GA: SBL Press, 2017), 483–533.
[16] Matthew D. C. Larsen, "Accidental Publication, Unfinished Texts and the Traditional Goals of New Testament Textual Criticism," *JSNT* 39 (2017): 362–87.
[17] E.g., the Oxyrhynchus papyri reveal circles of readers collecting works from particular genres such as lyric poetry or classical drama; for book collection at Oxyrhynchus, see William A. Johnson, *Readers and Reading Culture in the High Roman Empire: A Study of Elite Communities* (Oxford: Oxford University Press, 2010), 180–5; George W. Houston, *Inside Roman Libraries: Book Collections and Their Management in Antiquity* (Chapel Hill: University of North Carolina Press, 2014), 130–79. For sociology of reading, see, e.g., Harry Y. Gamble, *Books and Readers in the Early Church: A History of Early Christian Texts* (New Haven, CT: Yale University Press, 1995); Larry W. Hurtado, "Manuscripts and the Sociology of Early Christian Reading," in *The Early Text of the New Testament*, ed. Charles E. Hill and Michael J. Kruger (Oxford: Oxford University Press, 2012), 49–62. For manuscript materiality and the Gospels, see esp. Larry W. Hurtado, *The Earliest Christian Artifacts: Manuscripts and Christian Origins* (Grand Rapids, MI: Eerdmans, 2006).

one considers manuscript materiality. First and foremost, ancient books were built to last a very long time. From George Houston's stellar study of Roman libraries, "the evidence of these collections suggests that a roll might well be expected to last for 150 years, and that in some cases book rolls were kept for much longer than that."[18] Five hundred years was an exceptionally high age for a book, whereas fifty years was an exceptionally young age for a discarded book. It would have been unusual, then, for any author to write a book and throw away his sources. While it was physically possible to replace one's sources or rivals by effacement, this process would not ensue right away: there are rare examples of papyrus palimpsests, but the process was probably more trouble than it was worth;[19] parchment palimpsests are far more common, but underlying literary texts typically endured for a century or longer before being overwritten.[20] Besides material production, authors had relatively limited control over the circulation of their own works, let alone rival ones. More often than not, the loss of ancient literature was accidental, not intentional.

1.1 Greco-Roman Texts

The Greek Epic Cycle, encomia for Cato the Younger, and histories of the Jewish Revolt show how similar works would proliferate after a single work had established a market.

1.1.1 *The Greek Epic Cycle*

The so-called Epic Cycle consists of Homeric imitations that ipso facto supplement the Iliad and the Odyssey via prequels, interquels, and a sequel.[21] Although none rivaled the Iliad or Odyssey in length or prestige, "what Homer left out clearly appealed to a substantial number of Greeks."[22] The cycle began with the Titanomachy, according to which Zeus defeated Cronus and established the Olympian gods as rulers over the world. The Cypria described the Trojan war up to the commencement of the Iliad. Whereas the Iliad's ending anticipates the sack of Troy and the Odyssey's beginning presupposes it, the written Sack of Troy describes it in detail. Afterward, in imitation of the Odyssey, the Returns Home conveys the voyages of other heroes. Finally, the Telegony tells of Odysseus's adventures after the Odyssey. In addition to these five, at least five additional epics completed the cycle.

---

[18] Houston, *Inside Roman Libraries*, 174–5; there Houston discusses the Oxyrhynchus papyri, but the same figures apply also to the villa at Herculaneum (pp. 120–1).

[19] Thomas Schmidt, "Greek Palimpsest Papyri: Some Open Questions," *Proceedings of the 24th International Congress of Papyrology* 2 (2007): 979–90.

[20] This is particularly the case when both old and new texts are in the same language; via the Leuven Database of Ancient Books (http://www.trismegistos.org/tm/search_reuse.php), e.g., the old and new text of Russian National Library gr. 5 are in Greek, and the original text lasted at least 150 years before the MS became palimpsest.

[21] On the Epic Cycle, see Malcolm Davies, *The Greek Epic Cycle*, 2nd ed. (London: Bristol Classical Press, 2001); M. L. West, *Greek Epic Fragments from the Seventh to the Fifth Centuries BC*, LCL 497 (Cambridge: Harvard University Press, 2003); M. L. West, *The Epic Cycle: A Commentary on the Lost Troy Epics* (Oxford: Oxford University Press, 2013).

[22] Davies, *Greek Epic Cycle*, 10.

Each component of the cycle had likely been produced by the end of the sixth century BCE,²³ and the contents of the cycle were probably codified by the fourth century BCE.²⁴ The Epic Cycle was still being studied when Proclus summarized each work in the second century CE.²⁵ Proclus's summary intimates chronological and thematic coherence throughout the cycle, yet the extant fragments evince redundancy and incongruity.²⁶ As shown by the Cypria,²⁷ derivative works sometimes contradicted or reinterpreted Homer's original descriptions. And apparently there were rival sequels to the Iliad, for Lesches's Little Iliad probably overlapped considerably with Arctinus's Aethiopis and Sack of Troy.²⁸ Nonetheless, ancient scholars collected and studied these presumably rival works alongside one another, and they circulated together for centuries.

1.1.2 Encomia for Cato the Younger

Encomia for Cato the Younger proliferated immediately after his noble suicide at Utica in April of 46 BCE.²⁹ Cicero's letters attest the publication of at least five works within a year and a half. On June 13, 46 BCE, Cicero says that he is pleased with his own book on Cato (*Att.* 12.4). By May 9, 45 BCE, Aulus Hirtius had sent his book of Cato's defects (*vitia*) to Cicero; Cicero ordered it to be copied and published, because Cato's enemies' vituperations counterintuitively serve as praise (*Att.* 12.40, 41, 44, 45, 48). By August 12, 45 BCE, Caesar had read Brutus's book in praise of Cato (*Att.* 13.46). On August 20, 45 BCE, Cicero asked his friend Fadius Gallus to send his book on Cato, which Cicero expressly wanted to read (*Fam.* 7.24). By August 24, 45 BCE, Cicero had read Julius Caesar's books against Cato (*Att.* 13.50). At least two other contemporary works were published: Octavian wrote a response to Brutus's *Cato* (Suetonius *Aug.* 85); Munatius Rufus, a close friend of Cato, would have written his encomium around the same time (Plutarch *Cat. Min.* 25.1). A century later, Munatius's work was a source for Thrasea Paetus (Plutarch *Cat. Min.* 37.1), who wrote his own life of Cato before emulating Cato in death under Nero in 66 CE. Finally, Plutarch published his *Cato the Younger* in the late-first or early-second century CE.

Unfortunately, Plutarch's is the lone survivor of the nine lives of Cato. Accordingly, the extent to which subsequent works recapitulated or supplemented earlier ones cannot be determined. However, it can be determined that subsequent works did not

---

[23] West, *Epic Cycle*, 21.
[24] Ibid., 23; Aristotle refers to the Cypria and the Little Iliad (*Poet.* 1459ab).
[25] West, *Epic Cycle*, 8; West argues against identifying Proclus with the fifth-century CE Neoplatonist. Around the third century CE, Athenaeus mentions the Titanomachy (*Deipn.* 7.277) and the Thebais (*Deipn.* 11.465).
[26] Davies, *Greek Epic Cycle*, 7.
[27] Ibid., 40, 47.
[28] Ibid., 60; on the synchronization of subsequent installments to the Epic Cycle, see Marco Fantuzzi, "The Aesthetics of Sequentiality and Its Discontents," in *The Greek Epic Cycle and Its Ancient Reception: A Companion*, ed. Marco Fantuzzi and Christos Tsagalis (Cambridge: Cambridge University Press, 2015), 405–29, here 409.
[29] Richard A. Burridge (*What Are the Gospels? A Comparison with Graeco-Roman Biography*, 2nd ed. [Grand Rapids, MI: Eerdmans, 2004], 153) discusses encomia for Cato in the context of the Gospel genre.

replace their predecessors. Plutarch shows that after nearly 150 years, Cicero's *Cato* and Caesar's *Anti-Cato* were still being read, for each presently "has devotees" (σπουδαστὰς ἔχει; *Caes.* 54.3). Cicero apparently wrote the first life of Cato, yet he collected at least four other such books. Subsequent authors wrote directly in response to predecessors, so the term "competitive textualization" aptly captures the praise and blame oscillating between Cicero and Caesar and between Brutus and Octavian.[30]

1.1.3 Histories of the Jewish Revolt

Josephus begins his account of the Jewish War (*B.J.* 1.1) by contextualizing his history book among previously published second-hand accounts (οἱ μὲν οὐ παρατύχοντες τοῖς πράγμασιν) and first-hand accounts (οἱ παραγενόμενοι δέ). Josephus calls the second-hand accounts contradictory (ἀσύμφωνα), and he considers the first-hand accounts falsified either by flattery toward the Romans or by hatred toward the Jews (*B.J.* 1.1). Josephus published the Jewish War prior to Vespasian's death in 79 CE, so—if the plurals are taken seriously—Josephus's history was one of at least five such works produced within a decade of the temple's destruction. Josephus's might have been the first Jewish perspective on the war, for he praises his own accuracy (ἀκριβεία) in representing both sides of the conflict, even as he admits his sympathy (πάθος) for his countrymen (*B.J.* 1.4).

Justus of Tiberias later published another history of the War from a Jewish perspective. According to Josephus, Justus claimed to have surpassed his predecessors' histories of the war (*Vita* 357, 359), and he discredited Josephus in particular (*Vita* 340).[31] Josephus defended himself and disparaged Justus for waiting so long to publish his work—after Vespasian, Titus, and Agrippa had all died (*Vita* 359–360).[32] Justus's history cannot date before 90 CE, and Josephus's response appeared by either 93/94 or 97/98.[33] As authors, Justus and Josephus realistically expected readers to compare multiple accounts of the same war, and each author considered his own work superior to the other. A confident author could expect informed readers to recognize his book's superiority (as when Cicero himself published Hirtius's rival book); there was no need to suppress competition.

Since the works of Josephus's rivals did not endure, the extent to which subsequent histories overlapped or supplemented cannot be determined. It is clear, though, that rival works circulated alongside one another for decades, if not longer. Moreover, Josephus's works survived because of their usefulness to later Christians. Josephus hardly could have imagined such a wide Christian audience, let alone in an ascendant

---

[30] I owe the term "competitive textualization" to Chris Keith's 2016 *CBQ* article cited above in n. 15.
[31] Justus blamed Josephus and his fellow Galileans for instigating the city of Tiberias in the revolt against Rome.
[32] By contrast, Josephus shared his account with Titus and Agrippa, who approved of it (*Vita* 361–367).
[33] Regarding Justus, see Tessa Rajak, "Justus of Tiberias," *ClQ* 23 (1973): 345–68. Elsewhere Rajak (*Josephus: The Historian and His Society*, 2nd ed. [London: Duckworth, 2002], 237–8) dates *Antiquities* and *Vita*, together in a single edition, to 93/94; cf. Seth Schwartz, "The Composition and Publication of Josephus's *Bellum Iudaicum* Book 7," *HTR* 79 (1986): 373–86, here 385n. 45, who dates the *Vita* to 97/98.

Christian culture and polity in the fourth century. Thus it would be anachronistic to claim the eventual survival of Josephus's history as evidence of his initial intent.

1.2 Jewish Biblical Texts

Jewish biblical texts evince similar literary processes of proliferation and collection. Presumably rival works were read alongside one another or even canonized together; one did not replace another. Examples include the (eventually) canonical books of Deuteronomy and Chronicles, the (eventually) extracanonical books of *1 Enoch* and *Jubilees*, and Hebrew Scriptures in Greek translation.

1.2.1 Deuteronomy and Chronicles

The books of Deuteronomy and Chronicles exemplify a type of "rewritten Bible" within the Bible itself.[34] Some have claimed that Deuteronomy was intended to replace the earlier Book of the Covenant.[35] Conversely, both supplementary and documentary approaches to Pentateuchal criticism typically view Deuteronomy as intentionally complementary to the earlier legal and narrative collections.[36] Regardless of the writers' original intentions, early Jewish and Samaritan readers decisively included Deuteronomy as the fifth book of Moses prior to the turn of the era.[37] Simply put, the otherwise Tetrateuch turned into the extant Pentateuch.

Similarly, scholars typically argue that the Chronicler intended to supplement Samuel–Kings.[38] Obvious supplementation appears at the beginning and end of the book: 1 Chronicles lists genealogies from the creation of the world down to King Saul (chs. 1–9), and 2 Chronicles narrates the exiles' return from Babylon (36:20-23). Overall, though, Chronicles simply rewrites Samuel–Kings in approximately half as much space,[39] the most notable exceptions being omissions regarding the Northern Kingdom

---

[34] Sidnie White Crawford, *Rewriting Scripture in Second Temple Times* (Grand Rapids, MI: Eerdmans, 2008), 3.
[35] Frank Crüsemann, *The Torah: Theology and Social History of Old Testament Law*, trans. Allan W. Mahnke (Minneapolis, MN: Fortress, 1996), 202; Bernard M. Levinson, *Deuteronomy and the Hermeneutics of Legal Innovation* (Oxford: Oxford University Press, 1997), 152–4.
[36] For a supplementary approach, see Reinhard G. Kratz, *The Composition of the Narrative Books of the Old Testament*, trans. John Bowden (London: T&T Clark, 2005), 114–33; for a documentary approach, see Joel S. Baden, *The Composition of the Pentateuch: Renewing the Documentary Hypothesis*, AYBRL (New Haven, CT: Yale University Press, 2012), 146–8.
[37] Josephus mentions the five books of Moses in *C. Ap.* 1.8. The Samaritan Pentateuch likely emerged in the second or first century BCE; see Reinhard Plummer, "The Samaritans and Their Pentateuch," in *The Pentateuch as Torah: New Models for Understanding Its Promulgation and Acceptance*, ed. Gary N. Knoppers and Bernard M. Levinson (Winona Lake, IN: Eisenbrauns, 2007), 237–69, here 257.
[38] E.g., Mark Zvi Brettler, *The Creation of History in Ancient Israel* (New York: Routledge, 1995), 21–3; Ralph W. Klein, *1 Chronicles: A Commentary*, Hermeneia (Minneapolis, MN: Fortress, 2006), 37; Ralph W. Klein, *2 Chronicles: A Commentary*, Hermeneia (Minneapolis, MN: Fortress, 2012), 5; Gary N. Knoppers, *1 Chronicles*, 2 vols., AB 12–12A (New York: Doubleday, 2003), 1:129–34; Steven L. McKenzie, *1–2 Chronicles*, AOTC (Nashville: Abingdon, 2004), 33–40.
[39] According to BibleWorks 10, the Hebrew word count of 1 Samuel–2 Kings is 50,522, as compared with 24,566 for 1–2 Chronicles.

and King Saul. Emphasizing Chronicles's recapitulations and reinterpretations, some scholars argue that the Chronicler intended to replace Samuel–Kings.[40] In either case, Samuel–Kings and Chronicles were eventually canonized.

While the Chronicler's authorial intentions in the Persian or Hellenistic era are debatable, Jewish reading practices in the Hellenistic and Roman periods are much clearer. Portions of Samuel–Kings and Chronicles were discovered in Qumran Cave 4, and Josephus would have counted both books among his twenty-two authoritative Jewish Scriptures (*C. Ap.* 1.8). Josephus considered Samuel–Kings and Chronicles equally authoritative historical sources[41]; for example, in book 6 of *Antiquities*, he included extensive narratives about King Saul that are found in 1 Samuel (chs. 9–30) but omitted from 1 Chronicles, yet Josephus (*Ant.* 7.335–342) incorporated King David's preparations for building the temple from 1 Chronicles 22, material that has no parallel in Samuel–Kings. Similar to Chronicles' compression of Samuel–Kings, books 1–13 of Josephus's *Antiquities* total a bit more than 200,000 words—nearly two-thirds the length of his sources[42]; in approximately 100,000 additional words, Josephus could then relate the events of Jewish history down to his own day. Josephus's canon consciousness nonetheless implies that his own *Antiquities* were not intended to replace his biblical and historical sources.[43] So even if the Chronicler originally intended to replace Samuel–Kings, the possibility of replacement diminished over time, and replacement would have been practically impossible in Josephus's day.

1.2.2 First Enoch and Jubilees

The book of *Jubilees* depicts Moses retelling much of the content from Genesis and Exodus,[44] and *1 Enoch* fills a gap in the book of Genesis. Enoch, the great-grandfather of Noah, lived 365 years (Gen 5:23) before disappearing from the earth when God took (לקח) or transposed (μετατίθημι) him (Gen 5:24); as a Second-Temple spin-off, *1 Enoch*

---

[40] Bernard M. Levinson, *Deuteronomy and the Hermeneutics of Legal Innovation* (Oxford: Oxford University Press, 1997), 154–5. Other possibilities besides supplement/replace have been offered: for Chronicles and Samuel–Kings as rival works emerging simultaneously based on common sources, see Raymond F. Person, Jr., *The Deuteronomistic History and the Book of Chronicles: Scribal Works in an Oral World*, AIL 6 (Atlanta, GA: Society of Biblical Literature, 2010); for part of 2 Samuel actually depending on 1 Chronicles, see Kristin De Troyer, "The Final Verses of the Ammonite War Story in 2 Sam 22:26–31, and 1 Chron 20:1–3," in *Found in Translation: Essays on Jewish Biblical Translation in Honor of Leonard J. Greenspoon*, ed. James W. Barker, Joel N. Lohr, and Anthony Le Donne (West Lafayette, IN: Purdue University Press, 2018), 95–111.

[41] For Josephus's use of parallel stories in Samuel–Kings and Chronicles, see Michael Avioz, *Josephus' Interpretation of the Books of Samuel*, LSTS 86 (London: Bloomsbury T&T Clark, 2015), 175–83.

[42] Josephus's main sources for books 1–13 of *Antiquities* were Genesis–2 Kings, 1–2 Chronicles, Jonah, Esther, and 1 Maccabees, which total approximately 315,000 Greek words according to BibleWorks 10.

[43] Here I concur with Perrin, "Harmonization of the Gospel and the Question of Textual Authority," 601.

[44] *Jubilees* also alludes to laws from Leviticus and perhaps Numbers; see Jacques T. A. G. M. van Ruiten, *Abraham in the Book of Jubilees: The Rewriting of Genesis 11:26–25:10 in the Book of Jubilees 11:14–23:8*, JSJSup 161 (Leiden: Brill, 2012), 282–93; Perrin ("Harmonization of the Gospel and the Question of Textual Authority," 601–2) also adduced the complementarity of *Jubilees* as analogous to the Diatessaron.

describes the eponymous character's apocalyptic tour through the heavens. *Jubilees* (4.17–25) explicitly refers to the earlier book of Enoch.

The material remains of Qumran Cave 4 reveal that, in the Hasmonean and Roman eras, Genesis, Exodus, Leviticus, Numbers, Deuteronomy, *Jubilees*, *1 Enoch*, and others, were read alongside one another. The question arises whether this reading practice betrays the intentions of those who composed derivative works in the Second Temple period. According to one formulation, *1 Enoch* represents Enochic Judaism, the antithesis of Mosaic Judaism; the book of *Jubilees* self-consciously synthesizes Enochic and Mosaic Judaisms.[45] Others deny that Enochic Judaism was opposed to the Mosaic Torah and Zadokite Temple or that such a thing as Enochic Judaism even existed.[46] Overall, *Jubilees* is less than three-quarters the length of Genesis and Exodus,[47] but *Jubilees* could hardly replace the written Torah. Vis-à-vis the earlier Law, Eva Mroczek perceptively describes *Jubilees* as "neither subservient nor hostile"[48]; she continues,

> To ask the question about whether a new text intends to *replace* or merely *interpret* the Torah of Moses is already to assume a particular way of imagining the shape of sacred literature: the idea that it must be arranged around a single center. In this model, a nonbiblical text can either claim to take over the central, preeminent place or it can place itself in a derivative position in the service of the central text, as interpretation. But the prebiblical imagination was not structured this way. Scriptures took their place alongside other scriptures; proliferation was a value.[49]

I wholeheartedly concur with Mroczek on this point, not just for *Jubilees* in particular but—as her entire project incisively shows—for ancient Jewish "literary imagination" in general. But even if a writer intended one work as a replacement for a similar one, readers continued to collect similar works. Centuries after the destruction of Qumran,

---

[45] Gabriele Boccaccini (*Beyond the Essene Hypothesis: The Parting of the Ways between Qumran and Enochic Judaism* [Grand Rapids, MI: Eerdmans, 1998], 55) cautions not to confuse ownership with authorship; similarly, Andreas Bedenbender ("The Place of Torah in the Early Enoch Literature," in *The Early Enoch Literature*, ed. Gabriele Boccaccini and John J. Collins, JSJSup 121 [Leiden: Brill, 2007], 66–79) argues for a diachronic, increasing appreciation of Moses within the compositional stages of *1 Enoch*.

[46] Paul Heger, "1 Enoch—Complementary or Alternative to Mosaic Torah?" *JSJ* 41 (2010): 29–62; Helge S. Kvanvig, "Enochic Judaism—a Judaism without the Torah and the Temple?" in *Enoch and the Mosaic Torah: The Evidence of Jubilees*, ed. Gabriele Boccaccini and Giovanni Ibba (Grand Rapids, MI: Eerdmans, 2009), 163–77; George W. E. Nickelsburg, "Enochic Wisdom and Its Relationship to the Mosaic Torah," in *The Early Enoch Literature*, ed. Gabriele Boccaccini and John J. Collins, JSJSup 121 (Leiden: Brill, 2007), 82–94.

[47] According to Todd R. Hanneken (*The Subversion of the Apocalypses in the Book of Jubilees*, EJL 34 [Atlanta: Society of Biblical Literature, 2012], 1n. 1), James C. VanderKam's (*The Book of Jubilees*, CSCO 510–511 [Leuven: Peeters, 1989]) English translation of *Jubilees* is 48,337 words; according to BibleWorks 10, the RSV of Genesis and Exodus total 67,548 words.

[48] Eva Mroczek, *The Literary Imagination in Jewish Antiquity* (Oxford: Oxford University Press, 2016), 142.

[49] Mroczek, *Literary Imagination in Jewish Antiquity*, 142.

the Ethiopic Orthodox Church would canonize *Jubilees* and *1 Enoch* as complementary to one another and to the Pentateuch.[50] I modestly propose that writers were well attuned to contemporary reading practices. In other words, writers knew that readers were collecting similar works, so the likelihood of replacing a predecessor's text diminished as time passed and as similar works proliferated.

1.2.3 Greek Translations of Hebrew Scriptures

The *Letter of Aristeas* dates the seventy-two elders' Greek translation of the Torah to the reign of Ptolemy II (285–247 BCE). The rest of the books of the Tanakh were translated in the ensuing centuries before the Common Era. Although the term originally applied only to the translation of the Pentateuch, Septuagint (LXX) later became a catchall for the Greek Jewish Scriptures. As with any translation, the Septuagint diverged from its Hebrew sources, and full-scale revisions emerged very early.[51]

The earliest extant recension of the LXX is the Greek Minor Prophets Scroll from Naḥal Ḥever (8ḤevXIIgr), the physical copy of which dates just before the turn of the era.[52] The translation is very wooden and was designated *kaige* because of its tendency to translate וגם (also) as καίγε (even; at least).[53] *Kaige* clearly realigns the LXX toward the proto-Masoretic text (proto-MT). As I have explained elsewhere,[54] at times *kaige* corrects the LXX by matching the wording and even the word count of the proto-MT (e.g., spelling out יהוה τῶν δυνάμεων three times in Zech 1:3); yet *kaige* retains certain inexplicable translations from the LXX (e.g., σκοπ[ούς]/watchmen for בכורים/first fruits in Nah 3:12). Despite making numerous improvements to its predecessor, the Minor Prophets *kaige* circulated alongside the LXX for centuries, as evidenced by Justin Martyr's conflations of the two versions for his quotations of the Dodekapropheton in the Dialogue with Trypho ca. 165 CE.[55]

Furthermore, the Minor Prophets scroll is but one text within a wider (nonhomogeneous) *kaige*-tradition crossing numerous books, most notably Job and

---

[50] Leslie Baynes, "*Enoch* and *Jubilees* in the Canon of the Ethiopian Orthodox Church," in *A Teacher for All Generations: Essays in Honor of James C. VanderKam*, ed. Eric F. Mason et al., JSJSup 153 (Leiden: Brill, 2012), 2:799–818; R. W. Cowley, "The Biblical Canon of the Ethiopian Orthodox Church Today," *Ostkirchliche Studien* 23 (1974): 318–23.

[51] For up-to-date overviews of the Greek Jewish Scriptures, see Emanuel Tov, "Septuagint," and Peter J. Gentry, "Pre-Hexaplaric Translations, Hexapla, Post-Hexaplaric Translations," in *Textual History of the Bible*, vol. 1A, ed. Armin Lange (Leiden: Brill, 2016), 191–210, 211–34.

[52] Emanuel Tov, with the collaboration of R. A. Kraft and a contribution by P. J. Parsons, *The Greek Minor Prophets Scroll from Naḥal Ḥever (8ḤevXIIgr)*, DJD 8/The Seiyâl Collection 1 (Oxford: Clarendon Press, 1990), 26.

[53] Dominique Barthélemy, "Redécouverte d'un chaînon manquant de l'histoire de la Septante," *RB* 60 (1953): 18–29; Dominique Barthélemy, *Les Devanciers d'Aquila: Première publication intégrale du texte des fragments du Dodécaprophéton*, VTSup 10 (Leiden: Brill, 1963).

[54] James W. Barker, "Ancient Compositional Practices and the Gospels: A Reassessment," *JBL* 135 (2016): 109–21, here 115.

[55] Barthélemy, "Redécouverte d'un chaînon manquant"; James W. Barker, "The Reconstruction of Kaige/Quinta Zechariah 9,9," *ZAW* 126 (2014): 584–8; James W. Barker, "The Equivalence of *Kaige* and *Quinta* in the Dodekapropheton," in *Found in Translation: Essays on Jewish Biblical Translation in Honor of Leonard J. Greenspoon*, ed. James W. Barker, Joel N. Lohr, and Anthony Le Donne (West Lafayette, IN: Purdue University Press, 2018), 127–52.

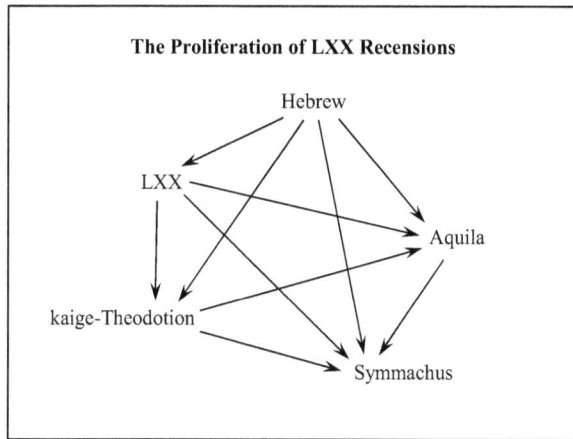

Figure 6.1 The proliferation of LXX recensions

Daniel. Standing squarely within the *kaige*-tradition, Theodotion's thoroughgoing recension is now dated near the turn of the era.[56] Aquila's recension is dated ca. 125 CE, and his translations are even more wooden than Theodotion's. Symmachus would reverse the trend, for his recension—dated ca. 200 CE—renders the Greek more idiomatically. Origen's Hexapla (ca. 250 CE) presented in parallel columns the Hebrew text, the Greek transliteration of the Hebrew, and the Septuagint alongside the recensions of Aquila, Symmachus, and Theodotion; besides the LXX and "the Three" main recensions, Origen occasionally preserved a fifth (*Quinta*) and a sixth (*Sexta*) version.

Within 500 years, then, at least four Greek translations of the entire Tanakh were published; within the same span, at least three other partial translations were also produced. In the century after Origen, the Christians Hesychius (ca. 300) and Lucian (ca. 312) made additional recensions, which Jerome attests. As shown in Figure 6.1 above, the interrelations among the three most prominent revisions ipso facto constitute one-upmanship: Theodotion intended to improve the LXX; Aquila intended to improve Theodotion; and Symmachus intended to improve both Aquila and Theodotion.[57] Yet improvement need not imply replacement.

Theodotion undoubtedly knew the widespread circulation of the LXX, so even if he intended to replace the LXX, replacement would have been difficult and would have taken considerable time—longer than a lifetime. Also, replacement would become

---

[56] Following Gentry ("Pre-Hexaplaric Translations"), the traditional dating of Theodotion ca. 180 CE should now be given up.
[57] For Symmachus's use of both Theodotion and Aquila, see, e.g., Michaël N. van der Meer, "Symmachus's Version of Joshua," in *Found in Translation: Essays on Jewish Biblical Translation in Honor of Leonard J. Greenspoon*, ed. James W. Barker, Joel N. Lohr, and Anthony Le Donne (West Lafayette, IN: Purdue University Press, 2018), 53–93.

an increasingly audacious goal as time passed and as similar works proliferated. Accordingly, it would have been more difficult for Aquila to replace the LXX *and* Theodotion, and it would have been more difficult still for Symmachus to replace all three of his predecessors. Symmachus's revision, instead, reveals an established market for Greek Jewish Scriptures; collectors of these texts would be Symmachus's likeliest audience, and they would not likely discard other versions. Origen's scholarship reveals an additive tendency to collect and compare all of these parallel versions of sacred Scripture. Justin had fewer versions from which to choose, but he too collected and compared what he could find; Tatian likely learned these habits directly from Justin.

1.3 In Lieu of Replacement: Loss, Revision, Absorption, and Destruction

Biblical scholars have questioned whether a subsequent text was intended to supplement or replace its predecessor(s). I do not consider such a dichotomy helpful, and I do not find many—if any—examples where replacement was clearly intended. There are, however, numerous examples of loss, revision and expansion, absorption, and destruction.

1.3.1 Eventual Loss

In addition to exemplifying literary proliferation, the previously adduced case studies demonstrate how relatively little ancient literature survived. Except for the Iliad and Odyssey, the entirety of the Greek Epic Cycle was lost; yet the cycle had taken a century or two to compile, and then it had circulated for another 500 years or more. Although Plutarch's life of Cato survived, eight other attested works perished; at the same time, multiple works survived for more than a century. Josephus's *Jewish War* endured unlike his predecessors' histories and that of his successor Justus; it cannot be determined how long Josephus's rivals maintained currency. The Septuagint persisted as its recensions disappeared, yet none of the recensions disappeared within a century, and some had clearly survived for multiple centuries.

None of these eventually surviving texts replaced its predecessor(s) within the author's lifetime. Furthermore, the survival of the LXX and Josephus's history depended on Christians' preferences, even though Christians could not have been the intended audience of either work. Publication and circulation lay largely beyond an author's control, and so the eventual survival or loss of a text is an accident of history that does not easily equate to authorial intent. Although there is insufficient data for Josephus's rivals, literary citations reveal that every other one of these texts circulated for at least a century. Such durations accord with archaeological evidence that both papyrus and parchment manuscripts of literary texts remained in use for 150 years on average.

1.3.2 Revision and Expansion

The previous examples of loss involved sets of texts that were similar to one another but were identified with different authors. By contrast, numerous works were revised and expanded, such that a text could circulate in different forms and still be identified by the same name. The proto-Masoretic Tanakh offers clear examples of textual expansion and revision. Whether supplementarian or documentarian in theory, the final form of the Pentateuch emerged after centuries of revision and expansion. The same goes for the Prophets: so-called Deutero- and Trito-Isaiah (chs. 40–55 and 56–66, respectively) were tacked on to the earlier book of Isaiah (chs. 1–39); similarly, so-called Deutero- and Trito-Zechariah (chs. 9–11 and 12–14, respectively) were added to the earlier book of Zechariah (chs. 1–8). The Writings reveal the same scribal processes, given the composite nature of books such as Job, Psalms, Proverbs, and Daniel; extracanonical texts, such as *1 Enoch*, are likewise composite works.

Processes of textual revision continued in the Greek Jewish Scriptures. Whereas the Masoretic text of Daniel already combined Aramaic (2:4b–7:28) and Hebrew (1:1–2:4a; 8:1–12:13) sections, the Greek version appended the detective stories of Bel and the Dragon as well as Susanna in addition to the pious Prayer of Azariah and Song of the Three Jews. The Greek version of Esther more intricately adds bookends concerning Mordecai's apocalyptic dream while interspersing the Persian emperor's decrees as well as prayers by Mordecai and Esther. The Greek versions of Daniel and Esther thus revised and extended—but did not replace or lose—the earlier Hebrew/Aramaic versions. The shorter and longer versions of both books circulated for centuries under the same title—down to the present. In these cases, "revision" is a more precise term than the "supplement or replace" dichotomy: earlier versions were supplemented by additional material at a later date; the earlier version was then "replaced," in a sense, but not "lost"; in some cases, the same scribal circles could have produced the earlier editions and the later revisions.

1.3.3 Absorption

Whereas subsequent "revisions" circulated under the same name as the source text, a subsequent work could subsume a source text and be known by a different name; I call this absorption. Absorption also overlaps with textual loss, but the loss was not total in cases of absorption. The books of 1–2 Kings repeatedly cite as separate sources the Annals of the Kings of Judah (e.g., 1 Kgs 14:29; 15:7, 23) and the Annals of the Kings of Israel (e.g., 1 Kgs 15:31; 16:5, 14, 20, 27). In the same narrative loci, 1–2 Chronicles repeat most of the citations for the Judahite kings. Conversely, the Chronicler usually unifies the name of the source as "the book of the kings of Israel and Judah" (e.g., 2 Chr 27:7); also, for particularly favorable kings, the Chronicler ascribes prophetic authorship to the source (e.g., 2 Chr 12:15).[58] There is little doubt that the Deuteronomistic Historian used actual sources that were then current. Yet these sources do not appear to have survived the respective conquests of Israel and Judah by the Assyrians and Babylonians; most likely, then, 1–2 Chronicles is simply citing 1–2 Kings in these instances. In terms of literary proliferation, portions of the earlier annals were absorbed into Samuel–Kings (and, by extension, Chronicles), but this process of absorption was only partial and did not imply intentional replacement.

---

[58] Klein, *2 Chronicles,* 39–42; Knoppers, *1 Chronicles,* 1:123–6; McKenzie, *1–2 Chronicles,* 40–1.

Without exception, the citations expressly refer to the "rest" (τὰ λοιπά/οἱ λοιποί; יתר) of a king's deeds being recorded in the source. Therefore, the Deuteronomistic Historian probably combined and condensed the sources with the expectation of being read alongside them.

Later Christian texts also evince the phenomenon of absorption. Eusebius of Caesarea lists the "Teachings (Διδαχαί) of the Apostles" among the spurious books that he rejects but other ecclesiastics accept (*Hist. eccl.* 3.25.4). Similarly, in his 39th Festal Letter, Athanasius refers to the "Teaching (Διδαχή) of the Apostles" among the noncanonical texts read by the church fathers. Eusebius's and Athanasius's canon lists approve of the *content* in the *Didache*, yet both church fathers deny apostolic *authorship* of the book. Attestation to the *Didache* diminished thereafter, but soon after Philotheos Bryennios rediscovered it in 1873, he detected that the fourth-century *Apostolic Constitutions* (7.1–32) had absorbed the *Didache*[59]; the author/compiler "silently copied out the entire text" and "continually commented on the text of the source, while also paraphrasing and altering it."[60]

I readily acknowledge that the *Apostolic Constitutions*' absorption of the *Didache* in the fourth century may indicate an attempt to remove the *Didache* from independent circulation, but two qualifications are necessary. One is that a much higher degree of canonical consciousness was operative in fourth-century Christianity; Dungan has argued compellingly that the Emperor Constantine's interest in Christianity creates the conditions for the possibility of a New Testament canon, in the sense of an authoritative list of authoritative books.[61] The second qualification is that the *Apostolic Constitutions*' absorption of the *Didache* only occurred after the *Didache* had already circulated for two centuries; that is, absorption did not commence right away, and even thereafter the *Didache* never completely stopped circulating, since the extant Greek manuscript was copied in the eleventh century.[62] Nevertheless, absorption represents a possible means of replacing an earlier text.

1.3.4 Destruction

There is evidence of Romans and Christians confiscating and burning magic books,[63] just as Christian Scriptures were destroyed during the Diocletian persecution (Eusebius *Hist. eccl.* 8.2.1). I do not presume that censorship of this kind pertained to Gospels in

---

[59] Ironically, the *Didache* itself (chs. 1–6) might have absorbed an originally independent "Two Ways" tractate; see Kurt Niederwimmer, *The Didache: A Commentary*, Hermeneia (Minneapolis, MN: Fortress Press, 1998), 30–41.

[60] Ibid., 17.

[61] David L. Dungan, *Constantine's Bible: Politics and the Making of the New Testament* (Minneapolis, MN: Fortress Press, 2007). Dungan does not mean that Constantine personally selected the individual books; while Dungan may overstate Eusebius's decisiveness and influence regarding the twenty-seven books, Dungan masterfully explains how the questions of how many books and which ones took on much greater importance and urgency after Constantine's "conversion."

[62] The *Didache* was also translated into Coptic and Ethiopic; see Niederwimmer, *Didache*, 19–27.

[63] Theodore De Bruyn, *Making Christian Amulets: Artefacts, Scribes, and Contexts*, OECS (Oxford: Oxford University Press, 2017), 68.

2. The Proliferation of Gospels before and after the Diatessaron

Before and after the work of Tatian, the proliferation of (eventually) canonical and extracanonical Gospels evinces imitation on the part of writers as well as collection on the part of readers. This section discusses the Synoptics; infancy Gospels; the Gospel of John, the *Gospel of Thomas* and other Gnostic Gospels; as well as Marcion's Gospel and the Ebionites' Gospel harmony. Key findings are that the Gospel of Mark continued circulating despite its potential loss via absorption; also, on rare occasions readers did use one Gospel exclusively, but exclusivity was the exception rather than the norm.

2.1 The Synoptics

Accepting Markan priority,[64] I question Matthew's and Luke's intentions in writing subsequent Gospels. I argue that Matthew and Luke did not necessarily intend to replace Mark's Gospel. Also, it is inaccurate to speak of Mark as though it barely survived the second century.

2.1.1 Matthew

The Gospel of Matthew reveals that "supplement and replace" are not mutually exclusive. Matthew undeniably supplements Mark by adding Jesus's genealogy and nativity at the beginning, more of his teachings throughout the middle, and his resurrection appearance at the end. The question is whether Matthew intentionally attempted to replace Mark. Highlighting Matthew's enduring respect for Mark, J. Andrew Doole argues that "Matthew's gospel replaces Mark in a spirit of respectful succession."[65] David Sim argues more strongly:

> The evidence of Matthew's treatment of Mark demonstrates that the former did not write to supplement his primary source and did not intend that his text would be read in conjunction with it. On the contrary, the conclusion is inescapable that Matthew specifically composed his Gospel to render Mark redundant. There was

---

[64] On the initial textualization of Mark's Gospel, see Chris Keith, "Early Christian Book Culture and the Emergence of the First Written Gospel," in *Mark, Manuscripts, and Monotheism: Essays in Honor of Larry W. Hurtado*, ed. Chris Keith and Dieter T. Roth, LNTS 528 (London: T&T Clark, 2015), 22–39; for a succinct defense of Markan priority, see Mark Goodacre, *The Case against Q: Studies in Markan Priority and the Synoptic Problem* (Harrisburg: Trinity Press International, 2002), 19–45.

[65] J. Andrew Doole, *What Was Mark for Matthew? An Examination of Matthew's Relationship and Attitude to His Primary Source*, WUNT 2/344 (Tübingen: Mohr Siebeck, 2013).

simply no place for Mark amongst the evangelist's readers once his own narrative saw the light of day.[66]

According to the taxonomy I have sketched, Matthew could be imagined as a revision of Mark,[67] but I do not think revision pertains since the two works circulated under different names. It would be more precise to say that Matthew had the potential to absorb Mark. Matthew absorbs approximately ninety percent of Mark, and one of the closest analogies is the Chronicler's use of Samuel–Kings. Given Matthew's opening genealogy, he might have self-consciously emulated the Chronicler's rewriting of a source text. I would not push the analogy too far, but it stands to reason that Matthew could have expected Mark to continue circulating, just as the Deuteronomistic History had endured alongside Chronicles. Among the Synoptics, the strongest case for literary replacement would indeed be Matthew's potential absorption of Mark. Even so, Matthew's intended replacement of Mark is hardly conclusive.

2.1.2 Luke

Sim acknowledges that Luke's prologue "appears to place his own work very much within the tradition of his sources."[68] Sim argues nonetheless that Luke rendered Mark superfluous and thus intended to replace his predecessor(s).[69] In the third person, Luke's verb that many have undertaken/attempted (ἐπιχειρέω; 1:1) can be interpreted as criticism of earlier works; yet Luke places himself alongside his forebears with the ensuing phrase, "it seemed to me too" (ἔδοξε κἀμοί; 1:3).[70] Loveday Alexander concludes, "Essentially these 'predecessors' are only there to reassure the reader that the subject is worth spending time on."[71] To someone who has never read a Jesus book before, Luke's preface presents his book as an excellent choice. To someone who has already read some Jesus books, Luke's preface makes a case for reading this book as well. I interpret Luke's "me too" as simply claiming equality with his predecessors.[72] He has added another book on the important subject of Jesus. Luke's preface need not entail his sense of superiority,[73] let alone his goal of replacement.[74]

---

[66] David C. Sim, "Matthew's Use of Mark: Did Matthew Intend to Supplement or to Replace His Primary Source?" *NTS* 57 (2011): 176–92, here 183.

[67] I agree with Larsen ("Accidental Publication," 378) that the Gospel of Matthew can be considered "a continuation of the same mushrooming textual tradition of the gospel," but I disagree that "it would be anachronistic to categorize Matthew as creating a separate piece of literature from Mark."

[68] Sim, "Matthew's Use of Mark," 188.

[69] Ibid., 189–90.

[70] Loveday Alexander, *The Preface to Luke's Gospel: Literary Convention and Social Context in Luke 1.1–4 and Acts 1.1*, SNTSMS 78 (Cambridge: Cambridge University Press, 1993), 115.

[71] Ibid., 116.

[72] By way of analogy, Luke calls Paul an apostle (Acts 14:14), even though Peter only counted as apostles those who had seen the risen Jesus *and* been present with him from the days of John the Baptist (Acts 1:21-22). The original apostle Peter had the right to deny Paul's apostleship; the sidling apostle Paul could never deny Peter's apostleship (e.g., 1 Cor 15:5, 9), although Paul could claim to be Peter's equal (e.g., 1 Cor 9:1).

[73] *Pace* Keith, "Competitive Textualization," 328.

[74] *Pace* Sim, "Matthew's Use of Mark," 189–90.

According to the Two-Source Hypothesis, Luke had the potential to absorb Mark and Q, but Luke's intentions look different according to the Farrer Hypothesis, which I endorse.[75] Luke (like Matthew) had the potential to absorb Mark, and Luke (like Matthew) omitted the same blind man, deaf man, and naked man from Mark. Even if Matthew had intended to replace Mark, Luke's indebtedness—and oftentimes preference—for Mark intimates its enduring authority.

It is even less likely that Luke would have intended to replace Matthew. At the beginning, Luke narrates the nativity from Mary's perspective, thereby supplementing Joseph's experience as narrated by Matthew.[76] At the end, Matthew had supplemented Mark's original ending by providing a resurrection appearance rather than a mere report that Jesus had risen. In so doing, Matthew made Jesus promise the disciples that he would be with them "all the days until the culmination of the aeon" (Matt 28:20)—the end. Matthew's ending raises the simple question of Jesus's whereabouts. Luke's ascension (24:50-51) clarifies that Jesus is no longer physically present—*deus in machina*, as it were; after Pentecost, though, Jesus would be with the disciples in Spirit (Acts 2:32-33).

2.1.3 The Myth of Mark's Survival

Sim asserts that the Gospel of "Mark slipped almost into oblivion" in the second century; accordingly, Mark's "demise" was not merely accidental but may actually reveal "the very intention of the later evangelists."[77] Like Sim, Michael Kok observes the numerical fact that Mark's was the least cited of the eventual fourfold gospel.[78] Yet it is fallacious for Kok to leap from "limited use" to "poor reception."[79] In the early second century, Ignatius attests Matthew, Luke, and John, but not Mark.[80] For the next century and a half, however, Mark is clearly attested by Justin Martyr, Tatian, Irenaeus, Tertullian, Clement of Alexandria, and Origen.[81] In other words, the very church

---

[75] That the Two-Source hypothesis demands such a short-lived Q may be more problematic than is usually supposed. E.g., Benedict Viviano (*What Are They Saying about Q?* [New York: Paulist, 2013], 86) says that Q "existed for a brief time (ca 40–50 years)." John S. Kloppenborg Verbin (*Excavating Q: The History and Setting of the Sayings Gospel* [Minneapolis, MN: Fortress, 2000], 367) admits: "In fact we do not know why Q disappeared"; he rightly notes that if Q disappeared via absorption, then it is odd that Mark did not likewise disappear.
[76] See esp. Goodacre, *Case against Q*, 54–9.
[77] Sim, "Matthew's Use of Mark," 190.
[78] Michael J. Kok, *The Gospel on the Margins: The Reception of Mark in the Second Century* (Minneapolis, MN: Fortress, 2015), 8–9.
[79] Pace Kok, *Gospel on the Margins*, 8–9.
[80] E.g., ca. 110 CE Ignatius refers to Jesus as "having been baptized by John in order that he would fulfill all righteousness by him" (*Smyrn.* 1.1), which constitutes Matthean redaction (Matt 3:15b). A juxtaposition of Pontius Pilate and Herod the Tetrarch only occurs in Luke 3:1, and Luke alone involves Herod Antipas in Jesus's condemnation; Ignatius says that Jesus was nailed by both of them (*Smyrn.* 1.2). Among other Johannine material, Ignatius says that the Lord did nothing without the Father (*Magn.* 7.1), which echoes Jesus's statement that "the Son can't do nothing by himself" (John 5:19b); regarding the Spirit, Ignatius says that God "knows from where it comes and where it goes" (*Phld.* 7.1), which agrees nearly verbatim with Jesus's saying in the dialogue with Nicodemus (John 3:8); and Ignatius's letters and the Gospel of John are the earliest Christian texts to call Jesus God, not just the Son of God (e.g., John 20:28; Ign. *Smyrn.* 1.1; *Eph.* inscription).
[81] E.g., Justin Martyr quotes Mark 3:17 in *Dial.* 106.3; Tatian includes Mark 7:31-37 in the Diatessaron (Arabic harmony 21.1–7; Liège harmony §114; Codex Fuldensis §87); Irenaeus includes Mark in

fathers whose fewer citations reveal Mark's "limited use" cannot, without contradiction, concomitantly show Mark's "poor reception." Kok finds it "astounding that (Mark) survived at all,"[82] but the language of survival connotes a threat of extinction, and extant evidence shows no such threat in the case of Mark's Gospel.

2.2 Infancy Gospels

Infancy Gospels provide insight into the intentions behind subsequent Gospels.[83] The *Protevangelium of James* narrates Mary's birth and childhood, offers proofs of her virginal conception and post-partum virginity, and clarifies that she did not give birth to Jesus's supposed siblings. In these regards, the *Protevangelium of James* intentionally supplements the canonical nativity stories. The *Protevanglium* also harmonizes Matthew and Luke to explain how the baby John the Baptist escaped Herod's slaughter of infants.[84] Only Luke makes Jesus and John blood relatives born within six months of each other, and only Matthew has Herod slaughter the Bethlehem children two years and younger shortly after Jesus's birth. When read alongside one another, the question arises as to how John the Baptist survived Herod's slaughter. The *Protevangelium of James* self-consciously resolves the seeming contradiction by constructing the angelic mountain rescue of the baby John the Baptist and his mother Elizabeth (ch. 22).

The intentions of the *Infancy Gospel of Thomas* are similar. The conclusion to its longer recensions overlap with Luke's narrative of the twelve-year-old Jesus in Jerusalem for Passover (2:41-52); the shortest recension does not include the Passover story, but—like the other recensions—this version does narrate events when Jesus was five, six, and eight years old.[85] In all cases, then, the *Infancy Gospel of Thomas* fills in the gaps of Luke's Gospel, which skips from Jesus's presentation when he was forty days old (2:22) to his return to the temple when he was twelve years old (2:42). Vernon Robbins describes this infancy gospel as "grounding" its narrative with Luke's, combining the familiar Lukan story with the new or unfamiliar infancy material.[86] At the same time, the *Infancy Gospel of Thomas* could not replace Luke's entire Gospel. The infancy Gospels stand on their own, but they do not stand alone. The written form of these (eventually) extracanonical Gospels reveals that the earlier Gospels were being read alongside one another and that others could be fit in as well.

---

the fourfold gospel (*Haer.* 3.11.8); Tertullian includes Mark in the fourfold gospel in *Marc.* 4.5.3; Clement of Alexandria quotes Mark 10:17-31 in *Quis div.* 4.4–10; and Origen's commentaries on Matthew and John are replete with comparisons to Mark (and Luke). Papias could be added to the list of second-century witnesses if he is the source behind Eusebius's testimony about the origins of the fourfold gospel (*Hist. eccl.* 3.24.5–8a); see, esp. T. Scott Manor, "Papias, Origen, and Eusebius: The Criticisms and Defense of the Gospel of John," *VC* 67 (2013): 1–21.

[82] Kok, *Gospel on the Margins*, 11.
[83] This paragraph and the next are adapted from James W. Barker, *John's Use of Matthew*, Emerging Scholars (Minneapolis, MN: Fortress, 2015), 31–3.
[84] Ronald F. Hock, *The Infancy Gospels of James and Thomas*, The Scholars Bible 2 (Santa Rosa, CA: Polebridge, 1995), 9.
[85] For a very helpful synopsis, see Tony Burke, *De infantia Iesu evangelium Thomae Graece*, CCSA 17 (Turnhout: Brepols, 2010), 466–539.
[86] Vernon K. Robbins, *Who Do People Say I Am? Rewriting Gospel in Emerging Christianity* (Grand Rapids, MI: Eerdmans, 2013), 185–6.

2.3 John, Thomas, and Gnostic Gospels

Hans Windisch's work on the Gospel of John brought the supplement or replace question to the fore. Windisch assumed—albeit without evidence—that early orthodox churches originally used a single Gospel, a practice that "only over the course of the second century gradually gave way to the two-, three-, or four-gospel system."[87] Windisch argued that the Gospel of John is dependent upon all three Synoptics but that John intended his Gospel as their replacement. Nearly one-fourth of John's Gospel has close parallels in the Synoptic Gospels,[88] even though John reinterprets his predecessors' stories.[89] Such Johannine rewriting exemplifies *oppositio in imitando*, while the majority of John's Gospel contains new stories and teachings. On balance, then, John supplements the Synoptics. John also "interlocks" with the Synoptics, and so it is unlikely that John intended to supplant the earlier Gospels.[90] If he did hope that his Gospel would be the only one, then John would be deleting approximately seventy-five percent of the Synoptic accounts. As I have argued elsewhere,[91] John likely intended his Gospel to be read alongside, not instead of, the Synoptics—as was the outcome in the early church.[92]

More than half of the *Gospel of Thomas* has close, verbal agreements in the Synoptic Gospels, and I am convinced by Mark Goodacre's demonstration of *Thomas*'s dependence on all three Synoptics.[93] *Thomas*'s unparalleled sayings supplement the teachings of Jesus found in the (eventually) canonical Gospels, and *Thomas* is attested along with Matthew, Mark, Luke, and John among the Oxyrhynchus Papyri. Apart from the *Gospel of Thomas*, the Nag Hammadi Codices reveal proliferation of Gnostic Gospels—for example, the *Gospel of Truth* and the *Gospel of Philip*. The material evidence incontrovertibly proves that readers considered multiple Gospels complementary, for *Thomas* and *Philip* stand back-to-back in Codex II. This is not just a later decision on the part of readers, since writers necessarily imitated their sources. Most notably, the Synoptics depict Simon Peter as the one disciple who knew Jesus's identity as the Messiah (Matt 16:16//Mark 8:29b//Luke 9:20cd), Simon Peter is outdone by Thomas in his eponymous Gospel (13); likewise, outside the Nag

---

[87] Hans Windisch, *Johannes und die Synoptiker: Wollte der vierte Evangelist die Älteren Evangelien ergänzen oder ersetzen?* UNT 12 (Leipzig: Hinrichs, 1926), 44.
[88] Synoptic parallels in the Gospel of John include, e.g., John the Baptist's testimony about Jesus (ch. 1), Jesus's disruption of the temple (ch. 2), healing the royal official's son (ch. 4), feeding the 5,000 and walking on water (ch. 6), being anointed at Bethany and entering Jerusalem (ch. 12), as well as Jesus's arrest, trial, crucifixion, burial, and resurrection (chs. 18–20).
[89] E.g., in the Gospel of John, Jesus is never said to have been baptized, and Jesus carries his own cross to Golgotha.
[90] On John's interlocking with the Synoptics, see D. A. Carson, *The Gospel According to John*, Pillar New Testament Commentary (Grand Rapids, MI: Eerdmans, 1991), 51–5; Leon Morris, *Studies in the Fourth Gospel* (Grand Rapids, MI: Eerdmans, 1969), 40–63.
[91] Barker, *John's Use of Matthew*.
[92] For a refutation of "the myth of orthodox Johannophobia," see Charles E. Hill, *The Johannine Corpus in the Early Church* (Oxford: Oxford University Press, 2004).
[93] Mark Goodacre, *Thomas and the Gospels: The Case for Thomas's Familiarity with the Synoptics* (Grand Rapids, MI: Eerdmans, 2012); cf. Thomas's use of Matthew and Luke according to Simon Gathercole, *The Composition of the Gospel of Thomas: Original Language and Influences*, SNTSMS 151 (Cambridge: Cambridge University Press, 2012).

Hammadi Codices, Mary Magdalene and Judas report their respective visions of Jesus in their eponymous Gospels.

The Gnostic Gospels contain only sayings and discourses, which did not replace narrative Gospels. Indeed, patristic testimonies attest the (eventually) canonical and extracanonical Gospels being read alongside one another. According to Hippolytus, the Gnostic Naassenes (cf. Hebrew נחש; a.k.a. Ophites, Greek ὄφις) use the *Gospel of Thomas* (*Haer.* 5.7.20, 21), but they also use the Gospels of Matthew and John.[94] Similarly, according to Irenaeus, Valentinians wrote the *Gospel of Truth* (*Haer.* 3.11.9), but they also read the Gospel of Luke (*Haer.* 3.14.4) and the Gospel of John (*Haer.* 3.11.7).

2.4 Marcion's Gospel and the Ebionites' Harmony: Exclusive Use of a Single Gospel

According to the terminology I have been employing, Marcion's Gospel could be considered a revision of the Gospel of Luke,[95] although Marcion's Gospel was not attributed to Luke.[96] To be sure, Marcion's Gospel comes the closest to revealing authorial intention of replacing one or more preceding Gospels.[97] Rather than "replacement," I prefer the terminology of "exclusive use" of a particular Gospel. Marcion could control what was read in his churches, and his Gospel was the only one. Marcion's exclusivity potentially limited his Gospel's readership, and yet his Gospel circulated for at least two centuries despite ardent opposition.

Tertullian's imagery implies that the fourfold gospel was firmly implanted in the church, yet "Marcion is seen to have uprooted [the Gospel of] Luke, which he chopped to pieces in the process" (*Marc.* 4.2.4).[98] Epiphanius says similarly that Marcion "has only the Gospel according to Luke, which he has chopped off from the beginning through the Savior's conception and his incarnate Parousia" (*Pan.* 42.9.1).[99] Epiphanius

---

[94] E.g., Hippolytus quotes the Parable of the Sower according to Matthew's hundredfold, sixtyfold, thirtyfold order (*Haer.* 5.8.29), and Hippolytus discusses the Naassenes' interpretation of Mary's virginal conception (5.8.45); Hippolytus also records Naassene quotations of John 1:3-4 (*Haer.* 5.8.5), John 2:11 (*Haer.* 5.8.7), John 3:3 (*Haer.* 5.7.40), John 4:10 (*Haer.* 5.9.18), John 6:53 (*Haer.* 5.8.11), John 8:21b (cf. 13:33; *Haer.* 5.8.11), and John 9:1 (*Haer.* 5.9.20).

[95] Marcion's Gospel includes the sine qua non of "minor agreements," namely that soldiers asked Jesus, "Who is the one who hit you?" (τίς ἐστιν ὁ παίσας σε). Accordingly, I find untenable arguments for the priority of Marcion's Gospel (e.g., Matthias Klinghardt, "The Marcionite Gospel and the Synoptic Problem: A New Solution," *NovT* 50 (2008): 1–27; Markus Vinzent, *Marcion and the Dating of the Synoptic Gospels*, StPatrSup 2 (Leuven: Peeters, 2014); Clare K. Rothschild (Review of *Marcion and the Dating of the Synoptic Gospels*, by Markus Vincent [sic: Vinzent], *Review of Biblical Literature* [March 2016]: 1–4, here 4) likens Vinzent's argument to "historical fiction."

[96] Tertullian remarks that Marcion ascribes no author to his Gospel (*Marc.* 4.2.3).

[97] For a recent overview of Marcion's Gospel, see Judith M. Lieu, *Marcion and the Making of a Heretic: God and Scripture in the Second Century* (Cambridge: Cambridge University Press, 2015), 183–233.

[98] Ernest Evans, *Tertullian: Adversus Marcionem*, 2 vols., OECT (Oxford: Clarendon Press, 1972), 2:262: *Lucam videtur Marcion elegisse quem caederet*.

[99] Karl Holl and Jürgen Dummer, *Epiphanius II: Panarion haer. 34–64*, 2nd ed., GCS 31 (Berlin: Akademie Verlag, 1980), 104: ἔχει εὐαγγέλιον μόνον τὸ κατὰ Λουκᾶν, περικεκομμένον ἀπὸ τῆς ἀρχῆς διὰ τὴν τοῦ σωτῆρος σύλληψιν καὶ τὴν ἔνσαρκον αὐτοῦ παρουσίαν (Epiphanius, *Pan.* 42.9.1).

also mentions numerous excisions from the middle and end (*Pan.* 42.9.2), and he lists differences between his version of Luke and Marcion's (*Pan.* 42.11.6, 17).[100]

Although Epiphanius did not have a copy before him when writing the *Panarion*, he does claim direct access to Marcion's Gospel a number of years ago (ἀπὸ ἐτῶν ἱκανῶν; *Pan.* 42.10.2), and he refers to "Marcion's still preserved Scripture" (τῷ Μαρκίωνι ἔτι σῳζομένης γραφῆς; *Pan.* 13.1).[101] Since the *Panarion* dates ca. 375, Epiphanius could find Marcion's Gospel approximately two centuries after it was produced. Epiphanius debated Marcionites academically without destroying copies of their Gospel or replacing it with the fourfold gospel. In the strongest possible terms, though, Epiphanius disapproved of the Marcionites' Gospel, and he would not have allowed it to be read in orthodox worship. The point is that literary "replacement" entails control, and it is important to qualify how limited or widespread one's influence extended: the orthodox could not control what Marcionites read and vice versa.

The Ebionite Gospel harmony provides another example of exclusivity. Epiphanius says that the Ebionites accept the Gospel according to Matthew, which they use exclusively (μόνῳ; *Pan.* 30.3.7). Epiphanius (*Pan.* 30.13.2) later refers to the Ebionites' "so-called Gospel according to Matthew" as incomplete (οὐχ ὅλῳ) and mutilated (ἠκρωτηριασμένῳ). Specifically, Epiphanius means: "For chopping off the genealogies by Matthew, they begin to make the beginning—as I said before—saying, 'It happened—it says—in the days of Herod king of Judea, in the high priesthood of Caiaphas, someone named John came baptizing a baptism of repentance in the Jordan River' and so forth" (*Pan.* 30.14.3). Epiphanius's quotations reveal that the Ebionites' Gospel was actually a harmony of the Synoptics.[102] The problem was not simply that the Ebionite harmony did not include the nativity, which Mark's Gospel also lacked. According to Epiphanius, the Ebionites believed Christ to be the biological son, the male seed (σπέρματος ἀνδρός), of Joseph (*Pan.* 30.2.2). In other words, the orthodox were more bothered by the Ebionites' interpretation than the text itself, and the orthodox were bothered by the Ebionites' exclusive use of one Gospel.

3. The Diatessaron amid the Proliferation of Gospels

As harmonies, the formal similarity between the Ebionite Gospel and the Diatessaron is undeniable. In terms of circulation, though, the Ebionite harmony is more similar to Marcion's Gospel, for each of these Gospels was used exclusively in churches deemed heretical. Early heresiologists did not talk about the Diatessaron in the same

---

[100] For discussion of Epiphanius's two, similar lists of variants, see Dieter T. Roth, *The Text of Marcion's Gospel*, NTTSD 49 (Leiden: Brill, 2015), 272–83.

[101] Epiphanius lists then-current, widespread sects of Marcionites at the beginning of his discussion (*Pan.* 42.1.2).

[102] E.g., the narrative of Jesus's baptism intricately harmonizes Matthew, Mark, and Luke; the Ebionite narrative includes no Johannine material and is incompatible with John the Baptist's statements about Jesus in the Gospel of John (*Pan.* 30.13.7–8).

way—even after Tatian himself had been labeled a heretic. I find no evidence that the Diatessaron was read exclusively or intended to be. Considerations include the relationship between the Old Syriac Gospels and the Diatessaron; Tatian's purported proselytizing and apologetic intentions; the Diatessaron's reception in Syria through the fifth century; the Diatessaron vis-à-vis the fourfold gospel; and Tatian's use of Mark. Assuming Tatian's awareness of ecclesiastic reading practices, he could have reasonably expected his Gospel to be read alongside—not instead of—his sources.

3.1 The Diatessaron and the Old Syriac Gospels

Scholars have long claimed that the Diatessaron predated the Old Syriac Gospels.[103] Key evidence comes from harmonizations in the Sinaitic and Curetonian manuscripts,[104] but it must be qualified that harmonizing and harmonistic variants could have arisen independent of Tatian.[105] A long-standing, and in my view more probable, dissent is that the Diatessaron actually depends on the Old Syriac Gospels, particularly the Sinaitic.[106] Regardless of which came first, posteriority merely indicates proliferation. On a related point, the Syriac terminology for the "Combined" (*Meḥallete*) Diatessaron Gospel and the "Separated" (*Mepharreshe*) Old Syriac Gospels does not indicate priority one way or another. That is, "separate" and "combined" are symbiotic terms; each one presupposes the existence of the other,[107] so Tatian's priority is by no means certain. And even if the Diatessaron were the first Syriac version of the Gospels, Ignatius shows that the Greek Gospels were hardly unknown in second-century Syrian churches. The Old Syriac Gospels do not clearly illuminate Tatian's authorial intent.

3.2 The Diatessaron, Evangelism, and Apologetics

Some have argued that the Diatessaron "was intended . . . for missionary purposes and came into official Church use only because at first it had no rival Gospels."[108] Since the

---

[103] Adolf von Harnack, "Tatian's Diatessaron und Marcion's Commentar zum Evangelium bei Ephraem Syrus," *ZKG* 4 (1881): 471–505; Peter J. Williams, "The Syriac Versions of the New Testament," in *The Text of the New Testament in Contemporary Research: Essays on the Status Quaestionis*, 2nd ed., ed. Bart D. Ehrman and Michael W. Holmes, NTTSD 42 (Leiden: Brill, 2013), 143–66, here 144.

[104] F. Crawford Burkitt, *Evangelion Da-Mepharreshe: The Curetonian Version of the Four Gospels with the Readings of the Sinai Palimpsest and the Early Syriac Patristic Evidence*, 2 vols. (Cambridge: Cambridge University Press, 1904), 2:220–3.

[105] George Howard, "Harmonistic Readings in the Old Syriac Gospels," *HTR* 73 (1980): 473–91; Peter J. Williams, *Early Syriac Translation Technique and the Textual Criticism of the Greek Gospels*, Texts and Studies 3/2 (Piscataway, NJ: Gorgias, 2004), 147; Theodor Zahn, *Tatian's Diatessaron*, FGNK 1 (Erlangen: Andreas Deichert, 1881), 232–4.

[106] E.g., Jeffrey Paul Lyon, *Syriac Gospel Translations: A Comparison of the Language and Translation Method Used in the Old Syriac, the Diatessaron, and the Peshitto*, CSCO 548 (Leuven: Peeters, 1994), 68, 196n. 18, 197n. 20, 203–6; H. S. Pelser, "The Origin of the Ancient Syriac New Testament Texts: A Historical Study," in *De fructu oris sui: Essays in Honour of Adrianus Van Selms*, ed. I. H. Eybers et al., Pretoria Oriental Series 9 (Leiden: Brill, 1971), 152–63, here 162.

[107] Matthew R. Crawford ("Diatessaron, A Misnomer? The Evidence from Ephrem's Commentary," *EC* 4 [2013]: 362–85, here 375) similarly describes "separate" and "combined" as "correlative terms."

[108] Daniel Plooij, *A Primitive Text of the Diatessaron: The Liège Manuscript of a Mediæval Dutch Translation: A Preliminary Study* (Leiden: A. W. Sijthoff, 1923), 73; similarly, Dungan, *History of the Synoptic Problem*, 39.

separate Gospels circulated in Syria—in Greek and perhaps Syriac—prior to Tatian, I am unpersuaded that the Diatessaron was intended for evangelism. Given the spread of Christianity by his time, Tatian had a ready-made audience for Gospel reading; he did not need to make converts to find readers.

Apologetics is another of Tatian's purported intentions.[109] The plurality of the Gospels engendered criticism of their veracity, and Celsus was quick to point out discrepancies in the Gospels. For example, Origen (*Cels.* 2.69) responds by extolling the "harmony" (συμφωνία) of the evangelists' statements that Jesus was buried in a "new tomb" (Matt 27:60//John 19:41), "in which no one had lain/been put" (Luke 23:53//John 19:41). Similarly, regarding the resurrection, Celsus did not understand why some say there were two angels but others say one; Origen responds that there were in fact two angels (Luke 24:4//John 20:12) at the tomb but that only one (Matt 28:5//Mark 16:5) moved the stone, so the multiple accounts are "not contrary" (οὐκ ἦν ἐναντία; *Cels.* 5.56). Baarda assumes that "Tatian tries to disarm such historical criticisms as those found in Celsus's refutation of Christianity."[110]

Tatian undoubtedly smoothed out discrepancies among the Gospels, but no Gospel harmony could overcome Celsus's main objections to Christianity. Celsus denied Jesus's virgin birth (*Cels.* 1.28) and accused Jesus of sorcery (*Cels.* 2.49). Celsus did not presume to know about the beginning and end of the world, but he thought it unreasonable for Christians to believe that God would create the world only to destroy it (*Cels.* 6.52–53). Celsus did not understand why Christians refused to participate in Roman festivals (*Cels.* 8.24), and above all Celsus ridiculed the resurrection of the flesh (*Cels.* 5.18). Tatian could pick a certain number of women and angels at the tomb, and Celsus would simply have yet another rendition of Jesus's resurrection. Tatian's revised Easter story would never change Celsus's opinion that a reanimated corpse was both impossible and undesirable. The apologetic intention of the Diatessaron is thus overstated. In my view, Tatian's second-century Gospel was more likely written for other Christians, a ready-made audience amenable to its contents.

3.3 Ecclesiastical Use of the Diatessaron in Fourth- and Fifth-Century Syria

The most important witnesses to the Diatessaron in fourth- and fifth-century Syria are Aphrahat, Ephrem, Theodoret, and Rabbula. In the fourth century, Aphrahat primarily cited the Diatessaron, but he might have known the separate Gospels as well.[111] A striking example comes from Aphrahat's two different quotations of Matt

---

[109] Baarda, "ΔΙΑΦΩΝΙΑ—ΣΥΜΦΩΝΙΑ."
[110] Ibid., 153.
[111] Tjitze Baarda (*The Gospel Quotations of Aphrahat, the Persian Sage: Aphrahat's Text of the Fourth Gospel*, 2 vols. [Meppel: Krips Repro, 1975]) does not rule out the possibility that Aphrahat knew the separate Gospels. Burkitt (*Evangelion Da-Mepharreshe,* 2:184–5) surmises that Aphrahat could keep the Synoptics separate, for in *Dem.* 14 he first alludes to a long string of Matthean material, then alludes to Mark's distinctive doorkeeper (13:34–5), and finally alludes to the wise king who makes peace from afar, a piece of Lukan *Sondergut* (14:31–2); here Aphrahat does not follow the sequence of the Diatessaron.

18:10.[112] In *Dem.* 2.20 Aphrahat quotes Jesus as saying not to "trample on those whose angels at all times see the Father who is in heaven."[113] In *Dem.* 6.15 Aphrahat quotes, "do not trample on one of these little ones who have faith in me, whose angels in heaven at all times see the face of my father."[114] Both of Aphrahat's quotations are abbreviated, so it is impossible to know the exact reading(s) of his source text(s). It is telling nonetheless that his two quotations of Matt 18:10 differ from one another, and yet each difference in wording matches a known variant in either the Old Syriac Gospels or other harmonies related to the Diatessaron.[115] To be sure, Aphrahat relied predominantly on the Diatessaron for his Gospel quotations, yet there are indications that he also knew the separate Gospels.

Aphrahat's contemporary Ephrem definitely used the separate Gospels in addition to writing a commentary on the Diatessaron.[116] Crawford has painstakingly shown that Ephrem knew the genealogies from Matthew and Luke as well as the prologue from the separate Gospel of John;[117] Ephrem even knew the *Protevangelium of James.*[118] The fourth-century writings of Aphrahat and Ephrem provide the clearest attestation to the text and significance of the Diatessaron, but neither Syrian father seems to have read the Diatessaron exclusively.

In 423 Theodoret became bishop of Cyrrhus in north-central Syria. He reports, "But I even found more than two hundred such books [i.e., the Diatessaron] having been revered in our churches, and having collected them all I put them away and introduced instead the Gospels of the four evangelists" (*Haer. fab.* 1.20).[119] Assuming Theodoret means one Gospel book per church, "over twenty-five per cent of the parishes in his diocese not only used the Diatessaron, but also lacked the separate gospels as late as

112 Lyon, *Syriac Gospel Translations,* 56–8.

113 William Wright, *The Homilies of Aphraates, the Persian Sage, vol. 1* (London: Williams & Norgate, 1869), 43: ܠܐ ܬܒܣܘܢ ܠܗܘܢ ܕܡܠܐܟܝܗܘܢ ܒܟܠܙܒܢ ܚܙܝܢ ܠܐܒܐ ܕܒܫܡܝܐ (*Dem.* 2.20); this quotation occurs in a string of Gospel material that closely follows the sequence of the Diatessaron.

114 Wright, *Homilies of Aphraates,* 127: ܠܐ ܬܒܣܘܢ ܚܕ ܡܢ ܗܠܝܢ ܙܥܘܪ̈ܐ ܕܡܗܝܡܢܝܢ ܒܝ ܕܡܠܐܟ̈ܝܗܘܢ ܒܫܡܝܐ ܒܟܠܙܒܢ ܚܙܝܢ ܦܪ̈ܨܘܦܗ ܕܐܒܝ (*Dem.* 6.15).

115 Aphrahat (*Dem.* 6.15) and the Arabic harmony (24.28) qualify "little ones" with "who believe in me"; this qualification also appears in Matt 18:10 according to the Curetonian MS and the Greek text of Codex Bezae. Conversely, Codex Fuldensis (§97), the Liège harmony (§133), and the Sinaitic MS do not include "who believe in me." Aphrahat's apparent *lectio brevior* "their angels" in *Dem.* 2.20 aligns with the Arabic harmony (24.28) and Matt 18:10 in the Sinaitic MS. Aphrahat's fuller "their angels in heaven" in *Dem.* 6.15 aligns with Ephrem (*Comm. Diat.* 14.24: ܕܡܠܐܟܝܗܘܢ ܒܫܡܝܐ ܚܙܝܢ ܦܪ̈ܨܘܦܗ ܕܐܒܝ), Codex Fuldensis (§97), the Liège harmony (§133), and the Curetonian MS. Aphrahat's quotation in *Dem.* 2.20 and Ephrem's quotation (*Comm. Diat.* 14.24) simply end with "Father," rather than "Father who is in heaven," as in the Arabic harmony (27.29), Codex Fuldensis (§97), the Liège harmony (§133), and the Sinaitic and Curetonian MSS.

116 Burkitt, *Evangelion Da-Mepharreshe,* 2:186–9; Lyon, *Syriac Gospel Translations,* 172.

117 Matthew R. Crawford, "The Fourfold Gospel in the Writings of Ephrem the Syrian," *Hugoye* 18 (2015): 9–51.

118 Ibid., 45; *pace* Francis Watson ("Towards a Redaction-Critical Reading of the Diatessaron Gospel," *EC* 7 [2016]: 95–112, here 106, 109–10), the *Protevangelium* material in Ephrem's *Commentary* does not derive from the Diatessaron.

119 See Migne, *PG* 83:372: εὗρον δὲ κἀγὼ πλείους ἢ διακοσίας βίβλους τοιαύτας ἐν ταῖς παρ' ἡμῖν ἐκκλησίαις τετιμημένας, καὶ πάσας συναγαγὼν ἀπεθέμην, καὶ τὰ τῶν τεττάρων εὐαγγελιστῶν ἀντεισήγαγον εὐαγγέλια.

the early fifth century."[120] Conversely, nearly three-quarters of the churches were using the fourfold gospel, and Theodoret seems to have had no difficulty procuring hundreds of additional copies. Some churches indeed used the Diatessaron as their standard Gospel text, but it is misleading to cite Theodoret as evidence that the Diatessaron was "the standard gospel in Syria as late as the fifth century."[121]

Around the same time and place as Theodoret, Bishop Rabbula of Edessa stipulated "that in every church the separate (*Mepharreshe*) Gospels be present and read."[122] Rabbula's promulgation has been taken as evidence that "when Rabbula became bishop of Edessa the form in which the Gospel was practically known to Syriac-speaking Christians was Tatian's Harmony;"[123] yet this is unsubstantiated. Granted, Rabbula would hardly have issued the canon if the Diatessaron were not being read in some places, but (unlike Theodoret) Rabbula does not tabulate how many churches were doing so. Moreover (like Theodoret) Rabbula's canon presumes that churches could easily procure copies of the fourfold gospel. The writings of Aphrahat, Ephrem, Theodoret, and Rabbula indicate the coexistence of the Diatessaron and the fourfold gospel in fourth- and fifth-century Syrian orthodox churches. Theodoret does mark the turning of the tide, yet his "putting away" (ἀποτίθημι) the Diatessaron need not connote destruction.[124]

3.4 Orthodox Use of the Fourfold Gospel: Diatessaron as Loophole

Irenaeus associates Tatian with those who renounce marriage, and Irenaeus says that Tatian was the first to deny Adam's salvation (*Haer*. 1.28.1; 3.23.8). Eusebius quotes Irenaeus on these points and adds that Tatian constructed a combination of the four Gospels and called it the Diatessaron, "which even by some is still until now transmitted" (ὃ καὶ παρά τισιν εἰς ἔτι νῦν φέρεται; *Hist. eccl.* 4.29.6). By "some," Eusebius means orthodox believers rather than heretics[125]; the Diatessaron is thus analogous to the *Didache*, which Eusebius approves for private study but not for public worship, and elsewhere Eusebius extols Tatian's refutation of Greek philosophy (*Hist. eccl.* 4.29.7).

Irenaeus nowhere mentions the Diatessaron, and he might not have known about it. It is thus debatable whether Irenaeus would have disallowed Tatian's harmony. To be sure, Irenaeus gives the earliest vigorous defense of the fourfold gospel, namely the Gospels of Matthew, John, Luke, and Mark—no more, no less, and no others (*Haer*. 3.11.8). Hence, the problem with Marcion is that he takes away parts of Luke and all of Matthew, Mark, and John (*Haer*. 3.11.7), and the problem with Valentinus is that he adds the *Gospel of Truth* (*Haer*. 3.11.9). By contrast, Tatian *does* use all four of Irenaeus's

---

[120] William L. Petersen, *Tatian's Diatessaron: Its Creation, Dissemination, Significance, and History in Scholarship*, VCSup 25 (Leiden: Brill, 1994), 42.
[121] E.g, Petersen, *Tatian's Diatessaron*, 1n. 5.
[122] Ibid., 42: ܟܬܒܐ ܕܡܦܪܫܐ ܢܗܘܘܢ ܐܝܬ ܒܟܠ ܥܕܬܐ.
[123] Burkitt, *Evangelion Da-Mepharreshe*, 2:164, cited approvingly by Petersen, *Tatian's Diatessaron*, 43.
[124] *Pace* Michael F. Bird, *The Gospel of the Lord: How the Early Church Wrote the Story of Jesus* (Grand Rapids, MI: Eerdmans, 2014), 306.
[125] Dungan, *Constantine's Bible*, 62.

Gospels. With respect to Irenaeus's insistence on the fourfold gospel, the Diatessaron is a loophole, since it incorporates virtually every word of Irenaeus's Gospels.

None of the orthodox opposed the Diatessaron until the fifth century, and then the opposition may be a case of mistaken identity. Theodoret calls Tatian an Encratite who "constructed the Gospel called Diatessaron, cutting off the genealogies and whatever other things indicate the Lord having been begotten according to the flesh from the seed of David" (*Haer. fab.* 1.20). Tatian probably did omit the genealogies,[126] but his motivation might simply have been their inherent contradictions, and it is unclear whether either genealogy was being read liturgically at this time.[127] Tatian undoubtedly harmonized Matthew's and Luke's nativity stories, so Theodoret's claim that Tatian denied the incarnation is perplexing—especially since the Diatessaron began with John's prologue. I consider it likely that Theodoret confused Tatian's harmony with the Ebionite harmony, for Epiphanius not only says that the Ebionites call their Gospel "according to the Hebrews" (*Pan.* 30.3.7) but also that some people call the Diatessaron the Gospel "according to the Hebrews" (*Pan.* 46.1.9). In any case, Theodoret does provide the earliest attested suspicion of the Diatessaron. Until then, it had been read in Syria alongside the fourfold gospel for centuries.[128]

3.5 Tatian's Use of Mark

I have cast doubt on Matthew's and Luke's intentions to replace Mark. Yet if these subsequent evangelists had held such aspirations, then they had proven profoundly unsuccessful as of the mid-second century. Tatian's onetime teacher Justin Martyr occasionally harmonized the Gospels,[129] and Justin clearly attests the Gospel of Mark; for example, Justin (*Dial.* 106.3) says that Jesus changed the names of the two Sons of Zebedee to "Boanerges, which is 'sons of thunder'" (Mark 3:17), and Justin says that King Herod put John the Baptist in prison (*Dial.* 49.4); Mark (6:14) says "King Herod," whereas the Matthean parallel (14:1) correctly labels Herod a "tetrarch." Compared with Justin, Tatian shows even more careful attention to include Markan material.

According to Mark 1:15, when Jesus began preaching, he declared that "the time is fulfilled," a declaration Tatian included (Ephrem, *Comm. Diat.* 5.13; Arabic harmony

---

[126] E.g., a recension of the Arabic harmony adds the genealogies as an appendix (Petersen, *Tatian's Diatessaron*, 136).

[127] Matthew's genealogy was read on the Sunday before Christmas according to the ninth- to eleventh-century Byzantine lectionary (Hughes Oliphant Old, *The Reading and Preaching of the Scriptures in the Worship of the Christian Church*, vol. 3: *The Medieval Church* [Grand Rapids: Eerdmans, 1999], 69), whereas Luke's genealogy was read on the Sunday of Epiphany according to the Gallican lectionary (p. 89).

[128] I acknowledge that in later centuries Codex Fuldensis became a single New Testament MS that replaced the fourfold gospel with the Vulgatized Diatessaron, yet Victor of Capua necessarily had the separate Gospels according to the Vulgate; also, Matthew Crawford helpfully pointed out to me via personal correspondence that Victor's preface and inclusion of the Eusebian Canon Tables explicitly presupposes that readers would compare the harmonized text with the fourfold gospel.

[129] *Pace* Nicholas Perrin's chapter (Chapter 5) in this volume as well as William L. Petersen, "Textual Evidence of Tatian's Dependence upon Justin's ΑΠΟΜΝΗΜΟΝΕΥΜΑΤΑ," *NTS* 36 (1990): 512–34, I find no evidence that Justin constructed a complete harmony of the Synoptics or the fourfold gospel.

5.43; Codex Fuldensis §18; Liège harmony §28).[130] Mark 4:26-29 relates a parable about seed growing secretly, which is repeated in the Arabic harmony (16.49-52) and Codex Fuldensis (§77) as well as the Stuttgart and Zurich harmonies (§87).[131]

In Mark 7:31-37, Jesus encounters a deaf man with a speech impediment in the Decapolis. To heal the man, Jesus puts his fingers in the man's ears and puts his spit on the man's tongue (v. 33). Mark also transliterates and translates Jesus's Aramaic command, "Ephphatha, that is, be opened" (v. 34). Both eastern and western witnesses to the Diatessaron sandwich this episode between the Canaanite woman and the Samaritan woman (Arabic harmony 21.1-7; Liège harmony §114; Codex Fuldensis §87). On the supposition of Markan priority, Matthew and Luke intentionally omitted this healing, yet Tatian reinserted it into his Gospel narrative.

It is more difficult to determine whether Tatian included the other relatively long piece of Markan *Sondergut*. In Mark 8:22-26, Jesus encounters a blind man in Bethsaida. Once again Jesus uses his spit to heal (v. 23a). At first the blind man sees unclearly, since people look like walking trees (v. 24), but he sees clearly after Jesus touches his eyes again (v. 25). This story appears in the Arabic harmony (23.26-30) between the Feeding of the 4,000 and Peter's confession at Caesarea Philippi, and Ephrem comments on the blind man at the same location (*Comm. Diat.* 13.13), but the episode does not appear in Codex Fuldensis (§§90-91) or the Liège harmony (§§122-123).

Diatessaron witnesses unanimously include Mark's unintentional streaker (14:51-52). When Jesus was arrested, one of his young followers was grabbed by the cloth he was wearing, and the man ran away naked. Tatian did not omit this brief episode (Arabic harmony 48.45-47; Codex Fuldensis §93; Liège harmony §225). Similarly, Salome is named only in Mark's Gospel, where she is present at the crucifixion on Friday (15:40) and at the tomb on Sunday (16:1). Tatian definitely included her somewhere in the Diatessaron, although extant witnesses are somewhat inconsistent: the Dura Europos fragment (line 1) places her at the crucifixion; so does the Arabic harmony (52.23), although she does not come to the tomb on Sunday; according to Codex Fuldensis (§§171, 174) and the Liège harmony (§§231, 233), Salome appears at the cross on Friday and at the tomb on Sunday. Finally, Tatian incorporated the Longer Ending of Mark into the Diatessaron: for example, according to Mark 16:17-18, believers will have the power to heal the sick, exorcise demons, and speak in tongues, as well as withstand serpents and poison; these promises are recorded in the Arabic harmony (55.9-10), Codex Fuldensis (§182), and the Liège harmony (§245).

These examples suffice to show that Tatian knew precisely how little of Mark's Gospel was unparalleled in Matthew and Luke. Although Matthew and Luke had the potential to absorb Mark, they had not done so after 50-100 years. Time and again,

---

[130] Ephrem's quotation awkwardly has a singular subject and a plural verb, "The time, they are themselves fulfilled" (ܙܒܢܐ ܠܗܘܢ ܫܠܡܘ; *Comm. Diat.* 5.13), most likely reflecting the plural "the times are fulfilled" (οἱ καιροί πεπλήρωνται) as attested in Codex Bezae and Old Latin MSS.

[131] This Markan parable is omitted from Liège harmony §§89-90, but editing is readily apparent in this section: a note about Luke's version of the parable of the sower was inserted in the bottom margin of f. 28r.

Tatian grafted Markan material into the Diatessaron. Tatian's use of Mark not only debunks the myth of Mark's second-century demise but also offers a glimpse of Tatian's intentions and expectations. Tatian intended to write a new Gospel, but doing so was not presumptuous in the second century. It would have been presumptuous, though, to think that his harmony could supplant his four primary source texts. Tatian's Diatessaron ipso facto reveals that the four separate Gospels were being read alongside one another. On the supposition that ancient authors were aware of their contemporary reading practices, Tatian could have considered it a reasonable success if his Gospel were read alongside the earlier ones. Tatian would achieve success in exactly this way.

4. Conclusion

Recent studies have effectively critiqued Romantic notions of authorship prevalent in Gospels research[132]; although the evangelists are often assumed to express the views of their relatively insular, individual Christian communities, a more plausible model situates Gospel writers among "fellow elite cultural producers."[133] Reciprocally, I apply the same insights to readers, thereby reformulating the collection of the Gospels. Regarding the intentions of subsequent evangelists, Windisch's "supplement or replace" assumed that each Christian community originally used a single Gospel[134]; by extension, the collection of multiple Gospels is assumed to be a gradual process.[135] I have shown, though, that exclusive use of a single Gospel was the exception rather than the norm, and the notion of such gradual Gospel collection is unfounded; for example, there is simply no basis for assuming that a decade elapsed before a subsequent Gospel appeared.[136]

---

[132] E.g., Last, "Social Relationships of Gospel Writers"; Stowers, "Concept of Community"; Walsh, "Q and the 'Big Bang.'"

[133] Walsh, "Q and the 'Big Bang,'" 498.

[134] Windisch, *Johannes und die Synoptiker*, 44; there Windisch supposes that the big churches in big cities like Ephesus or Antioch might have had more than one Gospel.

[135] E.g., Baarda ("ΔΙΑΦΩΝΙΑ—ΣΥΜΦΩΝΙΑ") likewise assumes a gradual process of collecting Gospels. By way of analogy, the Brothers Grimm—living at the peak of Romanticism—are nowadays imagined traveling the German countryside to collect folk tales from peasants, but the Grimms actually "collected their tales and variants primarily from educated friends and colleagues or from books" (Jack Zipes, "Introduction: Rediscovering the Original Tales of the Brothers Grimm," in *The Original Folk and Fairy Tales of the Brothers Grimm: The Complete First Edition*, ed. Jacob Grimm and Wilhelm Grimm, trans. Jack Zipes, 2 vols. [Princeton, NJ: Princeton University Press, 2014], 1:xix–xliv, here xxi).

[136] E.g., Bart D. Ehrman (*The New Testament: A Historical Introduction to the Early Christian Writings*, 6th ed. [New York: Oxford University Press, 2016]) dates Mark ca. 70 (p. 118), Matthew and Luke ca. 80–85 (pp. 147, 167), and John ca. 90–95 (p. 190). Although Paul N. Anderson (*The Fourth Gospel and the Quest for Jesus: Modern Foundations Reconsidered*, T&T Clark Biblical Studies [New York: T&T Clark, 2006]) does well to envision interconnected writing communities, he still dates Mark to 70, Luke to 85, Matthew to 90, and John to 100. Cf. Ellis's (*Making of the New Testament Documents*, 403) sense that Matthew could write between one and five years of Mark (albeit before the destruction of the temple) as well as Donald A. Hagner's (*Matthew*, 2 vols., WBC 33 [Dallas, TX: Word, 1993–5], lxxiv) reference to the "false assumption" of a decade-long gap between Gospels.

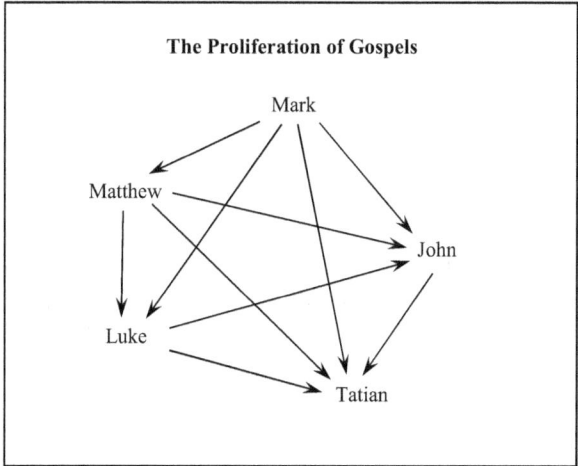

Figure 6.2 The proliferation of Gospels

I would date each of the canonical Gospels after the destruction of the temple but before the epistles of Ignatius, thus between 70 and 110 CE;[137] I do not think Justin Martyr knew Tatian's harmony, and so I would date the Diatessaron sometime after 165. Like encomia for Cato, the four canonical Gospels could have been written within a year and a half, and then Tatian could have resumed Gospel writing after nearly a century. Conversely, like histories of the Jewish War, multiple Gospels could have been written within one decade, with others emerging in the next decade or later. Either scenario is equally likely. I consider 70–110 CE a narrow range, not a broad one, and any further precision is mostly limited to relative dating based on one's source-critical commitments.

Gospel collection was constitutive to Gospel composition, and, as shown in Figure 6.2 above, source-critically I posit a simple, snowballing trajectory whereby each subsequent author copied, reworked, and retained each predecessor: Matthew used Mark; Luke used Matthew and Mark; John used Matthew, Mark, and Luke; and Tatian used Matthew, Mark, Luke, and John.[138] Based on papyrological evidence, it would have been highly unusual for any evangelist to discard any of his sources, especially if the manuscript were less than fifty years old; moreover, it would not have been unusual for an evangelist to have multiple copies of his source text(s).[139] Ignatius already has multiple Gospels in the early second century, and the fourfold gospel is attested by Justin, Tatian, Irenaeus, Clement of Alexandria, and Origen. By collecting and

---

[137] My former student Nicholas J. McGrory and I made this argument in "When Were the Gospels Written?" (paper presented at the annual meeting of the Midwest Region of the SBL, Bourbonnais, IL, February 7, 2016).

[138] My current book project fully develops this argument.

[139] E.g., the villa at Herculaneum contained multiple copies of Epicurus's *On Nature* as well as multiple copies (perhaps successive drafts) of several works by the Epicurean Philodemus of Gadara (Houston, *Inside Roman Libraries,* 91, 95–6).

comparing the Gospels, these church fathers mirror their contemporary connoisseurs' study of history, philosophy, astronomy, drama, or poetry.

Given that so few people could compose texts in the first place,[140] the most reasonable assumption is that writers were well attuned to their contemporary reading practices. Chris Keith's term "competitive textualization" is insightful, but one-upmanship need not entail hubris or anxiety. The Little Iliad was accompanied by Aethiopis and the Sack of Troy within the Epic Cycle. Cicero considered his praise of Cato superior to Aulus Hirtius's book of blame, yet Cicero himself arranged the publication of Hirtius's book. Josephus considered his history of the Jewish war superior to his predecessors and his successor Justus, yet Josephus wrote with the expectation that his book would be compared to these others. The LXX recensionists evince the same pattern, and to repeat Mroczek, "proliferation was a value."[141] Although many of these texts were eventually lost, they had circulated for centuries, during which similar works were read alongside one another; thus a text's eventual loss cannot be retrojected as a rival author's intent.

For the past century, biblical scholars have assumed evangelists' intentions to replace earlier Gospels, but literary replacement has remained an imprecise notion. One type of replacement could be absorption, whereby a subsequent text renders a predecessor superfluous. Mark's would have been the most likely Gospel to fall out of circulation via absorption, and Tatian knew better than anyone just how little unparalleled material Mark contained; yet Tatian extracted Markan *Sondergut* with surgical precision. Out of the fourfold gospel, Tatian left virtually nothing unparalleled in the Diatessaron, but it would have been unrealistic for Tatian to expect any one—let alone all four—of his sources to pass out of circulation any time soon. In other words, if Tatian intended to replace the fourfold gospel, then he was either ignorant of contemporary reading practices or defiant of them.

Another type of replacement could be exclusive use of a single Gospel, which vexed the orthodox. Irenaeus (*Haer.* 3.11.7), Tertullian (*Marc.* 4.2.4), and Epiphanius (*Pan.* 42.9.1) upbraid Marcion's excisions to, and exclusive use of, the Gospel of Luke. Likewise, Epiphanius (*Pan.* 30.3.7) and Eusebius (*Hist. eccl.* 3.27) chastise the Ebionites' exclusive use of the so-called Gospel of Matthew, a.k.a. the *Gospel according to the Hebrews*, which was a harmony of the Synoptics. The essential component of "exclusive use" is control: authors generally had little control over the transmission and reception of their works, but "heretics" could stipulate the reading of one Gospel, thereby suppressing others; of course, the "heretics" could not control which Gospels the orthodox read, and vice versa.

Among orthodox critiques of Tatian, exclusive use of the Diatessaron is attested nowhere. Regarding the maxim "absence of evidence is not evidence of absence," I consider lack of evidence to be a *measurable* absence in this case. Irenaeus and Tertullian are silent regarding the Diatessaron, and Epiphanius (*Pan.* 46.1.9) confuses

---

[140] A typical estimate of early Christian literacy is no more than ten percent; e.g., Gamble, *Books and Readers in the Early Church*, 5.

[141] Mroczek, *Literary Imagination in Jewish Antiquity*, 142.

it with the *Gospel according to the Hebrews*/Ebionite harmony—a confusion that probably led to Theodoret's and Rabbula's suppression of the Diatessaron. Eusebius does not list the Diatessaron in his canonical list (*Hist. eccl.* 3.25), but he does intimate that some contemporary, orthodox believers read the Diatessaron (*Hist. eccl.* 4.29.6). In fourth-century Syria, Aphrahat likely read the fourfold gospel in addition to the Diatessaron, and Ephrem definitely did so. I do not find this eventual outcome surprising, for I propose that Tatian adhered to the literary conventions of his day: the Diatessaron entered an established market for Gospels, and Tatian's Gospel mostly appealed to audiences well accustomed to collecting, reading, and studying the Gospels. For approximately two-hundred fifty years, then, the attested reception of the Diatessaron was the realization of Tatian's realistic intentions.

Part Three

The Witnesses to Tatian's Gospel

7

The Wrong Harmony

Against the Diatessaronic Character of the Dura Parchment

Ian N. Mills

Abstract

Dura Parchment 24 has assumed an undue importance in Diatessaronic scholarship. Recent studies by Matthew Crawford and Francis Watson, who both rely on Jan Joosten's argument for the Diatessaronic character of the text, treat the Dura fragment as if it were a piece of Tatian's Gospel itself. Joosten's argument, however, rests on a problematic analysis of Diatessaronic sources. Granting first the Petersen method championed by Joosten, no Tatianic reading can be identified in the Dura fragment. Then, apart from this now troubled methodology, a fresh reassessment of the pertinent witnesses weighs decidedly against identifying the Dura fragment as a piece of Tatian's Gospel. In so far as the relevant passage of the Diatessaron can be reconstructed, it contradicts the Dura fragment. Our limited evidence, therefore, indicates that Dura Parchment 24 is not a fragment of Tatian's lost work but another gospel harmony altogether.

1. Introduction

Dura Parchment 24 has assumed undue importance in scholarship on Tatian's gospel.[1] The Dura fragment, according to Matthew Crawford, is "of utmost significance in that it likely represents the purest form of Tatian's text yet available to us."[2] Similarly,

---

[1] The Dura fragment was published as Dura Parchment 24 by Carl Kraeling, but is cataloged as Dura Parchment 10 in the Beinecke Rare Book and Manuscript Library at Yale University and named Uncial 0212 in the Gregory-Aland system. It will be referred to as merely the "Dura fragment" henceforth. Carl H. Kraeling, *A Greek Fragment of Tatian's Diatessaron from Dura with Facsimile, Transcription and Introduction*, SD 3 (London: Christophers, 1935). For images of the fragment, see the two plates included in the present volume.

[2] Matthew R. Crawford, "The Diatessaron, Canonical or Non-Canonical? Rereading the Dura Fragment," *NTS* 62 (2016): 260.

Francis Watson calls it "the single extant piece of relatively intact Tatianic text."[3] These exalted judgments of the Dura fragment's value are predicated on a 2003 article by Jan Joosten.[4] Considered on its own methodological terms, Joosten's argument presents a dubious analysis of Diatessaronic sources. More importantly, a reassessment of the pertinent witnesses, apart from the problematic methodology employed by Joosten, reveals that the evidence weighs decidedly against identifying the Dura fragment as a witness to Tatian's Diatessaron.[5]

2. The Dura Fragment and the Diatessaron

The Dura parchment was first identified as a fragment of Tatian's gospel by Carl Kraeling in 1935 and his judgment went unchallenged for more than fifty years.[6] Kraeling cited the Diatessaron's importance in Syria and "the general coincidence" between the Dura fragment and the Arabic, Latin, and Dutch harmonies as evidence for identifying the former with Tatian's gospel.[7] Although he provides a two-page synopsis, Kraeling nowhere indicates precisely which textual phenomena ought to persuade the reader that the Dura fragment "without doubt" preserves Tatian's text "with a relatively high degree of fidelity."[8] Notably, the evidence from pseudo-Ephrem's *Commentary*, known at this time only in Armenian, is dismissed in a footnote.[9]

Subsequent twentieth-century scholarship would rely on Kraeling's judgment and concern itself with what could be learned about Tatian's composition from this fragment.[10] For instance, Daniel Plooij, the first to note the Dura fragment's deviation from the sequence of pseudo-Ephrem's *Commentary*, affirmed that "there is no reasonable doubt that the fragment is really Tatian."[11] Amidst these debates, however, no one sought to further demonstrate the fragment's Tatianic character.

---

[3] Francis Watson, "Harmony or Gospel? On the Genre of the (So-called) Diatessaron" (paper presented at the annual meeting of the SNTS Christian Apocryphal Literature Seminar, Perth, Australia, 2013), 2.

[4] Jan Joosten, "The Dura Parchment and the Diatessaron," *VC* 57 (2003): 159–75.

[5] The title "Diatessaron" is probably a misnomer but will nevertheless, for the sake of clarity, be adopted for the remainder of this chapter. See Matthew Crawford's excellent treatment of the subject in "Diatessaron, a Misnomer? The Evidence from Ephrem's Commentary," *EC* 4 (2013): 362–85.

[6] Kraeling, *Greek Fragment of Tatian's Diatessaron*.

[7] Ibid., 11–14.

[8] Ibid., 37.

[9] Ibid., 14 n. 1. See Christian Lange's compelling argument for the composite character of the *Commentary on the Gospel* traditionally attributed to Ephrem in Christian Lange, *The Portrayal of Christ in the Syriac Commentary on the Diatessaron*, CSCO 616, Subsidia 118 (Leuven: Peeters, 2005).

[10] Petersen provides a valuable summary of this research. William L. Petersen, *Tatian's Diatessaron: Its Creation, Dissemination, Significance, and History in Scholarship*, VCSup 25 (Leiden: Brill, 1994), 196–203, 224–5.

[11] D. Plooij, "A Fragment of Tatian's Diatessaron in Greek," *ExpTim* 46 (1935): 472. Here is one of the curiosities that fill Petersen's history of Diatessaronic scholarship. Petersen (*Tatian's Diatessaron*, 199–200) reports that Plooij "cautioned it was less than certain that the Fragment was from Tatian's Diatessaron." This is a peculiar summary in light of Plooij's emphatic affirmation of Kraeling's judgment.

3. Parker, Taylor, and Goodacre

At the close of the millennium, David Parker, David Taylor, and Mark Goodacre published a comprehensive study of the Dura fragment.[12] Their article reassesses the fragment's text, date, and relationship to the Dura-Europos house church. Most controversially, Parker, Taylor, and Goodacre challenge the identification of the Dura fragment with Tatian's Diatessaron.

Methodologically, they adopt William Petersen's first and third canons for identifying Diatessaronic readings:

1. To be considered Diatessaronic, a reading should be found in *both* Eastern *and* Western branches of the Diatessaronic tradition.
3. The genre of the sources should be the same. All should represent harmonized "Lives of Jesus," or traditions (e.g., the Vetus Latina, the Peshitta) which are acknowledged to have come under the influence of the harmonized tradition.[13]

The readings of the Arabic, Persian, Fuldensis, Liège, Stuttgart, and Tuscan harmonies are thus adduced for every unit of variation and the agreement of any eastern and western witness is taken to represent Tatian's text.

Petersen's second canon, however, proved more problematic for their approach.

2. The reading should not be found in any non-Diatessaronic texts, from which the Diatessaronic witnesses might have acquired it;

Parker, Taylor, and Goodacre reject this canon in a perplexing bit of argumentation:

> It is much harder to establish a continuous text of Tatian than it is to establish his reading in particular instances (not that the latter is easy). In other words, it is easier to demonstrate instances when Tatian deviated from common Gospel readings of the second century than to prove that in certain passages he was following them. For this reason the second of Petersen's criteria seems unnecessarily harsh, and whilst we have preserved it as a useful caveat we have not always felt it possible to adhere to it.[14]

Thus Parker, Taylor, and Goodacre rightly note that it is difficult (under the assumptions of the Petersen method) to identify Diatessaronic readings that agree with a "standard text" of the gospels.[15] This is due to the ubiquity of "vulgatization" in

---

[12] D. C. Parker, D. G. K. Taylor, and M. S. Goodacre, "The Dura-Europos Gospel Harmony," in *Studies in the Early Text of the Gospels and Acts*, ed. D. G. K. Taylor (Birmingham: University of Birmingham Press, 1999), 192–228.
[13] Petersen, *Tatian's Diatessaron*, 373. Parker, Taylor, and Goodacre ("The Dura-Europos Gospel Harmony," 217) likewise modify this third canon by restricting themselves to harmonized "Lives of Jesus."
[14] Parker, Taylor, and Goodacre, "The Dura-Europos Gospel Harmony," 217.
[15] Petersen uses this term repeatedly to clarify the second canon of his methodology. He seems to mean the Nestle-Aland critical text, Majority text, Latin Vulgate, and Syriac Peshitta. It should be

Diatessaronic witnesses—that is, harmonization toward the scribe's familiar text of the gospels. For this reason, Petersen argued, scholars can only be certain of a reading's Tatianic origin if that reading is not attested by corrupting influences.[16] Parker, Taylor, and Goodacre's verdict that, "For this reason [Petersen's second criterion] seems unnecessarily harsh" is a *non sequitur*. The authors recapitulate Petersen's own justification for the second canon and then reject it without counterargument.[17]

Proceeding on these principles, Parker, Taylor, and Goodacre reconstruct the Diatessaron at every point of variation and compare it with the Dura fragment.[18] The result is three agreements between Dura and their reconstruction of Tatian (one certain and two probable), five disagreements, and two units of variation where Tatian's text remains uncertain.[19] On this basis, Parker, Taylor, and Goodacre judge the Dura fragment to be non-Diatessaronic.

4. Joosten's Rebuttal

Four years later, Jan Joosten published a much-praised rebuttal.[20] Joosten rightly criticizes Parker, Taylor, and Goodacre's deviation from the Petersen method and identifies a feature in the Dura fragment that he believes will satisfy the criteria of the Petersen method, thus demonstrating the fragment's Diatessaronic character.[21] The description of Joseph of Arimathea evinces a harmonistic sequence that, according to Joosten, is attested in both eastern and western gospel harmonies and not derived from any non-Diatessaronic source. Joosten presents the evidence in the manner outlined in Table 7.1.

---

noted that the Old Latin and Syriac traditions as well as Codex Bezae (D05) are pointedly excluded as possible sources of corruption despite the fact that these latter textual traditions are precisely those which would have rivaled Tatian's text in Rome and the Far East.

[16] Petersen, *Tatian's Diatessaron*, 374–5.

[17] Joosten provides two helpful examples of this error. Joosten, "The Dura Parchment and the Diatessaron," 164–5.

[18] Criteria one and three are not applied with perfect consistency by Parker, Taylor, and Goodacre. Consider "item 4" ("The Dura-Europos Gospel Harmony," 220) where they cite Fuldensis, Pepys, and Zacharius (all Western witnesses) to support the inclusion of John 19:31-37 after Luke 23:49.

[19] Parker, Taylor, and Goodacre, "The Dura-Europos Gospel Harmony," 224–5.

[20] Joosten, "The Dura Parchment and the Diatessaron." For its praise, see Watson, "Harmony or Gospel? On the Genre of the (so-called) Diatessaron," 20; Charles E. Hill, *Who Chose the Gospels? Probing the Great Gospel Conspiracy* (Oxford: Oxford University Press, 2010), 274n. 15; Michael Peppard, *The World's Oldest Church: Bible, Art, and Ritual at Dura-Europos, Syria* (New Haven, CT: Yale University Press, 2016), 228n. 80. Ulrich Mell is apparently unaware of Joosten's rebuttal. Treating the debate over authenticity in a footnote, Mell argues that the Dura fragment is too brief for a meaningful textual analysis and that Parker, Taylor, and Goodacre's argument illustrates the unreliability of "aufgestellten Kriterienkatalogs"; see Ulrich Mell, *Christliche Hauskirche und Neues Testament: Die Ikonologie des Baptisteriums von Dura Europos und das Diatessaron Tatians* (Göttingen: Vandenhoeck & Ruprecht, 2010), 203–4, esp. 203 n. 47.

[21] Joosten articulates his method on p. 166 by paraphrasing the just defended methodology of William Petersen, but my use of "Petersen method" throughout refers to the school of thought and procedure described by Ulrich Schmid as the "Old Perspective," which was most forcefully articulated in the work of William Petersen. For Schmid's critique, see his "The Diatessaron of Tatian," in *The Text of the New Testament in Contemporary Research: Essays on the Status Quaestionis*, ed. Bart D. Ehrman and Michael W. Holmes, 2nd ed., NTTSD 42 (Leiden: Brill, 2013), 119–33.

Table 7.1 Joseph of Arimathea in the Dura Fragment, as Outlined by Joosten

Dura		Matt	Mark	Luke	John
A	ἄνθρωπος	1		(1)	
B	βουλευτὴς ὑπαρχων		(4)	3	
C	ἀπὸ Ἐρινμαθαιας πόλεως τῆς Ἰουδαίας	(3)	(2)	6	(2)
D	ὄνομα Ἰωσήφ	(4)	(1)	(2)	(1)
E	ἀγαθὸς δίκαιος			(4)	
F	ὢν μαθητὴς τοῦ Ἰησοῦ	(5)			3
G	κεκρυμμένος (...) Ἰουδαίων				(4)
H	καὶ αὐτὸς προσεδέχετο τὴν βασιλείαν τοῦ Θεοῦ		(5)	(7)	
I	οὗτος οὐκ ἦν συγκατατιθέμενος τῇ βουλῇ			5	
Not included: πλούσιος		2			
Not included: εὐσχήμων			3		

Source: Joosten, "The Dura Parchment and the Diatessaron," 167.

The Arabic, Liège, and Venetian harmonies, Joosten proceeds to argue, present the same information in the following sequences:

Arabic Harmony:	A + rich	+ B – C – D – E – F – G – I – H
Liège Harmony:	rich + A + noble	+ B – C – D – E – F – G – H – I
Venetian Harmony:	rich + A + noble	+ B – C – D – E – F – G – H – I

Much of the shared sequence is not explicable in terms of narrative logic or any known source. This agreement between western and eastern gospel harmonies copied a thousand years after the Dura fragment is, according to Joosten, only explicable by a common ancestor: Tatian's Diatessaron.

5. Reassessing the Dura Fragment

In order to dispute Joosten's argument on its own methodological terms, his analysis must be clarified on two points. First, his schema elides the different sources cited by the harmonists. Second, Joosten does not account for the counterevidence provided by Codex Fuldensis. Following these, it will be argued that Joosten has not identified a Diatessaronic feature on the Petersen method.

Before turning to this critique, it will be necessary to review the text and harmonistic sequence of the Dura fragment. A canonical source for nearly every phrase can be identified without ambiguity.[22] Table 7.2 presents the text of the Dura fragment divided

---

[22] The one exception is the phrase ονομα Ιωσηφ that does not correspond precisely to either Matthew or Luke. The Dura fragment's general adherence to the Matthean order and the nominative noun suggest Matt 27:57d, but none of my arguments hinge on this identification.

Table 7.2 Text of the Dura Fragment and Its Canonical Parallels

Unit	Dura Europos	Canonical Parallel	Source
1	[ζεβεδ]αιου	Ζεβεδαιου	Matt 27:56c[a]
2	και σαλωμη	και Σαλωμη	Mark 15:40c
3	κ[αι] αι γυναικες [εκ τω]ν ακολουθησαντων α[υ]τω απο της [γαλιλαι]ας ορωσαι τον στα[b]	και γυναικες αι συνακολουθουσαι αυτω απο της γαλιλαιας ορωσαι ταυτα και αι γυναικες αι συνακολουθουσαι [...] et mulieres eorum quae secutae erant [...] ⲚⲘⲚⲈ2ⲒⲞⲘⲈ ⲈⲚⲈⲨⲞⲨⲎ2 ⲚⲤⲰϤ [...]	Luke 23:49bc $\mathfrak{P}^{75}$ B 1241 (579 omits αι[2]) c Sahidic
4	ην δε [η ημερ]α παρασκευη σαββατον επεφω[σκεν	και ημερα ην παρασκευης και σαββατον επεφωσκεν και ημερα ην παρασκευη σαββατον επεφωσκεν ην δε η ημερα προσαββατου erat autem dies parasceue et sabbatum inlucescebat.	Luke 23:54 A C² *Byz* D d (c) r¹
5	ο]ψιας δε γενομενης επι τ[η Π]αρ[α]σ[κευη], ο εστιν προσαββατον	και ηδη οψιας γενομενης επει ην Παρασκευη ο εστιν προσαββατον serum autem cum factum esset, cene pure sabbati et cum sero esset factum, quoniam erat parasceue, quod est ante sabbati et cum iam sero esset factum, quae erat parasceue, quod est ante sabbatum	Mark 15:42c (cf. Matt 27:57 οψιας δε γενομενης)[d] k c d
6	προσ[ηλθεν] ανθρωπος	ηλθεν ανθρωπος πλουσιος ܒܪ ܓܒܪܐ ܗܘ ܥܬܝܪܐ	Matt 27:57b syrˢ syrᴺᶠ [e]
7	βουλευτη[ς υ]παρ[χων	βουλευτης υπαρχων	Luke 23:50c
8	α]πο ερινμαθαιας π[ο]λεως της [ιουδαι]ας	απο Αριμαθαιας πολεως των ιουδαιων ab Arimathia civitate Iudeae ܡܢ ܪܡܬܐ ܡܕܝܢܬܐ	Luke 23:51b e aur b ff² g¹ l q r¹ Vulgate syrˢ syrᶜ
9	ονομα Ιω[σηφ]	τουνομα Ιωσηφ ανηρ ονοματι Ιωσηφ	Matt 27:57d Luke 23:50b
10	α[γ]αθος δι[καιος]	ανηρ αγαθος και δικαιος ανηρ αγαθος δικαιος αγαθος και δικαιος (omit: ανηρ) ⲠⲢⲰⲘⲈ Ⲛ̅ⲀⲄⲀⲐⲞⲤ Ⲛ̅ⲆⲒⲔⲀⲒⲞⲤ	Luke 23:50d B D Γ e a b d ff² l q Sahidic
11	ων μαθητης τ[ο]υ ιη̅	ων μαθητης του Ιησου	John 19:38c
12	κε[κρυμ]μενος δε δια τον φοβον των [ιουδαιω]ν	κεκρυμμενος δε δια τον φοβον των Ιουδαιων	John 19:38d
13	και αυτος προσεδεχετο [την] β[ασιλειαν] του θυ̅	ος προσεδεχετο την βασιλειαν του Θεου ος και (αυτος) προσεδεχετο την βασιλειαν του Θεου	Luke 23:51c K P Γ 070 f¹³ q (K P αυτος)

Unit	Dura Europos	Canonical Parallel	Source
14	ουτος ουκ [ην συνκατατ]ιθεμεν[ο]ςτη β[ουλη]	ουτος ουκ ην συγκατατεθειμενος τη βουλη	Luke 23:51a (syr^s, syr^c, and c attest the variant sequence 23:51ca)

Notes: ^{a}The following analysis required dividing the canonical passages with unusual particularity. I have appended these verses with my atomistic partitioning in Table 7.12 in the addendum to this chapter.
^{b}I follow Parker, Taylor, and Goodacre here against Kraeling. The latter reconstructs the text to read κ[α]ι γυναικες [των συ]νακολουθησαντων α[υτ]ω (Kraeling, *Greek Fragment of Tatian's Diatessaron*, 28–30). The differences are immaterial to my argument.
^{c}While no singular Old Latin reading at Mark 15:42 corresponds exactly to the Dura fragment, every variation is attested. The "Frankenstein reading" *serum autem cum factum esset quae erat parasceue, quod est ante sabbatum* may be constructed from *k* and *d* to agree with the Dura fragment precisely. This, however, is unnecessary for my argument as the Dura fragment's reading is an unambiguous adaptation of Mark.
^{d}One hardly need suppose the harmonist's dependence on Matthew to account for an introductory δέ. The omission of introductory conjunctions and relative pronouns is to be expected in even the most literal ancient citations. Furthermore, *autem* in the Old Latin *k* may support the antiquity of the Dura fragment's text of Mark.
^{e}Transcribed from Syriac NF 39 f.11v. There is a larger-than-normal space before ܘ somewhat obscured by the over-text, but it appears to be empty. For more information on this third Old Syriac Gospel MS, see Sebastian Brock, "Two Hitherto Unattested Passages of the Old Syriac Gospels in Palimpsests from St Catherine's Monastery, Sinai," Δελτίο Βιβλικών Μελετών 31A (2016): 7–18.

into fourteen movable units.[23] All but one unit reflects a shift in the harmonist's source.[24] I have provided the text of the twenty-eighth edition of the Nestle-Aland for each parallel, followed by variant readings apparently supported by the Dura fragment. I make no attempt at an exhaustive catalog of supporting witnesses. Elements without parallel are underlined.

Joosten limited his analysis to nine of the fourteen source units extant in the Dura fragment (corresponding to my units 6–14 in Table 7.2). This does not correspond either to a pericope division or single-sense unit. Rather, this selection isolates the data amenable to his thesis. Since chance agreements are bound to appear between random data sets and the harmonization of common source material is far from perfectly randomized, any perceived agreement should be considered in light of the total data set to avoid misidentifying coincidences as meaningful.[25] Therefore, as I update Joosten's

---

[23] I have printed the text as reconstructed by Parker, Taylor, and Goodacre, "The Dura-Europos Gospel Harmony," 200–1. The differences between the three published reconstructions are immaterial for identifying the relevant source texts.
[24] The one exception is the separation of John 19:38c and 19:38d. This division is necessary because several harmonists reproduce only half of the verse, substituting a Matthean parallel for the other. Where this does not occur, verses 38c and 38d will be counted as one source unit and the total number of source units will be reduced to thirteen. This will be noted where relevant.
[25] It is difficult to imagine, for instance, a harmony of the gospels relating that Joseph was a secret disciple or that "he did not agree with their plans" before giving his name. The more succinct

Table 7.3 Joosten's Element B in the Dura Fragment and Western Parallels

		Nestle-Aland 28th	Stuttgart Vulgate	
Dura	βουλευτης υπαρχων	βουλευτὴς ὑπάρχων	qui erat decurio	Luke 23:50c
Liège	en edel die tine riddren hadde onder hem	εὐσχήμων βουλευτής	nobilis decurio	Mark 15:43c
Venetian	nobele decurione			
Fuldensis	nobilis decurio			

Source: The Middle Dutch text of Liège 232 is taken from C. C. de Bruin, translated by A. J. Barnouw, *Het Luikse Diatessaron* (Leiden: Brill, 1970), 270. The text of Venetian harmony 95v is taken from Venanzio Todesco, Alberto Vaccari, and Marco Vattasso, eds., *Il Diatessaron in volgare italiano*, StT 81 (Vatican City: Biblioteca Apostolica Vaticana, 1938), 157. Text of Fuldensis 172 from Nicholas J. Zola, "Tatian's Diatessaron in Latin: A New Edition and Translation of Codex Fuldensis" (Ph.D. diss., Waco, TX: Baylor University, 2014), 134. See also Ernst Ranke, *Codex Fuldensis: Novum Testamentum Latine Interprete Hieronymo ex Manuscripto Victoris Capuani* (Marburg: N. G. Elwert, 1868), 157. Latin gospel citations, unless otherwise noted, are quoted according to the Vulgate in Robert Weber et al., eds., *Biblia Sacra iuxta vulgata versionem*, 5th ed. (Stuttgart: Deutsche Bibelgesellschaft, 2007).

proposed nine-unit string, the agreements will be assessed in light of the total number of movable source units (fourteen or thirteen).

5.1 Source Text versus Concept

First, Joosten's schematization of the Dura fragment represents instances where two harmonies unambiguously cite different gospels as an agreement rather than a difference. This is accomplished by labeling elements in the several harmonies according to their conceptual content rather than the gospel cited. This method of representing the textual data not only makes the several harmonies appear more similar than they really are but masks two divergences between the Dura fragment and vernacular harmonies that betray the latter's dependence on Fuldensis or its text tradition. These two elided differences correspond to Joosten's elements B and F. First, I will tackle Joosten's element B in Table 7.3.

Joosten's element B is a verbatim citation of Luke 23:50c, βουλευτὴς ὑπάρχων, in the Dura fragment. The Liège harmony, however, reads "en edel die tine riddren hadde onder hem,"[26] reflecting the Latin *nobilis decurio*, a verbatim citation of Mark 15:43c. Note that the Liège harmony translates *decurio* with "who has ten riders under him" just as it elsewhere translates *centurio* with "who has one hundred riders under him."[27] Likewise, the Venetian harmony reads "nobele decurione." Both the Liège and

---

introduction of Joseph in the *Gospel of Nicodemus* (11), which is clearly not attempting to comprehensively harmonize the gospels, provides a helpful analog.

[26] Barnouw (in de Bruin, *Het Luikse Diatessaron*, 270 = Liège 232) provides the translation, "and noble man, who had ten soldiers under him," but note that "man" is a gloss. The adjective "edel" (noble) immediately precedes the paraphrase for Latin *decurio*.

[27] Liège 231 in de Bruin, *Het Luikse Diatessaron*, 270.

Table 7.4 Joosten's Element F in the Dura Fragment and Western Parallels

		Nestle-Aland 28th	**Stuttgart Vulgate**	
Dura	ων μαθητης του Ιησου	ὢν μαθητὴς τοῦ Ἰησοῦ	eo quod esset discipulus Iesu	John 19:38c
Liège	ende Ihesus ijongre was	ὃς καὶ αὐτὸς ἐμαθητεύθη τῷ Ἰησοῦ	qui et ipse discipulus erat Iesu	Matt 27:57e
Venetian	el quale era dispolo de Iesu			
Fuldensis	qui et ipse occultus discipulus erat ihesu			

Source: Text of Liège Harmony 232 from De Bruin, *Het Luikse Diatessaron*, 270. Text of Venetian Harmony 95v from Todesco et al., *Il Diatessaron in Volgare Italiano*, 157. Text of Fuldensis 172 from Zola, "Tatian's Diatessaron in Latin," 134. See also Ranke, *Codex Fuldensis*, 157.

Venetian harmonies omit anything corresponding to the Lukan participle ὑπάρχων and cite an equivalent of the Markan εὐσχήμων. As further discussed below, the Liège and Venetian harmonies agree with Codex Fuldensis here—all three cite Mark rather than Luke—against the Dura fragment. Joosten counts this unambiguous citation of different gospels as an agreement. This Dura–Liège/Venetian divergence reduces Joosten's string of nine agreements to C – D – E – F – G with the sequence F – G (John 19:38c and 38d), as Joosten acknowledges,[28] constrained by narrative logic. I move next to Joosten's element F in Table 7.4.

Similarly, Joosten's element F elides a difference between Dura's unambiguous citation of John 19:38c and the citation of Matthew 27:57e in both the Liège and Venetian harmony. Liège reads "ende Ihesus ijongre was,"[29] agreeing with Matthew's *qui et ipse discipulus erat Iesu* against John's *eo quod esset discipulus Iesu*. The Liège harmony elsewhere renders the causal phrase *eo quod esset* with "omdat" at Luke 1:7 and "want hi was" at Luke 2:4. The Venetian renders the same with "Imperço che" at Luke 1:7 and "per ço ch'eli era" at Luke 2:4. The use of only a finite past tense verb in both vernacular harmonies is, therefore, distinctly Matthean. Furthermore, "el quale" in the Venetian probably reflects the Matthean *qui (et) ipse*.[30] Both vernacular harmonies, therefore, attest uniquely Matthean terms and neither attests anything distinctively Johannine. Here again, as discussed below, the Liège and Venetian harmonies agree with Fuldensis against the Dura fragment. This disagreement further reduces the East-West-Dura agreement to C – D – E, a string of just three out of fourteen total source units.[31]

---

[28] Joosten, "The Dura Parchment and the Diatessaron," 167.
[29] De Bruin, *Het Luikse Diatessaron*, 271.
[30] The presence of the conjunction "ende" in Liège might also be cited as corresponding to the Matthean "et" but this may just as well be an artefact of harmonization.
[31] This evidence is presented in full in Table 7.2. Note that this metric does not represent the two additions in Liège (Mark 15:41ab and John 19:31-37) which further distance Dura from the Dutch harmony.

5.2 Codex Fuldensis as Counterevidence

The second problem on the Petersen method with Joosten's analysis is the omission of counter-evidence provided by Codex Fuldensis. Here, as elsewhere, the western vernacular harmonies depend upon/are corrupted by the vulgate Latin Fuldensis. To ascertain the force of this objection, one must first understand the role of Fuldensis in the reconstruction of the western Diatessaronic branch according to the Petersen method.

The Middle Dutch Liège harmony was introduced as a witness to Tatian's Diatessaron by Daniel Plooij.[32] Plooij argues that Liège's agreements with either the Old Latin gospels or eastern Diatessaronic witnesses *against* the Vulgate Fuldensis are evidence that Liège was derived from a lost Old Latin gospel harmony. This hypothetical Old Latin harmony, a pillar of the Petersen method, is supposed to have preserved Tatianic readings in the West into the second millennium. Scholars employing this methodology nevertheless acknowledge the ubiquity of corruption toward the Fuldensis-type Vulgate. As a result, the Old Latin harmony is only recoverable where the western harmony differs from Fuldensis in agreement with some eastern witness to Tatian's gospel.[33] Neither the Liège, the "single most important" western harmony,[34] nor the Venetian harmony are exceptions to this rule.[35] Petersen himself, acknowledging the influence of Fuldensis-type harmonies across the western tradition,[36] agreed with Plooij that readings from these western vernacular witnesses are valuable only where they differ from Fuldensis's vulgatized text.[37]

Joosten cites the studies of Plooij and Petersen as demonstrations of Liège's value in recovering the Old Latin harmony and thereby Tatian's Diatessaron.[38] A thoroughgoing application of the Petersen method, therefore, requires a presentation of Fuldensis for the sequence in question.[39] Only where the vernacular witnesses differ from Fuldensis can the former be used as a witness to Tatian's gospel. As shown in Table 7.5, Fuldensis, on the Petersen method, undermines the value of both the Liège and Venetian harmonies.

---

[32] Daniel Plooij, *A Primitive Text of the Diatessaron: The Liège Manuscript of a Mediæval Dutch Translation: A Preliminary Study* (Leiden: A. W. Sijthoff, 1923); Daniel Plooij, *A Further Study of the Liège Diatessaron* (Leiden: Brill, 1925).

[33] Elsewhere, Joosten too denies that Fuldensis has any value for reconstructing the text of Tatian's Gospel. Jan Joosten, *Language and Textual History of the Syriac Bible: Collected Studies*, TS 9 (Piscataway, NJ: Gorgias, 2013), 261n. 51; Jan Joosten, review of *Unum ex Quattuor: Eine Geschichte der lateinischen Tatianüberlieferung*, by Ulrich B. Schmid, Gnomon 80 (2008): 21.

[34] Petersen, *Tatian's Diatessaron*, 171.

[35] Plooij (*A Further Study of the Liège Diatessaron*, 2) states that "on one point of great importance there seems to be now general agreement: that behind the Liège Text lies an Old Latin form of the Diatessaron and that accordingly the Latin Diatessaron is ante-Hieronymic: that therefore the Vulgate forms (of which only the Fuldensis has been printed) are corrections, and, with regard to the fine structure of the harmonization, certainly deteriorations." On the Venetian harmony, see Petersen, *Tatian's Diatessaron*, 248.

[36] On vulgatization in the Liège harmony, see Petersen, *Tatian's Diatessaron*, 248. For the Venetian, see Petersen, *Tatian's Diatessaron*, 247–51.

[37] Petersen, *Tatian's Diatessaron*, 182.

[38] Joosten, review of *Unum ex Quattuor* (by Schmid), 21–2.

[39] Joosten comments on Fuldensis's rendering of Matthew 27:57e/John 19:38c in a footnote in "The Dura Parchment and the Diatessaron," 168n. 26.

Table 7.5 Sequence of Dura, Fuldensis, Liège, and Venetian Harmonies

Unit	Dura Fragment	Codex Fuldensis	Liège Harmony	Venetian Harmony
1	Matt 27:56c	Mark 15:40d	Mark 15:40d	
2	Mark 15:40d	Matt 27:56	Matt 27:56	Matt 27:56
		Mark 15:41a	Mark 15:41a	
			Mark 15:41b	
3	Luke 23:49b			
4	Luke 23:49c	Luke 23:49c		
		John 19:31-37	John 19:31-37	John 19:31-37
5	Luke 23:54			
6	Mark 15:42	Matt 27:57a	Matt 27:57a	Matt 27:57a
7	Matt 27:57b	Matt 27:57b (+dives)	Matt 27:57b (+rike)	Matt 27:57b (+richo)
8	Luke 23:50c	Mark 15:43c	Mark 15:43c	Mark 15:43c
9	Luke 23:51b	Luke 23:51b	Luke 23:51b	Luke 23:51b
10	Matt 27:57d/	Matt 27:57d/	Matt 27:57d/	Matt 27:57d/
	Luke 23:50b	Luke 23:50b	Luke 23:50b	Luke 23:50b
11	Luke 23:50d	Luke 23:50d (+vir)	Luke 23:50d (+man)	Luke 23:50d (+homo)
12	John 19:38c	Matt 27:57e	Matt 27:57e	Matt 27:57e
13	John 19:38d	John 19:38d	John 19:38d	John 19:38d
14	Luke 23:51c	Luke 23:51c	Luke 23:51c/	Luke 23:51c/
			Mark 15:43d	Mark 15:43d
15	Luke 23:51a	Luke 23:51a	Luke 23:51a	Luke 23:51a

Source: Text of Fuldensis 171-72 from Zola, "Tatian's Diatessaron in Latin," 132–4; Ranke, *Codex Fuldensis*, 156–7. Text of Liège Harmony 231-232/94r-95v from de Bruin, *Het Luikse Diatessaron*, 268–70. Text of Venetian Harmony 95v from Todesco et al., *Il Diatessaron in Volgare Italiano*, 156–7.

Before comparing the sequences *in toto*, it will be necessary to identify Codex Fuldensis's sources for Joosten's elements B and F. As shown in Table 7.3 for Joosten's element B, Fuldensis's verbatim citation of Mark 15:43c according to the Vulgate is hardly ambiguous. The Liège and Venetian harmonies, therefore, agree with Fuldensis here against the Dura fragment. Likewise, as shown in Table 7.4 for Joosten's element F, Fuldensis again provides an unambiguous citation of Matthew 27:57e according to the Latin Vulgate. This is not obscured by the occurrence of *occultus*, brought forward from the subsequent Johannine passage. Fuldensis attests every distinctively Matthean term and no distinctively Johannine vocabulary from the relevant passage. Here as well the Liège and Venetian harmonies agree with Fuldensis against the Dura fragment.

We can now compare the sequences of the Dura fragment, Fuldensis, and Liège in full, as outlined in Table 7.5. The Liège harmony and Dura fragment share a string of only three out of fourteen source units. More importantly, the Liège harmony reproduces the sequence of Fuldensis in its entirety. Where Fuldensis differs from Dura (two additions, two omissions, three substitutions, and one transposition), Liège follows Fuldensis. Where Liège differs from Fuldensis (one addition and one omission), Fuldensis agrees with Dura. Finally, Liège never agrees with Dura against Fuldensis.

Even if one isolates the description of Joseph—Joosten's Diatessaronic feature—Liège twice follows Fuldensis against the Dura fragment and never agrees with the Dura fragment against Fuldensis. Joosten has consistently championed the approach of Plooij and Petersen against its critics, but even according to this methodology, no part of the relevant passage in Liège can be identified as belonging to the (hypothetical) Old Latin Tatian.[40]

The Venetian harmony fares no better than the Liège. As illustrated in Table 7.5, the Venetian harmony and Dura fragment share a string of only three out of fourteen source units. Although the Venetian is parsimonious in its opening, citing Matt 27:56 but omitting several elements attested in Dura and Fuldensis, it subsequently reproduces Fuldensis in its entirety. Following the opening, the Venetian agrees five times with Fuldensis against Dura (one addition, one omission, and three substitutions) and never agrees with Dura against Fuldensis. Again, on the Petersen method, no part of the relevant passage in the Venetian harmony can be identified as belonging to the (hypothetical) Old Latin Tatian.

In conclusion, a closer examination of the harmonists' source texts and the counterevidence provided by Codex Fuldensis undermine Joosten's proposed Diatessaronic sequence. Without any western support for Joosten's proposed Diatessaronic feature, the Dura fragment fails the Petersen method.

6. Fuldensis *Redivivus*?

I have attempted to respond to Joosten's argument according to methodological principles that he and other advocates of the Petersen method might accept. This required compartmentalizing an important development in Diatessaronic studies—namely, the collapse of the Petersen method. This was effected by a series of articles and a monograph published by Ulrich Schmid and August den Hollander.[41] It would be superfluous to rehearse here the arguments adduced by Schmid and den Hollander against both the existence of an Old Latin harmony and the reliability of Petersen's three criteria. For those of us who accept the demise of Petersen's methodology, however, the question must be asked anew.

Perhaps Joosten's argument can be salvaged by abandoning the hypothetical Old Latin Diatessaron (and so the vernacular harmonies) and elevating Codex Fuldensis in its place? Although Fuldensis has traditionally been used to strain out non-Diatessaronic readings, some have recently suggested that Fuldensis might replace the bygone western

---

[40] See, for instance, his critique of Schmid's work in Joosten, review of *Unum ex Quattuor* (by Schmid).
[41] Ulrich B. Schmid, "In Search of Tatian's Diatessaron in the West," *VC* 57 (2003): 176–99; Ulrich Schmid, "Genealogy by Chance! On the Significance of Accidental Variation (Parallelisms)," in *Studies in Stemmatology II*, ed. August den Hollander, Margot van Mulken, and Pieter Th. van Reenen (Amsterdam: John Benjamins, 2004), 127–43; Ulrich Schmid, *Unum ex Quattuor: Eine Geschichte der lateinischen Tatianüberlieferung*, AGLB 37 (Freiburg im Breisgau: Herder, 2005); August den Hollander and Ulrich Schmid, "The *Gospel of Barnabas*, the Diatessaron, and Method," *VC* 61 (2007): 1–20.

Table 7.6 Placement of the Lance Piercing in Dura and Fuldensis

	Dura Fragment	**Codex Fuldensis**
Jesus's Death	Matt 27:56c	Mark 15:40d
	Mark 15:40d	Matt 27:56
		Mark 15:41a
	Luke 23:49b	
	Luke 23:49c	Luke 23:49c
Piercing		John 19:31-37
Jesus's Burial	Luke 23:54	
	Mark 15:42	Matt 27:57a
	Matt 27:57b	Matt 27:57b (+dives)
	Luke 23:50c	Mark 15:43c
	Luke 23:51b	Luke 23:51b
	Matt 27:57d/Luke 23:50b	Matt 27:57d/Luke 23:50b
	Luke 23:50d	Luke 23:50d (+vir)
	John 19:38c	Matt 27:57e
	John 19:38d	John 19:38d
	Luke 23:51c	Luke 23:51c
	Luke 23:51a	Luke 23:51a

Source: Text of Fuldensis 171-72 from Zola, "Tatian's Diatessaron in Latin," 132-4; Ranke, *Codex Fuldensis*, 156-7.

tradition. The relevant sequence of Fuldensis will be considered both on the inter-pericope or "block-by-block" level and the intra-pericope or "phrase-by-phrase" level below.[42] The former weighs decidedly against identifying the Dura Parchment as a fragment of Tatian's Diatessaron while the latter is shown to be without value.

6.1 Fuldensis's Inter-Pericope Sequence

Fuldensis's *inter*-pericope (block-by-block) sequence, owing to its similarity to pseudo-Ephrem's *Vorlage* and the Arabic Diatessaron, is widely accepted as a witness to Tatian's Gospel.[43] Unfortunately, the Dura fragment is extant only for a single shift between pericopes: "Jesus's Death" followed by "Jesus's Burial." In this sole inter-pericope datum, Codex Fuldensis differs from the Dura fragment by placing between these two stories the Johannine pericope of the lance piercing Jesus's side (19:31-37), as illustrated in Table 7.6.

---

[42] The distinction between "phrase-for-phrase" and "block-by-block" harmonization/conflation is borrowed from Sharon Lea Mattila, "A Question Too Often Neglected," *NTS* 41 (1995): 205. This roughly corresponds to the distinction between intra-pericope and inter-pericope sequence. For a helpful synopsis of the sequence of our sources, see Louis Leloir, *Le témoignage d'Éphrem sur le Diatessaron* (Leuven: Secrétariat du CorpusSCO, 1962), 2-11.

[43] The substantial agreement between these three witnesses is evident from the tables provided by Louis Leloir in *Le témoignage d'Éphrem*, 2-11.

As discussed below, pseudo-Ephrem's harmony corroborates Codex Fuldensis (against the Dura fragment) on this point. Since this is the only inter-pericope harmonization where the Dura fragment can be checked against Fuldensis, in so far as the latter is to be credited as a source for reconstructing Tatian's Gospel, it weighs decidedly against the Diatessaronic character of the Dura fragment.

6.2 Fuldensis's Intra-Pericope Sequence

The use of Fuldensis to evaluate Joosten's Diatessaronic feature would require the Latin harmony to be a reliable witness to Tatian's intra-pericope (phrase-by-phrase) sequence. Hort's dictum that "knowledge of documents should precede final judgment upon readings" is disregarded at the critic's peril.[44] Although scholars have long regarded the inter-pericope sequence of Codex Fuldensis as a witness to Tatian's Gospel (as assumed above), its text is that of Jerome's Vulgate.[45] It appears, therefore, that at an unknown stage in the manuscript's prehistory, Jerome's translation was inserted into the outline of Tatian's Gospel.[46] Unfortunately for those seeking to reconstruct Tatian's composition, a comparison of pseudo-Ephrem's *Commentary* with Codex Fuldensis reveals that the process of vulgatization that replaced Fuldensis's Tatianic text also rearranged—for our purposes, erased—its intra-pericope sequence. As such, Fuldensis is not a reliable witness for the level of variation necessary to assess Joosten's Diatessaronic feature.

This erasure of intra-pericope sequence is first evidenced in Fuldensis's frequent omission of phrases and narrative details attested by pseudo-Ephrem. Jesus's third temptation, for instance, is introduced in the *Commentary* with an adapted form of Matthew 4:8-9, distinguished from Luke by the mention of a very tall mountain.[47] Pseudo-Ephrem then indicates that "after this" his text of Tatian's Gospel included a phrase found only in Luke 4:6b, "To me (they have/it has) been handed

---

[44] Brooke Foss Westcott and Fenton John Anthony Hort, *The New Testament in the Original Greek: Introduction and Appendix* (New York: Harper, 1882), 31. Here I depart entirely from the methodologies championed by the last generation of Diatessaron scholars. If the text of Tatian's Gospel is to be established with anything approaching confidence, it must be on the basis of the text critical methods employed in every other field.

[45] Bruce M. Metzger, *The Early Versions of the New Testament: Their Origin, Transmission, and Limitations* (Oxford: Clarendon Press, 1977), 26–7. Bruce M. Metzger and Bart D. Ehrman, *The Text of the New Testament: Its Transmission, Corruption, and Restoration*, 4th ed. (New York: Oxford University Press, 2005), 108.

[46] This description probably underrates the degree of creativity involved in the vulgatization of Fuldensis. On the block-by-block level, pericopes absent in Tatian's Gospel were introduced (e.g., Lukan prologue, *Pericope Adulterae*) and others were relocated. On the phrase-by-phrase level, as argued below, fresh harmonization was undertaken.

[47] ܐܦ ܠܝ ܐܫܬܠܛܬ ܗܘܐ ܘܠܐ ܐܬܝܗܒܬ ܐܠܗܐ ܐܡܪ from *Comm.* 4.9 in Louis Leloir, *Saint Éphrem: Commentaire de l'Évangile concordant, texte syriaque (MS Chester Beatty 709): Folios additionnels*, CBM 8(b) (Leuven: Peeters, 1990), 26. Շարժեալ առ (ցսա/B omits) սծ հան ի լեառն մի բարձր յոյժ, և աստ ցսա. իմ են այս ամենայն թագաւորութիւնք from *Comm.* 4.9 in Louis Leloir, *Saint Éphrem: Commentaire de l'Évangile concordant, version arménienne*, CSCO 137, Scriptores Armeniaci 1 (Leuven: Imprimerie Orientaliste L. Durbecq, 1953), 51. For a Latin translation of the Armenian, see Louis Leloir, *Saint Éphrem: Commentaire de l'Évangile concordant, version arménienne*, CSCO 145, Scriptores Armeniaci 2 (Leuven: Peeters, 1954), 38.

over."⁴⁸ Fuldensis fails to incorporate this Lukan phrase and so does not here reflect the intra-pericope content of pseudo-Ephrem's Gospel.⁴⁹ Similarly, in the Cleansing of the Leper, pseudo-Ephrem thrice mentions Jesus's anger, a variant reading of Mark 1:41. Fuldensis, on the other hand, integrates both Matthean and Markan material in this pericope but omits any mention of Jesus's emotional response (anger or compassion) to the leper.⁵⁰ Again, in the discussion of divorce, the Pharisee's rejoinder from Mark 10:4 is attested by pseudo-Ephrem but omitted from Codex Fuldensis.⁵¹ Examples could be multiplied.

While such omissions from Fuldensis are easy to detect, our inability to identify omissions or determine phrase-by-phrase sequence in pseudo-Ephrem's *Vorlage* on the basis of the commentator's sparse—and typically brief—allusions presents a methodological obstacle to further assessing Fuldensis's intra-pericope sequence. One could imagine that the scribe responsible for vulgatizing Codex Fuldensis adhered to a Tatianic *Vorlage* on the phrase-by-phrase level necessary to assess Joosten's feature but frequently failed to note a shift in source gospel and thus often elided narrative details. In this speculative scenario, Fuldensis might be expected to omit elements attested by pseudo-Ephrem while sometimes remaining a credible witness to Tatian's intra-pericope sequence.⁵²

It is, however, occasionally possible to show that the vulgatizing scribe did not merely elide narrative details but exercised harmonistic creativity in composing the Fuldensis gospel harmony. This requires demonstrating that a phrase or narrative detail attested by Fuldensis in a complexly harmonized pericope was not present ad locum in pseudo-Ephrem's Gospel and so must have been introduced by the vulgatizing scribe. This creative intra-pericope harmonization, together with the omission of attested

---

⁴⁸ ܚܕܝ ܚܠܦ ܐܝܟܐ ܕܐܝܬܘܗܝ ܗܠܝܢ from *Comm.* 4.9 in Leloir, *Saint Éphrem* (1990), 26. Թէ այդպէս է, յորժամ աւետ զկնի նորա Թէ իւձ առեալ է from *Comm.* 4.9 in Leloir, *Saint Éphrem* (1953), 51.
⁴⁹ Fuldensis 15 from Ranke, *Codex Fuldensis*, 41.
⁵⁰ Pseudo-Ephrem, *Comm.* 12.22-23 in (Syriac) Louis Leloir, *Saint Éphrem: Commentaire de l'Évangile concordant, texte syriaque* (MS Chester Beatty 709), CBM 8 (Dublin: Hodges Figgis, 1963), 96–8; and (Armenian) Leloir, *Saint Éphrem* (1953), 173–5. Fuldensis 47 is in Ranke, *Codex Fuldensis*, 56. Nathan C. Johnson ("Anger Issues: Mark 1.41 in Ephrem the Syrian, the Old Latin Gospels and Codex Bezae," *NTS* 63 [2017]: 190) has recently argued that pseudo-Ephrem's references to "anger" do not support ὀργισθείς in Mark 1:41 but are instead alluding to the ἐμβριμησάμενος of Mark 1:43. This passage, too, is absent in Fuldensis.
⁵¹ ܕܠܐ ܢܦܩܝܢ ܐܢܬܘܢ. ܕܡܛܠ ܩܫܝܘܬ from *Comm.* 14.18 in Leloir, *Saint Éphrem* (1963), 130. Ասեն ցնա. Մովսէս հրամայեաց մեզ from *Comm.* 14.18 in Leloir, *Saint Éphrem* (1953), 196; Latin translation in Leloir, *Saint Éphrem* (1954), 141. This is quoted in the text form attested by the Sinaitic Syriac Palimpsest. The discussion of divorce in Fuldensis 154 follows Matthew 26:1-5; see Ranke, *Codex Fuldensis*, 136.
⁵² The fact that Fuldensis omits details in complexly harmonized pericopes (e.g., Mark 1:41), and not only where the Latin harmony follows at length a single gospel, weighs against the theory we are entertaining. In lieu of some independent corroboration, our inability to assess this proposed scenario in most pericopes (for the reasons described above) weighs against its admissibility. Shared material with pseudo-Ephrem in Fuldensis's complexly harmonized pericopes might be supposed to corroborate this theory, but these are, by definition, the very pericopes where Fuldensis will include the greatest amount of detail from the greatest number of sources. That the scant textual data (or their conceptual parallels) provided by pseudo-Ephrem should typically be among the large pool given by Fuldensis precisely where the latter is most inclusive is not especially meaningful.

Tatianic elements, effectively undermines Fuldensis's probative value for determining Tatian's intra-pericope sequence.

The most compelling evidence for the omission of a narrative detail from one pericope is its attestation elsewhere in the *Commentary*.[53] Indeed, passages situated in distant locales according to pseudo-Ephrem occasionally appear in Fuldensis as a single, complexly harmonized pericope. The *Commentary*, for instance, records two separate anointings of Jesus, once in the house of Simon the Pharisee (10.8-10) and again in the house of Simon the Leper (17.11-13). The former is reported in exclusively Lukan language while the latter is a harmonization of Markan/Matthean and Johannine elements.[54] Fuldensis, on the other hand, artfully conflates material from all four gospels into a single anointing: Mark 14:3[...]; John 12:2-3; Mark 14:3; Matt 26:7; John 12:3-6; Mark 14:4; Matt 26:10; Mark 14:7; Matt 26:12-13; Luke 7:39-50.[55] The scribe responsible for vulgatizing Fuldensis must, therefore, also have been responsible for harmonizing these two narratives.[56] This conclusion, considered alongside the frequent omission of details attested by pseudo-Ephrem, indicates that Fuldensis does not reliably preserve Tatian's intra-pericope sequence.[57] It cannot, therefore, be used to evaluate Joosten's Diatessaronic feature.

6.3 An Unexpected Agreement between Fuldensis and the Dura Fragment (Luke 23:51)

I have argued above that the intra-pericope sequence of Codex Fuldensis is not a reliable witness to Tatian's Gospel. Even apart from this, however, the agreement between Fuldensis and the Dura fragment on this intra-pericope level would not be particularly compelling. Fuldensis evinces two plusses, two minuses, three

---

[53] The *Commentary* frequently adduces passages drawn from elsewhere in the gospel in the course of exegesis. Reliably locating a passage typically requires lemmata or commentary specifically indicating that the narrative detail in question was part of the pericope in which it is cited.

[54] In 10.8-10, the commentator cites Luke 7:39, 41, 44, 45, and 47 but also describes the events of verses 36-38; for the texts, see Leloir, *Saint Éphrem* (1963), 42–6 (Syriac); Leloir, *Saint Éphrem* (1953), 98–9 (Armenian). In 17.11-13, the anointing is located in the home of "Simon the Leper" indicating the presence of either Matthew 26:6 or Mark 14:3. This is followed by an adaptation of Judas's objection to the anointing from John 12:5. For the texts, see Leloir, *Saint Éphrem* (1963), 201–3 (Syriac); Leloir, *Saint Éphrem* (1953), 180 (Armenian).

[55] Fuldensis 138-9 in Ranke, *Codex Fuldensis*, 123-4.

[56] In another instance, the question of James and John from Mark 10:35-37 in *Comm.* 10.1 is conflated with the passion predictions of Luke 18:31-33 in *Comm.* 14.4 by Fuldensis 113 into a single intricately interwoven pericope (Ranke, *Codex Fuldensis*, 101). The recurrence of the Zebedees' inquiry at *Comm.* 15.18-19 seems to be occasioned by their participation at the transfiguration. In any case, this latter section of the commentary is out of place and borrows verbatim from another section of the commentary (see Lange, *The Portrayal of Christ*, 53–8).

[57] Indeed, the data presented here are not incompatible with the supposition that the vulgatizing scribe copied out of his Tatianic *Vorlage* only a series of *capitula* (reflecting Tatian's inter-pericope sequence) and freely composed a harmony within that framework. It has been noted that Fuldensis's *capitula* agree more closely with pseudo-Ephrem's *Commentary* in phrasing and sequence than the actual text. See, for instance, Petersen, *Tatian's Diatessaron*, 127–9. Further study, especially comparison with the Arabic harmony, would be required to demonstrate or falsify this hypothesis. It has been demonstrated here only that the vulgatizing scribe exercised harmonistic creativity on the intra-pericope level.

Table 7.7 Luke 23:51 in Dura, Fuldensis, and the Syriac Peshitta

Luke 23:51 NA[28]	ªοὗτος οὐκ ἦν συγκατατεθειμένος τῇ βουλῇ καὶ τῇ πράξει αὐτῶν—ᵇἀπὸ Ἀριμαθαίας πόλεως τῶν Ἰουδαίων, ᶜὃς προσεδέχετο τὴν βασιλείαν τοῦ θεοῦ,	ªThis one did not agree with their plan and deed—ᵇfrom Arimathea, the city of the Jews—ᶜwho was expecting the kingdom of God
Dura Fragment	ᶜκαι αυτος προσεδεχετο την βασιλειαν του Θεου ªουτος ουκ ην συνκατατιθεμενος τη βουλη	ᶜand he was expecting the kingdom of God—ªhe was not agreeing with the plan
Codex Fuldensis	ᶜqui expectabat et ipse regnum dei· ªhic non consenserat concilio et actibus eorum·	ᶜwho was also himself anticipating the kingdom of God. ªHe had not consented to their decision and actions.
Luke 23:51 syrᵖ	ܗܢܐ ܠܐ ܫܠܡ ܗܘܐ ܠܨܒܝܢܗܘܢ ܘܠܥܒܕܗܘܢ ܘܡܣܟܐ ܗܘܐ ܠܡܠܟܘܬܐ ܕܐܠܗܐ	ªThis one did not agree with the plan and deed of them ᶜand he was expecting the kingdom of God.

Source: Text and translation of Fuldensis 172 from Zola, "Tatian's Diatessaron in Latin," 134; Ranke, *Codex Fuldensis*, 157.

substitutions, and one adjacent transposition. As Table 7.5 illustrates, the harmonies share a string of only three agreements out of fourteen less-than-randomly arranged source units.

Nevertheless, there remains a potentially remarkable agreement between Codex Fuldensis and the Dura fragment. Both harmonies place Luke 23:51b earlier in Joseph's introduction (after Luke 23:50c in the Dura fragment and Mark 15:43c in Fuldensis) and then, several clauses later, cite Luke 23:51c before 23:51a. This agreement is exhibited in Table 7.7.

Preliminarily, it should be reiterated that this is precisely the sort of intra-pericope variation for which Fuldensis is not a reliable witness to Tatian's Gospel.[58] If, therefore, Fuldensis and the Dura fragment are probably not witnesses (on the intra-pericope level) to the same Tatianic source, how is the agreement at Luke 23:51 to be explained? Although Ulrich Schmid's work has cautioned us against fixating on small agreements in larger bodies of divergent material, this shared reading is probably more than a mere coincidence but less than an indication of common Tatianic origin.[59] Rather, the shared rearrangement of Luke 23:51 likely arose independently as a solution to several otherwise attested "scribal irritants"—that is, stimuli for scribal emendation—in the text of Luke.

---

[58] As expected, based on the data provided above, Fuldensis fails to preserve other such intra-pericope sequences attested by pseudo-Ephrem that deviate from the standard gospel texts. For instance, the order of the "Two Sons" (Matt 21:28-32) in Pseudo-Ephrem, *Comm.* 16.18 and Fuldensis 124, for which see Leloir, *Saint Éphrem* (1990), 167; Ranke, *Codex Fuldensis*, 108. Similarly, pseudo-Ephrem's *Vorlage* apparently reversed the sequence of Jesus's benediction (from Matt 9:22/Mark 5:43/Luke 8:48) in *Comm.* 7.10, but Fuldensis 61 preserves the canonical sequence, for which see Leloir, *Saint Éphrem* (1963), 94–6 (Syriac); Leloir, *Saint Éphrem* (1953), 69 (Armenian); Ranke, *Codex Fuldensis*, 62.

[59] It should further be noted that the Arabic harmony does not support this reading.

The relocation of Luke 23:51b earlier in the passage is easily explicable as an attempt to remedy two such irritants. First, the conventional placement of a person's place of origin immediately after their name—as Matthew, Mark, and John do here—would tempt the harmonizing redactor to draw this piece of information forward from its place in Luke's Gospel. The force of this convention is evidenced by the interpolation of 23:51b or an equivalent phrase into Luke 23:50 by the Old Latin Codex Colbertinus, the Old Syriac gospels, the Syriac Peshitta, the Harklean passion harmony, and the Ethiopic version.[60]

Second, Luke 23:51b's prepositional phrase, "from Arimathea, the city of the Jews," creates an anacoluthon in its canonical location. This disjunction is indicated in the 28th edition of the Nestle-Aland by an *em dash* (see Table 7.7). Such a scribal irritant would also prompt the harmonizer to relocate v. 51b. The phrase's omission is, indeed, multiply attested in Luke's textual tradition—namely, Miniscule 713, the Old Latin Codex Colbertinus, the Old Syriac gospels, and the Syriac Peshitta.[61]

Finally, the reversed order of Luke 23:51a and 51c is plausibly explained as a shared stylistic and narrative improvement. In Codex Fuldensis and Lukan manuscripts, Luke 23:51c is a subordinate clause introduced by a relative pronoun while 51a is an independent clause beginning with an anaphoric demonstrative pronoun. With the anacoluthous 51b moved earlier, it makes sense for both harmonists to switch the sequence of 51a and 51c in order to place the relative pronoun closer to its antecedent subject, "Joseph," and avoid an awkward alternation between relative pronouns and demonstratives.[62] Furthermore, in both harmonies, 23:51a (Joseph's dissent) would intervene between the statement of Joseph's discipleship (Matt 27:57e/John 19:38) and

[60] Although the Old Syriac gospels and Peshitta have often been treated as a witness to Tatian's Diatessaron (e.g., Joosten, "The Dura Parchment and the Diatessaron," 169), these text traditions represent the Diatessaron's principal rivals among possible witnesses to Tatian's Gospel. Toward what text tradition is a fourth-century Syrian scribe supposed to vulgatize his MSS but the Old Syriac gospels or their Greek *Vorlage*? As J. P. Lyon has shown, not every harmonization and paraphrastic translation in the Old Syriac gospels is attributable to Tatian; see his *Syriac Gospel Translations: A Comparison of the Language and Translation Method Used in the Old Syriac, the Diatessaron, and the Peshitto*, CSCO 548 (Leuven: Peeters, 1994), 195. The Dura parchment, our only early Greek fragment from this region, unsurprisingly bears some significant relationship to the Old Syriac gospels but these rivals to the Diatessaron cannot be cited as evidence in favor of a reading's Tatianic origin. The text of Colbertinus may be found in Adolf Jülicher, Walter Matzkow, and Kurt Aland, eds., *Itala: Das neue Testament in altlateinischer Überlieferung*, 4 vols., 2nd ed. (Berlin: de Gruyter, 1963–76), 3:268. The text of the Ethiopic version may be found in The American and British Committees of the International Greek New Testament Project, eds., *The Gospel According to St. Luke*, 2 vols. (Oxford: Clarendon Press, 1984–7), 2:228. The text of the Harklean passion harmony Rubric 16 may be found in Morris A. Weigelt, "Diatessaric Harmonies of the Passion Narrative in the Harclean Syriac Version," (Th.D. diss., Princeton, NJ: Princeton Theological Seminary, 1969), 38*.

[61] Notably, this list is not coextensive with the interpolation of 23:51b in 23:50. Miniscule 713 (Codex Algerinae Peckover) is an eleventh-/twelfth-century minuscule that belongs to the Farrer group. Intriguingly, Harris identified a reading at Matthew 17:27 that is only elsewhere attested in pseudo-Ephrem's *Commentary*; see J. Rendel Harris, "Cod. Ev. 561: Codex Algerinae Peckover," *Journal of the Society of Biblical Literature and Exegesis* 6 (1886): 79–89; J. Rendel Harris, "The First Tatian Reading in the Greek New Testament," *Expositor* 8 (1922): 120–9.

[62] For Fuldensis, the awkward alternative would be four consecutive phrases alternating between relative and demonstrative pronouns: *qui* [...] (Matt 27:57), *hic* [...] (Luke 23:51a), *qui* [...] (Luke 23:51c), *hic* [...] (Matt 27:58). In the Dura fragment, Luke 23:51c begins with αυτος rather than a relative pronoun, so the arrangement in Dura needs to be explained by the two other proposed scribal stimulants.

his corollary expectation of the kingdom (Luke 23:51c). With 51b removed, reversing these makes better narrative sense. This transposition is also attested in the Old Latin Codex Colbertinus and the Old Syriac gospels—both of which also relocate 51b, reproducing the scribal irritant proposed above.[63]

In sum, Codex Fuldensis is not a reliable witness to Tatian's intra-pericope (phrase-by-phrase) sequence, and the brief agreement between the Dura fragment and Fuldensis at Luke 23:51 is explicable as a solution to several independently attested scribal irritants. Furthermore, the same reading is attested within the Diatessaron's rival textual traditions in both the Latin West and Syriac East and not supported by the Arabic harmony or any other witnesses to Tatian's intra-pericope harmonization. Most importantly, Fuldensis's inter-pericope sequence—a mostly reliable witness to Tatian's Gospel—differs from the Dura fragment.

7. Eastern Witnesses

All that remains are the Eastern Witnesses: pseudo-Ephrem's *Commentary* and the Arabic gospel harmony.[64] The former weighs decidedly against the Dura fragment's Diatessaronic character while the evidence of the latter is ambiguous.

7.1 Pseudo-Ephrem's *Commentary on the Gospel*

Pseudo-Ephrem's *Commentary on the Gospel* retains pride of place as the surest source for Tatian's Diatessaron.[65] Remarkably, its evidence for the relevant passage has been routinely disregarded in discussions of the Dura fragment. Kraeling dismisses pseudo-Ephrem's adaptation of Luke 23:51 in a footnote and fails to note the *Commentary*'s disagreement with the Dura fragment on the placement of John 19:31-37.[66] Plooij first noted this latter piece of counterevidence and used it to illustrate the relative freedom of the harmony's text tradition.[67] Pseudo-Ephrem's *Commentary* appears in Parker, Taylor, and Goodacre only in their discussion of the Dura fragment's language of composition,[68] and Joosten's rebuttal mentions it only in summarizing this section of their article.[69] Finally, Crawford notes pseudo-Ephrem's divergent placement of John 19:31-37 and suggests that rewriting must have already occurred between the Dura fragment and pseudo-Ephrem's *Commentary*.[70]

---

[63] See n. 72 on the problem with using the Old Syriac gospels as a witness to Tatian's Diatessaron.
[64] The edited works of Ephrem, Aphrahat's *Demonstrations*, pseudo-Ephrem's *Exposition of the Gospel* (not likely Diatessaronic), *The Book of Steps*, *Acts of Thomas*, *Doctrine of Addai*, and the fragments of Mar Aba preserve no relevant textual information.
[65] According to Petersen himself (*Tatian's Diatessaron*, 116), "Ephrem's *Commentary* remains the premier witness to the text of the Diatessaron."
[66] Kraeling, *Greek Fragment of Tatian's Diatessaron*, 14, 21.
[67] Plooij, "A Fragment of Tatian's Diatessaron in Greek," 472.
[68] Parker, Taylor, and Goodacre, "The Dura-Europos Gospel Harmony," 215.
[69] Joosten, "The Dura Parchment and the Diatessaron," 165.
[70] Crawford ("Diatessaron, Canonical or Non-Canonical?" 273n. 64) suggests that the difference in sequence between the Dura fragment and pseudo-Ephrem's *Vorlage* might have arisen during the

In *Comm.* 21, Pseudo-Ephrem discusses the relevant passages, citing four partial verses:[71]

(1)   *Comm.*   21.8   Luke 23:49a
(2)   *Comm.*   21.10–12   John 19:34
(3)–(4) *Comm.*   21.20   Luke 23:50d, 51a

Table 7.8 illustrates the sequence of these verses in relation to Dura, Fuldensis, and the Arabic Harmony.

The evidence for the sequence of pseudo-Ephrem's Gospel is slim but unambiguous. As Table 7.8 demonstrates, the *Commentary* places the lance piercing Jesus's side (John 19:31-37)—with Codex Fuldensis—after Jesus's death but before the introduction of Joseph of Arimathea.[72] Thus, the only sure unit of variation recoverable from the *Commentary* suggests that the Dura parchment is not a Greek fragment of the gospel harmony known to pseudo-Ephrem. Our best evidence for Tatian's Gospel, therefore, weighs decidedly against identifying the Dura fragment with the Diatessaron.

Table 7.9 illustrates a second piece of potentially relevant evidence from pseudo-Ephrem. The Syriac but not the Armenian recension of pseudo-Ephrem's *Commentary* omits Luke's mention of "the plan and the works" of the council. Furthermore, both the Syriac and the Armenian attest, with the Old Syriac gospels, the phrase "with the detractors." A number of methodological obstacles, however, preclude any attempt at using this passage of pseudo-Ephrem to evaluate Dura's relationship to the Diatessaron at Luke 23:51. First, until the relative reliability of the Syriac and Armenian texts can be determined, their conflicting testimonies effectively undermine the *Commentary*'s probative value.[73] Second, there is no indication that pseudo-Ephrem is providing a citation of his Gospel here. Rather, this would be classified as an "adaptation" according to the now-standard taxonomy for representing patristic evidence in

---

translation of the Diatessaron into Syriac. I discuss the reconstruction of this passage for Tatian's Gospel below.

[71] Pseudo-Ephrem's relevant citations are characteristically meager and paraphrastic. Only the paraphrase of Luke 23:50 and 51 overlap with the text of Dura. We are not, however, concerned here with precise wording or intra-pericope harmonization but the relative sequence of the episodes. The evidence for this inter-pericope sequence is unambiguous: pseudo-Ephrem discusses the onlookers first (*Comm.* 21.8), the piercing second (*Comm.* 21.10-12), and finally Joseph of Arimathea (*Comm.* 21.20). Text in Leloir, *Saint Éphrem* (1963), 212–15, 222–3 (Syriac); Leloir, *Saint Éphrem* (1953), 317–20, 325 (Armenian).

[72] Greek Miniscule 72 (Harley 5674 in the British Library) is an eleventh-century tetraevangelion with extensive marginalia. A scholion at Matthew 27:48-49 states that Diadore [sic], Tatian, and John Chrysostom placed a version of John 19:34 ad locum. This is contradicted by pseudo-Ephrem's *Commentary* and unsupported by any of the purported daughter versions. See the text and discussion in Petersen, *Tatian's Diatessaron*, 58–9.

[73] The relationship of these two recensions has been treated most fully in Louis Leloir, "Divergences entre l'original syriaque et la version Arménienne du commentaire d'Éphrem sur le Diatessaron," in *Mélanges Eugène Tisserant*, 7 vols., StT 231-37 (Vatican City: Biblioteca Apostolica Vaticana, 1964), 2:303–31. Also see William L. Petersen, "Some Remarks on the Integrity of Ephrem's Commentary on the Diatessaron," StPatr 20 (1989): 197–202; repr. Jan Krans and Joseph Verheyden, eds., *Patristic and Text-Critical Studies: The Collected Essays of William L. Petersen* (Leiden: Brill, 2012), 103–9; and see Lange, *The Portrayal of Christ*, 26–68.

Table 7.8 Sequence of Pseudo-Ephrem, Dura, Fuldensis, and Arabic

	Pseudo-Ephrem	Fuldensis	Dura	Arabic
Jesus's Death	Luke 23:49a	(Luke 23:49a)		(Luke 23:49a)
		Mark 15:40d	Matt 27:56c	Matt 27:56
		Matt 27:56	Mark 15:40d	Mark 15:40d
		Mark 15:41a		
			Luke 23:49b	Mark 15:41cd
		Luke 23:49c	Luke 23:49c	Luke 23:49c
Piercing		John 19:34		
		John 19:31-37		
Jesus's Burial			Luke 23:54	
		Matt 27:57a	Mark 15:42	Mark 15:42
				Luke 23:50a
		Matt 27:57b (+dives)	Matt 27:57b	Matt 27:57b
		Mark 15:43c	Luke 23:50c	Mark 15:43c
		Luke 23:51b	Luke 23:51b	Luke 23:51b
		Matt 27:57d/Luke 23:50b	Matt 27:57d/Luke 23:50b	Matt 27:57d/Luke 23:50b
	Luke 23:50d	Luke 23:50d (+vir)	Luke 23:50d	Luke 23:50d
		Matt 27:57e	John 19:38c	John 19:38c/Matt 27:57e
		John 19:38d	John 19:38d	John 19:38d
		Luke 23:51c	Luke 23:51c	Luke 23:51a
	Luke 23:51a	Luke 23:51a	Luke 23:51a	Luke 23:51c

Source: Text of Fuldensis 171-72 from Zola, "Tatian's Diatessaron in Latin," 132–4; Ranke, *Codex Fuldensis*, 156–7. Text of Arabic 52.21-27 from Augustinus Ciasca, *Tatiani Evangeliorum harmoniae arabice* (Rome: Typographia Polyglotta, 1888), 198 (Arabic), 93 (Latin); A.-S. Marmardji, *Diatessaron de Tatien: Texte arabe établi, traduit en français, collationné avec les anciennes versions syriaques* (Beyrouth: Imprimerie Catholique, 1935), 500-1.

textual criticism.[74] Even if the Syriac (rather than Armenian) text could be judged to reflect the initial form of pseudo-Ephrem's *Commentary*, the omission of τῇ βουλῇ καὶ τῇ πράξει αὐτῶν would probably be unreliable. Finally, the Dura fragment breaks off before indicating whether or not it agrees with the local variant "with the detractors."

7.2 Arabic Harmony

Finally, the Arabic Diatessaron must be consulted.[75] Our comparatively elementary understanding of this gospel harmony demands caution. The Arabic Diatessaron

---

[74] For methods of mitigating the uncertainties intrinsic to the use of patristic citations in textual criticism, see Carroll Osburn, "Methodology in Identifying Patristic Citations in NT Textual Criticism," *NovT* 47 (2005): 313–43.

[75] Thank you to Fady Atef Mekhael for his help in assessing the Arabic Diatessaron. Without his linguistic expertise and knowledge of the Arabic Bible, this project would not have been possible.

Table 7.9 Luke 23:51 in Dura, Pseudo-Ephrem, and the Old Syriac

Luke 23:51 NA[28]	οὗτος οὐκ ἦν συγκατατεθειμένος τῇ βουλῇ καὶ τῇ πράξει αὐτῶν—ἀπὸ Ἀριμαθαίας πόλεως τῶν Ἰουδαίων, ὃς προσεδέχετο τὴν βασιλείαν τοῦ θεοῦ,	This one did not agree with their plan and deed—from Arimathea, the city of the Jews—who was expecting the kingdom of God
Dura Fragment	και αυτος προσεδεχετο την βασιλειαν του Θεου ουτος ουκ ην συγκατατιθεμενος τη βουλη	and he was expecting the kingdom of God—he was not agreeing with the plan
Pseudo-Ephrem, *Comm.* 21:20 (Syr)	ܘܐܚܪܢܐ ܝܘܣܦ ܐܝܟܐ ܕܠܐ ܐܫܬܘܝ ܥܡ ܐܟܠܝ ܩܪܨܐ	The other [Joseph] was a just (man) who did not agree with the slanderers
Pseudo-Ephrem, *Comm.* 21:20 (Arm)	Եւ միւս եւ դարձեալ արդար էր,[a] զի ոչ եղեւ յար ի խորհուրդս և ի գործս նոցա ընդ չարախաւսսն.	And again the other [Joseph] was just, because he did not agree with their plan and works with the slanderers
Luke 23:51 syr[sc]	ܘܗܘ ܡܣܟܐ ܗܘܐ ܠܡܠܟܘܬܐ ܕܫܡܝܐ ܗܘ ܓܒܪܐ ܕܠܐ ܐܫܬܘܝ ܒܨܒܝܢܗܘܢ ܥܡ ܐܟܠܝ ܩܪܨܐ	And he was expecting the kingdom of heaven, this man who did not agree to the plan with the slanderers.

Source: Pseudo-Ephrem text from Leloir, *Saint Éphrem* (1963), 222 (Syriac); Leloir, *Saint Éphrem* (1953), 325 (Armenian).
[a]Armenian MS B omits the verb.

survives as two recensions in eight manuscripts, and no critical edition exists.[76] Unfortunately, the two quasi-diplomatic editions published by Augustinus Ciasca and A.-S. Marmardji are deeply flawed.[77] Most importantly, the Arabic Diatessaron's ardent defenders concede that it has undergone significant revision—frequently toward the Syriac Peshitta.[78] Further study is required to evaluate how much of the second-century gospel is preserved in these twelfth- to nineteenth-century manuscripts. Unsurprisingly, the text of the Arabic Diatessaron is not merely a translation of the Dura fragment. We will consider, therefore, the relevant inter- and intra-pericope sequences of the Arabic harmony in light of our other sources for Tatian's Gospel.

---

[76] The most up-to-date catalog of the manuscripts can be found in Giuliano Lancioni and N. Peter Joosse, "The Arabic Diatessaron Project: Digitalizing Encoding Lemmatization," *Journal of Religion, Media and Digital Culture* 5 (2016): 205–27. Also see N. Peter Joosse, "An Introduction to the Arabic Diatessaron," *OrChr* 83 (1999): 80–5.

[77] Ciasca, *Tatiani Evangeliorum Harmoniae*; Marmardji, *Diatessaron de Tatien*. For a discussion of their flaws, see Joosse, "An Introduction to the Arabic Diatessaron," 86–91.

[78] Tjitze Baarda, "An Archaic Element in the Arabic Diatessaron? (T^A 46:18 = John XV 2)," *NovT* 17 (1975): 151; repr. in *Early Transmission of Words of Jesus: Thomas, Tatian, and the Text of the New Testament*, ed. J. Helderman and S. J. Noorda (Amsterdam: VU Boekhandel/Uitgeverij, 1983), 173; Tjitze Baarda, "To the Roots of the Syriac Diatessaron Tradition (T^A 25: 1-3)," *NovT* 28 (1986): 3; Joosse, "An Introduction to the Arabic Diatessaron," 120.

7.3 Arabic Inter-Pericope Sequence

As shown in Table 7.8, on the inter-pericope level, the Arabic harmony and the Dura fragment agree against pseudo-Ephrem's *Commentary*[Syr+Arm] and Codex Fuldensis in not locating John 19:31-37, the piercing of Jesus's side, after the women at the cross.[79] A methodological digression is necessary. In order to determine whether the Dura fragment is a witness to Tatian's Gospel, the text of the latter must be reconstructed *ad locum* independent of the Dura fragment. To cite the coincidence of the Arabic and the Dura fragment against pseudo-Ephrem and Fuldensis would beg the question since the value of the Dura fragment for reconstructing Tatian's Gospel is precisely the matter under debate. Obviously, the Dura fragment cannot be used to reconstruct the very standard by which it is to be evaluated. Tatian's inter-pericope sequence must, therefore, be reconstructed on the basis of our relevant sources (i.e., pseudo-Ephrem, Codex Fuldensis, and the Arabic harmony) before comparing it with the Dura fragment.

Given this approach, the inter-pericope sequence of Tatian's Gospel weighs against identifying the Dura fragment as Tatianic. As all parties agree, pseudo-Ephrem's *Commentary* remains the surest source for Tatian's text. It is probably the oldest and least corrupt witness to the sequence of Tatian's Gospel. Two centuries later and halfway across the world, Codex Fuldensis provides an independent witness to Tatian's inter-pericope sequence. For the passage in question, these two witnesses from different ends of the Mediterranean agree against the solitary testimony of the Arabic harmony, translated from a vulgatized Syriac *Vorlage* half a millennium later.[80] It is only reasonable to reconstruct Tatian's inter-pericope sequence ad locum according to the joint testimony of pseudo-Ephrem and Codex Fuldensis against the Arabic. The only relevant datum recoverable from pseudo-Ephrem and Fuldensis, therefore, suggests that the Dura fragment is not a witness to Tatian's Gospel.

7.4 Arabic Intra-Pericope Sequence

The reliability of the Arabic harmony's intra-pericope sequence as a witness to Tatian's Gospel has not, to my knowledge, been systematically evaluated. Until a critical edition of the Arabic is available, any such study would probably be premature. We proceed,

---

[79] We do not, however, know if both the Dura and Arabic harmonies relocated John 19:31-37 to the same place.

[80] Since the Arabic harmony was translated from a Syriac Diatessaron which closely resembled the inter-pericope sequence of pseudo-Ephrem's *Vorlage*, the deviant sequence in the Arabic is probably the result of a later corruption in the Syriac-Arabic branch of the Diatessaron's textual history. As discussed above, the occurrence of such corruptions in the half millennium separating pseudo-Ephrem and the Arabic harmony is uncontroversial. Crawford ("The Diatessaron, Canonical or Non-canonical?" 273n. 64) seems to acknowledge the secondary position of the Arabic harmony in the eastern/Syriac branch of the text tradition by describing the Arabic's relocation of this pericope as "further editing [of the Syriac Diatessaron]." Even if one accepted Dura as Tatianic, therefore, the agreement of the Arabic sequence with Dura would not be genetic and so without probative value for reconstructing Tatian's sequence at this point of variation. On the Syriac origin of the Arabic Diatessaron, see Joosse, "An Introduction to the Arabic Diatessaron," 98–109.

Table 7.10 Joosten's Element B in the Dura Fragment and Arabic Diatessaron

		NA 28th	Peshitta	Old Syriac	
Dura	βουλευτης υπαρχων	βουλευτὴς ὑπάρχων	ܒܘܠܘܛܐ	ܒܘܠܘܛܐ ܗܘܐ	Luke 23:50c
Arabic	وجيه	εὐσχήμων βουλευτής	ܡܝܩܪܐ ܒܘܠܘܛܐ	ܡܝܩܪܐ ܒܘܠܘܛܐ[a]	Mark 15:43c

Source: Arabic text from Ciasca, *Tatiani Evangeliorum Harmoniae*, 198 (Arabic), 93 (Latin); Marmardji, *Diatessaron de Tatien*, 500–1. The Arabic texts in both Ciasca (MSS A & B) and Marmardji (MS E) have been consulted and there is no significant variation for any passage discussed here.

[a]The Curetonian Syriac and Sinai New Finds Palimpsest Gospels are not extant for this portion of Mark.

against the Hortian dictum, to consider in isolation the relationship of the intra-pericope sequence of the Arabic and Dura harmonies.

Let us first revisit Joosten's elements B and F since, as with the western harmonies, Joosten's presentation of the data elides the citation of different gospels in at least one place.[81] As above, this schema masks a substantive difference between the Greek and Arabic harmonies. Following this clarification, the remaining agreement must be considered in light of the complete data set.

As Table 7.10 illustrates, in Joosten's element B, the Dura fragment gives a verbatim citation of Luke 23:50c while the Arabic harmony reads وجيه = ܡܝܩܪܐ = εὐσχήμων from Mark 15:43c and provides no translation of the ambiguous element مجلس = ܒܘܠܘܛܐ = βουλευτής. Joosten's Diatessaronic sequence is thus reduced to "C – D – E – F – G" with "F – G" (John 19:38c and 19:38d) constrained by narrative logic—an agreement of only four out of thirteen movable source units.[82] We turn next to Joosten's element F.

As Table 7.11 likewise illustrates, the Dura fragment provides a verbatim citation of John 19:38c. Unfortunately, the source of the Arabic Diatessaron here is genuinely ambiguous. Although the Arabic more closely resembles the Johannine passage in Greek, the Arabic harmony is the translation of a Syriac *Vorlage*.[83] The Arabic attests a conjunction with some manuscripts of Matthew against John but both gospels in Syriac attest the copula ܗܘܐ and the noun ܬܠܡܝܕܐ = μαθητής rather than the distinctive passive verb ܐܬܬܠܡܕ = ἐμαθητεύθη. The Arabic lacks anything corresponding to the Matthean pronouns or the Syriac attempts at rendering the Johannine participle. The conjunction alone is insufficient evidence to identify the citation with Matthew rather than John and so I have left this undetermined in Table 7.8.

---

[81] The word وافي before Matthew 27:57b in the Arabic harmony should probably read وفي and may be a translation of ܘܗܐ = καὶ ἰδοὺ from Luke 23:50a (see Harklean ad locum; καὶ ἰδοὺ is omitted in the Peshitta and Old Syriac). This would introduce a further deviation from the Dura fragment not noted in my chart.

[82] The total number thirteen here again counts John 19:38c and 19:38d as a single unit, as seen in Table 7.8.

[83] Joosse, "An Introduction to the Arabic Diatessaron," 100–3.

Table 7.11 Joosten's Element F in the Dura Fragment and Arabic Diatessaron

		NA 28th	Peshitta	Old Syriac[a]	Harklean	
Dura	ων μαθητης του Ιησου	ὢν μαθητὴς τοῦ Ἰησοῦ	ܡܢ ܬܠܡܝܕܗ ܕܝܫܘܥ ܗܘܐ	–	ܕܐܝܬܘܗܝ ܗܘܐ ܬܠܡܝܕܗ ܕܝܫܘܥ	John 19:38c
		ὃς καὶ αὐτὸς ἐμαθητεύθη τῷ Ἰησοῦ	ܗܘ ܕܐܦ ܗܘ ܐܬܬܠܡܕ ܗܘܐ ܠܝܫܘܥ	(ܘ)ܐܦ ܗܘ ܬܠܡܝܕܗ ܗܘܐ ܕܝܫܘܥ	ܗܘ ܕܐܦ ܗܘ ܗܘܐ ܐܬܬܠܡܕ ܠܝܫܘܥ	Matt 27:57e
Arabic		وكان تلميذ ايسوع				John 19:38c/ Matt 27:57e

Source: Arabic text from Ciasca, *Tatiani Evangeliorum Harmoniae*, 198 (Arabic), 93 (Latin); Marmardji, *Diatessaron de Tatien*, 500–501.
[a] John 13:38 is not extant in the Old Syriac. Only the Syriac Sinaiticus and Sinai New Finds Palimpsest are extant for Matt 27:57. I have transcribed the latter from Sinai NF 39 f.11v and the only variant reading is an omitted conjunction, noted above in parentheses.

Considered in light of the complete data set, the Dura fragment and the Arabic harmony bear only a superficial similarity.[84] As shown in Table 7.8, Joosten's string of nine agreements is reduced to four out of thirteen source units. Collating the Arabic harmony against the Dura fragment reveals two substitutions, one addition, one omission, and one transposition. Some agreement is expected of any two attempts at harmonizing shared source material, but a string of four out of thirteen source units does not justify positing a genetic relationship between the Dura fragment and the Arabic Diatessaron more proximate than the canonical Gospels themselves.

8. Conclusion

A year after its discovery, the Dura fragment was uncritically accepted as Diatessaronic. Eighty years later, the Dura fragment is not considered merely Diatessaronic but treated as a fragment of the Diatessaron itself. I have attempted to demonstrate that, granting the assumptions of the Petersen method, Joosten has not identified a Diatessaronic feature in the Dura fragment. Then, apart from the Petersen method, I showed that the inter-pericope sequence of Codex Fuldensis weighs against identifying the Dura fragment as a piece of Tatian's Diatessaron. Finally, the two eastern witnesses were considered on their own merits. First, the only datum derivable from pseudo-Ephrem's *Commentary*, the most secure source for Tatian's text, corroborates Codex Fuldensis and weighs against the Dura fragment's Diatessaronic character. Second, the Arabic harmony, a much later and less certain source, offers a string of only four agreements out of thirteen. In conclusion, there is no firm evidence to support identifying the Dura fragment with Tatian's Diatessaron. The evidentiary basis for any judgment is

---

[84] The term "superficial" is intended to acknowledge real but not meaningful agreements.

undeniably slim and a new source may overturn our verdict. As it stands, however, our only reliable data for Tatian's text weigh against this identification.

Addendum: Gospel Parallels with the Dura Fragment

Table 7.12 Subdivision of NA[28] Gospel Texts that Overlap with Dura

Matt 27:55-57	Mark 15:40-43	Luke 23:49-51, 54	John 19:38
⁵⁵ᵃᵃἮσαν δὲ ἐκεῖ γυναῖκες πολλαὶ ἀπὸ μακρόθεν θεωροῦσαι, ᵇαἵτινες ἠκολούθησαν τῷ Ἰησοῦ ἀπὸ τῆς Γαλιλαίας διακονοῦσαι αὐτῷ· ⁵⁶ᵃἐν αἷς ἦν Μαρία ἡ Μαγδαληνὴ ᵇκαὶ Μαρία ἡ τοῦ Ἰακώβου καὶ Ἰωσὴφ μήτηρ ᶜκαὶ ἡ μήτηρ τῶν υἱῶν Ζεβεδαίου. ⁵⁷ ᵈὈψίας δὲ γενομένης ᵇἦλθεν ἄνθρωπος πλούσιος ᶜἀπὸ Ἀριμαθαίας, ᵈτοὔνομα Ἰωσήφ, ᵉὃς καὶ αὐτὸς ἐμαθητεύθη τῷ Ἰησοῦ·	⁴⁰ᵃἮσαν δὲ καὶ γυναῖκες ἀπὸ μακρόθεν θεωροῦσαι, ᵇἐν αἷς καὶ Μαρία ἡ Μαγδαληνὴ ᶜκαὶ Μαρία ἡ Ἰακώβου τοῦ μικροῦ καὶ Ἰωσῆτος μήτηρ ᵈκαὶ Σαλώμη, ⁴¹ᵃαἳ ὅτε ἦν ἐν τῇ Γαλιλαίᾳ ἠκολούθουν αὐτῷ ᵇκαὶ διηκόνουν αὐτῷ, ᶜκαὶ ἄλλαι πολλαὶ ᵈαἱ συναναβᾶσαι αὐτῷ εἰς Ἱεροσόλυμα. ⁴²ᵃΚαὶ ἤδη ὀψίας γενομένης, ᵇἐπεὶ ἦν παρασκευή, ὅ ἐστιν προσάββατον, ⁴³ᵃἐλθὼν Ἰωσὴφ ᵇὁ ἀπὸ Ἀριμαθαίας ᶜεὐσχήμων βουλευτής, ᵈὃς καὶ αὐτὸς ἦν προσδεχόμενος τὴν βασιλείαν τοῦ θεοῦ, ᵉτολμήσας εἰσῆλθεν πρὸς τὸν Πιλᾶτον καὶ ᾐτήσατο τὸ σῶμα τοῦ Ἰησοῦ.	⁴⁹ᵃεἱστήκεισαν δὲ πάντες οἱ γνωστοὶ αὐτῷ μακρόθεν, ᵇκαὶ γυναῖκες αἱ συνακολουθοῦσαι αὐτῷ ἀπὸ τῆς Γαλιλαίας, ᶜὁρῶσαι ταῦτα. ⁵⁰ᵃΚαὶ ἰδοὺ ᵇἀνὴρ ὀνόματι Ἰωσὴφ ᶜβουλευτὴς ὑπάρχων, ᵈἀνὴρ ἀγαθὸς καὶ δίκαιος ⁵¹ᵃοὗτος οὐκ ἦν συγκατατεθειμένος τῇ βουλῇ καὶ τῇ πράξει αὐτῶν ᵇἀπὸ Ἀριμαθαίας πόλεως τῶν Ἰουδαίων, ᶜὃς προσεδέχετο τὴν βασιλείαν τοῦ θεοῦ, ⁵⁴καὶ ἡμέρα ἦν παρασκευῆς, καὶ σάββατον ἐπέφωσκεν.	³⁸ ᵃΜετὰ δὲ ταῦτα ᵇἠρώτησεν τὸν Πιλᾶτον Ἰωσὴφ ἀπὸ Ἀριμαθαίας, ᶜὢν μαθητὴς τοῦ Ἰησοῦ ᵈκεκρυμμένος δὲ διὰ τὸν φόβον τῶν Ἰουδαίων, ᵉἵνα ἄρῃ τὸ σῶμα τοῦ Ἰησοῦ· καὶ ἐπέτρεψεν ὁ Πιλᾶτος. ἦλθεν οὖν καὶ ἦρεν τὸ σῶμα αὐτοῦ.

8

Before and After

Some Notes on the Pre- and Post-History of Codex Fuldensis

Ulrich B. Schmid

Abstract

Initially compiled by Victor of Capua in 546 CE, Codex Fuldensis has attracted special attention because its gospel text, while an early example of Jerome's Vulgate, is in the form of Tatian's Diatessaron, a second-century gospel harmony. This chapter concerns what Fuldensis's textual and paratextual clues reveal about its production (pre-history) and dissemination (post-history). The first part presents evidence from the *capitula* and Eusebian canons and sections to deduce that Victor likely had access to at least one non-harmonized Vulgate Gospel book whose text and form shared features with manuscripts like Codex Amiatinus and the Lindisfarne Gospels. The second part uses macrolevel sequence analysis to illustrate how a chain of "successive editorial interventions" that begin with Fuldensis as a base-text and propagate through its direct Latin offspring into the western vernacular harmonies can serve to establish the medieval vernacular harmonies' ultimate dependence upon Codex Fuldensis. The essay's conclusion proposes that the best avenue for identifying the nature of Fuldensis's unknown harmonized source lies in pursuing the origin of the non-Vulgate readings of its text and *capitula*.

1. Introduction

As a hand-written object consisting of about 1,000 pages, Codex Fuldensis[1] shares the main characteristic of every manuscript, that is, it is one of a kind. However, as a

---

[1] A full set of images is available under https://fuldig.hs-fulda.de/viewer/image/PPN325289808/1/. The only edition available is Ernst Ranke, *Codex Fuldensis: Novum Testamentum Latine Interprete Hieronymo ex Manuscripto Victoris Capuani* (Marburg: N. G. Elwert, 1868), available under http://reader.digitale-sammlungen.de/de/fs1/object/display/bsb10272027_00001.html.

Latin manuscript from the mid-sixth century containing all of the New Testament, it brings even more unique elements to the table, attracting the attention of scholars with different backgrounds and interests. In the context of the present collection of chapters, undoubtedly the interest lies almost exclusively with the unique feature of a gospel harmony found on 332 of Codex Fuldensis's pages, replacing the four Gospels in what otherwise appears to be a straight-forward New Testament manuscript encompassing all other twenty-three writings from the biblical canon.[2] This harmony is not just the oldest complete physical object of that sort that has come down to us today, but is also legitimately related to an even older gospel harmony from the second half of the second century, the original text of which is mostly lost: Tatian's Diatessaron. What exactly is this relationship? How can the two be linked? And eventually what light can Codex Fuldensis's harmony shed on the design and the text of its famous precursor?

These were and still are the questions of Diatessaronic scholarship when dealing with Codex Fuldensis and they revolve around the pre-history of its harmony text. However, since Codex Fuldensis consists of not only a harmony but also many paratexts accompanying the harmony, as well as other New Testament books with some paratexts of their own, there are more questions that have been asked and continue to be asked. Many of the additional questions come from students of the Latin Bible and involve codicology, the textual history of the Vulgate, as well as the art history of canon tables. The answers to these questions help a great deal to properly situate the unique artifact containing this harmony in time and space, especially when it comes to potentially reconstructing the logistics that went into actually producing the codex in general and the harmony more specifically. Hence, the first part of my chapter aims to take stock of where we stand concerning the immediate context of Codex Fuldensis: how were the individual elements found therein combined and arranged? What sources were used? And what can we reasonably know or infer about the characteristics of the harmony source in particular?

The second part of my chapter is devoted to the post-history of Codex Fuldensis. Its harmony has generated a substantial offspring in Latin through the ninth and especially in the twelfth and thirteenth centuries, whose filiation can be reasonably established. However, there is a substantial number of western vernacular harmonies from the thirteenth century onward that in the past have been viewed as useful for reconstructing Tatian's Diatessaron. Their relationship to Codex Fuldensis is up for debate. Can they be aligned with the harmony as it stems from Codex Fuldensis? Or is there reason to believe that the vernacular tradition, at least in part, may hark back to a harmony source prior to Codex Fuldensis?

In the first part, I will largely draw on and summarize previous scholarship that appears less accessible and therefore in danger of being overlooked.[3] The evidence discussed is mostly generated from the codicology of the manuscript and its paratexts. In the second part, I will try to engage in textual analysis of the harmony. When it

---

[2] Actually, Codex Fuldensis also includes Paul's letter to the Laodiceans, which is considered extracanonical in most churches.

[3] Bonifatius Fischer, "Bibelausgaben des frühen Mittelalters," in *La Bibbia nell'alto Medioevo*, Settimane di studio del centro italiano di studi sull'alto medioevo 10 (Spoleto: Presso la Sede del Centro, 1963), 519–600, esp. 545–57; repr. in B. Fischer, *Lateinische Bibelhandschriften im Frühen Mittelalter*, AGLB 11 (Freiburg im Breisgau: Herder, 1985), 35–100. Johannes Rathofer, "Zur Heimatfrage des althochdeutschen Tatian: Das Votum der Handschriften," *AION* (sezione germanica) 14

comes to comparing harmonies across language boundaries, the paratextual elements that are so rich in Codex Fuldensis rarely ever translate. Hence we have to utilize textual comparisons across harmonies in order to make our case. I will evaluate Nicholas Zola's "Leitfehler [method] to Test Dependence on Codex Fuldensis"[4] as a starting point from which to move on to a method that is more akin to the peculiarities of the harmony text. For lack of a better expression, I call it the "genealogy of successive editorial interventions." The method argues that ultimate dependence on Codex Fuldensis among western vernacular harmony texts is likely to be established through identifying chains of editorial changes that start off with Codex Fuldensis as a basetext, preferably include editorial modifications within Fuldensis's direct offspring, and eventually end up in the vernacular harmony with a special twist of its own. In my conclusion, I will sum up my findings and sketch a few methodological observations I find useful for utilizing Codex Fuldensis as a potential source to the Diatessaron.

2. The Pre-History of Codex Fuldensis

Codex Fuldensis is one of the few manuscripts from late antiquity that can be dated very precisely, that is, not just to a year or a year and a month but to a year and a month and a day. Actually, the manuscript carries three such dates that according to Bonifatius Fischer relate to three successive events of proofreading the manuscript.[5] Victor, bishop of Capua, who commissioned the manuscript, signed it for the first time after all three parts—(1) the harmony with its paratexts, (2) the Pauline Epistles with their paratexts, and (3) Acts, the Catholic Epistles, and the Apocalypse with incomplete paratexts—had been finished, on April 19, 546 CE; the signature is found at the end of the Apocalypse.[6] The chronologically second signature, dated May 2, 546, is found after the book of Acts and most likely relates to the addition of paratexts to this book inserted on a new quire before Acts, which caused all the subsequent quire numbers to be corrected and moved up by one. Victor's final signature is dated April 12, 547, and is, again, found after the Apocalypse. It took Victor almost a year to complete the second proofreading event pertaining to the entire manuscript. One of the reasons for this extended time period may be seen in the extra work that Victor and

---

(1971): 7–104; Donatien De Bruyne, "La préface du Diatessaron latin avant Victor de Capoue," *RBén* 39 (1927): 5–11; Franco Bolgiani, *Vittore di Capua e il "Diatessaron"* (Turin: Accademia delle Scienze, 1962); Theodor Zahn, *Tatians Diatessaron*, FGNK 1 (Erlangen: Andreas Deichert, 1881); Heinrich Joseph Vogels, *Beiträge zur Geschichte des Diatessaron im Abendland* (Münster: Aschendorff, 1919); Regina Hausmann, *Die theologischen Handschriften der Hessischen Landesbibliothek Fulda bis zum Jahr 1600: Codices Bonifatiani 1–3, Aa 1–145a* (Wiesbaden: Harrassowitz, 1992), 3–7; Patrick McGurk, "The Canon Tables in the Book of Lindisfarne and in the Codex Fuldensis of St. Victor of Capua," *JTS* 6 (1955): 192–8; John Chapman, *Notes on the Early History of the Vulgate Gospels* (Oxford: Clarendon Press, 1908), 78–95.

[4] See his "Tatian's Diatessaron in Latin: A New Edition and Translation of Codex Fuldensis" (PhD diss., Baylor University, 2014), esp. 154.

[5] Fischer, "Bibelausgaben," 546–8.

[6] Unfortunately it is no longer visible due to chemical treatment of the parchment. On the signatures, see also Kirsten Wallenwein, *"Subscriptiones* in karolingischen Codices," in *Karolingische Klöster: Wissenstransfer und kulturelle Innovation*, ed. J. Becker, J. Licht, and S. Weinfurter, Materiale Textkulturen 4 (Berlin: de Gruyter, 2015), 23–33, esp. 23 (ebook version is freely available).

his scribe likely decided to carry out before the manuscript achieved its status as final product. Fischer associates the completion of several additional paratexts that filled up empty pages to this phase.[7] But more importantly, a series of corrections to the Pauline Epistles that were executed by Victor himself appear to betray the use of a second copy of Paul's letters different from the copy that had been used for the transcription of the main text. Hence, it might be possible to imagine a time of diligent text comparison during this proofreading period that could have slowed down the entire process.

Moving on to the harmony part of Codex Fuldensis, we find it prefixed with a seven- page *praefatio* (ff. 1r–4r) and an excerpt from Jerome's *Novum Opus* (f. 4v) on an unnumbered quire. In addition, we find the canon tables (ff. 5–12) on two gatherings and a series of 182 numbered *capitula* on a quaternio (ff. 13–20). The harmony is then presented on 16 quinions (ff. 21–180), with the final 2.5 pages originally left empty but subsequently filled with a list of pericopes from the Pauline Epistles that follow. The harmony text is marginally equipped with chapter numbers referencing the *capitula* list and Eusebian section numbers referencing the canon tables. In addition, the running text is interspersed with abbreviated Gospel sigla indicating the Gospel source(s) for the following text portion.

In his *praefatio* Victor tells the readers two salient points concerning the harmony. First of all, he informs us that "by chance" (*fortuito*) he came across "a gospel harmony" (*unum ex quattuor euangelium*) and that "it lacked a title," which is why he could "not find the name of an author" (*absente titulo non inuenirem nomen auctoris*). To remedy this situation Victor researched the case and found in Eusebius of Caesarea (*Letter to Carpianus*[8] and *Ecclesiastical History*[9]) the necessary information to conclude that the author likely was Tatian, the pupil of Justin Martyr. Second, Victor mentions the fact that the harmony also lacked the Eusebian canon apparatus and that he himself took great pains to add the numbers and references for parallel passages with the intent of allowing easy comparison with the text of the canonical Gospels in order to settle cases of doubt concerning the exact wording at any given point in the harmony. Unfortunately, there is no further direct information to harvest from the *praefatio* that would help us uncover more context for Victor's extraordinary find. Hence, scholarship has sought instead to further elucidate the sources that Victor utilized and the logistics that were employed to craft this amazing piece of late antique Bible editing and book production.

Starting with the Eusebian apparatus[10]—after all, this is the only element that was clearly the work of Victor—we have basically two absolutely necessary elements: (1) the canon tables providing the collected numbers for the sets of parallel passages; and (2) the marginal numbers alongside the Gospel text that act as a referencing system,

---

[7] Fischer, "Bibelausgaben," 547, 553–4.
[8] Since D. De Bruyne's article in 1927 (see n. 3), we are aware of the fact that Victor was not using a Greek copy but a rare Latin translation of this letter.
[9] J. Chapman had already, in 1908, pointed out that Victor was using Rufinus's translation of Book 4 of Eusebius's *Church History*; cf. his "Notes," 93.
[10] This is terminology suggested by Thomas O'Loughlin, "Harmonizing the Truth: Eusebius and the Problem of the Four Gospels," *Traditio* 65 (2010): 1–29, esp. 6–7. O'Loughlin also offers an extended explanation of the entire Canon apparatus with examples (2–6).

allowing readers to find the same passages in a standard four-gospel codex. We also have one "bonus" element: an explanation of how to operate the system.[11] Eusebius of Caesarea, who authored this particular system, explains in his *Letter to Carpianus*[12] that there are nine categories (tables) of parallel passages[13] in the Gospels plus an additional tenth category (table) encompassing the leftovers, so to speak, the *Sondergut* of each Gospel. Each Gospel is subdivided into numbered passages of unequal length based on its placement in one of these categories. The respective numbers are added in the margins to the Gospels' texts and are accompanied by a second number penned in red (διὰ κινναβάρεως) that ranges from one to ten, indicating the respective table wherein the section number is found alongside the numbers representing the passages parallel to it. Jerome decided to include the Eusebian apparatus in his edition of the Vulgate Gospels. In his letter to Damasus that has become known by its opening words *Novum Opus*, he also explains the system very much like Eusebius did.[14] It is worth emphasizing that Eusebius as well as Jerome only mention two numbers in the margin, one for the Gospel section and one for the canon table. As a result, in the versions of Eusebius and Jerome, the canon tables serve as the navigational hub for the separate Gospels by listing the numbers for parallel passages from the individual gospels alongside one another. In other words, the user begins by reading one Gospel, then turns to the appropriate prefatory table to find the numbers for parallel passages, and finally flips to the other Gospels to read the parallels.

In order for this system to work for the harmony, Victor had to keep the numbers for the parallels exactly the same as he found them in his source, that is, every section of harmony text had to be identified according to its proper position in the Eusebian canon apparatus; otherwise no comparison between harmony and separate Gospels would be possible. As a source for these numbers, any Gospel book containing this system, whether in Greek or in Latin, would do. As for the design of the canon tables proper, the situation is different, because the sequence of the harmony has pushed the parallel passages out of their quasi-canonical positions within the tables. Equally troubling, some parallels found in the Eusebian apparatus are not applicable to the harmony, because the latter has omitted the respective passages. Even more confusing, quite a few parallels occur more than once in the harmony, because the Gospel text covered by them is repeated or chopped up into smaller units that appear nonconsecutively in the harmonized text. As a result, the canon tables had to be significantly modified.[15] For example, the first canon (Matt, Mark, Luke, John) typically contains 71 parallels and the second (Matt, Mark, Luke) contains 109. As a result of the text's harmonized sequence, Victor ended up with 124 entries for the first and 181 for the second canon.[16]

---

[11] It is quite conceivable, though, that users could have familiarized themselves with the system through thoroughly studying the manuscript in front of them when exploring all its elements.
[12] This letter functions as an introduction and often prefaces the canon tables in Greek Gospel books. It is reproduced in the introductory material of NA[28], pp. 89*–90*.
[13] Matt-Mark-Luke-John; Matt-Mark-Luke; Matt-Luke-John; Matt-Mark-John; Matt-Luke; Matt-Mark; Matt-John; Mark-Luke; Luke-John.
[14] Hence this *Novum Opus* introduction is found in many Latin Gospel books.
[15] J. Rathofer has studied this in some detail in his "Heimatfrage," 30–44.
[16] Numbers are taken from Rathofer, "Heimatfrage," 32.

Since repetition of parallels is also a dominant feature for the third and fourth canons of the Eusebian apparatus, Victor had to overcome two problems. The first problem is actually self-inflicted and has to do with the fact that he decided to follow a sixteen-page layout. P. McGurk[17] has demonstrated that this layout closely matches that of the Lindisfarne Gospels (British Library, Cotton, MS Nero D IV[18]) and thus partakes in a larger tradition that C. Nordenfalk has described in his classic *Die spätantiken Kanontafeln*.[19] What McGurk missed, however, is that Victor, by slavishly following this model, had to squeeze all these deviating concordances of the ten canons into the sixteen pages, arriving at a completely disproportionate arrangement of lines per table.[20] This is strong additional evidence that Victor indeed followed the sixteen-page layout despite it being designed for the canonical Gospels while not particularly suitable for the harmony requirements. The second problem has to do with recurring parallel passages in different parts of the harmony, and for this Victor found a decent solution by adding *capitula* numbers to the canon tables in order to assign any of the (recurring) parallels to their proper place within the sequence of the harmony. This is a clear indicator that the *capitula* served an important purpose for the usability of the canon tables in Victor's design.

Before we take a closer look at the *capitula* in Codex Fuldensis, we should deal first with the marginal numbers. As has been mentioned already, the system typically requires only two numbers in the margin, that is, a (sequential) number for the Gospel section (e.g., for Matt numbers 1–355) and a number for the canon (1–10), and this is what we find in normal Greek Gospel books, like, for example, GA 011, 026, 031. In the inner and outer margins of Codex Fuldensis, however, we have, in addition to those two numbers, all the numbers from the other Gospels that are part of a given set of parallel passages. In other words, the numbers for the parallel sections used in each passage of the harmony are not only found in the tables at the front of the codex but on each page right at the very spot. There is actually no need to consult the tables if one wishes to compare the harmony to the text of the Gospels in their usual form.

This feature of the Eusebian apparatus, however, is not restricted to Codex Fuldensis but is actually found in a surprising number of the earliest extant Vulgate Gospel books as well as in some Greek Gospel books.[21] The Latin and Greek examples I have seen so far suggest that for the most part there is a significant distinction in the design of the feature. On the one hand, we have a vertical design that is effectively expanding on the normal canon numbers that consist of section number (black ink) and table number (red ink) that are placed in the margins next to text passage they refer to. Additional numbers from the other Gospels that form a parallel are then simply written underneath the original pair, which is why this design is operated vertically

---

[17] "Canon Tables," 193.
[18] A full set of images is available under http://www.bl.uk/manuscripts/Viewer.aspx?ref=cotton_ms_nero_d_iv_fs001r.
[19] Carl Nordenfalk, *Die spätantiken Kanontafeln*, 2 vols. (Göteborg: Isacson, 1938), 218.
[20] McGurk relied on Ranke's edition of Codex Fuldensis that evened out the arrangement found in the manuscript. Rathofer exposes this problem in "Heimatfrage," 32–4.
[21] Cf. Matthew R. Crawford, "A New Witness to the 'Western' Ordering of the Gospels: GA 073 + 084," *JTS* 69 (2018): 481n. 15.

from top to bottom. By consequence, one finds the vertical design only in the inner and outer margins. On the other hand, we have a horizontal design that is effectively mirroring the design of the canon tables by aggregating the concordances needed for the canon numbers found on any given page of Gospel text into a small table at the bottom of the page. Like the canon tables these are operated from left to right, hence horizontally. The horizontal design is found in Latin, Greek, and Gothic manuscripts from the sixth century onward.[22]

The vertical design appears to be restricted to Latin Vulgate Gospel books, among them St. Gallen, Stiftsbibliothek Cod. Sang. 1395, which is considered to be the oldest Vulgate manuscript (first half of the fifth century), perhaps even produced during the lifetime of Jerome.[23] In addition, it is found in sixth-century Gospel books mostly from Italy, such as British Library, Harley MS 1775[24]; Cambridge, Corpus Christi College, MS. 286[25]; Würzburg, Universitätsbibliothek, Cod. M.P.Th.F. 68.[26] A special case is Milan, Biblioteca Ambrosiana, Cod. C. 39.inf.,[27] since it provides the marginal enumeration—both the section numbers and the canon number—with Greek letters instead of the normal Latin numerals; the Gospel sigla are given in Latin, however. Is this circumstantial evidence that the vertical design was also available in Greek Gospel books?

Even more importantly for what concerns us here, the vertical marginal concordances are found in the Lindisfarne Gospels and in Codex Amiatinus (Bibliotheca Laurenziana, MS Amiatinus 1).[28] The Lindisfarne Gospels have already been mentioned as a close parallel for the canon table layout in Fuldensis. Codex Amiatinus will become important when discussing the textual affiliation of the Fuldensis harmony below. It is now evident that the vertical marginal concordances are a common feature among a number of early Vulgate manuscripts, mostly from Italy (up to the sixth century). From the seventh or eighth centuries onward, it is also found in the British Isles. In my view, this suggests that Victor has not invented this feature but rather found it in the Vulgate Gospel book that he was using to prepare the canon apparatus for the harmony.

Functioning in concert with these marginal parallel section numbers are the Gospel sigla that are interspersed within the running text of the harmony, implying that in the process of transcribing the text, writing space has been left blank at the

---

[22] For the Greek and Gothic, see Crawford, "New Witness"; for the Latin, see H. A. G. Houghton, *The Latin New Testament: A Guide to its Early History, Texts, and Manuscripts* (Oxford: Oxford University Press, 2016), 216 (VL 10 and VL 11).

[23] Cf. O'Loughlin, "Harmonizing," 17–18, esp. 18n. 77; see also Christopher de Hamel, *The Book: A History of the Bible* (London: Phaidon, 2001), 25–6, with plate. The entire manuscript has been digitized and is available under https://www.e-codices.unifr.ch/de/list/one/csg/1395.

[24] de Hamel, *The Book*, 26, with plate; more sample images and references to relevant secondary literature are available under https://www.bl.uk/catalogues/illuminatedmanuscripts/record.asp?MSID=8348&CollID=8&NStart=1775.

[25] Full set of images available under https://parker.stanford.edu/parker/catalog/mk707wk3350.

[26] Full set of images available under http://vb.uni-wuerzburg.de/ub/mpthf68/index.html.

[27] de Hamel, *The Book*, 30, with plate.

[28] Full set of images available under http://mss.bmlonline.it/s.aspx?Id=AWOS3h2-I1A4r7GxMdaR&c=Biblia%20Sacra#/book.

appropriate positions for the sigla to be added later in a different (red) ink. The size of spaces initially left blank varies according to the number of Gospel sigla needing to be accommodated at a given position. Ranke thought that Victor inherited the sigla from the harmony source that he was using.[29] Fischer, and more assertively Rathofer, argued for Victor as their author.[30] Three observations are important for this question. First of all, Victor had a vested interest in the Gospel sigla, because in his proofreading of the manuscript he has personally added them when the scribe missed some.[31] Second, the sigla basically represent abbreviated versions of the aforementioned parallel section numbers in that they normally follow the sequence of the marginal parallels. Third, the sigla within the harmony text and the reference to the canon table (1-10) in the marginal parallels are both written in red ink, whereas the section numbers themselves are written in blackish ink, which suggests that from a logistical point of view these items fall into different phases of the work. The sigla and the canon numbers were probably added in one and the same production phase.[32] In other words, the interspersed Gospel sigla are intimately linked to Victor's project of incorporating the canon apparatus and should therefore be seen as part of it. If Victor found Gospel sigla in his harmony source, he surely reworked them to fit his edition of the Eusebian apparatus for the harmony.

To sum up our investigation of the Eusebian apparatus in Codex Fuldensis, it seems reasonable to assume that Victor has used a Latin Gospel book that included a sixteen-page canon table layout as well as a system of complete marginal parallel section numbers in the vertical design alongside the Gospel text. In addition, it probably also included Jerome's *Novus Opum*, since Fuldensis includes on folio 4v an excerpt of this letter.[33] In order to pay tribute to Occam's razor, one might ask what else this Latin Gospel book may have contributed to Codex Fuldensis.

According to experts on the history of the Latin Bible, the Vulgate harmony text of Codex Fuldensis is closely related to that of Codex Amiatinus.[34] This appears to be especially the case in longer passages solely containing text from John's Gospel, whereas in other passages Old Latin material or readings from Tatian's text may have been retained to some extent.[35] Fischer adds an interesting observation concerning Luke 5-9 in Codex Fuldensis, where he finds the relationship to Codex Amiatinus less pronounced. For these passages he sees a closer affinity with Codex Harleianus. Fischer

---

[29] Ranke, *Codex Fuldensis*, x.
[30] Fischer, "Bibelausgaben," 550; Rathofer, "Heimatfrage," 20-30.
[31] E.g., on f. 135r (left margin), on f. 142r (line 9), on f. 160r (line 4).
[32] Rathofer, "Heimatfrage," 22-3, actually suggests that the sigla were written first, before the parallel section numbers were added to the margin, and functioned as a guide for where the latter should be put. In my view, this is essentially correct, except that not only the red sigla but also the red canon numbers in the margin were added simultaneously, which provided an even better guide for the next step of adding the marginal parallel sections.
[33] R. Hausmann, *Handschriften*, 4.
[34] See Fischer, "Bibelausgaben," 552, with reference to previous scholarship.
[35] Fischer, "Bibelausgaben," 550: "Natürlich sind Victor bei dieser Umsetzung in Vulgata Fehler und Nachlässigkeiten unterlaufen. Nicht wenige Tatian-Lesarten oder altlateinische Lesarten sind stehen geblieben, am wenigsten in den längeren Johannes-Abschnitten, zu denen es keine Parallele gab." Fischer relies here on the work of H. J. Vogels, *Beiträge*, 18-24.

even ponders about the possibility that Harleianus might have been in the possession of Victor.[36] Did Victor possibly employ two early Vulgate Gospel books such as these? Apart from Luke 5–9 Fischer detects no influence from other Vulgate types that were around by that time.[37] For Fischer this is decisive evidence that there was only one editorial event that transformed the harmony into its current Vulgate dress, which is why he insists that, whatever Victor had found, it was not a Vulgate harmony.[38]

In sum, the Vulgate dress that Codex Fuldensis exhibits includes not just very specific features of the Eusebian apparatus (sixteen pages of tables and marginal enumeration for parallel passages) and Jerome's *Novum Opus*, but also clearly exhibits a textual blend that is closely akin to that of Codex Amiatinus, which is still today considered to be a very good early Vulgate text.

What about the set of 182 *capitula* that precede the harmony? Could they also derive from the Vulgate Gospel book that Victor was using? The answer is, in part. Chapman has studied this question for the first sixty chapters and concludes, "the result is that I find no striking likeness in F[uldensis] to any of the various summaries, except at the beginning, where Victor has used the Northumbrian summaries."[39] Here, Chapman refers to the *capitula* now accessible in D. De Bruyne's *Sommaires, divisions et rubriques de la Bible latine* under Type C.[40] This type is available at least in twenty-four Latin Gospel books, among them, again, Codex Amiatinus and the Lindisfarne Gospels. H. Houghton gives a concise assessment of the type C *capitula* (as found in Latin copies of the Gospel of John), concluding, "the full integration of Vulgate readings indicates that this series does not have Old Latin roots."[41] Chapman takes this finding as evidence that Victor created the Fuldensis *capitula* on his own, albeit with some limited influence from the Vulgate Gospel book that he was using to rework the harmony. This ties in with Chapman's overall perception that the harmony source was in Greek and translated by Victor. Vogels, while acknowledging Chapman's finding, nevertheless strongly disagrees with his conclusion.[42] He in turn assembles a long list of differences between the *capitula* and the harmony text for which the former exhibits Old Latin support, whereas the latter has a straightforward Vulgate text. This then suggests that those *capitula* were at least in part formed on the basis of an Old Latin

---

[36] "Bibelausgaben," 553.
[37] He builds on the work of H. J. Vogels (*Beiträge*, 18–20) who produced substantial collations of Fuldensis against the Irish Vulgate text tradition, showing that where they agree they usually have Old Latin support as well.
[38] Vogels tentatively suggested that Victor's harmony source might have reached him already in a Vulgate dress (*Beiträge*, 6–7).
[39] Chapman, *Notes*, 90.
[40] Donatien De Bruyne, *Sommaires, divisions et rubriques de la Bible latine* (Namur: Godenne, 1914), 270–311; repr. Donatien De Bruyne, P.-M. Bogaert, and T. O'Loughlin, *Summaries, Divisions and Rubrics of the Latin Bible* (Turnhout: Brepols, 2015).
[41] Cf. H. A. G. Houghton, "Chapter Divisions, Capitula Lists, and the Old Latin Versions of John," *RBén* 121 (2011): 316–56, 334–5, citation on 335.
[42] Vogels, *Beiträge*, 8: "Es ist freilich eine richtige und wichtige Beobachtung, daß einige Capitula (z.B. gleich das erste . . .) enge Berührung mit jenem Summarium aufweisen, allein noch wichtiger scheint mir die Feststellung, daß die Capitula offenbar nicht von Victor herrühren."

text, which Vogels takes to be the harmony in its Old Latin dress. Hence, the *capitula* were already part of Victor's harmony source and this harmony was in Latin.

This position was not only accepted by Fischer but happily embraced in Diatessaronic scholarship in particular, as it opened up the possibility for a Latin history of the harmony prior to Codex Fuldensis. While this is an entirely plausible scenario, the issue of the *capitula* is not so straightforward as it appears to be. First of all, the list of supposedly Old Latin readings in the *capitula*, by contrast to the Vulgate readings in the harmony text, is a mixed bag. It not only contains legitimate positive differences, such as, for example, lexical differences (*occidit* vs. *interfecit*[43]), but also encompasses simple omissions, such as, for example, the omission of *et bibit* in *capitulum* 56 as opposed to the full version, *manducat et bibit* in Mark 2:16 of the harmony.[44] Omissions such as this can occur for all sorts of reasons and should not be lumped with the positive lexical differences just exemplified. The mixed bag also contains cases in which the harmony has one version of a given story (e.g., Matt 12:46) while the *capitulum* (in this case, c. 59) refers to the synoptic parallel (Luke 8:20).[45] In my view, exchange of or attraction to synoptic parallel should not be counted among positive differences, since, again, they can occur for all sorts of reasons. As a result, we are left with legitimate positive differences between *capitula* and harmony text. But they are much fewer in number than the compilation of Vogels suggests. Second, Vogels acknowledges the fact that a series of Vulgate manuscripts have been equipped with Old Latin *capitula*.[46] This suggests two things. On the one hand, it appears that it is not uncommon for a Vulgate manuscript to circulate with a textually deviating (Old Latin) *capitula* list. On the other hand, instances such as this make it very likely that *capitula* lists are not required to conform to the main Gospel text and therefore do not need to be derived from the adjacent text as found in any given manuscript. Hence, the comparison between the two only reveals differences but no clear direction regarding how to reconfigure these differences historically. In other words, Vogels may have unjustly assumed that the *capitula* had to be derived from the harmony when it was in an Old Latin dress, since it might well be the case that *capitula* and harmony were quite independent.

Third, how should we conceptualize the creation of this particular *capitula* list as found in Codex Fuldensis? Chapman has already established that some *capitula* have been derived from a set of Vulgate *capitula* as found in Codex Amiatinus and the Lindisfarne Gospels (inter alia). Of special importance is the clear and verbatim parallel for the first *capitulum*: *in principio uerbum·deus apud deum per quem facta sunt omnia* (John 1:1-5).[47] Such parallels obviously make it possible to link the Fuldensis *capitula* series with the *capitula* found in the Vulgate Gospel book that Victor utilized to create Codex Fuldensis. But it seems to me that the implications of this observation have never been digested. Chapman's discovery clearly indicates that Victor was involved in

---

[43] Matt 2:16 vs. *capitulum* 10, cf. Vogels, *Beiträge*, 10.
[44] Vogels, *Beiträge*, 11.
[45] Ibid.
[46] Ibid., 9: "Bekanntlich gibt es eine Reihe von Vulgatahandschriften, die mit altlateinischen Summarien ausgestattet sind."
[47] Cf. Codex Amiatinus, f. 881v (http://mss.bmlonline.it/s.aspx?Id=AWOS3h2-I1A4r7GxMdaR&c=Biblia%20Sacra#/oro/1761).

shaping the *capitula*, at least to some degree. What exactly was his contribution? How did he go about it? Was he using multiple sources? Did he replace existing *capitula*? Did he expand a smaller set of *capitula*? Why did he interact with the *capitulum* for John 1:1-5 the way he did? Was the *capitulum* missing? Was John 1:1-5 missing in the harmony source? In my view, the *capitula*, their potential sources and prehistory, as well as Victor's contribution to them, require better understanding before we can accept them as uncontested evidence for an Old Latin pre-history of the harmony source in Victor's hands. To be sure, there is no positive evidence that this harmony was other than a Latin text. But so far there is equally no clear direct evidence that it necessarily must have been in Latin. Hence, I suggest we reopen this question and produce new evidence addressing this important issue. Other than tackling the *capitula* anew, we should also come to a better understanding of the non-Vulgate remnants that Vogels identified in the harmony text itself.[48] To what extent are they lexically "Old Latin" in nature, that is, to what extent do they display a more or less synonymous alternative rendering of the same underlying text? And to what extent do they exhibit variant readings that so clearly transgress language borders that one may posit a language other than Latin as the root? If such examples are found, one might potentially be dealing with remnants of the Diatessaronic version that lies at the heart of Codex Fuldensis's harmony source—in whatever language. After all, this is what we are most interested in, getting closer to the "initial" Diatessaron. Codex Fuldensis may provide us with some, albeit comparatively few, textual readings that should be assessed for their Diatessaronic status.

3. The Post-History of Codex Fuldensis

The Fuldensis harmony was copied at least twice independently in the ninth century CE. Subsequent copies from these ninth-century manuscripts peaked in the twelfth and thirteenth centuries, transforming Codex Fuldensis's offspring into a well-attested medieval text that was available in commentary editions by Zacharias Chrysopolitanus and Petrus Cantor, as well as in anonymous glossed harmony editions.[49] For the most part, the evidence for these relationships is derived from the paratextual features of Codex Fuldensis, such as the *capitula*, Victor's preface, and, to some extent, the excerpt from Jerome's *Novum Opus* found in Codex Fuldensis and handed down through time with telling differences. With these paratextual developments as guiding lines, the textual developments from the Fuldensis harmony down to its distant offspring in the thirteenth century fall neatly in place and are easily explained as either simple mistakes or textual changes inflicted by glossing material or comparison with local texts of the separate Gospels. Furthermore, close comparison of the characteristic Fuldensis harmony sequence with more harmonistic texts from the Middle Ages suggests that

---

[48] Vogels, *Beiträge*, 21–5.
[49] For the details, see U. Schmid, *Unum ex Quattuor: Eine Geschichte der lateinischen Tatianüberlieferung*, AGLB 37 (Freiburg im Breisgau: Herder, 2005), esp. 57–191.

another hugely popular text of the twelfth and thirteenth centuries, that is, Petrus Comestor's *Historia Scholastica*, also heavily draws on the Fuldensis harmony.[50] In this case, however, no paratextual features are available in Comestor's work, which leaves open the possibility that the harmony he was using might not be ultimately dependent on Codex Fuldensis itself but on a version that branched off of a common source prior to Codex Fuldensis. A priori this is an unlikely scenario given the many harmonies and harmony commentaries available in Comestor's time and locale (Paris) that clearly belong to the offspring of Codex Fuldensis and given the fact that we seem to have no indisputable evidence that any later harmony that is very close to Codex Fuldensis should not be considered part of its offspring. However, in comparisons of Gospel texts one is notoriously at a disadvantage in pinning down exact and irreversible stemmatic relationships. How can one demonstrate dependency and nondependency of later harmonies with regard to Codex Fuldensis across time, space, and even language borders?

A gospel harmony has basically two textual features that can be used to assess stemmatic relationships: (1) the macro-perspective of narrative sequence usually above the sentence level and (2) the micro-perspective of individual variant readings typically below the sentence level (done in comparison to the text of the separate Gospels). Although there is some blurring between these two categories, they work reasonably well to delineate textual features that have the potential of being comparatively unique or fairly common. In my opinion, the macro-perspective has a general advantage over the micro-perspective. For example, if we take a passage from the Synoptic Gospels, we may find harmonistic readings blending the text from different Gospels together not only in harmonies—which is to be expected—but also in almost any manuscript of the separate Gospels, albeit usually to a lesser extent. On the other hand, for example, we would clearly not expect to find a Johannine passage interspersed with synoptic material, not just once but repeatedly over a longer stretch of text, in normal manuscripts of the separate Gospels. Thus the macro-perspective of narrative sequence focuses on elements unique to gospel harmonies, whereas the micro-perspective of individual variant readings has to cope with parallels not just from harmonies but from gospel texts in general. In other words, with the macro-perspective we are hitting at editorial choices made by a harmonist, whether it is Tatian or a reviser of the original Diatessaron or an independent harmonizer, while with the micro-perspective we are in danger of drowning in the huge sea of the variant readings from the vast textual tradition of the Gospels.

A good example of the problems in dealing with the micro-perspective can be found in Nicholas Zola's unpublished doctoral thesis on Codex Fuldensis. Its fifth and final chapter almost exclusively deals with developing a test that allows for assessing whether or not a harmony text is ultimately derived from Codex Fuldensis. Zola's "*Leitfehler* test" starts from the desire to identify readings in the tradition that are not likely to have arisen multiple times independently.[51] From his detailed study of Codex

---

[50] Cf. ibid., 284–300 (Appendix I).
[51] Zola, "Tatian's Diatessaron," 153, with reference to Paul Maas.

Fuldensis, Zola aims at a list of "unique errors that Fuldensis may have introduced into the harmonized tradition. If these *Leitfehler* are present in later harmonies, it makes their ultimate dependence on Fuldensis evermore likely."[52] Although this is a reasonable assumption, it requires an awful lot of work when focusing on the micro-perspective of individual variant readings, which is exactly what Zola did. He undertook a huge screening process of Codex Fuldensis against the entire text tradition of the Gospels as available to him in critical editions, whether in Latin, Greek, or Syriac, in order to make sure that the former was not potentially influenced by the latter. From the selected parts of Fuldensis that his study is based upon, Zola arrives at a list of fifteen such readings that he deems suitable for performing the *Leitfehler* test. The test itself is performed on Codex Sangallensis (ninth-century Latin/Old High German bilingual harmony manuscript) and the Liège Diatessaron (thirteenth-century Middle-Dutch harmony manuscript), with the Arabic Diatessaron as a touchstone for assessing the potential Tatianic origin of any of the *Leitfehler* derived from Codex Fuldensis.[53] Zola's result is that Codex Sangallensis shares thirteen out of the fifteen *Leitfehler* from Codex Fuldensis, which is consistent with the conclusion that has been reached by Rathofer: Sangallensis is a direct copy of Fuldensis. On the other hand, the Liège Diatessaron shares only one out of fifteen. What conclusions can be drawn from this result? Zola is cautious enough to avoid a blatant logical error: "Of course, one cannot infer from this test that the Liège harmony is conclusively *independent* of Fuldensis."[54] Earlier he states that "disagreement on *Leitfehler* does not prove that a later manuscript is independent of an earlier manuscript, for it is always possible that the later manuscript is but a careful revision of the earlier one, with all the *Leitfehler* removed."[55] So what exactly can one learn from it? "Ultimately," Zola states, "these results suggest that there is still other work to be done in order to dislodge the Liège harmony from its Old Latin pedestal."[56]

The problem with Zola's test is not so much that it requires considerable work, but rather that he missed the really important witnesses in his screening process. In my own analysis of the later Latin harmony tradition clearly derived from Codex Fuldensis, I have already documented some of the textual developments concerning a number of Fuldensis's most awkward readings, which have largely been identified by Rathofer.[57] Zola is aware of Rathofer's test passages that were initially used to demonstrate the uniquely close relationship between Fuldensis and Sangallensis. Moreover, Zola acknowledges that "he [i.e., Rathofer] even uncovered some of the *Leitfehler* I am using for my test."[58] Unfortunately, Zola failed to digest the collation I did on those passages regarding the later Latin harmony manuscripts. Out of the fifteen *Leitfehler* from Zola's test a total of three are also covered by me: Matt 6:19 (*demolitur*) add.

---

[52] Ibid., 154.
[53] The list of readings is found in an Appendix (170–9) and discussed on 162–7.
[54] Ibid., 166–7.
[55] Ibid., 165.
[56] Ibid., 167.
[57] Schmid, *Unum ex Quattuor*, 308–23 (Appendix III).
[58] Zola, "Tatian's Diatessaron," 154.

ubi fures effodiunt et furantur)[59]; John 14:12 (*faciet*] add. *et maiora horum faciet*)[60]; John 15:11 (*meum*] add. *in vobis sit et gaudium vestrum*).[61] In all three cases, at least four later Latin harmony witnesses from the offspring of Codex Fuldensis testify to the respective textual development. In other words, the "careful revision" that Zola imagines is actually backed up by real data. Although the sample is fairly small, since it only affects three out of fifteen *Leitfehler* (20 percent), the matches are 100 percent (three out of three). This clearly suggests that the later Latin harmony tradition will exhibit similar developments for the remaining twelve *Leitfehler*. I am confident that most—if not all—of them will show similar patterns. As a result, one can expect that the huge gap between Codex Fuldensis and the Liège harmony, as suggested by the 93 percent disagreement in the *Leitfehler*, will be filled in by the testimony of the later Latin harmony tradition and will effectively cease to exist. This exercise shows once more that ignoring the later Latin harmony tradition is detrimental to understanding the medieval vernacular tradition, and that any attempt at comparing the latter directly to Codex Fuldensis is at best anachronistic. Screening Fuldensis's individual readings on the micro-level perspective against the textual tradition of the separate Gospels is distracting, so long as the rest of the Latin harmony tradition is left out of the equation. Therefore, I would like to shift attention to the macro-perspective of narrative sequence and harmonistic editorial activity in order to assess the intersection of the western harmony tradition, both Latin and vernacular. Are there ways in which we can use comparisons of sequence to find *Leitfehler* on the macro-perspective, that is, stretches of harmonistic text that are unlikely to have arisen independently?

For instance, when looking at Petrus Comestor's harmonistic *Historia Evangelica* in comparison with the Fuldensis harmony, the outline of both texts is very similar. However, there are differences as well, and this is where we likely encounter editorial choices altering the flow of the narrative and hence potential *Leitfehler* or smoking guns. One such example is the story (or stories) of the cleansing of the temple (Matt 21:12-13 par.; John 2:14-16). In the separate Gospels this story occupies very different positions in the respective flow of the narratives: in the Synoptics it is found after Jesus's triumphal entry into Jerusalem toward the end of his ministry, while in John it is found at the beginning of Jesus's public ministry. In Codex Fuldensis the two versions are textually conflated and presented after Jesus's triumphal entry. The most colorful trait from John (2:15) is the fabrication of the whip out of small ropes (*et cum fecisset quasi flagellum de funiculis*[62]) that John portrays Jesus using during his action in the entrance area to the temple. This conflation is a conscious editorial decision and makes perfect sense as long as one envisions only a single cleansing of the temple in the narrative. It becomes slightly awkward, however, once you have two cleansings of the temple as Comestor did[63]—one at the beginning (as John has it) and one toward the

---

[59] No. 5 in Zola's list ("Tatian's Diatessaron," 174) and Rathofer 5 in my list (*Unum ex Quattuor*, 309).
[60] No. 8 in Zola's list ("Tatian's Diatessaron," 176) and Rathofer 30 in my list (*Unum ex Quattuor*, 317).
[61] No. 10 in Zola's list ("Tatian's Diatessaron," 177) and Rathofer 32 in my list (*Unum ex Quattuor*, 318).
[62] Codex Fuldensis, f. 109v.
[63] Petrus Comestor, *Historia Evangelica*, *Cap. XL. De prima ejectione ementium et vendentium in templo* (PL 198:1560C); and *Cap. CXIX. De secunda ejectione ementium et vendentium de templo* (PL 198:1601A).

end (as the Synoptics have it)—*and* you retain that narrative element in your second, Synoptic cleansing event. In this case, the Johannine element functions as a smoking gun indicating that Comestor still drew on the conflated, Fuldensian version of the story. Interestingly enough, the singular cleansing event with its conflated version is also what is found in the Arabic Diatessaron, according to Marmardji's edition.[64] This, then, may well be a feature of the original Diatessaron[65] that is retained in Comestor's retelling of the gospel story, even though he actually reversed the decision of having only one temple cleansing event. Now, if we can invoke the original Diatessaron as a distributor of this feature, on purely textual historical grounds we surely cannot single out the Codex Fuldensis tradition as the sole possible avenue for mediating it to Comestor. After all, this feature must have been part of the harmony source in the hands of Victor, along with its ancestry all the way back to the Diatessaron. In other words, this is a classic *Leitfehler*, or smoking gun, for Tatian's Diatessaron and not for Codex Fuldensis, which is what we were looking for in the first place.

In order to find macro-level *Leitfehler* for Codex Fuldensis and later western harmonies, we have to look for passages that are limited to the western tradition and involve a series of editorial changes that apparently begins with Fuldensis. Subsequently, editorial reworkings should be evidenced within the offspring of Codex Fuldensis, preferably in successive steps, especially when vernacular harmonies are involved. Ideally, we would be able to group these events into a "genealogy of successive editorial interventions." One such example is the treatment of John 2:11c in the Fuldensis tradition. The data for the Latin Fuldensis tradition are published in my Teststellen under Schmid 5 and Schmid 6 and some of their implications are discussed in my section "Harmonie in Übersetzung."[66] I expand here on this with special emphasis on the diversity of editorial activity that is evidenced in the tradition on this verse far into the vernacular harmony tradition with the Liège harmony forming a stunning editorial end point.

The starting point is a peculiar editorial choice that is first documented in Codex Fuldensis. It has to do with the placement of the Wedding at Cana (John 2:1-11) in the harmony tradition. First off, Ephrem and the Arabic Diatessaron have the Wedding at Cana immediately after the first calling of disciples according to John 1:36-50[67] at the very beginning of Jesus's public ministry, while Codex Fuldensis and the Liège harmony have it after the Sermon on the Mount. This is a big difference between the eastern and western traditions and it seems likely that Codex Fuldensis and its offspring represent a secondary development for the following reason. In Ephrem and the Arabic Diatessaron, the Wedding at Cana indeed was the first miracle (*initium signorum*, John 2:11a) that Jesus performed, which provoked his disciples to believe in him (*et*

---

[64] A.-S. Marmardji, *Diatessaron de Tatien: Texte arabe établi, traduit en français, collationné avec les anciennes versions syriaques* (Beyrouth: Imprimerie Catholique, 1935), 303–5.
[65] This is not an isolated feature in this context, but the broad outline of the harmony narrative between the Arabic Diatessaron and Codex Fuldensis is very close from here on: cleansing of the temple; on the destruction of the temple (John 2:18-22); the woman with her small contribution (Luke 21:1-4); Pharisee and publican (Luke 18:9-14); retreat to Bethany (Mark 11:11; Matt 21:17).
[66] Schmid, *Unum ex Quattuor*, 323, 257–66, esp. 263–6.
[67] Cf. Louis Leloir, "Le Diatessaron de Tatien," *OrSyr* 1 (1956): 208–31, esp. 216.

crediderunt in eum discipulis eis, John 2:11c). This is fully consistent with Johannine theology and is a strong testimony to the theological preferences of this part of the harmony tradition. In contrast, the western tradition's transposition of John 2:1-11 to a later position disrupts the Johannine combination of Jesus's "sign" and the resulting "belief" of the disciples, since there are now other miracle stories before John 2:1-11, most notably the miraculous draught of fish (Luke 5:1-11), which now is the forerunner among the miracles in the Fuldensis tradition. However, a crucial detail in Fuldensis keeps the "original" Johannine combination alive: John 2:11c has been detached from its Johannine story and transposed as well, this time after Luke 5:10. In other words, the Fuldensis narrative retains Johannine theology—through means of transposing a small portion of text—which otherwise would have been discarded as a result of the transposition of the entire story of the Wedding at Cana. It does so by deemphasizing John 2:1-11b at its later position and balancing it with Luke 5:1-10, which has a similar function in the Gospel of Luke, that is starting off the relationship between Jesus and his early disciples with a powerful event that provokes a disciple-like reaction. In Luke 5:11, however, only the action that they followed Jesus is reported, whereas John 2:11c explicitly mentions that they believed in Jesus. Hence, by means of a small but decisive "upgrade," Luke 5:1-11 is now capable of transporting Johannine theology within the context of the harmony that has this story as its first powerful event. This is a purposeful and deliberate action. The editor of this small transposition (i.e., moving John 2:11c to follow Luke 5:10) in all likelihood was the editor of the large transposition of John 2:1-11 as well. The combination of both of them is a powerful testimony to the impact that the "original" Johannine sequence had on the person active here, and is therefore also a strong indication that the position of John 2:1-11 evident in Ephrem and the Arabic Diatessaron takes precedence over its placement in Codex Fuldensis.

Now, we cannot be sure that the aforementioned editorial activity originated with Codex Fuldensis; it might well have been in Victor's source already. It is clear, however, that eastern and western harmony traditions are split and that the Fuldensis version of it has not much claim to Tatianic origin. At the very least, then, we find ourselves firmly in the realm of the western Diatessaronic tradition in this case. Victor himself, by the way, has identified this Johannine piece inside of the Lukan story, since it has the appropriate Gospel siglum and canon number in the margin.

The next thing to realize is the fact that the Fuldensis narrative at this point was found to be perfectly acceptable by the copyists of the ninth century. In none of the four extant copies is a single shred of contemporaneous evidence visible to indicate otherwise. From the twelfth century onward the situation changes. One of the ninth-century copies from the Fuldensis offspring, kept in the cathedral library in Reims (France), was heavily glossed, and several more glossed and un-glossed harmony manuscripts were produced during the twelfth and thirteenth centuries that started to interact with the narrative sequence in Fuldensis. The glossator of the manuscript from Reims actually noticed that John 2:11c was wanting from its canonical position after 2:11b and simply added the missing words above the line. The same is true for a manuscript that is now kept at the Bodleian Library,[68] except that it was equipped

---

[68] Oxford, Bodl. Lib. 2761 (Auct. D. 1.8).

with glosses from the onset. Here, the missing words are treated like an interlinear gloss and placed at the appropriate position. Both these glossing events are actually editorial activities in their own right and testify to an awareness of the missing words. Judged by the massive glossing activity in both manuscripts, the addition of John 2:11c as a gloss at its appropriate place is but a minor event, although it is clear that it was the result of a detailed and thorough reading of the harmony text. The next phase in the editorial interaction with the passage is found in a group of seven manuscripts, consisting of glossed and un-glossed harmony manuscripts. In these, John 2:11c is present within the running text of the harmony narrative *twice*, once after Luke 5:10 and again after John 2:11b. In and of itself this is an unusual situation, since I am not aware of any other such clear reduplication of unique gospel passages within the framework of the Fuldensis harmony. It is, however, easy to understand how the reduplication came about. Most likely, it started out in the margin like the two previously mentioned manuscripts have it. Subsequently, as a result of yet another editorial event, the passage was taken over into the main text, effectively altering the narrative structure.

Despite the fact that quite a number of Latin harmonies seem to be content with this slightly odd, or at least unusual, reduplication of John 2:11c, this is not the end of editorial activity with this passage. Two manuscripts simply omitted John 2:11c from its position after Luke 5:11, thus retaining it only after John 2:11b. This editorial activity is clearly concerned with removing the doublet by removing it from its "noncanonical" position. The downside of such a solution is that it breaks the balance between the two miracle stories within the framework of the harmony. The reader now encounters the disciples' solemn reaction to Jesus's deeds long after the Sermon on the Mount and is left wondering how everything else that came before was actually received by the disciples, notably including the preaching of John the Baptist (John 3:22-36); Jesus in Galilee preaching and healing in the synagogues (Matt 4:23-25); and Jesus commissioning the twelve and delivering the Sermon on the Mount (Matt 5–7), with an additional speech to his disciples (Matt 9:35–11:1).

The final example of editorial activity comes from the vernacular tradition, in particular from the Middle-Dutch harmonies. We start off with a text that is fairly close to a Latin version that we have already encountered, namely the doublet of John 2:11c after Luke 5:10 and after John 2:11b. A manuscript housed at the Württembergische Landesbibliothek[69] reads,

> (cap. xxxii) . . . Doe sprac Jhesus tote Symone en vrese di niet. want vort ane saltu menschen werden vaende. *doe geloofden sine jongere in hem.* ende doe die scepe te lande quamen doe lieten si alle dinc ende volgeden hem.
>
> (cap. lvi) . . . Dit dede Jhesus in den beginne sire tekene in Cana Galilee ende oppenbarde sine glorie. *Ende sine jongere geloofden in hem.*

---

[69] Cod. theol. et philolol. 8° 140. Text available in the edition of Jan Bergsma, *De levens van Jezus in het Middelnederlandsch*, 3 vols. (Leiden: Sijthoff, 1895-8), which is available online at https://dbnl.org/tekst/_lev005leve03_01/.

This is a fairly straightforward translation of the aforementioned later Latin harmony tradition, and we should simply align this vernacular version with it. What about the Liège harmony? It belongs to the same trajectory but offers an advanced editorial attempt at dealing with the doublet. This is what it reads:[70]

> (cap. 30) Doe seide Ihesus tote Petre: En onssigh di nit; vanderre vren soutu menschen wesen vaende. *Daer begonsten sine ijongren te gheloeuene ane hem.* Alse die schepe te lande quamen, so liten si schep ende al ende volgden hem.
>
> (cap. 57) ... Dit was *ene der irsten* miraklen die Ihesus dede in Chana van Galileen, ende daer vertogde hi sine gotleke macht *ende dar met so worden sine ijongren ghesterkt in den gheloeue.*

First of all, at the first occurrence (Luke 5:10) it is said that disciples "started to believe in him," which clearly echoes John 2:11c, albeit reinterpreted to serve a larger narrative as well as theological purpose. This becomes, second, evident from the re-occurrence of John 2:11c after 2:11b which reads, "his disciples were strengthened in [their] belief," clearly referring back to the first occurrence. This is a deliberate attempt at balancing the doublet. From a narrative viewpoint it relates the two miracle stories by suggesting a development in the disciples' response to Jesus's deeds. Theologically and psychologically, *fides* becomes a layered experience that gradually evolves as more input becomes available that reinforces the initial experience. Third, the conscious editorial activity is amplified by the re-interpretation of *initium signorum* ("the first of the signs") into "one of the first miracles." This change is for obvious reasons, since the Wedding at Cana was not literally the first sign but has instead been displaced by the miraculous draught of fish (Luke 5:1-11) within the narrative framework of the Fuldensis harmony. No doubt the editor/translator of the Liège harmony took his or her liberties in dealing with the Latin source used. Yet the doublet must have been part of it, for otherwise the subtle, yet elaborate retelling just examined would not have been warranted. The textual history of the doublet is, however, sufficiently accounted for within the harmony tradition that started off with Codex Fuldensis, from which point each step is documented and straightforward to follow. Once the multifaceted editorial activity surrounding the placement of John 2:1-11b and 2:11c in the Latin part of the tradition is understood, it is obvious what the translator/editor of the Liège harmony did, as well as how he or she did it. Hence, the macro-perspective of narrative sequence, in my opinion, can serve as a background against which to detect and evaluate editorial activity on the harmony level. The example we have just looked at represents a series of "successive editorial interventions," and clearly suggests the Liège harmony is part of the Fuldensis offspring. Any other explanation would be special pleading; it would be to search for the elusive black swan as the key to unlocking the text of the vernacular harmonies while ignoring the fact that the black swan has already been found nesting

---

[70] I recommend the most recent edition, C. C. de Bruin, *Het Luikse Diatesseron*, trans. A. J. Barnouw (Leiden: Brill, 1970), also available online at https://www.dbnl.org/tekst/_lui001luik01_01/.

within the medieval Latin harmony tradition itself, a tradition that clearly derives directly from Codex Fuldensis.

4. Conclusion

Codex Fuldensis is a fascinating piece of late antique book production that sits at the crossroads of several avenues of historical inquiry. First, it is the oldest witness to a specific brand of early Vulgate Gospel text that is otherwise only known from manuscripts that are at least 150 years younger (e.g., Codex Amiatinus). In addition, it allows us not only to firmly place a Vulgate text but also a number of paratexts in time and space. Among them is a specific sixteen-page layout of the canon tables for which the second oldest representative is, again, about 150 years younger (i.e., the Lindisfarne Gospels). The same is probably also true for the *capitula* tradition of the C type that is at least echoed in a few of the Fuldensis *capitula*. For the special feature of marginal parallel section numbers added in Codex Fuldensis we have earlier or contemporaneous examples. The same is true for Jerome's *Novum Opus*. As such, all the above-mentioned textual and paratextual features add up to a robust understanding of the kind of early Vulgate Gospel book that Victor of Capua used for his edition of the Fuldensis harmony.

On the other hand, our understanding of the other main source, that is, the harmony that Victor came across, contains more unknowns. To begin with the most uncontroversial aspect, the harmony source indeed ultimately goes back to Tatian's Diatessaron. I have hinted at some striking parallels in narrative sequence with Ephrem's *Commentary* and the Arabic Diatessaron, for example, concerning the cleansing of the temple, which is exactly what is to be expected with a common ancestor. At the same time, however, there are differences between them as well, such as with the Wedding at Cana, which suggests that there have been editorial interventions adding their own narrative twist to the Diatessaronic tradition. For the positioning of the Wedding at Cana I have argued that Ephrem and the Arabic Diatessaron take precedence over the Fuldensis version. This may or may not be the case with other points of difference. (As a side note, Ephrem and the Arabic Diatessaron may differ as well on occasion.) In any case, I suggest that the macro-perspective of narrative sequence should be explored more courageously, and that hypotheses about relative priority when the main witnesses differ should be advanced and discussed. The good news is that the main players are only few in number. If my analysis of its post-history is essentially correct, Codex Fuldensis is the sole independent witness to Tatian's Diatessaron in the West. This is not only true when it comes to the microlevel of individual variant readings, but is also true with regard to the macro-perspective of narrative sequence. Hence Codex Fuldensis is the gem from the West when it comes to harking back to Tatian's Diatessaron. Previous scholarship has routinely dismissed its testimony due to the Vulgate dress in which it is cloaked. However, the time is ripe to go for its Old Latin remnants, and, in my opinion, the attention should shift away from the narrow focus on Old Latin versus Vulgate. This kind of framing of research was important for the old perspective in Diatessaronic scholarship, with its focus on the Old Latin

Diatessaron, bypassing Fuldensis and harvesting readings from comparatively late vernacular harmonies. A more adequate reframing of the research question might be to properly isolate the non-Vulgate—and in particular the non-Codex Amiatinus (and allies)—elements in the harmony text of Fuldensis, which in turn may provide the safest route for accessing the harmony source behind Codex Fuldensis. When working toward that goal we should make clear distinctions between readings that are likely to represent only developments bound by the Latin transmission process and readings that are likely to transgress language borders. The former readings may help us to identify any potential Old Latin dress of the harmony source that Victor was using, and, by implication, may provide evidence to argue for the existence of an Old Latin harmony prior to Codex Fuldensis. The latter readings may help us get back to Tatian's Diatessaron itself. After all, this text did not originate in Latin, and the safest way to start would seem to be to locate Codex Fuldensis's deviations from its Vulgate dress that are translatable into Greek.[71] Whether or not any such readings have to find parallels in either Ephrem or the Arabic Diatessaron in order to be vetted as Diatessaronic is not so clear-cut to me. If they are, fine! All the better! But, generally speaking, I would prefer to interpret readings from Codex Fuldensis that are likely older than Codex Fuldensis itself against their immediate context, as well as against the larger narrative context in which they are found. In my opinion, Fuldensis's readings should be assessed as parts of narrative units and then compared with the parallel narrative units from the Arabic Diatessaron and/or Ephrem. After all, as we have already seen with the macro-perspective, editorial activity has shaped the Diatessaronic tradition and we should not assume that the editors abstained from changing individual readings on the microlevel. To sum up, when comparing Codex Fuldensis to Ephrem and the Arabic Diatessaron, the entire package is worthy of study.

---

[71] Students of Codex Fuldensis are, of course, free to test the Syriac as well; however, it is much more difficult to argue for an exclusively Syriac source than simply to hunt for the Greek.

The Use of Tatian's Diatessaron in the Textual Criticism of the Gospels and the Future of Diatessaronic Studies

Nicholas J. Zola

Abstract

Diatessaronic studies in the modern period has largely been fueled by this tragically tantalizing task: if only we could reconstruct Tatian's "original" Diatessaron, we would gain access to a text of the Gospels that predates nearly all our surviving manuscripts. The current study traces the use of Tatian's Diatessaron in the textual criticism of the Gospels through fifteen editions of the Greek New Testament, from John Mill's edition in 1707 to the UBS[5] in 2014. As access to Diatessaronic witnesses grew, so too did Tatian's complicated and conflicting presence in the apparatus. But our discoveries outpaced our methodology. The Diatessaronic evidence in the apparatuses is often misguided, misleading, or simply misinformed, rendering the editions demonstrably unreliable when it comes to the Diatessaron. I conclude with seven recommendations for the future of the field, foremost of which is to *stop* citing the Diatessaron in the apparatus of the Greek NT until we can develop a full genealogical stemma of all the surviving Diatessaronic witnesses, in order to ascertain both their relation to each other and their relative weight for reconstructing what we can of Tatian's text. Only then can we determine what, if anything, Tatian can tell us about the text of the Gospels in the second century.

1. Introduction: The Elusive Text of Tatian's Diatessaron

In 1918, just as the field of Diatessaronic studies had begun to surge, Erwin Preuschen issued a vision and critique for the future textual criticism of the Gospels:

> It is without doubt one of the most astonishing phenomena in the field of text-critical work that research has turned with great urgency to producing as reliable a gospel text as possible, but that it has so far neglected to reconstruct the first edition of the Gospels, whose text is still in large extent to be determined. This edition, of course, is the Diatessaron of Tatian, whose reconstruction ... must be

attempted if the textual criticism of the Gospels…does not want to deprive itself of its primary pillar.[1]

Preuschen was neither the first nor the last to stress the magnitude of reconstructing Tatian's second-century composite gospel. Already in 1901, Frederick Kenyon had noted that "the *Diatessaron*, so far as we can recover its original form, provides us with a text that must go back to Greek MSS. of at least the middle of the second century, and possibly much earlier."[2] And as recently as 2012, Tjitze Baarda had quipped that "if we had this Greek Diatessaron in our hands, we would find in it readings that Tatian found in manuscripts of an earlier date than our earliest NT papyri."[3] William Petersen was, of course, fond of repeating the same assertion.[4] And it can be found even on the lips of those slightly more skeptical of Tatian's place in textual criticism.[5] In short, "the Diatessaron is of fundamental importance for the study of the text of the Gospels and for the study of the evolution of the gospel tradition."[6]

Preuschen eventually got his wish—kind of. Within a generation, reconstructing the Diatessaron would become central to the textual criticism of the Gospels. Nevertheless, a century after Preuschen, we have yet to reconstruct the Diatessaron even close to fully. The simple reason, of course—and the reason that necessitates its reconstruction in the first place—is that no copy of the "original" Diatessaron has survived.[7] Instead

---

[1] Erwin Preuschen, *Untersuchungen zum Diatessaron Tatians* (Heidelberg: C. Winter, 1918), 8: "Es ist ohne Zweifel eine der erstaunlichsten Erscheinungen auf dem Gebiet textkritischer Arbeit, daß die Forschung sich mit heißem Bemühen der Gewinnung eines möglichst zuverlässigen Evangelientextes zugewandt hat, daß sie es aber bisher verabsäumt hat, die erste Ausgabe der Evangelien, deren Text noch in erheblichem Umfang festzustellen ist, zu rekonstruieren. Diese Ausgabe ist eben das Diatessaron Tatians, dessen Wiederherstellung, wie sich aus dem Vorstehenden ergibt, versucht werden muß, wenn sich nicht die Textkritik der Evangelien—und nicht nur ihre Textkritik—der wichtigsten Stütze beraubt sehen will." All translations are my own unless otherwise noted.

[2] Frederic G. Kenyon, *Handbook to the Textual Criticism of the New Testament* (London: Macmillan, 1901), 128.

[3] Tjitze Baarda, "Tatian's Diatessaron and the Greek Text of the Gospels," in *The Early Text of the New Testament*, ed. Charles E. Hill and Michael J. Kruger (Oxford: Oxford University Press, 2012), 338.

[4] He features the claim in the opening pages of his grand treatise, *Tatian's Diatessaron: Its Creation, Dissemination, Significance, and History in Scholarship* (Leiden: Brill, 1994), 1–3. He repeats it, among other places, in the work cited at the beginning of n. 6 below.

[5] I was surprised, for instance, to discover it (with added caution) in D. C. Parker, *An Introduction to the New Testament Manuscripts and Their Texts* (Cambridge: Cambridge University Press, 2008), 334: "As a witness older than our oldest manuscripts, the Diatessaron is potentially a source of information about readings in manuscripts known to Tatian."

[6] William L. Petersen, "The Diatessaron of Tatian," in *The Text of the New Testament in Contemporary Research: Essays on the Status Quaestionis*, ed. Bart D. Ehrman and Michael W. Holmes (Grand Rapids, MI: Eerdmans, 1995), 77. Ulrich Schmid repeats this phrase verbatim in his update of Petersen's essay, just after Schmid also notes that "the Diatessaron antedates virtually all the MSS of the NT"; see Ulrich Schmid, "The Diatessaron of Tatian," in *The Text of the New Testament in Contemporary Research: Essays on the Status Quaestionis*, ed. Bart D. Ehrman and Michael W. Holmes, 2nd ed. (Leiden: Brill, 2013), 116.

[7] I place "original" in quotation marks because we are not even certain in what language Tatian composed his compilation (Greek or Syriac) or whether he initiated any revisions in his own lifetime (perhaps in the transition from west to east) that would complicate the matter of seeking an "original" in the first place. Despite its age, I still consider Bruce Metzger's chapter on the Diatessaron in his *The Early Versions of the New Testament: Their Origin, Transmission, and Limitations* (Oxford: Clarendon

we have a series of witnesses to the Diatessaron, either in the form of citations from those who used it, or in the form of later gospel harmonies somehow derived from it. Although there is broad agreement on the outline and approach among these witnesses, they diverge considerably in wording and detail, and their relationship to each other is complex. So we are left with a tragically tantalizing task: if only we could piece together Tatian's Diatessaron, we would gain access to a text of the Gospels that predates nearly all our surviving manuscripts. But Tatian's text remains just out of reach. Even so, Tatian has slowly crept his way into the developing apparatus of the Greek NT for the last three hundred years, which is the subject of my study.

How can we cite in a critical apparatus a work that no longer exists? In the following pages I have traced the presence of the Diatessaron in nearly every major printed Greek NT from the beginning of the eighteenth century (starting with John Mill in 1707) to today (ending with the UBS[5] in 2014).[8] My purpose is to chart the use of Tatian's Diatessaron in the textual criticism of the Gospels, as the field transitioned from having essentially no Diatessaronic witnesses to having more than it could handle. In the last three centuries, Tatian has enjoyed a rapid rise with a sudden fall, and the field is currently in a state of flux. After assessing Tatian's evolving face in fifteen editions of the Greek NT, I offer seven recommendations for the future direction of Diatessaronic studies and its place in NT textual criticism.

2. The Use of Tatian's Diatessaron in Printed Editions of the Greek NT

As an aid to the reader, I offer an outline of the printed editions of the Greek NT that I cover in the current section:[9]

Press, 1977), 10–36, as one of the most instructively balanced (and succinct) introductions to the complexity of Diatessaronic studies available; I commend it to the reader for further background.

[8] I am not aware of anyone who has performed such a survey on the Diatessaron before. The bulk of this information is not available in William Petersen's 1994 monograph *Tatian's Diatessaron*, although he certainly covers the discoveries of Diatessaronic witnesses that I mention along the way. Ulrich Schmid started along a path such as mine in "How Can We Access Second Century Texts? The Cases of Marcion and Tatian," in *The New Testament Text in Early Christianity: Proceedings of the Lille Colloquium, July 2000*, ed. C.-B. Amphoux and J. K. Elliott (Lausanne: Editions du Zèbre, 2003), 139–50, but only covered the UBS editions' changing approach to Tatian. I found initial guidance in a study by F. Neirynck, who briefly traces the Diatessaronic evidence for Luke 24:12 through several editions of the Greek NT in "Lk xxiv 12, Les témoins du texte occidental," in *Miscellanea Neotestamentica, Volume 1*, ed. Tjitze Baarda, A. F. J. Klijn, and W. C. van Unnik (Leiden: Brill, 1978), 49–52 (esp. p. 50n. 31). My survey, of course, is not exhaustive. Notable critical editions that I do not cover include those of Tregelles (1857–72), Weiss (1894–1900), and Bover (1943), both for the sake of space and because they overlap in time and approach with editions I already cover. I imagine that an even more exhaustive study could be done by tracing the discussion of the Diatessaron in handbooks on textual criticism, but my desire was to focus on those editors who had actually placed a critical apparatus in the hands of readers and therefore had to encounter Tatian in practice, not only in theory.

[9] Should the reader be more interested in my conclusions than my survey, I would suggest reading only my assessment of the UBS editions and then proceeding to my recommendations for the future.

1. John Mill (1707)
2. Johann Albrecht Bengel (1734)
3. Johann Jakob Wettstein (1751-2)
4. Johann Jakob Griesbach (1st ed. 1775-7; 2nd ed. 1796-1806)
5. Karl Lachmann (1st ed. 1831; 2nd ed. 1842-50)
6. Constantin von Tischendorf (8th ed. 1869-72)
7. B. F. Westcott and F. J. A. Hort (1st ed. 1881-2; 2nd ed. 1896)
8. Hermann Freiherr von Soden (1902-13)
9. Alexander Souter (1st ed. 1910; 2nd ed. 1947)
10. Heinrich Vogels (1st ed. 1920; 4th ed. 1955)
11. Augustin Merk (1st ed. 1933; 4th ed. 1942; 11th ed. 1992)
12. Interlude: S. C. E. Legg (1935, 1940), IGNTP's Luke (1984-7), Nestle-Aland (1st ed. 1898; 28th ed. 2012)
13. The United Bible Societies (1st ed. 1966; 5th ed. 2014)
    i. *The Deficiencies in UBS$^{1-3}$*
    ii. *The Changes—and Lingering Deficiencies—in UBS$^{4-5}$*
    iii. *The Effects of Bad Diatessaronic Data*

2.1 John Mill (1707)

John Mill's 1707 edition of the Greek New Testament is a fitting place to begin.[10] Mill's was one of the first major editions of the Greek NT to cite individual witnesses, including patristic citations, in the apparatus.[11] Mill devotes an impressively detailed section of his prolegomena to Tatian and the Diatessaron (pp. xxxviii-xl), where he discusses many of the key features of Tatian's biography and the Diatessaron (including Tatian's discipleship under Justin, Tatian's purported lapse into heresy, the association of the Diatessaron with the *Gospel of the Ebionites* and the *Gospel of the Hebrews*, Theodoret's systematic removal of the Diatessaron, and Victor's later discovery of an anonymous harmony). In particular, Mill uses Theodoret's statement that Tatian excised the genealogies as the litmus strip for testing a harmony's Diatessaronic status. Mill thereby concludes that Victor's harmony, since it includes the genealogies, is not in fact by Tatian but by Ammonius (to whom he devotes another long section of the prolegomena, pp. lxiii-lxiv).[12] Mill also has a section on Ephrem, but there is no mention of Tatian or the Diatessaron here (p. lxxvi).

---

[10] John Mill, Ἡ Καινὴ Διαθήκη: *Novum Testamentum: Cum lectionibus variantibus* (Oxford: Sheldonian Theatre, 1707).

[11] The London Polyglot Bible of 1655-7 included an appendix of variant readings derived from fifteen other sources, while John Fell's Greek NT of 1675 listed variants but grouped witnesses together rather than citing them individually. See Bruce M. Metzger and Bart D. Ehrman, *The Text of the New Testament: Its Transmission, Corruption, and Restoration*, 4th ed. (New York: Oxford University Press, 2005), 153-5.

[12] It is worth noting that whether Tatian or Ammonius composed the Diatessaron was a question that frustrated early research (see Petersen, *Tatian's Diatessaron*, 32-3, 98-9). Victor himself debates the question in his preface to Codex Fuldensis and ultimately settles on Tatian. Mill does not appear

Mill mentions Tatian a handful of times in his apparatus, often in conjunction with Ammonius (although sometimes he lists Ammonius by himself; cf. p. 79 vs. p. 100).[13] Of particular note is the statement that Mill makes regarding Tatian in reference to the *pericope adulterae* (John 7:53–8:11). Mill lists Tatian (along with Ammonius) as a witness for the passage's inclusion and then adds, "Now Tatian flourished before 160 AD, and indeed within sixty years, or thereabout, of the death of John himself."[14] In other words, Mill considers Tatian an especially authoritative witness to the text of John's Gospel because Tatian lived within a generation or so of the author. With this statement, Mill may well have kindled the modern text-critical enterprise of turning to Tatian for the earliest text of the Gospels. However, Mill's supposition that Ammonius was the author of Victor's harmony likely delayed the use of Tatian in the apparatuses of both Mill and his successors.

2.2 Johann Albrecht Bengel (1734)

Johann Albrecht Bengel published his Greek NT in 1734.[15] Although Bengel does not include Tatian (or Ammonius) in the list of early Christian writers that he intends to cite, he does include Ephrem (translated into Greek); but he does not yet associate Ephrem with Tatian.[16] Nonetheless, like Mill, he makes reference to Tatian, Ammonius, and Victor's harmony at various points in his apparatus.

---

to have direct access to Codex Fuldensis or even an edition thereof (which does not appear until 1868; see n. 31 below), but is reliant (see p. lxiii) on a 1524 edition of Michael Memler, *Quatuor evangeliorum consonantia, ab Ammonio Alexandrino congesta, ac a Victore Capuano episcopo translata* (Mainz: J. Schoeffer, 1524). In this edition, Memler reprints Victor's preface and the *capitula* of Fuldensis, so its base is clearly derived from a descendent of Fuldensis. But Memler concludes it is the work of Ammonius, not Tatian (hence his title). Furthermore, while Fuldensis has 182 chapters, Memler's edition has only 181. Thus it falls into Schmid's "Sa-recension" of the Latin Diatessaron, a recension that stems from the ninth-century Codex Sangallensis, on which see Ulrich Schmid, *Unum ex Quattuor: Eine Geschichte der lateinischen Tatianüberlieferung*, AGLB 37 (Freiburg im Breisgau: Herder, 2005), 100–4.

[13] Curiously, Mill (*Novum Testamentum*, 100 and elsewhere) refers to Ammonius's work as a *Monotessaron*, presumably meaning "one from four." This label will reappear frequently among the early modern editors of the Greek NT. Although it is not an ancient label for Tatian's or Ammonius's work so far as I can tell, it goes back at least to the fifteenth century, when Johannes Gerson uses it in 1420 as the title of his own gospel harmony; see Petersen, *Tatian's Diatessaron*, 189n. 137. It may also stem from the way Zacharias Chrysopolitanus referred to the Latin harmony on which he wrote a commentary in the twelfth century, on which see Petersen, *Tatian's Diatessaron*, 187–9.

[14] Mill, *Novum Testamentum*, 268: *Floruit autem Tatianus sub annum Christi 160, adeoque intra sexagesimum, aut circiter, ab ipsius Joannis morte*. I will take this moment to note that my primary concern in the following survey is to note when an editor cites a Diatessaronic reading in the critical apparatus. Although I will sometimes specify when an editor has adopted the alleged reading in the main text, not every edition includes a critically reconstructed text (some reprint an existing text, like the Textus Receptus), so the question is not always relevant. My ultimate aim is to trace the growing presence of the Diatessaron in the apparatus and assess its right to live there.

[15] Johann Albrecht Bengel, Ἡ Καινὴ Διαθήκη: *Novum Testamentum Graecum* (Tübingen: J. G. Cotta, 1734). Bengel even mentions Mill in the extended subtitle: *ita adornatum ut textus probatarum editionum medullam margo variantium lectionum in suas classes distributarum locorumque parallelorum delectum apparatus subiunctus criseos sacrae Millianae praesertim compendium, limam, supplementum ac fructum exhibeat.*

[16] Bengel, *Novum Testamentum Graecum*, 389. Bengel is presumably drawing on an edition of Ephrem's works that was published at Oxford in 1709 by Edward Thwaites. Ready access to Ephrem's

For instance, Bengel cites the *Harmonia Victoris Capuani* (or simply *Victor Capuanus*) directly for readings at Matt 1:11 (p. 452); Matt 4:16 (p. 456); and Matt 7:22 (p. 468), among others. In a discussion of John 1:1, Bengel adds the evidence of the "very ancient gospel harmony that Victor of Capua restored."[17] However, in an earlier note, Bengel makes clear that he is unsure to whom to attribute Victor's harmony. Commenting on the doxology appended to the Lord's Prayer at Matt 6:13, Bengel cites Victor of Capua as evidence for its omission, and then adds, "if not more accurately Ammonius of Alexandria himself, or whoever is the author of the Gospel Harmony that was restored through Victor, in which the full Lord's Prayer exists without the final line."[18] So Bengel considers the Victor harmony an important early witness to the gospel text, but he is not confident about its authorship.

Bengel's uncertainty does not keep him from citing Tatian directly on occasion. In a discussion of the ending of Mark, Bengel cites as evidence for the long ending, "the Monotessaron of Ammonius, the Harmony ascribed to Tatian, [and] the canons of Eusebius."[19] His reference to Ammonius's work as a *Monotessaron* draws upon the language of Mill (see n. 13 above). It is tempting to propose that Bengel is distinguishing between what is now termed a "synopsis" (a chart of gospel parallels) and a "harmony" (an interwoven narrative of the Gospels), but his earlier comments would preclude that conclusion, since he evidently thinks that Ammonius composed a complete gospel harmony, which Victor restored. What, then, is Bengel's source for Tatian's "Harmony"? The answer is likely found in the appendix of Mill's 1707 edition, where Mill adds supplementary evidence to his apparatus.[20] Under Mark 16:8, Mill likewise lists Ammonius's *Monotessaron* and Eusebius's canon tables as supporting evidence. In between those two, Mill mentions a work published in 1523 by Ottmar Luscinius (also called Ottmar Nachtigall). The work is Luscinius's Latin epitome of Greek gospel harmony fragments that he apparently thinks go back to Tatian.[21] Bengel is likely drawing

---

Commentary on the Diatessaron will not be available until 1836 (Armenian) and 1876 (Latin), on which see the discussion under Westcott and Hort below.

[17] Bengel, *Novum Testamentum Graecum*, 572: *Accedit antiquissima Harmonia evangelica, quam Victor Capuanus instauravit.*

[18] Bengel, *Novum Testamentum Graecum*, 461: *Silet etiam Victor Capuanus, nisi ipse potius Ammonius Alexandrinus, vel quisquis auctor est Harmoniae evangelicae per Victorem instauratae: in qua exstat tota, sine clausula, oratio dominica.* I can confirm that Codex Fuldensis does indeed omit the appended doxology of the Lord's Prayer at Matt 6:13, as does Jerome's Vulgate; see Nicholas J. Zola, "Tatian's Diatessaron in Latin: A New Edition and Translation of Codex Fuldensis" (PhD diss., Baylor University, 2014), 73. Memler's 1524 edition (p. 39), although not a direct edition of Fuldensis, also omits the doxology.

[19] Bengel, *Novum Testamentum Graecum*, 516: *Ammonii monotessaron, Harmonia Tatiano adscripta, Eusebii Canones.*

[20] This note appears under Mill's "Appendix ad Notas Superiores" (Appendix to the Notes Above), a section which follows p. 808 but whose page numbers restart. The note on Tatian is on p. 19 (col. 2, line 11).

[21] Ottmar Luscinius, *Evangelicae historiae ex quatuor Evangelistis perpetuo tenore continuata narratio* (Augsburg: n.p., 1523). Sadly, these Greek fragments are no longer extant. Although Luscinius initially attributes the fragments to Ammonius (whose name appears in the extended title), he apparently later concludes that they stem from Tatian, as do other scholars, including Theodor Zahn. On Luscinius's epitome, see esp. Theodor Zahn, *Tatian's Diatessaron*, FGNK 1 (Erlangen: Andreas Deichert, 1881), 313–28; John Mee Fuller, "Tatianus," *DCB* 4:797; and Samuel Hemphill, *The*

on this information to propose a separate harmony of Tatian from the *Monotessaron* of Ammonius. Thus Bengel recognizes that, even if he is not the author of Victor's harmony, Tatian would be a weighty early witness. The hunt for Tatian's harmony is on.

2.3 Johann Jakob Wettstein (1751-2)

With his Greek NT published in 1751-2,[22] Johann Jakob Wettstein more than doubled the number of manuscripts theretofore cited and amassed a compendium of citations from early Greek, Latin, and Hebrew writers.[23] In his section on Greek writers who cite the NT, Wettstein includes a paragraph on "Tatian the Syrian" that first lists Tatian's surviving *Oratio ad Graecos*,[24] then cites the basic information drawn from Eusebius's *Hist. eccl.* 4.29, and ends by noting Theodoret's removal of over two hundred copies of "such Gospels." What Wettstein appends to this description is instructive for the state of Diatessaronic studies in the mid-eighteenth century: "Today not one survives."[25] In Wettstein's opinion, there are no extant copies of the Diatessaron.

Accordingly, Wettstein does not associate Victor's harmony with Tatian; nor, however, does he associate it with Ammonius. In a discussion of Ammonius on the following page that is triple the size of his paragraph on Tatian, Wettstein comes to the surprising conclusion that Victor's harmony is the product of a harmonist working "not before Eusebius, but after."[26] Here Wettstein expressly parts from Mill's conclusion that Ammonius is the author of Victor's harmony, since it does not match Eusebius's description of Ammonius's work. Although Wettstein does not settle on Tatian as the author, he opens the door for reconsidering who lies behind the harmony that Victor found.

Wettstein also has a short paragraph on Ephrem but does not yet associate him with Tatian. Likewise, Wettstein does not mention the Diatessaron in his discussion of the Syriac versions of the NT and their editions.[27] Ephrem shows up on occasion in Wettstein's apparatus, but Tatian and Ammonius do not. Wettstein values the potential importance of Tatian but does not believe we have access to his text.

Diatessaron of Tatian: A Harmony of the Four Holy Gospels Compiled in the Third Quarter of the Second Century (London: Hodder & Stoughton, 1888), 63-9.

[22] Johann Jakob Wettstein, Ἡ Καινὴ Διαθήκη: *Novum Testamentum Graecum: Editionis receptae cum lectionibus variantibus*, 2 vols. (Amsterdam: Dommeriana, 1751-2).

[23] Kurt Aland and Barbara Aland, *The Text of the New Testament: An Introduction to the Critical Editions and to the Theory and Practice of Modern Textual Criticism*, trans. Erroll F. Rhodes, 2nd rev. and enl. ed. (Grand Rapids, MI: Eerdmans, 1989), 9; Metzger and Ehrman, *Text of the New Testament*, 160-1.

[24] Wettstein has access to this 1546 edition: Conrad Gesner, ed., *Tatiani Assyrii, Iustini martyris discipuli, Oratio contra Graecos* (Zürich: C. Froschoverus, 1546).

[25] Wettstein, *Novum Testamentum Graecum*, 1:67: *Theodoretus testatur, se plusquam ducentos tales Evangeliorum Codices deprehendisse atque seposuisse; hodie nec unus superest.*

[26] Wettstein, *Novum Testamentum Graecum*, 1:68: *Ex quibus omnibus conficitur, id quod sub Ammonii nomine nunc Latine circumfertur, scriptum esse Auctoris Eusebio non prioris sed posterioris.*

[27] Wettstein, *Novum Testamentum Graecum*, 1:70, 109. Wettstein (p. 1:66) does think that the author of the *Apostolic Constitutions* had access to Tatian's Diatessaron.

2.4 Johann Jakob Griesbach (1st ed. 1775–7; 2nd ed. 1796–1806)

In his edition of 1775–7 (second edition 1796–1806),[28] Johann Jakob Griesbach laid the groundwork for future labor on the Greek NT as one of the first to print a base text that differed from the Textus Receptus.[29] Despite his pioneering interest in synoptic criticism, Griesbach lists neither Tatian nor the Diatessaron in his Prolegomena as items he will consult; Ammonius is also absent, although Ephrem Syrus appears.[30] Nonetheless, Griesbach makes mention of Tatian, Ammonius, and Victor's harmony in his apparatus on occasion. Of particular note, Griesbach returns without discussion to Mill's opinion that Ammonius is the author behind Victor's harmony. For instance, in discussing an insertion at the end of John 1:36, Griesbach lists as evidence "Ammonius, according to Victor of Capua."[31] Griesbach accordingly will often cite simply "Victor of Capua" in the apparatus as a stand-in for Ammonius's authoritative harmony.[32]

It is fairly certain that Griesbach is accessing "Ammonius" through Memler's 1524 edition of the Victor harmony (as did Mill and Bengel), because at least two readings that Griesbach lists for Victor agree with Memler's edition *against* the actual Codex Fuldensis (and Ranke's 1868 edition thereof).[33] Consequently, while Griesbach thinks he is citing authoritative third-century readings for the Gospels, he is potentially citing early medieval readings instead.

Griesbach cites Tatian directly only rarely. One example is at Matt 27:49 regarding the famous *scholion* of minuscule MS 72 that says Tatian (among others) added here a line about Jesus being pierced in the side (cf. John 19:34) *before* he died, an interpolation that actually appears in several Greek and Latin manuscripts.[34] Griesbach also cites

---

[28] For this essay I have consulted an edition that was published in 1809 but which begins with Griesbach's preface from 1796 and so represents his second edition: Johann Jakob Griesbach, *Novum Testamentum Graece, Volumen 1: IV Evangelia*, 2nd ed. (London: J. Mackinlay; Cuthell and Martin, 1809).

[29] Metzger and Ehrman, *Text of the New Testament*, 165–7; Aland and Aland, *Text of the New Testament*, 9–11.

[30] Griesbach, *Novum Testamentum Graece*, xcvi–xcvii.

[31] Griesbach, *Novum Testamentum Graece*, 430: *Ammon. ap. Vict. capuan.* The discussion concerns the addition of ὁ αἴρων τὴν ἁμαρτίαν τοῦ κόσμου ("the one who takes away the sin of the world") at the end of John 1:36. I have consulted Codex Fuldensis, and indeed this insertion appears there at John 1:36 (see ch. 16 [fol. 35r]; Ernst Ranke, *Codex Fuldensis: Novum Testamentum Latine Interprete Hieronymo ex Manuscripto Victoris Capuani* [Marburg: N. G. Elwert, 1868], 41 line 27), although as will become clear below, Griesbach does not have direct access to Codex Fuldensis, but to Memler's 1524 edition of a recension of Fuldensis whose text is not identical to that of Fuldensis.

[32] As in Griesbach, *Novum Testamentum Graece*, 463, 513.

[33] The first reading is the omission of μὴ before πιστεύοντες in John 6:64 (Griesbach, *Novum Testamentum Graece*, 463). Codex Fuldensis actually omits the entire phrase in which these words occur (see ch. 83 [fol. 77v]; Ranke, *Codex Fuldensis*, 77 line 22). However, Memler (*Quatuor Evangeliorum Consonantia*, 93), includes the complete phrase and omits the *non* before *credentes* (as Griesbach reports). The second reading concerns the addition of καὶ before ἀνέπεσεν in John 13:12 (Griesbach, *Novum Testamentum Graece*, 513). Codex Fuldensis does not have *et* before *cum recubuisset* (see ch. 155 [fol. 147r]; Zola, "Codex Fuldensis," 87). Memler (*Quatuor Evangeliorum Consonantia*, 202), however, does read *et cum recubuisset* (as Griesbach reports). These two examples suffice to demonstrate that Memler's exemplar was a descendent of Fuldensis (since it includes Victor's preface and an altered 181-chapter scheme), but one whose text was altered along the way.

[34] Griesbach, *Novum Testamentum Graece*, 139. Griesbach is not the first editor of the Greek NT to mention this interpolation (Wettstein, for instance, also noted it). On this potential Diatessaronic reading see further Petersen, *Tatian's Diatessaron*, 58–59.

Tatian as evidence for the longer ending of Mark, but his citation is odd: "Ammonius and Tatian in [their] harmonies."[35] The word "harmonies" is clearly plural, suggesting that Griesbach is distinguishing between Ammonius's harmony (presumably found in Victor of Capua) and Tatian's harmony. His source for Tatian's harmony is unclear, but perhaps he is following Bengel's reference to Luscinius's 1523 edition described above. What is clear is that Griesbach desires to draw upon Tatian but is limited by his sources.[36] That will soon change.

2.5 Karl Lachmann (1st ed. 1831; 2nd ed. 1842–50)

Another early scholar to break from the Textus Receptus was Karl Lachmann, who published a Greek NT in 1831 and then an expanded edition in 1842–50.[37] Although Lachmann has a more selective manuscript base (he relies only on early majuscules, the Old Latin and Vulgate, a few early fathers, and no minuscules), he is the first in my survey to demonstrate direct awareness of Codex Fuldensis itself (and not reliance on Memler's 1524 edition of a later recension thereof). In his preface, Lachmann describes a trip he took to Fulda in autumn of 1839 with his coeditor Philip Buttmann in order to examine Fuldensis, to which he says they were given unprecedented access.[38] Lachmann considers Fuldensis his prime example of the Vulgate text; but he also recognizes the Gospels are in harmonized form and therefore less useful.[39] He discusses some of the harmonized readings in his preface; and he concludes (like Wettstein) that the harmony behind Fuldensis was composed by neither Tatian nor Ammonius, but by a Latin author post-Jerome, since the text is clearly dependent on

---

[35] Griesbach, *Novum Testamentum Graece*, 253: *Ammon. et Tatian. in harmoniis.*

[36] A final example is perhaps worth mentioning: Griesbach doubles down on a note he draws from Wettstein, which Wettstein drew from Mill, that concerns the interpolation of a line from Matt 10:15 at the end of Mark 6:11: "Latin Victor (according to Wettstein) and Zacharias Chrysopolitanus observe these [words] to be Matthew's, from the Monotessaron of Ammonius"; in Griesbach, *Novum Testamentum Graece*, 178: *Victor latinus (teste Wetst.) et Zacharias Chrysopolit. haec Matthaei esse notant ex Ammonii monotess.* What Griesbach seems to mean here, following his predecessors, is that Ammonius's harmony listed the source of this line not as Mark but as Matthew; Griesbach thinks we know this from both Victor's sixth-century harmony and Zacharias Chrysopolitanus's twelfth-century commentary. The important point here is that Griesbach is concerned about the source of interpolations into the Gospels, and he believes an ancient harmony may help shed light on the process by which they entered the text. We will see this pattern multiply with von Soden below.

[37] The first edition does not include an apparatus; I have consulted the second edition for this essay: Karl Lachmann, *Novum Testamentum Graece et Latine*, 2nd ed., 2 vols. (Berlin: G. Reimer, 1842–50). On Lachmann, see Metzger and Ehrman, *Text of the New Testament*, 170–1; Aland and Aland, *Text of the New Testament*, 11.

[38] Lachmann, *Novum Testamentum*, 1:xxvi–xxvii. Lachmann also notes his source for information on Codex Fuldensis, the 1723 work by historian Johann Friedrich Schannat, *Vindemiae literariae: Hoc est veterum monumentorum ad Germaniam sacram praecipue spectantium* (Fulda; Leipzig: M. G. Weidmann, 1723), 218–21. This work has a very complete description of Fuldensis, including images and transcriptions of Victor's subscriptions, some of which Lachmann repeats. A fascinating (if brief) account of Lachmann's trip to Fulda to examine Fuldensis may be found in Samuel Prideaux Tregelles, *An Account of the Printed Text of the Greek New Testament: With Remarks on Its Revision upon Critical Principles* (London: Samuel Bagster and Sons, 1854), 100. There Tregelles reports that Buttmann read Fuldensis aloud while Lachmann collated variant readings.

[39] Lachmann, *Novum Testamentum*, 1:xxvi, xxviii.

the Vulgate.⁴⁰ Lachmann is not yet in a position to consider what later Diatessaronic scholars will term "Vulgatization" (the conformation of the wording to the local "standard" gospel text), since he has no other versions of the Diatessaron with which to compare Fuldensis.⁴¹

In the edition itself, Lachmann prints his reconstructed Greek text on top, with a critical apparatus in the middle, and his reconstructed Latin Vulgate on the bottom.⁴² In his Vulgate text (even in the Gospels), Lachmann refers repeatedly to Fuldensis (as siglum F). Lachmann even has a special siglum (V) for places in which Victor of Capua corrects Fuldensis. Lachmann does not, however, list F (or any other Diatessaronic source) in the apparatus to his Greek text. So the Diatessaron has little impact on Lachmann's Greek NT, even while it inadvertently influences the Latin side. Nonetheless, Lachmann's personal examination of and heavy reliance on Fuldensis paves the way for its full inclusion in the critical apparatus of upcoming Greek editions.

2.6 Constantin von Tischendorf (8th ed., 1869-72)

Constantin von Tischendorf produced an unprecedented number of publications devoted to the text of the NT,⁴³ culminating in the eighth critical edition of his Greek NT published in 1869-72.⁴⁴ In between his seventh (1859) and eighth edition, Tischendorf updated a shorter work he entitled *When Were Our Gospels Written?*, which gives us a small preview of his approach toward Tatian's Diatessaron.⁴⁵ In it he discusses the harmonies of Theophilus of Antioch and Tatian but reports that "both of those works are lost."⁴⁶ Already then we have a clue for his coming assessment of Fuldensis, to which I will return below. Tischendorf goes on to discuss what is known

---

⁴⁰ Lachmann, *Novum Testamentum*, 1:xxviii–xxix.
⁴¹ See Petersen's explanation of "Vulgatization" in *Tatian's Diatessaron*, 127–9. Lachmann (1:xxviii) actually mentions J. A. Schmeller's 1841 edition of Codex Sangallensis (the ninth-century Latin-Old High German bilingual) as well. But Schmeller's title betrays his confusion over whether to attribute the harmony to Ammonius or Tatian—or whether they are one and the same: *Ammonii Alexandrini quae et Tatiani dicitur harmonia evangeliorum in linguam Latinam et inde ante annos mille in Francicam translata* (Vienna: Fr. Beck, 1841).
⁴² Recall that Lachmann only claims to be reconstructing the text as it was in the fourth century; see Metzger and Ehrman, *Text of the New Testament*, 170.
⁴³ See the discussions in Aland and Aland, *Text of the New Testament*, 11–14; Metzger and Ehrman, *Text of the New Testament*, 172–3.
⁴⁴ Constantin von Tischendorf, *Novum Testamentum Graece: Ad antiquissimos testes denuo recensuit*, 8th ed., 2 vols. (Leipzig: Giesecke & Devrient, 1869–1872). Tischendorf issued his eighth edition in two volumes. Unfortunately, he passed away in 1874 before he was able to complete the accompanying Prolegomena, which was consequently prepared as a third volume by his student Caspar René Gregory and issued in three parts (1884, 1890, 1894). Since I am tracing the text-critical use of Tatian's Diatessaron chronologically, I will limit myself to discussing only Tischendorf's first two volumes here. Gregory's third volume (particularly Part 3) discusses Tatian at several points, but many of these references draw upon works that were published after Tischendorf's death and which he therefore could not have consulted for the apparatus of his eighth edition.
⁴⁵ Published in German as *Wann wurden unsere Evangelien verfasst?* (Leipzig: J. C. Hinrich, 1865). The English translation that I cite was published under a different title (to distinguish it from a previous edition for a more popular audience): *Origin of the Four Gospels*, trans. William Leonard Gage, from the fourth German edition, revised and greatly enlarged (London: Jackson, Walford, & Hodder, 1868).
⁴⁶ Tischendorf, *Origin of the Four Gospels*, 46.

of Tatian and his Diatessaron, including the fact that Bar Salibi reports that Ephrem wrote a commentary on it. Tischendorf is the first in my survey to mention awareness of Ephrem's *Commentary*; sadly, he will not have easy access to it before he dies, so it will not be included in his apparatus.[47] Tischendorf ends his discussion of these two harmonies by arguing that their emergence just after the middle of the second century "points back conclusively to a time when the four Gospels were already accepted as a perfect record, and when the necessity had begun to be felt of deducing a higher unity and a more harmonious completeness from them than the diversity of the various books and the apparent discrepancies had rendered apparent." Tischendorf's statement is instructive for two reasons: (1) he invokes Tatian's Diatessaron as a demonstration that the fourfold gospel is already well established, rather than as a competing attempt to dethrone and replace the four—a debate that continues in this very volume; (2) he does not invoke Tatian's Diatessaron as a witness to the second-century text of the Gospels. He cannot, of course, since he has already said that the Diatessaron is lost. The implications for his Greek NT are that Tatian will play a diminishing role therein.

Just one year before Tischendorf completed volume one of his eighth edition, Ernst Ranke published the first printed edition of Codex Fuldensis, although probably not quite in time for Tischendorf to consult it directly.[48] Nonetheless, drawing on Lachmann's precedent, Tischendorf cites Fuldensis (as siglum "fu") very frequently throughout the apparatus to his Greek text (and not just to reconstruct a separate Vulgate text, as Lachmann had done).[49] Were it not for our awareness that Tischendorf already considers Tatian's harmony lost, we might expect that his ample use of Fuldensis reflects the growing weight he places on Tatian's early authority. His few direct references to Tatian in the apparatus demonstrate that such is not the case.

Tischendorf appends an extended note regarding Tatian at the end of his discussion of the *pericope adulterae* in John. Unlike his predecessors, he does not cite Tatian or Ammonius as evidence for the inclusion of the passage. But, he says, lest he should be accused of overlooking anything, those who cite these two as witnesses here do so in error. He goes on to summarize Victor's preface and how Victor found an untitled Latin harmony that Victor presumed, after consulting Eusebius, came either from Ammonius or Tatian (but probably Tatian). However, emphasizes Tischendorf, that

---

[47] A Latin translation of the Armenian text will be published in 1876, two years after Tischendorf dies. The Armenian edition had already been published in 1836. For the bibliographic details, see note 56 below.

[48] Ernst Ranke, *Codex Fuldensis: Novum Testamentum Latine Interprete Hieronymo ex Manuscripto Victoris Capuani* (Marburg: N. G. Elwert, 1868). Metzger (*Text of the New Testament*, 172) reports that Tischendorf issued his eighth edition in 11 parts beginning in 1864. I cannot find a direct reference to Ranke's edition of Fuldensis in Tischendorf's first volume. However, there is a reference to it in volume two (published 1872, p. 302) at 2 Pet 1:4. In the prolegomena to his seventh edition (1859), Tischendorf already highly anticipates Ranke's forthcoming edition with these words (p. ccxlviii): "Henceforth most gratefully there will be an accurate edition of Codex Fuldensis, which the most renowned Ernst Ranke has undertaken" (=*Hinc gratissima erit codicis Fuldensis accurata editio, quam suscepit clar. vir Ern. Ranke*). Ranke also mentions Tischendorf in his Prolegomena (p. v).

[49] Since Tischendorf's apparatus has been digitized, it is possible to count these references. Accordance reports that Tischendorf cites Fuldensis over 500 times in the Gospels and over 1,700 times in the whole NT.

was a "most unfortunate" guess, which "many even now repeat."[50] Tischendorf thus follows Lachmann in concluding that the harmony behind Fuldensis goes back neither to Tatian nor to Ammonius.

Tischendorf makes this conclusion explicit in a similar—and similarly harsh—statement in his discussion of the long ending of Mark. After listing the weighty evidence for omission, he discusses the early Christians who cite the long ending, including Irenaeus and Hippolytus. But, he says, those who appeal to the harmonies (plural) of Ammonius and Tatian do so "in vain" (*frustra*), for the harmonies that survive "have hardly anything in common with Tatian or Ammonius."[51] It is worth noting that among the Greek NT editions that I have surveyed so far, three (those of Mill, Bengel, and Griesbach) cite "the harmonies" (plural) of Ammonius and Tatian as individual witnesses—for this very passage! Tischendorf has launched a critique at his predecessors and a challenge to his successors: abandon references to Tatian's Diatessaron in the critical apparatus of the Greek NT.[52]

The renowned reputation that Tischendorf carried in the field of textual studies might well have closed the door on Tatian's foothold in the text once and for all. But several significant publications in the next two decades will jam the door wide open again and place Tatian square in the middle of the apparatus for the following century.

2.7 B. F. Westcott and F. J. A. Hort (1st ed., 1881–2; 2nd ed., 1896)

B. F. Westcott and F. J. A. Hort famously titled their trailblazing Greek NT of 1881 *The New Testament in the Original Greek*. As such, they elected not to include a critical apparatus. Instead they published an Introduction and Appendix in 1882 that explained their methodology and offered notes on select readings.[53] It is here that we witness a transition in the access and import of Tatian's Diatessaron.

While discussing those who intentionally tampered with the text for dogmatic purposes, Westcott and Hort begin with Marcion and move next to Tatian:

> The evidence which has recently come to light as to his [Marcion's] disciple Tatian's Diatessaron has shown that Tatian habitually abridged the language of the passages which he combined; so that the very few known omissions which might be referred to a dogmatic purpose can as easily receive another explanation.[54]

---

[50] Tischendorf, *Novum Testamentum Graece*, 1:834–5: *Quam coniecturam quamvis infelicissimam etiamnum sunt qui repetant* (p. 1:835).

[51] Tischendorf, *Novum Testamentum Graece*, 1:407: *quae enim supersunt, vix quicquam cum Amm[onio] aut Tat[iano] commune habent*.

[52] Tischendorf's only remaining references to Tatian are unrelated to the Diatessaron. He cites Tatian's *Oratio* 19 a few times at John 1:3 (*Novum Testamentum Graece*, 1:742); he even cites a reading of Tatian according to Clement of Alexandria at 1 Cor 7:5 (*Novum Testamentum Graece*, 2:489).

[53] Brooke Foss Westcott and Fenton John Anthony Hort, *The New Testament in the Original Greek: Introduction and Appendix* (New York: Harper, 1882). For a thorough description of their edition, see Metzger and Ehrman, *Text of the New Testament*, 174–83; Aland and Aland, *Text of the New Testament*, 14–19.

[54] Westcott and Hort, *New Testament in the Original Greek* (1882), 283. The reference to Tatian as Marcion's (and not Justin's) disciple is noteworthy, presumably drawn from Eusebius's description of

A significant shift has occurred. Westcott and Hort speak as though they have *access* to Tatian's harmonistic method—and, by implication, to his text. Despite the Diatessaron's omissions and abridgments, they do not believe Tatian willfully corrupted the text for theological purposes (notwithstanding his being a "disciple" of Marcion). What is this "evidence which has recently come to light"? The answer comes in the Appendix.

As they discuss their use of patristic citations at the beginning of the Appendix, Westcott and Hort end with this caveat:

> But it must suffice to notice once for all the complexity of the testimony obtained from the Armenian translation of Ephrem's Syriac commentary (or parts of it) on Tatian's Diatessaron, now made accessible by Moesinger's Latin rendering. It is often difficult to distinguish Ephrem's own (Syriac) readings from those which he found in the Syriac Diatessaron; and hardly ever possible to distinguish Tatian's own Greek readings from Old Syriac readings introduced by his translator.[55]

The "new evidence," then, is Moesinger's 1876 Latin translation of the Armenian manuscripts of Ephrem's *Commentary* on the Diatessaron.[56] Westcott and Hort's assessment of this work is instructive. On the one hand, they believe it provides access (essentially for the first time) to Tatian's text and method. On the other hand, the access is limited and complex. They consider that Tatian composed his Diatessaron in Greek, that someone else translated it into Syriac, and that Ephrem at times cites the Old Syriac and at times the Syriac Diatessaron.[57] Nonetheless, as evidenced by their previous reference to Tatian, Westcott and Hort think Ephrem's *Commentary* is a trustworthy and viable witness to the Diatessaron.[58]

Their newfound access to Tatian's text via Ephrem leads Westcott and Hort to cite the Diatessaron several times in their selective apparatus, typically under the siglum "Ephr.*Diat.*"[59] Here, for the first time in my survey, Ephrem functions as a witness to Tatian. At the same time, another note on the Diatessaron reveals the limitations Westcott and Hort place on Tatian's influence. As did several editors before them, Westcott and Hort discuss the *scholion* in MS 72 at Matt 27:49, which states that "the gospel of Tatian" inserted the piercing of Jesus's side (cf. John 19:34) at this point,

---

Tatian's Marcionite leanings (*Hist. eccl.* 4.29.2-3, quoting Irenaeus, *Adv. haer.* 1.28.1). As we will see below, Westcott and Hort do not have high regard for Tatian's orthodoxy.

[55] Westcott and Hort, *New Testament in the Original Greek* (1882), 3 (Appendix, where the page numbering restarts).

[56] Johann Baptist Aucher and Georg Moesinger, *Evangelii concordantis expositio facta a Sancto Ephraemo Doctore Syro* (Venice: Mechitarist Monastery of S. Lazzaro, 1876). Aucher had published the Armenian edition in 1836, but it was only accessible to those with a facility in that language; cf. Petersen, *Tatian's Diatessaron*, 114–15.

[57] Also see their discussion of the Syriac versions (pp. 84–5), which states that Ephrem cites the Old Syriac, but which does not mention the Diatessaron.

[58] A similar example comes later in the Appendix (p. 79, discussing the Passover of John 6:4), where Westcott and Hort consult Ephrem's *Commentary* to determine whether Tatian conceived of a one-year or three-year ministry for Jesus.

[59] For some examples, see p. 52 (at Luke 1:28 and 2:7); p. 59 (at Luke 9:54); and p. 88 (at John 10:8), among others.

before Jesus dies.[60] While several significant manuscripts of Matthew do insert the piercing here, Westcott and Hort note that Ephrem's *Commentary* does not support this sequence. They go on to cast a rather heavy stone upon both Tatian's orthodoxy and orbit. Even if this was the Diatessaron's sequence, they say, the Diatessaron could hardly be the root of the interpolation in so many ancient copies of Matthew. Why not? They go on:

> There is moreover no evidence that this obscure work was known out of Syria, where Tatian founded his sect; and the evil repute attached to his name renders the adoption of a startling reading from such a source highly improbable.[61]

In other words, the Diatessaron was too obscure to have had widespread influence on separated gospel texts, and Tatian's heretical reputation would have kept anyone from intentionally adopting his readings anyway. This damning declaration demonstrates an important point that I have not yet mentioned. Although they repeatedly draw upon Ephrem's *Commentary*, when Westcott and Hort cite Codex Fuldensis, it is never as evidence for Tatian's text. They do not even consider the Diatessaron to have circulated outside of Syria. By implication then, they do not consider Fuldensis to be Tatianic (perhaps following Tischendorf). Apparently, they have not yet realized that Ephrem's sequence correlates significantly with Fuldensis. Nor do they yet have the luxury of comparing these to the Arabic version, which is about to be published. All this will change before the second edition of their text.

Between the first edition (1881–2) and second edition (1896) of Westcott and Hort's Greek NT, several significant publications emerged in Diatessaronic studies that changed the face of the field. In 1881 (the same year as Westcott and Hort's initial edition) Theodor Zahn published his groundbreaking study entitled *Tatian's Diatessaron* in which he carefully compared the citations of the Diatessaron in Ephrem's *Commentary* (available as of 1876) with the citations in Aphrahat's *Demonstrations* (available as of 1869), along with Codex Fuldensis (available as of 1868), in order to produce an unprecedented reconstruction of the Diatessaron's outline and text.[62] Zahn's study was instrumental in convincing the scholarly world that Fuldensis was indeed a version of Tatian's Diatessaron.[63] Zahn was also aware of the forthcoming edition and Latin translation of the Arabic Diatessaron, published in 1888 by Augustin Ciasca.[64] The publication of the Arabic Diatessaron soon led to an English translation and in-depth study of the entire Diatessaronic tradition up to that point by J. Hamlyn Hill in 1894.[65]

Last, from Westcott's perspective (Hort had passed away by this point), the most significant find was the newly discovered Sinaitic palimpsest of the Old Syriac Gospels

---

[60] See the discussion under Griesbach and n. 34 above. We will return to this text again below.
[61] Westcott and Hort, *New Testament in the Original Greek* (1882), 22 (Appendix).
[62] Zahn, *Tatian's Diatessaron* (FGNK 1), introduced in n. 21 above. For an in-depth description of this work, see Petersen, *Tatian's Diatessaron*, 121–4.
[63] The articles in the 1887 *Dictionary of Christian Biography*, though obviously dated, are still remarkably informative in this regard. See esp. Fuller, "Tatianus," *DCB* 4:797; and F. H. Blackburne Daniell, "Victor of Capua," *DCB* 4:1124.
[64] Augustinus Ciasca, *Tatiani Evangeliorum harmoniae arabice* (Rome: Typographia Polyglotta, 1888).
[65] J. Hamlyn Hill, *The Earliest Life of Christ Ever Compiled from the Four Gospels Being the Diatessaron of Tatian: Literally Translated from the Arabic Version and Containing the Four Gospels Woven into One Story* (Edinburgh: T&T Clark, 1894). The Appendices in this work are still indispensable,

(syrˢ), which, Westcott notes, was part of the impetus for the second edition.[66] In this second edition, Westcott commissioned F. C. Burkitt to add significant notes on syrˢ and the Syriac tradition in general. These notes include many updated and amplified references to the Diatessaron (including the Arabic version) and its newly revised significance among the Syriac Gospels. While Burkitt doubts at this point that the Diatessaron was the first translation of the Gospels into Syriac (he would later change his mind), he does recognize significant interaction (even "disturbance") between the Diatessaron and the Old Syriac, which resulted in harmonizations corrupting the Old Syriac.[67] Thus Burkitt departs from Westcott and Hort's first edition, where they considered it hardly possible that the Diatessaron could affect the separated Gospels (albeit Burkitt is still limiting the Diatessaron's reach to a Syriac milieu). Burkitt, of course, will go on to publish in 1904 a highly influential study of the Old Syriac Gospels and their relation to the Diatessaron.[68]

This was the breakthrough period for Diatessaronic studies.[69] Between Tischendorf's eighth edition (1868–72) and Westcott and Hort's second edition (1896), four of the most foundational witnesses to the Diatessaron became widely accessible for the first time: Codex Fuldensis (1868), Aphrahat's *Demonstrations* (1869), Ephrem's *Commentary* (1876), and the Arabic Diatessaron (1888). The Diatessaron went from being lost and inaccessible (so Tischendorf) to recoverable and reconstructed (so Zahn).[70] As we enter the twentieth century, the Diatessaron will suddenly become central to the textual criticism of the Gospels.

2.8 Hermann Freiherr von Soden (1902–13)

Hermann Freiherr von Soden published his complex Greek NT in several installments from 1902–13.[71] Von Soden is notorious for his esoteric system of sigla as well as his

---

including a chart that outlines the comparative sequences of the Arabic, Fuldensis, and Ephrem (Appendix 1). Shortly after Hill's, another (slightly more accurate) English translation of the Arabic Diatessaron came out: Hope W. Hogg, "The Diatessaron of Tatian," in vol. 9 of *The Ante-Nicene Fathers*, ed. Alan Menzies (New York: Charles Scribner's Sons, 1896), 33–138.

[66] Brooke Foss Westcott and Fenton John Anthony Hort, *The New Testament in the Original Greek: Introduction and Appendix*, 2nd ed. (London: Macmillan, 1896), v.

[67] Westcott and Hort, *New Testament in the Original Greek* (1896), 326.

[68] F. C. Burkitt, *Evangelion Da-Mepharreshe: The Curetonian Version of the Four Gospels, with the Readings of the Sinai Palimpsest and the Early Syriac Patristic Evidence*, 2 vols. (Cambridge: Cambridge University Press, 1904). The very title of this work is the transliterated Syriac phrase used to distinguish the Gospel "of the separated" (*da-Mepharreshē*) from the Gospel "of the mixed" (*da-Meḥalleṭē*), that is, the Diatessaron. See 2:209–10 in this study for where Burkitt concludes that the Diatessaron preceded the Old Syriac Gospels.

[69] Indeed, I have not listed several other highly important studies that emerged in this same period, including others from Hill, Burkitt, and Zahn, as well as from Adolf von Harnack, J. Rendel Harris, Samuel Hemphill, and J. B. Lightfoot. See the selected bibliography in Hill, *The Earliest Life of Christ*, 378–9, for a list of pertinent works from the time. This truly was the watershed moment for the study of the Diatessaron.

[70] I will note that Zahn published two further influential studies in this period that advanced the field with additional Diatessaronic witnesses and insights: *Geschichte des neutestamentlichen Kanons*, 2 vols. (Erlangen: Andreas Dreichert, 1888–92); "Zur Geschichte von Tatians Diatessaron im Abendland," *NKZ* 5 (1894): 85–120.

[71] Hermann Freiherr von Soden, *Die Schriften des Neuen Testaments in ihrer ältesten erreichbaren Textgestalt hergestellt auf Grund ihrer Textgeschichte*, 2 vols. (Göttingen: Vandenhoek & Ruprecht,

impressively extensive but sadly unreliable apparatus.[72] His ill-fated proposal of three recensions (*I* = Jerusalem, *H* = Hesychian/Egyptian, and *K* = Koine) that stem from a lost archetype (*I-H-K*), which itself was already partly corrupted in the second century, has been rejected by modern text-critics. But perhaps more infamous than this is von Soden's unprecedented proposal for the source of that second-century corruption (at least, in the Gospels): none other than Tatian and his Diatessaron.[73] According to von Soden, Tatian was the primary source of widespread harmonizations and other contaminated readings in the surviving gospel manuscripts, not only in the Syriac tradition but also in the Greek and Latin traditions as well.[74] Von Soden concludes in his introduction: "Had Tatian not written a Diatessaron or had it not circulated so widely, we would have a very transparent textual tradition in the New Testament, as good as in the rest of literature preserved by manuscript."[75]

Recall that in their first edition Westcott and Hort had said precisely the opposite—the Diatessaron did not spread far and likely had little influence on separated gospel manuscripts. Von Soden, on the other hand, practically credits Tatian with single-handedly corrupting the text of the Gospels (especially his K recension).[76] In his edition, von Soden's aim is to discover and eliminate these Tatianic corruptions. Bruce Metzger summarizes two of von Soden's principles as they relate to Tatian, which are worth reproducing here:[77]

(1) The reading supported by Tatian is at once open to the suspicion of departing from the original text. Only in the event of two recensions agreeing with Tatian and the dissenting recension agreeing with a parallel is the latter to be adjudged

---

1911–13). Volume 1 (*Untersuchungen*) was originally published in Berlin in three parts: Part 1 (*Die Textzeugen*) in 1902; Part 2 (*Die Textformen: Die Evangelien*) in 1907; Part 3 (*Die Textformen: Der Apostolos mit Apokalypse*) in 1910. Volume 1 was then reprinted unchanged in Göttingen in 1911. (Rather frustratingly, the Table of Contents [which covers all three parts of Volume 1] does not appear until the end of Vol. 1, Pt. 3.) Volume 2 (*Text mit Apparat*) was published in 1913. Von Soden discusses Tatian's Diatessaron throughout, but the two most important sections are in Vol. 1, Pt. 2, pp. 1536–44 and pp. 1632–46. Hereafter the nomenclature *x.y:z* indicates Volume *x*, Part *y*, on page(s) *z*.

[72] Among others, see the devastating critiques in Metzger and Ehrman, *Text of the New Testament*, 185–9; Aland and Aland, *Text of the New Testament*, 22–3.

[73] von Soden, *Die Schriften des Neuen Testaments*, 1.2:1633: "Tatian's Diatessaron ist im Grund die einzige Quelle für alle irgend bedeutsameren Abwandlungen des Evv[= Evangelien]-Textes" (= Tatian's Diatessaron is basically the only source for any more significant modifications at all of the gospel text). For this section I have also drawn upon Petersen's treatment of von Soden in *Tatian's Diatessaron*, 155–8; and Baarda's treatment of von Soden in "The Diatessaron of Tatian: Source for an Early Text at Rome or Source of Textual Corruption?" in *The New Testament Text in Early Christianity: Proceedings of the Lille Colloquium, July 2000*, ed. C.-B. Amphoux and J. K. Elliott (Lausanne: Editions du Zèbre, 2003), 96–101.

[74] von Soden, *Die Schriften des Neuen Testaments*, 1.2:1544.

[75] von Soden, *Die Schriften des Neuen Testaments*, 1.2:1645: "Hätte Tatian kein Diatessaron geschrieben oder wäre dies nicht zu so weiter Verbreitung gelangt, so würden wir beim neuen Testament, so gut wie bei der übrigen handschriftlich erhaltenen Literatur, ... eine sehr durchsichtige Textüberlieferung besitzen." Von Soden does make exception for the likelihood that scribal knowledge of parallel passages would likely lead to more numerous errors than typically occur in other literature.

[76] von Soden, *Die Schriften des Neuen Testaments*, 1.2:1538, 1544.

[77] Metzger and Ehrman, *Text of the New Testament*, 188.

secondary, and this remains the case even when the former reading also agrees with a parallel.
(2) When early, certainly mutually independent witnesses—even though they may be only patristic writers or versions—agree in a reading that differs from Tatian, this reading requires serious consideration for adoption even when all three recensions agree with Tatian.

Von Soden's extreme distrust of Tatian's text, along with other idiosyncratic tendencies, drives him to produce an unlikely "original" text that is ironically slanted more toward the Textus Receptus than most other contemporary Greek NTs.[78] Tatian naturally features throughout the apparatus, primarily under the siglum Tα = Tatian's Diatessaron, which von Soden further subdivides into Tα^α = Arabic Text (based on Ciasca) and Tα^ε = Ephrem's (Armenian) text (based on Moesinger).[79] Von Soden is thus the first editor of the Greek NT in my survey to make a theoretical distinction between multiple witnesses to the Diatessaron in the apparatus (excluding Burkitt's supplemental notes to Westcott and Hort).[80] The nomenclature von Soden innovates here will continue in various adapted forms from this point forward, even up to today's Greek NTs.

Examples of how von Soden employs the Diatessaron in his apparatus abound. I will select only a few for illustration. Von Soden, for instance, considers Tatian a potentially better solution to explain the origin of Westcott and Hort's so-called "Western non-interpolations" (i.e., interpolations in their "Neutral text" that are not found in their "Western text"). One example is the insertion of the piercing of Jesus's side (cf. John 19:34) at Matt 27:49 in many manuscripts, which von Soden suggests may be due to Tatian (or even Ammonius!)—again, the very opposite of the conclusion reached by Westcott and Hort for the same variant.[81]

A pertinent example (already discussed above) is the doxology added to the end of the Lord's Prayer at Matt 6:13. In his apparatus, von Soden lists Tα as the first witness to the addition.[82] However, the actual evidence here is mixed. Fuldensis lacks the addition (following the standard Vulgate reading); but von Soden does not typically include Fuldensis in his Diatessaronic data. The Armenian translation of Ephrem does not cite this verse in the *Commentary* and thus is silent on the addition.[83] (Aphrahat is also

---

[78] Metzger and Ehrman, *Text of the New Testament*, 188.
[79] von Soden, *Die Schriften des Neuen Testaments*, 2:xxiii. Note that von Soden does not include Fuldensis, not because he does not think it is Tatianic, but because he recognizes it can only convey Tatian's sequence and not his wording (see 1.2:1537).
[80] I say "theoretical distinction" because, despite his subdivision, I could not find a single instance in which von Soden actually printed Tα^α or Tα^ε in the apparatus itself (as opposed to just "Tα"). Given the limited number of Ephrem's citations, the apparatus should in reality read Tα^α nearly all the time. Thus, it becomes clear (and see below) that von Soden essentially equates the Arabic Diatessaron with the text of Tatian himself.
[81] von Soden, *Die Schriften des Neuen Testaments*, 1.2:1570. I should note that in the apparatus itself at Matt 27:49 (on 2:113), von Soden does not list Tα, since neither Ephrem nor the Arabic Diatessaron has this interpolation.
[82] von Soden, *Die Schriften des Neuen Testaments*, 2:15. Recall that Bengel had cited Victor of Capua as evidence for the doxology's *omission*.
[83] Not until 1990 will it be discovered that the single surviving Syriac copy of Ephrem's *Commentary* does indeed cite Matt 6:13, without the added doxology. See the discussion under the UBS$^{4-5}$ below.

silent.) The Arabic Diatessaron 9:36 includes the addition; but the Arabic text has been conformed to the Syriac Peshitta, which also includes the addition, so its evidence may be of less value here. Syr^c includes the addition (but omits "and the power"), which von Soden notes (syr^s is lacunose here).[84] It would seem, then, that von Soden confidently reports the Diatessaronic reading, based largely on the Arabic Diatessaron, when in reality the evidence is quite slim. Von Soden will not be the last to misconstrue the Diatessaronic data for this verse; I will return to it again below.

Von Soden is not always confident in his ability to reconstruct Tatian's text, especially in the "surprisingly few" cases where the Arabic Diatessaron and Ephrem's *Commentary* diverge.[85] One such case occurs in the long ending of Mark, where the Arabic Diatessaron 55:5 appears to add οὖν after πορευθέντες in Mark 16:15 (cf. Matt 28:19), while Ephrem (19.15) does not. Although he largely trusts the Arabic's text, von Soden is unsure which is Tatian's reading here and therefore lists neither witness in his apparatus.[86]

To put it mildly, von Soden "certainly overestimated the impact of the Diatessaron."[87] No one today assigns Tatian the kind of corruptive influence on the transmission of the Gospels that von Soden attributed to him. Nonetheless, from this point forward nearly every editor of the Greek NT continued to set aside a special place in the apparatus for Tatian, some larger and some smaller. While von Soden likely represents the highpoint of the Diatessaron's perceived role in the transmission of the text, the emerging awareness of several additional witnesses to the Diatessaron will soon lead to a still more complicated apparatus for Tatian than even von Soden was able to assemble.

2.9 Alexander Souter (1st ed., 1910; 2nd ed., 1947)

At the same time as von Soden was producing his edition, Alexander Souter published his critical apparatus in 1910.[88] Although Souter elected not to produce his own critical text (he attached his apparatus to an existing Greek text), his apparatus added extensive patristic evidence (particularly among the Latin fathers). For this reason it holds promise for including more readings from the Diatessaron, and indeed it does. Souter includes a meager preface but a long list of witnesses, including the siglum "Diat. = Diatessaron Tatiani ([gr.]-syr.-[arm.]-arab.) (saec. ii)."[89] His list of languages suggests Souter is aware of Ephrem's *Commentary* (in Armenian) and the Arabic Diatessaron, but that he is not including Fuldensis (Latin), despite his penchant for

---

[84] Von Soden concluded in his earlier discussion of the Old Syriac that it was highly tainted by Diatessaronic readings; see *Die Schriften des Neuen Testaments*, 1.2:1582–85, 1593–94.

[85] von Soden, *Die Schriften des Neuen Testaments*, 1.2:1541.

[86] von Soden, *Die Schriften des Neuen Testaments*, 2:233.

[87] Petersen, *Tatian's Diatessaron*, 157. Coming from Petersen, this is a telling assessment.

[88] Alexander Souter, *Novum Testamentum Graece* (Oxford: Clarendon Press, 1910). Souter used Edwin Palmer's 1881 Greek text, in both this edition and his second edition in 1947. None of the Diatessaronic readings that I report below are modified in the second edition. On Souter, see Metzger and Ehrman, *Text of the New Testament*, 184–5.

[89] Souter, *Novum Testamentum Graece*, xix. Souter's list of languages for the Diatessaron is curious. Judging by the other items in his list (he does not explain his system), the dashes between languages indicate the direction of translation dependency and the square brackets indicate some question of

the Latin tradition. He also has sigla for Ephrem, Aphrahat, and even Tatian himself, whom he calls "the Syrian living in Rome" with a note to look under "Diat."

Despite the quasi-list of different sources for the Diatessaron, Souter only lists "Diat." in his apparatus; but it comes up quite frequently. For instance, in contrast to von Soden, Souter lists the Diatessaron as specifically *omitting* the interpolation at Matt 27:49 regarding the piercing of Jesus. (Recall that von Soden will leave the Diatessaron out of his apparatus here, but had suggested in his prolegomena that the Diatessaron was likely the original source of this addition.) Also in contrast to von Soden, Souter does not list the Diatessaron at all in his evidence concerning the doxology added to the end of the Lord's Prayer at Matt 6:13, whose addition von Soden will list confidently as a Diatessaronic reading. Although Souter could not have had access to von Soden's complete text (since Souter published his edition the same year as von Soden published Part 3 of his first volume), it is instructive to see how differently they interpret the same Diatessaronic data.

Souter also lists the Diatessaron for highly specific—and sometimes relatively trivial—variants (like the addition of a pronoun, the omission of a conjunction, the substitution of a word, and so forth).[90] There are also times when Souter places a question mark in parentheses following "Diat." (presumably to indicate his uncertainty). He does not mention the Diatessaron as a witness to the *pericope adulterae* in John (7:53–8:11, since the passage is not in the eastern witnesses), but he does list the Diatessaron as supporting the Long Ending of Mark (16:9-20, since it appears in the Arabic Diatessaron and Ephrem cites one partial verse).

A final reading worth mentioning is at Mark 2:14, where Souter lists "Diat." as supporting Ἰάκωβον (Jacob/James) in place of "Levi." Souter's choice is noteworthy because while Ephrem's *Commentary* does indeed mention a "James the tax-collector" (5.17), which would suggest Ephrem found this reading in his Syriac Diatessaron, Ciasca's edition and Latin translation of the Arabic Diatessaron reads "Levi" at the pertinent passage (7:9). Souter apparently elected to side with Ephrem over the Arabic, and his choice has been vindicated. It turns out that *all* the surviving manuscripts of the Arabic Diatessaron actually read "Jacob/James" for Mark 2:14. Ciasca, apparently uncomfortable with that reading, "corrected" his text and thereby misled a host of later scholars dependent on him.[91] Von Soden (p. 2:127), due to his heavy reliance on the

---

that dependency. Here that would suggest Souter believed that Tatian composed the Diatessaron (perhaps) in Greek, that the Greek was translated to Syriac, and that the Syriac was translated to Armenian and to Arabic (with the square brackets around the Armenian presumably indicating it was not the source of the Arabic). No other witness has two languages in square brackets, so the intended meaning is somewhat obscure.

[90] For a sampling, see Souter's apparatus at Matt 5:28; Mark 9:15; Luke 12:20; John 18:1. Von Soden, of course, does this to an even greater degree.

[91] So Baarda, "Tatian's Diatessaron and the Greek Text of the Gospels," 342. Following Ciasca, the English (both Hill and Hogg) and German (Preuschen) translations of the Arabic all printed "Levi" at Mark 2:14. Ciasca's "correction" was not corrected until A.-S. Marmardji's edition and French translation in 1935 (*Diatessaron de Tatien: Texte arabe établi, traduit en français, collationné avec les anciennes versions syriaques* [Beyrouth: Imprimerie Catholique, 1935]). Prior to Souter, Westcott and Hort in 1882 (Appendix, p. 23) had also listed "Ephr.Diat." as supporting Ἰάκωβον at Mark 2:14, but they did not yet have the Arabic version as a dissenting voice. (F. C. Burkitt did not add anything related to the Diatessaron to this reading in his 1896 supplements.)

Arabic text, will leave the Diatessaron out of his apparatus for this variant. But Souter's intuition to call this a Diatessaronic reading based on Ephrem was correct.[92] That being said, Souter continued to rely only on the *eastern* witnesses for establishing the text of the Diatessaron in his apparatus (even in his 1947 second edition). The Diatessaron's stake in the apparatus is about to experience a westward expansion.

2.10 Heinrich Vogels (1st ed. 1920; 4th ed. 1955)

H. J. Vogels is the first editor of a Greek NT in my survey who could also be labeled a Diatessaronic scholar in his own right. Vogels produced his first edition of the Greek NT in 1920, but prior to this he had already published numerous studies on the Diatessaron and would continue to produce more as he updated his text and apparatus through its fourth edition in 1955.[93] His focus was the early Latin versions and the so-called "Western text." In 1910 and 1911 he published two important studies arguing that the Diatessaron was the primary source of harmonizations in Codex Bezae and the "Western text," that therefore the Diatessaron preceded the separated Old Latin Gospels, and that the Diatessaron itself is the link between the Old Latin and Old Syriac. Thus rather than taking preexisting "Western" readings with him to the east (as Zahn had proposed), Tatian was the source of those readings and thereby the "Western text" itself (closer to von Soden).[94]

Critics were not keen on Vogels's proposal that the Diatessaron was the earliest form of the Gospels in Latin. In response he produced a major study in 1919 collating several gospel harmonies (mostly in Latin, but he also referenced Middle Dutch, Tuscan, and Old High German harmonies) and attempted to demonstrate how they were genetically related and, more importantly, how they shared readings with eastern witnesses.[95] He ended with two grand conclusions, that (1) "Fuldensis is not the oldest form of Latin gospel harmony, but has gone through a pre-history on Old Latin terrain"; and that (2) "Tatian's Diatessaron possessed a greater importance and circulation in the Western church than previously thought."[96] Vogels was not quite the

---

[92] I am also pleased to report that the newest discovery of a third Old Syriac Gospel text (also a Sinai palimpsest) is extant for Mark 2:14 (whereas syr^sc are lacunose here). It too reads the equivalent of Ἰάκωβον, further confirming the relatively ancient status of this reading, particularly in the Syriac milieu. For a description with some initial readings, see Sebastian P. Brock, "Two Hitherto Unattested Passages of the Old Syriac Gospels in Palimpsests from St Catherine's Monastery, Sinai," Δελτίο Βιβλικών Μελετών 31A (2016): 7–18.

[93] Vogels's first edition was titled *Novum Testamentum Graece* (Düsseldorf: L. Schwann, 1920). In 1922, Vogels added the Latin Vulgate on facing pages and updated the title appropriately. He published the third edition in 1949, and the fourth edition is *Novum Testamentum Graece et Latine*, 4th ed. (Freiburg: Herder, 1955). For Vogels's many contributions to Diatessaronic studies, see Petersen, *Tatian's Diatessaron*, 158–64.

[94] Petersen, *Tatian's Diatessaron*, 158–61. Vogels's two studies were *Die Harmonistik im Evangelientext des Codex Cantabrigiensis: Ein Beitrag zur neutestamentlichen Textkritik* (Leipzig: J. C. Hinrichs, 1910) and *Die altsyrischen Evangelien in ihrem Verhältnis zu Tatians Diatessaron* (Freiburg: Herder, 1911).

[95] Heinrich Joseph Vogels, *Beiträge zur Geschichte des Diatessaron im Abendland* (Münster: Aschendorff, 1919). Petersen assesses this work in *Tatian's Diatessaron*, 162–4.

[96] Vogels, *Beiträge zur Geschichte des Diatessaron*, 90: "1. . . . [dass] der Fuldensis nicht die älteste Form lateinischer Evangelienharmonie ist, sondern eine Vorgeschichte auf altlateinischem Boden

earliest scholar to propose the first conclusion—nor was he quite the one to make it stick—but in this conclusion he anticipates the next big movement in Diatessaronic studies, the hunt for an Old Latin Diatessaron.[97] His second conclusion reveals the growing weight of the Diatessaron in the twentieth-century study of the Gospels, a direct contrast to Westcott and Hort's assessment of this "obscure work."

Vogels's Greek NT naturally makes frequent reference to the Diatessaron. In his brief preface, he critiques von Soden's overreliance on the Arabic text as the "original text of the Diatessaron" without taking into account its well-known accommodation to the Syriac Peshitta. He goes on to say that he will only report readings of the Arabic Diatessaron that deviate from the Peshitta, a point which he hopes he does not need to justify.[98] He uses "Tat" as his siglum for Tatian, and (like von Soden), distinguishes between Tat[ephr] (= the Armenian edition of Ephrem's *Commentary*) and Tat[ar] (= Ciasca's edition of the Arabic Diatessaron) in the explanation of his apparatus. But, also like von Soden, Vogels almost never actually employs these subdivisions in his apparatus.[99]

In his first two editions (1920 and 1922), there is nothing of particular note in Vogels's apparatus that we have not already seen. At Matt 6:13, he does not list "Tat" as supporting the added doxology to the Lord's Prayer (as von Soden had done), since he refuses to cite the Arabic Diatessaron as evidence for Tatian when it agrees with the Syriac Peshitta (as it does here). He does not mention the Diatessaron at Matt 27:49. Like Souter, he does list "Tat" as supporting the reading of Ἰάκωβον in place of Levi at Mark 2:14. This variant would have been the ideal moment to employ the sub-siglum Tat[ephr], since as far as Vogels knew the Arabic text read "Levi" here (due to Ciasca's erroneous "correction"). But Vogels does not employ this more precise siglum here. There is no mention of "Tat" at the Long Ending of Mark or at the *pericope adulterae* in John.

A new Diatessaronic feature pops up beginning with Vogels's third edition (1949), but one that promises more than it delivers. In his description of Tatian (p. x), Vogels adds a third siglum: Tat[ned], a reference to the Middle Dutch versions of the Diatessaron.[100] Vogels's addition of a western Diatessaronic witness to his apparatus

---

durchlaufen hat. 2. . . . daß Tatians Diatessaron in der abendländischen Kirche größere Bedeutung und Verbreitung besessen hat, als man bisher annahm." There is a third conclusion that is specific to the texts under study, that although they are relatively young, they have preserved a number of important Diatessaronic readings.

[97] Petersen (*Tatian's Diatessaron*, 162n. 44) reviews how the concept of a missing "Old Latin" Diatessaron was independently "rediscovered" more than once. Before Vogels it was J. C. Zahn and Theodor Zahn, among others. After Vogels, it would be Daniel Plooij who would make it famous, as discussed below.

[98] Vogels, *Novum Testamentum* (1920), vi, viii. These points remain in all four editions of Vogels's preface.

[99] Vogels, *Novum Testamentum* (1920), xi. The siglum "Tat" appears on nearly every page of Vogels's apparatus in the Gospels. In my hunt through the apparatus, I only came across five instances where Vogels listed either Tat[ephr] or Tat[ar] separately (Mark 2:28; 10:35; Luke 1:45; 10:1; John 3:13; the last reference also lists Tat[afr[ahat]], whom Vogels had indicated he would list on his own, not under Tatian). In all five of these instances, the sub-sigla only appear in the third (1949) and fourth (1955) editions, not in the first two editions. In the third and fourth editions, I came across only one reference to Tat[ned], at John 20:31 (see the discussion below).

[100] Edited by Jan Bergsma, *De levens van Jezus in het Middelnederlandsch*, 3 vols. (Leiden: Sijthoff, 1895-8). On the announcement of the Middle Dutch harmonies and the contents of Bergsma's edition, see Petersen, *Tatian's Diatessaron*, 146, 175n. 88.

would appear novel, but it turns out that he was not quite the first to do so (more on which next). Moreover, the addition of Tat[ned] seems to have had little effect on Vogels's actual apparatus. I could find only one reference to Tat[ned] in the apparatus (at John 20:31), and Vogels says nothing more about it—or the momentous change it signaled—in his front matter.

Consequently, the next stage of our drama belongs not with Vogels (though he will reappear), but with his Roman Catholic contemporary (and competitor), Augustin Merk. Merk will incorporate more Diatessaronic evidence into his apparatus than any editor prior, elevating the Diatessaron to perhaps its highest height thus far—and at the same time setting it up for a devastating fall.

2.11 Augustin Merk (1st ed., 1933; 4th ed., 1942; 11th ed., 1992)

There are eleven editions of Augustin Merk's Greek NT published from 1933 to 1992, but he himself was editor of only the first five (1933-1944).[101] Merk's initial edition was largely based on von Soden's groupings and apparatus, whose sigla he translated to the more common Gregory system. Unfortunately, like von Soden, Merk's apparatus has not been praised for its accuracy.[102] Over time, however, it developed a flavor of its own, and perhaps none more distinctive than in its use of the Diatessaron.

As we might have expected, in his initial edition Merk cites evidence from the Arabic Diatessaron and Ephrem's *Commentary* (in Armenian) to represent Tatian, whom he considers an early witness to the gospel text. Less expected perhaps was the severely critical review Merk received from none other than Heinrich Vogels.[103] Vogels leveled the same critique at Merk that he had leveled at von Soden: Merk uncritically treats the Arabic text as a stand-in for Tatian's text,[104] even when it agrees with the Syriac Peshitta (to which it has been conformed). Merk thereby neglects the older and more valuable witnesses, Ephrem and Aphrahat, especially in that he labels the Arabic text "Ta" but Ephrem and Aphrahat merely "Ef" and "Af."[105] Given Merk's presentation

[101] The first edition is Augustinus Merk, *Novum Testamentum Graece et Latine* (Rome: Pontifical Biblical Institute, 1933). The following editions then emerged: 1935 (=2nd ed.); 1938 (=3rd ed.); 1942 (=4th ed.); 1944 (=5th ed.). Merk passed away in 1945. Thereafter, other editors took responsibility for the following editions: 1948 (=6th ed., S. Lyonnet; text unchanged, save corrections); 1951 (=7th ed., S. Lyonnet); 1957 (= 8th ed., J. P. Smith); 1964 (=9th ed., C. M. Martini); 1984 (=10th ed., C. M. Martini); 1992 (=11th ed., J. O'Callaghan). Much of this information may be garnered from the prefaces (re)printed in the 11th ed. (2*, 8*).
[102] Metzger and Ehrman, *Text of the New Testament*, 189–90; G. D. Kilpatrick, "Three Recent Editions of the Greek New Testament," *JTS* 50 (1949): 145–6.
[103] Heinrich Joseph Vogels, review of *Novum Testamentum Graece et Latine*, by Augustinus Merk, *TRev* 33 (1933): 473–8. To be fair, Merk had also reviewed both of Vogels's initial editions, but was far more praiseworthy than Vogels was a decade later; see Merk's reviews of Vogels in *Bib* 2.1 (1921): 78–87; and *Bib* 5.1 (1924): 85–8.
[104] This equation is still a problem today. I had a textbook in my first undergraduate religion class that cited Hill's English translation of the Arabic Diatessaron as though it were a perfect transmission of Tatian's wording and sequence. While I credit this textbook with igniting my curiosity for the Diatessaron, its treatment is woefully misleading. The oversimplification of the Diatessaron is in part what I am attempting to combat in this essay.
[105] Vogels, review of *Novum Testamentum Graece et Latine* (by Merk), 477. Vogels calls this "cluttering the crown": "Und um dem Wirrwarr die Krone aufzusetzen, hat man dem jungen Zeugen das Siglum Ta(tian) zuerkannt, während die alten in dem anspruchlosen Kleid Af und Ef erscheinen."

of Tatianic testimony, says Vogels, "one wonders if he would not have done better to follow the example of Erwin Nestle not even to venture with Tatian at all."[106]

Merk responds to Vogels's review the following year.[107] In fact, I would dare say that henceforth Merk designs his approach to Tatian as an implicit defense against Vogels's lingering critiques. First, Merk justifies his placement of Tatian in the apparatus. Merk lists Tatian first—before the Greek manuscripts—because Tatian (along with Marcion) is our oldest known "text."[108] It is worth pausing on this point for a moment to consider the evolution that Tatian has undergone. John Mill in his 1707 edition, although he had no real access to Tatian's text, pointed out that Tatian's early date would provide textual evidence within a generation of the last of the Evangelists. Now two hundred years later Merk cites Tatian first in his apparatus, ahead of essentially every other piece of evidence.[109] Mill's premonition has become a reality.

Next Merk responds to Vogels's critiques regarding his preference for the Arabic text. Merk is well aware of Vogels's distrust of the Arabic harmony (and even of Ephrem as a pure Tatianic source). Merk is simply not that pessimistic. He believes that the Arabic text *does* accurately represent Tatian. An observant reader of his apparatus, claims Merk, will not fail to see that it is the Peshitta that is dependent on Tatian, not the Arabic Diatessaron that has been conformed to the Peshitta. Merk references his own Prolegomena (p. 9*): when the Old Syriac is not extant and Tatian agrees with the Peshitta (the very reading Vogels omits), Merk reports that reading because it is likely older than the Peshitta.[110] Merk's language is illustrative. By "Tatian" he means the Arabic Diatessaron. He employs this circular metonym throughout his response. It comes down to a question of judgment (what Merk calls a "Geschmacksurteil").[111] Merk judges the Arabic Diatessaron as essentially equivalent to Tatian. Vogels does not.

Merk's real innovation, however, takes flight in his fourth edition (1942). There Merk goes from having cited two primary witnesses to Tatian (the Arabic Diatessaron and Ephrem) to citing *seven*, each with its own siglum, along with special sigla for

---

[106] Vogels, review of *Novum Testamentum Graece et Latine* (by Merk), 478: "Studiert man etwas eingehender, wie bei M[erk] das Tatianzeugnis auftritt, so fragt man sich, ob er nicht besser daran getan hätte, nach dem Vorbild von Erwin Nestle an Tatian sich gar nicht heranzuwagen." Incredibly, Vogels does not end there, but concludes the review citing a recent rejection he has received from a new publisher who is no longer interested in Vogels's own revised edition of the Greek-Latin NT because Merk's has been announced in Catholic circles as "the official edition of the New Testament…[that] will be the standard work for the world" (col. 478). The publisher does not think Vogels's revised edition can compete. Vogels bemoans that apparently "the Catholic world should no longer be wide enough to suffer two editions of the Greek-Latin N.T. side by side."

[107] Augustinus Merk, "Zur Ausgabe des Neuen Testaments des Bibelinstituts," *Bib* 15 (1934): 437–50. Merk's tone is remarkably gracious given Vogels's earlier acerbity.

[108] Merk, "Zur Ausgabe des Neuen Testaments," 444. Merk then adds, "or text-recension, if Vogels prefers that word." The full line is, "Tatian und Marcion sind die ältesten uns bekannten Texte oder Textrezensionen, wenn Vogels das Wort lieber ist."

[109] Von Soden also cited Tatian first, as did Vogels (despite his critique of Merk). What Vogels seems to have especially disliked was Merk's separation of Ephrem from Tatian in the first edition.

[110] Merk, "Zur Ausgabe des Neuen Testaments," 445–6: *si syra vetus vacat et Tatianus cum syp [=Peshitta] lectionem insolitam fert, eam allegamus, quia probabile est talem lectionem esse syp antiquiorem, maxime cum constet syp influxum syrae veteris aut Tatiani subiisse.*

[111] Merk, "Zur Ausgabe des Neuen Testaments," 446.

Table 9.1 Diatessaronic Sigla in Merk, 4th ed. (1942) to 11th ed. (1992)

Ta	Tatianus arab. ca. 170
Ta⁺	arab. et Taᵉ (Ef)
Taⁱ	italice
Taᵛ	venetus
Taᵗ	toscanus
Taᶠ	fuldensis
Taⁿ	neerland.
Taˡ	cod. leodiens.
Taˢ	cod. stuttgart.
Ta³	arab. ital. neerl.
Ta⁴	Ta³ + Taᵉ

Note: The Diatessaronic sigla are listed on p. 45* of Merk, from the 4th ed. (1942) through the 11th ed. (1992). Several points of Merk's scheme are noteworthy. First, note that he retains the designation of "Ta" for the Arabic Diatessaron (even misleadingly dating it to ca. 170). Second, note that the sigla overlap in more ways than he specifies here (but see p. 17*). So Taⁱ (Middle Italian) = Taᵛ + Taᵗ. Likewise, Taⁿ (Middle Dutch) = Taˡ + Taˢ. Third, note that Fuldensis is the only witness not part of any group. This omission renders Merk's apparatus inconclusive. When he cites Ta⁴, the theoretical "complete Tatian," does it include Fuldensis? Merk's intention is unclear (which becomes problematic, as we shall see).

denoting combinations, for a total of twelve possible ways of citing Diatessaronic witnesses (see Table 9.1).

Merk's Greek NT is unprecedented in its reporting of the Diatessaron. We are now in a position to explain Vogels's addition of Tatⁿᵉᵈ to his apparatus in 1949, which plainly pales in comparison to what Merk had created seven years earlier. What possessed either of them suddenly to add additional witnesses to their apparatus under Tatian? The decades from the 1920s to the 1950s turn out to be a second remarkably productive period that substantially alters the face of Diatessaronic studies. The catalyst came with Daniel Plooij's 1923 and 1925 landmark studies on the Liège Diatessaron, a Middle Dutch harmony in which he claimed to find eastern Diatessaronic readings not present in Fuldensis.[112] Their source, Plooij proposed, was a now-lost "Old Latin" Diatessaron that had survived into the Middle Ages and fed the Liège and other western harmonies real Tatianic readings. Suddenly the floodgates were opened to the possibility that medieval vernacular harmonies could have weight in determining Tatian's second-century text. Plooij's method of comparing eastern and western witnesses against Fuldensis to extract an "Old Latin" Diatessaron (what I will call the Plooij-Petersen method) dominated the field for the next generation. A slew of new witnesses and studies washed up between 1923 and 1951, of which I will name only a few: the Dura

---

[112] Daniel Plooij, *A Primitive Text of the Diatessaron: The Liège Manuscript of a Mediaeval Dutch Translation: A Preliminary Study* (Leiden: A. W. Sijthoff, 1923). He produced a follow-up study two years later: *A Further Study of the Liège Diatessaron* (Leiden: Brill, 1925). For Petersen's enamored assessment of Plooij, see *Tatian's Diatessaron*, 170–8, 189–203. Petersen, as a result of Plooij's work, declares the Liège Diatessaron "the single most important Western Diatessaronic witness" (p. 171).

fragment (1935); the Venetian and Tuscan Diatessarons (1938); the Persian Diatessaron (1942–3, 1951); and numerous studies by A. Baumstark (1929–39), C. Peters (1936–42), and several others (even Merk himself).[113] It is little wonder, then, that Merk and Vogels felt compelled to add Diatessaronic witnesses to their Greek NTs, even if simply to give notice to this tremendous progress.

Merk announced these ground-breaking additions in the front matter to his fourth edition (1942), with slight updates in the fifth edition (1944, one year before he died).[114] In the preface (p. 6*), he provides an extensive explanation of the changes, including a list of the additional witnesses he has consulted (as reflected in Table 9.1, plus some additional sources).[115] In the prolegomena (pp. 17*–18*), he explains his Diatessaronic method, some of which is worth citing:

> Tatian's Diatessaron, of which today a large part can be restored, we frequently cite on account of its age. [Merk goes on to list and explain his Diatessaronic sigla.] . . . Since the Arabic text of Tatian has many readings in common with syr^p, it is investigated whether these readings may be attributed to Tatian or rather belong to syr^p. First, we observe that Tatian often departs from syr^p and hence is independent from syr^p in many places. Next, where Tatian and syr^p agree, very often added [to the agreement] are the Old Syriac, Old Latin, Armenian, Georgian version, DWΘΦ among the Greek codices, or other codices—which are independent from syr^p. From which it is evident that these readings are older than syr^p and rightly attributed to Tatian. How often this happens is easy to recognize from our apparatus. Moreover, we do not at all deny that the Arabic text falls short of a primitive form in many places. We cite syr^p even if Tatian's text is established already from another source, not to demonstrate the Tatianic reading from it, but to reveal how often syr^p preserves ancient readings.[116]

---

[113] For the initial editions, see the following works: for the Dura fragment, see Carl H. Kraeling, *A Greek Fragment of Tatian's Diatessaron from Dura*, SD 3 (London: Christophers, 1935). Dura's Diatessaronic status, of course, has been repeatedly questioned, most recently in the present volume by Ian Mills in Chapter 7. For the Middle Italian harmonies, see Venanzio Todesco, Alberto Vaccari, and Marco Vattasso, eds., *Il Diatessaron in Volgare Italiano*, StT 81 (Vatican City: Biblioteca Apostolica Vaticana, 1938). For the Persian Diatessaron, see Giuseppe Messina, "Un Diatessaron persiano del secolo XIII tradotto dal siriaco," *Bib* 23.3 (1942): 268–305; 24 (1943), 59–106; Giuseppe Messina, *Notizia su un Diatessaron persiano: Tradotto dal siriaco*, BibOr 10 (Rome: Pontifical Biblical Institute, 1943); Giuseppe Messina, *Diatessaron Persiano*, BibOr 14 (Rome: Pontifical Biblical Institute, 1951). For the studies of Baumstark, Peters, Merk, and others, perhaps the most concentrated source is Petersen's bibliography in *Tatian's Diatessaron*, 491–521.

[114] Merk also announced these changes in a short notice in 1943: Augustinus Merk, "Nova editio Novi Testamenti graece et latine," *Bib* 24 (1943): 182–4. Curiously, there he adds a line about Codex Fuldensis (p. 184) that is not present in his actual preface: "The Fuldensis text, since it transmits the Vulgate version, is rarely included" (=*Textus fuldensis, cum tradat versionem vulgatam, raro apponitur*).

[115] In addition to the Middle Dutch and Middle Italian harmonies, Merk also says that he re-examined the Armenian version of Ephrem's *Commentary* and added other Syriac witnesses, including Aphrahat, the *Liber Graduum*, and the Syriac translation of Eusebius's *Theophania*. He also mentions the Pepysian harmony and the Persian Diatessaron but says he could not include them due to space constraints. These two witnesses are never ultimately added to the apparatus, but one wonders whether they might have been had Merk continued as editor.

[116] Here I cite the fifth edition (1944): Merk, *Novum Testamentum Graece et Latine*, 17*–18*: *Tatiani diatessaron, quod hodie magna ex parte restitui potest, propter eius antiquitatem frequenter*

One can almost see Vogels's shadow looming over Merk's shoulder as he writes. This is Merk's final defense for his decision to prioritize the Arabic Diatessaron (which, one notes, he continues to refer to simply as "Tatian"). Notable is the opening line, in which Merk's extreme optimism at our ability to reconstruct the Diatessaron shines through. Yet Merk's confidence is betrayed by the complicated data his new system reports. Where the Tatianic evidence diverges, how should a reader adjudicate? A single example will suffice.

In Merk's treatment of the *pericope adulterae* (John 7:53–8:11), he does not list Tatian initially as supporting the passage's presence. This is likely due to the fact that the Arabic Diatessaron (like most eastern witnesses) omits this passage. But then Merk goes on to cite Tatian for individual readings within John 7:53–8:11, always drawn from western Diatessaronic witnesses. Merk's apparatus cites Ta^{is} at 7:53; Ta^{i} at 8:5; Ta^{vl} at 8:9; Ta^{in} at 8:10; and Ta^{v} at 8:11. What is the reader supposed to make of this? Apparently the Middle Dutch and Middle Italian Diatessarons do support the *pericope adulterae* in John. But does that imply we have second-century evidence for the pericope from Tatian? However, Merk fails to mention that Fuldensis (ch. 121) also includes the passage (as does the Vulgate), which renders its presence in the Middle Dutch and Middle Italian harmonies essentially inconsequential. They could easily have drawn this passage directly from Fuldensis—which itself could have drawn it directly from the Vulgate—and *not* from Tatian. On top of that, Merk also fails to note that in two of his five "Tatianic" readings (7:53; 8:10), Fuldensis *supports* the reading, which renders those two readings inadmissible as Tatianic under the Plooij–Petersen method. This is a founding principle of the Plooij–Petersen approach: a reading shared by Fuldensis and the western vernaculars cannot be labeled Tatianic without some other support, since the Vulgatized Fuldensis (and not an independent "Old Latin" Diatessaron) would be the most likely source. To echo Vogels, Merk would have done better to leave Tatian out of this evidence.[117]

---

allegamus.... Quoniam textus arabicus Tatiani multas lectiones communes cum syp habet, quaeritur num hae lectiones Tatiano attribui possint an potius syp propriae sint. Primo notamus Tatianum frequenter a syp discedere et proinde in multis a syp esse independentem. Deinde ubi Tatianus et syp conveniunt, saepissime accedunt syv, vetus latina, armenia, georgica versio, ex codicibus graecis DWΘΦ vel alii codices, qui a syp sunt independentes. Unde patet has lectiones esse syp antiquiores et recte Tatiano attribui. Quam frequenter hoc accidat, ex apparatu nostro facile agnoscitur. Ceterum minime infitiamur textum arabicum in multis a forma primitiva deficere. Syp a nobis allegatur, etiam si de textu Tatiani iam aliunde constat, non ut lectio tatianea ex ea demonstretur, sed ut ostendatur quam frequenter syp conservaverit lectiones antiquas.

The fifth edition is identical here to the fourth, except in the last line, where Merk alters the wording slightly, but the meaning is the same. Merk then goes on to explain (p. 18*) that when "Tatian" (= Arabic Diatessaron) agrees with syr^p against the Old Syriac or other witnesses, he generally does not cite "Tatian," except in certain instances. But when the Old Syriac is absent, and "Tatian" agrees with syr^p, Merk still cites "Tatian," because he considers it probable that the reading is older than syr^p (as we have already seen in his response to Vogels).

[117] Merk does not typically cite divergent Tatianic evidence intentionally, but this hides the fact that it is usually present. Unless Merk lists Ta^4, his evidence for the Diatessaron is by definition mixed, even if he does not report the dissenting voices. And even when he does cite Ta^4, not all problems are solved. I return to this issue below (see Example 2 under UBS$^{1-3}$).

To Merk's credit, his comprehensive approach to the Diatessaron drew early praise from at least a few text-critics. In a 1949 review, G. D. Kilpatrick could say, "While we cannot commit ourselves to all that M[erk]'s literal use of the symbol Ta (Tatian) implies, it is valuable to have the medieval Gospel harmonies cited so often."[118] And Bruce Metzger could write in 1950: "For a sane and balanced statement of the correct methodology of Tatianic-Forschung, which is drawn up with lapidary succinctness, see August Merk."[119] Metzger, of course, would soon serve on the editorial committee for the United Bible Societies' upcoming edition, where Merk's influence likely reached its height. For, in 1966, the UBS Committee chose to adopt Merk's Diatessaronic approach wholesale—indeed, with added detail—for its first edition of the Greek NT. If I have especially belabored Merk's contribution, it is because his precedent likely placed Tatian in the hands of every Bible translator from 1966 to today.

2.12 Interlude: S. C. E. Legg (1935, 1940), IGNTP's Luke (1984–7), Nestle-Aland (1st ed., 1898; 28th ed., 2012)

Before moving to the UBS editions, I should add a brief word on three intervening editions whose publications remain influential but whose treatments of the Diatessaron less so. S. C. E. Legg produced a critical apparatus of Mark (1935) and Matthew (1940) using Westcott and Hort's text.[120] Legg includes "Tat.$^{\text{diat.}}$" (with no subdivisions) in his list of ecclesiastical writers that he will cite, but he only actually cites Tatian in his apparatus on occasion. Legg's project was sadly abandoned after it became clear that his apparatus had too few manuscripts and too many errors.

A somewhat reimagined version of Legg was initiated by the International Greek New Testament Project (IGNTP) for Luke, finally published in 1984–7 (2 vols.) after significant delays.[121] The committee was intentional in its approach to the Diatessaron

---

[118] Kilpatrick, "Three Recent Editions," 142. Incidentally, Kilpatrick will go on to edit his own Greek NT, the *Greek-English Diglot for the Use of Translators*, sponsored by the British and Foreign Bible Society, which would later abandon the project in favor of the UBS's forthcoming edition; on Kilpatrick see Aland and Aland, *Text of the New Testament*, 25, 32.

[119] Bruce M. Metzger, "Tatian's Diatessaron and a Persian Harmony of the Gospels," *JBL* 69 (1950): 266n. 18. Metzger goes on to cite Merk's sixth ed. (1948), but the text is the same as the fifth.

[120] *Novum Testamentum Graece: Secundum textum Westcotto-Hortianum: Euangelium secundum Marcum* (Oxford: Clarendon Press, 1935); and *Novum Testamentum Graece: Secundum textum Westcotto-Hortianum: Euangelium secundum Matthaeum* (Oxford: Clarendon Press, 1940). On Legg's editions, see Metzger and Ehrman, *Text of the New Testament*, 191–2; Aland and Aland, *Text of the New Testament*, 23–4. I could find only two references to Tatian in Legg's apparatus for Mark (1:41; 9:1); he cites Tatian more often in Matthew, on average once or twice per chapter.

[121] The American and British Committees of the International Greek New Testament Project, eds., *The Gospel According to St. Luke*, 2 vols. (Oxford: Clarendon Press, 1984–7). For a fascinating narrative of the transition from Legg to the IGNTP, see the well-documented article by Eldon Jay Epp, "The International Greek New Testament Project: Motivation and History," *NovT* 39 (1997): 1–20. Tjitze Baarda has also produced an extended review of the IGNTP edition of Luke, with a specific focus on Luke 23:48 and its Diatessaronic addition, in Tjitze Baarda, "What Kind of Critical Apparatus for the New Testament Do We Need? The Case of Luke 23:48," in *New Testament Textual Criticism, Exegesis, and Early Church History: A Discussion of Methods*, ed. Barbara Aland and Joël Delobel (Kampen: Pharos, 1994), 37–97. Baarda covers in brief how some previous Greek NTs reported

and more limiting than Merk. Only the Arabic Diatessaron (Ciasca and Marmardji's editions) and Persian Diatessaron (Messina's edition) are cited as full witnesses, while Syriac citations are drawn from Ephrem's *Commentary* (now also available in Syriac[122]), Aphrahat's *Demonstrations*, and the *Liber Graduum*. Many scholars were involved in the collation of Diatessaronic evidence, including J. N. Birdsall, L. Leloir, S. P. Brock, A. J. B. Higgins, and T. Baarda (among others).[123] The decision to include the Persian Diatessaron (not directly derived from Tatian's Diatessaron, but recognized as containing Diatessaronic readings)—and not other witnesses—is surprising.[124] The exclusion of the western Diatessaronic witnesses may either indicate the committee's skepticism of their value or simply reflect that decisions were made regarding what to include before the western witnesses achieved their surge in scholarship.[125] The IGNTP continues to partner with the Institut für neutestamentliche Textforschung (INTF) in the production of the *Editio Critica Maior* (*ECM*) of John and the Pauline Epistles.[126]

Finally, the Nestle-Aland (NA) Greek NT has, of course, enjoyed a rich history of editions, beginning with Eberhard Nestle's 1st ed. in 1898 and arriving most recently at the 28th ed. in 2012.[127] Although it began as something of a consensus text with

---

Luke 23:48, similar to my own study thus far. It is also worth noting how many of Baarda's suggestions for the ideal apparatus were eventually taken up in the Institut für neutestamentliche Textforschung's (INTF) *Editio Critica Maior* (*ECM*), described below.

[122] In 1957, a remarkable find occurred: Sir Chester Beatty acquired what turned out to be a considerable portion of Ephrem's *Commentary* in Syriac. Since Louis Leloir had recently produced a new edition and translation of the Armenian version, Beatty invited him to edit the Syriac text as well, which he published in 1963: *Saint Éphrem: Commentaire de l'Évangile concordant, texte syriaque (MS Chester Beatty 709)*, CBM 8 (Dublin: Hodges Figgis, 1963). Some twenty years later, additional Syriac folios were found, and Leloir edited these as well: Louis Leloir, *Saint Éphrem: Commentaire de l'Évangile concordant, texte syriaque (MS Chester Beatty 709): Folios additionnels*, CBM 8(b) (Leuven: Peeters, 1990). (Of course, the IGNTP edition of Luke was not able to take this second Syriac find into account.) For a brief description of the finds, see Carmel McCarthy, *Saint Ephrem's Commentary on Tatian's Diatessaron: An English Translation of Chester Beatty Syriac MS 709*, JSSSup 2 (Oxford: Oxford University Press, 1993), 25–7.

[123] For a full list of those involved with all the Diatessaronic and Syriac evidence, see *The Gospel According to St. Luke* (IGNTP), 1:xiv, xv. A. J. B. Higgins prepared the evidence for the Arabic and Persian Diatessarons. Higgins subsequently published a short article in 1986 with additional details for the evidence cited: "The Arabic Diatessaron in the New Oxford Edition of the Gospel According to St Luke in Greek," *JTS* 37 (1986): 415–19. J. K. Elliott issued a small correction to that article the following year in *JTS* 38 (1987): 135. There is also considerable additional evidence for the Arabic and Persian Diatessarons in the Appendix to Vol. 2 of the edition (2:258–61).

[124] For information on the Persian Diatessaron, see Petersen, *Tatian's Diatessaron*, 259–63.

[125] Despite the IGNTP edition's relatively recent publication date, much of the plans were laid in the 1940s and 1950s. I note that William Petersen joined the Committee in 1989 (so Epp, "The International Greek New Testament Project," 19). One wonders what Diatessaronic witnesses he would still advise for inclusion in the upcoming *ECM*, were he still with us.

[126] The INTF intends to complete the *ECM* for the entire NT by 2030, on which see H. A. G. Houghton, "Recent Developments in New Testament Textual Criticism," *EC* 2 (2011): 246–8. For my own assessment of how the *ECM* should handle the Diatessaron, see my answer to question six in Section 3.

[127] The first edition is Eberhard Nestle, *Novum Testamentum Graece cum apparatu critico ex editionibus et libris manuscriptis collecto* (Stuttgart: Privilegierte Württembergische Bibelanstalt, 1898). The most recent edition is Barbara Aland et al., eds., *Novum Testamentum Graece*, 28th ed. (Stuttgart: Deutsche Bibelgesellschaft, 2012). A history of the edition may be found in Metzger and

apparatus, it transitioned to a critical text with the work of Kurt Aland and later the UBS Committee in the 1950s and 1960s. Beginning with the 26th ed. (1979) its text has been identical with the concurrent UBS edition (starting with UBS³ in 1975), although the apparatuses are strikingly different. One major difference is that the NA has consistently opted *not* to include Diatessaronic evidence at all in its apparatus (even after joining forces with the UBS for its text). Reading the Introduction to the NA (whether the 28th ed. or the 25th ed., the last edition for which Aland was single editor), one would not even know that Tatian or his Diatessaron had ever existed, much less had had any bearing on the text of the Gospels.[128]

Although the Diatessaron garners no mention in the list of early versions or church fathers in NA²⁸, the NA²⁸ does list Ephrem among potential early writers it will cite. However, my exhaustive search of the NA²⁸ apparatus in the Gospels revealed not a single citation of Ephrem (even in some of the classic verses where he supports an Old Syriac reading, like the added "woe" at Luke 23:48).[129] Readings from Ephrem had been reported on occasion in NA²⁵ (e.g., at Matt 11:27; 17:26; etc.), but all of these references have now been expunged in the Gospels.[130] While I am sympathetic to the NA's total boycott of the Diatessaron, future editions might do well at least to mention why the Diatessaronic evidence is absent, rather than omit any mention of the Diatessaron at all.

2.13 The United Bible Societies (1st ed., 1966; 5th ed., 2014)

My survey culminates with the *Greek New Testament* of the United Bible Societies (UBS), first published in 1966, and most recently in 2014 (fifth edition).[131] I will begin with an outline of how UBS¹⁻³ reports the Diatessaron and the resulting deficiencies (with four illustrations). Then I will cover the modifications that UBS⁴⁻⁵ made in

---

Ehrman, *Text of the New Testament*, 190–1; Aland and Aland, *Text of the New Testament*, 20–2, 31–6. Hereafter I will refer to each edition as NAˣ, with the edition number superscripted.

[128] Despite the NA's total omission of the Diatessaron, the Alands do consider it to be the earliest translation of the Gospels into Syriac; see Aland and Aland, *Text of the New Testament*, 18, 192–3.

[129] The only reference to Ephrem in the *entire* apparatus of NA²⁸ appears at Acts 12:8.

[130] This is my best explanation for the otherwise cryptic report by Petersen in 1984 that "it is disturbing to discover that Diatessaronic readings have been deleted from the apparatus of the latest (twenty-sixth) edition of Nestle-Aland," as first read in a paper for the Annual Meeting of the SBL (1984), then published in "New Evidence for the Question of the Original Language of the Diatessaron," in *Studien zum Text und zur Ethik des Neuen Testaments: Festschrift zum 80. Geburtstag von Heinrich Greeven*, ed. Wolfgang Schrage (Berlin: de Gruyter, 1986), 325; reprinted as ch. 5 in Jan Krans and Joseph Verheyden, eds., *Patristic and Text-Critical Studies: The Collected Essays of William L. Petersen*, NTTSD 40 (Leiden: Brill, 2012). To my knowledge, the Nestle-Aland has *never* cited the Diatessaron (and certainly not the NA²⁵, which I have examined carefully), unless Petersen means the few references to Ephrem.

[131] Kurt Aland, Matthew Black, Bruce M. Metzger, and Allen Wikgren, eds., *The Greek New Testament* (New York: United Bible Societies, 1966). The following editions were subsequently published under an updated editorial committee: 2nd ed. in 1968; 3rd ed. in 1975, with corrected printing in 1983; 4th ed. in 1993; and 5th ed. in 2014. The history of the edition is outlined well in Metzger and Ehrman, *Text of the New Testament*, 192–4; Aland and Aland, *Text of the New Testament*, 31–6. Hereafter I will refer to each edition as UBSˣ, with the edition number superscripted.

Table 9.2 Diatessaronic Sigla in UBS[1-3] (1966–83)

	Special abbreviations used in connection with the Diatessaron include:
a	Arabic
e	quotation by Ephraem
e[arm]	quotation preserved in the Armenian version of Ephraem's commentary.
e[syr]	quotation preserved in the Syriac text of Ephraem's commentary.
f	Fulda
i	Italian (the agreement of [t] and [v])
l	Liège
n	Old Dutch (the agreement of [l] and [s])
p	Persian
s	Stuttgart
t	Tuscan
v	Venetian

Note: For this list of witnesses, see p. xxxv in UBS[1-2] and p. xli in UBS[3]. The thirteenth "siglum" is simply to cite "Diatessaron" by itself, with no superscript, which serves as a stand-in for the Arabic version, as described in the caveat that precedes this list (which I discuss in the text).

reporting the Diatessaron and the remaining deficiencies (with two illustrations). I will end with the ill effects those deficiencies have had on an actual textual commentary.

2.13.1 *The Deficiencies in UBS[1-3]*

An editorial committee forms the UBS text, and the first committee consisted of Kurt Aland, Matthew Black, Bruce Metzger, and Allen Wikgren, "with the participation of Arthur Vööbus during the first part of the work."[132] I note Vööbus's participation in particular, because it was Vööbus who penned the following opening line to his 1954 monograph on the early versions of the NT:

> In the history of the versions, as well as in the early phase of textual developments of the New Testament as a whole, there is no greater and more important name than Tatian. This is not an overstatement.[133]

If Vööbus had any sway on the Committee's patristic guest-list, then an invitation would be forthcoming for Tatian's new home in the UBS. Indeed, the lavish accommodations that UBS[1-3] initially establishes for Tatian go beyond even Merk's generous hospitality.[134]

---

[132] Aland et al., *Greek New Testament* (UBS[1]), vi.
[133] Arthur Vööbus, *Early Versions of the New Testament* (Stockholm: Estonian Theological Society in Exile, 1954), 1. Petersen also reproduces this statement as the first line of his own monograph in Petersen, *Tatian's Diatessaron*, 1. Bruce Metzger will go on to update Vööbus's work in his own *Early Versions* (see n. 7 above).
[134] I will also note that the Roman Catholic scholar (and later cardinal) Carlo M. Martini, who was responsible for revisions to Merk's Greek NT from 1964 (9th ed.) to 1984 (10th ed.), had also joined the UBS Committee by 1968 (on which see Aland and Aland, *Text of the New Testament*,

Where Merk listed seven individual Diatessaronic witnesses, UBS[1-3] lists *eight*, along with added sigla for combinations and subdivisions, for a total of *thirteen* different ways to list Diatessaronic evidence (see Table 9.2).

In light of this complicated Tatianic infrastructure, the UBS editors also prefaced it with something of a warning label:

> The problem of the Diatessaron of Tatian is particularly complex due to the indirect nature of the evidence, and the resulting diversity of theories and opinions concerning the tradition. When the term Diatessaron is used without superscript designation (see below) it usually refers to the Arabic version, which has been extensively accommodated to the Syriac Peshitta. However, rather than eliminate evidence traditionally cited for the Diatessaron, the Committee has included it, though with this word of caution.[135]

It can hardly be coincidence that the UBS takes over nearly the same sigla system as Merk and at the same time uses the generic reference "Diatessaron" as a stand-in for the Arabic version—precisely as Merk had used "Ta." The editors presumably have Merk in mind when they refer to "evidence traditionally cited," since no other Greek NT cited evidence to this degree. But where Merk would generally list only one side of the Diatessaronic evidence for a given variant, UBS[1-3] will sometimes list opposing readings, which puts the reader in a tensioned position. Beyond being of questionable value, the extra evidence in UBS[1-3] is also not always accurate. Consider the following four examples.

Example 1: *Conflicting Evidence.* In their introduction to textual criticism, the Alands select a sample page from UBS[3] (the current edition at the time) to highlight some of its features. The page they select comes from Mark 8, and it serves—with some bit of irony—as a fitting example to demonstrate the confusing state of Diatessaronic evidence that UBS[1-3] reports.[136] For Mark 8:15, UBS[1-3] lists several variant readings for the printed words "ὁρᾶτε, βλέπετε," and parts of the Diatessaron fall under three of these:

ὁρᾶτε, βλέπετε	Diatessaron[a]
ὁρᾶτε καὶ βλέπετε	Diatessaron
βλέπετε	Diatessaron[p]

What is a reader supposed to do with this evidence? For one, there is the confusing issue that "Diatessaron" without superscript is supposed to refer to the Arabic version (see the citation above), but here we have Diatessaron[a] (= Arabic version) cited separately

---

33). Although Martini obviously did not persuade the initial Committee to include Diatessaronic evidence (since he was not yet a member), it is possible that he helped maintain Tatian's presence in UBS[2-3], even as he did the same for Merk's editions.

[135] This caveat appears on p. xxxiv in UBS[1-2] and on p. xl in UBS[3], in identical form. It is replaced in UBS[4-5], as we shall see.

[136] The page is reproduced on Aland and Aland, *Text of the New Testament*, 226, with discussion on pp. 224–32. They select the page because it is one of those with "the most variants" in the UBS[3]. To be fair to the Alands, they themselves question the value of including the abundance of Diatessaronic evidence on p. 227, as I will note below in my discussion of UBS[4-5].

from "Diatessaron" (with no superscript). Does the Arabic Diatessaron support both readings?[137] Even ignoring that conflict, there is the next issue that the Arabic Diatessaron is now pitted against the Persian Diatessaron. Is the reader expected to referee between these witnesses and judge which can topple the other? This is not the only case in which such a conflict occurs.[138]

This example illustrates a major flaw in the way UBS[1-3] (and accordingly Merk) presents Diatessaronic evidence. When Diatessaronic witnesses diverge for a particular reading, what good does it do to present this information to the reader? The text-critic, of course, wishes to see the range of variants for a given reading, but when conflicting variants are listed under the umbrella of a single witness, then that witness ceases to function as a single witness.[139] The reader must now perform "second-order" textual criticism on the witness itself in order to use that witness for the "first-order" textual criticism of the reading in question.

Perhaps it would be more fair to say that this example illustrates a flaw in the state of Diatessaronic research itself, in that while the witnesses to the Diatessaron have multiplied several fold in the last three centuries, their frequent divergence has rendered a full reconstruction even more problematic. It is inappropriate to require the reader of a Greek NT apparatus to decide first what the Diatessaron read before being able to rely on the Diatessaron. If the reading of the Diatessaron is not relatively secure (and I use that word with some trepidation), then the Diatessaron should *not* be cited for a given variant.

Example 2: *Misleading Evidence.* The divergence of Diatessaronic witnesses is not the only issue in UBS[1-3], for an inverse problem can occur when the witnesses are all in agreement. For example, at Luke 23:34, the famous variant of Jesus's prayer of forgiveness for his crucifiers, UBS[1-3] provides a compelling swath of Diatessaronic evidence for its inclusion: Diatessaron$^{a,\,e^{arm,\,i,\,n}}$ = the Arabic Diatessaron, the Armenian version of Ephrem's *Commentary*,[140] the Middle Italian harmonies, and the Middle

---

[137] As it turns out, it does!—however, the conflicting citations in UBS[3] are obviously not the proper way to indicate this tension, and I doubt that was the intent. One recension of the Arabic Diatessaron (MSS B and E) includes the conjunction; the other recension (MS A) does not. The resulting editions and translations are thus quite confused. The reading occurs at 23:18 in the Arabic text. Ciasca's Latin reads "Videte, *et* cavete" (p. 41); Ciasca's Arabic (p. 89 from the back) likewise prints the conjunction between the two words; and he includes a textual note that MS A omits the conjunction. Both Hill (p. 135: "Take heed, and beware") and Hogg (p. 79: "Take heed, and guard yourselves") therefore print the conjunction. But Marmardji's French reads "Voyez, guardez-vous" and his corresponding Arabic omits the conjunction (pp. 220–1); a textual note in Marmardji explains that MSS B and E include the conjunction. Ephrem, unfortunately, is silent on this verse.

[138] Another conflict, among others, occurs at John 3:13, where the reader is asked to weigh Ephrem and the Venetian Diatessaron together against the Arabic Diatessaron.

[139] I consider this example different than the practice of noting divergent variants cited by the same early Christian writer (i.e., when a patristic author cites the same text in two different ways). In that case (assuming the manuscripts are trustworthy and the variants are authorial, not scribal) the data reveal that the same individual knew more than one variant. That is helpful information, since it represents a reality, not a conjecture. Such is not the implication of divergent Diatessaronic data. When Diatessaronic witnesses diverge, the expectation is not that Tatian had multiple variants in front of him, but that he had one variant—except we are not certain which one.

[140] Luke 23:34 also appears in the Syriac version of Ephrem's *Commentary*, in the folios already edited by Leloir in 1963 (see n. 122 above). I am not certain why UBS[3] does not reflect that fact. It is fixed in UBS[4-5].

Dutch harmonies. In short, the Diatessaron's major witnesses, both eastern and western, agree that Tatian included this prayer, which would thereby suggest it goes back at least to the second century.[141] But what UBS[1-3] leaves out is Codex Fuldensis, which also includes the prayer. And an informed reader will note that the Syriac Peshitta and the Latin Vulgate also include the prayer. Now suddenly the situation is less compelling.

The Arabic Diatessaron (as the UBS Committee acknowledged) has been accommodated to the Peshitta, which renders its evidence here less weighty, since it could have gotten this reading directly from the Peshitta. Likewise, the Middle Italian and Middle Dutch harmonies are most significant only when they diverge from Fuldensis (at least, under the "Old Latin" Diatessaron thesis), so their value is now diminished, since they could have gotten this reading directly from Fuldensis. And Fuldensis itself has been conformed to the Vulgate, so its independent value is likewise diminished. Suddenly what looked like a multiply-attested Diatessaronic reading, when filtered against the potential of "Vulgatization," is reduced to a single witness: Ephrem's *Commentary*. Ephrem is still a weighty witness (perhaps the weightiest), but the picture is different than when we started. The information UBS[1-3] has provided is misleading; it suggests a more compelling situation for the Diatessaron than truly exists. This is not the only case in which such a misrepresentation occurs.[142]

Example 3: *Incorrect Evidence.* In addition to the issues of divergent or misleading evidence, sometimes UBS[1-3] is simply wrong in its reporting of Diatessaronic evidence. At John 7:53–8:11, UBS[1-3] reports that Diatessaron[a, f] (=Arabic Diatessaron and Codex Fuldensis) both omit the *pericope adulterae*. This is one of the few times that UBS[1-3] reports the individual reading of Fuldensis, and here it is sadly mistaken. While the Arabic Diatessaron omits the *pericope adulterae*, Fuldensis *includes* it at ch. 121.[143] Not only that, the pericope is listed in the Fuldensis *capitula* as well (as ch. 120), which are likely older than Fuldensis since they contain some Old Latin readings and do not always match the wording or sequence of the harmonized text (as here, where the numbering is different).[144] So it is incorrect to say that Fuldensis omits the *pericope adulterae*, and therefore misleading to imply that the Diatessaron is unified on

---

[141] I should note that the Diatessaron is not the only second-century evidence for this verse that UBS[3] cites. It also includes Hegesippus, Marcion, Justin, and Irenaeus[lat]. The UBS[5] significantly reduces this number, though, to just Diatessaron, Jacobus-Justus[acc. to Hegesipp], and Irenaeus[lat].

[142] Another case, among others, of full Diatessaronic evidence that ultimately reduces to Ephrem alone occurs at Luke 1:28.

[143] In fact, the pericope begins at the end of ch. 120 and continues into ch. 121. Admittedly, the placement of the *pericope adulterae* in Fuldensis is odd. It does not appear between John 7:52 and 8:12 (which would place it in Fuldensis chs. 130–2). Instead, it appears directly following the Nicodemus episode of John 3, which is itself placed in between the cursing and withering of the fig tree from Matt 21 // Mark 11, in a mid-ministry visit to Jerusalem that the Diatessaron apparently creates. The Arabic Diatessaron and Fuldensis agree on this sequence, save for the inclusion of the *pericope adulterae*, which the Arabic omits. So, it may well be that a Latin precursor to Fuldensis (and not Tatian himself) added the *pericope adulterae* sometime in the transmission stream. But it is certainly not correct to say that Fuldensis omits the pericope. Incidentally, both the Arabic and Fuldensis do insert a passage between John 7:52 and 8:12, but it comes from Matt 22 // Mark 12 // Luke 20 and concerns how the son of David can also be the Messiah.

[144] On the *capitula* of Fuldensis, see Zola, "Codex Fuldensis," 15–16.

this omission. The reality, again, is mixed. As we shall see below, this error (and its propagation in UBS[4-5]) has misinformed at least one reader.

Example 4: *Misconstrued Evidence*. In my last example, the evidence is not so much incorrect as it is misconstrued. For the addition of Jesus's piercing following Matt 27:49 (which we have discussed more than once above), UBS[1-3] lists the Diatessaron (no superscript) as explicitly omitting this addition. This is a curious listing. For one, a *scholion* in Greek minuscule MS 72 explicitly states that Tatian added this line, which ought to make us at least pause here, even though it is true that no extant Diatessaronic witness (including the Arabic version) has the piercing of Jesus precede his death. However, if we imagine for the sake of argument that Tatian found this additional piercing in his copy of Matthew, but also knew the "traditional" piercing of John 19:34 that follows Jesus's death, then Tatian would have more than one harmonistic option available to him. He could insert both readings and have Jesus pierced twice, or he could select one reading or the other.[145] If he opted to go with the Johannine version, we would have little way of knowing whether his copy of Matthew had included the piercing. The only way we could ascertain Tatian's Matthean text is if Tatian explicitly included it. Since none of our extant witnesses include it, it is better to remain agnostic on Tatian's awareness of this Matthean addition. In general, one must hesitate to cite the Diatessaron for an omission, since a harmony can always omit a reading without the implication that it was absent in the source text.

2.13.2 *The Changes—and Lingering Deficiencies—in UBS[4-5]*

I am not the first to point out the deficiencies in how UBS[1-3] treats the Diatessaron. I was intrigued to discover a similar assessment by Tjitze Baarda, who apparently turned down the offer to prepare the Diatessaronic evidence for UBS[1]:

> A long time ago, I was asked by W. C. van Unnik of Utrecht and R. P. Markham of the American Bible Society to provide all the textual Diatessaronic data for the apparatus of the first edition of the UBS Greek New Testament. I really tried to fulfill that task, but after several months of study I had to withdraw: my investigation of the various texts involved led me to the conclusion that it was not—or hardly—possible to arrive at a decisive conclusion about the precise text of the Diatessaron in many of the cases where it was required for the GNT apparatus. The reason was that I found too many conflicting readings in the witnesses of the Diatessaron. Others have done the work that I had abandoned with more or (rather) less success.[146]

---

[145] Tatian could also, of course, select neither reading, or he could create his own reading. But I am bracketing those options for the sake of this argument.

[146] Baarda, "Tatian's Diatessaron and the Greek Text of the Gospels," 345. Baarda does not say who replaced him in compiling the Diatessaronic data for UBS[1], and the UBS preface does not specify either. In the preface to the first edition (p. vii), it does note in general that N. Joseph Kikuchi supplied the Syriac evidence; that A. F. J. Klijn supplied the Armenian evidence; and that M. Black supervised the collations of Syriac data. But it does not mention who worked on the Diatessaron directly. Regarding the deficiencies in UBS[1-3] and the changes in UBS[4], I also found a similar assessment to my own in Schmid, "How Can We Access Second Century Texts?" 141–2, 149–50.

Baarda goes on to list three examples (different than my own) where UBS[1-3] falls short in its citation of the Diatessaron. Baarda then describes the improvements made in UBS[4], and these are noteworthy.

There was already a hint that the UBS Committee had recognized its unsatisfactory approach in UBS[1-3] when the Alands wrote the following (while UBS[4] was still in production): "Whether it is useful to identify the textual traditions of the Diatessaron in such detail (especially for translators) is questionable, and it has been decided negatively for the fourth edition of *GNT*. The secondary traditions will be eliminated, and the apparatus will cite only the most important witnesses [namely, the two versions of Ephrem's *Commentary*]."[147]

Once UBS[4] emerged, these changes were made explicit in a lengthy addition to the Introduction (which replaced the original "warning label" of UBS[1-3]), portions of which are worth repeating here:

> As a witness to the text of the New Testament, Tatian's harmony of the Gospels known as the Diatessaron is burdened with particularly complex problems. Among the more serious are the circumstances that the work itself has not survived in its original form, the language of the original is in dispute (Greek or Syriac), and neither the sources nor the methods used by Tatian in compiling it are known. The available translations (especially a 6th century [*sic*!] Arabic translation) and numerous revisions made in many different languages and cultures admittedly permit the scholar to obtain a fairly precise impression of the work's profile, but they do not provide the textual critic with verifiable readings in the sense defined above on p. 3*f. The necessary definitive research is lacking here just as for Marcion's New Testament. But as the Committee wished to offer as accurate a view of the data as possible rather than ignore this early (though indirect) witness completely, the following principles were agreed upon for its citation.[148]

The description goes on to note that since the UBS apparatus does not cover any variant readings that overlap with the Dura fragment, only Ephrem's *Commentary* will be considered. It notes that Louis Leloir (who produced the modern editions of the Armenian and Syriac versions of Ephrem's *Commentary*) accepted editorial responsibility for its inclusion. The description ends with the following statement:

> Thus the reader has access to the earliest appearance of the Diatessaron (possibly in its original language) in the form of the commentary used in the region of the church where it was for centuries regarded as the standard form of the Gospels. The data provided here are as authentic as the present state of scholarly research

---

[147] Aland and Aland, *Text of the New Testament*, 227. This statement appears just after the description of Diatessaronic evidence for Mark 8:15 in my first example above.

[148] This description appears in UBS[4] on pp. 39*–40* and is reproduced unchanged (except for internal page references) in UBS[5] on pp. 44*–46*. At the time of the fourth edition, the UBS Committee consisted of Barbara Aland, Kurt Aland, Johannes Karavidopoulos, Carlo M. Martini, and Bruce M. Metzger. It is especially noteworthy to see how the editors have downgraded the Diatessaron to the status of "early (though indirect) witness."

Table 9.3 Diatessaronic Sigla in UBS⁴⁻⁵ (1993–2014)

The following abbreviations are used in connection with the Diatessaron.	
Diatessaron	a citation from Ephraem's commentary on the Diatessaron where the Syriac original and the Armenian translation are in agreement.
Diatessaron^syr	a citation from the Syriac original of Ephraem's commentary where it differs from the Armenian version.
Diatessaron^arm	a citation from the Armenian version of Ephraem's commentary where it differs from the Syriac original.

in the field can yield. In contrast, information derived from later translations and revisions of the Diatessaron is often lacking in consistency, and in default of any reliable principles for dealing with such materials their inclusion in the present edition could only lead to confusion. The reader would be well advised, however, even for the citations derived from Ephraem's commentary, to be cautious in using the Diatessaron as a witness to the text of the New Testament, especially in citations from parallel pericopes in the synoptic gospels.[149]

Finally, the introduction notes the new sigla employed for the Diatessaron (see Table 9.3).

First, allow me to return to the glaring blunder in the opening paragraph on the Diatessaron, which states that the available translations include "a 6th century Arabic translation." A date this early for an Arabic Christian work would be remarkable; it is clearly a typographical error. A conflation seems to have occurred between Codex Fuldensis, which is a sixth-century *Latin* translation, and the Arabic version, which was likely translated in the eleventh century. Somewhat shocking is that this mistake is repeated in UBS⁵, after the Committee had had over twenty years to notice it. It must be corrected for the next edition.[150]

Blunder aside, the editors have done a commendable job identifying and attempting to rectify the confusing state of affairs that UBS¹⁻³ had created for the Diatessaron. The Committee aptly outlines the complexities that plague Diatessaronic research, and their statements at the end concerning the present state of the field and the caution it warrants are appropriate caveats. In this revised warning of 1993, the Committee anticipated the major shift that Diatessaronic studies was about to undergo in the next decade. For in the late 1990s and early 2000s, Ulrich Schmid and others began publishing essays that signaled the deflation of the "Old Latin" Diatessaron construct and the end of the Plooij–Petersen method for identifying Diatessaronic readings from medieval western witnesses. The face of Diatessaronic studies was entering a third

---

[149] This conclusion appears in UBS⁴, 39*–40*; and UBS⁵, 45*.

[150] The editors have three options in how to adjust their current reading. They can change it to (1) "especially a 6th-century Latin translation," (2) "especially an 11th-century Arabic translation," or (3) "especially a 6th-century Latin translation and an 11th-century Arabic translation" (which is my preference, since both principal witnesses to the Diatessaron deserve mention).

phase, where assumptions of the past were becoming questions again, and where the once abundant number of witnesses to the Diatessaron was being stripped down to but a few key specimens.[151]

While UBS[4-5] made laudable efforts in its revision of Diatessaronic evidence, some deficiencies remain. I will note only two examples for illustration, but they could be multiplied.

Example 1. In the first example we return to John 7:53–8:11, where UBS[5] *still* lists "Diatessaron" as omitting the *pericope adulterae.* Now, of course, "Diatessaron" no longer stands for the Arabic Diatessaron, but for the combined Syriac and Armenian evidence of Ephrem. But what can it mean that Ephrem "omits" this pericope? Ephrem's work is a commentary, in which he cites the Diatessaron on occasion but neither exhaustively nor consistently. While his sequence generally matches the sequence of the Arabic Diatessaron, Ephrem's lack of commentary on a particular passage is by no means proof that it was absent from his copy of the Diatessaron. Although I consider it highly unlikely that Ephrem's Diatessaron had the *pericope adulterae,* this is an argument from silence. There is no way to prove that Ephrem's Diatessaron *lacked* this passage—or most any passage. If we are to limit ourselves only to Ephrem's *Commentary* for citations of the Diatessaron in the apparatus, then we no longer (or at least rarely) have the luxury of reporting omissions. The nature of the evidence simply precludes it.

Example 2. In the second example we turn back once again to the doxology appended to the end of the Lord's Prayer in Matt 6:13. Here UBS[1-3] had listed "Diatessaron" (no superscript) for the inclusion of the addition, implying that the Arabic version includes the doxology, which it does at 9:36. But UBS[4-5] has reversed course. Now it lists Diatessaron[syr] as *omitting* the addition, implying that Ephrem cites the verse, but with the shorter reading (without the doxology), which he does in 6.16a.[152] However, as indicated by the superscript, this reading only appears in the Syriac version of Ephrem's *Commentary.* This entire section (6.16a), in which Ephrem works through the Lord's

---

[151] This most recent phase of Diatessaronic studies, which Schmid has labeled "the new perspective on the Diatessaron," is well documented in his *Status Quaestionis* essay "The Diatessaron of Tatian" (see n. 6 above). The three most important studies are Ulrich Schmid, "In Search of Tatian's Diatessaron in the West," *VC* 57 (2003): 176–99; August den Hollander and Ulrich Schmid, "The *Gospel of Barnabas,* the Diatessaron, and Method," *VC* 61 (2007): 1–20; and Schmid's monograph *Unum ex Quattuor: Eine Geschichte der lateinischen Tatianüberlieferung* (Freiburg im Breisgau: Herder, 2005). I also provide a summary of this major course correction in Zola, "Codex Fuldensis," 19–26, where I note two important precursors by Johannes Rathofer in 1972 and 1973: "'Tatian' und Fulda: Die St. Galler Handschrift und der Victor-Codex," in *Zeiten und Formen in Sprache und Dichtung: Festschrift f. Fritz Tschirch z. 70. Geburtstag,* ed. Karl Heinz Schirmer and Bernhard Sowinskii (Köln: Böhlau, 1972), 337–56; and "Die Einwirkung des Fuldischen Evangelientextes auf den althochdeutschen 'Tatian': Abkehr von der Methode der Diatessaronforschung," in *Literatur und Sprache im europäischen Mittelalter: Festschrift f. Karl Langosch z. 70. Geburtstag,* ed. Alf Önnerfors, Johannes Rathofer, and Fritz Wagner (Darmstadt: Wissenschaftliche Buchgesellschaft, 1973), 256–308. Rathofer's studies may well have contributed to the UBS Committee's sense that the western Diatessaronic witnesses were not as valuable as once purported.

[152] Despite my previous cry against citing Ephrem for omissions, I think it is reasonable to conclude that the Syriac version of Ephrem's *Commentary* omitted the added doxology here, since Ephrem cites each line of the prayer one by one followed by commentary, ending with the shorter reading of Matt 6:13. If he had had the doxology, he almost certainly would have continued. Of course, there is the (remote) possibility that he simply decided to move on at this point without commenting on the last line of the prayer.

Prayer line by line, is absent in the Armenian translation. Now what does the reader do? Did the Armenian translator skip a section, or did a Syriac scribe add a section? We are back to battling witnesses. And despite the UBS Committee's frequent appeal to the "Syriac original" of Ephrem's *Commentary* in the sigla description, it is not always clear which is more original when the Syriac and Armenian diverge.[153]

I should note that UBS[4-5] does fix many references to the Diatessaron as well. The bulk of such references once present in UBS[1-3], of course, have now disappeared entirely, simply by nature of the more limited evidence. For instance, our example above of divergent witnesses in Mark 8:15 is now gone (in fact, the entire variant reading is no longer listed). Likewise, in UBS[4-5] the Diatessaron is no longer listed as omitting the piercing of Jesus at Matt 27:49 (even though Ephrem would technically support that omission). And in UBS[4-5], "Diatessaron" is still listed as including Jesus's prayer of forgiveness at Luke 23:34, which is accurate, since Ephrem cites it on more than one occasion (10.14; 21.3; 21.18). The question of whether the UBS should still label any of this evidence as "Diatessaron" I will leave for Section 3.

2.13.3 *The Effects of Bad Diatessaronic Data*

As I close my review of the UBS edition, I offer a short demonstration of how poor Diatessaronic evidence can mislead even an informed reader, using Philip W. Comfort's *New Testament Text and Translation Commentary*, a textual commentary designed to provide an educated audience with information on the variants that most affect translation and interpretation.[154] Comfort references the Diatessaron in about fourteen of the readings he discusses, and in about half of these he cites the Diatessaron correctly as far as the current available evidence goes. But the other half of his readings contain serious issues in his treatment of the Diatessaron. I will review two examples.

Example 1. Comfort erroneously cites the Diatessaron as omitting the *pericope adulterae* (John 7:53–8:11)[155]; but, as we have already seen, so do both UBS[1-3] and UBS[4], Comfort's sources. Unfortunately, Comfort specifically points to the Diatessaron's omission as early evidence (among others) that the Gospel of John did not include

---

[153] Christian Lange, among others, has investigated the possibility that not all of the *Commentary* is attributable to Ephrem, but that it may contain later interpolations. For his discussion of the Syriac passages that are not in the Armenian, see his *The Portrayal of Christ in the Syriac Commentary on the Diatessaron* (Leuven: Peeters, 2005), 42–8.

[154] Philip W. Comfort, *New Testament Text and Translation Commentary* (Carol Stream, IL: Tyndale House, 2008), vii. Comfort relies on the UBS[4] and NA[27], among other text-critical resources, so his treatment is up-to-date for his day. It is not my intention to disparage Comfort or his textual commentary. Though it has its shortcomings, it contains many helpful discussions of significant textual variants and is laudably dedicated to making textual criticism accessible to a general audience. As an informed textual scholar, Comfort is in a better position than many to understand the complexities of the Diatessaron. The fact that he misreads the evidence on several occasions illustrates my point that the evidence itself is misleading and confusing. I imagine that were I instead to survey exegetical commentaries on the Gospels that incorporate some amount of textual criticism in their discussions, I would find equally confused accounts of the Diatessaronic evidence.

[155] Comfort, *New Testament Text and Translation Commentary*, 285–6.

this passage, which is beyond what the Diatessaronic evidence can do at this point. Comfort has been deceived by bad data.[156]

Example 2. Mark 1:41 contains the notorious variant in which Jesus is "angry" (ὀργισθείς) rather than "compassionate" (σπλαγχνισθείς). Startlingly, Comfort lists the Diatessaron as supporting σπλαγχνισθείς rather than ὀργισθείς,[157] when in fact Ephrem's *Commentary* is one of the few ancient witnesses that appears to support the "angry" reading. How could Comfort cite the Diatessaron on the wrong side of this debate? The answer probably lies in the poor way that the UBS presents the evidence. In UBS[3], the apparatus lists Diatessaron[a] in support of σπλαγχνισθείς, then lists Ephrem in support of ὀργισθείς. Again we have divergent Diatessaronic witnesses; note, however, that UBS[3] lists Ephrem's *Commentary* here simply as "Ephraem," and not as "Diatessaron[e]," as the Introduction had promised it would. An inattentive reader might easily miss this veiled Diatessaronic reference, as apparently Comfort did. When we come to UBS[4], the reading remains opaque: the apparatus now lists "(Diatessaron)"—in parentheses—in support of ὀργισθείς. What do the parentheses signify?[158] Does Ephrem only kind of say "angry"? Whatever the intent, it does not help Comfort correctly interpret the reading, since he erroneously lists the Diatessaron on the side of σπλαγχνισθείς. This time he is the victim of bad form.[159]

My purpose in this final section has been to demonstrate that misrepresenting Diatessaronic evidence in the apparatus of a Greek NT has real consequences. Scholars rely on the apparatus to present reliable and readable information, neither of which has the UBS consistently demonstrated in its current presentation of Diatessaronic data. Comfort's textual commentary is but one real-world example of how easily poor information can mislead an otherwise informed reader. If the Diatessaron is ever to be a meaningful witness in the textual criticism of the Gospels, we need to get this right.

3. Recommendations and Conclusions: The Future of Diatessaronic Studies

In the preceding pages I have traced the use of Tatian's Diatessaron in the textual criticism of the Gospels from John Mill's 1707 Greek NT to the fifth edition of the

---

[156] Another example where Comfort takes weak Diatessaronic evidence offered by UBS[3] and presents it as solid occurs at John 9:6 (*New Testament Text and Translation Commentary*, 292–3).

[157] Comfort, *New Testament Text and Translation Commentary*, 98. A recent study by Nathan Johnson has made a worthwhile argument that Ephrem's Syriac Diatessaron in fact read "compassionate" and that Ephrem's reference to "angry" derives from Jesus's rebuke of the leper and not from the presence of the word in the text; see "Anger Issues: Mark 1.41 in Ephrem the Syrian, the Old Latin Gospels and Codex Bezae," *NTS* 63 (2017): 188–92. Should Johnson be correct, Comfort has still misread the evidence that was available to him at the time.

[158] Baarda asks the same question in "Mark 1:41: ὀργισθείς: A Reading Attested for Mar Ephraem, the Diatessaron, or Tatian," *ZNW* 103 (2012): 292n. 16.

[159] Placing the Diatessaron on the correct side of this debate also would have complicated Comfort's argument, for he (unconvincingly) blames the scribe behind Codex Bezae for the creation of the "angry" variant, which he could not have done had he understood its antiquity in the Diatessaron. Another example in which Comfort misreads the UBS Diatessaronic evidence occurs at Mark 7:3 (*New Testament Text and Translation Commentary*, 118).

UBS Greek NT published in 2014—over three hundred years of references to the Diatessaron. My survey has led me to three primary observations:

1. There were three major phases (each spanning three to four decades) in modern Diatessaronic studies that significantly affected the presence of the Diatessaron in the apparatus of the Greek NT:
    i. The 1860s–1890s, in which Codex Fuldensis, Ephrem's *Commentary*, and the Arabic Diatessaron (among others) first became widely accessible.
    ii. The 1920s–1950s, in which the Middle Dutch, Middle Italian, Persian, and Dura harmonies (among others) first took on a central role in the Diatessaron's reconstruction.
    iii. The 1990s–present, in which the alleged relationship between those witnesses discovered in the first phase and those identified in the second phase was called back into question.
2. As awareness of and access to Diatessaronic witnesses grew, so too did the Diatessaron's complicated and conflicting presence in the apparatus. Yet as new data became available, the assessment and approach of the editor significantly affected how that data was reported in the apparatus. Editions emerged side by side in which Tatian was blamed for everything (von Soden) and nothing (Westcott and Hort). Even today an edition exists that cites seven individual Diatessaronic witnesses (Merk's 11th ed.) alongside an edition that cites only one witness (UBS[5]) alongside an edition that refuses to cite the Diatessaron at all (NA[28]).
3. The Diatessaronic evidence that does appear in the apparatus is often misguided, misleading, or simply misinformed. The Diatessaronic status of the same variant reading (for instance, the end of Matt 6:13) has often changed from edition to edition, depending on the available witnesses and the editor's approach. These inconsistencies render the editions demonstrably unreliable. One has to understand something of the editor's presuppositions before one can properly assess a purported Diatessaronic reading.

My three observations lead me to this single declaration: direction is needed in the field of Diatessaronic studies. To conclude, I offer responses to seven questions on the future of Tatian's Diatessaron and its role in the textual criticism of the Gospels. These responses comprise my recommendations and vision for the discipline. As an aid to the reader, I offer a list of the seven questions I will address:

1. Should the critical apparatus still cite Tatian's Diatessaron?
2. What are the next steps in Diatessaronic research?
3. What can we do to make Diatessaronic research more accessible?
4. Can we ever reconstruct Tatian's Diatessaron?
5. Would reconstructing Tatian's Diatessaron give us access to the text of the Gospels in the second century?
6. How should future editions of the Greek NT (including the UBS, NA, and *ECM*) cite the Diatessaron?

7. If we may never be able to reconstruct Tatian's Diatessaron, and if reconstructing it still might not provide us with the earliest text of the Gospels, should the entire enterprise simply be abandoned?

3.1 Should the Critical Apparatus Still Cite Tatian's Diatessaron?

My answer to this question is, in essence, not yet. Tatian's Diatessaron is not ready for public display. As my survey has shown, our method has not caught up to our sudden wealth of information. There was a time when we longed for a witness to Tatian's text. Now we have an abundance—but with conflicting ideas of where they come from and how they relate. Before we can cite these in an apparatus, we need to assess where we stand.[160]

3.2 What are the Next Steps in Diatessaronic Research?

We need reliable and accessible editions of all the major witnesses to the Diatessaron. Too many mistakes have been made in the past based on faulty editions or misconstrued evidence.[161] For some witnesses, excellent editions already exist. For others, they are in progress or awaiting production.[162] Once accurate editions of Fuldensis and the Arabic version, in particular, are available, we need to create a detailed comparison of their sequences, section by section and verse by verse. From there we can begin to assess the other surviving Diatessaronic harmonies and fit them into a grand Diatessaronic

---

[160] The voice of Petersen (from 1986!) echoes in my ears: "The result of this new exclusion is that we will soon be awash with a generation of NT scholars who do not even think of the Diatessaron when considering the NT text: out of sight, out of mind. The Diatessaron must now struggle to be readmitted to the apparatus" (Petersen, "New Evidence," 67; see n. 130 above). My answer to Petersen would be, "Yes. Diatessaronic studies has not shown itself worthy of the apparatus. It must earn its way back in, once it has developed a sound methodology that can withstand the criticisms of Schmid's 'new perspective.'" I was surprised to discover that Baarda was even more reticent than I. In 2000 he opined, "In my view there are serious doubts as to whether one should include the data of the Diatessaron in a critical apparatus to the Gospels" ("Source for an Early Text at Rome," 134). Then a decade later he confirmed, "And, indeed, it is my conviction that it is not possible to make the Diatessaron a standard witness in any apparatus" ("Tatian's Diatessaron and the Greek Text of the Gospels," 348).

[161] The classic examples are those identified by Rathofer in "'Tatian' und Fulda" and "Die Einwirkung des Fuldischen Evangelientextes" (see n. 151), which are well outlined by Petersen, *Tatian's Diatessaron*, 301–9.

[162] A prime example of an excellent edition is Leloir's multipart edition of Ephrem's *Commentary* (see n. 122). Two faulty editions of the Arabic Diatessaron exist: Ciasca's (see n. 64) and Marmardji's (see n. 91). Fortunately, a new critical edition is in the works, on which see Giuliano Lancioni and N. Peter Joosse, "The Arabic Diatessaron Project: Digitalizing, Encoding, Lemmatization," *Journal of Religion, Media and Digital Culture* 5.1 (2016): 205–77. The subject of my doctoral dissertation was to produce a new edition and translation of Codex Fuldensis (see n. 18), which I am currently revising for publication. New witnesses are also emerging. In 2011, an edition of a hitherto overlooked Anglo-Norman gospel harmony was published, which is likely the long-sought "Old French" exemplar of the Pepysian harmony; see Brent A. Pitts, ed., *Estoire de l'Evangile (Dublin, Christ Church Cathedral, MS. 6.1.1)*, Medium Ævum Monographs 28 (Oxford: Society for the Study of Medieval Languages and Literature, 2011). The field is still ripe for harvest.

stemma.¹⁶³ I believe minute oddities in sequence, as well as indicative errors in wording, will help us trace genealogical relationships. This in turn will help us gauge the value of the western vernacular harmonies, whose status is currently in flux, and fit them in among the eastern witnesses.¹⁶⁴

3.3 What Can We Do to Make Diatessaronic Research More Accessible?

Diatessaronic studies has become something of an exclusive club.¹⁶⁵ There is indeed a heavy linguistic demand, but the overly complicated methodology of the past has often barred outsiders from stepping into or even comprehending the field. I propose we create a central repository of information related to Tatian's Diatessaron, hosted online, and accessible to all would-be investigators and seasoned text-critics alike. This repository would include a database of Diatessaronic witnesses, an annotated bibliography of research, a catalog of ostensible Diatessaronic readings and their evidence, and—crucially—digital transcriptions of the available editions. When a researcher wishes to inquire about a particular witness or see the evidence for a particular reading, this repository will be the first stop. Ideally, the repository would also contain a list of desiderata for future work, as a benefit to graduate students or others interested in pursuing Diatessaronic studies.

3.4 Can We Ever Reconstruct Tatian's Diatessaron?

We must contend with the serious possibility that the answer is no. Our available evidence may never allow us to reconstruct the wording of the Diatessaron as issued from Tatian's hand—at least, not a full reconstruction.¹⁶⁶ Indeed, we must contend

---

[163] There is some irony in my proposing we construct a grand genealogy for a work that is supposed to have excised Jesus's genealogies. Here I am suggesting we build upon the previous genealogical work that Ulrich Schmid began in his *Unum ex Quattuor* (see n. 151). I am also echoing a proposal I made in a previous essay that served as a precursor to the SBL sessions from which the current volume emerged; see my "Evangelizing Tatian: The *Diatessaron*'s Place in the Emergence of the Fourfold Gospel Canon," *PRSt* 43 (2016): 412–14.

[164] Metzger recognized our crucial need to assess the western Diatessaronic witnesses as early as 1950 when he wrote, "Whether any of them are grandsons or merely great-nephews of Tatian, or bear no discernible relationship at all, are questions which demand further attention by critics," in "The Evidence of the Versions for the Text of the New Testament," in *New Testament Manuscript Studies: The Materials and the Making of a Critical Apparatus*, ed. Merrill M. Parvis and Allen Paul Wikgren (Chicago, IL: University of Chicago Press, 1950), 29.

[165] Baarda was fond of noting how Jülicher referred to the field as a "Tatiankultus"; for the reference, see Baarda's "Op zoek naar de tekst van het Diatessaron," *Vox Theologica* 17 (1962): 107, which is reprinted as "In Search of the Diatessaron Text," in *Early Transmission of Words of Jesus: Thomas, Tatian the Text of the New Testament*, ed. J. Helderman and S. J. Noorda (Amsterdam: VU Boekhandel/Uitgeverij, 1983), 65. But my preferred notice of Diatessaronic obscurity comes from a paper presentation I heard Bart Ehrman deliver: "Diatessaronic studies are among the most arcane, complex, and convoluted subfields within our discipline, or rather a minefield that on which even seasoned text-critical angels fear to tread" (in his "Response to Charles Hill, The Four Gospel Canon in the Second Century" [paper presented at the Annual Meeting of the SBL, San Francisco, CA, 21 November 2011], 8).

[166] Here I am primarily concerned with the pursuit of a full reconstruction. I am still hopeful that individual readings of the Diatessaron can be reconstructed with some reliability in certain cases. But

with the possibility that there is no *single* Diatessaron to reconstruct. Already there is significant evidence of separate eastern and western branches of the Diatessaron. Later scribe-harmonists have clearly revised the Diatessaron as they translated and transcribed it in their own vernaculars.[167] Tatian himself may have initiated these revisions as he brought his Diatessaron from west to east. We are not dealing with a static text, but a living Gospel.[168] To speak of *the* Diatessaron may no longer be accurate. Once we have achieved our complete stemma of the tradition, we will better be able to say whether reconstructing an "initial" Diatessaron is ever feasible.

3.5 Would Reconstructing Tatian's Diatessaron Give Us Access to the Text of the Gospels in the Second Century?

Despite the many claims for "yes" at the outset of this chapter, we must now seriously consider the possibility that Tatian was far less constrained with his text than we have previously assumed. If Tatian understood himself as a gospel-writer, and not a gospel-harmonizer, then reconstructing his composition may give us more of his creative end-product than its underlying sources.[169] There has long been evidence that the

---

[the] the alluring feature of the Diatessaron (for text-critics especially) is the potential access it allegedly grants to huge portions of the early gospel text, if only we could reconstruct Tatian's "original" (a situation that is different than what reconstructing Marcion's or another early Christian's gospel text can provide, since these others are far less complete). Theodor Zahn receives credit for the first attempt at a major reconstruction of the Diatessaron, and his results are remarkable given his limited resources in 1881 (see n. 21; not even the Arabic version was fully accessible to him yet). No one has quite accomplished a full reconstruction. Baarda, "In Search of the Diatessaron Text," 66-7, reviews some more recent attempts. In 1997-8, a team of six researchers (T. Baarda, W. Petersen, U. Schmid, A. den Hollander, P. Joosse, and H. Bakker) assembled at the *Netherlands Institute for Advanced Studies* (NIAS) in an attempt to reconstruct John 1-5 from all the major Diatessaronic witnesses. Despite promises of a forthcoming monograph, no publication emerged following the ten-month project. Instead, the team ultimately determined that an effort to integrate all the extant witnesses into a critical edition is simply too ambitious and complicated. Schmid describes the project briefly in his *Status Quaestionis* essay ("The Diatessaron of Tatian," 116-17), but my primary source of information comes from the participants' synopses of the fellowship year, once available on the NIAS website (https://nias.knaw.nl/), but sadly no longer accessible. If a team consisting of these Diatessaronic luminaries could not accomplish the task, one wonders whether a full reconstruction will ever be feasible.

[167] These scribal modifications are easily demonstrable simply by comparing the general sequences of the various extant harmonies. Petersen, at the end of his grand monograph, attempts to account for the different eastern and western streams of the Diatessaronic tradition with the solution that it was Justin's harmony that initially circulated in the west, which, since Tatian integrated it into his own, also had affinities with the Diatessaron that circulated in the east (*Tatian's Diatessaron*, 428-37). In either case, there is a separate eastern and western tradition. Francis Watson's study in Chapter 4 of the current volume makes important inroads into delineating the different sequence approaches of the eastern and western branches.

[168] Here I am echoing the language of D. C. Parker, *The Living Text of the Gospels* (Cambridge: Cambridge University Press, 1997).

[169] Baarda has raised this issue before: "This might imply that Tatian is a first class witness to the Greek Gospel texts that were at his desk, if only we could by way of reconstruction rediscover not only the text which he wrote but also the text which he read. However, one cannot always immediately conclude from such a reconstruction that the text which he produced was, indeed, the text that he read in his copies of the various Gospels" ("Source for an Early Text at Rome," 96). Baarda goes on to note that in harmonizing, Tatian may have constituted "a new text that in detail differed from that of

Diatessaron contained "nontraditional" material that does not derive directly from a *written* gospel text.[170] However, the evidence is now growing thinner for Tatian's use of "noncanonical" *written* sources as well.[171] Consequently, the oddities traceable in the Diatessaron may stem from Tatian himself (and not from written copies of either "canonical" or "extracanonical" Gospels). The question of whether Tatian desired to supplement or supplant the fourfold gospel thus remains a pertinent one, even if his authorial intent lies ultimately beyond our reach.[172]

3.6 How Should Future Editions of the Greek NT (Including the UBS, NA, and *ECM*) Cite the Diatessaron?

I have an extended answer to this question. Never again can we cite *the* Diatessaron with a single siglum (as, e.g., von Soden, Souter, and even Vogels did), as though it were a unified extant manuscript with secure readings like its neighbors in the apparatus. *The* Diatessaron no longer survives; many witnesses to the Diatessaron exist, not all of equal value, and not all in agreement.[173]

Neither, however, is the answer to cite some or all of the divergent witnesses to the Diatessaron at once and let the reader work things out (as, e.g., Merk or UBS[1-3] did). As I have illustrated, that erases any potential value the Diatessaron may have as a witness. The selectivity of this method also tends to hide or ignore dissenting evidence.[174]

---

his source texts" and that Tatian's "specific understanding of Christian faith" may also have influenced his redactional work. Francis Watson has also recently argued that Tatian operates as a gospel writer, not a harmonizer; see his "Towards a Redaction-Critical Reading of the Diatessaron Gospel," *EC* 7 (2016): 95–112; and his *Gospel Writing: A Canonical Perspective* (Grand Rapids, MI: Eerdmans, 2013), 28–61, 78–91. Matthew Crawford has argued for the same (Tatian as evangelist) in "Diatessaron, a Misnomer? The Evidence from Ephrem's Commentary," *EC* 4 (2013): 362–85.

[170] I have in mind here some of the classic passages that once apparently stood in the Diatessaron but which are unlikely to have come directly from Tatian's written sources (whether "canonical" or not), like Jesus's airborne flight to Capernaum, on which see Tjitze Baarda, "'The Flying Jesus': Luke 4:29–30 in the Syriac Diatessaron," *VC* 40 (1986): 313–41. Baarda describes another expanded variant at Matt 17:26 that Tatian may well have invented in "Tatian's Diatessaron and the Greek Text of the Gospels," 342–3. I describe a potential example of Tatian's creativity regarding the second cock-crow at Mark 14:72 in my essay "Evangelizing Tatian," 412. If Crawford is correct about identifying the Dura fragment as Tatianic, it contains several innovative readings; see Matthew R. Crawford, "The Diatessaron, Canonical or Non-Canonical? Rereading the Dura Fragment," *NTS* 62 (2016): 253–77. Petersen (*Tatian's Diatessaron*, 78–82) provides a list of potential Encratite readings Tatian may have inserted into the Diatessaron, and there are several studies that investigate whether Tatian's theology has affected his composition; see, for one example among many, J. Rendel Harris, "Was the Diatessaron Anti-Judaic?," *HTR* 18 (1925): 103–9. The point is that none of these readings is attributable to a *written* source of Tatian; rather, they are attributable to Tatian himself.

[171] On whether Tatian actually used additional sources beyond the four Gospels, see Chapter 2 by Charles Hill in the present volume.

[172] Several chapters in the current volume address this issue, which is one of the volume's central questions; see Chapter 5 by Nicholas Perrin and Chapter 6 by James Barker.

[173] On this point, Baarda agrees: "This relative uncertainty in the evaluation of the textual data should make it clear that we should be very cautious in using the name Tatian or Diatessaron in any apparatus to the Greek New Testament" ("Tatian's Diatessaron and the Greek Text of the Gospels," 345).

[174] As a case in point, the IGNTP's decision for its edition of Luke to include only the Arabic and Persian Diatessarons comes across as arbitrary. Why the Persian Diatessaron (which is only

Instead I propose that before the Diatessaron in any form may reenter the apparatus, we first create a *Textual Commentary on Tatian's Diatessaron*, which will serve as a running annotated apparatus for potential Diatessaronic readings. This textual commentary (also initially hosted online) can discuss all the relevant evidence of each Diatessaronic witness for each potential Diatessaronic reading.[175] Of course, we could not compile such a commentary until after we have reliable editions of the witnesses and an accurate understanding of their origins and relations with one another.

In the meantime, I propose that future editions of the UBS continue the current practice of citing Ephrem's *Commentary* alone as a witness to the Diatessaron,[176] with one significant modification: the UBS should no longer label Ephrem's *Commentary* as *the* "Diatessaron" in the apparatus. This change is vital. Just because Ephrem is likely citing the Diatessaron does not make his fourth-century Syriac citations somehow equivalent to a second-century Greek text (which is the implication when the UBS includes the Diatessaron under its "List of Greek Church Fathers"); we do not know where Ephrem's Syriac Diatessaron came from or what revisions it underwent before he got it. To label Ephrem as *the* "Diatessaron" in the apparatus is misleading and inaccurate. The UBS apparatus should either label Ephrem simply as "Ephrem," in keeping with its established practice for other early Christian writers, or (preferably) it may adopt Ephrem$^{Comm.Diat.}$ as a more precise siglum.[177] The reader may then decide what additional value, if any, to place on Ephrem's citations, without confusing them for direct references to *the* Diatessaron.

For future editions of the NA, I consider it wise to continue omitting the Diatessaron from the apparatus, as it has traditionally done. I would, however, prefer to see a short paragraph in the Introduction explaining its reasoning for doing so, so that the reader is aware that bracketing Tatian is a conscious decision of the editors.

---

distantly related to Tatian) and not the western witnesses? I was pleased to discover that Baarda makes the same critique of the IGNTP's decision in "What Kind of Critical Apparatus," 59–60. The same critique could be extended to the UBS$^{1-3}$. Why not include the Pepysian harmony? Or the Heliand? Or the Old High German Diatessaron? Or other representatives of the Middle Dutch beyond just the two selected? If we are to be selective, we must develop criteria for our selectivity.

[175] The model for such a textual commentary would be the majestic edition of the Liège Diatessaron initiated by Plooij in 1929 and finally brought to completion by A. H. A. Bakker in 1970: D. Plooij et al., *The Liège Diatessaron*, 8 vols., VKNAW 31.1-8 (Amsterdam: Koninklijke Akademie van Wetenschappen, 1929–70). In addition to being an edition and English translation of the Liège Diatessaron, it contains a running apparatus that cites the variant readings of most of the major Diatessaronic witnesses, along with the major Greek manuscripts and early versions of the Gospels. It is a remarkable undertaking and indispensable for Diatessaronic work (although it lacks a Scripture index, which makes it extremely difficult to find a particular verse). Unfortunately, it was never bound as a single volume (it appeared as eight fascicles, the first five of which are often grouped together separately from the last three) and is therefore not easy to obtain.

[176] Leloir's editions of the Armenian and Syriac versions of the *Commentary* are excellent and reliable, and it is usually (though not always) possible to tell when Ephrem is citing his gospel text.

[177] Baarda makes a similar suggestion, and prefers the sigla Ephraem$^{com.arm}$ and Ephraem$^{com.syr}$ ("Tatian's Diatessaron and the Greek Text of the Gospels," 348). My own position is that the UBS should refrain from listing variant readings where the Armenian and Syriac versions of Ephrem's *Commentary* disagree, since it is not always clear which is more original (especially when the Syriac version includes material that is absent from the Armenian). Where the Syriac text is not extant, however, it would still be appropriate to list the Armenian version and label it as such.

For the upcoming *ECM* of the Gospels, it is unlikely that Diatessaronic research will have advanced enough in time to make including data from the Diatessaron a viable option at all. Supposing for a moment that it does (or that a later edition of the *ECM* wishes to include the Diatessaron), the Diatessaron obviously does not deserve a position among the Greek manuscripts or even the versions (*pace* von Soden, Vogels, and Merk). At best it could be classified among the church fathers (as in the UBS), since that is indeed what Tatian was (any heretical notions notwithstanding). Instead, however, I would propose that the *ECM* create an "additional apparatus" dedicated to the Diatessaron in its supplementary volumes to the Gospels (in the same way it has created an additional apparatus for additional Greek readings and ambiguous versional evidence in the supplementary volume to the Catholic Letters[178]). This apparatus could draw key readings from my proposed *Textual Commentary on Tatian's Diatessaron*, once available, and distill them for significance and relevancy. It will be a momentous day indeed when the state of Diatessaronic studies has progressed enough to earn a spot (even supplementary) in the apparatus of the *ECM*.

3.7 If We May Never Be Able to Reconstruct Tatian's Diatessaron, and If Reconstructing It Still Might not Provide Us with the Earliest Text of the Gospels, Should the Entire Enterprise Simply Be Abandoned?

Μὴ γένοιτο! Tatian's Diatessaron and its reception is a window into how the church has historically wrestled with a unified life of Jesus.[179] Despite the diversity and divergence of the four Gospels, most Christians throughout history have traditionally interpreted them as pointing to one Jesus, not four. Tatian's Diatessaron is one of the earliest testaments to that fascinating aspect of historical theology, whatever his intentions or even his additional sources may have been. It is further remarkable, and perhaps not coincidental, how often a version of the Diatessaron turns out to be one of the oldest surviving pieces of literature we have for a given written language.[180] The Diatessaron spoke to people. It encapsulates the comprehensive Jesus narrative. Whether or not it can ever get us back to the second-century text of the Gospels or ever finds its way back into the critical apparatus, to study the evolution of the Diatessaron is to study the reception history of Jesus himself, spanning culture, language, and time. That is a worthy study in its own right.

---

[178] See Barbara Aland, Kurt Aland, Gerd Mink, Holger Strutwolf, and Klaus Wachtel, eds., *Novum Testamentum Graecum Editio Critica Maior: Vol. IV: Catholic Letters / Part 2: Supplementary Material*, 2nd ed. (Stuttgart: Deutsche Bibelgesellschaft, 2013). This supplementary volume contains (among other items) an additional apparatus for additional Greek readings, patristic quotations and allusions, and further information on versional witnesses that had been marked as ambiguous in the apparatus of Part 1. The INTF has also issued a supplementary volume for Acts in the *ECM* (listed as Vol. III / Part 2) with similar content.

[179] Here I am echoing the language of Bart Ehrman in "The Text as Window: New Testament Manuscripts and the Social History of Early Christianity," in *The Text of the New Testament in Contemporary Research: Essays on the Status Quaestionis*, ed. Bart D. Ehrman and Michael W. Holmes, 2nd ed. (Leiden: Brill, 2013), 803–30.

[180] Petersen makes this point, among other additional reasons to study the Diatessaron, in *Tatian's Diatessaron*, 3–4.

4. Concluding Thoughts

The irony of my proposal to remove the Diatessaron from the apparatus for the time being has not escaped me. I am, in a sense, advocating a return to the beginning of the eighteenth century, when we had practically no access to Diatessaronic witnesses.[181] So we have come full circle in my survey. I hope, however, that the setback is only temporary and that through the efforts that I propose, Tatian's Diatessaron may soon again be useful to the textual criticism of the Gospels.

As I close, I am reminded of how Vogels assessed the state of Diatessaronic studies in his own day, in the mid-twentieth century:

> It is very regrettable that we no longer possess this work in its original form, because the knowledge of the exact wording would be of the utmost importance to us, not only for questions on the history of the New Testament canon, but also for the problems of the textual criticism of the Gospels.[182]

He goes on to say that, unlike some of his contemporaries, he does not hold out hope that we will ever recover the Diatessaron's original form, due in large part to the unending revisions that all of its surviving witnesses have undergone. He then quips:

> Und es ist gewiß, daß dieses Buch dazu reizte wie kaum ein anderes.

Vogels is referring to how the Diatessaron lends itself to ongoing revisions, but his statement's potential for wordplay strikes me. The German verb *reizen* can mean both "to stimulate" and "to irritate," "to attract" and "to provoke."[183] Vogels is correct: "And it is certain that this book to that end has stimulated/irritated/attracted/provoked like hardly any other"—and like hardly any other in our discipline ever will.[184]

---

[181] I suppose in the case of the UBS I am only advocating a return to the end of the nineteenth century, when Westcott and Hort cited Ephrem's *Commentary* as their sole witness to the Diatessaron.

[182] Heinrich Joseph Vogels, *Handbuch der Textkritik des Neuen Testaments*, 2nd ed. (Bonn: Hanstein, 1955), 144: "Es ist sehr bedauerlich, daß wir dieses Werk in der ursprünglichen Form nicht mehr besitzen, denn nicht allein für Fragen der neutestamentlichen Kanongeschichte, sondern auch für die Probleme der Textkritik der Evangelien wäre die Kenntnis des genauen Wortlautes uns von allerhöchsten Bedeutung." The line that I cite next comes from this same page.

[183] Cf. *Collins German Unabridged Dictionary*, 7th ed. (Glasgow: HarperCollins, 2007), 1755.

[184] I will take this moment to thank my colleagues who were willing to read and comment on sections or drafts of this chapter, including Matt Crawford, Ian Mills, Grant Edwards, David Dowdey, Mike Parsons, Hugh Houghton, and Mike Holmes. I am grateful for the feedback and improvements that each of them provided.

Bibliography

Aland, Barbara, Kurt Aland, Johannes Karavidopoulos, Carlo M. Martini, Bruce M. Metzger, and Holger Strutwolf, eds. *Novum Testamentum Graece*. 28th ed. Stuttgart: Deutsche Bibelgesellschaft, 2012.

Aland, Barbara, Kurt Aland, Gerd Mink, Holger Strutwolf, and Klaus Wachtel, eds. *Novum Testamentum Graecum Editio Critica Maior: Vol. IV: Catholic Letters / Part 2: Supplementary Material*. 2nd ed. Stuttgart: Deutsche Bibelgesellschaft, 2013.

Aland, Kurt, and Barbara Aland. *The Text of the New Testament: An Introduction to the Critical Editions and to the Theory and Practice of Modern Textual Criticism*. Translated by Erroll F. Rhodes. 2nd rev. and enl. ed. Grand Rapids, MI: Eerdmans, 1989.

Aland, Kurt, Matthew Black, Bruce M. Metzger, and Allen Wikgren, eds. *The Greek New Testament*. New York: United Bible Societies, 1966.

Alexander, Loveday. "Ancient Book Production and the Circulation of the Gospels." In *The Gospels for All Christians: Rethinking the Gospel Audiences*. Edited by Richard Bauckham, 71–105. Grand Rapids, MI: Eerdmans, 1998.

Alexander, Loveday. *The Preface to Luke's Gospel: Literary Convention and Social Context in Luke 1.1–4 and Acts 1.1*. SNTSMS 78. Cambridge: Cambridge University Press, 1993.

The American and British Committees of the International Greek New Testament Project, eds. *The Gospel According to St. Luke*. 2 vols. Oxford: Clarendon Press, 1984–7.

Anderson, Paul N. *The Fourth Gospel and the Quest for Jesus: Modern Foundations Reconsidered*. T&T Clark Biblical Studies. New York: T&T Clark, 2006.

Andrade, Nathanael. "Assyrians, Syrians and the Greek Language in the Late Hellenistic and Roman Imperial Periods." *JNES* 73 (2014): 299–317.

Aucher, Johann Baptist, and Georg Moesinger. *Evangelii concordantis expositio facta a Sancto Ephraemo Doctore Syro*. Venice: Mechitarist Monastery of S. Lazzaro, 1876.

Avioz, Michael. *Josephus' Interpretation of the Books of Samuel*. LSTS 86. London: Bloomsbury, 2015.

Augustine. *De consensu evangelistarum*. See F. Weihrich.

Baarda, Tjitze. "An Archaic Element in the Arabic Diatessaron? (T^A 46:18 = John XV 2)." *NovT* 17 (1975): 151–5. Repr. pages 173–7 in Tjitze Baarda, *Early Transmission of Words of Jesus: Thomas, Tatian, and the Text of the New Testament*. Edited by J. Helderman and S. J. Noorda. Amsterdam: VU Boekhandel/Uitgeverij, 1983.

Baarda, Tjitze. "On the Author of the Arabic Diatessaron." In *Miscellanea Neotestamentica*. Edited by T. Baarda, A. F. J. Klijn, and W. C. van Unnik, vol. 1, 61–103. Leiden: Brill, 1978.

Baarda, Tjitze. "ΔΙΑΦΩΝΙΑ—ΣΥΜΦΩΝΙΑ: Factors in the Harmonization of the Gospels, Especially in the Diatessaron of Tatian." In *Gospel Traditions in the Second Century: Origins, Recensions, Text, and Transmission*. Edited by William L. Petersen, 133–54. Notre Dame: University of Notre Dame Press, 1989. Repr. pages 29–47 in Tjitze Baarda, *Essays on the Diatessaron*. CBET 11. Kampen: Kok Pharos, 1994.

Baarda, Tjitze. "The Diatessaron of Tatian: Source for an Early Text at Rome or Source of Textual Corruption?" In *The New Testament Text in Early Christianity: Proceedings of the Lille Colloquium, July 2000*. Edited by C.-B. Amphoux and J. K. Elliott, 93–138. Lausanne: Editions du Zèbre, 2003.

Baarda, Tjitze. *Essays on the Diatessaron*. Kampen: Kok Pharos, 1994.

Baarda, Tjitze. "'The Flying Jesus': Luke 4:29–30 in the Syriac Diatessaron." *VC* 40 (1986): 313–41. Repr. pages 59–85 in Tjitze Baarda, *Essays on the Diatessaron*. CBET 11. Kampen: Kok Pharos, 1994.

Baarda, Tjitze. *The Gospel Quotations of Aphrahat the Persian Sage: Aphrahat's Text of the Fourth Gospel*. 2 vols. Meppel: Krips Repro, 1975.

Baarda, Tjitze. "John 1:5 in the Oration and Diatessaron of Tatian, Concerning the Reading καταλαμβάνει." *VC* 47 (1993): 209–25.

Baarda, Tjitze. "Mk 1:41: ὀργισθείς: A Reading Attested for Mar Ephraem, the Diatessaron, or Tatian." *ZNW* 103 (2012): 291–5.

Baarda, Tjitze. "To the Roots of the Syriac Diatessaron Tradition (T^A 25: 1–3)." *NovT* 28 (1986): 1–25.

Baarda, Tjitze. "In Search of the Diatessaron Text." In *Early Transmission of Words of Jesus: Thomas, Tatian the Text of the New Testament*. Edited by J. Helderman and S. J. Noorda, 65–78. Amsterdam: VU Boekhandel/Uitgeverij, 1983. Repr. and trans. from "Op zoek naar de tekst van het Diatessaron," *Vox Theologica* 17 (1962): 107–19.

Baarda, Tjitze. "Tatian's Diatessaron and the Greek Text of the Gospels." In *The Early Text of the New Testament*. Edited by Charles E. Hill and Michael J. Kruger, 336–49. Oxford: Oxford University Press, 2012.

Baarda, Tjitze. *VIER=EEN, Enkele bladzijden uit de geschiedenis van de harmonistiek der Evangeliën*. Kampen: J. H. Kok, 1969.

Baarda, Tjitze. "What Kind of Critical Apparatus for the New Testament Do We Need? The Case of Luke 23:48." In *New Testament Textual Criticism, Exegesis, and Early Church History: A Discussion of Methods*. Edited by Barbara Aland and Joël Delobel, 37–97. Kampen: Pharos, 1994.

Baden, Joel S. *The Composition of the Pentateuch: Renewing the Documentary Hypothesis*. AYBRL. New Haven, CT: Yale University Press, 2012.

Baldus, Aloys. *Das Verhältnis Justins des Märtyrers zu unsern synoptischen Evangelien*. Münster: Aschendorff, 1895.

Barker, James W. "Ancient Compositional Practices and the Gospels: A Reassessment." *JBL* 135 (2016): 109–21.

Barker, James W. "The Equivalence of *Kaige* and *Quinta* in the Dodekapropheton." In *Found in Translation: Essays on Jewish Biblical Translation in Honor of Leonard J. Greenspoon*. Edited by James W. Barker, Joel N. Lohr, and Anthony Le Donne, 127–52. West Lafayette, IN: Purdue University Press, 2018.

Barker, James W. *John's Use of Matthew*. Emerging Scholars. Minneapolis, MN: Fortress Press, 2015.

Barker, James W. "The Reconstruction of *Kaige/Quinta* Zechariah 9,9." *ZAW* 126 (2014): 584–8.

Barker, James W. "Written Gospel or Oral Tradition? Patristic Parallels to John 3:3, 5." *EC* 6 (2015): 543–58.

Barker, James W., and Nicholas J. McGrory. "When Were the Gospels Written?" Paper presented at the annual meeting of the Midwest Region of the SBL. Bourbonnais, IL, February 7, 2016.

Barthélemy, Dominique. *Les Devanciers d'Aquila: Première publication intégrale du texte des fragments du Dodécaprophéton*. VTSup 10. Leiden: Brill, 1963.

Barthélemy, Dominique. "Redécouverte d'un chaînon manquant de l'histoire de la Septante." *RB* 60 (1953): 18–29.

Barton, John. "Marcion Revisited." In *The Canon Debate*. Edited by Lee Martin McDonald and James A. Sanders, 341–54. Peabody: Hendrickson, 2002.

Bauckham, Richard. "For Whom Were the Gospels Written?" In *The Gospels for All Christians: Rethinking the Gospel Audiences*. Edited by Richard Bauckham, 9–48. Grand Rapids, MI: Eerdmans, 1998.

Bauckham, Richard, ed. *The Gospels for All Christians: Rethinking the Gospel Audiences*. Grand Rapids, MI: Eerdmans, 1998.

Bauckham, Richard. "Introduction." In *The Gospels for All Christians: Rethinking the Gospel Audiences*. Edited by Richard Bauckham, 1–7. Grand Rapids, MI: Eerdmans, 1998.

Bauer, Walter. *Rechtgläubigkeit und Ketzerei im ältesten Christentum*. Tübingen: J. C. B. Mohr, 1934.

Baumstark, Anton. *Geschichte der syrischen Literatur*. Bonn: A. Marcus und E. Webers Verlag, 1922.

Baynes, Leslie. "*Enoch* and *Jubilees* in the Canon of the Ethiopian Orthodox Church." In *A Teacher for All Generations: Essays in Honor of James C. VanderKam*. Edited by Eric F. Mason, et al., 2:799–818. 2 vols. SJSJ 153. Leiden: Brill, 2012.

Bedenbender, Andreas. "The Place of Torah in the Early Enoch Literature." In *The Early Enoch Literature*. Edited by Gabriele Boccaccini and John J. Collins, 66–79. JSJSup 121. Leiden: Brill, 2007.

Bellinzoni, Arthur J. *The Sayings of Jesus in the Writings of Justin Martyr*. NovTSup 17. Leiden: Brill, 1967.

Belsheim, Johannes. *Codex Vercellensis. Quatuor evangelia ante hieronymum latine translata ex reliquiis codices vercellensis, saeculo ut videtur quarto scripti et ex editione iriciana principe*. Christiania: Libraria Mallingiana, 1894.

Bengel, Johann Albrecht. Ἡ Καινὴ Διαθήκη: *Novum Testamentum Graecum*. Tübingen: J. G. Cotta, 1734.

Bergsma, Jan. *De levens van Jezus in het Middelnederlandsch*. 3 vols. Leiden: Sijthoff, 1895–8.

Bird, Michael F. *The Gospel of the Lord: How the Early Church Wrote the Story of Jesus*. Grand Rapids, MI: Eerdmans, 2014.

Blomberg, Craig L. "The Gospels for Specific Communities *and* All Christians." In *The Audience of the Gospels: The Origin and Function of the Gospels in Early Christianity*. Edited by Edward W. Klink III, 111–33. LNTS 353. New York: T&T Clark, 2010.

Bobichon, Philippe. "Composite Features and Citations in Justin Martyr's Textual Composition." In *Composite Citations in Antiquity: Volume 1: Jewish, Graeco-Roman and Early Christian Uses*. Edited by Sean A. Adams and Seth M. Ehorn, 158–81. LNTS 525. London: T&T Clark, 2016.

Boccaccini, Gabriele. *Beyond the Essene Hypothesis: The Parting of the Ways between Qumran and Enochic Judaism*. Grand Rapids, MI: Eerdmans, 1998.

Bolgiani, Franco. *Vittore di Capua e il "Diatessaron."* Turin: Accademia delle Scienze, 1962.

Borret, Marcel. *Origène: Contre Celse, Tome III: Livres V-VI*. SC 147. Paris: Les Éditions du Cerf, 1969.

Bousset, Wilhelm. *Die Evangeliencitate Justins des Märtyrers in ihrem wert für die Evangelienkritik*. Göttingen: Vandenhoeck & Ruprecht, 1891.

Brettler, Mark Zvi. *The Creation of History in Ancient Israel*. New York: Routledge, 1995.

Brock, Sebastian. *The Bible in the Syriac Tradition*. 2nd ed. Piscataway, NJ: Gorgias Press, 2006.

Brock, Sebastian. "Two Hitherto Unattested Passages of the Old Syriac Gospels in Palimpsests from St Catherine's Monastery, Sinai." Δελτίο Βιβλικών Μελετών 31A (2016): 7–18.
Brooke, A. E. *The Commentary of Origen on St. John's Gospel*. Cambridge: Cambridge University Press, 1896.
de Bruin, C. C. *Diatessaron Cantabrigiense*. Leiden: Brill, 1970.
de Bruin, C. C. *Diatessaron Haarense*. Leiden: Brill, 1970.
de Bruin, C. C. *Het Luikse Diatessaron*. Translated by A. J. Barnouw. Leiden: Brill, 1970.
Burke, Tony. *De infantia Iesu evangelium Thomae Graece*. CCSA 17. Turnhout: Brepols, 2010.
Burkitt, F. C. "The Dura Fragment of Tatian." *JTS* 36 (1935): 255–9.
Burkitt, F. C. *Evangelion Da-Mepharreshe: The Curetonian Version of the Four Gospels with the Readings of the Sinai Palimpsest and the Early Syriac Patristic Evidence*. 2 vols. Cambridge: Cambridge University Press, 1904.
Burkitt, F. C. "Tatian's Diatessaron." *The Times*, May 21, 1934, 11.
Burkitt, F. C. "Tatian's Diatessaron and the Dutch Harmonies." *JTS* 25 (1924): 113–30.
Burridge, Richard A. *What Are the Gospels? A Comparison with Graeco-Roman Biography*. 2nd ed. Grand Rapids, MI: Eerdmans, 2004.
von Campenhausen, Hans. *The Formation of the Christian Bible*. Translated by J. A. Baker. Philadelphia, PA: Fortress Press, 1972.
Carson, D. A. *The Gospel According to John*. The Pillar New Testament Commentary. Grand Rapids, MI: Eerdmans, 1991.
Chapman, John. *Notes on the Early History of the Vulgate Gospels*. Oxford: Clarendon Press, 1908.
Charlesworth, James H. "Tatian's Dependence upon Apocryphal Traditions." *HeyJ* 15 (1974): 5–17.
Ciasca, Augustinus. *Tatiani Evangeliorum harmoniae arabice*. Rome: Typographia Polyglotta, 1888.
Cirafesi, Wally V., and Gregory P. Fewster. "Justin's Ἀπομνημονεύματα and Ancient Greco-Roman Memoirs." *EC* 7 (2016): 186–212.
Collins German Unabridged Dictionary. 7th ed. Glasgow: HarperCollins, 2007.
Comfort, Philip W. *New Testament Text and Translation Commentary*. Carol Stream, IL: Tyndale House, 2008.
Cook, John Granger. "A Note on Tatian's *Diatessaron*, Luke, and the Arabic Harmony." *ZAC* 10 (2006): 462–71.
Cowley, R. W. "The Biblical Canon of the Ethiopian Orthodox Church Today." *Ostkirchliche Studien* 23 (1974): 318–23.
Crawford, Matthew R. "Ammonius of Alexandria, Eusebius of Caesarea, and the Origins of Gospel Scholarship." *NTS* 61 (2015): 1–29.
Crawford, Matthew R. "Diatessaron, A Misnomer? The Evidence from Ephrem's Commentary." *EC* 4 (2013): 362–85.
Crawford, Matthew R. "The Diatessaron, Canonical or Non-canonical? Rereading the Dura Fragment." *NTS* 62 (2016): 253–77.
Crawford, Matthew R. "The Fourfold Gospel in the Writings of Ephrem the Syrian." *Hugoye* 18 (2015): 9–51.
Crawford, Matthew R. "A New Witness to the 'Western' Ordering of the Gospels: GA 073 + 084." *JTS* 69 (2018): 477–83.
Crawford, Matthew R. "Rejection at Nazareth in the Gospels of Matthew, Mark, Luke— and Tatian." In *Connecting Gospels: Beyond the Canonical/Non-canonical Divide*.

Edited by Francis Watson and Sarah Parkhouse, 97–124. Oxford: Oxford University Press, 2018.

Crawford, Matthew R. "'Reordering the Confusion': Tatian, the Second Sophistic, and the So-Called *Diatessaron*." *ZAC* 19 (2015): 209–36.

Crawford, Sidnie White. *Rewriting Scripture in Second Temple Times*. Grand Rapids, MI: Eerdmans, 2008.

Credner, K. A. *Beiträge zur Einleitung in die biblischen Schriften*. 2 vols. Halle: Buchhandlung des Waisenhauses, 1832–8.

Crüsemann, Frank. *The Torah: Theology and Social History of Old Testament Law*. Translated by Allan W. Mahnke. Minneapolis, MN: Fortress, 1996.

Cullmann, Oscar. "Die Pluralität der Evangelien als theologisches Problem im Altertum (1945)." In *Vorträge und Aufsätze 1925–1962*. Edited by K. Fröhlich, 548–65. Tübingen: Mohr Siebeck, 1966.

Cumont, Franz. *Oriental Religions in Roman Paganism*. Chicago: The Open Court Publishing Company, 1911.

Daniell, F. H. Blackburne. "Victor of Capua." In *Dictionary of Christian Biography*. 4 vols. Edited by W. Smith and H. Wace, vol. 4, 1123–6. London: John Murray, 1877–87.

Davies, Malcolm. *The Greek Epic Cycle*. 2nd ed. London: Bristol Classical Press, 2001.

De Bruyne, Donatien. *Sommaires, divisions et rubriques de la Bible latine*. Namur: Godenne, 1914. Repr. Donatien De Bruyne, P.-M. Bogaert, and T. O'Loughlin, *Summaries, Divisions and Rubrics of the Latin Bible*. Turnhout: Brepols, 2015.

De Bruyne, Donatien. "La préface du Diatessaron latin avant Victor de Capoue." *RBén* 39 (1927): 5–11.

De Bruyn, Theodore. *Making Christian Amulets: Artefacts, Scribes, and Contexts*. OECS. Oxford: Oxford University Press, 2017.

De Troyer, Kristin. "The Final Verses of the Ammonite War Story in 2 Sam 22:26–31, and 1 Chron 20:1–3." In *Found in Translation: Essays on Jewish Biblical Translation in Honor of Leonard J. Greenspoon*. Edited by James W. Barker, Joel N. Lohr, and Anthony Le Donne, 95–111. West Lafayette, IN: Purdue University Press, 2018.

Donfried, Karl P. *The Setting of Second Clement in Early Christianity*. NovTSup 38. Leiden: Brill, 1974.

Doole, J. Andrew. *What Was Mark for Matthew? An Examination of Matthew's Relationship and Attitude to His Primary Source*. WUNT 2/344. Tübingen: Mohr Siebeck, 2013.

Drijvers, H. J. W. "Facts and Problems in Early Syriac-Speaking Christianity." *The Second Century* 2 (1982): 157–75.

Dungan, David L. *Constantine's Bible: Politics and the Making of the New Testament*. Minneapolis: Fortress, 2007.

Dungan, David L. *A History of the Synoptic Problem: The Canon, the Text, the Composition, and the Interpretation of the Gospels*. ABRL. New York: Doubleday, 1999.

Edwards, James R. *The Hebrew Gospel and the Development of the Synoptic Tradition*. Grand Rapids, MI: Eerdmans, 2009.

Ehrman, Bart D. *The New Testament: A Historical Introduction to the Early Christian Writings*. 6th ed. New York: Oxford University Press, 2016.

Ehrman, Bart D. "Response to Charles Hill, The Four Gospel Canon in the Second Century." Paper presented at the Annual Meeting of the SBL. San Francisco, CA, November 21, 2011.

Ehrman, Bart D. "The Text as Window: New Testament Manuscripts and the Social History of Early Christianity." In *The Text of the New Testament in Contemporary*

Research: Essays on the Status Quaestionis. Edited by Bart D. Ehrman and Michael W. Holmes, 2nd ed., 803–30. Leiden: Brill, 2013.

Elliott, J. K. *The Apocryphal New Testament: A Collection of Apocryphal Christian Literature in an English Translation.* Oxford: Clarendon Press, 1993.

Elliott, J. K. "The Arabic Diatessaron in the New Oxford Edition of the Gospel according to St Luke in Greek: Additional Note." *JTS* 38 (1987): 135.

Ellis, E. Earle. *The Making of the New Testament Documents.* Biblical Interpretation. Leiden: Brill, 1999.

von Engelhardt, Moritz. *Das Christentum Justin Märtyrers: Eine Untersuchung über die Anfänge katholischen Glaubenslehre.* Erlangen: Deichert, 1878.

Epiphanius. *The Panarion.* See F. Williams; see K. Holl.

Epp, Eldon Jay. "The International Greek New Testament Project: Motivation and History." *NovT* 39 (1997): 1–20.

Eusebius. *Gospel Problems and Solutions.* See R. Pearse.

Eusebius. *Historia ecclesiastica.* See E. Schwartz.

Evans, Ernest. *Tertullian: Adversus Marcionem.* 2 vols. OECT. Oxford: Clarendon Press, 1972.

Fantuzzi, Marco. "The Aesthetics of Sequentiality and Its Discontents." In *The Greek Epic Cycle and Its Ancient Reception: A Companion.* Edited by Marco Fantuzzi and Christos Tsagalis, 405–29. Cambridge: Cambridge University Press, 2015.

Ferguson, Everett. "Factors Leading to the Selection and Closure of the New Testament Canon." In *The Canon Debate.* Edited by Lee Martin McDonald and James A. Sanders, 295–320. Peabody, MA: Hendrickson, 2008.

Fischer, Bonifatius. "Bibelausgaben des frühen Mittelalters." In *La Bibbia nell'alto Medioevo*, 519–600, 685–704. Settimane di studio del centro italiano di studi sull'alto medioevo 10. Spoleto: Presso la Sede del Centro, 1963. Repr. pages 35–100 in Bonifatius Fischer, *Lateinische Bibelhandschriften im Frühen Mittelalter.* AGLB 11. Freiburg im Breisgau: Herder, 1985.

Fuller, John Mee. "Tatianus." In *Dictionary of Christian Biography.* 4 vols. Edited by W. Smith and H. Wace, vol. 4, 783–804. London: John Murray, 1877–87.

Gamble, Harry Y. *Books and Readers in the Early Church: A History of Early Christian Texts.* New Haven, CT: Yale University Press, 1995.

Gamble, Harry Y. "The New Testament Canon: Recent Research and the Status Quaestionis." In *The Canon Debate.* Edited by Lee Martin McDonald and James A. Sanders, 267–94. Peabody, MA: Hendrickson, 2008.

Gathercole, Simon. *The Composition of the Gospel of Thomas: Original Language and Influences.* SNTSMS 151. Cambridge: Cambridge University Press, 2012.

Gathercole, Simon. "The Titles of the Gospels in the Earliest New Testament Manuscripts." *ZNW* 104 (2013): 33–76.

Gentry, Peter J. "Pre-Hexaplaric Translations, Hexapla, Post-Hexaplaric Translations." In *Textual History of the Bible, vol. 1A.* Edited by Armin Lange, 211–34. Leiden: Brill, 2016.

Gerhardt, Christoph. *Diatessaron Theodiscum: Das Leben Jhesu.* Leiden: Brill, 1970.

Gesner, Conrad, ed. *Tatiani Assyrii, Iustini martyris discipuli, Oratio contra Graecos.* Zürich: C. Froschoverus, 1546.

Goates, Margery. *The Pepysian Gospel Harmony.* London: Oxford University Press, 1922. Repr., New York: Kraus, 1971.

Goodacre, Mark. *The Case against Q: Studies in Markan Priority and the Synoptic Problem.* Harrisburg, PA: Trinity Press International, 2002.

Goodacre, Mark. *Thomas and the Gospels: The Case for Thomas's Familiarity with the Synoptics*. Grand Rapids, MI: Eerdmans, 2012.
Goodenough, E. R. *The Theology of Justin Martyr*. Jena: Walter Beidermann, 1923.
Goodspeed, Edgar J. *Die ältesten Apologeten: Texte mit kurzen Einleitungen*. Göttingen: Vandenhoeck & Ruprecht, 1914.
Gregory, Andrew. "Prior or Posterior? The Gospel of the Ebionites and the Gospel of Luke." *NTS* 51 (2005): 344–60.
Gregory, Andrew. "Jewish Christian Gospels." In *The Non-canonical Gospels*. Edited by Paul Foster, 54–67. London: T&T Clark, 2008.
Gregory, Andrew. *The Gospel According to the Hebrews and the Gospel of the Ebionites*. Oxford: Oxford University Press, 2017.
Griesbach, Johann Jakob. *Novum Testamentum Graece, Volumen 1: IV Evangelia*. 2nd ed. London: J. Mackinlay; Cuthell and Martin, 1809.
Haelewyck, Jean-Claude. "Les Vieilles versions syriaques des Évangiles." In *Le Nouveau Testament en syriaque*. Edited by Jean-Claude Haelewyck, 67–113. Études Syriaques 14. Paris: Geuthner, 2017.
Hagner, Donald A. *Matthew*. 2 vols. WBC 33. Dallas: Word, 1993–5.
Hahneman, Geoffrey Mark. *The Muratorian Fragment and the Development of the Canon*. Oxford: Clarendon Press, 1992.
Halliwell, Stephen. *Aristotle: Poetics*. LCL 199. Cambridge: Harvard University Press, 1995.
de Hamel, Christopher. *The Book: A History of the Bible*. London: Phaidon, 2001.
Hannah, Darrell D. "The Four-Gospel 'Canon' in the *Epistula Apostolorum*." *JTS* 59 (2008): 598–633.
Hanneken, Todd R. *The Subversion of the Apocalypses in the Book of Jubilees*. EJL 34. Atlanta: Society of Biblical Literature, 2012.
von Harnack, Adolf. *Die Geschichte der altchristlichen Literatur bis Eusebius*. 2 vols. Leipzig: Hinrichs, 1897.
von Harnack, Adolf. *Marcion: Das Evangelium vom fremden Gott*. 2nd ed. Leipzig: Hinrichs, 1924.
von Harnack, Adolf. "Tatian's Diatessaron und Marcion's Commentar zum Evangelium bei Ephraem Syrus." *ZKG* 4 (1881): 471–505.
Harris, J. Rendel. "Cod. Ev. 561: Codex Algerinae Peckover." *Journal of the Society of Biblical Literature and Exegesis* 6 (1886): 79–89.
Harris, J. Rendel. *The Diatessaron of Tatian, A Preliminary Study*. London: C. J. Clay, 1890.
Harris, J. Rendel. "The First Tatian Reading in the Greek New Testament." *Expositor* 8 (1922): 120–9.
Harris, J. Rendel. *Fragments of the Commentary of Ephrem Syrus on the Diatessaron*. London: C. J. Clay, 1895.
Harris, J. Rendel. "Presbyter Gaius and the Fourth Gospel." In *Hermas in Arcadia and Other Essays*. 43–57. Cambridge: Cambridge University Press, 1896.
Harris, J. Rendel. "Some Notes on the Gospel-Harmony of Zacharias Chrysopolitanus." *JBL* 43 (1924): 32–45.
Harris, J. Rendel. "Was the Diatessaron Anti-Judaic?" *HTR* 18 (1925): 103–9.
Hausmann, Regina. *Die theologischen Handschriften der Hessischen Landesbibliothek Fulda bis zum Jahr 1600: Codices Bonifatiani 1–3, Aa 1–145a*. Wiesbaden: Harrassowitz, 1992.
Head, Peter M. "Tatian's Christology and Its Influence on the Composition of the Diatessaron." *TynBul* 43 (1992): 121–37.
Heger, Paul. "1 Enoch—Complementary or Alternative to Mosaic Torah?" *JSJ* 41 (2010): 29–62.

Hemphill, Samuel. *The Diatessaron of Tatian: A Harmony of the Four Holy Gospels Compiled in the Third Quarter of the Second Century*. London: Hodder & Stoughton, 1888.

Hengel, Martin. *The Four Gospels and the One Gospel of Jesus Christ*. London: SCM, 2000.

Higgins, A. J. B. "The Arabic Diatessaron in the New Oxford Edition of the Gospel according to St Luke in Greek." *JTS* 37 (1986): 415–19.

Hilgenfeld, Adolf. *Kritische Untersuchungen über die Evangelien Justin's, der Clementinischen Homilien und Marcion's*. Halle: Schwetschke, 1850.

Hill, Charles E. "A Four-Gospel Canon in the Second Century? Artifact and Arti-fiction." *EC* 4 (2013): 310–34.

Hill, Charles E. *The Johannine Corpus in the Early Church*. Oxford: Oxford University Press, 2004.

Hill, Charles E. "'The Orthodox Gospel': The Reception of John in the Great Church Prior to Irenaeus." In *The Legacy of John: The Second Century Reception of the Fourth Gospel*. Edited by T. Rasimus, 233–300. NovTSup 132. Leiden: Brill, 2010.

Hill, Charles E. "Was John's Gospel among Justin's Apostolic Memoirs?" In *Justin Martyr and His Worlds*. Edited by Sara Parvis and Paul Foster, 88–94. Minneapolis, MN: Fortress, 2007.

Hill, Charles E. *Who Chose the Gospels? Probing the Great Gospel Conspiracy*. Oxford: Oxford University Press, 2010.

Hill, J. Hamlyn. *The Earliest Life of Christ Ever Compiled from the Four Gospels Being the Diatessaron of Tatian: Literally Translated from the Arabic Version and Containing the Four Gospels Woven into One Story*. Edinburgh: T&T Clark, 1894.

Hock, Ronald F. *The Infancy Gospels of James and Thomas*. The Scholars Bible 2. Santa Rosa, CA: Polebridge, 1995.

Hogg, Hope W. "The Diatessaron of Tatian." In *The Ante-Nicene Fathers*. Edited by Alan Menzies, vol. 9, 33–138. New York: Charles Scribner's Sons, 1896.

Holl, Karl. *Epiphanius: Ancoratus und Panarion, Vol. II: Panarion haer. 34–64*. GCS 31. Leipzig: Hinrichs, 1922.

Holl, Karl and Jürgen Dummer. *Epiphanius II: Panarion haer. 34–64*. 2nd ed. GCS 31. Berlin: Akademie Verlag, 1980.

den Hollander, August. *Virtuelle Vergangenheit: Die Textrekonstruktion einer verlorenen Mittelnieder-ländischen Evangelienharmonie*. Leuven: Leuven University Press, 2007.

den Hollander, August and Ulrich Schmid. "The *Gospel of Barnabas*, the Diatessaron, and Method." *VC* 61 (2007): 1–20.

den Hollander, August and Ulrich Schmid. "Middeleeuwse bronnen van het Luikse 'Leven van Jezus.'" *Queeste* 6 (1999): 127–46.

Holmes, Michael W. *The Apostolic Fathers: Greek Texts and English Translations*. 3rd ed. Grand Rapids, MI: Baker, 2007.

Houghton, H. A. G. "Chapter Divisions, Capitula Lists, and the Old Latin Versions of John." *RBén* 121 (2011): 316–56.

Houghton, H. A. G. *The Latin New Testament: A Guide to its Early History, Texts, and Manuscripts*. Oxford: Oxford University Press, 2016.

Houghton, H. A. G. "Recent Developments in New Testament Textual Criticism." *EC* 2 (2011): 245–68.

Houston, George W. *Inside Roman Libraries: Book Collections and Their Management in Antiquity*. Chapel Hill: University of North Carolina Press, 2014.

Howard, George. "Harmonistic Readings in the Old Syriac Gospels." *HTR* 73 (1980): 473–91.

Hurtado, Larry W. *The Earliest Christian Artifacts: Manuscripts and Christian Origins.* Grand Rapids, MI: Eerdmans, 2006.
Hurtado, Larry W. "Manuscripts and the Sociology of Early Christian Reading." In *The Early Text of the New Testament.* Edited by Charles E. Hill and Michael J. Kruger, 49–62. Oxford: Oxford University Press, 2012.
Johnson, Nathan C. "Anger Issues: Mark 1.41 in Ephrem the Syrian, the Old Latin Gospels and Codex Bezae." NTS 63 (2017): 183–202.
Johnson, William A. *Readers and Reading Culture in the High Roman Empire: A Study of Elite Communities.* Oxford: Oxford University Press, 2010.
Joosse, N. Peter. "From Antioch to Bagdad, From Bagdad to Cairo: Towards an Archetype of the Arabic Diatessaron." *Parole de l'Orient* 37 (2012): 67–84.
Joosse, N. Peter. "An Introduction to the Arabic Diatessaron." *OrChr* 83 (1999): 72–129.
Joosten, Jan. "The Date and Provenance of the *Gospel of Barnabas.*" *JThS* 61 (2010): 200–15.
Joosten, Jan. "Le Diatessaron syriaque." in *Le Nouveau Testament en syriaque.* Edited by Jean-Claude Haelewyck, 55–66. Études Syriaques 14. Paris: Geuthner, 2017.
Joosten, Jan. "The Dura Parchment and the Diatessaron." *VC* 57 (2003): 159–75.
Joosten, Jan. "The *Gospel of Barnabas* and the Diatessaron." *HTR* 95 (2002): 73–96.
Joosten, Jan. *Language and Textual History of the Syriac Bible: Collected Studies.* TS 9. Piscataway, NJ: Gorgias, 2013.
Joosten, Jan. Review of *Unum ex Quattuor: Eine Geschichte der lateinischen Tatianüberlieferung*, by Ulrich B. Schmid. *Gnomon* 80 (2008): 21–2.
Joosten, Jan. *The Syriac Language of the Peshitta and Old Syriac Versions of Matthew: Syntactic Structure, Inner-Syriac Developments and Translation Technique.* SSLL 22. Leiden: Brill, 1996.
Joosten, Jan. "Tatian's *Diatessaron* and the Old Testament Peshitta." *JBL* 120 (2001): 501–23.
Joosten, Jan. "Two West Aramaic Elements in the Old Syriac and Peshitta Gospels." *BN* 61 (1992): 17–21.
Joosten, Jan. "West Aramaic Elements in the Old Syriac and Peshitta Gospels." *JBL* 110 (1991): 271–89.
Jülicher, Adolf. "Der echte Tatiantext." *JBL* 63 (1924): 132–71.
Jülicher, Adolf, Walter Matzkow, and Kurt Aland, eds. *Itala: Das neue Testament in altlateinischer Überlieferung.* 4 vols. 2nd ed. Berlin: de Gruyter, 1963–76.
Justin Martyr. *First Apology and Dialogue with Trypho.* See M. Marcovich.
Keith, Chris. "The Competitive Textualization of the Jesus Tradition in John 20:30–31 and 21:24–25." *CBQ* 78 (2016): 321–37.
Keith, Chris. "Early Christian Book Culture and the Emergence of the First Written Gospel." In *Mark, Manuscripts, and Monotheism: Essays in Honor of Larry W. Hurtado.* Edited by Chris Keith and Dieter T. Roth, 22–39. LNTS 528. London: T&T Clark, 2015.
Kenyon, Frederic G. *Handbook to the Textual Criticism of the New Testament.* London: Macmillan, 1901.
Kilpatrick, G. D. "Three Recent Editions of the Greek New Testament." *JTS* 50 (1949): 10–23, 142–55.
Kiraz, George Anton. *Comparative Edition of the Syriac Gospels.* 4 vols. Leiden: Brill, 1996.
Klein, Ralph W. *1 Chronicles: A Commentary.* Hermeneia. Minneapolis, MN: Fortress, 2006.
Klein, Ralph W. *2 Chronicles: A Commentary.* Hermeneia. Minneapolis, MN: Fortress, 2012.
Klijn, A. F. J. *Jewish-Christian Gospel Tradition.* VCSup 17. Leiden: Brill, 1992.

Klijn, A. F. J. "The Question of the Rich Young Man in a Jewish-Christian Gospel." *NovT* 8 (1966): 149–55.
Klijn, A. F. J. *A Survey of the Researches into the Western Text of the Gospels and Acts. Part Two: 1949–1969.* Brill: Leiden, 1969.
Kline, Leslie Lee. "Harmonized Sayings of Jesus in the Pseudo-Clementine Homilies and Justin Martyr." *ZNW* 66 (1975): 223–41.
Kline, Leslie Lee. *The Sayings of Jesus in the Pseudo-Clementine Homilies.* SBLDS 14. Missoula, MT: Scholars Press, 1975.
Klinghardt, Matthias. "The Marcionite Gospel and the Synoptic Problem: A New Solution." *NovT* 50 (2008): 1–27.
Kloppenborg Verbin, John S. *Excavating Q: The History and Setting of the Sayings Gospel.* Minneapolis, MN: Fortress, 2000.
Knoppers, Gary N. *1 Chronicles.* 2 vols. AB 12–12A. New York: Doubleday, 2003.
Koester, Helmut. *From Jesus to the Gospels: Interpreting the New Testament in Its Context.* Minneapolis, MN: Fortress, 2007.
Koester, Helmut. "From the Kerygma-Gospel to Written Gospels." *NTS* 35 (1989): 361–81.
Koester, Helmut. *Synoptische Überlieferung bei den Apostolischen Vätern.* TU 65. Berlin: Akademie Verlag, 1957.
Kok, Michael J. *The Gospel on the Margins: The Reception of Mark in the Second Century.* Minneapolis, MN: Fortress Press, 2015.
Koltun-Fromm, Naomi. "Re-imagining Tatian: The Damaging Effects of Polemical Rhetoric." *JECS* 16 (2008): 1–30.
Kraeling, Carl H. *A Greek Fragment of Tatian's Diatessaron from Dura.* SD 3. London: Christophers, 1935.
Krans, Jan, and Joseph Verheyden, eds. *Patristic and Text-Critical Studies: The Collected Essays of William L. Petersen.* NTTSD 40. Leiden: Brill, 2012.
Kratz, Reinhard G. *The Composition of the Narrative Books of the Old Testament.* Translated by John Bowden. London: T&T Clark, 2005.
Kvanvig, Helge S. "Enochic Judaism—a Judaism without the Torah and the Temple?" In *Enoch and the Mosaic Torah: The Evidence of Jubilees.* Edited by Gabriele Boccaccini and Giovanni Ibba, 163–77. Grand Rapids, MI: Eerdmans, 2009.
Lachmann, Karl. *Novum Testamentum Graece et Latine.* 2 vols. 2nd ed. Berlin: G. Reimer, 1842–50.
Lafontaine, G. *La version Arménienne des oeuvres d'Aphraate le Syrien, I.* Louvain: CSCO, 1977.
Lake, Kirsopp. "Tatian's Diatessaron." *The Times*, May 16, 1934, 17.
Lampe, P. *Die Stadtrömischen Christen in den ersten beiden Jahrhunderten.* WUNT 2/18. Tübingen: Mohr Siebeck, 1982.
Lancioni, Giuliano, and N. Peter Joosse. "The Arabic Diatessaron Project: Digitalizing Encoding Lemmatization." *Journal of Religion, Media and Digital Culture* 5.1 (2016): 205–77.
Lange, Christian. *The Portrayal of Christ in the Syriac Commentary on the Diatessaron.* CSCO 616, Subsidia 118. Leuven: Peeters, 2005.
Larsen, Matthew D. C. "Accidental Publication, Unfinished Texts and the Traditional Goals of New Testament Textual Criticism." *JSNT* 39 (2017): 362–87.
Last, Richard. "Communities that Write: Christ-Groups, Associations, and Gospel Communities." *NTS* 58 (2012): 173–98.
Last, Richard. "The Social Relationships of Gospel Writers: New Insights from Inscriptions Commending Greek Historiographers." *JSNT* 37 (2015): 223–52.

Legg, S. C. E., ed. *Novum Testamentum Graece: Secundum textum Westcotto-Hortianum: Euangelium secundum Marcum.* Oxford: Clarendon Press, 1935.
Legg, S. C. E., ed. *Novum Testamentum Graece: Secundum textum Westcotto-Hortianum: Euangelium secundum Matthaeum.* Oxford: Clarendon Press, 1940.
Lehto, Adam. *The Demonstrations of Aphrahat, the Persian Sage.* Piscataway, NJ: Gorgias Press, 2010.
Leloir, Louis. "Le Diatessaron de Tatien." *OrSyr* 1 (1956): 208–31.
Leloir, Louis. "Divergences entre l'original syriaque et la version Arménienne du commentaire d'Éphrem sur le Diatessaron." In *Mélanges Eugène Tisserant*, 7 vols, 2:303–31. StT 231–7. Vatican City: Bibliotheca Apostolica Vaticana, 1964.
Leloir, Louis. *L'Évangile d'Éphrem d'après les oeuvres éditées: Recueil des textes.* Leuven: Secrétariat du CorpusSCO, 1958.
Leloir, Louis. *Saint Éphrem: Commentaire de l'Évangile concordant, version arménienne.* CSCO 137, Scriptores Armeniaci 1. Leuven: Imprimerie Orientaliste L. Durbecq, 1953.
Leloir, Louis. *Saint Éphrem: Commentaire de l'Évangile concordant, version arménienne.* CSCO 145, Scriptores Armeniaci 2. Leuven: Peeters, 1954.
Leloir, Louis. *Saint Éphrem: Commentaire de l'Évangile concordant, texte syriaque (MS Chester Beatty 709).* CBM 8. Dublin: Hodges Figgis, 1963.
Leloir, Louis. *Saint Éphrem: Commentaire de l'Évangile concordant, texte syriaque (MS Chester Beatty 709): Folios additionnels.* CBM 8(b). Leuven: Peeters, 1990.
Leloir, Louis. *Le témoignage d'Éphrem sur le Diatessaron.* Leuven: Secrétariat du CorpusSCO, 1962.
Levinson, Bernard M. *Deuteronomy and the Hermeneutics of Legal Innovation.* Oxford: Oxford University Press, 1997.
Lieu, Judith M. *Marcion and the Making of a Heretic: God and Scripture in the Second Century.* Cambridge: Cambridge University Press, 2015.
Lindemann, Andreas. *Die Clemensbriefe.* Tübingen: Mohr Siebeck, 1992.
Lippelt, E. *Quae fuerint Justini Martyris ΑΠΟΜΝΗΜΟΝΕΥΜΑΤΑ quaque ratione cum forma Evangeliorum syro-latina cohaeserint.* Halle: Karras, 1901.
Luomanen, Petri. *Recovering Jewish-Christian Sects and Gospels.* VCSup 110. Leiden: Brill, 2012.
Luomanen, Petri. "Where Did Another Rich Man Come from? The Jewish-Christian Profile of the Story about a Rich Man in the '*Gospel of the Hebrews*' (Origen, *Comm. in Matth.* 15.14)." *VC* 57 (2003): 243–75.
Luscinius, Ottmar. *Evangelicae historiae ex quatuor Evangelistis perpetuo tenore continuata narratio.* Augsburg: n.p., 1523.
Lyon, Jeffrey Paul. *Syriac Gospel Translations: A Comparison of the Language and Translation Method Used in the Old Syriac, the Diatessaron, and the Peshitto.* CSCO 548. Leuven: Peeters, 1994.
MacKnight, James. *Harmony of the Four Gospels, in Which the Natural Order of Each Is Preserved.* 2 vols. London: [Printed for the Author], 1756.
Manor, T. Scott. "Papias, Origen, and Eusebius: The Criticisms and Defense of the Gospel of John." *VC* 67 (2013): 1–21.
Marcovich, Miroslav, ed. *Iustini Martyris Apologiae pro Christianis, Dialogus cum Tryphone.* PTS 47. Berlin: de Gruyter, 2005.
Marmardji, A.-S. *Diatessaron de Tatien: Texte arabe établi, traduit en français, collationné avec les anciennes versions syriaques.* Beyrouth: Imprimerie Catholique, 1935.
Massaux, Edouard. "Le texte du sermon sur la montagne de Matthieu utilisé par Saint Justin: Contribution à la critique textuelle du premier évangile." *ETL* 28 (1952): 411–48.

Mattila, Sharon Lea. "A Question Too Often Neglected." *NTS* 41 (1995): 199–217.
McCarthy, Carmel. *Saint Ephrem's Commentary on the Diatessaron: An English Translation of Chester Beatty Syriac MS 709 with Introduction and Notes*. JSSSup 2. Oxford: Oxford University Press, 1993.
McCullough, W. Stewart. *A Short History of Syriac Christianity to the Rise of Islam*. Chico, CA: Scholars Press, 1982.
McDonald, Lee Martin. "The Gospels in Early Christianity: Their Origin, Use, and Authority." In *Reading the Gospels Today*. Edited by Stanley E. Porter, 150–78. Grand Rapids, MI: Eerdmans, 2004.
McGurk, Patrick. "The Canon Tables in the Book of Lindisfarne and in the Codex Fuldensis of St. Victor of Capua." *JTS* 6 (1955): 192–8.
McKenzie, Steven L. *1–2 Chronicles*. Abingdon Old Testament Commentaries. Nashville: Abingdon, 2004.
van der Meer, Michaël N. "Symmachus's Version of Joshua." In *Found in Translation: Essays on Jewish Biblical Translation in Honor of Leonard J. Greenspoon*. Edited by James W. Barker, Joel N. Lohr, and Anthony Le Donne, 53–93. West Lafayette, IN: Purdue University Press, 2018.
Mell, Ulrich. *Christliche Hauskirche und Neues Testament: Die Ikonologie des Baptisteriums von Dura Europos und das Diatessaron Tatians*. Göttingen: Vandenhoeck & Ruprecht, 2010.
Memler, Michael. *Quatuor evangeliorum consonantia, ab Ammonio Alexandrino congesta, ac a Victore Capuano episcopo translata*. Mainz: J. Schoeffer, 1524.
Merk, Augustinus. "Nova editio Novi Testamenti graece et latine." *Bib* 24 (1943): 182–4.
Merk, Augustinus. Review of *Novum Testamentum Graece*, by Heinrich Joseph Vogels. *Bib* 2.1 (1921): 78–87.
Merk, Augustinus. Review of *Novum Testamentum Graece* and *Novum Testamentum Graece et Latine*, by Heinrich Joseph Vogels. *Bib* 5.1 (1924): 85–8.
Merk, Augustinus. *Novum Testamentum Graece et Latine*. Rome: Pontifical Biblical Institute, 1933.
Merk, Augustinus. "Zur Ausgabe des Neuen Testaments des Bibelinstituts." *Bib* 15 (1934): 437–50.
Merkel, H. *Die Widersprüche zwischen den Evangelien: Ihre polemische und apologetische Behandlung in der Alten Kirche bis zu Augustin*. WUNT 13. Tübingen: Mohr Siebeck, 1971.
Messina, Giuseppe. *Diatessaron Persiano*. BibOr 14. Rome: Pontifical Biblical Institute, 1951.
Messina, Giuseppe. *Notizia su un Diatessaron persiano: Tradotto dal siriaco*. BibOr 10. Rome: Pontifical Biblical Institute, 1943.
Messina, Giuseppe. "Un Diatessaron persiano del secolo XIII tradotto dal siriaco." *Bib* 23.3 (1942): 268–305.
Messina, Giuseppe. "Un Diatessaron persiano del secolo XIII tradotto dal siriaco." *Bib* 24 (1943): 59–106.
Metzger, Bruce M. *The Canon of the New Testament: Its Origin, Development, and Significance*. Oxford: Oxford University Press, 1987.
Metzger, Bruce M. *Chapters in the History of New Testament Textual Criticism*. Grand Rapids, MI: Eerdmans, 1963.
Metzger, Bruce M. *The Early Versions of the New Testament: Their Origin, Transmission, and Limitations*. Oxford: Clarendon Press, 1977.

Metzger, Bruce M. "The Evidence of the Versions for the Text of the New Testament." In *New Testament Manuscript Studies: The Materials and the Making of a Critical Apparatus*. Edited by Merrill M. Parvis and Allen Paul Wikgren, 25–68. Chicago, IL: University of Chicago Press, 1950.

Metzger, Bruce M. "Tatian's Diatessaron and a Persian Harmony of the Gospels." *JBL* 69 (1950): 261–80.

Metzger, Bruce M., and Bart D. Ehrman. *The Text of the New Testament: Its Transmission, Corruption, and Restoration*. 4th ed. New York: Oxford University Press, 2005.

Mill, John. *Ἡ Καινὴ Διαθήκη: Novum Testamentum: Cum lectionibus variantibus*. Oxford: Sheldonian Theatre, 1707.

Miller, Carolyn R. "Genre as Social Action." *The Quarterly Journal of Speech* 70 (1984): 151–67.

Mitchell, Margaret M. "Patristic Counter-Evidence to the Claim that 'The Gospels Were Written for All Christians.'" *NTS* 51 (2005): 36–79.

Moore, George Foote. "Tatian's Diatessaron and the Analysis of the Pentateuch." *JBL* 9 (1890): 201–15.

Morris, Leon. *Studies in the Fourth Gospel*. Grand Rapids, MI: Eerdmans, 1969.

Mroczek, Eva. *The Literary Imagination in Jewish Antiquity*. Oxford: Oxford University Press, 2016.

Neirynck, F. "Lk xxiv 12, Les témoins du texte occidental." In *Miscellanea Neotestamentica, Volume 1*. Edited by Tjitze Baarda, A. F. J. Klijn, and W. C. van Unnik, 45–60. Leiden: Brill, 1978.

Nestle, Eberhard. *Novum Testamentum Graece cum apparatu critico ex editionibus et libris manuscriptis collecto*. Stuttgart: Privilegierte Württembergische Bibelanstalt, 1898.

Nickelsburg, George W. E. "Enochic Wisdom and Its Relationship to the Mosaic Torah." In *The Early Enoch Literature*. Edited by Gabriele Boccaccini and John J. Collins, 82–94. SJSJ 121. Leiden: Brill, 2007.

Niederwimmer, Kurt. *The Didache: A Commentary*. Hermeneia. Minneapolis, MN: Fortress Press, 1998.

Nilson, Jon. "To Whom is Justin's *Dialogue with Trypho* Addressed?" *TS* 38 (1977): 538–46.

Nordenfalk, Carl. *Die spätantiken Kanontafeln*. 2 vols. Göteborg: Isacson, 1938.

Old, Hughes Oliphant. *The Reading and Preaching of the Scriptures in the Worship of the Christian Church, vol. 3: The Medieval Church*. Grand Rapids, MI: Eerdmans, 1999.

O'Loughlin, Thomas. "Harmonizing the Truth: Eusebius and the Problem of the Four Gospels." *Traditio* 65 (2010): 1–29.

Olson, S. Douglas. *Athenaeus: The Learned Banqueters*, vols. 3, 5. LCL 224, 274. Cambridge: Harvard University Press, 2008–9.

Origen. *Contra Celsum*. See M. Borret.

Origen. *Commentarii in evangelium Joannis*. See A. Brooke.

Ortiz de Urbina, Ignacio. *Vetus evangelium Syrorum et exinde excerptum Diatessaron Tatiani*. Biblia Polyglotta Matritensia VI. Madrid: CSIC, 1967.

Osiander, Andreas. *Harmoniae Evangelicae libri quatuor, in quibus Evangelica historia ex quatuor Evangelistis ita in unum est contexta, ut nullius verbum ullum omissum, nihil alienum immixtum, nullius ordo turbatus, nihil non suo loco positum: omnia vero litteris et notis ita distincta sunt, ut quid cujusque Evangelistae proprium, quid cum aliis, et cum quibus commune sit, primo aspectu deprehendere queas*. Basel: H. Froben and N. Episcopius, 1537.

Osburn, Carroll. "Methodology in Identifying Patristic Citations in NT Textual Criticism." *NovT* 47 (2005): 313–43.
von Otto, J. K. Th. *Ivstini Philosophi et Martyris Opera*. 4 vols. Jena: Dufft, 1876–81.
Parker, D. C. *An Introduction to the New Testament Manuscripts and Their Texts*. Cambridge: Cambridge University Press, 2008.
Parker, D. C. *The Living Text of the Gospels*. Cambridge: Cambridge University Press, 1997.
Parker, D. C., D. G. K. Taylor, and M. S. Goodacre. "The Dura-Europos Gospel Harmony." In *Studies in the Early Text of the Gospels and Acts*. Edited by D. G. K. Taylor, 192–228. Birmingham: University of Birmingham Press, 1999.
Parisot, J. *Aphraatis Sapientis Persae Demonstrationes*. 2 vols. PS 1–2. Paris: Firmin-Didot, 1894–1907.
Patrologia Graeca. Edited by J.-P. Migne. 162 vols. Paris, 1857–86.
Patrologia Latina. Edited by J.-P. Migne. 217 vols. Paris, 1844–64.
Pearse, Roger, ed. *Eusebius of Caesarea, Gospel Problems and Solutions*. Ipswich: Chieftain Publishing, 2010.
Pelser, H. S. "The Origin of the Ancient Syriac New Testament Texts: A Historical Study." In *De fructu oris sui: Essays in Honour of Adrianus Van Selms*. Edited by I. H. Eybers et al., 152–63. Pretoria Oriental Series 9. Leiden: Brill, 1971.
Peppard, Michael. *The World's Oldest Church: Bible, Art, and Ritual at Dura-Europos, Syria*. New Haven, CT: Yale University Press, 2016.
Perrin, Bernadotte. *Plutarch: Lives*, vols. 7, 8. LCL 99, 100. London: William Heinemann, 1919.
Perrin, Nicholas. "The *Diatessaron* and the Second-Century Reception of the Gospel of John." In *The Legacy of John: The Second-Century Reception of the Fourth Gospel*. Edited by T. Rasimus, 301–18. NovTSup 132. Leiden: Brill, 2010.
Perrin, Nicholas. "Hermeneutical Factors in the Harmonization of the Gospel and the Question of Textual Authority." In *The Biblical Canons*. Edited by J.-M. Auwers and H. J. de Jonge, 599–605. BETL 163. Leuven: Leuven University Press, 2003.
Person, Jr., Raymond F. *The Deuteronomistic History and the Book of Chronicles: Scribal Works in an Oral World*. AIL 6. Atlanta, GA: Society of Biblical Literature, 2010.
Peters, Curt. "Nachhall ausserkanonischer Evangelien-Überlieferung in Tatians Diatessaron." *Acta Orientalia* 16 (1938): 258–94.
Petersen, William L. "Canonicity, Ecclesiastical Authority, and Tatian's *Diatessaron*." In *Patristic and Text-Critical Studies: The Collected Essays of William L. Petersen*. Edited by Jan Krans and Joseph Verheyden, 489–516, NTTSD 40. Leiden: Brill, 2012. English original of "Canonicité, autorité ecclésiastique et *Diatessaron* de Tatien," in *Le canon du Nouveau Testament: Regards nouveaux sur l'histoire de sa formation*. Edited by Frédéric Amsler, 87–116. Le monde de la Bible 54. Geneva: Labor et Fides, 2005.
Petersen, William L. "The Diatessaron and the Fourfold Gospel." In *The Earliest Gospels: The Origins and Transmission of the Earliest Christian Gospels—The Contribution of the Chester Beatty Gospel Codex P45*. Edited by Charles Horton, 50–68. London: T&T Clark, 2004.
Petersen, William L. "The Diatessaron of Tatian." In *The Text of the New Testament in Contemporary Research: Essays on the Status Quaestionis*. Edited by Bart D. Ehrman and Michael W. Holmes, 77–96. Grand Rapids, MI: Eerdmans, 1995.
Petersen, William L. "From Justin to Pepys: The History of the Harmonized Gospel Tradition." *StPatr* 30 (1997): 71–96.
Petersen, William L. "The Genesis of the Gospel." In *New Testament Textual Criticism and Exegesis: Festschrift J. Delobel*. Edited by A. Denaux, 33–65. Leuven: Leuven University Press, 2002.

Petersen, William L. "New Evidence for the Question of the Original Language of the Diatessaron." In *Studien zum Text und zur Ethik des Neuen Testaments: Festschrift zum 80. Geburtstag von Heinrich Greeven*. Edited by Wolfgang Schrage, 325–43. Berlin: de Gruyter, 1986. Repr. pages 67–87 in *Patristic and Text-Critical Studies: The Collected Essays of William L. Petersen*. Edited by Jan Krans and Joseph Verheyden. Leiden: Brill, 2012.

Petersen, William L. "Some Remarks on the Integrity of Ephrem's Commentary on the Diatessaron." *StPatr* 20 (1989): 197–202. Repr. pages 103–9 in *Patristic and Text-Critical Studies: The Collected Essays of William L. Petersen*. Edited by Jan Krans and Joseph Verheyden. Leiden: Brill, 2012.

Petersen, William L. "Tatian the Assyrian." In *A Companion to Second-Century Christian "Heretics."* Edited by A. Marjanen and P. Luomanen, 125–58. VCSup 67. Leiden: Brill, 2005. Repr. pages 437–69 in *Patristic and Text-Critical Studies: The Collected Essays of William L. Petersen*. Edited by Jan Krans and Joseph Verheyden. Leiden: Brill, 2012.

Petersen, William L. *Tatian's Diatessaron: Its Creation, Dissemination, Significance, and History in Scholarship*. VCSup 25. Leiden: Brill, 1994.

Petersen, William L. "Textual Evidence of Tatian's Dependence upon Justin's ἈΠΟΜΝΗΜΟΝΕΥΜΑΤΑ." *NTS* 36 (1990): 512–34. Repr. pages 130–51 in *Patristic and Text-Critical Studies: The Collected Essays of William L. Petersen*. Edited by Jan Krans and Joseph Verheyden. Leiden: Brill, 2012.

Phillips, C. A. "Diatessaron—Diapente." *Bulletin of the Bezan Club* 9 (1931): 6–8.

Phillips, George. *The Doctrine of Addai, the Apostle*. London: Trübner, 1876.

Pierre, M.-J. *Aphraate le Sage Persan: Les Exposés, I*. SC 349. Paris: Les Éditions du Cerf, 1988.

Pitts, Brent A., ed. *Estoire de l'Evangile (Dublin, Christ Church Cathedral, MS. 6.1.1)*. Medium Ævum Monographs 28. Oxford: Society for the Study of Medieval Languages and Literature, 2011.

Plooij, Daniel. "A Fragment of Tatian's Diatessaron in Greek." *ExpTim* 46 (1935): 471–6.

Plooij, Daniel. *A Further Study of the Liège Diatessaron*. Leiden: Brill, 1925.

Plooij, Daniel. *A Primitive Text of the Diatessaron: The Liège Manuscript of a Mediæval Dutch Translation: A Preliminary Study*. Leiden: A. W. Sijthoff, 1923.

Plooij, D., A. J. Barnouw, C. A. Phillips, and A. H. A. Bakker. *The Liège Diatessaron*. 8 vols. VKNAW 31.1–8. Amsterdam: Koninklijke Akademie van Wetenschappen, 1929–70.

Plummer, Reinhard. "The Samaritans and Their Pentateuch." In *The Pentateuch as Torah: New Models for Understanding Its Promulgation and Acceptance*. Edited by Gary N. Knoppers and Bernard M. Levinson, 237–69. Winona Lake, IN: Eisenbrauns, 2007.

Preuschen, Erwin. *Untersuchungen zum Diatessaron Tatians*. Heidelberg: C. Winter, 1918.

Quispel, Gilles. "The Gospel of Thomas and the New Testament." *VC* 11 (1957): 189–207.

Quispel, Gilles. "L'Évangile selon Thomas et le Diatessaron." *VC* 13 (1959): 87–117.

Rajak, Tessa. *Josephus: The Historian and His Society*. 2nd ed. London: Duckworth, 2002.

Rajak, Tessa. "Justus of Tiberias." *ClQ* 23 (1973): 345–68.

Ranke, Ernst. *Codex Fuldensis: Novum Testamentum Latine Interprete Hieronymo ex Manuscripto Victoris Capuani*. Marburg: N. G. Elwert, 1868.

Rathofer, Johannes. "Die Einwirkung des Fuldischen Evangelientextes auf den althochdeutschen 'Tatian': Abkehr von der Methode der Diatessaronforschung." In *Literatur und Sprache im europäischen Mittelalter: Festschrift f. Karl Langosch z. 70. Geburtstag*. Edited by Alf Önnerfors, Johannes Rathofer, and Fritz Wagner, 256–308. Darmstadt: Wissenschaftliche Buchgesellschaft, 1973.

Rathofer, Johannes. "'Tatian' und Fulda: Die St. Galler Handschrift und der Victor-Codex." In *Zeiten und Formen in Sprache und Dichtung: Festschrift f. Fritz Tschirch z. 70. Geburtstag*. Edited by Karl Heinz Schirmer and Bernhard Sowinskii, 337–56. Köln: Böhlau, 1972.

Rathofer, Johannes. "Zur Heimatfrage des althochdeutschen Tatian: Das Votum der Handschriften." *AION (sezione germanica)* 14 (1971): 7–104.

Robbins, Vernon K. *Who Do People Say I Am? Rewriting Gospel in Emerging Christianity*. Grand Rapids, MI: Eerdmans, 2013.

Rolfe, J. C. *Suetonius: Lives of the Caesars*. 2 vols. LCL 31, 38. London: William Heinemann, 1913–14.

Roth, Dieter T. *The Text of Marcion's Gospel*. NTTSD 49. Leiden: Brill, 2015.

Rothschild, Clare K. Review of *Marcion and the Dating of the Synoptic Gospels*, by Markus Vincent [sic: Vinzent]. *Review of Biblical Literature* (March 2016): 1–4.

van Ruiten, Jacques T. A. G. M. *Abraham in the Book of Jubilees: The Rewriting of Genesis 11:26–25:10 in the Book of Jubilees 11:14–23:8*. JSJSup 161. Leiden: Brill, 2012.

Sanday, William. *The Gospels in the Second Century: An Examination of the Critical Part of a Work Entitled Supernatural Religion*. London: Macmillan, 1876.

van de Sande Bakhuyzen, W. H. *Der Dialog des Adamantius*. Leipzig: Hinrichs, 1901.

Schannat, Johann Friedrich. *Vindemiae literariae: Hoc est veterum monumentorum ad Germaniam sacram praecipue spectantium*. Fulda; Leipzig: M. G. Weidmann, 1723.

Scharb, Egbert, and Dieter Lührmann. *Fragmente apokryph gewordener Evangelien in griechischer und lateinischer Sprach*. MTS 50. Marburg: Elwert, 2000.

Schmeller, Johann Andreas. *Ammonii Alexandrini quae et Tatiani dicitur harmonia evangeliorum in linguam Latinam et inde ante annos mille in Francicam translata*. Vienna: Fr. Beck, 1841.

Schmid, Ulrich B. "The Diatessaron of Tatian." In *The Text of the New Testament in Contemporary Research: Essays on the Status Quaestionis*. Edited by Bart D. Ehrman and Michael W. Holmes, 2nd ed., 115–42. NTTSD 42. Leiden: Brill, 2013.

Schmid, Ulrich B. "Genealogy by Chance! On the Significance of Accidental Variation (Parallelisms)." In *Studies in Stemmatology II*. Edited by August den Hollander, Margot van Mulken, and Pieter Th. van Reenen, 127–43. Amsterdam: John Benjamins, 2004.

Schmid, Ulrich B. "How Can We Access Second Century Texts? The Cases of Marcion and Tatian." In *The New Testament Text in Early Christianity: Proceedings of the Lille Colloquium, July 2000*. Edited by C.-B. Amphoux and J. K. Elliott, 139–50. Lausanne: Editions du Zèbre, 2003.

Schmid, Ulrich B. "In Search of Tatian's Diatessaron in the West." *VC* 57 (2003): 176–99.

Schmid, Ulrich B. *Unum ex Quattuor: Eine Geschichte der lateinischen Tatianüberlieferung*. AGLB 37. Freiburg im Breisgau: Herder, 2005.

Schmidt, Thomas. "Greek Palimpsest Papyri: Some Open Questions." *Proceedings of the 24th International Congress of Papyrology* 2 (2007): 979–90.

Schwartz, Eduard, and Theodor Mommsen. *Eusebius Werke 2: Die Kirchengeschichte*. GCS 9.1–3. Leipzig: Hinrichs, 1903–9.

Schwartz, Seth. "The Composition and Publication of Josephus's *Bellum Iudaicum* Book 7." *HTR* 79 (1986): 373–86.

Semisch, Karl G. *Die apostolischen Denkwürdigkeiten des Märtyrers Justinus: Zur Geschichte und Aechtheit der Kanonis*. Hamburg: Perthes, 1848.

Shackleton Bailey, D. R. *Cicero: Letters to Atticus*. 4 vols. LCL 7, 8, 97, 491. Cambridge: Harvard University Press, 1999.

Shackleton Bailey, D. R. *Cicero: Letters to Friends*. 3 vols. LCL 205, 216, 230. Cambridge: Harvard University Press, 2001.
Shodu, E. L. *La mémoire des origines chrétiennes selon Justin Martyr*. Paradosis 50. Fribourg: Fribourg Academic Press, 2008.
Siker, Jeffrey S. Review of *The Proof from Prophecy: A Study in Justin Martyr's Proof-Text Tradition: Text-Type, Provenance, Theological Profile*, by Oskar Skarsaune. *CBQ* 52 (1990): 365-6.
Sim, David C. "The Gospels for All Christians? A Response to Richard Bauckham." *JSNT* 84 (2001): 3-27.
Sim, David C. "Matthew's Use of Mark: Did Matthew Intend to Supplement or To Replace His Primary Source?" *NTS* 57 (2011): 176-92.
Skarsaune, Oskar. "Justin and His Bible." In *Justin Martyr and His Worlds*. Edited by Sara Parvis and Paul Foster, 53-76. Minneapolis, MN: Fortress Press, 2007.
Skarsaune, Oskar. *The Proof from Prophecy: A Study in Justin Martyr's Proof-Text Tradition: Text-Type, Provenance, Theological Profile*. NovTSup 56. Leiden: Brill, 1987.
Smith, William, and Henry Wace, eds. *A Dictionary of Christian Biography, Literature, Sects and Doctrines during the First Eight Centuries*. 4 vols. London: John Murray, 1877-87.
von Soden, Hermann Freiherr. *Die Schriften des Neuen Testaments in ihrer ältesten erreichbaren Textgestalt hergestellt auf Grund ihrer Textgeschichte*. 2 vols. Göttingen: Vandenhoek & Ruprecht, 1911-13.
Souter, Alexander. "Francis Crawford Burkitt." *JTS* 36 (1935): 225-54.
Souter, Alexander. *Novum Testamentum Graece*. Oxford: Clarendon Press, 1910.
Stanton, Graham N. "The Fourfold Gospel." *NTS* 43 (1997): 317-46.
Stanton, Graham N. "Jesus Traditions and Gospels in Justin Martyr and Irenaeus." In *The Biblical Canons*. Edited by J.-M. Auwers and H. J. de Jonge. BETL 163, 353-70. Leuven: Leuven University Press, 2003.
Stöver, H. D. *Christenverfolgung im Römischen Reich*. Düsseldorf/Vienna: Antiquariat Walter Nowak, 1984.
Stowers, Stanley. "The Concept of Community and the History of Early Christianity." *MTSR* 23 (2011): 238-56.
Strack, Hermann L., and Paul Billerbeck. *Kommentar zum Neuen Testament aus Talmud und Midrasch*. 6 vols. Munich: Beck, 1922-61.
Tatian. *Oratio ad Graecos*. See J. Trelenberg.
Tertullian. *Adversus Marcionem*. See E. Evans.
Thackeray, Henry St. John. *Josephus: Jewish War, vol. 3*. LCL 210. London: William Heinemann, 1928.
Thackeray, Henry St. John. *Josephus: The Life; Against Apion*. LCL 186. London: William Heinemann, 1926.
Thackeray, Henry St. John, and Ralph Marcus. *Josephus: Jewish Antiquities, vol. 7*. LCL 281. London: William Heinemann, 1934.
Tischendorf, Constantin von. *Novum Testamentum Graece: Ad antiquissimos testes denuo recensuit*. 2 vols. 8th ed. Leipzig: Giesecke & Devrient, 1869-72.
Tischendorf, Constantin von. *Origin of the Four Gospels*. Translated by William Leonard Gage. From the 4th German ed., rev. and greatly enlarged. London: Jackson, Walford, & Hodder, 1868.
Tischendorf, Constantin von. *Wann wurden unsere Evangelien verfasst?* Leipzig: Hinrichs, 1865.
Todesco, Venanzio, Alberto Vaccari, and Marco Vattasso, eds. *Il Diatessaron in Volgare Italiano*. StT 81. Vatican City: Biblioteca Apostolica Vaticana, 1938.

Tov, Emanuel. "Septuagint." In *Textual History of the Bible, vol. 1A*. Edited by Armin Lange, 191–210. Leiden: Brill, 2016.
Tov, Emanuel, with the collaboration of R. A. Kraft and a contribution by P. J. Parsons. *The Greek Minor Prophets Scroll from Naḥal Ḥever (8ḤevXIIgr)*. DJD 8/The Seiyâl Collection 1. Oxford: Clarendon Press, 1990.
Tregelles, Samuel Prideaux. *An Account of the Printed Text of the Greek New Testament: With Remarks on Its Revision upon Critical Principles*. London: Samuel Bagster and Sons, 1854.
Trelenberg, Jörg. *Tatianos, Oratio ad Graecos*. Tübingen: Mohr Siebeck, 2012.
Tuckett, C. M. *2 Clement: Introduction, Text, and Commentary*. Oxford Apostolic Fathers. Oxford: Oxford University Press, 2012.
Ulrich, Daniel W. "The Missional Audience of the Gospel of Matthew." *CBQ* 69 (2007): 64–83.
VanderKam, James C. *The Book of Jubilees*. CSCO 510–511. Leuven: Peeters, 1989.
Vinzent, Markus. *Marcion and the Dating of the Synoptic Gospels*. StPatrSup 2. Leuven: Peeters, 2014.
Viviano, Benedict. *What Are They Saying about Q?* New York: Paulist, 2013.
Vogels, Heinrich Joseph. *Beiträge zur Geschichte des Diatessaron im Abendland*. Münster: Aschendorff, 1919.
Vogels, Heinrich Joseph. *Die altsyrischen Evangelien in ihrem Verhältnis zu Tatians Diatessaron*. Freiburg: Herder, 1911.
Vogels, Heinrich Joseph. *Die Harmonistik im Evangelientext des Codex Cantabrigiensis: Ein Beitrag zur neutestamentlichen Textkritik*. Leipzig: Hinrichs, 1910.
Vogels, Heinrich Joseph. *Handbuch der Textkritik des Neuen Testaments*. 2nd ed. Bonn: Hanstein, 1955.
Vogels, Heinrich Joseph. *Novum Testamentum Graece*. Düsseldorf: L. Schwann, 1920.
Vogels, Heinrich Joseph. *Novum Testamentum Graece et Latine*. 4th ed. Freiburg: Herder, 1955.
Vogels, Heinrich Joseph. Review of *Novum Testamentum Graece et Latine*, by Augustinus Merk. *TRev* 33 (1933): 473–8.
Vööbus, Arthur. *Early Versions of the New Testament*. Stockholm: Estonian Theological Society in Exile, 1954.
Vööbus, Arthur. *Studies in the History of the Gospel Text in Syriac*. Louvain: Peeters, 1951.
Wallenwein, Kirsten. "*Subscriptiones* in karolingischen Codices." In *Karolingische Klöster: Wissenstransfer und kulturelle Innovation*. Edited by J. Becker, T. Licht, and S. Weinfurter, 23–37. Materiale Textkulturen 4. Berlin: de Gruyter, 2015.
Walsh, Robyn Faith. "Q and the 'Big Bang' Theory of Christian Origins." In *Redescribing the Gospel of Mark*. Edited by Barry S. Crawford and Merrill P. Miller, 483–533. SBLECL 22. Atlanta, GA: SBL Press, 2017.
Watson, Francis. *Gospel Writing: A Canonical Perspective*. Grand Rapids, MI: Eerdmans, 2013.
Watson, Francis. "Harmony or Gospel? On the Genre of the (So-Called) Diatessaron." Paper presented at the annual meeting of the SNTS Christian Apocryphal Literature Seminar, Perth, Australia, 2013.
Watson, Francis. "Towards a Redaction-Critical Reading of the Diatessaron Gospel." *EC* 7 (2016): 95–112.
Weber, Robert, et al., eds. *Biblia Sacra iuxta vulgata versionem*. 5th ed. Stuttgart: Deutsche Bibelgesellschaft, 2007.

Wengst, Klaus. *Didache (Apostellehre), Barnabasbrief, Zweiter Klemensbrief, Schrift an Diognet.* Schriften des Urchristentums 2. Munich: Kösel, 1984.

Weigelt, Morris A. "Diatessaric Harmonies of the Passion Narrative in the Harclean Syriac Version." Th.D. diss. Princeton, NJ: Princeton Theological Seminary, 1969.

Weihrich, Franz, ed. *Augustine, De consensu evangelistarum.* CSEL 43. Vienna: Österreichische Akademie der Wissenschaften, 1904.

West, M. L. *The Epic Cycle: A Commentary on the Lost Troy Epics.* Oxford: Oxford University Press, 2013.

West, M. L. *Greek Epic Fragments from the Seventh to the Fifth Centuries BC.* LCL 497. Cambridge: Harvard University Press, 2003.

Westcott, Brooke Foss. *A General Survey of the Canon of the New Testament.* London: Macmillan, 1870.

Westcott, Brooke Foss, and Fenton John Anthony Hort. *The New Testament in the Original Greek: Introduction and Appendix.* New York: Harper, 1882.

Westcott, Brooke Foss, and Fenton John Anthony Hort. *The New Testament in the Original Greek: Introduction and Appendix.* 2nd ed. London: Macmillan, 1896.

Wettstein, Johann Jakob. Ἡ Καινὴ Διαθήκη: *Novum Testamentum Graecum: Editionis receptae cum lectionibus variantibus.* 2 vols. Amsterdam: Dommeriana, 1751–2.

Williams, Frank, trans. *The Panarion of Epiphanius of Salamis.* 2 vols. 2nd ed. Leiden: Brill, 2000.

Williams, Peter J. *Early Syriac Translation Technique and the Textual Criticism of the Greek Gospels.* Texts and Studies 3/2. Piscataway, NJ: Gorgias, 2004.

Williams, Peter J. "The Syriac Versions of the New Testament." In *The Text of the New Testament in Contemporary Research: Essays on the Status Quaestionis.* Edited by Bart D. Ehrman and Michael W. Holmes, 2nd ed., 143–66. NTTSD 42. Leiden: Brill, 2013.

Windisch, Hans. *Johannes und die Synoptiker: Wollte der vierte Evangelist die Älteren Evangelien ergänzen oder ersetzen?* UNT 12. Leipzig: Hinrichs, 1926.

Wright, William. *The Homilies of Aphraates, the Persian Sage, Vol. 1.* London: Williams & Norgate, 1869.

Wright, W., and N. McLean, eds. *The Ecclesiastical History of Eusebius in Syriac.* Cambridge: Cambridge University Press, 1898.

Yates, JoAnne, and Wanda Orlikowski. "Genre Systems: Chronos and Kairos in Communicative Action." In *The Rhetoric of Ideology and Ideology of Genre.* Edited by Richard Coe, Lorelei Lingard, and Tatiana Teslenko, 103–22. Cresskill, NJ: Hampton Press, 2002.

Zahn, Theodor. *Geschichte des neutestamentlichen Kanons.* 2 vols. Erlangen: Andreas Deichert, 1888–92.

Zahn, Theodor. *Tatian's Diatessaron.* FGNK 1. Erlangen: Andreas Deichert, 1881.

Zahn, Theodor. "Zur Geschichte von Tatians Diatessaron im Abendland." *NKZ* 5 (1894): 85–120.

Zipes, Jack. "Introduction: Rediscovering the Original Tales of the Brothers Grimm." In *The Original Folk and Fairy Tales of the Brothers Grimm: The Complete First Edition,* by Jacob Grimm and Wilhelm Grimm. Translated by Jack Zipes, vol. 1, xix–xliv. Princeton, NJ: Princeton University Press, 2014.

Zola, Nicholas J. "Tatian's Diatessaron in Latin: A New Edition and Translation of Codex Fuldensis." Ph.D. diss. Waco, TX: Baylor University, 2014.

Zola, Nicholas J. "Evangelizing Tatian: The *Diatessaron*'s Place in the Emergence of the Fourfold Gospel Canon." *PRSt* 43 (2016): 399–414.

Index of Ancient Sources

Page numbers with an appended italic *t* or *f* indicate a table or figure.

Hebrew Scripture

Genesis
- 4:24 — 39 n.66
- 5:23 — 118

Leviticus 18:5 — 65

1 Samuel 9–30 — 118

1 Kings
- 14:29 — 123
- 15:7, 23 — 123
- 15:31 — 123
- 16:5, 14, 20, 27 — 123

1 Chronicles
- 1–9 — 117
- 22 — 118

2 Chronicles
- 12:15 — 123
- 27:7 — 123
- 36:20–23 — 117

Psalms
- 2:7 — 46
- 77:21 LXX — 43 n.86

Isaiah
- 1–39 — 123
- 40–55 — 123
- 56–66 — 123
- 61 — 89

Daniel
- 1:1–2:4a — 123
- 2:4b–7:28 — 123
- 8:1–12:13 — 123

Nahum 3:12 — 120

Zechariah
- 1:3 — 120
- 9–11 — 123
- 12–14 — 123

New Testament

Matthew
- 1:1, 18 — 86 n.57
- 1:1–6 — 80
- 1:11 — 196
- 1:18–25 — 80
- 1:21 — 86 n.60
- 3:11 — 44
- 3:13 — 82
- 3:14–15 — 82
- 3:14–17 — 82
- 3:15b — 127 n.80
- 3:16 — 44
- 4–10 — 91
- 4:1–11 — 82, 105
- 4:5 — 33, 37
- 4:8–9 — 158
- 4:10 — 104, 105
- 4:10b — 105
- 4:12 — 83
- 4:12–16 — 83
- 4:13–16 — 83
- 4:15–16 — 83
- 4:16 — 196
- 4:17 — 83, 89
- 4:18–22 — 81, 83
- 4:23–24 — 83
- 4:23–25 — 81, 83, 187
- 5–6 — 103
- 5–7 — 91, 187
- 5:1 — 84, 103
- 5:1–7:27 — 81
- 5:3–11 — 84
- 5:3–12 — 84
- 5:14–16 — 30
- 5:27–30 — 102
- 5:28 — 102, 209 n.90
- 5:29–30 — 102
- 5:31–32 — 102
- 5:32 — 102–103
- 5:34, 37 — 104, 105
- 5:40 — 103
- 5:40–6:1 — 104*t*
- 5:44, 46 — 103

6:1	104	18:23–35	40 n.75
6:2	103	19:3–12	102-3
6:13	105, 196, 207, 209, 211, 227, 230	19:10	60
		19:11–12	102-3
		19:16	65, 105
6:16a	227	19:16, 17	105
6:19	183	19:16–22	41
6:25	104	19:16–30	41
6:26	104	19:17	105
6:32	104	19:22	41
7:22	196	21	223 n.143
7:28	103	21:12–13	184
8–9	91	21:17	185 n.65
8:1, 18	103	21:28–32	161 n.58
8:4	62, 63, 64, 65	22	223 n.143
8:14–16	81	22:37	104, 105
9:1–8	81	23:35	33, 36
9:8	103	25:46	65
9:9	83	26:6	160 n.54
9:9–10	83	26:7	160
9:9–13	81	26:10	160
9:13	103	26:12–13	160
9:22	161 n.58	26:26	77 n.32
9:35–11:1	187	26:27	77 n.32
9:36	227	26:28	77 n.32
10:1–4	91	27:49	198, 203, 207, 209, 211, 224, 228
10:15	199 n.36		
11:27	219		
12:1, 2, 5	84	27:51	33
12:1–8	81 n.47, 84	27:53	37
12:9–14	33	27:55–57	170t
12:11–12	84	27:56	155t, 156, 157t, 165t
12:46	180		
13:19, 38	105	27:56c	150t, 157t, 165t
13:55	90	27:57	150t, 162 n.62, 169t
14:1	136		
15:2	63–5	27:57a	155t, 157t, 165t
16:16	129	27:57b	150t, 155t, 157t, 165t, 168 n.81
17:26	219, 234 n.170		
17:27	162 n.61		
18:10	51, 134	27:57d	150t, 155t, 157t, 165t
18:10–11	40 n.75		
18:15–17	40 n.75	27:57e	153t, 154 n.39, 155, 155t, 157t, 162, 165t, 169t
18:15–22	40		
18:20	51		
18:21	43	27:58	162 n.62
18:21–22	38, 40	27:60	133
18:21f.	33, 38	28:5	133
18:22	40 n.75	28:19	208

Index of Ancient Sources

28:20	127	9:49	28 n.19
Mark		10:4	159
1:1	16	10:17	65
1:12	82	10:17–22	41
1:14–15	83, 89	10:21	59–60, 61
1:15	83, 136	10:30	65
1:21–28	81, 83	10:35	211 n.99
1:29–34	83	10:35–37	160 n.57
1:35–39	83	11	223 n.143
1:41	159, 217 n.120, 229	11:11	185 n.65
		12	223 n.143
2:1–12	84	13:34–35	133 n.111
2:13–17	84	14:3	160, 160 n.54
2:14	84, 209, 209 n.91, 210 n.92, 211	14:4	160
		14:7	160
		14:51–52	137
2:16	180	14:72	234 n.170
2:17	103	15:40	137
2:18–22	84	15:40–43	170t
2:19	84	15:40c	150t
2:23–28	84	15:40cd	165t
2:27	84	15:40d	155t, 157t, 165t
2:28	211 n.99	15:41a	155t, 157t, 165t
3:1–6	33, 37, 84	15:41ab	153 n.31
3:7–12	84	15:41b	155t
3:13–14	84	15:42	150t, 151t, 155t, 157t, 165t
3:13–19	81		
3:17	127 n.81, 136	15:43c	152, 155, 155t, 157t, 161, 165t, 168
3:21	84		
4:21	30		
4:26–29	137	15:43d	155t
5:43	161 n.58	16:1	137
6:11	199 n.36	16:5	133
6:14	136	16:8	196
7:3	63, 64, 229 n.159	16:9–20	209
		16:15	208
7:5	63, 64	16:17–18	137
7:31–37	127 n.81, 137	Luke	
7:33	137	1:1	19, 126
7:34	137	1:1–3	81
8	221	1:1–4	19 n.46, 20, 23, 80
8:15	221, 228		
8:22–26	137	1:2	19
8:23a	137	1:3	75 n.25, 77
8:24	137	1:7	153
8:29b	129	1:28	203 n.59
9:1	217 n.120	1:31	86 n.60
9:15	209 n.90	1:45	211 n.99
9:43	102	2:1–7	80

2:4	153	5:27–32	81, 84
2:4–5	86	5:30, 32–33	84
2:7	203 n.59	5:32	103
2:9	46 n.101	5:33–39	84
2:22	128	6	103
2:35	58	6:1–5	84
2:41–52	128	6:4	28 n.19
3:1	127 n.80	6:6–12	84
3:16	44	6:12–16	81, 91
3:19–20	83	6:12–17	84
3:21–22	82	6:13–16	84
3:22	46	6:17	103
3:23	82, 85	6:17–49	81
3:23–38	85	6:22	84
3:34–38	80	6:24	84
4:1–13	105	6:24–26	84
4:5–6	82	6:28	103
4:6	82	6:30, 34	103
4:6b	158	7:36–38	160 n.54
4:8	104	7:39, 41, 44, 45, 47	160 n.54
4:8b	105	7:39–50	160
4:14–15	82	8:16	30
4:14–21	89	8:20	180
4:14–22	83	8:48	161 n.58
4:14a	82	9:20cd	129
4:14b-15	83	9:54	203 n.59
4:16–21	89	10:1	211 n.99
4:16–30	90	10:25	65 n.38
4:20–21	89 n.70	10:28	65 n.38
4:21–24	89–90	11:33	30
4:22	89, 90	12:13–21	41
4:23–30	90	12:20	209 n.90
4:25–27	90	12:47–50	40 n.75
4:28–29	90	13:1–17	40 n.75
4:31–37	81	13:26–27	98
4:31–38	83	14:31–32	133 n.111
4:38–39	81	16:10–12	99
4:38–41	83	16:18	102
4:42–44	83	16:19–31	41
4:42–45	83	17:3–4	40
5–9	178–179	17:3f.	33, 38
5:1–6:19	103	17:4	39, 40, 41, 43
5:1–10	186	18:9–14	185 n.65
5:1–11	81, 83, 186, 188	18:18	65
5:2, 5, 7	83	18:18–23	41
5:10	186, 187, 188	20	223 n.143
5:11	186, 187	21:1–4	185 n.65
5:17–26	81, 84	21:19a	77 n.32
5:20, 22–23	84	21:19ba	77 n.32

21:19c	77 n.32	1:19–23	87
22:20	77 n.32	1:24–28	87
23:34	222, 228	1:29–31	82, 87
23:44	48	1:30	88
23:48	49, 217–18 n.121, 219	1:32	88
		1:32–34	82, 87
23:49	148 n.18	1:33–34	82
23:49–51, 54	170t	1:34	82
23:49a	164, 165t	1:35	88
23:49b	155t, 157t	1:35–37	87
23:49bc	150t	1:35–37, 41, 46–47	82
23:49c	155t, 157t, 165t	1:35–51	82
23:50	164 n.71	1:36	198
23:50a	165t, 168 n.81	1:36–50	185
23:50b	150t, 155t, 157t, 165t	1:43–51	89, 90
		2	129 n.88
23:50c	150t, 152, 155t, 157t, 161, 165t, 168	2:1–10	83
		2:1–11	83, 90, 91, 185–6
23:50d	150t, 155t, 165t	2:1–11b	186, 188
23:50d, 51a	164	2:11	90, 130 n.94
23:51	160–163, 161t, 163, 164, 166t	2:11a	185
		2:11b	186, 187, 188
23:51a	151t, 155t, 157t, 161, 162, 162 n.63, 165t	2:11c	185, 186–7, 188
		2:14–16	184
		2:15	184
23:51b	150t, 155t, 157t, 161, 162, 163, 165t	3	223 n.143
		3:3	130 n.94
		3:3–5	100
23:51c	150t, 155t, 157t, 161, 162, 162 n.62, 163, 165t	3:8	127 n.80
		3:13	211 n.99, 222 n.138
		3:22–4:2	81
23:53	133	3:22–4:3	81 n.47, 83, 91
23:54	150t, 155t, 157t, 165t	3:22–36	90, 187
		4	129 n.88
24:4	133	4:4–42	91
John		4:10	130 n.94
1	88, 129 n.88	4:45–54	91
1–5	233 n.166	4:46–54	83, 90, 91
1:1	13, 15–17, 23–4, 196	4:54	91
		6	129 n.88
1:1–5	16, 23, 29 n.24, 80, 180, 181	6:53	130 n.94
		7:1	40 n.75
1:1f.	22	7:52	223 n.143
1:3	22, 202 n.52	7:53	216
1:3–4	130 n.94	7:53–8:11	28 n.19, 216, 195, 209, 223, 227, 228
1:9	22		
1:15–18	87		

8:1–11	81	26:15	46
8:5	216	Romans 1:1	20 n.49
8:9	216	1 Corinthians	
8:10	216	7:5	202 n.52
8:11	216	9:1	126 n.72
8:12	223 n.143	9:18	15 n.17
8:17	63	15:5, 9	126 n.72
8:21b	130 n.94	2 Corinthians 11:7	15 n.17
9:1	130 n.94	Ephesians 4:26	40 n.73
9:6	229 n.156	Hebrews 11:12	103 n.37
10:8	203 n.59		
10:34	62–3	**Other Jewish Writings**	
12	129 n.88		
12:2–3	160	Babylonian Talmud,	
12:3–6	160	b. Sukkah 46a	64 n.35
12:5	160 n.54	1 Enoch	118–20
13:38	169t	Josephus	
14:12	184	Antiquities	
15:11	184	1–13	118
15:25	63	7.335–342	118
18–20	129 n.88	Against Apion 1.8	118
18:1	209 n.90	Jewish War	
19:31–37	148 n.18, 153 n.31, 155t, 157, 157t, 163, 164, 165t, 167	1.1	116
		1.4	116
		Vita	
		340	116
19:34	164, 164 n.72, 165t, 198, 203, 207, 224	357	116
		359	116
		359–360	116
19:38	162, 170t	361–367	116 n.32
19:38c	150t, 151 n.24, 153, 154 n.39, 155t, 157t, 165t, 168	Jubilees 4.17-25	119
		Testament of Benjamin 7.4	39 n.66
		Early Christian Writings	
19:38d	150t, 151 n.24, 153, 155t, 157t, 165t, 168	Aphrahat, Demonstrations	
		1.1	14 n.3
19:41	133	1.8	15 n.17
20:12	133	1.10	13–14, 15 n.17
20:28	127 n.80	2.20	134
20:31	211 n.99, 212	4.10	14 n.5
21:24	77	6.1	15 n.17
21:25	23	6.15	134
Acts		8.3	14 n.5
1:21–22	126 n.72	14	133 n.111
2:32–33	127	14.9	14 n.5
9:5	46	14.26	49
14:14	126 n.72	14.31	14 n.4, 15 n.17
22:8	46	14.44	38, 39

20.11	14 n.4, 15 n.17	5.18	83
20.20	134	5.19–20b	84
21.1	14 n.5	5.21	84
22.18	14 n.4, 15 n.17	5.22	84
23.1	14 n.5	5.23–24	84
23.9	15 n.17	6.1a-1b	84
23.53	14 n.5	6.2	84

Apostolic Constitutions

7.1–32	124	7.10	161 n.58

Augustine, *De consensu evangelistarum*

		10.1	160 n.56
2.21.51	70 n.2	10.8–10	160 n.54
3.24.69	75 n.25	10.14	228

2 Clement

		11.23, 26, 27	90 n.72
		12.21, 23	62
4.5	98	12.22–23	159 n.50
5.4	98	13.13	137
8.5	99	14.4	160 n.56

Clement of Alexandria

		14.18	159 n.51
Quis dives salvetur		14.22	38, 39
1.5	28 n.17,	14.24	50–1,
	53 n.130		134 n.115
4.4–10	128 n.81	15.1	65
Stromata		15.1–11	41 n.78
3.12.81	85 n.53	15.6, 7, 8	59
3.13.93	28 n.16,	15.12–13	41 n.78
	53 n.130	15.18–19	160 n.56
Didache 1–6	124 n.59	16.18	161 n.58

Ephrem (attrib.), *Commentary on the Gospel* (i.e. *Commentary on the Diatessaron*)

		17.11–13	160 n.54
		19.15	208
		20.28	48
1.2	17 n.27	21.3	228
1.3	17 nn.26–7	21.8	164
1.4	17 nn.26–7	21.10–12	164
1.5	17 nn.26–7	21.18	228
1.7	83	21.20	164, 166t
1.25	86 n.58,	21.27	58
	86 n.60	Epiphanius of Salamis, *Panarion*	
1.25–26	86 n.58	13.1	131
1.26	86 n.58	13.2	42 n.81
4.1–5	82	14.3	42 n.81
4.2	47 n.106	20.3.7	42 n.81
4.4–16	82	30.2.2	131
4.5	43–8, 87 n.62	30.3.7	131, 136, 140
4.9	159 n.48	30.13	45–8
4.17–20	82	30.13.2	131
5.1–12	83	30.13.7–8	131 n.102
5.13	83, 136,	30.14.3	131
	137 n.130	31.7.1–2	19 n.41
5.17	209	42.1.2	131 n.101
5.17a	83	42.9.1	130, 140

42.9.2	131	inscription	127 n.80
42.11.6, 17	131	*Letter to the Magnesians*	
46.1	41, 42	7.1	127 n.80
46.1.6–9	85 n.54	*Letter to the Philadelphians*	
46.1.9	73 n.17, 136, 140	7.1	127 n.80
		Letter to the Smyrnaeans	
51.4.7–10	87 n.64	1.1	127 n.80
51.12.1–21.17	88 n.66	1.2	127 n.80
51.18.1	87 n.65	Irenaeus of Lyon, *Adversus haereses*	
51.21.15	22 n.59	1.28.1	135, 203 n.54
Eusebius, *Historia ecclesiastica*		3.1.1	53 n.130
3.24.5–8a	128 n.81	3.4.3	19 n.41
3.25	141	3.11.7	130, 135, 140
3.25.4	124	3.11.8	53 n.130, 127–8 n.81, 135
3.27	140		
3.39.4	78 n.36	3.11.9	28 n.16, 53 n.130, 130, 135
3.39.15	75 n.25		
3.39.15–16	78 n.36	3.14.4	130
3.39.17	28 n.19	3.23	72 n.12
4.16	18 n.38	3.23.8	135
4.16.7	72 n.11	5.7.20, 21	130
4.29	197	Jerome	
4.29.2	72 n.12, 203 n.54	*Commentary on Matthew*	
		23:35	36
4.29.6	14 n.9, 72 n.13, 75 n.24, 135, 141	27:51	36
		De viris illustribus	
		23	18 n.38
4.29.7	72 n.11, 85 n.55, 135	54, 61	88 n.67
		Against the Pelagians 3.2	38, 39
6.14.10	88 n.67	Justin	
6.25.4	28 n.18	*Dialogue with Trypho*	
8.2.1	124	1.7	20 n.51
Gospel of Peter		35.3	96
7	49–50	45.4	86 n.59
23	31–2	49.4	136
Gospel of Thomas		76.5	98
13	129	88.3	43–4, 87 n.62
30	50–1	100.4	86 n.59
Hippolytus of Rome, *Refutation of All Heresies*		101.2	41 n.77
		103	46
5.7.40	130 n.94	103.8	107
5.8.5	130 n.94	106.3	127 n.81, 136
5.8.7	130 n.94	*First Apology*	
5.8.11	130 n.94	15–16	100, 101, 102, 105
5.8.29	130 n.94		
5.8.45	130 n.94	15–17	96
5.9.18	130 n.94	15.1	102
5.9.20	130 n.94	15.1, 9	102
Ignatius of Antioch		15.1–8	102
Letter to the Ephesians,		15.2	102

15.3–4	102–3	Romanos the Melodist, *First Hymn on the*	
15.4	102–3	*Epiphany* XVI.14.7–10	44 n.89
15.7	103	Tatian, *Oratio ad Graecos*	
15.8	103	5.1	22
15.9	103	11.1	17
15.9, 10, 13, 17	104t	13.2	22
15.9–16	102	18.6	18
15.10	103	19	202 n.52
15.14, 15, 16	104	19.2	18 n.36
15.17	104	19.4	22
16.1, 5	102	21.5	21
16.1–4	102	29	21 n.54
16.5	105, 105 n.40	29.1	17
16.5–7	104	29.2	17
16.5–14	102	29.2–3	18
16.6a	105	35.1	17
16.6b	105	42.1	17
16.6b-7	105	Tertullian, *Adversus Marcionem*	
16.7	41 n.77, 105	4.2.1–2	76 n.28
16.11	98	4.2.3	76 n.29,
33.5	86 n.60		130 n.96
61.4–5	100	4.2.4	130, 140
66.3	77	4.5.3	128 n.81
	nn.31–2, 106–7	Theodoret of Cyrrhus, *Hæreticarum*	
67.3	106	*fabularum compendium* 1.20	15 n.14, 29
Second Apology 3	18 n.37		n.25, 78 n.38,
Origen			79 n.42,
Against Celsus			80 n.45,
1.28	133		134, 136
2.27	77 n.34	Zacharias Chrysopolitanus, *Commentary*	
2.49	133	ch. 141	35
2.69	133	ch. 170	36
5.18	133	third preface	35 n.48
5.56	133		
5.59	18 n.39	**Classical Authors**	
5.61	19 n.40		
5.62	19 n.42	Aristides of Athens, *Apology*	
6.52–53	133	2.4	99
8.24	133	Aristotle, *Poetics* 1459ab	115 n.24
Commentary on John		Athenaeus, *Deipnosophistae*	
2.29–30	87 n.63	7.277	115 n.25
5.7	21 n.52	11.465	115 n.25
10.1–2	88 n.67	Cicero	
10.2	88 n.68	*Epistulae ad Atticum*	
10.3.2	21 n.52	12.4	115
Commentary on		12.40, 41, 45, 48	115
Matthew 15.14	41	13.46	115
Protevangelium of James		13.50	115
11.3	86 n.60	*Epistulae ad familiares*	
22	128	7.24	115

Plutarch		25.40	60 n.23
Caesar 54.3	116	27	40 n.75
Cato Minor		27.29	134 n.115
25.1	115	28–29	41
37.1	115	48.45–47	137
Suetonius, *Augustus* 85	115	52.21–27	165t
		52.23	137
Diatessaronic Witnesses		55.5	208
		55.9–10	137
Arabic Diatessaron		Codex Fuldensis	
1.1–5.21	90	1–17	90
2.12–13	86 n.58	5	86 n.58
4.28–41	82	14	82
4.41	89	15	82
4.42–5.3	82	15–63	91
5.4–20	82	16–17	82
5.21–32	83	16–20	81
5.33–43	83	17	90
5.43	136–7	17–23	89
5.44–6.4	83	18	83, 89, 137
6.5–25	83	19–20	83
6.5–34	91	21	81, 81 n.47, 83
6.25–35	83	22	83
6.34	91	22–43	81
6.36–39	83	23	83–4, 91
6.40–8.25	81	23–44	91
6.40–45	83	24	84
6.46	83	45	91
6.47–54	83	46	91
7.1–6	83	46–62	91
7.7–10	83	48	90 n.71
7.9	209	49	90 n.71
7.11–24	84	50	91
7.25–30	84	55	90 n.71
7.31–36	84	56	90 n.71, 91
7.37–46	84	69	81 n.47
7.47–53	84	70	81 n.47
8.9–25	84	77	137
8.26–36	84	79	90
8.37–39	84	87	81 n.47, 127 n.81, 137
9.36	208		
11.4–16	90 n.71	88	81 n.47
16.49–52	137	90–91	137
17.36–53	90	93	137
21.1–7	127 n.81, 137	97	134 n.115
23.18	222 n.137	103	81 n.47
23.26–30	137	104	81 n.47
24.27	134 n.115	105	81 n.47
24.28	134 n.115	113	160 n.56

120	223	59	180
121	81 n.48, 223	67	81 n.47
124	161 n.58	68	81 n.47
138–139	160 n.55	72	81 n.47
154	159 n.51	86	81 n.47
158	81 n.47	87	81 n.47
171	137	102	81 n.47
171–172	155*t*, 157*t*, 165*t*	103	81 n.47
172	152*t*, 153*t*, 161*t*	104	81 n.47
174	137	120	81 n.48
182	137	157	81 n.47
capitula		158	81 n.47
1	180	Liège harmony	
5	80	28	137
10	180 n.43	89–90	137 n.131
14	82	114	127 n.81, 137
15	82	122–3	137
16	82	133	134 n.115
18	83	225	137
19	83	231	137, 152 n.27
20	81 n.47	231–232	155*t*
21	83	232	152 n.26,
22	83–4		152*t*, 153*t*
23	84	233	137
56	180	245	137

Index of Modern Authors

Aland, Barbara 219 n.128, 221, 225
Aland, Kurt 219 n.128, 221, 225
Alexander, Loveday 126
Anderson, Paul N. 138 n.136
Andrade, Nathaniel 56 n.4
Aucher, Johann Baptist 16, 203 n.56
Avioz, Michael 118 n.40

Baarda, Tjitze 2, 3, 7, 13, 52 n.127, 94
  n.2, 112, 133, 138 n.135, 192, 206 n.73,
  217–18 n.121, 218, 224–5, 229 n.158,
  231 n.160, 233–4 nn.169–70, 233 n.166,
  234 n.173, 235 n.177
Baden, Joel S. 117 n.36
Bakker, A. H. A. 235 n.175
Bakker, H. 233 n.166
Barker, James 4, 7, 8, 111, 128 n.83
Barnouw, A. J. 152 n.26
Bauckham, Richard 112
Bauer, Walter 21–2 n.56
Baumstark, Anton 215
Beatty, Sir Chester 218 n.122
Bedenbender, Andreas 119 n.45
Bellinzoni, Arthur J. 21 n.56, 96–7, 98, 99,
  105 n.40
Bengel, Johann Albrecht 194, 195–7, 199,
  202
Bergsma, Jan 211 n.100
Birdsall, J. Neville 218
Black, Matthew 220, 224 n.146
Bobichon, Philippe 103 n.18
Boccaccini, Gabriele 119 n.45
Bousset, Wilhelm 96
Brock, Sebastian P. 47 n.104, 218
Brothers Grimm 138 n.135
Bryennios, Philotheos 124
Burkitt, F. C. 1, 5, 7, 8–9, 58 n.17, 205, 207,
  209 n.91
Burridge, Richard 115 n.29
Buttmann, Philip 199

Campenhausen, Hans von 29 n.25
Chapman, J. 174 n.9, 179, 180
Charlesworth, James H. 27 n.13, 45 n.93,
  45 n.96, 52–3 n.129
Ciasca, Augustin 16, 166, 204, 207, 209,
  211, 218, 222 n.137, 231 n.162
Cirafesi, Wally V. 106 n.41
Comfort, Philip W. 228–9
Cook, John Granger 29, 100 n.29
Crawford, Matthew R. 1, 27–8, 30, 50, 75–6
  n.27, 94 n.2, 109 n.47, 111, 132 n.107,
  134, 136 n.128, 138, 145, 146 n.5, 163–4
  n.70, 167 n.80, 234 nn.169–70
Credner, K. A. 95

De Bruyne, D. 174 n.8, 179
De Troyer, Kristin 118 n.40
den Hollander, August 61, 156, 233 n.166
Doole, J. Andrew 125
Drijvers, H. J. W. 27 n.7
Dungan, David 112, 124

Elliott, J. K. 218 n.123
Ellis, E. Earle 138 n.136
Elze, M. 94 n.2
Engelhardt, Moritz von 95

Fantuzzi, Marco 115 n.28
Fell, John 194 n.11
Ferguson, Everett 26 n.1
Fewster, Gregory C. 106 n.41
Fischer, Bonifatius 173, 174, 178–9, 180

Gamble, Harry Y. 26 n.1
Gathercole, Simon 129 n.93
Gentry, Peter J. 121 n.56
Gerson, Johannes 195 n.13
Goodacre, Mark 129, 147–8, 151 n.23, 163
Gregory, Andrew 34–5, 37–8
Gregory, Caspar René 200 n.44, 212

Index of Modern Authors

Griesbach, Johann Jakob 194, 198–9, 202
Grotius, Hugo 58

Hagner, Donald A. 138 n.136
Harnack, Adolf von 98 n.23
Harris, J. Rendell 15 n.11, 36 n.50, 234 n.170
Head, Peter M. 23 n.61
Higgins, A. J. B. 218
Hilgenfeld, Adolf 95 n.3
Hill, Charles E. 3–4, 7, 25, 88 n.64, 99 n.27, 111
Hill, J. Hamlyn 204, 209 n.91, 212 n.104, 223 n.137
Hogg, Hope W. 205 n.65, 209 n.91, 223 n.137
Hollander, August den 61, 156, 233 n.166
Hort, F. J. A. 158, 168, 194, 202–5, 206, 207, 209 n.91, 211, 217, 230, 237 n.181
Houghton, H. A. G. 44 n.92
Houston, George 114

Johnson, Nathan C. 159 n.50, 229 n.157
Joosse, Peter 29 n.22, 32 n.34, 233 n.166
Joosten, Jan 4, 6, 7, 8, 35 n.46, 55, 85 n.56, 146, 148–9, 151–6, 158–60, 163, 168–9
Jülicher, Adolf 3, 94 n.2

Karavidopoulos, Johannes 225 n.148
Keith, Chris 140
Kenyon, Frederick 192
Kikuchi, N. Joseph 224 n.146
Kilpatrick, G. D. 217
Klijn, A. F. J. 34, 37, 224 n.146
Kline, Leslie L. 96–7, 98, 99
Koester, Helmut 96, 97, 98, 99
Kok, Michael 127
Koltun-Fromm, Naomi 56 n.3
Kraeling, Carl H. 1 n.2, 85 n.56, 145 n.1, 146, 163
Kratz, Reinhard G. 117 n.36

Lachmann, Karl 194, 199–200
Lake, Kirsopp 1
Lange, Christian 146 n.9, 228 n.153
Larsen, Matthew D. 113, 126 n.67
Legg, S. C. E. 194, 217
Leloir, Louis 6 n.10, 16 n.20, 157 n.43, 218, 222 n.140, 225, 231 n.162, 235 n.176

Lightfoot, J. B. 98 n.23
Lippelt, E. 95
Luomanen, Petri 35 n.44, 42
Luscinius, Ottmar (Ottmar Nachtigal) 196, 199
Lyon, J. P. 162 n.61

MacKnight, James 70
Markham, R. P. 224
Marmardji, A.-S. 166, 185, 209 n.91, 218, 222 n.137, 231 n.160
Martini, Carlo M. 220–1 n.134, 225 n.148
McGurk, P. 176
Mell, Ulrich 148 n.20
Memler, Michael 195 n.12, 198, 199
Merk, Augustin 194, 212–17, 220 n.134, 221, 222, 230, 234, 236
Messina, G. 27 n.12
Metzger, Bruce M. 27 n.12, 192–3 n.7, 217, 220, 225 n.148
Mill, John 193, 194–5, 196, 197, 199 n.36, 202, 213, 229
Mills, Ian N. 5, 6, 28, 145
Moesinger, Georg 16, 203, 207
Moore, George Foote 52
Mroczek, Eva 119, 140

Nachtigal, Ottmar (Ottmar Luscinius) 196, 199
Nestle, Eberhard 218
Nestle, Erwin 213
Nordenfalk, C. 176

O'Loughlin, Thomas 174 n.10
Orlikowski, Wanda 108
Osiander, Andreas 70 n.1

Palmer, Edwin 208 n.88
Parker, David C. 147–8, 151 n.23, 163, 192 n.5, 233 n.168
Perrin, Nicholas 4, 7, 8, 93, 109 n.47, 112, 118 nn.43–4
Person, Raymond F., Jr. 118 n.40
Peters, C. 52–3 n.129, 215
Petersen, William L. 2–3, 5, 8, 15 n.11, 25, 26, 27, 31 n.30, 31 n.32, 33–8, 40, 42, 46, 47, 48 n.109, 49–50, 52, 56, 61–4, 85 n.56, 97–8, 109 n.46, 112, 135 n.123, 146, 147–8, 154, 156, 160 n.57, 163 n.65,

169, 192, 206 n.73, 211 n.97, 214 n.112, 216, 218 n.125, 219 n.130, 220 n.133, 226, 231 n.160, 233 nn.166–7, 234 n.170, 236 n.180
Phillips, C. A. 33–8, 41, 42, 43, 51
Plooij, Daniel 61, 94 n.2, 146, 154, 156, 163, 211 n.97, 214, 216, 226
Preuschen, Erwin 94 n.2, 191–2, 209 n.91

Quispel, Gilles 50 n.124, 61, 64

Rajak, Tessa 116 n.33
Ranke, Ernst 201
Rathofer, Johannes 178, 178 n.32, 183, 227 n.151

Sanday, William 95
Schmeller, J. A. 200 n.41
Schmid, Ulrich B. 3, 5, 6, 32–3, 35 n.48, 61, 75 n.24, 148 n.21, 156, 161, 183–4, 185, 192 n.6, 195 n.12, 224 n.146, 226, 227 n.151, 233 n.166
Schmidtke, Alfred 34
Semisch, Karl 95
Shodu, E. L. 106 n.41
Siker, Jeffrey S. 101 n.32
Sim, David 125–6, 127
Skarsaune, Oskar 100, 101
Soden, Hermann Freiherr von 194, 205–8, 209, 211, 212, 213 n.109, 230, 234, 236
Souter, Alexander 1 n.1, 194, 208–10, 211, 234
Stanton, Graham 107

Taylor, David 147–8, 151 n.23, 163
Thwaites, Edward 195–6 n.16

Tischendorf, Constantin von 194, 200–2, 205
Tregelles, Samuel Prideaux 193 n.8, 199 n.38
Tuckett, C. M. 99 n.26

van Unnik, W. C. 224
Vielhaur, Philipp 34
Vogels, Heinrich J. 179–80, 194, 210–13, 215, 216, 234, 236, 237
von Harnack, Adolf 98 n.23
von Soden, Hermann Freiherr 194, 205–8, 209, 211, 212, 213 n.109, 230, 234, 236
von Tischendorf, Constantin 194, 200–2, 205
Vööbus, Arthur 220

Watson, Francis 4, 6, 7, 69, 112, 134 n.118, 145–6, 233 n.167, 234 n.169
West, M. L. 115 n.25
Westcott, B. F. 194, 202–5, 206, 207, 209 n.91, 211, 217, 230, 237 n.181
Wettstein, Johann Jacob 194, 197, 199
Wikgren, Allen 220
Windisch, Hans 129

Yates, JoAnne 108

Zahn, J. C. 211 n.97
Zahn, Theodor 16, 94 n.2, 95, 98 n.23, 196 n.21, 204, 205, 210, 211 n.97, 233 n.166
Zipes, Jack 138 n.135
Zola, Nicholas J. 1, 5, 7, 30, 36 n.52, 52 n.127, 111–12, 173, 182–4, 191, 231 n.162

Index of Subjects

Page numbers with an appended italic *t* or *f* indicate a table or figure.

'Abd Iso' 15 n.15
absorption of earlier texts 123–4, 140
Abu-l-Faraj Abdullah ibn-aṭ-Ṭayyib 71
accessibility of Diatessaronic research 232
Acts of Thomas 163 n.64
Agrippa II 116
allegorical interpretation 21
Alogi 22, 23, 87 n.64
Ambrose of Milan 85
Ammonian section numbers. *See under* Eusebian Canon Tables
Ammonius of Alexandria
   genre issues and 72–3, 75
   harmony tradition and 35 n.48
   in printed editions of Greek NT 194, 195, 196–7, 198, 199, 200 n.41, 201, 202
   status of fourfold gospel and 26 n.1
Anglo-Norman gospel harmony 231 n.162
Annals of the Kings of Israel/Annals of the Kings of Judah 123
anonymity, gospel convention of 74–9
"another rich man," reference to Hebrew gospel beginning with 33, 41–3
Anti-Montanists 22 n.59, 23
antinomianism 62
Apelles 19
Aphrahat, *Demonstrations*
   Dura Parchment and 163 n.64
   ecclesiastical use of Diatessaron by 133–4
   extracanonical influences and 29, 32, 35, 38, 40–1, 43, 49, 50, 52 n.127
   fourfold gospel, knowledge of 133 n.111
   John's Gospel and 13–14, 15–16
   on opening of Diatessaron with John's prologue 80 n.44
   printed editions of Greek NT and 204, 205, 207–8, 209, 212, 215 n.115, 218

   textual evidence for Syriac origins of Diatessaron and 59
apologetics/polemics
   Celsus on multiple gospel revisions 77 n.34
   intent of Diatessaron and 133
   Justin's Roman school, purpose of 18
   opening of Diatessaron with prologue of John and 23
   philosophical texture, providing Christianity with 18, 22–3
   problem of multiple gospels in second century 20–1, 133
Apostolic Constitutions 124, 197 n.27
Aquila, Greek recension of 122
Arabic Diatessaron
   access to text of 231, 233 n.166
   Codex Fuldensis and 157, 160 n.57, 161 n.59, 165*t*, 167, 183, 185, 186, 189, 190
   Dura Parchment and 147, 149, 165–9, 165*t*, 168*t*, 169*t*
   Egyptian origins and Coptic milieu of 29 n.22
   as evidence of original text of the Diatessaron 29, 30, 205, 207–8, 212–17, 218, 221–3
   extracanonical material, [lack of] evidence for 32, 33, 40 n.75, 41, 42, 51
   genre, evidence of 71–4
   as gospel harmony 71
   inter-pericope sequence 167
   intra-pericope sequence 167–9, 168*t*, 169*t*
   John 1:1-5 as opening verses of 29 n.24
   John 21:25 as closing verse of 23
   length compared to fourfold gospel 79 n.41
   Lukan prologue absent from 80

manuscripts B, E, O, and A 16 n.25, 41 n.76, 71 nn.4–5, 74 n.22, 80 n.46, 222 n.137
Peter's question about forgiveness in 40
printed editions of Greek NT and 204, 205, 207–13, 214*t*, 215, 216, 221–4, 226, 230, 234–5 n.174
publication and study of 16, 204–5, 209 n.91, 231 n.162
representation of fourfold gospel in 52
sequence issues in 6, 51, 80–5, 167–9
sigla within 71
Syriac source for 56, 167 n.80
"Vulgatization" and 32 n.33
Aramaic
Matthew, Aramaic version of 34–5, 38
western Aramaic gospel tradition 58, 59, 65
Arctinus, *Aethiopis* 115, 140
Aristides of Athens, *Apology* 99
Armenian version of Ephrem's *Commentary* 16, 17, 29, 45, 48, 146, 164–5, 166*t*, 201 n.47, 203, 207, 208, 211, 212, 218 n.122, 220*t*, 226*t*, 228, 235 n.177
Armenian Vulgate 17 n.27
Assyrian origins of Tatian 17–18, 56
Athanasius, *39th Festal Letter* 124
Augustine of Hippo 70 n.2, 75 n.25
Aulus Hirtius 116, 140

baptism of Jesus, fire/light at 43–8
Bar Bahlul 15 n.15
Bar Hebraeus 15 nn.15–16, 80 n.44
Bar Kepha 15 n.15
Bel and the Dragon 123
Bengel edition of Greek NT (1734) 194, 195–7, 199, 202
The Book of Steps 163 n.64
bookrolls, length of survival of 114
Bover edition of Greek NT (1943) 193 n.8
Brutus, *Cato* 115, 116
Byzantine lectionary 136 n.127

Cambridge, England
Corpus Christi College MS. 286 25, 177
Dutch harmony manuscript 24
Cana, wedding feast at 6, 83, 87, 89, 90 n.71, 91, 185–9

Catholic Letters, editions of 236
Cato the Younger, encomia for 115–16, 122, 139, 140
Celsus 19, 77 n.34, 133
Christian of Stavelot 36 n.56
Chronicle of Seʿert 15 n.15
Chronicles, biblical books of 117–18, 123
Cicero 115, 116, 140
1 Clement 18 n.39
2 Clement 98–9
Clement of Alexandria 41 n.77, 77 n.30, 96, 127, 139, 202 n.52
Clementine Homilies 41 n.77, 96, 97
Codex Algerinae Peckover (Greek Minuscule 713) 162
Codex Amiatinus 177, 178–9, 180
Codex Bezae 28, 46, 134 n.115, 137 n.130, 148 n.15, 210, 229 n.159
Codex Colbertinus 162, 163
Codex Fuldensis 5, 171–90. *See also* Dura Parchment and Codex Fuldensis
access to text of 195 n.12, 198, 199, 205, 231
Arabic Diatessaron and 157, 160 n.57, 161 n.59, 165*t*, 167, 183, 185, 186, 189, 190
Canon Tables apparatus in 5, 30, 71, 79 n.40, 174–6, 178, 179
capitula 80–1, 174, 176, 179–81, 189, 223
Codex Amiatinus and 177, 178–9
contents of 173–4
dating of 173–4
doxology of Lord's Prayer omitted by 196 n.18
Dutch and German harmonies compared 24
editorial activity in descendant works 185–9
Ephrem's *Commentary* and 157–60, 161 n.58, 165*t*, 167, 185, 186, 189, 190
Eusebius's *Letter to Carpianus* and 174, 175
as evidence of original Diatessaron text 29, 33, 189–90
extracanonical material, [lack of] evidence for 32, 34, 43
fourfold gospel and 136 n.128, 172
genre of Diatessaron, evidence of 71–4
as gospel harmony 71

intra-pericope sequence in 6
Jerome's *Novum Opus* in 174, 175, 178, 179, 181, 189
John 1:1 in 23
Leitfehler in 173, 182–5
Liège harmony and 183, 184, 185, 188
Liège/Venetian harmonies and 154–6, 155*t*
manuscript of (Fulda, Bonifatianus I) 26 n.5, 171–2
marginal numbers and *sigla* in 174, 176–8, 189
Memler edition of later reception of 195 n.12, 198, 199
"old perspective" on Diatessaronic studies and 32
paratexts of 172, 173, 174, 181
Peter's question about forgiveness in 40
post-history (copying and dissemination) of 172, 181–9
preface of Victor 30 n.26, 35 n.48, 74–5, 80 n.43, 136 n.128, 174, 181, 194–5 n.12, 198 n.33, 201
pre-history (production) of 172, 173–81
in printed editions of Greek NT 194, 195–6, 198, 199, 200, 201, 205, 207, 208, 214*t*, 215 n.115, 216, 223, 226, 230
sequencing issues 80–5
Tatian's Diatessaron, relationship to 172, 189–90
Vulgate and 75, 175, 177, 179, 189, 190
Vulgatization of Diatessaronic text in 31 n.30, 31 n.32, 32 n.33
western vernacular harmonies and 172–3
Zacharias Chrysopolitanus, harmony used by 35 n.48
Codex Harleianus (London, British Library, Harley MS 1775) 177, 178–9
Codex Sangallensis (St. Gallen, Stiftsbibliothek Cod. Sang. 1395) 177, 183, 195 n.12, 200 n.41
Codex Sangermanensis 44–5, 46, 49
conflict of traditions, Diatessaron resolving 85–7
Constantine I (Roman emperor) 124
coordination of adjacent narratives 87–9
Crescens 18

Cypria 114, 115

Damasus (pope) 175
Daniel, Book of 121, 123
destruction of texts 124–5
Deutero-Isaiah and Deutero-Zechariah 123
Deuteronomistic Historian 123–4, 126
Deuteronomy 117
Diadore 164 n.72
Diapente, as name for Diatessaron 26–7, 72, 111 n.1
Diatessaron. *See* Tatian's Gospel
"Diatessaron," as title 27–8, 72–4, 85, 146 n.5
Diatessaronization of deviating canonical texts 48 n.107
Didache ("Teaching of the Apostles") 124, 135
Diocletian, persecutions under 124
Dionysius bar Ṣalībī 15 nn.15–16, 80 n.44, 87 n.64, 88 n.66, 201
docetism 80
Doctrina Addai 48–9, 163 n.64
Dodekapropheton 120
doxology of Lord's Prayer 196, 211, 227–8
Dura Parchment 5, 145–70
  Arabic Diatessaron and 147, 149, 165–9, 165*t*, 168*t*, 169*t*
  canonical sources for 149–51, 150–1*t*
  dating of 47 n.104, 56–7
  disagreement about text represented in 5, 31 n.31, 85 n.56, 145, 146, 215 n.113
  discovery and publication of 1, 146, 215
  Ephrem's *Commentary* compared 42 n.78, 146, 158, 163–5, 165*t*, 166*t*, 169
  establishment of precise wording of Diatessaron and 28
  gospel texts overlapping with 170*t*
  Greek Diatessaron, evidence for 85
  initial identification with Diatessaron 146
  Joosten's rebuttal of Parker/Taylor/Goodacre study 148–9, 149*t*, 169
  Joseph of Arimathea passage in 30, 31–2, 50
  Mark and 137
  Old Syriac gospel texts and 150*t*, 151*t*, 162 n.60, 166*t*

original language of Diatessaron and 56–7
Parker/Taylor/Goodacre study of 147–8, 151 n.23, 163
"Petersen method" and 135 n.123, 146, 147–8, 154, 156, 169
printed editions of Greek NT and 215, 225, 230, 234 n.170
reassessment of 149–56, 150–3*t*, 155*t*
sequence and 6
Syriac or eastern tradition and 163–9, 165*t*, 166*t*, 168*t*, 169*t*
treatment of fourfold gospel in 30
"Vulgatization" and 32 n.33
Dura Parchment and Codex Fuldensis
Arabic Diatessaron and 165*t*, 167
collapse of Petersen method and 156–7
counter-evidence of Fuldensis for relationship between Dura and Diatessaron 149, 152, 153, 154–6, 155*t*
Ephrem, Dura, Fuldensis, and Arabic harmony sequences compared 165*t*
inter-pericope or block-by-block sequence in 157–8, 157*t*, 164
intra-pericope or phrase-by-phrase sequence in 158–60, 161
in Parker/Taylor/Goodacre study 147, 148 n.18
unexpected agreement between (on Luke 23:51) 160–3, 161*t*

early Christianity
canonical consciousness of 124
canonical status of fourfold gospel in 25–6, 28, 53
gospel harmony, literary tradition of 94, 100
liturgy, use of Gospels and Hebrew prophets in 106–7
oral versus written tradition in 19–20, 28, 101 n.34
philosophical texture of 18, 22–3
Roman Christian groups in second century 18–19
status and acceptance of John in second century 21–3, 87 n.64
writing and reception of gospel literature in 7, 9, 19–20

eastern tradition. *See* Syriac or eastern tradition
Ebionite gospel harmony. *See Gospel of the Ebionites*
Ebionites' exclusive use of Matthew 131, 140
Editio Critica Maior (ECM) of Greek NT 218, 230, 236
Encratite heresy, association of Tatian with 14 n.10, 60, 64, 72, 73, 136, 234 n.170
1 Enoch 118–20
Ephrem the Syrian, *Commentary on the Diatessaron* (attrib.)
access to text 195–6 n.16, 205, 231 n.162
Arabic Diatessaron and 157–60, 161 n.59, 165*t*, 167
Codex Fuldensis and 157–60, 161 n.58, 165*t*, 167, 185, 186, 189, 190
Dura Parchment and 42 n.78, 146, 158, 163–5, 165*t*, 166*t*, 169
ecclesiastical use of Diatessaron by 134
extracanonical influences and 32, 32 n.33, 33, 35, 38–41, 41–2 n.78, 43–9, 50–1
genre of Diatessaron and 74, 82, 91
Jewish law in Diatessaron and 65–6
John's Gospel and 16, 17
in printed editions of Greek NT 194, 195, 197, 198, 201, 203–5, 207–13, 215 n.115, 218, 219, 222, 223, 225, 226*t*, 227–30, 235, 237 n.181
sequence in 6 n.10, 82
textual evidence for Syriac origins of Diatessaron and 59
western Diatessaronic tradition and 61
Ephrem the Syrian, *Exposition of the Gospel* (attrib.) 163 n.65
Epic Cycle 114–15, 122, 140
Epicurus, *On Nature* 139 n.139
Epiphanius of Salamis, *Panarion* 19 n.41, 22, 34, 41, 42, 45–6, 47, 56 n.6, 88, 130–1, 140–1
Epistula Apostolorum 53 n.130
eschatology 65
Esther, Book of 123
eternal life 65
Ethiopic tradition
Didache in Ethiopic 124 n.62
Jubilees and *1 Enoch* as canonical in 120

Luke 23:51b in 162
Eusebian Canon Tables
  in Codex Fuldensis 5, 30, 71, 79 n.40, 136 n.128, 174–6, 178, 179
  Jerome on 79 n.40, 175
  Letter to Carpianus 73 n.16, 75, 174, 175
  Matthew as base text for 73, 91
  in post-Diatessaronic Syriac gospel books 78
  purpose and use of 78–9
  section numbers 30, 71, 72–3, 79 n.40, 91, 174–6, 178, 179
Eusebius of Caesarea
  on Ammonius 197
  on conflicts in gospel traditions 85–6
  eastern knowledge of Diatessaron and 56 n.6
  Ecclesiastical History 15, 26, 73–5, 174, 197
  extracanonical sources of Tatian and 26, 27 n.13
  Irenaeus and 78
  lost texts referred to by 124
  in printed editions of Greek NT 197, 202–3 n.54
  Syriac translation of *Ecclesiastical History* 15, 73–4
  on Tatian and Diatessaron 14–15, 26, 72–4, 141
  Theophania 215 n.115
  Victor of Capua on 26, 72
evangelical intent of Diatessaron 132–3
expansions and revisions of texts 122–3
extracanonical influences 3–4, 25–53
  "another rich man," reference to Hebrew gospel beginning with 33, 41–3
  canonicity of fourfold gospel in second century and 25–6, 28, 53
  on *2 Clement* 99
  defined 57–8 n.11
  disagreement about 4, 7, 26–8, 57–9
  evidence for/significance of 51–53, 57–9
  "fire/light at the baptism" variant 43–8
  forgiveness, Peter's question about 33, 38–41
  Gospel of Peter 31–2, 48, 49–50
  Justin and 96

  "old perspective" versus "new perspective" on Diatessaronic studies and 32–8
  proliferation theory and 128–31
  sequence issues 41–2 n.78
  treatment of fourfold gospel in Diatessaron and 28–31
  Vulgatization in Diatessaronic tradition and 31, 32 n.33, 40, 43, 48, 52 n.127
  "where there is one, there I am" saying 50–1
  "woes at the crucifixion" passage 48–50, 58

Fadius Gallus 115
Fell edition of Greek NT (1675) 194 n.11
"fire/light at the baptism" variant 43–8
"flying Jesus" variant 52 n.127, 90 n.72, 234 n.170
forgiveness, Peter's question about 33, 38–41
fourfold gospel. *See also* John; Luke; Mark; Matthew
  Aphrahat's knowledge of 133 n.111
  Arabic Diatessaron, representation in 52
  canonical status in early Christianity 25–6, 28, 53
  2 Clement's knowledge of 98–9
  dating of 138–9
  Dura Parchment texts overlapping with 170t
  Hebrew scriptures, status of gospels equated with 106
  Justin's knowledge of 53 n.130, 101 n.35, 106–8, 139
  length compared to Arabic Diatessaron 79 n.41
  maintaining even treatment of, in Diatessaron 90–1
  as "memoirs of apostles," 106–7
  status of Diatessaron as supplementing versus supplanting 1, 4, 8–9, 25–6, 69–71, 74, 79, 91–2, 109, 111–14
  in Syriac 57, 74
  Tatian's use of all of 135–6, 139
  treatment of, in Diatessaron 28–31
future of Diatessaronic studies 5, 229–36

Gaius of Rome 23, 87–8
Gallican lectionary 136 n.127

genealogies, treatment of 29–30, 36, 42 n.81, 45 n.97, 80, 85–7, 99, 117, 125, 126, 131, 134, 136, 194, 232 n.163
genre of Diatessaron 4, 69–92
    anonymity, gospel convention of 74–9
    applying contemporary genre theory to ancient gospel harmony 108
    Codex Fuldensis and Arabic Diatessaron, evidence from 71–4
    as gospel rather than gospel harmony 4, 69–71, 74, 79, 91–2
    Greek Diatessaron, evidence for 73–4, 81, 85
    redactional strategies and 85–91
    redaction-critical approach to 79–85
Glossa Ordinaria 32, 35
Gnostic Gospels 129, 130
Gnosticism 22
gospel harmony. *See also specific harmonies*
    applying contemporary genre theory to 108
    2 Clement, evidence of gospel harmony in 98–9
    defined 70
    as early Christian literary tradition 94, 100
    Justin's gospel hypothesized as 95–100, 136
    purpose of, for Justin 107–8
    status of Tatian's Gospel as 4, 69–71
    textual features used to assess stemmatic relationships for 182
Gospel of Barnabas 55 n.1
Gospel of the Ebionites/Ebionite Gospel Harmony 20, 27, 34, 42 n.81, 45–6, 47, 131, 136, 140, 141, 194
Gospel of the Egyptians 20
Gospel of the Hebrews/Gospel According to the Hebrews 20, 25, 27, 28 n.19, 34, 36 n.54, 36 nn.49–50, 37 n.57, 38–41, 42 n.81, 43, 52–3 n.129, 65, 97 n.19, 99 n.28, 140, 141, 194
Gospel of Judas 130
Gospel of Mary Magdalene 130
Gospel of the Nazarenes 20, 34, 36, 37
Gospel of Nicodemus 152 n.26
Gospel of Peter 20, 25, 27, 31–2, 48, 49–50, 77, 95
Gospel of Philip 129

Gospel of Thomas 25, 27, 60, 129–30
Gospel of Truth 129, 130, 135
Gospels, canonical. *See* fourfold gospel; John; Luke; Mark; Matthew
Greco-Roman texts, proliferation of 114–17
Greek Diatessaron, evidence for 73–4, 81, 85
Greek Epic Cycle 114–15, 122, 140
Greek Majuscule 011 176
Greek Majuscule 026 176
Greek Majuscule 031 176
Greek Minuscule 72 (London, British Library, Harley 5674) 164 n.72, 198, 203, 224
Greek Minuscule 566 33, 35 n.44, 37–8
Greek Minuscule 713 (Codex Algerinae Peckover) 162
Greek Minuscule 1424 35 n.44
Greek NT editions, citation of Diatessaron in 193–229. *See also* textual criticism of Gospels, use of Diatessaron in; *specific editions*
Greek translations of Hebrew scriptures 120–1, 121f, 123
Griesbach edition of Greek NT (1775–7/1796–1806) 194, 198–9, 202

Haaren manuscript of Dutch harmony 24
Hadrian (Roman emperor) 99
Harklean passion harmony 162
Harmoniae Evangelicae (Andreas Osiander, 1537) 70 n.1
harmonies. *See* gospel harmony
Harmony of the Four Gospels (James MacKnight, 1756) 70
Hebrew Gospels. *See* Jewish-Christian/Hebrew Gospels
Hebrew scriptures. *See also specific books*
    absorptions of earlier texts 123–4
    Greek translations of 120–1, 121f, 123
    proliferation of 117–21
    proto-Masoretic text 120
    revisions and expansions of 123
    status of Gospels equated with 106
Hegesippus 223 n.141
Heliand harmony 235 n.174
Herculaneum papyri 114 n.18, 139 n.139
heresy. *See also specific heresies*

Index of Subjects

association of Tatian with 14 n.10, 60, 64, 72, 73, 74, 75, 132, 136, 194, 203–4, 234 n.170
heresiologists on Diatessaron 131–2, 135–6
Hesychius 121
Himmelgarten Fragments 37
Hippolytus of Rome 88, 130, 201
Historia passionis Domini 36 n.56
Homer 114, 115
Hugo of St. Cher 36 n.56

Ignatius of Antioch 127, 139
Iliad 114, 115, 122
Infancy Gospel of Thomas 128
infancy Gospels 128
Institut für neutestamentliche Textforschung (INTF) 218
International Greek New Testament Project (IGNTP) 194, 217–18, 234–5 n.174
Irenaeus of Lyon 9, 78, 127, 130, 135–6, 139, 140, 202, 223 n.141
Isho'dad 15 nn.15–16, 58 n.15
Isho' bar Ali/Isā ibn 'Alî 15 nn.15–16, 71 n.5

Jerome
  Commentary on Matthew 36
  Jewish-Christian Gospel known to 33–7, 38, 51, 52
  on marginal section and canon numbers 79 n.40, 175
  Novum Opus, in Codex Fuldensis 174, 175, 178, 179, 181, 189
  Vulgate 75, 136 n.128, 158, 175, 177, 179, 189, 190, 196 n.18, 210 n.93, 223
  Zacharias Chrysopolitanus and 36–7
Jesus
  as author of one true Gospel 14, 78
  Diatessaron's reconstruction of life of 89–90
Jewish biblical texts, proliferation of 117–21
Jewish law in Diatessaron 4, 62–6
Jewish Revolt, histories of 116–17, 139
Jewish scriptures. *See* Hebrew scriptures
Jewish-Christian/Hebrew Gospels
  attraction of idea of lost Ur-Judaic gospel 52–3

  "fire/light at the baptism" variant and 47
  known to Jerome 33–7, 38, 51, 52
  used by Origen in *Commentary on Matthew* 41–3
  "where there is one, there I am" saying 50
  "woes at the crucifixion" variant and 50
Job, Book of 120, 123
John
  authorial persona in 77
  Justin's knowledge of 21–2, 99–100
  proliferation theory and 129
  realized eschatology of 65
  sequence of Diatessaron and 29
  status and acceptance of, in second century 21–23, 87 n.64
  Synoptic parallels in 120 n.88
John, Tatian's use of Gospel of 3, 13–24
  Aphrahat's *Demonstrations* on 13–14
  apologetic/polemical purpose of 20–1, 23
  breaking dominance of Matthean sequence 90–1
  Eusebius's *Ecclesiastical History* on 14–15
  extracanonical influence, lack of evidence of 53
  geographic/historical context of Tatian and 17–18
  importance of opening Diatessaron with John 1:1, 23
  Mill's edition of Greek NT (1707) on 195
  origins of Gospel writing and 19–20
  philosophical texture of early Christianity and 18, 22–3
  problem of multiple Gospels in second century 20–1
  status and acceptance of John in second century 21–3, 87 n.64
  western tradition, John 1:1 in 23–4
John Chrysostom 164 n.73
John the Baptist, coordinating testimony of 87–9
Joseph of Arimathea 30, 31–2, 50, 148–9, 149t, 151–2 n.26, 156, 161, 162, 164 n.71
Josephus 21, 116–17, 118, 122, 140
  Antiquities 116 n.33, 118
  Jewish War 116, 118, 122, 140
  Vita 116

Jubilees 118–20
Julius Caesar, *Anti-Cato* 115, 116
Justin and Justin's gospel 4, 93–109
  anonymity, gospel convention of 77
  apologetic/polemical purpose of Roman school of 18
  challenges of gospel harmony hypothesis 100–106, 104t
  Dialogue with Trypho 18, 43–4, 46, 77, 120
  Diatessaron, Justin's lack of knowledge of 139
  Dodekapropheton quoted by 120
  Eusebius on 72 n.11
  "fire/light at the baptism" variant and 43–4
  First Apology 18, 77
  fourfold gospel, knowledge of 53 n.130, 101 n.35, 106–8, 139
  geographic/historical context of Diatessaron and 8, 18
  gospel harmony hypothesis of 95–100, 136
  influence on Tatian 97–8, 106, 108–9
  John, knowledge of 21–2, 99–100
  Mark, knowledge of 101 n.35, 127, 136
  martyrdom of 8, 18
  Matthew privileged by 84 n.52, 96, 101 n.35, 103–5 n.39
  plurality of textual sources for 101, 122
  purpose of gospel harmony for 107–8
  Roman school, catechisms and church manuals used in 96, 108
  Second Apology 18
  synoptic gospel harmony possibly created in Roman school of 21
  teacher of Tatian, Justin as 3, 8, 18
  UBS edition of Greek NT and 223 n.141
Justus of Tiberius 116

kaige tradition 120–1
Kings, biblical books of 117–18, 123

Lachmann edition of Greek NT (1831/1842-50) 194, 199–200
lance-piercing, placement of 157–9, 157t, 164, 167, 207, 224
Laodiceans, Paul's letter to 172 n.2
Latin Diatessaron. *See* Codex Fuldensis

Legg edition of Greek NT (1935/1940) 194, 217
Leitfehler test 173, 182–5
Lesches, *Little Iliad* 115, 140
Letter of Aristeas 120
Leuven Database of Ancient Books 114 n.20
Liber Graduum 215 n.115, 218
Liège harmony 33, 37, 61, 62, 64, 134 n.115, 147, 149, 152–3, 154–6, 155t, 183, 184, 185, 188, 214, 235 n.175. *See also* Middle Dutch harmonies
life of Jesus, Diatessaron's reconstruction of 89–90
Lindisfarne Gospels (London, British Library, Cotton MS Nero D IV) 176, 177, 179, 180
liturgy
  early Christian use of Gospels and Hebrew prophets in 106–7
  genealogies, reading of 136 n.127
Logos
  Justin's Logos theology 100
  status and acceptance of John in second century and 22
London, British Library
  Cotton MS Nero D IV (Lindisfarne Gospels) 176, 177, 179, 180
  Harley MS 1775 (Codex Harleianus) 177, 178–9
  Harley MS 1915 35 n.47
  Harley MS 5674 (Greek Minuscule 72) 164 n.73, 198, 203, 224
London Polyglot Bible (1655) 194 n.11
Lord's Prayer, doxology of 196, 211, 227–8
lost ancient literature 122
Lucian, Christian translation of Hebrew scriptures by 121
Luke
  Arabic Diatessaron, prologue absent from 80
  authorial persona in 77
  2 Clement and 99
  Justin's knowledge of 101 n.35, 103–5 n.39
  Marcionite Gospel based on 14, 20, 76, 130–1
  Papias's knowledge of 19 n.46
  Paul, Luke as disciple of 76

proliferation theory and 126–7
sequence of Diatessaron and 29, 75, 84
Theophilus in 92
"woes at the crucifixion" passage and 49
LXX (Septuagint) 101, 120–2, 121*f*, 122, 140

macro-level sequence 6
Mar Aba fragments 163 n.65
Marcion, Marcion's Gospel, and Marcionites 8, 9, 14, 19, 20, 52 n.127, 76, 78, 130–1, 135, 202–3, 213, 223 n.141, 225, 233 n.166
Mari ibn Sulaiman 15 n.15
Mark
 authorial persona, lack of 77
 Justin's knowledge of 101 n.35, 127, 136
 longer ending of 137, 199, 202, 209
 Matthew's relationship to 70
 Papias's knowledge of 19
 Peter, Mark as disciple of 76
 priority of 125
 proliferation theory and 125–8, 136–8, 140
 treatment of, in Diatessaron 30, 84, 136–8
Matthew
 Aramaic version of 34–5, 38
 authorial persona, lack of 77
 as basis for Ammonius's gospel synopsis 73, 91
 2 Clement and 99 n.26
 Ebionites' exclusive use of 131, 140
 "fire/light at the baptism" variant and 46–7, 49
 Justin privileging 84 n.52, 96, 101 n.35, 103–5 n.39
 lost Greek text of 62
 Mark, relationship to 70
 medieval Hebrew version of (twelfth c.) 61
 Papias's knowledge of 19
 proliferation theory and 125–6, 127
 sequence of Diatessaron, as main guide for 29, 30, 84–5
 use of John in Diatessaron breaking dominance of Matthean sequence 90–1
Megethius (follower of Marcion) 14

"memoirs of apostles," fourfold gospel as 106–7
Merk edition of Greek NT (1933/1942/1992) 194, 212–17, 214*t*, 220 n.134, 221, 222, 230, 234, 236
Michael the Syrian 15 nn.15–16
Middle Dutch harmonies 24, 33, 37, 147, 210, 211–12, 214, 216, 222–3, 230, 234 n.174
Middle Italian harmonies 61, 62, 64, 147, 149, 152–53, 154–6, 155*t*, 210, 214*t*, 215, 216, 222–3, 230
Milan, Biblioteca Ambrosiana, Cod. C. 39. inf. 177
Mill edition of Greek NT (1707) 193, 194–95, 196, 197, 199 n.36, 202, 213, 229
missionizing intent of Diatessaron 132–3
Monotessaron, as term 195 n.13, 196
Montanus and Montanism 22 n.59
Munatius Rufus 115
Muratorian Fragment 53 n.130

Nag Hammadi texts 129–30
Naḥal Ḥever Greek Minor Prophets Scroll, 8ḤevXIIgr 120
narrative criticism 80
Nassenes 130
nature of Tatian's Gospel 1, 4, 8–9, 25–26. *See also* genre of Diatessaron; Justin and Justin's gospel; proliferation of Gospels
Neoplatonism 22 n.57
Nero (Roman emperor) 115
Nestle-Aland editions of Greek NT (1898/2012) 194, 218–19, 221, 230
Netherlands Institute for Advanced Studies (NIAS) 233 n.166
"new perspective" versus "old perspective" on Diatessaronic studies 32–8
New Testament Text and Translation Commentary (Comfort) 228–9

Octavian (Roman emperor) 115, 116
Odyssey 114, 122
Old French exemplar of Pepysian harmony 24 n.70, 231 n.162
Old High German harmonies 24, 210, 235 n.174

Old Latin Gospels/gospel harmonies 75 n.26, 154, 162, 163, 178, 179–81, 189–90, 210–11, 214, 215, 216, 223, 226
"old perspective" versus "new perspective" on Diatessaronic studies 32–8
Old Syriac gospel texts
  Curetonian manuscript 49, 58 n.14, 60, 64, 132, 134 n.115, 150–51*t*, 166*t*, 208, 210 n.92
  Dura Parchment and 150*t*, 151*t*, 162 n.60, 166*t*
  Jewish law in 64
  Luke 23:51b in 162
  printed editions of Greek NT and 203 n.58, 204–5, 210, 215, 216 n.116
  relationship to Diatessaron 56, 59–60, 61, 64 n.33, 132, 162 n.60
  Sinai New Finds manuscript 151*t*, 168*t*, 169*t*, 210 n.92
  Sinaitic manuscript 49, 58–62, 64, 86, 132, 134 n.115, 150–51*t*, 159 n.51, 166*t*, 204–5, 208, 210 n.92
Old Testament. *See* Hebrew scriptures
Ophites 130
oppositio in imitando 129
oral versus written tradition in early Christianity 19–20, 28, 101 n.34
Origen
  Against Celsus 19, 133
  Commentary on Matthew 28 n.18, 33, 41–3, 51, 66
  fourfold gospel known to 139
  Hexapla 73 n.16, 121–2
  Jewish law in Diatessaron and 65
  on John the Baptist traditions 87, 88
  Mark attested by 127, 129 n.81
  primitive Christian catechism, knowledge of 96
  on problem of multiple gospels 20–1
orthodoxy and the Diatessaron 135–6, 140–1
Oxford, Bodleian Library
  MS 209 35 n.47
  MS 2761 (Auct. D. 1.8) 186
Oxyrhynchus papyri 113 n.17, 114 n.18, 129

palimpsests 114, 159 n.51, 204–5, 210 n.92
Papias 19–20, 28 n.19, 53 n.130, 75, 78 n.36, 128 n.81

papyri
  P.Egerton 2, 99 n.28
  P.Oxy. 1 50, 51
paratexts. *See also* Eusebian Canon Tables
  of Codex Fuldensis 172, 173, 174, 181
  Petrus Comestor's *Historia Scholastica* void of 182
Paschasius Radbertus 36, 37
Paul
  as apostle in New Testament 126 n.72
  Laodiceans, letter to 172 n.2
  Luke as disciple of 76
  Marcion and 20
  question put to Jesus by, on road to Damascus 46
  on single gospel 15 n.17, 20
Pepysian harmony 24, 61, 148 n.18, 235 n.174
Persian Diatessaron 16, 215, 218, 230, 234–5 n.174
Peshitta
  Arabic Diatessaron and 166
  Diatessaron's influence on 56, 59–60, 162 n.61
  Dura Parchment and Codex Fuldensis on Luke 23:51 compared 161*t*
  Luke 23:51b in 162
  Old Testament, Tatian's use of 57, 59
  printed editions of Greek NT and 211, 212, 213, 223
Peter
  apostleship of Paul and 126 n.72
  forgiveness, question about 33, 38–41
  in *Gospel of Thomas* 129
  Mark as disciple of 76
Petrus Cantor 181
Petrus Comestor
  Historia Evangelica (in *Historia Scholastica*) 184–5
  Historia Scholastica 36, 182
Philo of Alexandria 22 n.57
Philodemus of Gadara 139 n.139
philosophical texture of early Christianity 18, 22–3
Plato and Platonism 22
Plutarch 115–16
  Cato the Younger 8, 122
polemics. *See* apologetics/polemics
Prayer of Azariah 123

printed editions of Greek NT, citation of Diatessaron in 193–229. *See also* textual criticism of Gospels, use of Diatessaron in; *specific editions*
Proclus 114
proliferation of Gospels 4, 111–41
    analogies in other types of works 113–21
    defined 112
    diagram of 139*f*
    early Christian Gospels before and after Diatessaron 125–31
    gospel collection and 138–40
    loss, revision, absorption, and destruction of texts 121*f*, 122–5, 140
    problem of multiple Gospels 20–1
    purposes and intentions of multiple Gospels 112–13
    single gospel theory and 113, 129, 130–1, 138, 140
    supplement/supplant theories and 111–14
    Tatian's Diatessaron and 131–8
Protevangelium of James 27, 128, 134
proto-Masoretic text of Hebrew scriptures 120
Proverbs, Book of 123
Psalms 123
pseudo-Ephrem. *See* Ephrem the Syrian
Ptolemy II 120

Q 127
Qumran scrolls 118, 119

Rabanus Maurus 37
Rabbula of Edessa 15 n.15, 74, 135, 141
reconstruction of Diatessaron 16, 55–61, 158 n.44, 191–3, 205, 232–4, 236
redaction-critical approach to Diatessaron 79–85
Reims, cathedral library, copy of Codex Fuldensis 186
Returns Home 114
revisions and expansions of texts 122–3
Rhetorical Genre Studies school 108
Romanos the Melodist 44, 62
Rome, Tatian's context in 8
Rufinus 15 n.13, 75, 174 n.9
Russian National Library gr. 5, 114 n.20

Sack of Troy 114, 115, 140
Samaritan Pentateuch 117 n.37
Samuel, biblical books of 117–18, 123
scriptura sui ipsius interpres 103
section numbers, Eusebian 30, 71, 72–3, 79 n.40, 91, 174–6, 178, 179
Septuagint (LXX) 101, 120–2, 121*f*, 122, 140
sequence issues 6–7. *See also under* Dura Parchment and Codex Fuldensis
    in Arabic Diatessaron 6, 51, 80–5, 167–9, 168*t*, 169*t*
    Diatessaron as effort to solve problem of 75
    Ephrem's *Commentary* and 6 n.10, 82
    evidence for original sequence of the Diatessaronic text 29
    extracanonical influences and 41–2 n.78, 51
    in Justin 106
    macro-perspective of narrative sequence 182, 188
    in redaction-critical approach to Diatessaron 79–85
Sermon on the Mount/Plain 100, 101, 102, 103, 105, 106, 185, 187
shema 105
single gospel theory and proliferation of Gospels 113, 129, 130–1, 138, 140
Society of Biblical Literature (SBL) sessions on Diatessaron 1–3, 25–6, 52 n.127, 112 n.11
von Soden edition of Greek NT (1902–13) 194, 205–8, 209, 211, 212, 213 n.109, 234, 236
Song of the Three Jews 123
source criticism 80
sources of Tatian's Gospel 3–4, 7–8, 21, 57–59. *See also* extracanonical influences; John, Tatian's use of Gospel of
Souter edition of Greek NT (1910/1947) 194, 208–10, 211, 234
St. Gallen, Stiftsbibliothek Cod. Sang. 1395 (Codex Sangallensis) 177, 183, 195 n.12, 200 n.41
Stoics and Stoicism 22
Stuttgart harmony 24, 33, 37, 147. *See also* Middle Dutch harmonies
Susanna and the Elders 123

Symmachus 122
Syriac or eastern tradition. *See also* Old Syriac gospel texts; Peshitta
   Arabic Diatessaron, Syriac source for 56, 167 n.80
   commonness of Diatessaron in Syria 15, 29 n.25, 74
   dating of translation of Greek Diatessaron into Syriac 47 n.104
   Diatessaron as Syriac text 56–7, 59, 61
   Dura Parchment and 163–9, 165t, 166t, 168t, 169t
   ecclesiastical use of Diatessaron, fourth and fifth c. 133–5
   Ephrem's *Commentary*, version of Diatessaron used in 41–2 n.78, 47 n.105
   Eusebius's *Ecclesiastical History* in Syriac, on Diatessaron 15, 73–4
   evidence of original Diatessaron text in 29
   "flying Jesus" variant from 52 n.127, 90 n.73, 234 n.170
   fourfold gospel, first Syriac translation of 57
   "Gospel of the Mixed" versus 'Gospel of the Separated" in 15, 29 n.25, 73, 75–6 n.27, 132, 205 n.68
   missionary work of Tatian among Syriac speakers 8
   primary status of Diatessaron in 93–4
   Rome, cultural connections with 100 n.31
   Tatian's Assyrian origins 17–18, 56
   textual evidence for Syriac origins of Diatessaron 59–60
   "Vulgatization" and 32 n.33

Tatian
   biographical information about 17–18, 56
   heresy, association with 14 n.10, 60, 64, 72, 73, 74, 75, 132, 136, 194, 203–4, 234 n.170
   Oratio ad Graecos 56, 64, 73, 197
Tatian's Gospel (Diatessaron) 1–9
   access to 203
   authorship of 56 n.3
   base text, lack of 55–6
   composition, language and dating of 17, 42 n.84, 56–7, 59, 139, 192 n.7, 208–9 n.89
   Diapente, as name for 26–7, 72
   "Diatessaron," as title 27–8, 72–4
   early Christianity, writing and reception of gospel literature in 7, 9 (*See also* early Christianity)
   editorial techniques and strategies 7–8, 28, 85–91
   Eusebius on 14–15, 26, 72–4
   first mention of 14–15
   future of studies of 5, 229–36
   geographic/historical context of 8, 17–18 (*See also* Syriac or eastern tradition; western tradition)
   Jesus viewed as author of 14
   Jewish law in 4, 62–6
   Justin's influence on 97–8, 106, 108–9 (*See also* Justin and Justin's gospel)
   nature of 1, 4, 8–9, 25–26 (*See also* genre of Diatessaron; Justin and Justin's gospel; proliferation of Gospels)
   orthodox on 135–36, 140–1
   purposes and intentions of 7–8, 21, 26, 59, 94, 132–3
   reconstruction of 16, 55–61, 158 n.44, 191–3, 205, 232–4, 236
   sequence issues 6–7 (*See also* sequence issues)
   single gospel book, usefulness of 78–9
   sources of 3–4, 7–8, 21, 57–9 (*See also* extracanonical influences; John, Tatian's use of Gospel of)
   state of scholarly study of 1–3
   as supplementing or supplanting fourfold gospel 1, 4, 8–9, 25–6, 69–71, 74, 79, 91–2, 109, 111–14
   two editions of 71, 84–5
   witnesses to 5, 55 n.1 (*See also* Codex Fuldensis; Dura Parchment; textual criticism of Gospels, use of Diatessaron in)
"Teaching of the Apostles." *See Didache*
Telegony 114
Tertullian 76–8, 127, 130, 140
textual criticism of Gospels, use of Diatessaron in 5, 191–237

differences between Tatian's sources and extant editions 7
future of Diatessaronic studies and 5, 229–36
list of printed editions of Greek NT 194
in printed editions of Greek NT (1707–2014) 193–229 (*See also specific editions*)
proper citation of Diatessaron 234–6
propriety of critical apparatus citing Diatessaron 231
reconstruction of Diatessaron and 158 n.44, 191–3, 205, 232–4, 236
Thebais 115 n.25
Theodoret of Cyrrhus 15, 29, 56 n.6, 74, 78, 79, 80, 94, 134–5, 136, 141, 194, 197
Theodorus bar Koni 15 n.15
Theodotion 121–2
Theophilus, in Luke's Gospel 92
Theophilus of Antioch, *Harmony* 26 n.1, 31 n.31, 53 n.130, 200
Thrasea Paetus 115
Tischendorf edition of Greek NT (1869–72) 194, 200–2, 205
Titanomachy 114, 115 n.25
Titus (Roman emperor) 116
Tregelles edition of Greek NT (1857–72) 193 n.8
Trito-Isaiah and Trito-Zechariah 123
Tuscan harmony 64, 147, 210, 214*t*, 215. *See also* Middle Italian harmonies
"Two Ways" tractate 124 n.59
Two-Source hypothesis 127

United Bible Societies (UBS) editions of Greek NT (1966/2014) 194, 219–29
changes and continuing deficiencies in 4th-5th editions 224–8
deficiencies of 1st-3rd editions 220–4
Diatessaronic *sigla* in 220*t*, 226*t*
effects of poor Diatessaronic evidence on 228–9, 237 n.181
future of Diatessaronic studies and 230, 235
Merk edition and 217
Nestle-Aland edition and 219
proper citation of Diatessaron and 234

unum ex quattuor euangelium 29, 33, 36, 72, 75
Utrecht manuscript of Dutch harmony 24 n.69

Valentinus and Valentinians 19, 22, 130
Venetian harmony 61, 62, 149, 152–3, 152*t*, 153*t*, 154–6, 155*t*, 214*t*, 215, 222 n.138. *See also* Middle Italian harmonies
Vespasian (Roman emperor) 116
Vetus Latina MS *a* (Vercellensis) 44–5, 46
Victor Codex. *See* Codex Fuldensis
Victor of Capua 24, 26–7, 29–30, 35 n.48, 71–2, 74–5, 78, 79, 111 n.1, 136 n.128, 173–4, 178, 179, 189, 194. *See also* Codex Fuldensis
Vogels edition of Greek NT (1920/1955) 194, 210–12, 215, 234, 236
von Soden edition of Greek NT (1902-13) 194, 205–8, 209, 211, 212, 213 n.109, 234, 236
Vulgate 75, 136 n.128, 152*t*, 153*t*, 158, 175, 177, 179, 189, 190, 196 n.18, 210 n.93, 223
Vulgatization 31, 32 n.33, 40, 43, 48, 52 n.127, 56, 147–8, 154 n.36, 158 n.46, 160 n.57, 200

Weiss edition of Greek NT (1894–1900) 193 n.8
Westcott/Hort edition of Greek NT (1881–2/1896) 194, 202–5, 206, 207, 209 n.91, 211, 217, 230, 237 n.181
western tradition. *See also* Codex Fuldensis; Vulgate
Christian groups in second-century Rome 18–19
Eusebius's *Ecclesiastical History* on Diatessaron 14–15
evidence of original Diatessaron text in 29, 32–3
John 1:1 in 23–4
Justin's school in Rome, Tatian's connections to 8
Old Latin gospel text 75 n.26
printed editions of Greek NT and 210–12, 214, 216, 218
reconstruction of Diatessaron using 61

"Vulgatization" and 32 n.33
Wettstein edition of Greek NT (1751–2) 194, 197, 199
"where there is one, there I am" saying 50–1
"wildest form" principle 31 n.32
Winchester Cathedral MS of Zacharias Chrysopolitanus 35 n.47
"withered hand" story added to Mark and Matthew 33, 37
witnesses to Tatian's Gospel 5, 55 n.1. *See also* Codex Fuldensis; Dura Parchment; textual criticism of Gospels, use of Diatessaron in
"woes at the crucifixion" passage 48–50, 58
written versus oral tradition in early Christianity 19–20, 28, 101 n.34
Württembergische Landesbibliothek, Cod. theol. et philolol. 8° 140 187–8
Würzburg, Universitätsbibliothek, Cod. M.P.Th.F. 68, 177

Zacharias Chrysopolitanus, commentary of 33, 35–7, 148 n.18, 181, 199 n.36
Zurich harmony 64

www.ingramcontent.com/pod-product-compliance
Lightning Source LLC
Chambersburg PA
CBHW070019010526
44117CB00011B/1635